Regenerating
British Columbia's Forests

Regenerating
British Columbia's Forests

Editors: D.P. Lavender, R. Parish, C.M. Johnson,
G. Montgomery, A. Vyse, R.A. Willis, and
D. Winston

Sponsored by

UBC PRESS / VANCOUVER

Printed in Canada

ISBN 0-7748-0352-5

Funding for this book was provided by the Canada-British
Columbia Forest Resource Development Agreement – a five-
year (1985-1990) $300 million program cost-shared equally by
the federal and provincial governments.

Design and typesetting
T.D. Mock and Associates Inc., Victoria, Canada

CANADIAN CATALOGUING IN PUBLICATION DATA

   Main entry under title:

   Regenerating British Columbia's forests

   Includes bibliographical references.
   ISBN 0-7748-0352-5

   1. Reforestation – British Columbia.
   I. Lavender, D.P. (Denis Peter), 1926 –
   SD409.R44   1990   634.9'56'09711   C90-091082-8

UBC Press
University of British Columbia
6344 Memorial Rd.
Vancouver, BC
V6T 1Z2
(604) 822-3259
Fax: 1-800-668-0821
E-mail: orders@ubcpress.ubc.ca

Mention of trade names or products does not constitute
endorsement by the authors, the editors, the publisher, or
the sponsoring agencies.

CONTENTS

SECTION THREE

SECTION FOUR

SECTION FIVE

AFFILIATIONS

P.N. Affleck
T.M. Thompson and Associates
Victoria, B.C.

L.P. Atherton
Brinkman and Associates
  Reforestation Ltd., Burnaby

J.Otchere-Boateng
B.C. Ministry of Forests, Victoria

P.G. Comeau
B.C. Ministry of Forests, Victoria

T.G. Daniels
Weyerhaeuser Canada, Armstrong

I.H. Davis
B.C. Ministry of Forests, Merritt

D. DeYoe
Ministry of Natural Resources
Sault Ste. Marie, Ont.

P.K. Diggle
B.C. Ministry of Forests, Victoria

G. Dunsworth
MacMillan Bloedel Ltd., Nanaimo

R.D. Eremko
Silvastream Forest Services, Kamloops

M.C. Feller
University of British Columbia
Vancouver

K.E. Finck
Forestry Canada, Victoria

J.W. Gates
Pacific Regeneration
  Technologies Inc., Victoria

R.N. Green
B.C. Ministry of Forests, Burnaby

M.J. Hadley
M.J. Hadley & Associates Ltd.
Vancouver

D.L. Handley
MacMillan Bloedel Ltd., Nanaimo

A.S. Harestad
Simon Fraser University, Burnaby

B.C. Hawkes
Forestry Canada, Victoria

I.B. Hedin
Forest Engineering Institute
  of Canada, Vancouver

L.J. Herring
B.C. Ministry of Forests, Prince George

R.S. Hunt
Forestry Canada,Victoria

C.M. Johnson
Pacific Regeneration
  Technologies Inc., Victoria

R.C. Jones
Formerly with Silviculture Branch
B.C. Ministry of Forests, Victoria

J.P. Kimmins
University of British Columbia
Vancouver

K. Klinka
University of British Columbia
Vancouver

E. Knight
Formerly with Silviculture Branch
B.C. Ministry of Forests, Victoria,

J.D. Konishi
B.C. Ministry of Forests, Victoria

D.P. Lavender
University of British Columbia
Vancouver

C.L. Leadem
B.C. Ministry of Forests, Victoria

D.T. Lester
University of British Columbia
Vancouver

A. Macadam
B.C. Ministry of Forests, Smithers

R.G. McMinn
Forestry Consultant, Victoria

D. Meehan
Weyerhaeuser Canada, Vavenby

D.V. Meidinger
B.C. Ministry of Forests, Victoria

W.K. Mitchell
B.C. Ministry of Forests, Victoria

G. Montgomery
G. Montgomery and Associates, Victoria

M. Newton
Oregon State University
Corvallis, Oregon

R. Parish
Forest Resource Development Agreement
Victoria

C. Pearce
Forestry Consultant, Vancouver

J.R. Revel
B.C. Ministry of Forests, Prince George

G.M. Shrimpton
B.C. Ministry of Forests, Surrey

D.G. Simpson
B.C. Ministry of Forests, Vernon

D.L. Spittlehouse
B.C. Ministry of Forests, Victoria

R.J. Stathers
Forestry Consultant, Penticton

T.P. Sullivan
Mammal Pest Management Ltd., Langley

D.W. Summers
B.C. Ministry of Forests, Victoria

J.R. Sutherland
Forestry Canada, Victoria

R. Trowbridge
B.C. Ministry of Forests, Smithers

E. Van Eerden
Pacific Regeneration
  Technologies Inc., Victoria

A. Vyse
B.C. Ministry of Forests, Kamloops

G. Weetman
University of British Columbia
Vancouver

B.M. Wikeem
B.C. Ministy of Forests, Kamloops

W.G. Williams
Pacific Regeneration
  Technologies Inc.,Prince George

R.A. Willis
Weyerhaeuser Canada, Armstrong

D.Winston
Forestry Canada, Victoria

J. Worrall
Faculty of Forestry, Vancouver

M.H. Wyeth
B.C. Ministry of Forests, Victoria

C.C. Ying
B.C. Ministry of Forests, Victoria

DEDICATION

Robert C. (Bob) Jones (1927-1989)

Bob Jones graduated in forestry from the University of British Columbia in 1950, and devoted his forestry career to the British Columbia Forest Service. From 1972 until his retirement in July 1986, Bob was Manager of Silviculture with the Silviculture Branch. During this period, Bob was instrumental in ensuring the success of various Federal/Provincial co-operative agreements and in the development of the silviculture portion of the Five Year Forest and Range Resource Program.

Bob was a gentleman and a gentle manager who led by example, who was always willing to listen to others or to provide a word of encouragement and support to new recruits and old-timers alike.

This book is dedicated to Bob Jones, who will always be appreciated for his quiet manner, his abundance of goodwill, and his love of silviculture.

FOREWORD

This edition of *Regenerating British Columbia's Forests* has been sponsored by the Forest Resource Development Agreement through the British Columbia Ministry of Forests and Forestry Canada.

This publication is meant as a reference on methods and principles for establishing new forests through both natural and artificial regeneration methods. In the last ten years there has been a great increase in knowledge for re-establishing new forests and understanding the large number of forest ecosystem types within this very diverse province of British Columbia. *Regenerating British Columbia's Forests* presents much of this new knowledge and provides the principles that must be considered when planning the establishment of new forests.

A number of leading silviculturalists, forest research scientists, and university staff in British Columbia have contributed to this book. We are grateful to all who have donated their time, efforts, and knowledge to this project. We are confident this publication can assist everyone involved in the establishment of new forests for the use and benefit of all British Columbians.

We would like to thank Dr. Denis P. Lavender of the University of British Columbia for the leadership he has shown and the intelligent advice he has provided in bringing this significant publication to press.

C.M. Johnson, R.P.F.
Former Director
Silviculture Branch

PREFACE

Regenerating British Columbia's Forests is an outgrowth of what has long been recognized as the need for a comprehensive educational text on the theory and practice behind forest renewal in British Columbia. This book organizes the experience gained from reforestation projects and scientific investigations and presents it as a guide for the practicing regeneration forester and silviculturist in the province. It is designed to be a reference that both identifies possible problems and suggests potential solutions.

Unlike the many prescriptive manuals currently available, *Regenerating British Columbia's Forests* aims first at increasing the reader's understanding of the historical, financial, physiological, and ecological aspects underlying regeneration. It then goes on to show how this knowledge can be applied in the field to ensure the successful establishment of future forests.

Section One is devoted to material that is basic to the planning and conduct of a reforestation program in British Columbia. Background is laid out in Chapter 1, which presents a brief history of forest land ownership and responsibility in the province. Chapter 2 discusses the role played by various parties in forest renewal – the public, forestry professionals, and forestry workers – and the information or training requirements of each. Chapter 3 outlines the general procedures for performing a financial analysis and applying it to forest regeneration planning. It is aimed primarily at helping the forester select the most cost-effective option at the stand level. The physiological and ecological principles governing the establishment, survival, and growth of crop tree seedlings are discussed in the remaining section chapters. Chapter 4 describes basic principles of seedling physiology and the effect of both internal cycles and environmental factors on the vigor of seedlings. The role of ecological principles in the reforestation process is discussed in Chapter 5; the application of the principles to species and stock type selection is presented in Chapter 6. Understanding these ecological aspects of forest establishment can allow the silviculturist to prepare plans that will improve natural and artificial regeneration.

Planning is a crucial but often neglected step in regeneration programs. While reforestation necessarily involves solving biological problems, poor planning is often the principal cause of regeneration failures. **Section Two** focuses on the importance of program planning and monitoring. Chapter 7 explains how regeneration plans must fit into the broader scheme of silviculture and forest plans at regional and provincial levels. It also provides practical advice on how useful plans can be developed for coordinating and evaluating the many interrelated regeneration activities that must take place before a healthy forest grows on a single block.

The first contact many foresters have with the regeneration planning process is when they are asked to prepare a pre-harvest prescription for a block. This prescription sets the course for all future activities on that piece of forest ground. Chapter 8 explains the steps involved in making a sound prescription with the available information. Even sound prescriptions are not always the right ones, however. Goals change and knowledge expands. Chapter 9 addresses monitoring, which, if carried out with care, allows foresters to assess their decisions and modify or correct their regeneration activities.

Section Three presents a range of techniques that have been developed to modify the post-harvest site. First Chapter 10 discusses natural regeneration and indicates regeneration options for each major biogeoclimatic zone in British Columbia, to give the reader a guide for selecting the most appropriate natural or artificial systems for effective reforestation. Chapters 11 to 13 describe a range of fire, mechanical/manual, and chemical site preparation techniques which will provide an optimum number and spacing of microsites favorable for establishment of natural and planted seedlings. These chapters also discuss the short- and long-term impact of site preparation upon the basic productivity of the treated area.

Section Four is concerned with the production of vigorous propagules well suited to areas to be reforested. Chapter 14 describes the potential for increased growth—as well as the risk of greater damage—represented by the use of seeds of selected species and ecotypes. Maps of seed zones of the major British Columbia timber species are also included, in addition to general guides that govern seed transfer in the province. The biological sequence involved in the flowering and fruiting of forest trees is outlined in Chapter 15. The methodology to assure vigorous seed crops are identified, harvested, processed, and stored with a minimum loss of quality is also described. Chapters 16 and 17 present the nursery scenarios necessary to produce vigorous seedlings. The final chapter examines the procedures that should be followed during plantation establishment to assure high survival and vigorous growth of planted stock, and explores direct seeding as a reforestation option.

The final section in the book (**Section Five**) is concerned with how the impact of non-crop plants, disease organisms, insects, and animal clipping or browsing on crop seedlings and saplings can be minimized. Although many plantations have been well established, they can still be lost through the failure of proper maintenance schedules. Chapters 19 to 22 provide diagnostic guides to help the reader identify which, if any, destructive agents are present in a given plantation, and what methods are necessary to prevent reduction in seedling growth and survival.

ACKNOWLEDGMENTS

Regenerating British Columbia's Forests has been styled after the landmark publication *Regenerating Oregon's Forests*, by B.C. Cleary, R.D. Greaves, and R.K. Hermann (editors) and the Oregon State University, Extension Service. Although the content, organization and presentation of this book differs, we gratefully acknowledge the role model provided by *Regenerating Oregon's Forests*.

This book has been three years in the making. During this time, many people have contributed with planning and coordination, by reviewing chapters, or by providing information or technical assistance. George Krumlik of the Ministry of Forests, Research Branch and a former FRDA Extension, Demonstration, Research and Development (E, D,R & D) chairperson, coordinated the efforts of the editorial committee until February, 1989. Margot Spence, a FRDA contractor with the Ministry of Forests, Research Branch, inherited the coordinator role from George and was responsible for securing a complete first draft from the busy and hard-to-pin-down chapter authors.

Much of the information on cone crop monitoring, seed crop evaluation, and post-harvest handling in Chapter 15 was provided by Heather Rooke of the Ministry of Forests, Surrey Seed Centre. Dirk Brinkman of Brinkman and Associates and Peter Saunders of University of British Columbia Research Forest in Maple Ridge provided material included in Chapter 18.

Chapter drafts were revised at each review stage and on numerous other occasions during the past nine months. Susan Bannerman, Elizabeth Nutting and Lana Knapp of T.D. Mock and Associates carried out this important work with care and diligence. Laurice Mock and Linda Patterson of T.D. Mock & Associates proofread the manuscript.

Throughout production, numerous citations were checked for accuracy and completeness. This service was skillfully and cheerfully provided by Susan Barker, Roxanne Smith, and Denise Van Ryswyk of the B.C. Ministry of Forests Library. Most figures were prepared by Susan Bowen and Dave Butcher of T.D. Mock & Associates. Jennifer Tan of the Forest Engineering Research Institute of Canada (FERIC) illustrated the mechanical site preparation implements shown in Chapter 12. Paul Nystedt of the Ministry of Forests, Research Branch was most helpful in locating and redrawing a number of figures.

A special thank you is extended to Susan Bowen who designed and typeset the book and has worked tirelessly through many overtime hours accommodating revisions and last minute changes.

Special appreciation is extended to Tim Mock of T.D. Mock & Associates, production manager for the book. Despite the problems, the frustrations, and the rewrites, Tim's enthusiasm and commitment to the project never faltered. His experience and expertise has been a considerable help in bringing the manuscript to publication.

D.P.L. & R.P

SECTION ONE

1

REFORESTATION IN BRITISH COLUMBIA: A BRIEF HISTORY

E. Knight

British Columbia's reforestation policies and programs have evolved through four distinct stages, each reflecting the political view of forest management at the time.

In the pioneer period, dating from the earliest European settlement up to passage of the first Forest Act in 1912, timber was sold and cutting rights were granted without any regard for forest regeneration. During a transition period between 1912 and 1947, forest administration was authorized by the 1912 Forest Act and amendments under the direction of a provincial Forest Branch. The Forest Act also designated Crown lands as forest reserves to ensure the continuous production of timber. This legislation showed some concern with forest regeneration.

In the third stage, from 1947 to 1978, regulations were developed to restrict the cut from designated areas to estimated sustainable yields. This marked the beginning of the forestry industry. In the era since 1979, the tenure system has been overhauled to reflect the decision that forest regeneration after logging is the harvester's responsibility. According to the new policy, any system of logging that fails to provide for adequate regeneration is unacceptable to the public interest and will not be tolerated.

THE PIONEER PERIOD, PRE-1912

The Land Ordinance of 1865 introduced the principle that the Province should retain ownership and control of the forest land, granting only the right to cut timber. This policy has continued to the present, with the result that only 5% of the productive forest land in British Columbia is held privately.

The relative merits of the policy have been reviewed from time to time, most recently by the Royal Commission on Forest Resources, P.H. Pearse, Commissioner. In his 1976 report, "Timber Rights and Forest Policy," Pearse recommended that there be "no change in the general policy of retaining Crown title to unalienated forest lands." The significance of this policy to forest regeneration is that public ownership of forest land requires the government to accept direct responsibility for reforestation. The decision to make an investment in reforestation thus becomes political, and reflects the current attitudes and policy preferences of the majority. During the pioneer period, the forest resource was considered to be limitless. The forests were a resource to be exploited as a source of public revenue and employment. Forest regeneration was thought to be a naturally occurring phenomenon that would somehow happen on its own. Without a basis of scientific knowledge, there was no reason to question the logic of policies that treated the forests as a "cut out and move on" resource.

The end of the pioneer period was preceded by the first of a succession of Royal Commissions of Inquiry into Forest Policy (Table 1.1). The 1909-10 commission chaired by F.J. Fulton was appointed because of concern with the longer term implications of the then current timber alienation policy. The final report of that Royal Commission (the Fulton Report) led to the passage of the first Forest Act in 1912.

THE TRANSITION PERIOD, 1912-47

The 1912 Forest Act established a Forest Branch (later renamed the Forest Service in 1945). Its responsibilities included conservation of existing forests, reforestation, and prevention of forest fires. As well, it provided for the establishment of forest reserves, which were placed under the control and management of the forestry minister. Through a series of amendments to the Forest Act between 1923 and 1927, the Forest Reserve Account was set up to fund the development and replanting of forest reserves.

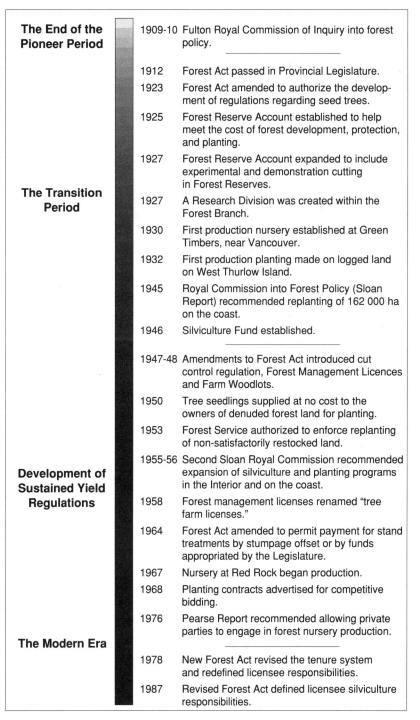

The End of the Pioneer Period	1909-10	Fulton Royal Commission of Inquiry into forest policy.
	1912	Forest Act passed in Provincial Legislature.
	1923	Forest Act amended to authorize the development of regulations regarding seed trees.
	1925	Forest Reserve Account established to help meet the cost of forest development, protection, and planting.
	1927	Forest Reserve Account expanded to include experimental and demonstration cutting in Forest Reserves.
The Transition Period	1927	A Research Division was created within the Forest Branch.
	1930	First production nursery established at Green Timbers, near Vancouver.
	1932	First production planting made on logged land on West Thurlow Island.
	1945	Royal Commission into Forest Policy (Sloan Report) recommended replanting of 162 000 ha on the coast.
	1946	Silviculture Fund established.
	1947-48	Amendments to Forest Act introduced cut control regulation, Forest Management Licences and Farm Woodlots.
	1950	Tree seedlings supplied at no cost to the owners of denuded forest land for planting.
	1953	Forest Service authorized to enforce replanting of non-satisfactorily restocked land.
Development of Sustained Yield Regulations	1955-56	Second Sloan Royal Commission recommended expansion of silviculture and planting programs in the Interior and on the coast.
	1958	Forest management licenses renamed "tree farm licenses."
	1964	Forest Act amended to permit payment for stand treatments by stumpage offset or by funds appropriated by the Legislature.
	1967	Nursery at Red Rock began production.
	1968	Planting contracts advertised for competitive bidding.
	1976	Pearse Report recommended allowing private parties to engage in forest nursery production.
The Modern Era	1978	New Forest Act revised the tenure system and redefined licensee responsibilities.
	1987	Revised Forest Act defined licensee silviculture responsibilities.

TABLE 1.1. Chronology of significant dates and events in reforestation history in British Columbia.

Because of the large trees and generally difficult topography on the coast, the logging method used there during this period was predominantly high lead. It was devastation logging, destroying the understory together with any trees considered unmerchantable. The standard of utilization was also sufficiently low that, after logging was completed, logging slash could impede natural regeneration and create a long-lasting fire hazard.

BCARS Photo H99204

On July 5, 1938, a spark from a yarding engine ignited the Campbell River Fire. It burned 30 184 ha of forest land from Campbell River to Courtenay. In spring 1939, the largest reforestation program in the province's history began, with 763 550 seedlings planted on more than 400 ha of provincial forest.

In the Interior, topography and tree size allowed a variety of logging methods including some selective logging. However, although logging was often selective and included only stems larger than a specified diameter of the preferred species, no attention was paid to spacing or forest regeneration. After logging was finished, forest lands were left with a poorly spaced residual stand made up mainly of the less commercially attractive species.

There is no evidence to suggest that the public was particularly concerned about the way their forest resource was being treated. Except for fire losses, the forests of the Interior were still largely untouched. Timber harvest on the coast was remote from the settled areas and, in most cases, visible only to those directly involved in the operations. The pressure to encourage more responsible forest management came from the technical forestry staff employed in the Forest Branch and from the larger forest industry companies. In 1930, the first production nursery was established at Green Timbers, near Vancouver. With Douglas-fir stock from that nursery, the first production planting was made in 1932 on logged land on West Thurlow Island.

Although throughout this period provincial forest policy was clearly concerned with preserving the forest resource, very little real progress was made beyond the development of a legislative framework. Still missing was the assurance of adequate funding over the long term to meet research and staffing requirements. In the 1937 Forest Branch report, "Forest Resources of British Columbia," author F.D. Mulholland bluntly described the impact of the years of neglect: "Until recently public indifference to forestry would almost lead one to believe that America has been regarded as a place for temporary residence while its treasures were rifled as quickly as possible; that there would always be somewhere else for the 'pioneers' to go, leaving a trail of devastated forests behind them." He continued: "In British Columbia it has been evident for some time that the forests with protection only will not continue indefinitely to support the great industries already established, to say nothing of the increased production which is now being actively planned. It is time to institute active measures providing for more successful reforestation."

This report, issued while the provincial economy remained crushed by the Great Depression, had no immediate impact. Nevertheless, its publication was a significant step toward developing the political will that led the provincial government (when no doubt they were also anticipating post-Second World War expansion) to initiate the second Royal Commission into Forest Policy, with Hon. G. McG. Sloan as Commissioner.

The report of that commission (the Sloan Report 1945) was the catalyst for subsequent amendments to the forest act. The 1946 amendment established the Silviculture Fund, into which went an amount, earned from each sale of Crown timber in the Interior, estimated to be necessary to reduce the hazard created or to ensure the growth of a second forest crop. The 1947 and 1948 amendments introduced a period of cut control regulation.

DEVELOPMENT OF THE SUSTAINED YIELD REGULATION, 1947-78

Amendments to the Forest Act in 1947 and 1948 introduced a period of cut control regulation. The forest policy objective was to achieve sustained yields of commercially usable wood from defined forest areas.

For the first time, both private forest land owners and the forest industry were to have a role through the new Forest Management Licence and Farm Woodlot Licence tenure. The new policy required a change in the timber sales policy, from unrestricted sale with no limit on the rate of cutting and only incidental concern with regeneration, to a planned and regulated timber sales program with a controlled annual and periodic rate of cutting and assured regeneration. This signalled the beginning of an enhanced commitment to forest regeneration.

The Sloan Report of 1945 had estimated that 162 000 ha of the 405 000 ha of not satisfactorily stocked productive forest land on the coast could be economically replanted. It also recommended that those lands be planted at the earliest possible date — certainly within 25 years. The Commissioner did not consider it necessary to replant any of the estimated 7.7 million ha of productive forest land not satisfactorily restocked in the Interior because, "Interior increment is exceeding depletion and, assuming fire-protection, the situation is not as critical there as on the Coast." The Forest Service accepted that reasoning and nursery capacity was expanded on the coast in 1947, with the first production coming from the Duncan nursery. An experimental nursery was established for the Interior East Kootenay region, but was abandoned after a few years.

To encourage the replanting of denuded privately owned forest land on the coast, the Forest Act was amended in 1950 so that tree seedlings could be supplied at no cost to the owners for planting on such land. In 1953, the Forest Service was authorized to examine denuded private forest land and to require the planting of areas found to be not satisfactorily stocked. This situation applied to private forest land where the owners had not opted to include their lands in the tree farm licence tenure or to elect classification as a tree farm.

For logging operations in the Interior, the emphasis was on the application of silviculture systems that would not make planting necessary after logging.

BCARS Photo H99203

The Sayward Forest District in June 1964, looking across John Hart Lake 25 years after the area was planted.

Such systems protected the understory, maintained a healthy, well-spaced residual stand, or left a satisfactory seed source and suitable seedbed after logging.

Between 1947 and 1954, public concern heightened over the quality of forest management both on the coast and in the Interior. The government responded in 1955 by again appointing Hon. G. McG. Sloan to examine the forest resource. In his report a year later, Commissioner Sloan recommended a major expansion in the silviculture and planting programs. In particular, he rejected the argument that regeneration by planting could not be economic in the Interior of the province: "We are trustees of our forest wealth and it seems to me that if the Government continues to be influenced unduly by the profit motive, it is inevitable we will pass on to future generations an impaired and diminished forest resource." As a result of the Commissioner's recommendations, government funding for reforestation increased. Forest tree seedling nurseries were expanded, a seed extraction plant was established at the Duncan nursery, and the seed registration program was started.

With the cooperation of foresters employed by companies holding forest management licences (renamed "Tree Farm Licences" by an amendment in 1958), the Plus Tree Board was organized as the first step toward the production of genetically improved seed. In addition, pilot scale plantations were established in the Interior and small nurseries were started at Ranger Stations in the central Interior, with technical staff supplied from headquarters.

Reforestation by planting became an option in the Interior in the 1960's, initially using seedlings grown at Forest Service nurseries on the coast. The nursery at Red Rock, close to Prince George, began production in 1967, supplying seedlings for planting in the region. At the same time, nurseries already established on the coast were expanded to supply seedlings for the Interior planting program.

Planting was just one option. Other silvicultural systems also remained in widespread use in the Interior, notably strip clearcutting with mechanical scarification in spruce-balsam types and drag scarification in lodgepole pine stands. To ensure that payment would not be made before the work was done, the Forest Act was amended in 1964 to allow payment for silvicultural treatments either by an offset against stumpage or by payment from funds appropriated by the Legislature. The licensee was required to pay full stumpage as the timber was cut, being compensated only after the post-logging treatment had been satisfactorily completed. Payment by stumpage offset was later restricted by an internal policy directive, because it involved the use of funding that had not been specifically appropriated by the Legislature.

By 1968, the Forest Service planting program had increased so much that it could no longer be accomplished totally in-service. Planting contracts were advertised for competitive bidding, with the work subject to Forest Service quality control. This initiative marked the beginning of a silviculture or forestry industry as distinct from a forest industry in British Columbia.

The holders of Tree Farm Licences were required to take on the responsibility for forest regeneration as a condition of the licence. The costs of regeneration were recovered through reduced stumpage payments. Although that form of tenure had become a political liability in the early 1950's (with no new applications being processed after the 1956 Sloan Report), the Forest Service developed a new form of timber sale in 1969. The Timber Sale Harvesting Licence required that the holder become involved in reforestation on areas approved for harvest. The licensee was compensated on the same "payment by reduced stumpage" basis that was applied to the tree farm licence tenure.

Planting was not a requirement for licensees cutting on Crown land under other tenures. That continued to be a Forest Service responsibility. In 1972, however, the Forest Act was amended such that the holders of the other tenures could also be held responsible for regeneration. Although this requirement was never administered in this period (because the Regulations were never made), the 1972 amendment showed the direction in which the government was intending to move, presumably in response to public concern.

In June 1975, the government appointed P. H. Pearse to inquire into matters relating to forest policy in the province, including, "The provisions for conservation, management, utilization, protection and development of the forest resources allocated." The report of that Commission (the Pearse Report 1976) was followed by an external policy review process that climaxed with the passage by the Legislature in 1978 of a new Forest Act.

THE MODERN ERA, 1978-PRESENT

The new Act completely overhauled the tenure system and redefined licensee responsibilities. One new tenure was created, the Forest Licence, which replaced the Timber Sale Harvesting Licence that the Forest Service had developed to give the forest industry an opportunity to be involved in forest management. The Forest Licence requires the holder to submit a management and working plan — which includes a regeneration commitment — prepared by a professional forester. Such a commitment is also called for under the Timber Licence and the Tree Farm Licence. The Timber Sale Licence was retained to be small scale and short term, and is the only tenure that does not require a regeneration commitment by the licensee. Regeneration on those licences was carried out by the Forest Service until 1987.

From 1978 to 1987, the cost of basic silviculture work carried out by the licensee was credited against their stumpage payable. A major change to the Forest Act in 1987, transferred the cost of basic silviculture to the holders of major licenses. On Timber Sale Licences the Crown continues to carry out the silviculture work with funding from the Small Business Forest Enterprise Account.

Other significant changes to the Forest Act in 1987 include the requirement that the holder of a major licence submit a pre-harvest silviculture prescription (PHSP) for every site. The PHSP, prepared by a professional forester, is the licensee's contract with the Ministry of Forest to ensure that a free growing crop of trees will be established after harvesting. The PHSP requirement reflects an increase in stewardship which is characteristic of the Modern Era of forest management.

The Pearse Report had recommended that the government consider allowing private parties to engage in forest nursery production. That has been done. Private forest nurseries now compete to supply tree seedlings grown from seed collected for and registered by the Forest Service. In 1988, a large part of the nursery capacity built up by the Forest Service was sold to private parties. The combined public and private nursery capacity in 1988 exceeded 200 million seedlings.

The changes in forest administration made since the Pearse Report, combined with the increased nursery capacity, should secure satisfactory regeneration of Crown forest land as it is logged. The regeneration of those denuded lands that pre-dated the new tenure system — the backlog — is being worked on with funds voted for that purpose by the Province and through a cost-shared program under the Forest Resource Development Agreement (1985-90) with the federal government.

The uncertainty about "who pays" that goes back to the Land Ordinance of 1865 now seems to have been resolved. The cost of regeneration is a part of the cost of logging, something that has to be taken into account when the price for standing timber is being determined. In the final analysis, the provincial government, as the owner of the resource, pays the cost by accepting a lower price for its timber than it could otherwise demand. However, this also secures regeneration at a relatively low cost, by giving the forest industry the incentive to use silviculture systems that are making planting less costly or even unnecessary.

Forestry is an art born of necessity, as opposed to arts of convenience and of pleasure. Only when a reduction in the natural supplies of forest products under the demands of civilization, necessitates a husbanding of supplies or necessitates the application of art or skill or knowledge in securing a reproduction, or when unfavorable conditions of soil or climate induced by forest destruction make themselves felt does the art of forestry make its appearance. Hence its beginnings occur at different times and its development proceeds at different paces.

History of Forestry
B.E. Fernow
Dean, Faculty of Forestry
University of Toronto, 1911

PEOPLE: THE VITAL RESOURCE

2

R.C. Jones

People—the public, politicians, forestry professionals, and field workers—play a significant and interractive role in forest renewal.

In the last few years, public demand has grown for meaningful involvement in management decisions that affect the forest resource. As a result, forestry conduct is now subject to major challenges from both public and private interest groups. Although politicians are the ultimate decision makers, they respond to "people power." Sustained, concerted public pressure can bring about stability or change in policies and programs. The forestry professional's response to the actions of these various decision-making groups must be threefold: to respect the demands for public participation, to establish credibility with the public, and to ensure that important information is presented to the public clearly and accurately. Once management descisions are made, it is then the skilled workforce in the silviculture industry that ensures the decisions are carried out successfully.

THE ROLE OF THE PUBLIC IN FOREST RENEWAL

A study conducted in 1986 to assess public perception about forestry/environmental issues in the province showed that the public was greatly concerned about how well forestry management practices were being handled in British Columbia (Decima Research Ltd. 1986). The public recognized the importance of the forestry sector to the provincial economy, but also supported the need for "environmentally sensitive" measures in forest practices. They rated reforestation as the highest priority for industry and government.

The resulting political awareness of reforestation needs, coupled with the growing knowledge amongst forestry professionals of how to address the problem, has led to an expanding silviculture program in British Columbia over the last decade.

Forest Land Ownership and Responsibility

Provincial responsibility

Under the Canadian Constitution, management of forest resources is vested with the provinces. In British Columbia, legislation for managing forest and range is contained in three provincial acts: the Ministry of Forests Act, the Forest Act, and the Range Act. The area of productive forest land in British Columbia is approximately 43 million hectares. This total excludes 6

TABLE 2.1. Allowable cut by tenure in British Columbia, as of March 31, 1989

Tenure	Volume (1000's m³)	%
Tree Farm Licence (TFL)	18 584	25.3
Woodlot Licence (WLL)	448	0.6
Forest Licence[a]	42 530	57.9
Timber Sale Licence[b]	9 208	12.5
Timber Sale Licence (Major)	461	0.6
Forest Service Reserve	662	0.9
Pulpwood Agreements	1 624	2.2
Total	73 517	100.0

[a] Forest Licence: a long-term, volume-based tenure which includes a regeneration commitment. Includes non-replaceable Forest Licences.

[b] Small Business Program. Includes non-replaceable Timber Sale Licences.

million hectares that are dedicated to parks and ecological reserves. Of the 43 million hectares only 22 million are available for forest management. The balance contains areas of inoperable forest sites or problem forest types. Of that 22 million, 3.19 million ha are within Tree Farm Licences (TFL's) — a long-term, area-based tenure which can include a mix of the private and Crown lands or be solely Crown lands. Recent legislation has also allowed smaller area-based tenures, in the form of over 400 Woodlot Licences (WLL's) which average about 300 ha in size.

The allowable annual cut for British Columbia is 74 million m³. Volumes committed by tenure to March 31, 1989, are shown in Table 2.1.

Industry responsibility

Harvesting rights on provincial Crown lands are issued under a number of tenures, either as area-based (in the case of TFL's and WLL's) or volume-based (for Forest Licences, Timber Sale Licences, and Special Licences in Timber Supply Areas [TSA's]). Licensees are committed to a wide range of responsibilities according to the type of tenure and terms of the Licence Agreement. Typically, they must submit management and working plans, development plans, cutting permits, and pre-harvesting silviculture prescriptions.

Recent amendments to the Forest Act and Silviculture Regulations require the holders of all Major Licences to be fully responsible for carrying out basic silviculture on areas where harvesting began after September 30, 1987. In meeting the requirement to establish a "free growing" stand at their expense, licensees must follow an approved pre-harvest silviculture prescription (see Chapter 8).

Federal responsibility

Forestry matters in the federal government are primarily the responsibility of Forestry Canada (formerly the Canadian Forestry Service). Among its key roles are:

- to develop and coordinate national forest policy;
- to administer forest development agreements negotiated with the provinces;
- to undertake and support research, development, and technology transfer;
- to monitor disease and insect pests;
- to promote public awareness; and
- to promote employment, training, and educational opportunities in the forest sector.

Federal/provincial forestry agreements

Cooperative federal/provincial support for silviculture in British Columbia has been significant during the 1980's. The 5-year Intensive Forest Management Subsidiary Agreement (1980-85) devoted $50 million to backlog reforestation and intensive silviculture treatments on provincial Crown lands. It was extended for a year, and then the Forest Resource Development Agreement (FRDA) followed in 1985. This 5-year, $300 million agreement (1985-90) has involved three main programs:

1. Backlog Reforestation ($199.5 million)
2. Intensive Forest Management ($86.0 million)
3. Implementation, Communication, Evaluation ($14.5 million)

A significant component, $27 million, has been directed to Extension, Demonstration, Research and Development.

The major goals of FRDA were to rehabilitate 150 000 ha of backlog not satisfactorily restocked lands (NSR) including the planting of 180 million seedlings and surveying of 250 000 ha; to juvenile space and fertilize 66 700 ha; and to conduct other silvicultural treatments on 36 000 ha.

Public Access to Information

Information on forestry matters is available from many sources in government and other agencies and organizations. As well, the Forest Service has several policies and procedures to ensure there is public involvement in forestry issues. Much of the problem for any concerned citizen, therefore, is not getting access to information; it is understanding what the "real" facts are from the often conflicting sources and complicated reports and analyses available. The forestry sector's goal must be to ensure that a variety of information is disseminated through a range of reliable outlets. If the public has a reasonable understanding of how the forests are being managed, it will be able to make balanced judgments about resource use.

The role and efficiency of public involvement are sometimes questioned. Concern has been voiced that the emergence of skilled individuals who can eloquently argue public positions has lessened the opportunity for ordinary citizens to participate, and that "loud" pressure groups can persuade politicians to make popular decisions contrary to sound technical advice. Nevertheless, the public has come to expect to participate in forest management planning at various levels. Obviously a well-informed public is a valuable asset to the forestry sector, helping to keep elected representatives aware of public sentiment and influencing political decisions.

The Forest Service and Public Participation

The Ministry of Forests Act requires that information on program goals and achievements be reported at regular intervals. In compliance with this, the Forest Service publishes three important documents concerning its management of forests on provincial Crown lands:

1. A Forest and Range Resource Analysis, updated periodically, describes in detail the resource's condition, management, and future uses. This analysis enables the government to set overall priorities and long-term objectives.
2. A 5-Year Forest and Range Resource Program, prepared and presented annually to the legislature, sets schedules, methods, and priorities for resource management and improvement. This program, which presents the

government's resource management intentions, describes the silviculture goals for various treatments. The most recent 5-year program submitted is for the period 1988-93.

3. An annual report reviews the use and management of the resource, and monitors the performance of the Forest Service in its 5-year program.

Other procedures in the Forest Service are also aimed at ensuring information about forestry matters is widely and easily available to the public. For example:

- Revisions to the Forest Act and Silviculture Regulations require the preparation of a Pre-Harvest Silviculture Prescription (PHSP) and notice of the silviculture prescription must be advertized in the Provincial Gazette and a local paper at least 7 weeks before harvesting begins.

- Forest service policy requires that managers and technical staff at all levels of the Forest Service be, as part of their regular work assignment, responsible for communicating with groups and agencies outside the Service.

- Senior management positions at all levels of the Forest Service carry formal responsibility for ensuring that appropriate public involvement activities are carried out.

The public is thus provided with several opportunities to evaluate and comment on the contents of new or revised plans for Timber Supply Areas (TSA's). They have access to the TSA data and reports generated by the Forest Service; they can be involved in identifying resource issues within a TSA that have a bearing on forest and range rates of harvest; and they can comment on the draft final plan before it is implemented and the allowable annual cut for the TSA is set.

As well, all holders and approved applicants of TFL's must provide for public review of their 5-Year Management and Working Plans.

Other public advisory agencies and organizations

In addition to the government bodies that provide information and opportunities for public involvement, several other professional and public interest organizations also prepare and disseminate forestry information. These include:

- B.C. Forestry Association (BCFA)

- Canadian Institute of Forestry (CIF)

- Association of B.C. Professional Foresters (ABCPF)

- Industry associations such as the Council of Forest Industries (COFI), the Northern Interior Lumber Manufacturer's Sector (COFI - NILS), the Cariboo Lumber Manufacturer's Association (CLMA), and the Interior Lumber Manufacturer's Association (ILMA)

Summary of Regular Forestry Information Publications	
Publication	**Organization**
B.C. Professional Forester	Association of Professional Foresters
Forestry Chronicle	Canadian Institute of Forestry
Forest Report	B.C. Ministry of Forests
Information Forestry	Forestry Canada
Renewal Solutions	Forestry Canada/B.C. Ministry of Forests FRDA
Silviculture	McLean Hunter Ltd.
Screef	Pacific Reforestation Workers Association
Update	B.C. Forestry Association
WSCA News	Western Silviculture Contractors Association

THE ROLE OF THE PROFESSIONAL AND TECHNICAL WORKFORCE IN FOREST RENEWAL

Renewing and tending the forests is a complex process. It involves professional and technical personnel, specialists from a wide range of allied science disciplines, and forestry workers. The heightened involvement of well-organized interest groups in challenging "professional" decisions and competency also means that forestry personnel must develop the skills and specialized knowledge to address public concerns. At the same time, they must recognize the limits of their expertise and know when to seek specialist consultation in complex situations.

Recent provincial legislation requiring professional foresters to prepare and implement silviculture prescriptions places the foresters' performance, legitimacy, and accountability under closer scrutiny than ever before. Forestry professionals must manage the forest in an arena of mounting challenges to forestry decisions from other resource users and the general public.

The Forest Service employs nearly 800 people in the silviculture program. Of these, approximately 150 are in professional positions and the balance are in forest technical, other technical, and clerical positions.

About one-third of the approximately 1700 Association of British Columbia Professional Foresters are employed by industry and another third by the provincial government.

The Association of Applied Science Technologists and Technicians has over 450 members registered as Forest Technologists. This number, it estimates, represents only one-fifth to one-quarter of all graduates eligible for registration.

Educational Opportunities

University and technical colleges

The University of British Columbia has the only forestry degree granting program in the province. The Faculty offers 4-year programs leading to a Bachelor of Science in Forestry (B.S.F.) (Forest Resources Management or Forest Harvesting) or a B.Sc. (Forest Sciences or Wood Science and Industry), as well as programs leading to M.Sc., M.A.Sc., M.F., and Ph.D. degrees in most fields of Forest and Wood Sciences.

Four colleges offer diploma programs in forest technology; two also offer horticulture programs in nursery culture.

The British Columbia Institute for Technology in Burnaby has a 2-year program in forest resource technology and a post-diploma/degree program in natural resources management.

Malaspina College in Nanaimo, Selkirk College in Castlegar, and the College of New Caledonia in Prince George also offer similar 2-year forest technology programs.

Advanced educational opportunities

Numerous opportunities are available to foresters in British Columbia who want to enhance their competence in silviculture:

Silviculture Institute of British Columbia   Patterned after the U.S. Forest Service Certified Silviculturist Program, the Institute offers professional foresters (from government, industry, and consulting) advanced education in silviculture, to help them develop and refine their ability in making sound silvicultural prescriptions.

Continuing Education   A number of agencies, institutions, and organizations regularly offer courses around the province. The Continuing Education Committee of the Professional Foresters Association often sponsors or assists in presenting these courses and workshops. The University of British Columbia's Guided Independent Study also offers a wide range of university level forestry courses by correspondence.

Silviculture Committees   Three Silviculture Committees in the province provide a forum for field practitioners from all agencies to meet and study solutions to operational and technical facets of silviculture. They include the Coastal Silviculture Committee (CSC), the Southern Interior Silviculture Committee (SISCO), and the Northern Silviculture Committee (NSC).

FRDA - Extension and Demonstration   Through three technical advisory committees and the Nursery Technical Committee, the Extension and Demonstration component of FRDA is aimed at ensuring that research results are presented to field practitioners and program branches responsible for standards and procedures. This is accomplished through courses, seminars, workshops, videos, and research publications.

Professional and Technical Registration Requirements

Professional   The Foresters Act (1979) requires that anyone practising professional forestry in British Columbia be registered through the Association of British Columbia Professional Foresters. Upon registration, a member is entitled to use the title of Registered Professional Forester (RPF).

Certain forestry documents can be signed and sealed only by an RPF.

Technical   The Applied Science Technologists and Technicians Act of 1985 established a registering body for technicians and technologists in British Columbia. (A certified technician is entitled to use the title A. Sct. or C. Tech.) Fourteen disciplines are recognized, including Forest Resources. The membership in the organization is 5000, of which 465 are in the Forest Resource category.

Professional biologists

The Association of Professional Biologists is an organization of Registered Professional Biologists (RPBio) under the Societies Act. The minimum academic requirement for an RPBio is a B.Sc. degree, and the registrant must have worked at the professional level in research, education, or management for at least 3 years.

The Association's role is to ensure high standards of professional conduct among its members; to advise government on biological issues; to promote sound management of biological resources; and to advise educational institutions on biology curricula.

Special certification

The Pesticide Control Act and regulations of British Columbia, administered by the B.C. Ministry of Environment, Pesticide Control Branch, apply to the sale, transportation, preparation, application, and disposal of pesticides.

A pesticide use permit is required when restricted commercial or domestic schedule pesticides are applied for forestry use on public or private lands. Any individual or company that provides a service in applying pesticides must have a valid service licence, and the licenced operator must have one or more employees certified as applicators.

Forestry is a designated applicator category and includes three applicator subcategories:

- Forestry General (for herbicides and insecticides)
- Forest Nursery (for production of planting stock)
- Forestry, tree injection, hack and squirt, etc.

The Pesticide Control Branch is responsible for administering and certifying various categories of applicators through an examination. A certificate is currently granted for 1 year to a candidate achieving 60-74% in the examination, and 5 years for those who achieve over 74%. Several courses are given throughout the province to assist prospective applicants in preparing for the exam, but attendance is not a prerequisite to writing it.

Silviculture surveyor

The Forest Service offers a silviculture surveying course for foresters, technicians, and contractors, aimed at ensuring that everybody involved understands the basis of silviculture surveys and their linkage with other systems, and appreciates their role in decision-making.

Those who successfully pass the course exam are certified with the Silviculture Branch, Ministry of Forests, as technically competent in the basics of silviculture surveys and their use. Ministry Silviculture Survey contracts stipulate that each crew engaged in the contract shall have at least one person who is a certified silviculture surveyor. However, certification is not mandatory for licensee surveys, unless the project is funded by the Forest Service.

THE ROLE OF FORESTRY WORKERS IN FOREST RENEWAL

Most silvicultural activities are highly labor-intensive, requiring considerable physical effort, often under adverse climatic and terrain conditions. Since the early 1970's, most field silviculture activities — such as planting, spacing, cone collecting, and other tending treatments — have been carried out by silviculture contractors. More recently, silviculture surveys and site preparation projects have also been contracted out. Forest Service information shows that over 800 contractors conduct a variety of silviculture activities in the province.

Until 1988, most contracts conducted on Crown land were issued under a competitive bid system. Since forest companies are now no longer reimbursed for silvicultural activities on Crown lands, the choice of contractors is at the full discretion of the companies. Forest Service contracts issued for work on Crown land still use the competitive bid system.

Of the almost 12 000 people employed in the silviculture industry in British Columbia, the overwhelming majority are planters. The following discussion focuses on the general working conditions of this workforce in the province.

"Working between two variables — speed and precision — there's only motion. This is all you'll ever know, all you'll ever hold: this shovel."

In a Canvas Tent, Robert MacLean

Characteristics of the Tree Planting Workforce

Contractor crews range from 35 to 400 workers, about half of whom are either university students or graduates. One-third to one-half are estimated to have at least three seasons of experience. Most contracts are single activity, short duration, with a typical field season lasting 13-19 weeks. Recent ergonomic studies conducted by Drs. Tom Smith and Eric Bannister of Simon Fraser University show that tree planting requires intensive physical exertion and sustained elevated work rates. As a consequence, a significant number of planters experience planters "burn out."

Until recently, camp conditions were generally poor. They have improved significantly since the Ministries of Health and Forests implemented Camp Standards. Additional improvements are still required, however, including dry floors, sanitary kitchens, clothes drying areas, and better personal hygiene facilities. Because access to project worksites often involves transport over difficult terrain, better vehicle safety checks are also needed to ensure compliance with standards.

Most planters are paid on a piece rate basis (per planted tree or per hectare) — a method of payment that they well accept. Nearly 40% are also covered by some form of bonus system. Workers are not usually compensated for time lost because of travel, snow, and camp setup and dismantling.

Future prospects

Much has to be done to make the forest worker's job a more attractive proposition as a full-time vocation. The formation of the Silviculture Joint Adjustment Committee early in 1987, with representation from contractors, workers, government, and industry, heralds a more comprehensive approach to human resource issues in the industry. Efforts are continuing, aimed at improving camp facilities, developing proper hire agreements with employment conditions clearly spelled out, improving training for workers and supervisors, and improving worker safety. Research is examining the physical demands of planting and ways of mitigating fatigue and reducing health problems (T.J. Smith 1987).

At the same time, opportunities are being investigated for changing contracts from short-term single activity to multi-year single activity or multi-year multi-activity, to extend the annual employment period and provide greater business stability to the contracting community.

The Silviculture Joint Adjustment Committee's recommendations envisage a very different type of workforce — one with longer periods of employment, more career-oriented workers, increases in knowledge and skill level, and greater local employment.

Associations and Training Opportunities for Forestry Workers

Pacific Reforestation Workers Association (PRWA)
The PRWA was registered as a society in 1979, with members drawn from workers in the silviculture industry, primarily in planting. Its main purpose is to represent the interests of workers and to act on their common concerns.

Western Silviculture Contractors Association (WSCA)
The WSCA was formed in 1981 to improve the standards of conduct in the contracting industry. An Ethics Committee has been established to review all complaints about the conduct of any member. Chapters of the WSCA operate in each of the six forest regions of the province.

B.C. Ministry of Forests

FIGURE 2.1. Planters make up the overwhelming majority of the almost 12 000 people employed in the silviculture industry in British Columbia.

Forest Worker Training

Survey results indicate that most contractors prefer to train inexperienced workers on the job, rather than hire those trained by other contractors or institutions. Because of the competitive nature of the industry, however, contractors acknowledge that the quality and amount of on-the-job training is not high. With the continuing increase in the scope and size of the silviculture program, the need for a greater number of acceptable outside training facilities will also grow in the coming years. Credible training programs developed in cooperation with contractors and experienced workers are needed to develop a stable workforce. Currently the Ministry of Advanced Education and Job Training offers only two courses for forestry crew persons and tree planters.

An industry aim in British Columbia is to stabilize this workforce by developing occupational satisfaction among workers involved in forest renewal. Together, these people — a well-informed and active public, responsive politicians, and skilled forestry professionals and field workers — are working to ensure the regeneration of our forests.

3 FINANCIAL EVALUATION OF REGENERATION ACTIVITIES

R.A. Willis and P.N. Affleck

Practicing foresters are often faced with a confusing number of management opportunities and conflicts that complicate the decision-making process. One approach that can help them make better decisions is financial analysis. This chapter describes general procedures for performing financial analysis and applying it to forest regeneration planning. The primary focus is on analysis of options at the stand level. The advantage of evaluation at this level is that where strong local data are lacking, personal judgment and observation can usually fill information gaps, allowing the objective analysis of alternatives.

Financial analysis is concerned with monetary factors. Economic analysis has a much larger context, in that it includes non-market values and social impacts as well as financial considerations. For the reader interested in doing so, the general procedure described in this chapter can be expanded and used for economic analysis. Gunter and Haney (1984) provide an in-depth review of forestry investment analysis.

TYPES OF REGENERATION DECISIONS

In making regeneration decisions, the forester must select options from among a number of different projects, various levels of treatment within a project, and various treatments within a management regime for an area. To aid the decision-making process, these options can be grouped and evaluated as follows:

1. Project Feasibility
    - What regeneration options are feasible, given known constraints such as budgets, seedlings, manpower, and access?
    - Will the option meet the minimum required standard for the area?
    - Will treatment investment beyond the minimum standard meet financial return standards?
2. Choice of Options
    - What is the preferred option biologically and financially for a given area?
    - What regime of site preparation, species mix, stock type, planting density, and brush treatment will most successfully meet the landowner's objectives?

3. Project Ranking
    *   How can projects be ranked to meet the landowner's objectives most effectively? Limited resources such as budget or seedling supply may mean that some feasible projects cannot be undertaken.

GENERAL PROCEDURE

Financial analysis to guide field foresters in determining whether prescriptions and plans are meeting the desired financial objectives involves the following steps:

*   defining objectives
*   selecting criteria
*   identifying constraints
*   determining appropriate options
*   collecting information and identifying costs and benefits
*   deriving cash flows
*   calculating values for criteria
*   interpreting results

These steps are discussed below and related to the example shown on page 21, which includes three regeneration options. In practice, some of the steps may be simplified if procedures for project evaluation already exist within an organization.

Defining Objectives

Forest management objectives are the goals that the owner or manager has for the land under care. Some benefit is expected from the investment of time and money in the property. It is essential, therefore, that objectives be well defined, as they determine what costs, benefits, and criteria are included in an economic analysis.

These objectives can vary substantially between landowners. A small landowner's objective may be to maximize profits on the current harvest operation. The next rotation may be of little interest. An industrial forest landowner, however, may have a longer-term view. If profit maximization is the objective, financial costs and revenues throughout the rotation will have to be estimated so that regeneration investment opportunities can be analyzed.

The public forest manager has a broader mandate. Public concerns include social issues — such as employment and regional development — as well as financial return. These concerns may have to be included in the objectives of economic analyses for public forest land. Relevant benefits and costs, therefore, may be substantially different from those determined for private land.

Selecting Criteria

Criteria are standards against which the relative success of alternatives in meeting an objective may be compared. To be useful, the criteria must be consistent with the objectives. If the management objective is to increase employment, an appropriate criterion might be the number of jobs generated or the net cost per job created. An organization with the objective of maximizing profit will use financial criteria such as net present value (NPV), benefit-cost ratio (B/C), and internal rate of return (IRR). These three criteria are used to evaluate the management options in the example.

Net present value (NPV)

Net present value is the sum of the discounted revenues minus the sum of the discounted costs for a defined analysis period. If the NPV is positive, revenues exceed costs and the project is acceptable at the chosen discount rate. It is an appropriate criterion for selecting the preferred stand option. It is not, however, recommended for ranking projects to meet budget constraints because it provides an absolute value, not an index of returns, in relation to the size of the investment.

Benefit-cost ratio (B/C)

The benefit-cost ratio is the ratio of discounted benefits to discounted costs. It expresses the relative efficiency of a project in terms of dollars of present benefits generated per dollar of present costs. Definition of costs and benefits depends on the objectives for the exercise. In its pure form, "costs" covers all items throughout the investment period, including final harvest costs. Fraser (1985) uses this form in his analysis. Projects are attractive at the defined discount rate if the B/C is greater than or equal to 1.

The B/C is useful for ranking independent projects according to their relative efficiency. However, ranking by this strict definition of B/C may be misleading in an annual capital budgeting exercise where funds are limited. Davis and Johnson (1987) suggest that the net revenue/cost ratio (NR/C) be used instead.

The NR/C relates cost in the current year to future net revenues generated by the investment. Ranking according to this ratio and selecting projects in descending order will maximize the present net worth of the capital program or annual plan.

For forest regeneration, a useful variation of the benefit-cost ratio is relating incremental net harvest benefits to regeneration costs (see example). This method has the advantage of highlighting the feasibility of the incremental investment of one option over another.

Internal rate of return (IRR)

The internal rate of return is the discount rate that results in a zero net present value. The IRR is a measure of the rate of growth of capital invested in a project. It has the advantage of not requiring an interest rate for calculation. To test project feasibility, however, a "hurdle" rate is needed for comparison. If the IRR is greater than or equal to the hurdle rate, the project is acceptable.

One disadvantage of IRR is the possibility of multiple interest rate solutions where a project has frequent alternating negative and positive cash flows. Fortunately, this is not a common occurrence in regeneration analyses.

Financial Analysis for Stand Regeneration: An Example

The example is based on a site located in the CWHd1 ecosystem association[1]. The site index is estimated to be 27 m on a 50-year base.

Large accumulations of slash will restrict the distribution of seedlings, and the number of plantable spots is limited. If the area is left to regenerate naturally, 500 stems per hectare of western hemlock and western redcedar can be expected at 50% distribution. It is further expected that existing patches of salal and later invasion of red alder will slow stand growth by 19 years if they go untreated. Without treatment, a harvest volume of 307 m³/ha is expected in 87 years.

For ease of illustration, only three management options are presented in this example. Some management is assumed to be required to meet a minimum regeneration standard.

Option 1. Minimum Regeneration Standards

In this example, minimum regeneration standards are defined as having 600 well-distributed, free-growing seedlings in 12 years. To achieve this, an estimated minimum planting of 300 stems per hectare are required at a cost of $255 per hectare, followed by one $400/ha brush treatment at age 5 years. The patches of salal are expected to slow growth by an average of 4 years. The expected harvest in 72 years is 440 m³/ha.

Option 2. Discretionary Investment in Slashburning

To improve the distribution of natural seedlings, increase the number of plantable spots, and reduce the impact of salal, a discretionary investment in slashburning could be planned. The cost of the burning treatment will be $150/ha. The treatment is expected to result in natural regeneration of 600 stems per hectare with 70% distribution. A further discretionary investment in planting 900 stems per hectare will cost $540/ha. Brush control in year 5 will cost $400/ha. As a result of these treatments, the expected harvest in 69 years is 683 m³/ha.

Option 3. Discretionary Investment in Higher Density Planting

This option is the same as Option 2, except 1200 stems per hectare are planted rather than 900 stems per hectare. The expected harvest in 69 years is 776 m³/ha.

Notes on Harvest Values

Timber prices and harvest costs are based on schedules reported by the Sterling Wood Group Inc. (1988) and Nawitka Resource Consultants (1987). Both gross stand value and harvesting costs are calculated according to stand volume and average diameter (DBH).

The example site is assumed to be on easy terrain a short distance from the mill. Species composition is 50% western hemlock and 50% western redcedar.

Alternative	Harvest age	Volume (m³/ha)	Average price ($/m³)	Average harvest cost ($/m³)	Net value of stand ($/ha)
Unmanaged	87	307	42.85[a]	19.50	7 168
Option 1	72	440	42.38	19.50	10 067
Option 2	69	683	40.78	19.75	14 363
Option 3	69	776	40.45	19.75	16 063

[a] Average price in this analysis is based primarily on tree size. Because of decreased stocking and wider spacing, individual tree size will be greater in the unmanaged stand and in Option 1.

Summary

Situation	-	private industrial forest owner
Objective	-	profit maximization
Discount rate	-	4%
Constraints	-	minimum regeneration standard of 600 stems per hectare
Rotation age	-	calculated on a financial basis. Selected rotation ages yield the highest NPV at a discount rate of 4%.

[1] See Chapter 6.

Identifying Constraints

Constraints are those factors that may limit the achievement of an objective. They can be imposed from within or without the organization. Internal constraints include budget restrictions, end product goals, and operating procedures. External constraints include laws, regulations, biological and technical limitations, and social standards.

Another useful subdivision identifies resource and policy constraints. Resource constraints such as budget, seedling, and manpower availability affect the priority of regeneration investment opportunities within an overall plan. Where managers have several objectives, they may even include some of the objectives as policy constraints. These often take the form of minimum performance or production levels, such as minimum regeneration standards and environmental guidelines. The unmanaged situation in the example is not feasible because it fails to meet the minimum regeneration standards.

In the example, Options 2 and 3 may not be realistic alternatives if smoke management rules limit the use of broadcast burning. Options favoring mechanical or no site treatment would be favored if this constraint existed.

Objectives, criteria, and constraints can vary markedly between organizations — and, thus, so can the results of the financial analysis of similar situations.

Determining Appropriate Options

Chapters 7, 8, and 9 discuss the numerous alternatives in each step of the regeneration process. Each alternative leads to choices and consequences later in the regeneration cycle. Selective logging, for example, leads to an entirely different set of regeneration costs and final products than does clearcut logging. To help the forester select appropriate options from this multitude of choices, an analytical approach based on the "decision tree" is often used.

A decision tree is a schematic diagram that displays optional paths from project initiation to completion. It ensures that the forester pays attention to stand treatments throughout the rotation; and it helps the forester to define costs and benefits, and to evaluate uncertainty through the use of probabilities.

Figure 3.1 is a simplified decision tree for the chapter example. It and the sequence of treatments develop from left to right, starting with the first post-harvest decision. Four site preparation alternatives are identified in the example: no treatment, scarification, slashburning, and windrowing. Option 1 prescribes no treatment; Options 2 and 3 prescribe slashburning. Each site preparation treatment can be followed by a number of planting treatments. For example, a number of planting densities between 0 and 1200 stems per hectare are identified following slashburning. Option 2 takes the 900 stems per hectare path; Option 3, the 1200 stems per hectare path. Other planting decisions that may be important but not shown here include selection of stock type, species, and seedling protection systems.

At the brushing level, the example shows three alternatives of no brushing, mechanical brushing, and chemical brushing. All options include one mechanical brushing at 5 years after planting.

Further treatments such as spacing, fertilizing, or pre-commercial thinning could be added to the diagram as additional decision points. Generally, the final level is harvesting or the point at which gross returns are realized. Logging may be the initial decision level, where planning precedes harvesting and there are harvest alternatives that produce different regeneration conditions or costs.

The decision tree in Figure 3.1 is drawn as if the decision-maker knows precisely

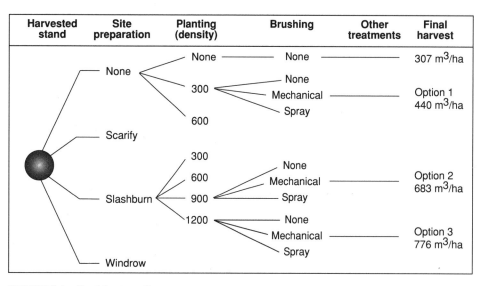

FIGURE 3.1. Decision tree diagram.

what future stand conditions will occur. Most analysis of forest management is portrayed this way even though decision-making under certainty is not typical. The actual path may differ significantly from the average or expected path. For example, although the average stocking from natural regeneration might be 500 stems per hectare, experience may show that stocking can range from zero to several thousand stems per hectare. Each of the extreme conditions may trigger changes in subsequent activities, costs, and benefits.

Where this variety of possible outcomes is known and can be predicted, the analyst can expand the decision tree diagram to recognize these other possibilities within each option. Costs and benefits of these possible outcomes can be prorated by their chance of occurring, and summed to give average expected values. This method of prorating possible costs and benefits is appropriate where the option being analyzed may be applied over many stands. Davis and Johnson (1987) address this technique in detail.

Collecting Information and Identifying Costs and Benefits

Information needs for financial analysis fall into four broad categories: treatment costs, stand yields, harvest costs and benefits, and financial parameters. Information on treatment costs is generally good, but a great deal of uncertainty surrounds future yields and benefits. Despite this uncertainty, foresters must attempt to estimate volume impacts of proposed treatments. Pearse et al. (1986), for example, chose to rank rehabilitation opportunities for backlog lands by the cost per cubic meter of timber volume produced, rather than to speculate about future value of timber stands.

Stand growth projections

At the time of this writing, managed stand yield data are available in British Columbia only for coastal Douglas-fir (*Pseudotsuga menziesii*). Projections for western hemlock (*Tsuga heterophylla*), lodgepole pine (*Pinus contorta* var. *latifolia*), and white spruce (*Picea glauca*) are being prepared. In the interim, estimates for these species can be obtained from the Ministry of Forests, Research Branch.

Because they are designed for use with site index curves developed from stem analysis, these estimates must be applied cautiously. The curves have not yet been fully integrated into the provincial inventory classification system. Other yield projection systems are also available, such as the Stand Projection System (SPS) (Arney 1986), but without local calibration they should only be used to estimate incremental changes between management regimes. Marshall (1988) discusses this problem of estimating treatment response, and proposes a method for integrating conflicting estimates from a number of sources.

Stand values

Species, log size, wood density, juvenile wood content, and other qualitative factors can be important considerations when stand value is estimated. These factors are modified by regeneration decisions, particularly those involving species choice and stand density. Nawitka Resource Consultants (1987) and the Sterling Wood Group (1988) provide examples of wood price estimates by species and tree size.

Other values

The broad mandate and objectives of the public forest manager were discussed earlier. This mandate demands that public forest managers consider other values as well as financial costs and benefits. Krutilla (1986) discusses the treatment of some of these other values in economic analysis. The accounting procedures used by public managers may differ substantially from those used by private landowners. Benefits may include fees and taxes as well as direct stumpage revenues. To handle social, environmental, and other impacts, separate accounts for each value can be kept. To compare projects, these accounts or criteria can be combined into a single index, with each criterion provided a weight according to its relative importance. Where impacts are difficult to quantify — aesthetics, for example — they may be qualitatively described and included with quantitative results for consideration.

Sunk costs

Costs incurred previously in the management of a stand are referred to as "sunk costs." They cannot be changed by choices among current options and therefore should be excluded in an analysis of these options.

An example is a choice between treating brush on a planted block or on a naturally regenerated block. It is irrelevant if the previous investment in the planted block is higher than in the naturally regenerated block. Of importance are the brush control costs and the impact of treatment on the future value of the two alternatives.

Financial parameters

Financial parameters include discount rates, inflation, and real cost and price trends. Typically, these are defined by policy within an organization and need not be derived for each analysis. Society gives a time value to money. One hundred dollars paid today is worth more than the same sum promised in 10 years' time. Investments differ as to when costs and revenues occur over time. For comparison, the values of future costs and revenues are discounted and expressed as present values. In the chapter example, all costs and revenues are discounted to a common year, year (0)

1989, the year of the first treatment decision. Fraser (1985) and Brumelle et al. (1988) discuss the rationale for discounting and list interest rates commonly used by public institutions.

Inflation is the continuing rise in the level of prices in the economy. The general rule is either to include inflation in both the discount rate and the estimates of future costs and revenues, or to exclude it from both. A "nominal" or market interest rate includes inflation; a "real" rate excludes inflation. For example, the 9% received from a savings deposit is nominal because it includes inflation. If the rate of inflation is 4%, the real rate of interest is approximately 5% (9%-4%). A real interest rate is frequently used for discounting, as it avoids the need to include inflation in estimates of future costs and benefits.

Real price and cost trends are used when changes in prices or costs are expected to vary from the average inflation rate. For example, as clear wood becomes more scarce, it may be expected to increase in price at a faster rate than inflation. It will appreciate in real terms relative to the general level of prices in the economy. Similarly, a decreasing real cost trend may be used to portray real cost savings from technological change.

Deriving Cash Flows

When the treatment costs and the harvest costs and revenues for each alternative have been determined, the next step is to derive cash flows.

A cash flow charts the costs and benefits occurring throughout the analysis period, and forms the basis for investment analysis. Correct time relationships and all relevant costs and benefits must be included.

A time line shows the sequence of events and identifies the base year of the analysis. Table 3.1 shows a time line for Option 2 of the chapter example.

When costs and benefits are added to the time line, a cash flow table is formed (Table 3.1). Summing costs and revenues for each time period creates a net cash flow table. Net cash flows for each option are shown in Table 3.2.

Calculating Values for Criteria

Cash flows form the basis for calculating the three common financial criteria used in the chapter example: NPV, B/C, and IRR. Table 3.3 shows the discounted net cash flows and resultant NPV's for the three options under consideration.

The main objective in the example is to evaluate the attractiveness of the incremental investment between the options. For instance, how attractive is slashburning and planting an additional 600 trees per hectare (Option 2 compared to Option 1), or planting a further 300 trees per hectare (Option 3 compared to Option 2)? In this application, it is important that the difference between an absolute measure like NPV and relative measures like B/C and IRR be recognized.

TABLE 3.1. Time line for Option 2[a]

Chronological time	1989	1990	1995	2059
Analytical time	0	1	6	69
	Site preparation	Planting	Brushing	Harvest
Cash flow				
Time (years)	0	1	6	69
Cost ($/ha)	150	540	400	
Revenue ($/ha)				14 363
Net cash flow	(150)	(540)	(400)	14 363

[a] Bracketed numbers are minus.

TABLE 3.2. Net cash flows[a]

		Net cash flows ($/ha)		
Year	Analytical Time	Option 1	Option 2	Option 3
1989	0	(255)	(150)	(150)
1990	1		(540)	(720)
1994	5	(400)		
1995	6		(400)	(400)
2058	69		14 363	14 363
2061	72	10 067		

[a] Bracketed numbers are minus.

TABLE 3.3. Total stand discounted cash flows. Discount rate: 4%, discounted to 1989 (year 0)[a]

	Discounted net cash flows ($/ha)			
Year	Analytical Time	Option 1	Option 2	Option 3
1989	0	(255)	(150)	(150)
1990	1		(519)	(692)
1994	5	(329)		
1995	6		(316)	(316)
2058	69		959	1073
2061	72	598		
Net present value		14	-26	-85
Benefit-cost ratio		1.02	0.97	0.93

[a] Bracketed numbers are minus.

In Table 3.4, the additional investment in Option 2 over that in Option 1 is assessed. When the NPV of each option is calculated separately (Table 3.3), the difference between the two NPV's is the NPV of the additional investment. The same result will be achieved if the NPV is calculated for the difference in cash flows between the options (Table 3.4). For the relative measures, B/C and IRR, these two approaches will not necessarily provide the same result. The correct procedure is to calculate the value of the criterion from the cash flow difference between the options (Table 3.4).

Net present value

The calculation of NPV is shown in Table 3.3. All cash flow items are discounted to analytical time 0, according to the basic present value equation:

$$V_o = V_n / (1+i)^{**n}$$

where V_o = value of an amount at present (n=o)

V_n = value of an amount n periods in the future

n = number of periods (years) over which discounting occurs

i = interest rate stated as a decimal

For example, the brushing cost of $400/ha is discounted 6 years at 4%. Therefore,

Discounted Brushing Cost = $400/(1.04)^6$ = $316/ha

The discounted cash flow items are then summed to determine the NPV. For Option 2, this is:

-150 - 519 - 316 + 959 = -$26/ha

From Table 3.3, the NPV for Option 1 is $14/ha. The NPV of the difference between Option 2 and Option 1 is:

-26 - 14 = -$40/ha

As already mentioned, this is the same as the NPV calculated from the cash flow difference between Options 2 and 1 in Table 3.4.

Benefit-cost ratio

The calculation of the B/C is shown in Table 3.4. Column 4 is the cash flow difference between Option 2 and Option 1. This net cash flow is discounted (Column 5) as described under the net present value section. The sum of the discounted costs are then divided into the sum of the discounted net harvest revenues:

$$B/C = \frac{959 - 598}{519 + 316 - 329 - 105} = 0.91$$

TABLE 3.4. Incremental analysis of Option 2 in relation to Option 1 values. Discount rate: 4%, discounted to 1989 (year 0)[a]

Net cash flows ($/ha)			(Option 2 - Option 1)	
Analytical time	Option 1	Option 2	Net cash flow ($/ha)	Discounted net cash flow ($/ha)
0	(255)	(150) =	105	105
1		(540)	(540)	(519)
5	(400)		400	329
6		(400)	(400)	(316)
69		14 363	14 363	959
72	10 067		10 067	(598)
Net present value				-40
Benefit-cost ratio				0.9
Internal rate of return				3.8

[a] Bracketed numbers are minus.

Internal rate of return

In Table 3.4, the IRR on the additional investment in slashburning and planting in Option 2 is compared to the investment in Option 1. Calculation of IRR is a trial and error process, during which different discount rates are tried until a zero NPV is achieved. This process is best handled by computer.

Table 3.4 shows that the NPV at 4% is -$40/ha. This indicates that a zero NPV (IRR) is achieved at a discount rate somewhat less than 4%. At a trial discount rate of 3.5%, an NPV of $87/ha is achieved. The two results show that the IRR is closer to 4% than to 3.5%. If the process is continued, 3.83% is determined to be the IRR.

Interpreting Results

Interpretation of analysis results depends on a clear understanding of the intent of the analysis, the organization objectives, and the criteria used. The financial results may, of course, be only one component of the final decision-making process.

Project feasibility

In the chapter example, the "no treatment" regime is not feasible as it does not meet minimum regeneration standards. At the least, Option 1 should be selected to meet these standards.

What about financial feasibility? Does the additional investment in either Option 2 or 3 return at least 4% — the minimum financial requirement in the example?

Table 3.5 shows the incremental NPV's of Options 2 and 3, relative to Option 1, to be $-40/ha and $-99/ha. The negative NPV's mean that Options 2 and 3 are not attractive (i.e., the additional expenditure earns less than 4%). The results for the B/C and IRR calculations presented in Table 3.5 also show that Options 2 and 3 are not financially acceptable. Incremental B/C's are less than 1 and IRR's are less than the 4% hurdle rate.

Choice of options

In the example, the decision about which alternative to choose is straightforward. Option 1 is preferred. Options 2 and 3 do not meet financial requirements.

If Options 2 and 3 had positive NPV's (were feasible), then NPV would be the preferable criterion for selecting between the two options. The option with the highest NPV would be chosen. Using the other criteria might give inconsistent results. This process is discussed below under "sensitivity analysis."

Project ranking for capital budgeting

Assume a budget of $1 million has been allocated for investment in management beyond the minimum regeneration standards. It is insufficient to cover all the available feasible projects. Which projects should be chosen? The usual procedure would first be to calculate the B/C's for all the projects and then rank them from highest to lowest B/C. Projects would be selected from the top of the list until the budget was

TABLE 3.5. Summary of incremental analysis[a]

	Net present value[b] ($/ha)	Benefit-cost ratio[b]	Internal rate of return(%)
Option 2	-40	0.9	3.8
Option 3	-99	0.8	3.7

[a] Analysis is of investment above that in Option 1.
[b] Calculated at a 4% discount rate.

used. The resulting projects would achieve the highest NPV from the given budget at the defined discount rate.

Ranking of projects becomes more complex when there are a number of constraints such as budget and seedling limitations, or a requirement for discreteness (all or none of a stand is treated). Mathematical programming techniques are suitable for solving such problems. Refer to examples in Davis and Johnson (1987).

Costs minimization

In some instances, several options may achieve a defined level of regeneration or stand condition at the free-growing stage. If the final benefits are the same, minimizing regeneration costs will maximize net return. The most effective option can be chosen by discounting the costs of each option to the present and selecting the least-cost alternative.

Uncertainty

Silvicultural decision-making involves uncertainty. Investment periods are long, forest conditions are variable, and knowledge is imperfect on yields, future technologies, costs, and prices.

Field data and local experience provide information on the range and likelihood of possible post-silviculture outcomes. Assigning probabilities as discussed in the section on the decision tree is one way of recognizing the probable variations. Payandeh and Field (1985) developed a computer simulation model for comparing relative financial desirability of forestry investments subject to risk.

Sensitivity analysis

Sensitivity analysis is a common procedure for coping with uncertainty. It measures the amount of change required in one or more factors of an analysis to change a decision. Often sensitivity analysis is used to test internal policy on forest management investments. The sensitivity of results to changes in assumptions on yields, prices, and costs are of particular interest.

Consider timber prices, for instance. It is postulated that timber supply will be constrained by increasing demand for other forest uses and that demand for forest products will continue to grow. As timber becomes increasingly scarce, real prices for timber will increase. To simulate this effect, timber prices in the chapter example were increased by 1% per year in real terms. Average price of timber for Options 2 and 3 would rise to $81.03/m^3 and $80.37/m^3 from $40.78/m^3 and $40.45/m^3, respectively. Resulting incremental NPV's would be $637/ha for Option 2 over Option 1, and $810/ha for Option 3 over Option 1. These positive NPV's show that the financial feasibility of Options 2 and 3 is sensitive to real price trend assumptions. The preferred option under this new price scenario is Option 3, because its NPV is the highest. For the capital budgeting exercise described above, Option 3 would be ranked with projects for other areas based on its B/C of 2.4.

Once the sensitivity of results to changes in specific information is known, emphasis can be placed on refining the most sensitive data sources. If the certainty of data cannot be improved, other users of the analysis must be told so its weaknesses are recognized.

FOREST LEVEL ANALYSIS

The information presented so far in this chapter is designed to help the forester select the best treatment alternative for an individual stand. This type of analysis tends to concentrate on stand variables and ignore forest level factors. When the impact of individual stand treatment is considered on the forest level, the "best" prescription may be considerably different from that suggested by stand level analysis.

Forest level factors that can influence stand level decisions include policy constraints, other resource uses, and forest age class profiles. Reed (1984) discusses the major impact of some of these forest and provincial level considerations on the viability of forestry investments.

Harvest regulation policies can have a significant effect on forestry investment. The allowable cut effect (ACE), for example, is the increase in today's allowable cut attributed to increases in yield expected from current investments in silviculture. It favors treatments that have a significant impact on volume (from many regeneration treatments) over those that predominantly affect timber quality or value (from pruning and often from spacing). With the ACE, volume-producing treatments become more attractive because benefits in the form of allowable cut increases are expressed annually over the period from treatment to harvest, rather than solely at harvest. For further information on the ACE and constraints on its use, refer to Haley (1972), Pearse (1976), and Fraser (1985).

The interaction of harvest policies and the forest age class distribution may also affect rotation lengths and preferred options. For example, a stand level analysis may show that the preferred option for a 15-year-old stand is precommercial thinning and a rotation age of 100 years. Suppose at the forest level, however, an age class imbalance will result in a timber supply shortage in 30-50 years. Reassessing the stand level analysis, or running a forest level analysis including the timber supply constraints and an evenflow goal, may change the preferred option to one commercial thinning and a shorter final rotation. The complexity of this type of analysis lends itself to the use of timber analysis or strategic planning computer models. Models currently in use in British Columbia are generally maintained by specialists and are not available to most regeneration practitioners.

Despite the critical impact that forest level decisions can have on the stand, financial analysis at the stand level is a valuable tool. Forest level analyses and capital budgeting exercises rely on optimum stand level treatments as a starting point. In an industry where capital, land, and human resources are often limited, efficient use of resources is only prudent.

4

PHYSIOLOGICAL PRINCIPLES OF REGENERATION

D.P. Lavender

Successful reforestation requires high quality site preparation, planting stock, and planting. However, as Sutton (1988) notes, "The term *quality* derives from the Latin *qualis*, meaning 'of what kind.' In relation to planting stock, quality is the degree to which any designated stock proves to be suited to the purpose for which it was produced. Clear expression of objectives is therefore prerequisite to any determination of planting stock quality." He goes on to say that:

> *The field performance of outplants is determined by the interaction between planting stock performance potential at the time of planting and the environment experienced by the outplant. Planting stock quality is the degree to which that stock achieves the purpose, enunciated in the objectives of management, for which it was produced and planted. The determination of planting stock quality therefore requires not just the determination of performance but the determination of performance in relation to the objectives of management.*

Thus, discussing seedling physiology means discussing the factors that affect stock performance potential rather than stock quality.

The importance of the physiology of coniferous seedlings, as reflected by their potential to survive and grow after outplanting, was first recognized in North America by Wakeley (1948), although he was unable to distinguish between the preplanting physiological grades he hypothesized. Several studies have since tried to find parameters that reflect seedling vigor, such as root regeneration (Stone et al. 1962; Lavender 1964; Burdett 1979b; Sutton 1983; Ritchie 1985; Feret et al. 1985; McCreary and Duryea 1987) and root respiration (McCreary and Zaerr 1987). Such work has shown that very good and very poor seedlings might be identified, but it, too, failed to distinguish quality differences (as reflected by field performance) among the great majority of seedling populations. Our ability to predict coniferous seedling performance in plantations, according to a physiological assessment before planting, therefore, remains little advanced over that of Wakeley (Lavender 1989).

On the more positive side, however, our understanding of the physiological principles governing the survival and growth of seedlings has expanded considerably in recent years. This chapter discusses these principles, both in terms of the environmental factors that influence seedling growth and in terms of the seedling response to the environment.

ENVIRONMENTAL FACTORS

Light

Intensity

Light is the term commonly given to the portion of the sun's radiation which is perceived by the human eye. It represents a relatively small part of the solar spectrum, being bounded by ultraviolet radiation with a wavelength of about 390 nm and infrared light with a wavelength of about 760 nm. Approximately 45% of the sun's radiant energy is found in the visible spectrum, with a peak around 500 nm (green light). The color of an object represents that portion of the spectrum which is *reflected* or transmitted and not *absorbed* under white light. Therefore, chlorophyll, the pigment which modulates photosynthesis (the process by which plants convert radiant energy to chemical energy), does not absorb energy in the green wavelengths, but rather in the red region of the spectrum (wavelengths of about 660 nm).

Under laboratory conditions, photosynthesis in forest trees is saturated at approximately 40% of full sunlight (800 μmol m^{-2} s^{-1}). Under natural conditions, however, because of the mutual shading of foliage by adjacent branches, some tree species require light levels of at least 75% of full sunlight for optimum growth. While full sunlight is ideal for species such as coastal Douglas-fir (*Pseudotsuga menziesii* and lodgepole pine (*Pinus contorta*), it may be less than ideal for recently planted seedlings of species such as white spruce (*Picea glauca*). Foliage of all species may be "burned" by sudden exposure to full sunlight if the needles have developed in a shaded location. This response is frequently seen in the loss of crop tree foliage after the midsummer slashing of competing vegetation, or in the loss of lower crown foliage by seedlings grown under crowded conditions in the nursery and then outplanted.

Duration

Plant populations or ecotypes are known to adapt to particular environments. This "adaption" refers to a plant's ability to recognize cues provided by changes in environmental factors, and to adjust its phenology or growth cycle so that it achieves maximum growth during favorable weather and avoids damage during adverse weather (such as drought and frost).

By far the most reliable of such cues is the length of the day which, for any given location and date, is constant every year. Perennial plants, particularly those indigenous to high latitudes or elevations (sub-boreal or boreal forests), use daylength — or more properly, length of the unbroken night (nycto-period) — to trigger changes from active growth to the state of stress resistance commonly associated with dormancy. The plant measures the length of a dark period by the extent to which a pigment, phytochrome, changes from a form which absorbs light with a wavelength of about 735 nm (near infrared), to one which absorbs light of about 660 nm wavelength. This chemical change is sufficiently precise that plants can easily detect changes in nightlength between successive days in late summer (Pollard and Ying 1979). The length of night necessary to stimulate dormancy in photoperiodically sensitive species varies with location and ecotype, but it is generally correlated with the incidence of frost. The chemical system involved is so sensitive that less than 0.01% of full sunlight is enough to stimulate a response of the phytochrome. Light from the headlights of passing cars, for example, may interfere with the dormancy induction of seedlings in greenhouses built near highways. Nursery night security lighting may cause the same problem.

Light quality

In addition to affecting quantity and duration of growth, light may affect plant morphology and seed germination. For example, light under living shade is relatively rich in blue, a color shown to stimulate extreme elongation or etiolation. Plants affected this way typically have weak stems, which leave them subject to snow press, and poor root systems, which make them vulnerable to drought and windthrow.

Light quality also plays an important role in controlling germination in the seed both from trees and from competing vegetation. Light under a foliage canopy is richer in near infrared radiation than is light in non-shaded areas (Pons 1983). Consequently, some seeds will germinate only when incident light has a relatively high red:infrared ratio. Such light indicates to the germinants that the microsite is not occupied by competing plants (Pons 1983).

Temperature

Plant life occurs only in a very narrow temperature range, from 0 °C to about 50 °C (with the exception of those organisms indigenous to hot springs or polar regions). Yet, within this very restricted zone, relatively small temperature differences are associated with dramatic changes in animal and plant life. Temperatures affect plant growth and development in three distinct ways:

1. Most enzymes, the chemicals responsible for metabolism, have distinct temperature optima. Accordingly, the growth rate of plants is closely controlled by ambient temperatures.

2. The annual growth cycle of most temperate zone plants is largely regulated by temperature. Buds and seeds have distinct, genetically determined requirements for discrete quantities of heat (heat sums) to prepare them for resumption of growth. A perennial temperate zone species cannot grow where the environment does not satisfy these requirements.

3. Either high or low temperatures may physically injure seedlings. Most proteins are denatured at 55 °C and the ability to tolerate temperatures below -3 to -5 °C without cold injury differs dramatically with species, ecotype, and season of the year.

Heat

Seedlings are at risk of damage from high temperatures primarily in a zone about a centimeter above and below the ground line. Although the principal concern has been for areas in the southern mainland and Vancouver Island (Ballard et al. 1977), potentially damaging soil surface temperatures (i.e., above 55 °C), can occur in the northern Interior (Draper et al. 1985). Air temperature measured at the standard height of 1.3 m above the ground never rises high enough to damage seedling tissues.

The forester should recognize that soil temperatures are a function of the heat input into the soil, the specific heat of the soil material, and the ability of the soil to transmit heat downward.

The heat input is a function of the slope and aspect — maximum heating by the sun occurs when its rays are perpendicular to the soil surface — and of the reflectivity of the soil surface. Light-colored soils reflect much of the incoming radiation, while blackened, charred surfaces are highly absorptive.

Specific heat is largely a function of the water-holding capacity of soil because water has the highest specific heat of any known substance. Clay soils, particularly when moist, resist changes in temperature much more so than do soils of coarse texture.

Finally, the ability of soil material to transmit heat downward dramatically affects soil surface temperature for any given air temperature and radiation load. Rock has a high capacity to transmit heat; organic materials have a low capacity.

In summary, maximum soil temperatures are likely to occur on moderate southerly aspects with a blackened litter and duff layer. Germinants and seedlings on such sites, especially 1-year-old container stock, are frequently damaged or killed by excessive soil temperatures (Helgerson 1988). Survival, therefore, may be significantly increased through the use of site preparation techniques such as scarification or shading devices, which lower maximum soil surface temperatures around the base of the seedling stem.

Frost

Temperatures below freezing are prevalent at the higher elevations throughout British Columbia. Such temperatures may limit plantation success in two ways:

1. directly, by resulting in frost damage to planting stock; and

2. indirectly, by reducing the growth of coniferous seedlings so that competing vegetation dominates the site.

Frost damage *per se* may be minimized by site preparation, choice of microsite, and correct choice of species and ecotype (Figure 4.1). For example, lodgepole pine has greater frost resistance during the growing season than Douglas-fir; Douglas-fir from the Babine Mountains has greater fall frost resistance than Douglas-fir from the southern Kootenays. Suitable nursery culture may also increase stock frost resistance (Weiser 1970).

Cold injury can occur at any time of the year in some areas of British Columbia, but it is most frequent in the spring or fall, not in midwinter. It is, therefore, important that stock be outplanted in a physiological state which will allow the seedlings to develop the required cold hardiness before frost events. The timing and degree of cold hardiness attained by seedlings is a function of their genetic potential

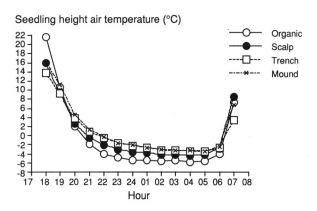

Seedling height air temperature (°C)

— Organic
— Scalp
— Trench
— Mound

FIGURE 4.1. Seedling height air temperatures in a forest clearcut in the Esperson Lake area (MSb) near Kelowna, B.C., under typical summer radiation frost conditions. The burned area had a 15 cm deep surface organic layer, the scalp was a 50 cm diameter mineral soil patch, the steep-walled trench was 30 cm deep, and the mineral mound was 20 cm high (Stathers 1989).

and of the nursery culture. Plants that are growing actively in August or early September are at much greater risk than those stimulated to form buds in midsummer (Blake et al. 1979). Seedlings grown at favorable spacing in the nursery (i.e., less than 700 per square meter) have the capacity to harden to a greater degree than similar plants grown under crowded conditions (Timmis and Tanaka 1976). It is imperative, then, that planting stock destined for plantations on frost-prone sites be of the correct genetic material *and* have undergone nursery culture techniques known to favor cold hardiness.

Although all cold injury produces damage or death to seedling tissues and, possibly, death to the seedling, the pattern of such damage is specific to the nature of the injury:

- Cold injury as a result of convection commonly occurs in early fall or spring, when seedlings are exposed to unseasonably low temperatures during periods that they lack maximum cold hardiness. Such events are rare in winter but can occur when a period of above-freezing temperatures is followed by a sharp freeze. This result is a function of the labile nature of cold hardiness (i.e., a relatively brief exposure to warm temperatures can cause loss of cold resistance). Characteristic symptoms of this injury include brown foliage and possible death of apical buds. The seedling may die if it is exposed to sufficiently low temperatures.

- Cold injury as a result of radiation may occur at any time during the year, but is most common during the growing season. It results from exposure of seedling tissues to sub-freezing temperatures as a result of radiation cooling during nights with clear skies. It is most common at higher elevations and affects those portions of the seedling which have direct exposure to the sky (i.e., terminal bud and shoot, ends of branches). Such damage rarely occurs where the seedling is protected by an overstory.

- Cold injury as a result of desiccation during the winter has been observed in northeastern British Columbia, particularly on recently planted seedlings. It is a result of extreme evaporative stress during periods of sub-freezing temperatures when frozen tissues prevent plants from replacing moisture lost.

- Cold injury as a result of desiccation caused by the death of the phloem and lateral meristem of the lower stem can occur when extremely low temperatures accompany a very shallow layer of snow. Such conditions result in extreme cold immediately above the snow. Symptoms of this damage are frequently confused with drought, as seedlings may initiate shoot elonga-tion the following spring before the roots die and the seedling shoots dry out.

Snow may act as an insulating blanket to protect seedlings. Consequently, it is not uncommon to see seedlings with cold-injured upper crowns and healthy lower crowns which were protected by snow during the damaging cold event.

The recent increasing reliance on "hot planting" white spruce seedlings in July and August has added to the potential for low temperature damage to seedlings. White spruce seedlings in midsummer may appear to be dormant, yet not be significantly cold-hardy. Such material should not be planted in areas where it will be at risk of exposure to freezing temperatures during the growing season (Stathers 1989; Revel et al. 1990). Furthermore, summer frosts may damage even spring-planted seedlings, especially on sites where herbicides have left a dead organic layer to insulate the soil surface.

Low soil temperatures are considered to be a major obstacle to successful plantation establishment in much of interior British Columbia (Butt 1988). Development of site preparation machines has addressed this problem (see Chapters 11-13), and current research of seedling handling and storage methodology may result in planted seedlings with greater tolerance of cold soils (Husted and Lavender 1990).

Moisture

Drought

Droughty sites in British Columbia occur primarily on southern exposures in the southern portion of the province (areas which also experience high soil temperatures) and where coarse, excessively drained soils exist. Research conducted by the FIR (Forestry Intensified Research) program in southwest Oregon has shown that even very harsh sites may be successfully reforested if reforestation is carefully planned and conducted (Hobbs et al. 1982).

In British Columbia, pre-harvest prescriptions for droughty sites should describe the necessary requirements for drought-hardy propagules, including shoot:root ratio, species and ecotype, nursery culture, harvest, storage, and shipment. Planting and vegetation management procedures should specify proper placement of seedling roots and techniques to ensure minimal competition by weed species. *Careful attention to detail is always necessary for optimum plantation establishment and growth; on harsh sites, only careful planning and conduct of reforestation will prevent plantation failure.*

Excess moisture (high water tables)

Current research suggests that high water tables may be at least as responsible as low soil temperatures for limiting white spruce establishment. Von der Gonna and Lavender (1989) found that roots which grew on white spruce seedlings planted in wet soil in late spring frequently died by late summer. Similarly, a greenhouse trial (Mueller-Dombois 1964) demonstrated that the growth of white spruce seedlings was depressed when the water table was less than 30 cm below the soil surface for either sandy or loamy sand soils.

Nutrients

Although mineral nutrients make up less than 5% of a coniferous seedling's total dry weight, they are essential to all metabolic processes. The regeneration specialist should recognize that forest stands predominantly occupy sites whose soils are low in mineral nutrients, and that the fertility present is found largely in the litter layer and the upper 10-20 cm of the soil's horizon. Reforestation should, therefore, ensure that these materials remain on site so that mineral nutrients are available to seedlings (Utzig and Walmsley 1988).

Fertilization

Although coniferous seedlings do not have high nutrient demands, it is essential for good growth that they have access to balanced nutrient supplies. Brockley (1988) reported that nutrients applied to white spruce seedlings at the time of planting may reduce planting shock, and that maximum response depends on good site preparation and adequate moisture. Similarly, Arnott and Burdett (1988) found a short-lived but notable response of western hemlock (*Tsuga heterophylla*) seedlings to the application of nitrogenous fertilizer; and van den Driessche (1988a) recorded a positive growth response by Douglas-fir seedlings fertilized with a slow release nitrogen compound. However, while we have a fair understanding of the empirical growth responses which may result from fertilization, data describing the economic efficiency of such treatment are lacking.

There are, nevertheless, relatively inexpensive techniques the reforestation forester may use to determine seedling nutrient status if a plantation's growth appears to be limited by mineral deficiencies (Weetman et al. 1984).

MECHANISMS OF UPTAKE

Nutrients

The soil-plant-atmosphere-continuum   Under natural environments, all the elements in Table 4.1 are absorbed to clay minerals or organic compounds as either negatively or positively charged ions (i.e., NH_4^+, $PO_4^=$, Ca^{++}, $SO_4^=$). The uptake of ions by plants involves the exchange of a cation (usually H^+) for a positively charged mineral ion, or of an anion (usually OH^-) for a negatively charged mineral ion and the expenditure of energy.

The movement of ions through the soil, from zones of high concentration to zones of lower concentration, occurs primarily by diffusion and secondarily by mass flow when the soil is saturated. The total of such movement accounts for about 95% of the total nutrients taken up by the root-mycorrhizae complex (Mengel and Kirkby 1978). The relative importance of mass flow or diffusion in moving ions to the root surface depends on the seedling's use of water and the water availability. Rapid uptake of water allows for movement of large quantities of ions to the root by mass flow. Low water use, characteristic of plants in dry soils, means that most ion movement will be by diffusion. However, this diffusion to the root varies with specific ions. For example, nitrate (NO_3^-), calcium (CA^{++}), and sulfate ($SO_4^=$) are supplied primarily by mass flow. Ammonium (NH_4^+), potassium (K^+), and phosphate ($H_2PO_4^-$), on the other hand, normally present in soil solutions at much lower concentrations, reach the plant root mainly by diffusion. Barber (1977) estimates that over 95% of the phosphate ions taken up by plants reach the root surface this way.

The soil volume from which ions may diffuse to the root (depletion zone) varies with specific ions. Phosphate, for example, diffuses for no more than the length of a root hair, a distance only a tenth of that diffused by potassium and one-hundredth of the distance of nitrate (Mengel and Kirby 1978).

TABLE 4.1. The function of mineral nutrients in conifers (after Lavender and Walker, 1979)[a]

Element	Content of healthy foliage (% dry weight)	Role in plant metabolism	Deficiency symptoms
	Macro-elements		
Nitrogen	1.6 - 2.0	Prime constituent of amino acids, nucleic acids, plant hormones, and chlorophyll.	General chlorosis and stunting of needles increasing with severity of deficiency; in most severe cases, needles short, stiff, yellow-green to yellow; in some cases, purple tipping followed by necrosis of needles at end of growing season.
Phosphorus	0.15 - 0.35	Forms pyrophosphate bonds important in energy transfer; is a constituent of phospho-lipids, phosphorylated sugars, co-enzymes, nucleic acids, nucleoproteins, and nucleotides.	Youngest needles green or yellow-green; older needles distinctly purple-tinged; purple deepens with severity of deficiency; in very severe cases in seedlings, all needles purple.
Potassium	0.6 - 1.2	Participates in many enzymatic reactions.	Symptoms vary; usually needles short, chlorotic, with some green near base; in some severe cases, purpling and necrosis with top dieback, or little or no chlorosis of needles but purpling, browning, or necrosis.
Calcium	0.1 - 0.2	Constituent of the middle lamella and of certain enzymes.	General chlorosis followed by necrosis of needles, especially at branch tips; in severe cases, death of terminal bud and top dieback; resin exudation.
Magnesium	0.1 - 0.2	Constituent of chlorophyll; important in enzyme binding and activation, particularly of those involved in carbohydrate metabolism.	Yellow tipping of current needles followed in severe cases by tip necrosis.
Sulfur	0.1 - 0.2	Constituent of certain amino acids, thus in proteins and enzymes; involved in electron transfer.	General chlorosis of foliage followed in severe cases by necrosis. Severe needle twisting in some cases.
	Micro-elements		
Iron	0.005 - 0.01	Constituent of oxidizing enzymes, heme proteins of the electron transport chain, and important nonheme enzymes.	More or less diffuse chlorosis confined in milder cases to new needles; in more severe cases, bright yellow discoloration with no bud development.
Manganese	0.01 - 0.5	Serves as an activator for a wide variety of enzymes, especially those important in oxidating-reduction, decarboxylations, and hydrolysis. Major role is in the citric acid cycle and photosynthesis.	Needles slightly chlorotic; in severe cases, some necrosis of needles.
Molybdenum	0.00005 - 0.0001	Essential component of two major enzymes, nitrogenase and nitrate reductase.	Chlorosis of leaves followed by necrosis of tissue, beginning at tip and eventually covering whole leaf.
Boron	0.0020 - 0.0050	Important in carbohydrate transport, and in synthesis of nucleic acids, lignin, and cytokinins.	Reduced or absent needles near apex, tip dieback late in growing season with associated chlorotic-to-necrotic foliage, intergrading to dieback of leading shoot with characteristic crooking.
Copper	0.0004 - 0.0012	Constituent of chlorophyll protein and of enzymes that reduce molecular oxygen (i.e., ascorbic acid oxidase, cytochrome oxidase, polyphenol oxidase). Probably important in both protein and carbohydrate metabolism.	Needles twisted spirally, yellowed or bronzed; "tipburn" or necrosis of needle tip evident; in severe cases, young shoots twisted or bent.
Zinc	0.001 - 0.01	Constituent of several enzymes including carbonic anhydrase, glutamic acid dehydrogenase, lactic acid dehydrogenase, and alcohol dehydrogenase. Important in RNA synthesis, synthesis of tryptophane, and indole-acetic acid.	Extreme stunting of trees with shortening of branches; needles yellow, short, crowded together on twig; sometimes bronze-tipped; older needles shed early, with resultant tufting of foliage; in severe cases, trees rosetted with top dieback.

[a] These data are based on foliage of mature trees. Nursery-grown seedlings frequently have higher nutrient contents, but values more than 25% greater than those shown represent excessive fertilizations.

The extension of roots

Another way in which roots contact nutrient ions is through extension of the roots or the hyphae of associated mycorrhizae. Plants vary widely in their ability to explore new volumes of soil in this manner. For example, a rye (*Secale cereale*) plant may contact a cylinder of soil 2 mm in diameter and as much as 5 km long every day. In contrast, the roots of *Populus trichocarpa* seedlings may undergo a maximum total daily elongation of about 50 mm, and the seedlings of species such as *Larix leptolepsis* or *Pinus silvestris*, a daily total of 25 mm (Lyr and Hoffmann 1967). The diameter of even the fine roots of these plants precludes their exploring the fine interstices of soil particles.

The low growth rate of tree roots seems to be responsible for the relatively low density of roots under forest stands. Data describing the density of herbaceous roots suggest that root density (centimeters of roots per cubic centimeter of soil) may be as high as 30-50 in the upper 15 cm of grassland soils, and only 2 in the upper 8 cm of soil under *Pinus radiata* (Barber 1977). This low density reflects the great dependence of coniferous seedlings on mycorrhizae to take up nutrients, particularly phosphorus and boron, and the relatively small role that root extension plays in seedling establishment.

This last statement seems to contradict the common belief that rapid production of new roots is essential to seedling survival after planting (Stone et al. 1962). In fact, the new roots produced shortly after a coniferous seedling is planted may contribute little to the total moisture and nutrient uptake (Chung and Kramer 1975). The open, spreading root system of a wildling is more efficient than the closely spaced roots of a planted seedling, which are confined either to the shape of the container or to the small planting slit in the soil. Actually, the spreading of fungal mycelia associated with mycorrhizae is perhaps more important to increased moisture and nutrient uptake than root growth is.

However, if the production of even low numbers of new roots is interpreted as a measure of high seedling vigor (Burdett 1987), then it is logical to associate new roots with high seedling survival (Burdett et al. 1983). As Sutton (1983) points out, though, root growth potential in the laboratory and root growth in plantations may not be well correlated. Recent field observations have suggested that, although shoot growth of white spruce during the growing season after planting is not correlated with root growth that year, the shoot growth of the following season definitely is. This observation may reflect the well-established horticultural principle that, for a given environment, a plant species is committed to a specific shoot:root ratio. A second explanation of why root growth after planting is a poor predictor of seedling survival is that differences in forest sites and climates may have a greater effect on survival and growth of seedlings than does seedling physiology. Nevertheless, data describing the volume and fibrosity of the seedling root system at time of planting (which represent 95% of the plant's ability to absorb nutrients and water) correlate strongly with subsequent survival and growth (Lavender 1989).

As noted above, a large body of research has established that plants are flexible in their allocation of carbon and will direct resources to compensate environmental stress. For example, a seedling grown in shade will channel most growth to elongation of the shoot — even to the detriment of its roots. Conversely, a seedling on a droughty or nutrient-poor site will use much of its photosynthate to extend its root system. In fact, such carbon allocation can account, at least in part, for the commonly observed "planting check" of plantation seedlings. It may well be that such plants are using photosynthate initially for root growth and that vigorous height growth occurs only after an appropriate root system is established.

The nurseryman will be guided by carbon allocation principles in designing nursery environments that create the desired seedling morphology. This will require "correctly" allocating resources to favor a fibrous root system and a stocky (ht:diam ratio of 50 or less), well-lignified stem.

Mycorrhizae

The symbiotic association between higher plants and fungi (mycobionts) is extremely important for the survival and growth of tree seedlings.

Mycorrhizae (from the New Latin *myco* = fungus and the Greek *rhiza* = root, literally "fungus-root") have been described as the ultimate in reciprocal parasitism (symbiosis). The fungus supplies the higher plant partner with mineral nutrients and plant growth hormones and protects the roots against pathogens; the higher plant supplies the fungus with energy substrates (Figure 4.2). Virtually all higher plants depend on a mycorrhizal association. Only crucifers, chenopods, sedges, and aquatic plants are thought to be non-mycorrhizal. However, there are wide differences in the extent of mychorrhizal infection of root systems, with the hairy, fine roots of grasses being less dependent on this habit than the coarse roots of many trees (Baylis 1974).

Mycorrhizal forms include endomycorrhizae and ectomycorrhizae. The distinction between the two is based on the morphology of the structure formed by the fungus and higher plant. Ectomycorrhizae-forming fungi are able to penetrate between, but not into, the cortical cells of the host root, thus forming a network of fungal strands within the cortex commonly called the "Hartig net." The fungus also normally makes a mantle that completely encloses the infected root tip, from which fungal hyphae extend into the soil. This network of hyphae increases the ability of the root to take up nutrients in several ways:

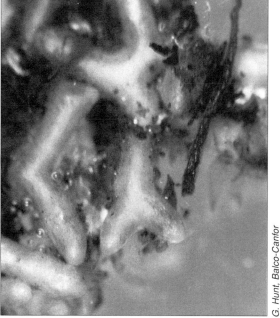

1. the surface area in contact with soil particles is increased and the high density of the fungal hyphae network provides for depletion zones that use the entire soil mass rather than the small fraction occupied by roots alone;

2. the much smaller hyphae can penetrate fissures in soil particles too small for roots;

3. the fungus excretes enzymes that dissolve soil nutrients otherwise unavailable to the roots;

4. the relatively high respiratory rates of fungi release large quantities of carbon dioxide, which is converted to HCO_3^- and H^+, stimulating solution of nutrients; and

5. the fungus extends the life of an absorbing root from a few days to a year or more (Harley 1974).

Endomycorrhizae differ from the above primarily in that the fungus hyphae penetrate directly into the cortical cells of the roots, and the external hyphae generally do not form as densely around the root. Endomycorrhizae are generally considered to be more

FIGURE 4.2. Mycorrhizae on seedling roots. The symbiotic relationship between the fungus and seedlings is extremely important for seedling survival and growth.

G. Hunt, Balco-Canfor

primitive than the ectomycorrhizae, and there is evidence that higher plants are gradually evolving away from this type of mutualism (Pirozynski 1981).

Because neither endo- nor ectomycorrhizae-forming fungi are able to penetrate beyond the cortical region, the vascular tissues of the root are not infected.

Water

Because water makes up most of the fresh weight of seedlings, and because plant metabolism requires an aqueous medium in all living cells, water is *the* most important substance taken up by seedling roots. In British Columbia, where forest environments range from warm and dry during the growing season in the southern Interior to cool and wet for the same period in the northern Interior, a seedling may be stressed by either too much or too little moisture. The following seedling water relations are basic to the planning of reforestation in British Columbia:

- Movement of water through the soil-seedling-atmosphere continuum is mediated by stress at the seedling-atmosphere interface. That is, moisture is pulled through the seedling by the evaporative potential of the atmosphere.

- No coniferous seedling can survive for a prolonged period without a source of moisture. If such a seedling were in equilibrium with an atmosphere containing 95% relative humidity, the desiccation would be lethal. Seedlings avoid drought by closing their stomata, thus limiting both water loss and photosynthesis. In the case of white spruce, about 1.7 MPa of plant moisture stress is sufficient to stimulate stomatal closure (Figure 4.3). Therefore, on exposed clearcuts, this species frequently conducts maximum photosynthesis only in the morning (Figure 4.4).

- A second major moisture-induced stress may affect seedlings as a result of high water tables. In this case the adverse environment is a result of too much, not too little, water. Saturated soils affect seedling roots adversely because (1) root metabolism requires oxygen not available in an anaerobic environment, and (2) soil micro-organisms release toxic substances which are very damaging to seedling root systems.

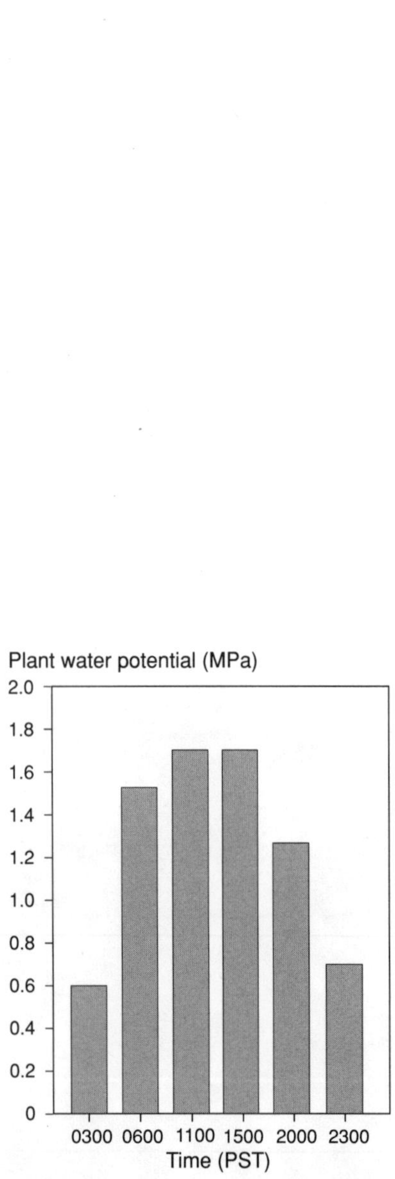

Among British Columbia conifers, Douglas-fir is most sensitive to high water tables; lodgepole pine and western redcedar (*Thuja plicata*) are most tolerant.

THE SIGNAL-RESPONSE PATHWAY BETWEEN SEEDLINGS AND THEIR ENVIRONMENT

Environmental Cues

Unlike animals, which cope with annual changes in temperate zone climates by migrating or seeking shelter, perennial plants must remain exposed. As a result, tree seedlings have evolved a succession of physiological states and morphological forms that allow them to make the best use of site resources during periods of favorable weather, and provide them with

Plant water potential (MPa)

FIGURE 4.3. Plant water potential (MPa) of a white spruce seedling on a sunny day near Prince George. Plant water potential is maintained at about 1.7 MPa for most of the daytime. Nighttime recovery is to a potential about 0.55 MPa drier than the soil. (D.A. Draper, D.L. Spittlehouse, and W.D. Binder, Research Branch, B.C. Forest Service, Victoria, B.C., unpublished data.)

a high resistance to damage during unfavorable weather. Transitions between periods of active growth and stress resistance (dormancy) are mediated by such external signals as:

- accumulation of "heat sums" which is associated with resumption of growth in the spring. Plant response includes resumption of cell division in apical and lateral meristems and, in the case of determinate plants, enlargement of tissues initiated the previous year.

- moisture stress or lengthening nights in midsummer which stimulate the initiation of dormancy in the apical meristems and the formation of resting buds.

- mild temperatures and long nights in early fall which promote "rest" in the apical meristems and initiate cold hardiness in the entire plant.

- low temperatures and very long nights in late fall which terminate rest in the apical meristems and maximize cold hardiness.

Terms Defined

Heat sums

A heat sum is the summation, with time, of degree hours or degree days based on the difference between the mean hourly or daily temperature and a given "base" temperature at which biological activity is very low. That is, if the base temperature is designated as 3 °C, then a day with a mean temperature of 15 °C would be credited with 12 degree days. Resumption of growth in the spring is triggered by the accumulation of a given number of degree days. This number is under strong genetic control and varies among seedlings of a given species and among species. Generally the "heat sum" of a given genotype in a given location will permit the earliest possible growth resumption compatible with the normal incidence of spring frost.

Dormancy

The classical definition of dormancy (Lavender 1990) is "when an organ or tissue, predetermined to elongate or grow in some other manner, does not do so." With woody, temperate perennials, "dormancy" is confined to the apical meristems. It has several stages:

1. Quiescence: earliest stage of dormancy commonly occurring in mid- to late summer. Growth is controlled by environment, not by internal plant physiology.

2. Rest: commonly occurs in midfall. Growth is controlled by the physiology of the bud and will not occur under even very favorable conditions. Stress resistance at this time is very low.

3. Post-dormancy (quiescence): once again, growth is controlled by the environment rather than by the physiology of the bud. Transition from rest to post-dormancy is mediated by exposure of the plant to temperatures of about 5 °C. The number of days of such temperature needed to complete the transition depends on species (e.g., white spruce, about 6 weeks; Douglas-fir, about 14 weeks). It is termed the "chilling requirement." Seedlings

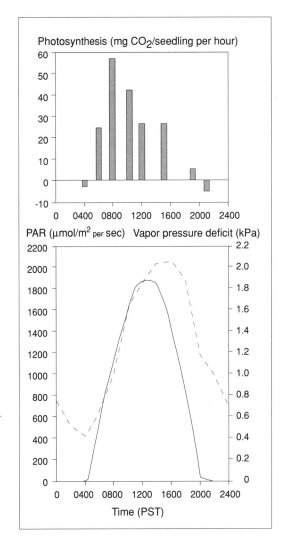

FIGURE 4.4. Comparison of the photosynthesis of a white spruce seedling (upper graph), and photosynthetically active radiation (PAR) (solid line) and vapor pressure deficit (vpd) (dashed line) (lower graph). (D.A. Draper, D.L. Spittlehouse, and W.D. Binder, Research Branch, B.C. Forest Service, Victoria, B.C., unpublished data.)

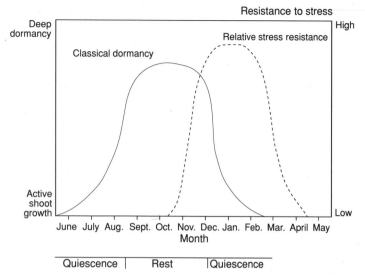

FIGURE 4.5.   Relationship between classical dormancy and dormancy as defined by stress resistance ("hardening off") in Douglas-fir. (The curve defining stress resistance is based on data for the period early October to early March.)

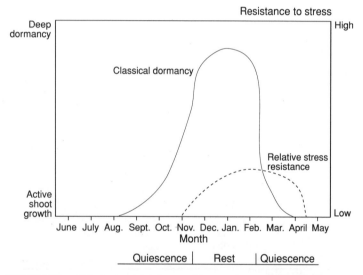

FIGURE 4.6.   Effect of maintaining seedlings under a growth-inducing environment after midsummer. Classical dormancy curve is moved forward in time and seedlings do not achieve the level of stress resistance that develops if they are in phase with the natural weather sequence.

are highly resistant to stress in this stage (Figure 4.5) until stem elongation is initiated.

The forester should be aware that coniferous seedlings have evolved to respond to cues in the normal weather sequence experienced each season. If a seedling is exposed to environments that differ from the normal, it may be out-of-phase with its regular environment. The result may be that normal stress resistance does not develop during the late fall, and the seedling's subsequent survival and growth may be poor. For example, in Douglas-fir seedlings irrigated too long during the summer months, quiescence might not be initiated until late August or September. The dormancy curve for such plants (Figures 4.5 and 4.6) moves forward in time. Also, because dislocation of the normal physiological sequence occurring during dormancy is correlated with reduced vigor and stress resistance (Figure 4.6), such plants have a significantly reduced survival and growth potential the following spring.

Growth Regulation

In reviewing the various mechanisms of growth regulation in temperate perennial plants, Lavender (1981) noted that low or deficient quantities of nutrients and water may stimulate dormancy, while plentiful supplies of both nutrients and water may result in extended growth periods. Warm temperatures appear to accelerate the transition to dormancy in the first case and increase growth rate in the second. Such results may be interpreted as straightforward responses to the availability of essential substrates.

More difficult to explain, however, is the plant response to the length of day or, more properly, the length of the unbroken dark period. This environmental factor has been known to have a profound effect on plant physiology, since the pioneering research of Garner and Allard (1920) with mammoth tobacco. Early work showed that a wide range of species would flower only when exposed to short nights — about 8 hours of unbroken dark period per day (long day plants) — while other species would flower only after a series of long, unbroken dark periods — about 16 hours per day (short day plants). Similar research with perennial woody plants (Nitsch 1957) has shown that many temperate zone trees, particularly boreal species, will initiate dormancy if exposed to uninterrupted dark periods of 10 hours or more each day. This photoperiodic response is believed to be mediated by phytochrome, the pigment in the foliage (Nooden and Weber 1978). Exposing this pigment to light will keep it in the physiologically active 730-nm absorbing form, though it will gradually revert to the inactive 660-nm absorbing form in darkness. A long unbroken daily dark period, then, will ensure that the pigment is predominantly in the inactive state. This state has been correlated with dormancy, but the physiological mechanisms producing this response are not clear.

Plant growth regulators are organic substances capable of influencing plant physiological events in extremely low (nanograms/gram dry weight) concentrations. Compounds such as auxins, cytokinins, and gibberellins have generally been associated with active growth (Lavender and Silim 1987; Doumas and Zaerr 1988), whereas abscisic acid concentrations have been related to dormancy. However, as Lavender and Silim (1987) point out, the extreme experimental difficulties in plant growth regulator research have prevented clear definition of the role of these substances in the annual growth cycle.

Interpretation, Decisions, and Action

The nursery manager, by manipulating the environment, can effect various growth responses in seedlings. Several guidelines should be followed in the production and handling of seedlings:

1. Germination of seeds and culture of seedlings should be scheduled so that desired minimum size is achieved by no later than mid-July. Seedlings should then be exposed to a dormancy-inducing environment.

2. Nutrition of seedlings should be tailored to induce well-balanced plants that have a maximum size compatible with the capacity of the container. A large body of research has shown that the mass of effective roots is the seedling parameter most correlated with survival and growth after outplanting (Lavender 1989).

3. Photosynthesis is essential to the development of cold hardiness. Seedlings should be spaced to permit the illumination of the crown; not crowded so that the lower crown is dead (Timmis and Tanaka 1976).

4. Throughout the processing sequence and during transport to plantation and planting site, seedlings should be handled like a carton of eggs, not like a sack of potatoes. Even minor damage is cumulative and can greatly reduce survival and growth. *Moisture and temperature stress should be minimized at all times.*

5. *Cold, dark storage is a stress.* Therefore, seedlings should be stored only when the alternative is more stressful, and then for as brief a time as possible.

6. Figure 4.5 shows the annual growth cycle of coniferous seedlings. As much as it is logistically possible, the principles used in this diagram should be used to guide the schedule of seedling production and handling.

7. The seedling must be considered a balanced system. Emphasis on any one part is not valid. Culling standards, in the absence of appropriate physiological measures, should reflect overall seedling vigor through such morphological parameters as well-formed buds, healthy foliage, a low (about 50) shoot length:diameter ratio, and a well-developed fibrous root system.

SUMMARY: HANDLING SEEDLINGS WITH CARE

Unlike animals, plants must tolerate rather than avoid environmental stress. To do so, they have developed distinct daily and annual rhythms which permit them to take advantage of favorable growing conditions during spring and summer, and then to develop a resistance to adverse weather. Any procedures that disrupt these basic controlling rhythms may have more serious consequences for the plants than even physical damage such as a torn root or broken branch. Care must be taken at all stages of growth, handling, and storage to ensure that seedling physiology is not harmed by either a series of "minor" insults or a single major destructive event.

ECOLOGICAL PRINCIPLES: BASIC CONCEPTS

5

R.J. Stathers, R. Trowbridge, D.L Spittlehouse,
A. Macadam, and J.P. Kimmins

The plants, animals, and soils in our forests interact with one another and with abiotic environmental factors — such as topography and climate — to yield forest ecosystems. In a geographical context, a forest ecosystem is a segment of landscape that is relatively uniform in abiotic factors and biotic (plant, animal, and microorganism) communities.

Seedling survival and growth are influenced by all of these ecosystem components. The response of a seedling to any one component and to the interaction of components depends on its genotype, morphology, and physiology.

Vegetation and soils are readily observed components of an ecosystem. They can be used to help the forester recognize different ecosystems and delineate their boundaries. However, vegetation changes over time, and plant communities can be significantly modified by natural disturbance or management. Soils and climate (site factors), on the other hand, tend to be more stable within the period associated with forest management.

This chapter describes some of the basic concepts related to climate, soil, and vegetation — three broad categories of interacting ecological factors that affect crop tree establishment, survival, and growth.

CLIMATE

Climate directly affects plants through solar radiation, air temperature and humidity, precipitation, and wind; and indirectly through the soil moisture and thermal regimes. Climate can be evaluated at the seedling, plant community, local, or regional level (Major 1951, 1963):

- Regional climates (macroclimates) are characteristic of large areas (10 to hundreds of kilometers in extent) and are not affected by either local vegetation cover or topography.
- Local climates (about 1-10 km in extent) result from the local topography modifying the impact of the regional climate.
- Plant community climates (microclimates) are modified by local topography, soil, and vegetation, and can be characterized by the vegetation of a particular site (0.001-1 km in extent).

Seedling environments should be assessed on the basis of regional climate characteristics, local topography, microtopography (see the section on Microsites), and vegetation.

Solar radiation relative to flat ground (flat ground = 1.0)

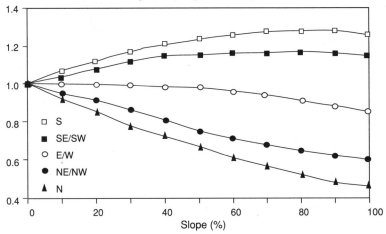

FIGURE 5.1. Effect of slope on solar irradiance at 50° north latitude.

Solar Radiation and Light

Light, or photosynthetically active radiation (PAR), is the visible portion of the solar radiation spectrum. These wavelengths are absorbed by plants and used in photosynthetic reactions and account for only about 45% of the energy from the sun. Photosynthesis uses less than 5% of this energy. Most of the energy of solar radiation that is absorbed at the ground surface heats the seedlings' environment and evaporates water.

Slope and aspect have a major influence on the amount of solar radiation received above a vegetation canopy (Figure 5.1). Their effect, however, is greater on site warming than on photosynthesis.

Latitude affects day length and the intensity of solar radiation. At higher latitudes, longer days during the summer tend to compensate for the lower solar intensity. Such days can be particularly beneficial for seedling growth, since less than full sunlight is required for maximum photosynthesis.

TABLE 5.1. Macroclimatic, site, vegetation, and soil factors that determine air temperature (Spittlehouse and Stathers 1990)

Category	Factor	Influences
Macro-climate	Cloud cover, air temperature, and air humidity	- solar radiation receipt, longwave radiation emission, and heat release by condensation
	Wind speed	- mixing of the air
Site	Elevation	- atmospheric conditions
	Slope angle	- cold air drainage
	Topography	- cold air drainage and wind
	Slope position	- size of uphill cold air source
	Slope and aspect	- solar radiation receipt for air and soil heating
	Latitude	- day length, weather conditions
Vegetation	Cover	- wind speed, cold air drainage, longwave radiation emission from the ground, and soil heating
Soil	Composition	- soil heat storage and release
	Water content	- evaporative cooling and heat storage

Air Temperature and Humidity

Air temperature near the ground surface has a wide diurnal and annual variation. The largest temperature variation usually occurs at the ground surface and around the seedling where radiant energy is absorbed and emitted. Air temperatures 2 m above the ground can often be 5-10°C cooler during the day and 2-5°C warmer at night than at the surface (Figure 5.2), especially under calm, clear conditions. The major factors affecting air temperature are summarized in Table 5.1.

Solar radiation absorbed at the ground surface heats the air during the day. At night, when there is no solar heating, the ground surface and overlying air cool through a net loss of longwave radiation toward the cold sky. Cloud cover reduces both daytime solar heating and nighttime longwave cooling and, as a result, reduces diurnal temperature variation. Air temperatures near the ground are also influenced by wind, which increases mixing of the surface air with the air higher up in the atmosphere.

The regional air mass largely determines the vapor pressure and relative humidity near the seedling. The humidity of the air mass is modified by the land and water surfaces over which it has passed. The source of the air mass also affects its temperature. Water vapor in the air increases longwave radiation emission from the atmosphere toward the ground surface. Humid air is more likely to show less diurnal temperature variation than dry air.

Site factors influence air temperature through their effect on the local surface energy balance. Geographic location influences the climatic regime of the site. Air temperature generally decreases with increasing elevation, partly in response to the changes in weather conditions that occur with increasing elevation. Slope and aspect significantly influence the amount of solar energy received (Figure 5.1), with southerly aspects usually being warmer and drier than any other.

Vegetation that shades the surface moderates air and soil temperature extremes for seedlings. Shading reduces daytime solar heating and nighttime longwave radiation cooling at the soil surface by shifting most of the radiative transfer from the surface into the vegetative canopy. Heavy brush cover can result in seedling and soil surface temperatures that are close to that of the air at 2 m above the surface.

The *albedo* (or reflectivity) of the surface also affects temperatures around the seedling. Dark-colored surfaces absorb more radiation and tend to be warmer than lighter surfaces.

The energy balance of the ground surface determines how much of the absorbed solar radiation is transferred into the soil profile and how much is dissipated into the atmosphere as heat or water vapor. Mineral soil surfaces allow more heat to be conducted into the underlying profile than do organic soil surfaces. As a result, air temperatures just above organic surfaces get hotter during the day and colder at night than air temperatures do above mineral surfaces.

The moisture content of the soil surface also influences air temperatures by altering the surface energy balance. When the surface is wet, a larger proportion of the absorbed solar energy is used to evaporate the surface soil moisture than to increase soil and air temperatures. Similarly, when root zone soil is moist, a vegetated surface can be cooler than when the soil is dry because of the greater evapotranspirational cooling.

Frost Occurrence

Frost occurs when the surface temperature of the ground or the seedling drops to 0°C or lower. Two different processes cause frost and affect its occurrence throughout the landscape. *Radiation frosts* occur when the ground surface cools to below 0°C through the net loss of longwave radiation to the atmosphere. *Advection frosts* occur when air, which has radiatively cooled to below the freezing point at another location, flows or is "advected" onto a site. An air mass with a sub-zero temperature is a macroclimatic scale advection frost.

The amount of longwave radiation (thermal radiation) emitted from any surface increases with increasing temperature. Since the night sky is colder than the ground surface, more longwave

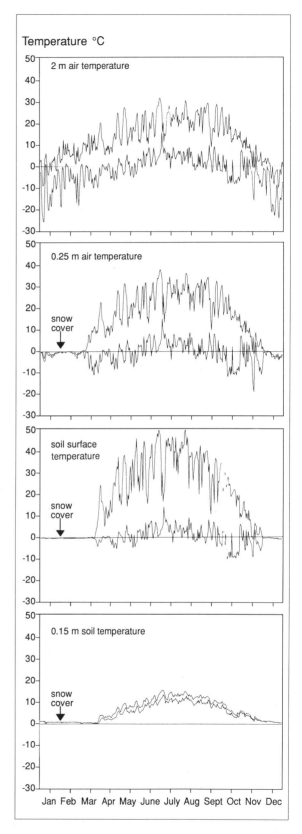

FIGURE 5.2. Annual variation in the daily maximum and minimum air and soil temperatures in a clearcut in the Montane Spruce Zone in the Hurley River valley near Gold Bridge. (D.L. Spittlehouse and M.J. Goldstein, unpublished data, B.C. Forest Service, Victoria, B.C.)

radiation is emitted from the ground toward the sky than vice versa. The net loss of longwave radiation from the ground surface causes it to cool. This, in turn, causes the heat stored in the soil profile and overlying atmosphere to be transferred toward the cooling ground surface. The result is a reduction in soil and air temperatures during the night, with the coldest temperature occurring at the surface.

Unlike the ground, the atmosphere does not behave like a simple radiating surface. A clear sky is partially transparent to the longwave radiation from the ground. This can produce an effective sky temperature that is well below 0°C. Water, carbon dioxide, and other gases at different heights in the atmosphere contribute to the longwave radiation from the sky. Under cloudy conditions, the water droplets in the clouds close the atmospheric radiative window. As a result, there is more downward longwave radiation, less net longwave loss from the ground surface, and a reduced chance of frost occurring.

Wind influences frost occurrence by mixing cold surface air with warmer air aloft. Consequently, the chance of frost is reduced under windy conditions. Local topography disposes some sites to a higher frost risk than others. Air that is radiatively cooled at higher elevations flows down slopes and accumulates on flat or low-lying areas, where it ponds to increasing depths while continuing to cool radiatively. Only slight depressions or changes in microtopography may be sufficient to cause cold air ponding.

The ground surface temperature can continue to drop as long as there is a net radiative loss of heat from the ground toward the sky. Thus, daily minimum temperatures usually occur just before sunrise with the coldest temperatures occurring at the ground surface. In the spring and fall when the nights are longer, more radiative cooling can occur and the risk of frost increases. As well, less heat is stored in the soil and overlying air during the day in these seasons, and this further compounds the frost hazard. Information on frost and treatments to minimize frost damage can be found in Stathers (1989).

Precipitation

The type of storm, whether frontal or convective, determines the amount and areal extent of the precipitation. Convective storms usually occur in the summer and can be localized, whereas frontal storms are larger and provide more uniform rainfall over the landscape. The time of year affects amount of precipitation received and whether it is in the form of rain or snow.

The site factors that affect precipitation are:

- *geographic location* (e.g., distance from the coast or other large bodies of water).
- *elevation* (e.g., precipitation generally increases with elevation in any one area. Snow depth and snow cover duration also usually increase with elevation).
- *topography* (e.g., windward slopes that face prevailing storms or leeward rain shadows). Depressions, lee slopes, and other areas where drifting occurs can have higher snow accumulations than ridges where wind scour reduces accumulation. Wind scour can also reduce snow accumulation near stumps, logs, and brush. In the spring, these darker surfaces increase the rate of

snow melt by absorbing solar radiation and becoming sources of heat that melt the surrounding snow.

Snow accumulation on a site can be both beneficial and detrimental to seedlings. Snow cover provides insulation and, on many of the drier sites, provides water to recharge the soil. Snow press, down-slope movement of the snow pack, and the late melting of deep snow packs or snow drifts can harm seedlings by deforming stems and increasing a plant's vulnerability to shrub competition and snow molds. Snow press depends on the degree of settling of the snow pack. The down-slope movement of the snow pack is determined by the depth and density of snow, the slope angle, and the slope roughness. There is a low risk of down-slope movement on sites with slopes of less than 20°, at lower elevations in areas where less snow occurs, and on sites that have rough surfaces such as rock outcrops, stumps, mounds, and brush cover. Steep, smooth, grassy surfaces with few large surface irregularities are at a higher risk for snow movement (Megahan and Steele 1987).

Wind

The wind speed at a site is determined by large scale meteorological processes. Differences in the solar heating of areas of the earth create large scale temperature variations which result in air pressure variations. The air moves (winds blow) in response to these differences in pressure. The greater the temperature range, the greater the difference in pressure and the stronger the wind.

Local topography can reduce or increase ground level winds. For example, wind can be channelled by valleys, and wind speed can increase as air flows over a ridge, but remain much reduced in the lee of the ridge. Daytime heating in valleys can generate up-slope (anabatic) winds as the warm, less dense valley air rises up through the cooler air. The winds generated during a forest fire are an example of the extreme effect of the upward movement of warm air. Down-slope and down-valley (katabatic) winds occur at night as the cooler, denser up-slope air flows down the slope. A glacier at the head of a valley can create strong katabatic winds during the day.

The concept of wind chill only applies to objects that generate heat such as animals or houses. Leaves and stems of plants (just like thermometers) cannot be wind-chilled. Wind increases mixing of the air so that the temperature of the plant more closely approaches that of the surrounding air.

Extremes in the Weather

Weather conditions at a site vary from year to year. Extremes in the weather may be more influential to growth than the average weather conditions (the climate). Temperature extremes, for example, can physically damage seedlings in any climate. Freezing temperatures can result in frost heaving or, if seedlings are not hardy, frost damage. High temperatures, particularly on water-deficient sites, can increase seedling moisture stress and reduce seedling growth. A year with low spring and summer rainfall can drastically affect plantation performance. Although such extreme conditions do not occur often, they need only happen once to cause serious damage.

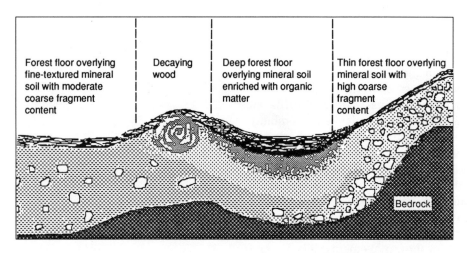

Forest floor overlying fine-textured mineral soil with moderate coarse fragment content

Decaying wood

Deep forest floor overlying mineral soil enriched with organic matter

Thin forest floor overlying mineral soil with high coarse fragment content

Bedrock

FIGURE 5.3.   Cross-sectional diagram depicting a variety of surface substrates commonly associated with forest soils.

SOILS

The surface soil material includes the upper soil solum, from the ground surface to a depth of approximately 30 cm (Figure 5.3). There are two basic types of soil material, organic and mineral. In the organic layer (forest floor), decaying wood is recognized as a separate type of organic material. The mineral layer is made up of both fine soil material and coarse fragments. Surface water and exposed bedrock may also be present on the ground surface, and will detract from a site's suitability for seedling establishment. Each of these materials affects the soil temperature (Table 5.2), moisture (Table 5.3), and nutrient regimes of microsites, and ultimately their appropriateness as planting spots.

Surface Organic Layer

The surface organic layer is typically more heterogeneous than the underlying mineral layer. In addition to the differences in the depth and coverage of forest floor and decaying wood materials, variation in the rate of their decomposition frequently occurs within a site. This is manifested in the presence of different humus forms, which indicate differences in nutrient availability. The profile and differentiating characteristics of the three humus form orders are shown in Figure 5.4 (consult Klinka et al. 1981 for humus form classification). In general, microsites with Moder and Mull humus forms indicate greater nutrient availability than do those with Mor humus forms.

The surface organic layer insulates the underlying mineral soil from moisture and temperature conditions at the soil surface. The magnitude of this effect is related to forest floor depth: soil temperature and moisture levels beneath deep forest floors fluctuate to a lesser degree and less rapidly throughout the season than beneath thin forest floor layers. This effect may be undesirable in cold climates where seedling root growth may be inhibited by low soil temperature in the growing season, but beneficial in warm climates where the presence of the deep forest floor may help to conserve soil moisture.

Mineral Soil

Mineral soil is a suitable planting substrate, and is generally preferred over organic material for planting nursery stock. Soil texture (particle size composition of the mineral soil fraction < 2 mm) is one of the most important interpretive soil properties and is easily estimated in the field. Coarse-textured (sandy and/or gravelly) soils typically have a low water- and nutrient-holding

TABLE 5.2.   Macroclimatic, site, vegetation and soil factors that determine soil temperature (Spittlehouse and Stathers 1990)

Category	Factor	Influences
Macro-climate	Solar radiation, air temperature, precipitation, and wind speed	- heat transfer into the soil, and soil water content
Site	Latitude, elevation, slope, and aspect	- solar radiation air temperature, soil water content, growing season, and day length
Surface	Vegetation cover, snow cover, albedo, and surface roughness	- solar radiation heat transfer into the soil
Soil	Soil composition	- thermal conductivity
	Bulk density, and soil water content	- volumetric heat capacity, and heat transfer into the soil

capacity, but good water drainage and aeration. Fine-textured (silty and clayey) soils have high water- and nutrient-holding capacity, but poorer drainage and aeration. Although clayey soils can have a higher water-holding capacity, much of the water is held so tightly as to be unavailable to plants. In addition, soil compaction and frost heaving of seedlings occur more frequently in finer-textured soils. Loamy soils are generally ideal because they are intermediate in the above properties.

Coarse fragments (the mineral soil fraction > 2 mm) reduce the quality of the textural properties by lessening the water- and nutrient-holding capacity. Bedrock close to the surface decreases moisture and nutrient content. Organic matter in the mineral soil will increase water- and nutrient-holding capacity, improve soil structure, and enhance biological activity. Well-drained and well-structured mineral soil enriched with organic matter is a good indicator of productive microsites and planting spots.

Microsite Concept

A forest is a mosaic of sites and each site is usually a complex of microsites. A microsite is a portion of a site that is uniform in microtopography and surface soil materials. It can range in size from less than 1 m^2 to occasionally over 5 m^2. Microsites are dynamic in that their characteristics are ever-changing, imperceptibly or suddenly. These changes occur through aggradation or degradation processes associated with water, wind, mass wasting, blowdown, and wildfire, as well as with forest management, harvesting, and site preparation.

Most sites have several types of microsites, and some of these may be more appropriate for tree establishment than others. While site quality is used as a criterion for tree species selection, microsites should be the criterion for the selection of actual planting spots. Furthermore, an understanding of the relationship between microsites and seedling survival and growth on a particular site is essential to the selection of the most appropriate site preparation method.

TABLE 5.3. Macroclimatic, site, vegetation, and soil factors that determine soil moisture (Spittlehouse and Stathers 1990)

Category	Factor	Influences
Macro-climate	Solar radiation, air temperature, air humidity, and wind speed	- transpiration and soil evaporation
	Precipitation	- input of water
Site	Geographic location, elevation, aspect, and slope angle	- solar radiation air temperature, relative humidity, and precipitation
	Slope position	- soil drainage and runoff
Vegetation	Height and cover	- interception of precipitation and transpiration
	Species and rooting depth	- transpiration
Soil	Texture, coarse fragments, bulk density, and organic matter	- available water storage capacity, drainage, and soil evaporation
	Profile depth	- soil water storage
	Profile discontinuities	- drainage

FIGURE 5.4. Typical examples of Mor, Moder, and Mull humus forms and their distinguishing characteristics.

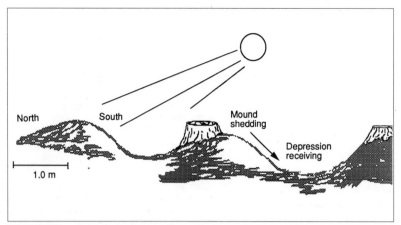

FIGURE 5.5. Schematic diagram illustrating some features of forest microtopography.

Microtopography

Mounds and depressions are two principal expressions of microtopography (surface shape) (Figure 5.5). The primary influences on the climatic regimes of mounds and depressions are height and frequency, along with slope and aspect.

In general, mounds are drier and warmer than depressions. However, the magnitude of the difference depends on the local climate, relief, and aspect of a site, in addition to the material composition of the mounds and depressions. Because of the accumulation of fine organic and mineral materials, depressions often have greater concentrations of nutrients than do the apices of mounds.

On sites with no major water deficit in the growing season and high precipitation in fall and winter, depressions can have temporary surface ponding or a high water table. In such situations, they are less suitable for seedling establishment and growth than mounds. On sites in dry and warm climates, where a water deficit is expected early in the growing season, depressions can provide more suitable planting spots than mounds, especially south-exposed mounds. The latter, however, can be appropriate microsites in cold and snowy climates, while north-exposed mounds can be suitable in warm climates, particularly on steep, south-facing slopes.

The type and frequency of mounds and depressions can restrict the stocking level and uniformity of spacing on some sites. A mixed-species plantation can be used to obtain full site occupancy where this occurs.

VEGETATION

Successful regeneration of forests depends on how associated vegetation affects the establishment and growth of the crop species. The composition, structure, and function of plant communities change over time. This process is termed succession, and understanding the way it influences forest environments is critical to sound forest management.

Primary Succession

Primary succession occurs in environments that have not been previously altered by living organisms. It occurs over long time periods, as organisms colonize freshly exposed, unaltered parent materials. Early stages of primary succession can be observed on rock outcrops, on recently deposited or exposed soil parent material, and in shallow lakes, ponds, and wetlands. Primary succession in a particular type of environment tends to follow predictable rates of change, sequences of communities, and rates of plant growth.

Secondary Succession

Secondary succession occurs after a disturbance removes an existing community while leaving the physical, chemical and biological characteristics of the soil largely intact. The patterns of change in plant communities following wildfire or forest harvesting are normally described as secondary succession. Unlike primary succession, secondary succession tends to be variable and unpredictable in its rates and patterns of change and in the productivity of the communities. It may occur over tens or hundreds of years, while primary succession generally occurs over hundreds or thousands of years.

Factors Affecting Pattern and Rate of Succession

A diversity of patterns of secondary succession and early-seral communities are found in British Columbia. Patterns of early-secondary succession cannot yet be predicted from the biogeoclimatic ecosystem classification, because sampling to date has dealt mainly with maturing-seral and old-growth ecosystems.

The composition of early-seral plant communities is influenced by the survival of species that were present before disturbance (bud banks); by seed stored within the ecosystem (seed banks); by seed arriving from adjacent areas (seed rain); and by the germination and growth of each species.

Harvesting operations that cause little damage to aboveground parts of understory vegetation (such as winter logging on snow) may result in communities dominated by the species which were present in the understory before harvesting (e.g., white-flowered rhododendron (*Rhododendron albiflorum*) in Interior high-elevation forests). Similarly, activities such as slashburning that remove aboveground parts but cause minimal damage to buds or underground organs like roots and rhizomes may result in the regrowth of many of the existing shrubs and forbs (e.g., thimbleberry (*Rubus parviflorus*), salmonberry (*Rubus spectabilis*), and fireweed (*Epilobium angustifolium*)). Some plants may resprout in abundance from extensive root systems following the cutting of stems (e.g., trembling aspen (*Populus tremuloides*)). Viable rhizomes of some herbs and shrubs may be maintained in stands where most of the shoots have been eliminated by shading. This can result in surprisingly rapid colonization of the site by these species following clearcutting.

Seed banks (viable seeds accumulated in the forest floor or the upper mineral soil, or stored in unopened cones in the vegetation canopy) can contribute to the establishment of trees, shrubs, and herbs following disturbance. Lodgepole pine stands typically regenerate from seed banks following disturbance. Shrubs that may germinate from seed stored on-site include small-seeded species such as thimbleberry and salmonberry, and other species such as red elderberry (*Sambucus racemosa*), vine maple (*Acer circinatum*), and Douglas maple (*Acer glabrum*). Seed of some species may remain viable in the forest floor for long periods of time after all live plants of the species have disappeared from the ecosystem. The seed bank of some species is stimulated to germinate by fire providing the fire is not so hot that it kills the seeds.

Several million seeds may arrive annually in 1 ha of disturbed land (Archibold 1980). This seed rain is likely to make the largest contribution to community characteristics on sites where seed banks and bud banks have been destroyed. Most conifers regenerate in this fashion. Species such as fireweed and red alder produce abundant quantities of seed which can be carried by wind for several hundred meters over adjoining areas. Seeds from thimbleberry, salmonberry, raspberry (*Rubus idaeus*), elderberry, huckleberry (*Vaccinium parvifolium*), and salal (*Gaultheria shallon*) may be transported by animals and deposited with their excrement. Germination of some of these seeds may be aided by the action of the digestive enzymes of the animals. Plant establishment and growth from seed depend on the seedbed conditions and the presence of other plants.

Under favorable conditions, plant communities develop rapidly following harvesting. In the Sub-Boreal Spruce Zone, both the rate of site invasion and the total vegetation cover after logging and burning were found to increase with increasing soil moisture (Eis 1980; Hamilton and Yearsley 1988). Eis (1980) found that shrub and herb cover totalled 100% within 3 years after logging on moist to very moist alluvial sites, while on slightly dry to fresh upland sites, total vegetation cover was only 46% within 6 years after logging and burning.

The maximum leaf area that can be supported by mature stands growing on a particular site (the leaf area carrying capacity of the site) is largely determined by moisture availability, nutrient availability, and the efficiency with which the species in the community use water and nutrients. The leaf area carried by early-seral communities may be lower than that found in later successional stages because of differences in the ability of plants to use site resources and in the ability of different species to capture and use light, water, and nutrients. Once a portion of a site's leaf area carrying capacity has been captured by early seral species (herbs, shrubs), the development of leaf area by crop trees may be slowed, possibly resulting in delayed canopy closure and reduced rotation-length yields.

ECOLOGICAL PRINCIPLES: APPLICATIONS

6

K. Klinka, M.C. Feller, R.N. Green,
D.V. Meidinger, J. Pojar, and J. Worrall

Forest site quality has been defined as the sum total of all the many environmental factors affecting the biotic community (Daniels et al. 1979; Spurr and Barnes 1980). It is measured by the maximum tree biomass the land can produce in a given time. While it is fairly easy to list individual site factors, it is very difficult to evaluate and predict their integrated effect on plants. Different combinations of site factors can have similar influences because of compensating effects.

SITE QUALITY ASSESSMENT

Site quality can be assessed directly or inferred from certain site features. It is generally difficult and time consuming to measure light, temperature, moisture, and nutrients directly, or the site characteristics that influence these factors. Many of these measurements need to be taken regularly over several years to account for seasonal and annual differences. However, such site factors can also be evaluated from indicator plants and selected topographic and soil properties, through the application of the biogeoclimatic ecosystem classification.

This classification system delineates site units — groups of biologically equivalent sites with similar potential vegetation and productivity. Similar vegetation potential implies that, in the course of time and in the absence of further disturbance, similar types of plant communities will develop on similar sites. The potential productivity can be attained only if the actual forest community is capable of using the site completely. Otherwise, the productivity of a site will depend on tree species and stand management. Sites with similar climate, soil moisture, and soil nutrient characteristics have the same site quality and are expected to have similar vegetation and productivity potentials.

If a forest, which consists of many different and complex ecosystems, is classified into site units, then management of that forest can be simplified and, at the same time, given a sound ecological foundation. Forest regeneration can be achieved in any given site unit by the application of the ecological knowledge and experience relevant to that unit.

Biogeoclimatic Ecosystem Classification

Ecosystem studies carried out from 1950 to 1975 by Dr. V. J. Krajina and his students at the University of British Columbia resulted in the development of the biogeoclimatic ecosystem classification (BEC) system (Krajina 1969, 1972, 1977). The B.C. Forest Service adopted this system and began a province-wide program to develop a site classification that could be used operationally. In the past decade, the BEC system has become firmly entrenched in forest management, and is also being used by wildlife, range, and park managers.

Several modifications and amendments to the system have been made over the years. The most recent account of the BEC system, which is summarized here, was provided by Pojar et al. (1987). All reports since then refer to site rather than ecosystem units. This change reflects a "site approach" in which ecosystems are classified and identified on the basis of their site characteristics.

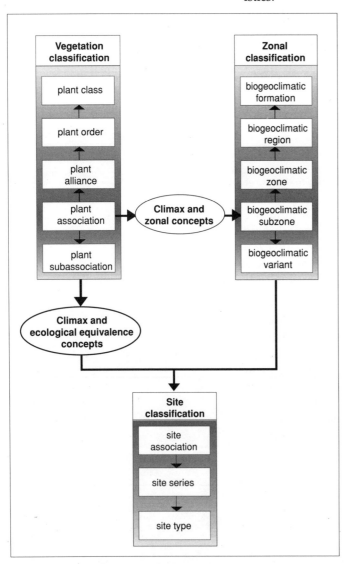

FIGURE 6.1. Categories and relationships of vegetation, zonal, and site classifications in the system of biogeoclimatic ecosystem classification.

The BEC system organizes ecosystems to show their relationships in form, space, and time. The local level organizes ecosystems according to their similarities in form: that is, the structure and composition of their vegetation and sites (Figure 6.1). At the regional level, stable vegetation on zonal (intermediate) sites is used to infer regional climate (Figure 6.1). The result of this zonal or climatic classification are biogeoclimatic units. At a chronological level, ecosystems are organized according to their successional relationships. To do this, the vegetation units recognized for a particular site unit (association) are arranged into chronosequences by disturbance/treatment and successional status.

Zonal Features

The BEC system uses zonal vegetation to delineate biogeoclimatic units — specifically zones, subzones, and variants. These units define a group of geographically related ecosystems that are distributed within, and influenced by, the same regional climate. Each biogeoclimatic unit can be characterized by a set of climatic parameters, for example, temperature and precipitation means, standard deviations, and ranges.

Zones are more general units than subzones or variants. The 14 zones in British Columbia are characterized in Table 6.1 by their vegetation, soils, and some climatic parameters.

Subzones and variants are more specific units of regional climate and are mapped at larger scales (the actual scale depends on terrain, access, and available base maps). Identification of the biogeoclimatic unit is the first step in the assessment of site quality.

Table 6.1. Summary information on Biogeoclimatic Zones of British Columbia

Zone	Code	Zonal vegetation	Zonal soils	Monthly temp. range	Selected climatic characteristics			
					°days >5C	°days <0C	May-Sept. ppt (mm)	Oct.-April ppt (mm)
Alpine Tundra	AT	*Cassiope* spp., *Phyllodoce* spp., *Luetkea pectinata, Loiseleuria procumbens, Dryas* spp., *Salix* spp., *Silene acaulis, Poa* spp., *Festuca* spp., *Carex* spp., *Cetraria* spp., *Stereocaulon* spp., *Polytrichum piliferum*	Regosols, Humic Regosols, Brunisols, Humo-Ferric Podzols	-11.1 - 9.5	427	1763	287	469
Boreal White and Black Spruce	BWBS	White spruce, lodgepole pine, black spruce, *Rosa acicularis, Viburnum edule, Mertensia paniculata, Pyrola asarifolia, Cornus canadensis, Vaccinium vitis-idaea, Ptilium crista-castrensis, Pleurozium schreberi*	Gray Luvisols, Dystric and Eutric Brunisols	-24.5 - 16.6	709 - 1268	1692 - 2742	145 - 305	182 - 198
Bunchgrass	BG	*Agropyron spicatum, Artemisia tridentata, Artemisia frigida, Poa sandbergii, Koeleria macrantha, Festuca scabrella, Festuca idahoensis, Chrysothamnus nauseosus*	Brown and Dark Brown Chernozems	-10.8 - 22.4	1771 - 2516	230 - 878	98 - 175	108 - 208
Coastal Douglas-fir	CDF	Douglas-fir, grand fir, bigleaf maple, western flowering dogwood, *Holodiscus discolor, Gaultheria shallon, Mahonia nervosa, Rosa gymnocarpa, Symphoricarpos albus, Trientalis latifolia, Rubus ursinus, Pteridium aquilinum, Kindbergia oregana, Rhytidiadelphus triquetrus*	Dystric Brunisols	1.8 - 18.0	1794 - 2121	9 - 43	107 - 238	540 - 1107
Coastal Western Hemlock	CWH	Western hemlock, amabilis fir, Sitka spruce, yellow-cedar, *Vaccinium alaskaense, Vaccinium parvifolium, Menziesia ferruginea, Gaultheria shallon, Polystichum munitum, Pteridium aquilinum, Blechnum spicant, Clintonia uniflora, Rhytidiadelphus loreus, Hylocomium splendens*	Ferro-Humic and Humo-Ferric Podzols	-6.6 - 18.7	1059 - 2205	5 - 493	159 - 1162	695 - 3225
Engelmann Spruce Subalpine Fir	ESSF	Subalpine fir, Engelmann spruce, *Rhododendron albiflorum, Menziesia ferruginea, Vaccinium (membranaceum, ovalifolium, scoparium), Rubus pedatus, Gymnocarpium dryopteris, Tiarella unifoliata, Valeriana sitchensis, Orthilia secunda, Streptopus roseus, Veratrum viride, Barbilophozia lycopodioides, Pleurozium schreberi, Rhytidiopsis robusta*	Humo-Ferric Podzols	-10.9 - 13.3	629 - 801	879 - 1189	205 - 425	271 -1597
Interior Cedar-Hemlock	ICH	Western hemlock, western redcedar, hybrid white spruce, Douglas-fir, subalpine fir, *Vaccinium ovalifolium, Oplopanax horridus, Vaccinium membranaceum, Rubus parviflorus, Paxistima myrsinites, Smilacina racemosa, Streptopus (amplexifolius, roseus), Chimaphila umbellata, Goodyera oblongifolia, Gymnocarpium dryopteris, Ptilium crista-castrensis, Pleurozium schreberi, Hylocomium splendens, Rhytidiadelphus triquetrus*	Humo-Ferric Podzols, Gray Luvisols, and Dystric Brunisols	-10.7 - 20.8	1267 - 2140	238 - 820	200 - 439	294 - 1098

Table 6.1. (Continued)

Zone	Code	Zonal vegetation	Zonal soils	Monthly temp. range	°days >5C	°days <0C	May-Sept. ppt (mm)	Oct.-April ppt (mm)
					Selected climatic characteristics			
Interior Douglas-fir	IDF	Douglas-fir, lodgepole pine, ponderosa pine, Spiraea betulifolia, Amelanchier alnifolia, Juniperus communis, Symphoricarpos albus, Mahonia aquifolium, Paxistima myrsinites, Calamagrostis rubescens, Arctostaphylos uva-ursi, Agropyron spicatum, Pleurozium schreberi	Gray Luvisols, Eutric and Dystric Brunisols	-13.1 - 21.3	903 - 2366	235 - 1260	107 - 291	149 - 1022
Montane Spruce	MS	Hybrid white spruce, subalpine fir, lodgepole pine, Douglas-fir, Vaccinium scoparium, Lonicera utahensis, Shepherdia canadensis, Paxistima myrsinites, Vaccinium membranaceum, Alnus viridis, Linnaea borealis, Empetrum nigrum, Calamagrostis rubescens, Pleurozium schreberi	Dystric Brunisols and Humo-Ferric Podzols	-12.5 - 17.4	891 - 1310	847 - 890	158 - 252	223 - 469
Mountain Hemlock	MH	Mountain hemlock, amabilis fir, yellow-cedar, Vaccinium (ovalifolium, membranaceum, alaskaense), Menziesia ferruginea, Rhododendron albiflorum, Rubus pedatus, Phyllodoce empetriformis, Rhytidiopsis robusta, Rhytidiadelphus loreus, Hylocomium splendens	Ferro-Humic Podzols and Folisols	-2.3 - 13.2	919 - 933	307 - 352	694 - 707	1857 - 2260
Ponderosa Pine	PP	Ponderosa pine, Agropyron spicatum, Balsamorhiza sagittata, Festuca (saximontana, idahoensis), Koeleria macrantha, Lithospermum ruderale, Achillea millefolium	Eutric and Dystric Brunisols	-8.6 - 21.6	1505 - 2442	258 - 861	86 - 270	170 - 334
Spruce - Willow - Birch	SWB	White spruce, subalpine fir, Salix glauca, Betula glandulosa, Potentilla fruticosa, Shepherdia canadensis, Festuca altaica, Lupinus arcticus, Pedicularis labradorica, Epilobium angustifolium, Empetrum nigrum, Vaccinium (vitis-idaea, caespitosum), Hylocomium splendens, Cladina spp., Nephroma arcticum	Eutric or Dystric Brunisols, Humo-Ferric Podzols	-19.2 - 14.0	534 - 933	2036 - 2298	275 - 280	179 - 424
Sub-Boreal Pine - Spruce	SBPS	Lodgepole pine, white spruce, Shepherdia canadensis, Spiraea betulifolia, Rosa acicularis, Calamagrostis rubescens, Arctostaphylos uva-ursi, Vaccinium caespitosum, Linnaea borealis, Pleurozium schreberi, Peltigera spp., Cladina spp.	Gray Luvisols and Dystric Brunisols	-13.8 - 14.3	697 - 1044	1140 - 1405	243 - 300	218 - 222
Sub-Boreal Spruce	SBS	Hybrid white spruce, subalpine fir, lodgepole pine, Vaccinium membranaceum, Rubus parviflorus, Viburnum edule, Lonicera involucrata, Rubus pedatus, Spiraea betulifolia, Rosa acicularis, Aralia nudicaulis, Cornus canadensis, Linnaea borealis, Arnica cordifolia, Clintonia uniflora, Aster conspicuus, Osmorhiza chilensis, Oryzopsis asperifolia, Smilacina racemosa, Gymnocarpium dryopteris, Pleurozium schreberi, Ptilium crista-castrensis, Hylocomium splendens, Dicranum polysetum, Rhytidiadelphus triquetrus, Peltigera spp.	Gray Luvisols, Dystric Brunisols, and Humo-Ferric Podzols	-14.6 - 16.9	884 - 1510	792 - 1369	189 - 353	250 - 1383

Selected climatic characteristics summarized from AES Long-term Stations. Prepared by D. Meidinger.

Soil Moisture and Nutrient Classification

Soil moisture and nutrient characteristics are incorporated into the assessment of site quality through the classification of soil moisture and nutrient regimes.

Soil moisture regime (SMR) is the average amount of soil water available for evapotranspiration over several years. Krajina (1969) adopted nine classes (0-8) of SMR's and applied them in different climates. The driest soil in any climate is always very xeric (0) and the wettest is always hydric (8). A synthesis of topographic and soil characteristics, aided by indicator plants, has been used to estimate the relative SMR's of forest sites (e.g., Walmsley et al. 1980; Pojar 1983).

Despite the ease of identifying relative SMR's in the field, the actual amount of available soil water can vary widely throughout British Columbia for any given relative SMR. As a result, quantitative classifications of SMR's have also been developed (Soil Survey Staff 1975; Klinka et al. 1984; Agriculture Canada Expert Committee on Soil Survey 1987). Where the information is available, the relationships between actual and relative SMR's are shown on the edatopic grids prepared for each biogeoclimatic subzone.

Soil nutrient regime (SNR) refers to the amount of essential soil nutrients that are available to vascular plants over a period of several years. Krajina (1969) adopted six classes of SNR's (A to F — F being a hypereutrophic class used to designate saline soils) — and applied them in different climates. The poorest soil in any climate is always oligotrophic (A) and the richest is always eutrophic (E). A synthesis of soil characteristics and indicator plants has been used to estimate the relative SNR's of forest sites (e.g., Walmsley et al. 1980; Pojar 1983; Klinka et al. 1989). As with relative SMR, relative SNR does not indicate the actual amount of available soil nutrients.

Levels of available soil moisture and soil nutrients are influenced by several site properties which have been used for the field identification of SMR's and SNR's (Figures 6.2 and 6.3). However, because these properties do not behave independently, indicator plants again offer the best means of estimating the position of a site on climatic, soil moisture, and soil nutrient gradients.

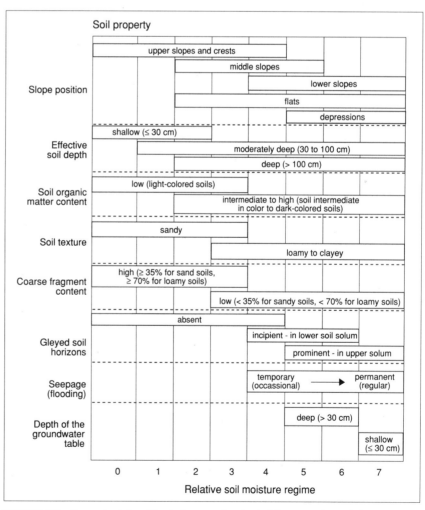

FIGURE 6.2 General relationships between soil water-holding capacity and site properties selected for the diagnosis of relative soil moisture regimes.

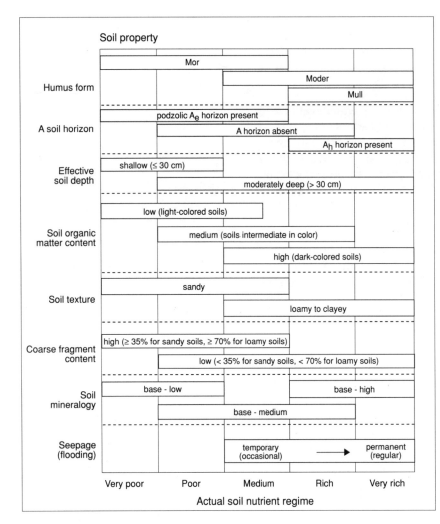

FIGURE 6.3. General relationships between available soil nutrients and site properties selected for the diagnosis of actual soil nutrient regimes.

Site Classification

Figure 6.4 illustrates some relationships among climatic, soil moisture, and soil nutrient gradients and vegetation, zonal, and site units. A section of predominantly undisturbed forest landscape shows the location of three biogeoclimatic subzones (1, 2, and 3), distinguished according to zonal climax plant associations (the middle diagram). The floristic pattern, which reflects variation in local climate, topography, and soils, distinguishes several azonal climax plant associations (e.g., *a* to *c* and *e* to *g* in the top diagram). The vegetation on many of these sites can be in various stages of succession (see bottom diagram), but the basic quality and vegetation potential of the sites are not expected to change significantly. Therefore, all seral plant associations (including the climax one) with the same site quality are grouped into one site association.

For operational application, a forester need only be concerned with the zonal and site classifications, in particular the biogeoclimatic subzones and variants, and the site associations and series (occasionally site types). It is still important, however, for the forester to understand how the site classification is linked to both the vegetation and zonal classifications.

Site units are groups of ecosystems, regardless of present vegetation, that have the same or equivalent environmental properties and vegetation and productivity potentials. The basic category in site classification is the *site association*. Site series and types are divisions of associations. Environmentally, site associations correspond to the plant associations derived from ecosystems with "stable" (mature, old-growth) vegetation. The plant association is characterized and identified by a combination of diagnostic plant species. The site association is identified by a range of climatic, soil moisture, and soil nutrient regimes, and, if appropriate, by an additional environmental factor or property strongly influencing the development of vegetation. For example, two site associations can occur on sites with the same range of climate (i.e., in the same biogeoclimatic subzones), soil moisture regime, and soil nutrient regime, although one may be subject to periodic flooding and the other to temporary seepage, resulting in two different vegetation types.

For the user's convenience in making generalizations, site associations can be combined into site groups according to similarities in climatic, soil moisture, and soil nutrient gradients. For example, all wet, nutrient-

medium to nutrient-rich sites within the cool mesothermal and submaritime cool temperate climates can be represented by the Western Redcedar - Skunk Cabbage site group.

Site series are the basic units used to make pre-harvest silviculture prescriptions (Chapter 8). They result from site associations being divided (using biogeoclimatic subzones and variants) into climatically, and therefore usually edaphically, more uniform units whose response to management is fairly predictable. Readers of older literature such as Annas and Coupé (1979) or Pojar (1983) should note that the site series is equivalent to the former ecosystem association.

Site types are divisions of site series, separated according to one or more topographic and soil properties which are thought to affect ecosystem response to management. The site type is the most edaphically consistent site unit.

The names of site units are intended to show categorical rank and to be connotative. The name of a site association (s.a.) usually consists of the generic name of a major pioneer and/or climax tree species and one or two generic names of indicator plants that are expected to be nearly always present on the site (e.g., Western Redcedar - Oak Fern s.a.). Site series (s.s.) are named by prefixing the name of the site association with the symbol for a biogeoclimatic subzone (e.g., ICHvk/Western Redcedar - Oak Fern s.s.; ICHvk designates the Very Wet Cool Interior Cedar - Hemlock subzone). The name of the site type (s.t.) consists of the name of the site series modified by one or more diagnostic edaphic adjectives (e.g., ICHvk/Western Redcedar - Oak fern/Sandy s.t.). Table 6.2 gives a synopsis of the site classification for the Hybrid White Spruce - Black Huckleberry s.a. in central British Columbia.

Site Identification

Identification of site units is necessary for the application of the classification system. The first step is determining the biogeoclimatic subzone or variant from the small scale biogeoclimatic maps. The next step involves collecting environment and vegetation data. This is usually done after division of a stand or "opening" into segments that are uniform in local topography and soil parent materials (landforms). Data collection procedures are detailed in all regional field guides (e.g., Mitchell and Green 1981; Klinka et al. 1984; Pojar et al. 1984; DeLong et al. 1986; Utzig et al. 1986; B.C. Ministry of Forests 1987).

Analysis of the data — topographic and soil properties and, if present, indicator plants — requires using the edatopic grids, keys, and supplementary descriptive materials from the field guides. Correct identification of a site initially requires the user to follow the keys or tables for identifying soil moisture and nutrient regimes. The intersection of the SMR and SNR values on the edatopic grid indicates the site series (see Figure 6.5). This identification can be checked, if undisturbed mature vegetation is present on the site, against the lists of plant species characteristic of mature vegetation that are presented in the guides.

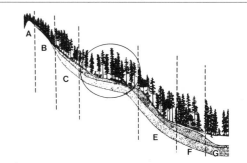

A topographic sequence showing location of vegetation units along the local climatic, soil moisture, and soil nutrient gradients. The circled area represents the zonal site.

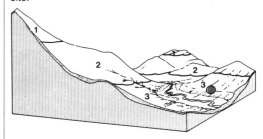

A section of landscape showing locations of three biogeoclimatic subzones (1,2,3) recognized on the basis of distribution of zonal ecosystems. Each segment features a variety of ecosystems (as shown above) where vegetation may be in various successional stages (as shown below).

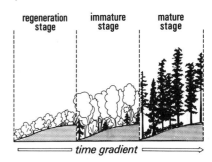

A site-specific chronosequence of vegetation units along the time gradient.

FIGURE 6.4. Schematic diagrams illustrating relationships among vegetation, zonal, and site units.

TABLE 6.2. Synopsis of proposed site series and types[a] of the Hybrid White Spruce - Black Huckleberry (Sx - Black Huckleberry) site association in central British Columbia

Site series
Site type
SBSmc1[b]/Sx - Black Huckleberry
SBSmc1/Sx - Black Huckleberry/Typic[c]
SBSmc1/Sx - Black Huckleberry/Skeletal[d]
SBSmc2/Sx - Black Huckleberry
SBSmc2/Sx - Black Huckleberry/Typic
SBSmc2/Sx - Black Huckleberry/Sandy[e]
SBSmc3/Sx - Black Huckleberry/Clayey[f]
SBSmc3/Sx - Black Huckleberry/Skeletal
SBSmc3/Sx - Black Huckleberry
SBSmc3/Sx - Black Huckleberry/Typic
SBSmc3/Sx - Black Huckleberry/Sandy
SBSmc3/Sx - Black Huckleberry/Skeletal

[a] The methodology for identification of site types follows Pojar et al. (1987). This system is presently under review and may result in modifications.

[b] SBSmc - Moist Cold Sub-Boreal Spruce subzone, 1 - Moffat variant, 2 - Babine variant, 3 - Kluskus variant.

[c] Typic - the central edaphic concept of the particular site association. In this case, moderately deep, well to moderately well-drained, loamy, with <35% coarse fragments, Brunisolic Gray Luvisols on gently sloping morainal materials.

[d] Skeletal - soils with 35% or more but <90% coarse fragments (gravel, stones, or boulders) by volume.

[e] Sandy - sandy (sand or loamy sand) soils, with <35% coarse fragments by volume.

[f] Clayey - fine-textured soils (silty clay, clay, or heavy clay), with <35% coarse fragments by volume.

Keys to site series are prepared for each biogeoclimatic unit (or occasionally groups of units, to avoid repetition). The keys can be based on vegetation or environmental features, or a combination of both (Table 6.3). Environmental keys use topographic and soil properties of a site; vegetation keys use diagnostic species or indicator species groups to differentiate among all site series included in the key. Vegetation keys, however, should only be applied when understory vegetation is well developed (i.e., in the late-immature and older successional stages). If site types are described (Table 6.2), the diagnostic edaphic properties must be determined to identify the unit.

Once the site classification has been determined for the field data points, the boundaries on the initial site map can be verified. Following this, users can consult the management interpretations for each site unit to help them prepare the prescriptions.

Site units are given a numerical symbol so they can be coded into data bases. The symbols are appended after the biogeoclimatic code and separated by slashes. Site series and types are each given two-digit codes; for example, SBSmc1/01/01 refers to the SBSmc1/Sx - Black Huckleberry/Typic site type.

PRINCIPLES OF TREE SPECIES SELECTION

Selecting appropriate tree species to manage on a site is one of the most important decisions a forester makes (e.g., Anderson 1950; Packee 1976; Mayer 1977; Blatchford 1978; Daniels et al. 1979; Hobbs 1984; Klinka and Feller 1984; Smith 1986). The long-term implications of such decisions in the management costs and value of the final crop are significant. A poor choice of tree species can cost thousands of dollars per hectare to correct, for site preparation, replanting, and delayed production; and substantially more if the problem is left unchecked. In British Columbia, obvious examples of inappropriate species choice can be found, often in association with an "over-used" species such as Douglas-fir (Carter and Klinka 1986; Middleton et al. 1989).

Several options are usually available for the regeneration of a new forest. The forester may simply reestablish the original tree species composition on the site or select one or more of the original species. However, species previously found on the site are not necessarily the most appropriate for management. For example, a few large individuals of a particular species in the original stand may mislead the forester into establishing a stand composed only of this species. In fact, species that were absent in the original stand but present in the general area may do equally well. Establishing species that were absent in both the original stand and the general area is another option. The correct option depends on many factors, one of which is the ecological suitability of the species for the site.

In British Columbia, site-specific tree species selection guidelines have been developed within the framework of the BEC system (Pojar et al. 1987). The development and application of these guidelines should be based on: 1) ecological factors; 2) management factors; and 3) selection criteria (Klinka and Feller 1984) (Figure 6.6).

Ecological Factors

Successful reforestation requires the forester to understand not only the silvics of each tree species being dealt with, but also the quality of each forest site to be reforested. Established in unfavorable environments, a species may not realize its growth potential, it will be more susceptible to damaging agents, and it will require more effort to establish and grow. Reforestation also creates a new interaction between the forest community and site, such as in the way a species affects forest floor development and nutrient cycling.

Management Factors

Viable crop species are evaluated to determine which reforestation option best meets the management objectives. Maximum sustained yield depends on the site's natural carrying capacity. A site may be suitable for one of several different management objectives, such as maximizing piece size or merchantable fiber. The preferred species may change with the management objectives, although such change could likely be accommodated through the modifications of silvicultural regimes. Management factors must not override ecological factors in the final selection of tree species, unless considerable funds are spent to modify the environment to suit the species.

Selection Criteria

Given a number of species options that conform to ecological and management factors, the forester should use three criteria to guide species selection: maximum sustainable productivity, crop reliability, and silvicultural feasibility. Making the final choice of suitable tree species for a site will also require information on growth and yield, ecosystem function, future costs of silvicultural treatments, and future markets.

Maximum sustainable productivity

The most productive tree species or combination of tree species should be selected for a given site. Productivity of different species is based on yield. However, a lack of site-specific yield tables in British Columbia means site index should be used as an estimate of forest productivity. Other aspects influencing stand yield — for example, a species' shade tolerance, crown spatial requirements, and form factor — also help in productivity ranking. For example, a management objective of maximum fiber production may result in a shade-tolerant species being ranked above a shade-intolerant species of a similar site index because of the former's higher density and potential yield.

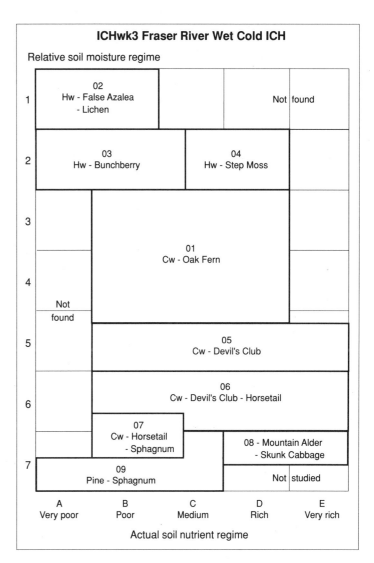

FIGURE 6.5. An edatopic grid showing relationships among ICHwk3 site series, soil moisture regimes, and soil nutrient regimes. The blank cells indicate absence of particular combinations of soil moisture and nutrient regimes in the ICHwk3 variant. The abbreviations used for tree species in the names of site series are: Cw - *Thuja plicata*, Hw - *Tsuga heterophylla*, Pl - *Pinus contorta*.

TABLE 6.3. Key to site series of the Goat Wet Cool Interior Cedar - Hemlock (ICHwk3) variant. Figure 6.5 presents soil moisture and soil nutrient regimes for each site series.

1a	Black spruce in canopy, *Sphagnum* spp. dominant; organic soils, groundwater table close to surface, bogs	ICHwk3/09
1b	Black spruce absent from canopy, *Sphagnum* spp. low cover (<2%) or absent; mineral soils, groundwater table variable	2
2a	Lodgepole pine in canopy, with western hemlock, moderate to high cover (>30%) of lichens; dry rock outcrops	ICHwk3/02
2b	Lodgepole pine absent, lichens low cover (<10%)); not on a dry rock outcrop	3
3a	Very uneven and open canopy, moderate to high cover of *Lysichitum americanum*; narrow drainage channel, groundwater table close to surface	ICHwk3/08
3b	Well-developed canopy, *Lysichitum americanum* low cover (<1%) or absent; not a narrow drainage channel, groundwater table variable	4
4a	*Oplopanax horridus* present, usually moderate to high cover (>10%), herb layer well developed (>60% cover); mid to lower slopes or level	5
4b	*Oplopanax horridus* absent; upper slope to crest	8
5a	Tree canopy often stunted and with poor form, *Sphagnum* spp. moderate to high cover (>10%); groundwater table close to surface (within 50 cm), level, lacustrine parent materials	ICHwk3/07
5b	*Sphagnum* spp. low cover (<1%) or absent; groundwater table usually at depths >50 cm, parent materials variable	6
6a	Hybrid white spruce and subalpine fir >50% of tree canopy; *Equisetum* spp. moderate to high cover (>5%); groundwater table present, often within 50 cm of surface	ICHwk3/06
6b	Western redcedar and western hemlock dominate canopy, *Equisetum* spp. low cover (<1%) or absent; groundwater table deeper, seepage water often present	7
7a	*Oplopanax horridus* high cover (>20%); lower slope to level, seepage water often present	ICHwk3/05
7b	*Oplopanax horridus* low to moderate cover (<20%) if present; slope position variable, seepage water rarely present	ICHwk3/01
8a	*Gymnocarpium dryopteris* moderate to high cover (>10%); generally not occurring on steep (>50%) slopes and soils not shallow (>1 m deep)	ICHwk3/01
8b	*Gymnocarpium dryopteris* usually low cover (<10%) or absent; occurring on steep slopes or shallow soils	9
9a	*Gymnocarpium dryopteris* absent; occurring on steep (>50%) slopes, aspect usually SE to SW	ICHwk3/04
9b	*Gymnocarpium dryopteris* present; occurring on gentle slopes (<10%), aspect variable	ICHwk3/03

Mixed species stands on suitable sites have the potential to increase yield through the complete exploitation of available above- and belowground space. Fresh to moist, nutrient-medium to nutrient-rich sites, particularly in cool temperate and cool mesothermal climates, generally support several tree species and are better suited to managing mixed-species stands. Species in mixtures should be compatible in their shade tolerance so that a stratified canopy reduces interspecific competition. Even-aged mixed-species stands of no more than two or three species are most desirable.

Crop reliability

Stand resistance and resilience to potential hazards aid its survival through the rotation. Susceptibility to hazards such as animals, insects, disease, wind, snow, frost, drought, and flooding depends on stand composition. A species that is very productive on a site but susceptible to hazards (e.g., sites where western white pine is susceptible to blister rust, Sitka spruce to spruce weevil, or Douglas-fir to root rot) should not be a major component of the stand. On the other hand, stand resistance to windthrow can be enhanced by certain species, such as western redcedar and yellow-cedar, which have characteristically dense root systems.

Silvicultural feasibility

Some species on certain sites require more complicated and expensive silvicultural regimes than others. From this perspective, the most productive and reliable options may not be the most suitable overall. Generally, species requiring the fewest and most economical treatments are ranked as silviculturally most feasible. For example, species that can be regenerated naturally may be chosen over an otherwise equally suitable species that must be planted. The recommended option should, however, still meet management objectives.

SILVICAL CHARACTERISTICS AND REGENERATION IMPLICATIONS OF MAJOR TREE SPECIES

As a guide to species selection, the most important silvical characteristics for the major tree species in British Columbia are summarized in Table 6.4. Fowells (1965), Krajina (1969), Minore (1979), and Krajina et al. (1982) were the main sources used to outline ecological amplitudes of species in relation to climate (represented by biogeoclimatic zones), soil moisture, soil nutrients, light (shade tolerance), and often characteristics including potential for natural regeneration, spatial requirements, and special adaptations. For each commercial species, there are also highlights on ecologically suitable sites, suitable companion tree species, regeneration, and major potential hazards. Comments on advanced regeneration are based on McCaughey and Ferguson (1988).

Greater detail can be obtained from the sources cited above, and from Atkinson and Zasoski (1976) for western hemlock, Smith et al. (1976) for western larch, Ruth and Harris (1979) for Sitka spruce, Oliver and Kenady (1982) for the true firs, Minore (1983) for western redcedar, Baumgartner et al. (1985) for lodgepole pine, DeByle and Winokur (1985) for trembling aspen, and Oliver et al. (1986) for Douglas-fir.

The following synopsis of silvical characteristics is necessarily generalized. The reader should also be mindful of:

- genetic variation within a species (particularly those with wide geographic, altitudinal, and edaphic ranges);
- differences between young and mature trees; and
- the confounding effect of climate, soil moisture, and soil nutrients on the survival, shade tolerance, and growth performance of a particular species.

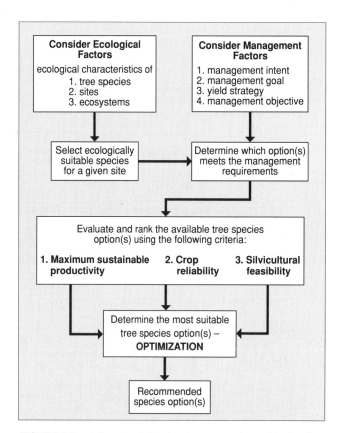

FIGURE 6.6. A flow chart showing the approach used to develop tree species selection guidelines for regenerating forest sites in British Columbia (from Klinka and Feller [1984]).

Softwoods

Pacific silver fir (*Abies amabilis* (Dougl. *ex* Loud.) Forbes)

Suitable on fresh to very moist sites in the wetter CWH subzones and MH zone, in pure or mixed-species stands (with western hemlock or mountain hemlock). Consider extension to Queen Charlotte Islands. Shade tolerance, high form factor, and low spatial crown requirements contribute to high timber yields. Advanced regeneration responds well to overstory removal, but is often delayed for several years following release; logging damage allows entry of decay organisms. Major potential hazards are: heart rots, balsam woolly aphid (only in south coastal British Columbia), and western balsam bark beetle.

Avoid moisture-deficient sites, waterlogged sites, and warm-aspect slopes. Favor the species over western and mountain hemlock on nitrogen-rich sites (e.g., river terraces and seepage sites). Prefer suitable natural regeneration to planting (organic materials are acceptable planting substrates).

TABLE 6.4. Synopsis of selected silvical characteristics of major tree species of British Columbia

Species	Climatic gradient: MH	ESSF & MS	BWBS	SBS	SBPS	IDF	ICH	PP	CDF	CWH	Moisture: very dry	dry	fresh	moist	wet	ranking*	Nutrient: very poor	poor	medium	rich	very rich	ranking*	Shade: very shade-tolerant	shade-tolerant	moderately shade-tolerant	shade-intolerant	very shade-intolerant	ranking*	Reg. in shade	Reg. in open	Spatial requirements	Special adaptations and indicative values
Pacific silver fir	●	○					○			•		○	●	●	○	16	○		•	●	○	8	•	•	●			1	H	L	L	heavy snow cover- & flood-tolerant; indicator of maritime, wet (snowy) climates
Grand fir						•	•		•	○		○	●	●	○	16		○	•	●	●	18		•	●	●	○	8	L	L	M	fluctuating water table & flood-tolerant; indicator of nutrient-rich sites
Subalpine fir	○	●	○	○	○	○	○			○	○	•	●	●	○	18	○	•	●	●	•	9	●	●	●	○	○	3	H	L	L	frost-, heavy snow cover- & flood-tolerant; at high elevations, vegetative reproduction by layering
Tamarack		•	●	○									○	●	●	26		○	○	●	○	16				●	●	26	L	M	H	frost- & flood-tolerant; indicator of continental boreal, moist to wet & nutrient-rich sites
Subalpine larch	•	●									○	●	•	○		4	○	•	●	●	•	6				○	●	22	L	M	H	frost-tolerant; indicator of continental subalpine boreal climates
Western larch		●		•		●	•	○			○	●	●	•		5		•	●	●	•	14					●	18	L	M	H	frost-tolerant; deep & wide-spreading root system; indicator of continental temperate climates
Engelmann spruce	○	●		•	○	•	•			○	○	•	●	●	•	18	○	•	●	●	○	12	•	•	●	•		12	L-M	M	M	frost-, heavy snow cover- & flood-tolerant
White spruce		●	●	●	○	○	•				○	•	●	●	•	15		•	●	●	○	18	○	○	●	•	•	11	L-M	M	H	frost- & flood-tolerant; indicator of continental boreal climates
Black spruce		•	●	●	●		○			○	•	•	●	●	●	23	●	●	•			2	•	•	●	•	•	6	M	L	L	persistent & semi-serotinous cones; vegetative reproduction by layering; frost-tolerant; indicator of continental boreal climates & nutrient-poor sites
Sitka spruce	○						○		○	●	○		○	●	●	21		•	●	●	●	25	○	○	●			14	L	H	H	frost & snow-intolerant; ocean spray-, brackish water- & flood -tolerant; indicator of wet mesothermal climates
Whitebark pine	○	•		•			•				•	●	●	○		5	●	●	•			7				•	●	18	L	L	H	regeneration largely from seed caches of Clark's nutcracker; frost-tolerant indicator of subalpine boreal climates
Jack pine			●	●	○						•	●	●	○		3	●	●	•			1				•	●	22	L	L	H	serotinous cones; frost-tolerant; indicator of continental boreal climates and dry & nutrient-poor sites
Lodgepole pine	○	●	●	●	●	●	•	○		○	•	●	●	•	○	7	•	●	●	•	○	3			○	●	●	17	L	L-H	L-M	serotinous cones; frost-tolerant
Limber pine		○				●		•			●	●	•			2		○	●	●		15			•	●	•	18	L	L	H	regeneration largely from seed caches of Clark's nutcracker; frost-tolerant, calciphytic; indicator of continental subalpine boreal climates
Western white pine		○		•		●	●		●	●	○	•	●	•	○	12		•	●	●	●	18	•	•	●	•		9	L-M	H	H	moderately frost- & flood-tolerant; calciphytic
Ponderosa pine						●	•	●			○	●	•	○		1	•	●	●	●	○	18			○	●	•	15	L	H	H	flood- & heavy snow cover-intolerant
Douglas-fir	○	•		•	○	●	●	●	●	●	○	•	●	•	○	8	○	•	●	●	•	9		•	●	●	•	10	L-M	M-H	M	flood- & heavy snow cover-intolerant
Western hemlock	○	○		•			●		•	●		○	●	●	•	10	•	●	●	•		3	●	●	●	○		2	H	H	L	indicator of acid substrates
Mountain hemlock	●	○		○			○			•			○	●	○	10	•	●	●	•		3	●	●	●	○		4	H	M	M	heavy snow cover-tolerant; indicator of acid substrates
Alaska yellow-cedar	●	○		•			○	○		●		○	●	●	•	23	○	•	●	●	•	9	●	●	●	○		6	L-M	M	L	frost-intolerant, heavy snow cover-tolerant; indicator of maritime wet (snowy) climates
Western redcedar	○	○		○		○	●		•	●			○	●	●	18	○	•	●	●	•	17	●	●	●	○		4	M	M-H	H	flood-tolerant
Balsam poplar & black cottonwood	○	○	•	•	○	○	•	•	○	•			•	●	●	25		○	•	●	○	18				•	●	22	L	H	H	vegetative reproduction from root & stump sprouts; frost- & flood-tolerant; indicator of fresh to moist & nutrient-rich (alluvial) sites
Trembling aspen			•	•	•	•	•	○			•	●	●	•	○	13		○	•	●	●	18			○	●	•	16	L	H	H	vegetative reproduction from root suckers & sprouts & stump sprouts
Red alder							○		•	●		○	●	●	•	22		•	●	●	●	18			○	●	○	18	L	H	H	in symbiosis with N-fixing *Actinomyces alni*; vegetative reproduction from stump sprouts; frost- & snow-intolerant, flood-tolerant; indicator of mesothermal climates
Bigleaf maple									•	•	○	•	●	•	○	14		•	●	●	●	25	○	•	●	•	○	13	L	L	H	vegetative reproduction from stump sprouts; frost-intolerant, flood-tolerant; indicator of maritime climates & nutrient-rich sites
Paper birch		○	•	•		•	•	○	○	•	○	•	●	●	•	9		•	●	●	•	13			○	●	●	22	L	H	H	vegetative reproduction from stump sprouts; frost- & flood-tolerant

Legend:

Distribution along the climatic gradient: ● very frequent, • frequent, ○ less frequent, □ absent

Distribution along the soil moisture gradient / nutrient gradient: ● very frequent, • frequent, ○ less frequent, □ absent

Shade tolerance: ● very frequent, • frequent, ○ less frequent, □ absent

Potential for natural regeneration / Spatial requirements: L low, M medium, H high

* Approximate comparative ranking of the species along the gradients (± 2 or 3 of the 26 species listed); i.e. 1 – driest soils, nutrient-poorest soils, or most shade-tolerant to 26 – wettest soils, nutrient richest soils, or most shade-intolerant

Preserve forest floor materials and advance regeneration, particularly on montane and subalpine sites.

Grand fir (*Abies grandis* (Dougl. *ex* D. Don) Lindl.)

A neglected species, suitable on slightly dry to very moist, nutrient-medium to nutrient-very rich sites in the southern IDF subzones, southern drier ICH and CWH subzones, and CDF zone, in pure or mixed-species stands (with Douglas-fir or western redcedar). Low spatial crown requirements and high form factor can result in timber yields comparable or superior to those for Douglas-fir. Advanced regeneration survives release well, but growth response is highly variable; poor response to release is associated with older regeneration tall trees with low pre-release vigor, and logging damage. Major potential hazards are: heart rots, root rots, balsam woolly aphid, spruce budworm, western balsam bark beetle, fire, frost, and snow.

Avoid very dry, moderately dry, and nutrient-poor sites. Favor the species on alluvial and winter-wet/summer-slightly dry to moist sites (usually gleyed soils). Prefer planting to natural regeneration on moist sites (plant in mineral substrates); select shaded microsites on slightly dry sites.

Subalpine fir (*Abies lasiocarpa* (Hook.) Nutt.)

Suitable on slightly dry to wet sites in the ESSF zone, northern snowy ICH subzones, southern BWBS subzones, and moister SBS subzones mainly in mixed-species stands (with Engelmann, white, or hybrid spruce, occasionally in pure stands on upper subalpine sites). Aim for a high component of spruce in these mixed-species stands. Low spatial crown requirements, high shade tolerance, and high form factor contribute to high timber yields. Advanced regeneration responds well to overstory removal, but is often delayed for several years following release; logging damage allows entry of decay organisms. Major potential hazards are: heart rots, root rots, spruce budworms, western blackheaded budworm, western balsam bark beetle, and fire.

Favor the species on moist to very moist sites (usually gleyed soils); avoid nutrient-very poor sites. Prefer suitable natural regeneration to planting (well-decomposed organic materials are acceptable planting substrates). Preserve forest floor materials and advance regeneration, particularly on subalpine sites.

Tamarack (*Larix laricina* (Du Roi) K. Koch)

A potential crop species in pure stands on fresh to wet, nutrient-medium to nutrient-very rich sites in the BWBS and SBS zones. Avoid very acid substrates. Major potential hazards are: larch casebearer, larch sawfly, and fire.

Western larch (*Larix occidentalis* Nutt.)

Suitable in pure stands on moderately dry to moist, nutrient-medium to nutrient-very rich sites in the southern MS and IDF zones, and southern drier ICH subzones; consider extension to the central ICH, subcontinental IDF, and submaritime CWH subzones. Because of its very rapid growth rate, favor the species in short-rotation management. Natural regeneration can be very successful on mineral substrates. Major potential hazards are: larch casebearer, needlecast, and dwarf mistletoe.

Avoid nutrient-poor, high brush hazard, very moist to wet, and frost prone sites. Plant in mineral substrates; use shaded or wetter microsites on dry sites.

Engelmann spruce (*Picea engelmannii* Parry *ex* Engelm.)

Suitable on slightly dry to wet sites in the submaritime MH subzones, ESSF, MS, and SBS zones (where it commonly occurs as hybrid with white spruce), upper IDF and ICH subzones, and upper submaritime CWH subzones in mixed-species stands (with Pacific silver fir, subalpine fir, Douglas-fir, or western redcedar). Low spatial crown requirements and high form factor result in high timber yields. Advanced regeneration responds well to release but there is some delay; decay organisms are a major problem with older larger stems. Major potential hazards are: root rots, spruce bark beetle, spruce budworms, white pine weevil, fire, wind, and frost.

Avoid very to moderately dry and nutrient-very poor sites and microsites with frost in the growing season. On slightly dry sites, seek shaded or wetter microsites and plant in mineral substrates. In the warmer subzones of the ICH, IDF, and CWH zones, favor the species on alluvial and cold air drainage sites. Prefer planting to natural regeneration on most sites. Preserve forest floor materials and acceptable advance regeneration on the subalpine sites.

White spruce (*Picea glauca* (Moench) Voss) (includes *P. glauca* x *engelmannii*)

Suitable on a range of sites in several montane boreal and cool temperate zones in pure or mixed-species stands (mainly with subalpine fir). Advanced regeneration qualities similar to those for Engelmann spruce. Major potential hazards are: root rots, spruce bark beetle, spruce budworm, white pine weevil, fire, wind, and frost damage.

Avoid very to moderately dry, wet, and nutrient-very poor sites and microsites with frost in the growing season. Favor the species (or its hybrids with Engelmann spruce) on alluvial sites, in the IDF and ICH zones on cold air drainage and gleyed sites.

Black spruce (*Picea mariana* (Mill.) B.S.P)

Suitable on slightly dry to wet, nutrient-very poor to nutrient-medium sites in the BWBS zone and the northern portion of the SBS zone (particularly on cool-aspect slopes). High shade tolerance and very low spatial crown requirements may result in timber yields comparable to short rotation lodgepole pine. Regenerates naturally following fire disturbance or can be planted if the species was a minor component in the original stand. Advanced regeneration qualities similar to those in Engelmann spruce, but information is limited. Major potential hazards are: butt, heart, root rots, and fire.

Sitka spruce (*Picea sitchensis* (Bong.) Carr.)

Suitable on fresh to wet, nutrient-medium to nutrient-very rich sites in the hypermaritime and northern wet maritime CWH subzones in pure or mixed-species stands (most commonly with western hemlock). Use white-Sitka spruce hybrids in the northern submaritime CWH subzones and Engelmann-Sitka spruce hybrids in the southern submaritime CWH subzones. Major potential hazards are: heart rots, aphids, white pine weevil, frost, and wind.

Avoid water- and nitrogen-deficient sites. Favor the species on alluvial sites and winter-wet — summer-moist sites. Prefer planting to natural regeneration on moist sites. On high brush hazard sites, black cottonwood or red alder can be used as a temporary nurse species.

Lodgepole pine (*Pinus contorta* Dougl. *ex* Loud.)

Suitable in pure stands on a variety of sites in all forested zones, except the PP zone. In the CDF and CWH zones, its suitability is extended to very dry or wet, nutrient-poor sites. Regenerates naturally following fire disturbance or drag-scarification or can be planted (in mineral substrates). Advanced regeneration in dry SBPS and SBS subzones will respond to release, but it is not acceptable because of risk of mistletoe infection. Major potential hazards are: blister rusts, needleblight, western gall rust, lodgepole pine terminal weevil, northern lodgepole pine needleminer, and pitch moths.

Favor the species on moisture-deficient, nutrient-poor, and frost-prone sites. In the Interior, maintain nitrogen-fixing Sitka or green alder in the understory.

Western white pine (*Pinus monticola* Dougl. *ex* D. Don. *in* Lamb.)

Suitable as a minor species on slightly dry to wet, nutrient-medium to nutrient-very rich sites in southern IDF subzones, southern IWH subzones, and southern maritime and submaritime CWH subzones. The major hazard is blister rust which limits suitability. Other potential hazards are: heart rots, root rots, and mountain pine beetle. Avoid moisture-deficient and nutrient-very poor sites; favor alluvial and base-rich sites; plant in mineral substrates.

Ponderosa pine (*Pinus ponderosa* Dougl. *ex* P. & C. Lawson)

Suitable in pure stands on very to moderately dry, nutrient-medium to nutrient-very rich sites in the southern IDF subzones, southern drier ICH subzones, and PP zone. Consider extension to the CDF zone and southern submaritime drier CWH subzone. Major potential hazards are: root rots and bark beetle.

Avoid acid, base-poor sites; outside the PP zone, prefer warm-aspect sites. Favor the species over Douglas-fir in southern drier IDF subzones. Regenerates naturally or can be planted (in mineral substrates); use shaded or wetter microsites in the warmest climates.

Douglas-fir (*Pseudotsuga menziesii* (Mirb.) Franco)

Suitable on very dry to moist sites in the lower MH subzones, southern SBS subzones, IDF zone, ICH zone, CDF zone, and southern maritime and submaritime CWH subzones, in pure or mixed-species stands. Consider the establishment of mixed Douglas-fir - western hemlock stands because of contrasting nutrient adaptations. Accept and maintain a component of western redcedar in the lower tree stratum (as a crop species) or shrub stratum (as a nurse species). Advance regeneration responds well to release; diameter growth response is immediate but height growth response is delayed. Has few decay problems, but the presence of dwarf mistletoe in the southern Interior limits acceptability. Root rots may restrict natural regeneration option in some areas. Major potential hazards are:

heart rots, root rots, Douglas-fir beetle, Douglas-fir tussock moth, dwarf mistletoe, western spruce budworm, browsing, frost, and snow damage.

Avoid subalpine-boreal, winter-wet (gleyed), flooded, and waterlogged sites; also avoid moist to very moist, nutrient-rich sites in southern parts of the Very Wet Maritime CWH subzone. Favor the species over western hemlock on base-rich sites. Regenerates naturally or can be planted. Protect advanced regeneration in IDF, MS, and SBS zones. In general, plant in mineral substrates, on warm and moisture-deficient sites, select shaded or wetter microsites, or plant close to decaying, coarse woody debris.

Western hemlock (*Tsuga heterophylla* (Raf.) Sarg.)

Suitable on fresh to very moist, nutrient-very poor to nutrient-medium sites, in the wetter ICH subzones and hypermaritime and maritime CWH subzones, in pure or mixed-species stands (mainly with Pacific silver fir, Sitka spruce, yellow-cedar, or western redcedar). Consider the establishment of mixed Douglas-fir - western hemlock stands because of contrasting nutrient adaptations. Accept and maintain a component of western redcedar in the lower tree stratum. Consider crop reliability in the ICH zone, with its high incidence of Indian paint fungus; decay risk greatly increases in older stands but may be acceptable up to age 90-100 years. Advanced regeneration releases after a delay of several years but there is often substantial mortality; the risk of decay is high. Major potential hazards are: heart rots (especially in the ICH zone), root rots, hemlock loopers, hemlock sawfly, western blackheaded budworm, dwarf mistletoe, and wind.

Avoid dry sites. Favor the species over Douglas-fir, Pacific silver fir, Sitka spruce, or western redcedar on base-poor sites. Prefer natural regeneration to planting (well-decomposed organic materials are acceptable planting substrates). Preserve forest floor materials and acceptable advance regeneration, particularly on montane sites.

Mountain hemlock (*Tsuga mertensiana* (Bong.) Carr.)

Suitable on fresh to very moist, nutrient-very poor to nutrient-medium sites in the hypermaritime and maritime MH subzones in pure or mixed-species stands (mainly with Pacific silver fir or yellow-cedar). Advanced regeneration releases well both in height and diameter; decay organisms and dwarf mistletoe reduce acceptability. Accept and maintain a component of Pacific silver fir or yellow-cedar to ameliorate humus forms. Major potential hazards are: heart rots, root rots, hemlock loopers, hemlock sawfly, western blackheaded budworm, dwarf mistletoe, and wind.

Avoid moisture-deficient sites. Favor the species over Pacific silver fir on nitrogen-poor sites. Prefer natural regeneration to planting (well-decomposed organic materials are acceptable planting substrates). Preserve forest floor materials and acceptable advance regeneration.

Yellow-cedar (*Chamaecyparis nootkatensis* (D. Don) Spach)

Suitable on wide range of sites in the hypermaritime and maritime MH subzones and wetter CWH subzones in pure or mixed-species stands (commonly with lodgepole pine, mountain hemlock, Pacific silver fir, western hemlock, or western redcedar). Low spatial crown requirements and relatively high shade tolerance contribute to high timber yields. Relatively free of damaging agents.

Favor the species over mountain hemlock on nitrogen-rich sites; and over Pacific silver fir on colluvial and waterlogged sites. Both mineral and well-decomposed organic materials are acceptable planting substrates.

Western redcedar (*Thuja plicata* Donn *ex* D. Don *in* Lamb.)

Suitable on slightly dry to wet, nutrient-poor to nutrient-very rich sites in the wetter IDF subzones, and ICH, CDF, and CWH zones in pure or mixed-species stands (commonly with Douglas-fir, Sitka spruce, yellow-cedar, or western hemlock). Accept and maintain a component of western redcedar in Douglas-fir and western hemlock stands to ameliorate humus forms. Low spatial crown requirements and shade tolerance contribute to high timber yields. Advanced regeneration responds to release. Little information is available on risk. Major potential hazards are: heart rots (more in the interior than coastal zones), fire, frost, and browsing.

Avoid moisture-deficient sites; favor the species in ravines and gullies, and on floodplain, steep slope-seepage, and waterlogged sites. Prefer planting to natural regeneration, on moist, very moist, and wet sites. Advanced and natural regeneration acceptable especially in wetter ICH subzones. Plant in mineral materials on upland sites and in well-decomposed organic materials on wetland sites.

Hardwoods

Accounting for less than 2% of British Columbia's inventory and about 0.5% of the annual cut, the province's hardwood species have traditionally been considered weeds. This is particularly the case with red alder, which invades high-productivity coastal sites. Only cottonwood has been grown in managed forests to any extent, and only on certain sites. Recently, attention has also been given to the commercial use of aspen. These and the other species discussed below are not likely to be encouraged by foresters until specialty markets open up or local British Columbia-based secondary industries appear. Nevertheless, these hardwoods often have ameliorative effects on the environment of conifers.

The species are discussed here in descending order of the size of their inventory in British Columbia. As a proportion of the timber cut, cottonwood outweighs the other hardwoods combined, by a factor of four or five.

Trembling aspen (*Populus tremuloides* Michx)

Aspen is easy to regenerate and will provide good yields on a short rotation basis on slightly dry to moist, nutrient-medium to nutrient-rich sites in the BWBS and SBS zones (perhaps 35 years). Sawlogs may require twice this long. However, biological and economic maturity occur early in this species.

The species displays wide genetic diversity including polyploidy, which may be used in root cutting and future breeding programs to produce individuals with superior form, wood properties, and growth rate.

Balsam poplar (*Populus balsamifera* L.) and black cottonwood (*Populus trichocarpa* Torr. & Gray *ex* Hook.)

Suitable in pure stands on fresh to wet, nutrient-rich to nutrient-very rich sites in all forested zones. These species produce high yields of wood suitable for mechanical pulping. Both species can be regenerated naturally (vegetative reproduction from root sprouts, stump sprouts, or buried branches) or by being planted from shoot cuttings (whips). Relatively free of seriously damaging agents.

Favor the species for a short rotation management on alluvial floodplains, winter-wet/summer-fresh to moist upland sites (usually gleyed soils), and high brush hazard upland sites, where the establishment of conifers is difficult. Avoid sites affected by brackish water. Prefer planting to natural regeneration on high-productivity sites.

Birch (*Betula papyrifera* Marsh.)

Suitable on moderately dry to very moist, nutrient-poor to nutrient-rich sites in the BWBS, SBS, IDF, and ICH zones. In countries with intensive management, birches have been bred for high quality furniture and use in the manufacture of pulp. Regenerates from seed on most surfaces except drier moss- and broad-leaved litter, where its small radical cannot penetrate to moisture. Easily grown in nurseries, either bareroot or in containers, and the supply of wildings is more than adequate.

Red alder (*Alnus rubra* Bong.)

Occurs in the CDF zone and in submontane CWH subzones on all but the driest sites. Prolific annual fruiting ensures abundant regeneration on disturbed sites with exposed mineral soil, even in the wettest CWH subzones. Direct seeding on mineral soil yields good results. For other soils, wildlings, which are always in copious supply, can be planted where required. These usually show good survival. Has been suggested as a nurse species for Sitka spruce, as its shade and visual diversion will deter the spruce weevil. It will also enrich the soil with nitrogen, although the more shrubby Sitka and mountain alders may be more appropriate.

Bigleaf maple (*Acer macrophyllum* Pursh.)

In some individuals, the grain patterns are unsurpassed, even by walnuts, suggesting a potential for use in furniture. Perhaps some maple should be grown on fresh to moist, nutrient-rich sites in the CDF zone and drier southern CWH subzones (skeletal alluvial fans, very steep, fragmental colluvial slopes, stream-edge sites, or floodplains).

SECTION TWO

7 REFORESTATION PLANNING

W.C. Williams, J.R. Revel, and L.P. Atherton

Silviculture planning occurs on a wide range of levels, from provincial strategic to local operational . Reforestation planning is a subset of silviculture planning; that is, it is only one of a number of potential silviculture activities that may be employed to meet strategic goals. In British Columbia, reforestation is classified as both a basic and an incremental silviculture activity — the incremental activity being the rehabilitation of backlog, "not satisfactorily restocked" (NSR) forest land. The basic silviculture component of reforestation is a legislated requirement of the forest industry in British Columbia (Chapter 1).

Silviculture activities are conducted to support other strategic goals, such as a future target harvest level. Recently, silviculture activities have also been undertaken in support of goals for other resources such as fish, wildlife, and aesthetics. If these higher level goals are unclear, and if sound operational plans are not in place, sound strategic silviculture planning becomes difficult. Without a solid operational planning and administrative process to support it, reforestation goals cannot be achieved cost effectively.

This chapter discusses reforestation planning in British Columbia, which has a unique mixture of government and industry responsibilities for funding and undertaking the task. First the broad "planning spectrum" is discussed, and then strategic and operational planning processes are reviewed. The chapter is not intended to provide "how to" guidelines; rather it aims to give the reader sufficient planning detail to understand the concepts associated with each planning level.

THE PLANNING SPECTRUM

Every planning process operates within a unique environment which gives the process its own shape. British Columbia's reforestation planning process is shaped by such elements as the Ministry of Forests designated planning hierarchy, the Ministry's organizational structure, company organizational structures, funding sources, the land tenure system, and political influences. These elements, except political influences, and their interactions are shown in Figure 7.1.

No aspect of the planning spectrum can function independently of the others. Each one relies on information from the others. Often the information flow is iterative, with information from a lower level plan affecting a higher level plan, which in turn results in change to the original lower level plan.

The Planning Hierarchy

The B.C. Ministry of Forests uses a hierarchical approach to forest planning. It begins with a general strategic overview of goals and objectives, and moves down to very specific operational plans. Four basic planning levels are recognized:

- provincial
- regional
- management unit (forest)
- operational (stand)

Silviculture plans are generated at each level. Of all the elements that affect the planning process in British Columbia, this planning hierarchy exerts the strongest influence.

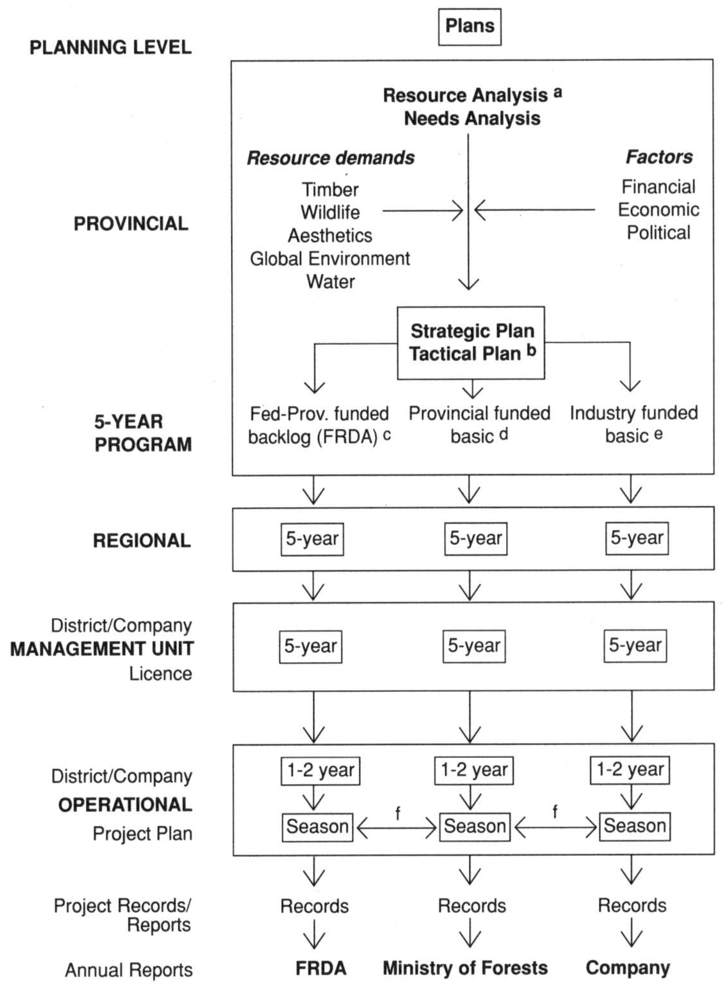

[a] Data typically analyzed at management unit or licence levels by region and district. Required at least every 10 years by legislation.

[b] Typically the Five-Year Forest and Range Resource Program submitted annually to the Legislature.

[c] Areas harvested prior to 1982.

[d] Areas harvested between 1982 and September 1987 or destroyed after 1982 by fire, insects, or disease and not salvaged under major tenure or by Small Business Forest Enterprise Program.

[e] Areas harvested after September 1987.

[f] Individual projects often amalgamate areas having different funding sources.

FIGURE 7.1. British Columbia's reforestation planning spectrum.

Ministry of Forests Organization

The Ministry is organized into three levels: provincial, regional, and district. The first two correspond exactly with levels in the planning hierarchy, but the district level may or may not correspond with the hierarchy's management unit level of planning. Sometimes there are several districts within one Timber Supply Area (TSA), or several portions of different TSA's within one district. Often there is both a TSA and one or more Tree Farm Licences (TFL's) within a district. When any of these situations occur, a new dimension must be added to the strict hierarchical planning process so that district operational planning can be connected to both the regional planning process and the management unit planning process.

Company Organization

Much of British Columbia's forest is harvested by large, integrated forest companies. These companies have multiple divisions, often operating as separate cost centers, which may have several Crown forest tenures under the management of a single division. Again, as noted above for district structures, it is often necessary for a company to add a dimension to the planning process to enable it to connect the operational process internally and externally to higher level plans.

Funding

Funding for reforestation comes from four sources. One is the forest companies, which pay for areas harvested under a major Crown licence since October 1, 1987, and for their own private lands. Another is the Ministry of Forests' Small Business Forest Enterprise Program, which generates revenues for reforestation from areas harvested under the program. (The government considers this to be "industry funding" and therefore it is not differentiated on Figure 7.1.) A third funding source is the provincial government, which pays for reforestation on Crown land harvested between January 1, 1982, and September 30, 1987. The fourth source is the Canada-British Columbia Forest Resource Development Agreement (FRDA), which pays for backlog NSR areas harvested before January 1, 1982.

Each of these funding sources requires a separate plan, but each plan must complement the others. For operational efficiency a number of areas being funded differently are often combined into one project. A single planting contract covering four openings, for example, may consist of two areas funded by the Ministry of Forests and two areas funded under FRDA.

Tenures

Two types of tenure — TFL's and Woodlot Licences — constitute management units themselves, while others, notably Forest Licences, constitute only part of a harvest within the TSA management unit ("management unit" being defined as an area on which an allowable annual cut is *calculated*).

Major tenures, as defined in the Forest Act, are required to have a Management and Working Plan approved by the Ministry of Forests. This plan must include a silviculture component, broadly outlining the company's silviculture and reforestation plans. Particulars for these plans are contained in the Ministry of Forests *Resource Planning Manual*.

Political Influences

At higher planning levels, political influences may directly affect the planning process. One of the greatest examples of this is the impact of the recent Canada - U.S. Memorandum of Understanding on softwood lumber, which resulted indirectly in the British Columbia government shifting cost and responsibility for reforestation to the forest industry. Other "political" factors are the Economic Development Regions instituted by the provincial government and the boundaries of both federal and provincial electoral districts. Any planning and information processes must be capable of responding to new and sometimes unforeseen influences from the political arena.

STRATEGIC REFORESTATION PLANNING

Provincial/Regional Level Planning

In British Columbia, the first stage of planning strategies begins at the provincial level. Legislation requires that a review of the whole provincial forest and range resource take place periodically, at least every 10 years.

Such a review is reported in a document entitled the "Forest and Range Resource Analysis." It is used by government to shape future management programs, policies, and long-range plans.

The Ministry of Forests is also required to submit a Five-Year Forest and Range Resource Program (Plan) to the provincial cabinet. This plan, which is updated annually, is strongly influenced by the Forest and Range Resource Analysis report. It includes strategies and tactical plans for managing the provincial forest resource for a 5-year period, and gives a broad overview to all forest managers of the resources and dollars that will be required to maintain or enhance the forest resources.

The resource analysis report, although adequate for establishing strategic direction, soon becomes outdated for refining the provincial tactical silviculture goals as defined in the Five-Year Program. To fill this gap, the Ministry of Forests conducts a thorough "Needs Analysis" every 3 years. This analysis defines basic silviculture needs for reforestation by activity and by year, to meet government-funded obligations. It details these needs by analysis unit (a grouping of similar site types), ecosystem subzone (optional), tenure, company, district, management unit, and region.

To assist provincial strategic planning, a variety of computer-based analysis models have been used. No one modelling system has yet been established as the standard. Even if one were, however, most use of models is restricted by the lack of growth and yield information for managed stands. This lack of data particularly limits the investigation of the effects of different levels of silviculture investment on future harvest levels. Province- or region-wide models often have the disadvantage of masking local timber supply shortages.

Some forest companies have begun to study options to increase investment in incremental silviculture. This strategy, however, is unlikely to be fully implemented until the benefits of incremental silviculture on Crown land have been recognized.

Management Unit (Forest) Level Planning

The management unit level of planning is the pivotal point between strategic planning and operational planning. This section discusses the strategic aspects of management unit planning. The next section discusses operational aspects.

A forest is a collection of stands of trees, and is generally the smallest unit for which logical plans can be drawn for maintaining a continuous supply of timber. In British Columbia, forest-level planning addresses the long-range requirements (20-100 years) of the regional or local forest resource users. This stage of planning allocates resources and responsibilities to the users of the forest resource. Forest-level plans are generally developed for area-based management units such as TSA's, TFL's, and Woodlot Licences. These plans require that environmental concerns and other resource uses be integrated with Timber Harvest and Development Plans. Long-run sustainable yields and allowable annual cuts are calculated for these management units. The plans also specify what amount of silviculture activity is required to maintain or enhance timber production and other resource values. To this end, a management unit plan should reflect the general strategic directions and priorities already established at higher planning levels.

A TSA boundary is usually drawn according to the pattern of wood flow from management units to the primary timber-processing facilities. One or more forest companies as well as the Ministry's Small Business Forest Enterprise Program can operate within a TSA boundary. The right to harvest specific volumes within a TSA is usually given under Forest Licences or Timber Sale Licences. The B.C. Forest Service develops a TSA Plan, incorporating the comments from all resource users including the forest industry.

Each Forest Licensee is allocated 20-year operating areas within a TSA, and develops a Management and Working Plan for each. These plans contain long-range goals and objectives for managing the licence, and must fulfill the intent of the TSA plan. They must also address long-term research needs and tree improvement programs, if these are required. The Management and Working Plans must be prepared and submitted for approval every 5 years or as required by the Chief Forester. Holders of TFL's are also required to submit a Management and Working Plan.

OPERATIONAL REFORESTATION PLANNING

The operational reforestation planning process has three main planning components: 1) a broad Five-Year Plan for a licence or for a reforestation program (as in the case of FRDA); 2) an Annual Operating Plan; and 3) Project (Activity) Plans. Essential to all of these stages is the Pre-Harvest Silviculture Prescription, which generates the work activities that are organized into a plan (see Chapter 8). Also prerequisite to sound operational planning is a reliable information system (see "Managing Information" in this chapter).

Five-Year Plans

For most major tenures in British Columbia, a Five-Year Development Plan must be submitted annually to the Ministry of Forests for approval, as required by the Management and Working Plan. These development plans provide information about the areas to be harvested during the plan period and about the silviculture treatments the areas will receive. Forest cover maps, which locate present and future cutblocks and show silviculture treatment units, are a part of the plan. Pre-Harvest Silviculture Prescriptions must also be supplied for areas scheduled for harvesting within the first 2-3 years of the plan.

The Ministry prepares similar 5-year plans for the Small Business Forest Enterprise Program and for backlog NSR reforestation under FRDA. Such plans are usually district-oriented because of their operational nature, but they must still be in keeping with regional goals and TSA strategic plans.

This planning process also considers other resource uses in the management unit, such as trapping, wildlife and fisheries, recreation, and cattle grazing. The manager assesses how these other uses might affect the development plan and how the development plan might affect them. The plan may have to be altered, but in the process the manager may be able to enhance the other resource values through silviculture activities.

As well, the 5-year plan gives managers a guide to the number and type of seedlings they will have to order, often well before harvesting occurs. Table 7.1 shows a Five-Year Silviculture Plan.

TABLE 7.1. An example of a Five-Year Silviculture Plan (data for the first two years shown)

MULTI USE SUPPLY AREA 5 YEAR SILVICULTURE MANAGEMENT PLAN

Year: _____
Review Date: _____

Developed by: D. Forester

Activity		Year 1				Summary		Year 2				Summary	
Operations Silviculture	**Method**	**Project #**	**Unit(s)**	**Costs**		**Unit(s)**	**Costs**	**Project #**	**Method**	**Unit(s)**	**Costs**	**Unit(s)**	**Costs**
1) Prescriptions	Pre Harvest		(Ha)						Pre Harvest	(Ha)			
		OP101	50	500				OP1211		200	1000		
		OP211	200	2000				OP1022		150	750		
		OP102	100	1000				OP1110		300	10003		
		OP103	125	1250				OP1001		300	1500		
		OP212	75	750		550	5500	OP1001		350	1750	1200	6000
	Site Prep.	OP205	75	250				OP102	Site Prep.	100	175		
		OP203	100	250				OP211		200	500		
		OP202	80	250				OP600		150	200		
		OP105	200	500				OP550		300	300		
		OP201	200	250		655	1500	OP551		250	325	1000	1500
	Plant	OP089	300	750				OP400	Plant	300	800		
		OP210	200	500				OP320		200	500		
		OP099	200	500				OP420		200	500		
		OP089	100	250				OP901		100	300		
		OP215	150	375		950	2375	OP181		150	250	950	3850
	Brushing	OP060	200	800				OP013		200	800		
		OP070	150	600		350	1400	OP007		300	1200	500	2000
Total						**2505**	**10775**					**3650**	**13350**
2) Sowing Request (Needs)			Seedlings							(Ha)			
	Spruce	OP201	250000	42500				OP400	Spruce	300	93750		
	Spruce	OP260	125000	20000				OP320	Spruce	200	42500		
	Pine	OP150	240000	33600				OP420	Pine	200	57500		
	Pine	OP203	160000	19200		775000	115300	OP901	Pine	100	22400		
								OP131	Pine	150	28800	950	244950
3) Site Prep.	Broadcast	OP400	300	66000				OP205	Broadcast	75	18750		
	Broadcast	OP320	200	37000				OP203	Broadcast	100	22500		
	Windrow	OP420	200	70000				OP202	Broadcast	80	24000		
	Windrow	OP901	100	30000				OP105	Windrow	200	70000		
	Mound	OP181	150	22500		950	225500	OP201	Disc trench	200	30000	655	165250
4) Planting	Hand	OP199	200	77500				OP174	Hand	250	100000		
	Hand	OP204	300	129600				OP244	Hand	250	78125		
	Hand	OP500	400	145000		900	352100	OP501	Hand	100	37500		
								OP333	Hand	400	175000	1000	390625

TABLE 7.1. (Continued)

Year: _____
Review Date: _____

MULTI USE SUPPLY AREA 5 YEAR
SILVICULTURE MANAGEMENT PLAN

Developed by: D. Forester

Year 1

Activity / Operations Silviculture	Method	Project #	Unit(s) (Ha)	Costs	Summary Unit(s)	Summary Costs
5) Brushing Spot	Aerial Chem.	OP030	300	105000		
	Backpack	OP055	500	175000	800	280000
6) Surveys	Stocking	OP180	125	1500		
	Stocking	OP200	200	2400		
	Stocking	OP45	70	840	295	4740
	Perform	OP011	250	3750		
	Perform	OP006	100	1500	350	5250
	Brush	OP187	200	3000	200	3000
	Prespace	OP005	250	3000	250	3000
	Free grow	OP050	125	1875		
		OP014	75	1125		
		OP016	80	1200	280	4200
Total					**1375**	**20190**
7) Spacing	Brush saw	OP007	300	135000		
	Brush saw	OP009	150	45000	450	180000
8) Research	Growth & Yield	R111		30000		
	Stock Trial			10000		40000
9) Other	Fence			15000		
	Grass Seeding			5000		20000
Total						**$1,243,265**

Year 2

Activity / Operations Silviculture	Method	Project #	Unit(s) (Ha)	Costs	Summary Unit(s)	Summary Costs
5) Brushing Spot	Aerial Chem.	OP060	200	50000		
	Aerial Chem.	OP070	150	37500	350	87500
6) Surveys	Stocking	OP099	200	2400		
	Stocking	OP233	150	1800		
	Stocking	OP001	100	1200	450	4400
	Perform	OP003	75	1125		
	Perform	OP008	250	3750	325	4875
	Brush	OP113	300	3600		
	Brush	OP417	200	2400	500	6000
	Free grow	OP922	100	1500		
	Free grow	OP516	50	500	150	2000
Total					**1425**	**2000**
7) Spacing	Brush Saw	OP005	250	125000	250	125000
8) Research	Growth & Yield	R111		20000		
	Stock Trial			2000		
	Remeasure			8000		30000
9) Other	Grass Seeding			4000		4000
Total						**$1,077,950**

Annual Operating Plan: stand level

While the Five-Year Plan is concerned with planning at the tenure, management unit, or district level, the Annual Operating Plan deals with the stand level. A stand is defined as a group of trees that have similar growth and age characteristics. In British Columbia, a stand is generally considered to be the same as a cutblock, an area to be harvested.

The Annual Operating Plan is taken directly out of the Five-Year Development Plan. It specifies the operational plans for the first year of the 5-year period. It is therefore much more detailed than the five-year plan, identifying dollars, activities, goals, resources, and timing. The detail of the Annual Operating plan organizes daily activities and dictates whether project plans are also required. It is developed in the fall or winter before the year it is to be implemented. Since many planting contracts are awarded in the fall, plans for planting must be well advanced by early September. Table 7.2 shows a sample format of an Annual Operating Plan.

TABLE 7.2. Format for recording the Annual Operating Plan

Year:_____
Review date:_____   **Multi Use Supply Area Annual Operating Plan**

Silviculture activity and method	Project	Location	Resources	Persons requ'rd (days)	Project leader	Contract	Start date	Finish date	Units	Costs	Notes
1)Prescriptions Pre-Harvest	OP101	McGregor			B. Green	Yes	Apr 15	May 15	50	500	B.Green to
	OP211	Bowron			B. Green	Yes			200	2000	administer
	OP102	Torpy			B. Green	Yes			100	1000	contract
	OP103	Otter Cr.			B. Green	Yes			125	1250	
	OP212	Davie Lk.			B. Green	Yes			75	750	
Inspection			(1) Truck @ 10 days	(1)@10	B. Green	No	Apr 15	May 20		2000	
Site Preparation	OP201	Bowron I		1@3	B. Green	No	June 15	June 15	200	250	To verify
	OP205	Pass	(1) 4x4 @ 3 days		B. Green	No	June 15	June 15	75	250	PHSP
	OP203	Willow			B. Green	No	June 16	June 16	100	250	
	OP202	Bowron II			B. Green	No	June 16	June 16	80	250	
	OP105	McGregor			B. Green	No	June 17	June 17	200	500	
Planting	OP098	McGregor	(1) 4x4 @ 2 days	(1)@2	T. Field	No	Sept 10	Sept 10	300	750	To verify
	OP210	Pass Lk			T. Field	No	Sept 11	Sept 11	200	500	PHSP
	OP099	McGregor	(1) 4x4 @ 3 days	(1)@3	T. Field	No	Aug 15	Aug 15	200	500	
	OP089	W.Torpy			T. Field	No	Aug 16	Aug 16	100	250	
	OP215	Pass Lk			T. Field	No	Aug 17	Aug 17	150	375	
Brushing	OP060	Bowron	(1) 4x4 @ 4 days	(2)@4	T. Field	No	July 2	July 3	200	800	To verify
	OP070	Bowron			T. Field	No	July 4	July 5	150	600	PHSP brushing survey
Prescription Totals			(1) 4x4 @ 20	24		1			2505	10775	Avg/ha cost $15.20

Project Plan

The Project Plan is the last phase in the silviculture planning system. Prepared by the project leader, it is project-specific and very detailed. It is developed to ensure that nothing is left to chance, scheduling and listing every detail from dates to flagging tape. Table 7.3 shows how the necessary information might be recorded.

REFORESTATION LIABILITIES PLANNING

In 1987, forest legislation was passed requiring that reforestation after harvesting be a legal obligation of major licensees and the Small Business Forest Enterprise Program. Immediately following a harvest, therefore, a silviculture liability exists. The new financial implications posed by this legislation to companies and the government requires an additional form of silviculture financial plan. Such a plan should generally incorporate a risk management plan to ensure losses — and therefore expenses — are minimized.

Financial Plans

At the time of harvest, licensees should set aside sufficient funds from current revenues to cover the cost of future silviculture activities on the site. The amount can be determined from detailed information in the Pre-Harvest Silviculture Prescription which schedules expected treatments; or it can more simply be determined as an average cost for silviculture for a particular site type.

For large companies or the Small Business Forest Enterprise Program, the total silviculture liability can become a substantial amount, potentially many millions of dollars. At some time, however, the total outstanding liability will stabilize as silviculture operations in a given year extinguish existing liabilities and so offset newly incurred liabilities.

Establishing current silviculture liability is a relatively simple exercise if a good record system is in place (see "Managing Information" in this chapter). Total outstanding silviculture operations, by activity, are multiplied against planned costs per hectare. This provides a total liability estimate. Projecting liabilities to some point in the future (for example, annually for the next 5 years) is more complex, as it requires both a good harvest plan (for determining new liabilities to be incurred in a given year) and a good silviculture operations plan (to determine the extinguishment of liability in a given year). To calculate the net liability in a given year, new liabilities are added to the net liability carried forward from the previous year and the extinguished liability is subtracted.

Risk Management

Another new form of silviculture planning needed as a result of the recently legislated reforestation obligation is the risk management plan. This plan requires forest managers to anticipate potential threats to successful reforestation by any agent, notably fire, insects, or disease. It can be cutblock-specific or more general, describing broad goals and objectives for a license.

TABLE 7.3. Example of the information included in a Project Plan

PROJECT PLAN			
Aerial Cone Collection			
OBJECTIVE: To increase seed supply			
GOAL: Collect (100) hectoliters of white spruce cones.			
DATES: Start: January 10th; Finish: September 30th.			
Date	**Activity**	**Resources**	**Cost**
Nov. 15-16	Develop Project Plan		
Jan. 10	Discuss to see if a pre-cooperative collection is feasible. Prepare office in for cone collection.		
Jan. 15	Check seed register Seed zone maps superior provenances Seed transfer rules Review literature	Seed register Reproduction of conifers Guidelines to collecting	
Jan. 20	Prepare flight lines	Air photos, forest cover maps	
Jan. 30	Survey potential stands - collect twig samples	Helicopter	$1000
Feb. 1	Dissect bud	Hand lens, cone knife	
Feb. 2	Analyze male:female ratio Check promising areas		
March 10	Order cone sacks and tags		
May 20	Revisit potential areas - check flowering to verify potential - choose best stand with alternatives	Truck or helicopter, binoculars	$1000
June 10	Check weather records for frost and rain during flowering stage		
July 10	Cone crop survey of selected areas - cone crop rating - areas A, B & C	Sample bags, cone crop survey book, truck, rifle, binoculars, bullets, knife, marking pen, hand lens	$250
July 20	Cone crop survey of selected areas - cone crop rating - check for insects and disease - stands A, B & C - if area still acceptable, start arranging cone collection - choose picking and field storage sites	Sample bags, cone crop survey book, truck, rifle, binoculars, bullets, knife, marking pen, hand lens	$250
July 21	Prepare contract and maps		
July 22	Advertise contract		$100
July 23	Arrange for transport		
Aug. 1	Revisit A, B & C cone crop survey sites - cone crop rating - collect cone sample - dissect cones, do seed count, and check for insect and disease - decide whether to go or not with collection - arrange for seed extraction		
Aug. 5	- arrange for delivery of racking material (2 x 4's) - arrange for one staff member to turn sacks and monitor cone condition		
Aug. 7	Open and award cone collection contract - contact contractor - give him estimated dates for collection - send start-up letter and contract for signature		

Aug. 15	Cone survey
	- cone rating
	- dissect cones and check for insects,
	  disease & embryo elongation
	- check weather forecast if it is warm and dry.
	  Seed could mature quickly.
		Hand lens, knife, truck, rifle, etc.	$250

For further information about reforestation planning in British Columbia, the following sources are recommended:

B.C. Ministry of Forests. 1980. Forest and range resource analysis technical report. Vol. 1. Resource Analysis Branch, Victoria, B.C. 511 p.

B.C. Ministry of Forests. 1984. Forest and range resource analysis. Resource Analysis Branch, Victoria, B.C. 400 p.

B.C. Ministry of Forests. 1989. Five Year Forest and Range Resource Program 1989 - 1994. Victoria, B.C. 15 p.

B.C. Ministry of Forests
   - Resource Planning Manual.
   - Timber Management Manual.
   - Ministry Policy Manual.
   - Silviculture Manual.
   Technical and Administrative Services Branch, Victoria, B.C.

B. C. Ministry of Forests and Canadian Forestry Service. 1988. Managing your woodland: a non-foresters guide to small-scale forestry in British Columbia.Victoria, B.C.

Forestry Handbook for British Columbia. 1983. 4th ed. by S.B. Watts (editor). Univ. B.C., Faculty of Forestry, Forestry Undergraduate Society. Vancouver, B.C. 611 p.

MANAGING INFORMATION

Effective plans at any planning level cannot be made without good information on which to base them. Other than for the smaller forms of licence (e.g., Woodlot Licences), vast amounts of data are usually necessary. The only efficient way of handling this information is with computer-based inventory and history record systems. Strategic analyses, AAC calculations, and silviculture benefit-cost evaluations are also best performed by computers.

Some examples of the types of information that must be organized and managed are as follows:

Inventory

- forest cover maps and inventory data
- site types
- ecological maps and data
- NSR areas

Operational

- numbers of blocks and locations of planned harvests
- planned silviculture activities
- survival and growth performance
- Pre-Harvest Silviculture Prescriptions

Strategic Planning/Analysis

- expected annual harvests in both the short and long terms
- frequency and extent of wildfires or other damaging agents
- growth and yield estimates
- age class distribution
- overstocked areas
- silviculture activities to be carried out
- other users and their locations

History Record Systems

Since the late 1970's, the Ministry of Forests has maintained silviculture records for Crown land on a computer based information system called the "History of Crop Establishment and Tending" system (commonly referred to as the "history record" system). With the transfer of reforestation responsibility to the forest industry in 1987, however, the onus for primary record-keeping has also been transferred to the industry. Information is to be reported once annually by industry to the Ministry through the "Major Licence Silviculture Information System" (MLSIS). Data from this system will eventually mesh with the history record system to generate one provincial data base.

Inventory Systems

Forest inventories contain data on all forest stands and openings. Silviculture information has generally not been recorded in as much detail in the Ministry's forest inventory as it has in their history record system. In fact, inventory information for recently disturbed or regenerated areas, is usually obtained from the silviculture history records.

As Geographic Information Systems (GIS) become more common, it is expected that they will eventually be used to generate both forest cover maps and associated data.

PRE-HARVEST ASSESSMENT AND PRESCRIPTION

8

M.J. Hadley, P.K. Diggle, D.L. Handley, and M.H. Wyeth

INTRODUCTION

A forest is an expression of the physical and biological capabilities of a site, shaped by outside forces such as climate and people. As the most visible, living product of these interactions, forests provide a great deal of information about a site, its productive capacity for growing trees, and its ability to adapt to modification. The best time to assess the character and condition of a site, therefore, is before cutblock boundaries are finalized and harvesting takes place.

In the forested state it is easier to determine the ecological classification of a site, identify the natural forces at work, and assess the sensitivity of the site and its various resources to the impacts of timber harvesting. For planning purposes, this is also the most effective time to identify the key biological and site-specific factors to be addressed in the management of that site, and to establish prescriptions to guide the harvesting, regeneration, and silvicultural activities that will be carried out over the next rotation.

The system of assessing planned logging sites and developing overall guidelines for their management is referred to as the pre-harvest prescription.

This chapter outlines the conceptual framework of the pre-harvest prescription, and addresses the types of information and treatment and management regimes that are considered in its development.

What is a Pre-Harvest Prescription?

The pre-harvest prescription is a framework for collecting information and making decisions about how best to use the natural productivity and potential of a site to serve specified management goals. Pre-harvest prescriptions are the forerunners to detailed operational plans for harvesting, regeneration, and silviculture on a site. In effect, they are site-specific management strategies.

The prescription process begins with the assessment of a site and its resource values, to identify the significant site and resource variables that must be considered in the development of operational plans. The pre-harvest assessment also identifies the sensitivity of the site and its resources to impacts from harvesting and other forest management operations. It does not require a full inventory of all resources on-site, but focuses on the key elements that must be incorporated into management plans for timber production and other resources.

The resource values and site sensitivities identified in the field assessment are addressed in discussions with local experts and in consideration of the prescriptions for other resource uses, to develop a forest management strategy for the site that reflects all resource-use concerns and includes the necessary provisions to maintain site productivity. Based on this information, a pre-harvest prescription (PHP) is developed for the area. The prescription sets out the forestry activities, the methods that will be used, and the proposed constraints necessary to protect the site and its resource values.

Why is a Pre-Harvest Prescription Required?

The objective of the pre-harvest prescription is to establish an integrated plan for the management of a piece of forest land, prior to harvesting, that sets all management activities in an ecological context. This plan should also ensure that the site is managed to achieve the objectives established in higher level management plans in such a way as to safeguard the integrity of the site.

Assessing the status and sensitivities of a site before harvesting means that potential problems and conflicts can be reduced and planning steps coordinated. As well, activities such as harvesting and protection can be integrated, and administrative tasks such as sowing requests and pesticide application permits can be initiated well before implementation. By considering all steps together — such as harvesting, hazard abatement, pest management, site preparation, regeneration, and maintenance — and by assessing their potential impacts on other resources, forest managers can find an overall optimum solution rather than simply one optimum step. The coordination of operations on-site can significantly reduce site damage and unnecessary or conflicting activities, and reduce the overall costs of forest land management.

The informal assessment of logging sites before cutting was often part of the 5-year Management and Development Plans. The process was formalized in a 1987 amendment to the provincial Forest Act (1979), and pre-harvest prescriptions are now a legal prerequisite to harvesting on Crown lands. The content and standards for pre-harvest prescriptions are defined in the Silviculture Regulation (B.C., Reg. 147/88) and subsequent interpretive documentation prepared by the Forest Service. While the prescriptions are formally identified as *pre-harvest silviculture prescriptions* in the regulation, in this chapter we will refer to them as *pre-harvest prescriptions* in recognition of the fact that they address harvesting methods, protection, and other resources in addition to silvicultural concerns.

The Planning Hierarchy

The pre-harvest prescription acts as the vehicle through which the higher level objectives of Timber Supply Area plans, Tree Farm Licence plans, and other area-based management plans are communicated into site-specific forestry operations. This connection between on-site operations and the overriding management objectives of the Timber Supply Area, Tree Farm

Licence, or Woodlot Licence is vital in the long-range planning of the forest resource. It is a means of ensuring that short-term actions planned on individual sites collectively serve the long-term strategies for the larger management area.

The pre-harvest prescription provides a mechanism for monitoring short-term operations and their effectiveness in achieving short-term production goals, and at the same time acts as the link with the longer term management goals and objectives for the area.

When is a pre-harvest prescription prepared?

In general, pre-harvest prescriptions are prepared 2-3 years before harvesting. Ideally, they are used to define the cutblock boundaries, and to identify the considerations and constraints that must be incorporated into the cutting permit application.

Pre-harvest prescriptions are carried out at a time of year when the site conditions allow for site characteristics and resource status to be assessed. It is important that the area be free of snow, that the ground not be frozen, and that the vegetation can be identified.

Who is responsible for pre-harvest prescription?

Pre-harvest prescriptions are required for all Crown lands on which harvesting is planned. Where the licensee pays for silviculture, the pre-harvest prescription is the responsibility of the licensee. Where the government pays for silviculture, as is the case in the Small Business Forest Enterprise Program, the responsibility rests with the Forest Service.

A pre-harvest prescription must be developed for each cutblock, and be signed and sealed by a British Columbia registered professional forester. By affixing a professional seal to the prescription, foresters certify the technical aspects of the management prescriptions and their appropriateness to the particular site. Once a pre-harvest prescription has been completed, an advertisement is placed inviting the public to review and comment on its content.

The prescription, along with responses to any comments from the public, is submitted to the district manager for approval. Once it has been approved, the licensee is responsible for implementation. The performance of the licensee in meeting the obligations set out in the pre-harvest prescription must be detailed in an annual report and submitted to the district manager.

THE PRE-HARVEST PRESCRIPTION FRAMEWORK

The development of ecologically and economically sensitive prescriptions is a process of observation, analysis, and synthesis. The person collecting the field data must be able to identify the forces at work on the site, and assess the sensitivity of the site and other resource values to the impacts of harvesting and other forest management activities. Using this information, he must prescribe the forestry operations necessary to achieve the management objectives while protecting the long-term productivity of the site. This process relies heavily on the informed judgment and innovation of the forester designing the prescription.

The pre-harvest prescription provides guidelines for on-site operations. It is not a comprehensive development plan for a site, but an integration of all the factors that should be considered and addressed in the development of specific operational plans, such as those for harvesting, regeneration, and post-establishment activities.

An ecological basis for assessments

The biogeoclimatic ecosystem classification used in British Columbia groups ecosystems with similar vegetation and productivity potential into site units that are biologically equivalent. This grouping simplifies the management of a forest, and at the same time provides a strong ecological foundation for management decision-making. It establishes a framework to help understand how specific site units respond to different treatments. This experience can then be transferred from one site unit to other, biologically equivalent site units.

For operational purposes, a forester needs information on the characteristics of a site and its vegetation. Since biogeoclimatic information is used at the site level, it is important that the forester understand how the site classification is linked to the vegetation and zonal classifications. (For more detail see Chapter 6, and the Forest Service ecosystem guides.)

The correct ecological classification of the site is the crux of the pre-harvest prescription. It integrates the biological, geological, and climatic forces on-site, and indicates the site's inherent capabilities and limitations. The ecological classification provides the key to forest management, including such issues as species selection, productivity, stocking standards, site protection, and habitat values.

Consideration of resource values

Since the intent of the pre-harvest prescription is to prescribe a treatment schedule that integrates resource uses and safeguards site productivity, the pre-harvest assessment must first identify the site and resource characteristics. This can be done through a preliminary study of the available information about the site and its resources, as well as referral to handbooks available for managing these.

Foresters should develop a working familiarity with both the plans and the resource guidelines applicable to the site before collecting field data. This will help them focus attention on what to look for, and to assess what is relevant in determining management impacts. Resource guidelines will also help in the development of the prescription. It should be emphasized that handbooks and guidelines are designed to acquaint and sensitize personnel to the needs and special considerations in protecting and managing resources for specified goals. These materials must be used as tools for prescription development, rather than as prescription "cookbooks."

Site sensitivity issues

The sensitivity of a site to timber harvesting depends on a range of on-site and off-site considerations, including wildlife, range, fisheries, water, soil stability, aesthetics, and economics, as well as site productivity. In addition to the handbooks available to help individuals assess these, local studies and local specialists should be consulted during prescription development. The level of sensitivity of the site will help the forester determine the priorities to be addressed in the pre-harvest prescription.

THE PROCESS OF PRE-HARVEST PRESCRIPTION DEVELOPMENT

The development of pre-harvest prescriptions involves six steps undertaken in three major stages (Table 8.1). The first stage includes the preliminary organization of all background information, the collection of field data, and the development of an initial prescription. The second stage involves the identification of the major factors that influence the management of a particular area, and the related resource management options. In the third stage, all the information collected is analyzed and synthesized into the final pre-harvest prescription for the site. The entire pre-harvest prescription package consists of field data, the initial prescription, the final prescription, and a base map.

TABLE 8.1. The process of pre-harvest prescription development

Pre-harvest assessment	1. determine management objectives and priorities for the site
	2. collect field data
Identifying issues and options	3. refer to applicable standards (Ministry of Forests or Management Working Plan)
	4. refer to prescription guidelines

Developing the prescription	5. make treatment decisions for each phase of the regime
	   - species to regenerate
	   - method of regeneration
	   - silvicultural system and harvesting method
	   - site preparation
	   - brushing and weeding
	   - spacing, thinning, release, fertilization, pruning

	6. ensure that silviculture phases are compatible with other disciplines and resource uses

The Pre-Harvest Assessment

Preliminary organization

Informed judgment is crucial in developing the pre-harvest prescription. Before a field assessment is done, all the information relevant to the area must be reviewed. This includes management plans and objectives, resource documents, inventories and guidelines, maps, aerial photographs, pest inventories, Forest Service Silviculture and Protection Branch manuals, and Regional ecological classification guides. The information will enable the field data and initial prescription forms to be partially completed in the office, and will help focus attention on the data that needs to be collected in the field.

The next task is to identify tentatively the biogeoclimatic ecosystem classification for the area, which will later be confirmed on the ground. The purpose of the classification is to facilitate forest management. Consequently, the classification is carried only to the level of significance required for treatment differences on the site. Depending on its size, configuration, and site uniformity, a single site unit may become a "treatment unit": an area for which uniform prescriptions can be made. Where it is too small to form a logical treatment unit, it should be grouped with compatible neighbors. When this is done, the final prescription for that treatment unit will synthesize the varying field prescriptions made for the individual components.

A proposed cutblock may include more than one treatment unit. This is commonly the case in old-growth forests. As British Columbia moves into more intensive forest management and undertakes greater effort in shaping its forests, treatment units will more often correspond to individual cutblocks.

Field data collection

The intent of field data collection is to identify the significant limiting factors of the site and to collect sufficient information to develop a site prescription accommodating all resources. Additional information will be available from local specialists, so enough data should be gathered to acquaint them with the site. Making a detailed inventory of each resource, however, is inappropriate at this stage.

The Forest Service has developed forms to assist in the collection of data and the development and presentation of pre-harvest prescriptions. The forms provide a standard format for recording data, and a standard procedure that can help ensure interpretations and prescriptions are consistent throughout the province. The amount and range of information necessary in pre-harvest assessments vary between regions as well as sites. The principles for data collection in pre-harvest prescription are to observe widely and record selectively. The intensity of data collection should depend on site complexity and management requirements. Only information that is significant for treating the particular situation should be collected.

Before leaving the site, the forester should make an initial field prescription for each tentative treatment unit. This allows a quick check to ensure that data have been collected for all the factors that might constrain the choice of treatments. This initial prescription should include both preferred and alternative treatment options to allow for treatment failures or changing circumstances.

The following sections shows the type of questions the pre-harvest assessment must help the forester to answer, and outlines the kinds of information to be collected.

Physical and climatic characteristics of the site

How steep is the site? Is skidding, grapple, or high lead yarding preferable? Is there evidence of sloughing or slope failure? Should cutblocks be aligned with contours? What are the climatic considerations? What are the site implications for regeneration (species, scheduling, site preparation, stock)?

The physical features of a site (such as elevation, aspect, slope, and terrain) all affect the ways in which harvesting and silvicultural activities are implemented. They determine the susceptibility of a site to erosion, and influence the distribution of heat and water on the site. These characteristics will influence prescriptions for the size, shape, and alignment of cutblocks, as well as for the silvicultural system, logging methods, and regeneration program. A combination of topographical and climatic factors determines cold air pooling and the potential for frost pockets, and these in turn affect seedling survival and growth. Weather patterns also play a part in the development of protection plans, regeneration plans (such as the timing of planting, stock transportation, and storage), access, and the scheduling of logging.

Soils assessment

How vulnerable are these soils to compaction and traffic? Will logging have to be scheduled for frozen or dry conditions only? Will high impact burns be detrimental? Are the soils sensitive to erosion or sloughing? Is high lead logging preferable to skidding? Will skid trails need to be constructed and heavy equipment movements restricted? What species will the site support?

Soil is a critical element in the development of the pre-harvest prescription, determining in particular the methods of harvesting, site preparation, and planting. Soil texture affects nutrient status, drainage, compaction and trafficability, potential for erosion, and frost heave. The type and depth of humus influence soil nutrient status and its ability to withstand compaction and erosion.

Vegetation description

What major and minor vegetation is currently on-site and what is the site capability? Should the current crop be renewed or converted to species more suited to the management objectives for the site? Is there advance regeneration of the desired species; and is it of acceptable abundance and quality? Is brush encroachment likely after harvesting? What species exist and what is the potential forage value?

The vegetation description is used to help identify the ecosystem association, the potential for brush encroachment, and the potential browse material for ungulate species. The status of advance regeneration may affect the methods and timing of logging, as well as the reforestation prescription. The composition and condition of overstory vegetation will influence reforestation strategies (the vegetation being a seed source to encourage or discourage) and also site preparation (in terms of how much residual wood should be left on-site after harvesting).

Ecological classification

How will this site respond to different treatments? What species are best suited to the site? What are the water table implications? What type of site preparation is recommended? What is the potential for wildlife on this site?

The site's ecosystem association is one of the keys to prescription development. Since site classification groups ecosystems into silviculturally equivalent units, it is possible to apply the treatment experience gained in one site to similar sites. The Forest Service ecological handbooks provide guidelines for species selection, site productivity, and post-treatment vegetation development.

Assessment of fire hazard and risk

What is the nature of the fuel complex: windthrow? snags? What is the fuel loading? Are there obvious sources of ignition? How will harvesting affect the fuel management plan?

The presence of campsites and major access routes and the incidence of lightning in the area influence the fire risk. The incidence of lightning strikes can be obtained from regional protection staff. Slash loading and climate affect the hazard and how the site fits into the fuel management plan for the area.

Assessment of pest hazards and risks

What pests, especially of young stands, are a problem in this area? Are there any signs of pests that pose a particular threat to subsequent crops, such as the presence of root disease or dwarf mistletoe?

Pest information collected at this early stage in planning can help prevent some problems and reduce the risk of others. Pest management staff should be consulted before field assessment to provide some basic information on pest identification and the assessment of risk. At the field level, data should be collected on the type of damage, level of incidence, and stage of infestation.

Presence of other resource values

How is the area used by wildlife? Is it being used as rangeland? What is the source of water on the site? Are the streams or lakes important to salmonids or other fish? Is the water on-site a source of domestic water? How visible is the area from major viewing sites such as highways or wilderness vantage points? What are the recreational and heritage features of the area?

The pre-harvest prescription is one of many stages at which non-timber resource values are considered in forest planning. This is the time to think about all resource values and how their needs can be incorporated in the development of the site. Data are gathered on the current status and condition, as well as the potential use, of streams and lakes, wildlife habitat, recreation areas, and range. The visibility and sensitivity of the landscape are also assessed.

Since the pre-harvest assessment provides the baseline information for prescription development, the status of all resources on-site must be considered. The conditions of rangeland tenures — the timing of grazing, presence of fencing, and location of watering holes — can affect forestry operations and wildlife habitat. The impacts of water licenses and fisheries enhancement activities should also be considered.

Data collected on-site, combined with information from resource inventories and specialists, are used to determine how non-timber resource needs affect harvesting and silviculture treatments. Based on the identified requirements for protecting or enhancing certain resource values, the prescription will contain the necessary modifications or constraints to forest development activities.

Economics

How productive is the site? How much will it cost to treat, manage, and log? How long before the trees can be harvested? How far from the mill? How would the stand rank?

In assessing each site, the forester must give thought to economics. The prescription should tailor cost-effective means of achieving the goals for the area, and consider probable future management options.

Identifying the Issues and Management Options

In the office, the field data and initial prescriptions are reviewed along with the reference materials, so that the site sensitivity, the management objectives, and any potential site conflicts can be identified. When the issues have been noted, the next task is to determine the management and treatment options that will address these needs. Here, the forester may need to seek the advice of specialists. For instance, if wildlife and recreation factors were identified as significant elements within the treatment unit, then additional information on the management options for these two resources should be sought from the local wildlife and recreation specialists.

Some of the site issues and management options that are commonly incorporated into the pre-harvest prescription are described below.

Site degradation

Soil is the foundation of the forest. It shapes the type and quality of forest that can be achieved on a site and the extent to which a site can be manipulated without severe consequences. Harvesting, by nature of its requirement for roads, landings, and fireguards, results in some reduction to the productive area of forest sites. Inappropriate site preparation may also reduce site productivity. The extent and severity of soil degradation related to these actions can be limited by the careful planning of operations. The pre-harvest prescription provides an excellent vehicle for the early identification of a site's sensitivity to disturbance and of the modifications required to forestry practices, so that degradation can be minimized.

The susceptibility of a site to degradation is determined by the site's physical, climatic, biological, and ecological character. Slope, soil depth, and frequency of watercourses and gullies are the major indicators of sensitivity to degradation. In British Columbia, the major types of site degradation are soil compaction, soil displacement, soil erosion, and loss of soil nutrients. The careful planning of water movement and placement of skid roads reduces the potential for both compaction and soil displacement damage. As a site's sensitivity increases, harvesting and site preparation practices that minimize disturbance may be required. Such practices include skidding over frozen ground or snow, limiting excavation during road construction, using high flotation skidders or high lead logging systems, and conducting low intensity burns.

Site degradation is recognized as a major element of the pre-harvest prescription. The sidebar lists several guides for minimizing site disturbance caused by ground skidding and other forestry practices.

Watershed and fisheries

Impacts on fish habitat, water quality, water temperature, and streambank stability must be assessed wherever fish are present or a stream flows into fish-bearing waters. On the coast the British Columbia "Coastal Fisheries Forestry Guidelines" (B.C. Ministry of Forests et al. 1987) must be consulted.

Where a watershed provides water for domestic use or irrigation, the need for special management must be evaluated. Control of sedimentation through partial cutting or limitations on rate of cut should be discussed with a hydrologist.

Range and wildlife

The seasonal provision of foraging areas and the protection of calving and wintering areas are of primary concern for wildlife habitat management. For domestic stock, management issues

B.C. Ministry of Forests and Lands, Timber Harvesting Methods Committee and Terry Lewis. 1988. Guidelines for timber harvesting prescriptions for Interior sites of various degradation sensitivities. Available from the Ministry of Forests, Victoria, B.C. 65 p.

B.C. Ministry of Forests and Lands. 1987. Ground skidding guidelines. Engineering and Silviculture Branches, Victoria, B.C. 58 p.

Carr, W.W. 1980. A handbook for forest roadside erosion control in British Columbia. B.C. Min. For., Victoria, B.C. Land Manage. Rep. No. 4. 43 p.

Coates, D. and S. Haeussler. 1987. A guide to the use of mechanical site preparation equipment in Northern British Columbia. 2nd ed. For. Can. and B.C. Min. For., Victoria, B.C. FRDA Handb. No. 002.

Forest Engineering Research Institute of Canada (FERIC). 1980. Site classification system promises reduced costs, efficient logging. Can. Pulp and Paper Industry 1980 (6):26-29.

Johnson, W. and G.V. Wellburn (editors). 1976. Handbook for ground skidding and road building in British Columbia. FERIC, Vancouver, B.C. FERIC Handb. No. 1.

Krag, R.K. and S.R. Webb. 1988. Cariboo Lake logging trials: production, performance and costs of rubber tired skidder, small crawler tractor and cable yarding systems on steep slopes in the central interior of British Columbia. FERIC, Vancouver, B.C. 48 p.

Lousier, J. D. and G. Still (editors). 1988. Degradation of forested lands: forest soils at risk. Proc. 10th B.C. Soil Science Workshop. B.C. Min. For., Victoria, B.C. Land Manage. Rep. No. 56.

Utzig, G.F. and M.E. Walmsley. 1988. Evaluation of soil degradation as a factor affecting forest productivity in British Columbia: problem analysis. Phase I. For. Can. and B.C. Min. For., Victoria, B.C. FRDA Rep. No. 25.

will relate to the terms of the grazing tenures on the land, and will be influenced by the timing and movement of cattle over a licence area. For both domestic stock and wildlife, management options should include appropriate combinations of forage, water, and cover.

Recreation and landscape

Management options for recreation and landscape values may vary from restricted access and no harvesting, to the maintenance of forested buffer zones around clearcuts, depending on the recreational values of an area, the proximity of users, the level of use, and the visual impact to the public of forestry operations. Such considerations should be reflected in the choice of silvicultural system and harvesting method, in the location and design of cutblocks, and in the designation of campsites or other recreational facilities.

Engineering constraints

Access is a critical link in forestry operations — and also a potential major source of site degradation. Management options must address ways to limit the risk of erosion, soil displacement, and mass-wasting, and to minimize the total affected area of the site. Comprehensive planning of access is important to prevent the creation of pockets of inaccessible timber, and to reduce the amount of non-productive area created on a site, such as that tied up in roads or landings.

Regeneration and harvesting method

The choice of regeneration method (clearcut, shelterwood, selection, see Chapter 10) to be followed in harvesting, regeneration, and tending is a major element of the prescription. Having chosen the silvicultural system, the options for harvesting methods and site preparation will depend on the sensitivity of the soils to compaction, displacement, and erosion. It may be necessary to schedule logging to times of year when impact is low because the ground is either very dry or frozen and covered with snow. Logging may be restricted from highly sensitive areas, or modified where possible through the use of high flotation equipment, smaller skidders, or high lead systems.

Trees remaining

Trees may be left on a site for silvicultural reasons, such as to provide a shelterwood or to act as seed trees. They may also be left to provide browse and cover for wildlife, nesting sites for birds, food and protection for fisheries values, or a buffer for recreation or landscape purposes. It is important to consider what dangers the trees left on-site might pose for other users of the site. No less important is the consideration of trees that must **not** remain on site, lest they provide an unsuitable seed source for regeneration or contribute to subsequent fire or pest-related protection problems.

Wood residue

The type and condition of current forest cover, as well as the harvesting method, affect the amount of post-logging residue on-site. This in turn will affect prescriptions for protection, site preparation, and planting. Consideration must be given to what should be left on-site to preserve microsites or nutrients, weighed against the potential protection costs or other disadvantages of doing so.

Silviculture planning

Where there is a possibility of treatment failure, the prescription must include a preferred treatment and an alternative. Treatment standards — such as minimum regeneration delays, stocking standards, or the maximum acceptable impact rank from slashburning — must be indicated where appropriate. The species and method of regeneration, along with decisions on stock type, size, and timing of planting, must be addressed. The potential for brush encroachment will determine the treatments required to ensure that trees reach a free-growing state within the acceptable period. Logistical considerations, such as the transport and storage of stock, may further influence decisions on the timing and methods of silviculture treatments.

Protection

Fire and pest protection issues focus on reducing the hazards on-site. For fire, some of the management options include: modifying the shape, size, and orientation of cutblock openings, particularly where burning will be required; scarifying to break up and distribute slash, or windrowing and burning slash; and leaving areas of standing timber as firebreaks. Pest management options may include selecting species that are less susceptible to local insect or disease problems, or thinning to maintain stand vigor.

Boundary determination

Determining the boundaries for a treatment unit will involve a wise compromise of the boundaries for access, management and treatment purposes. The size and shape of a cutblock opening must be determined by such factors as:

- the merchantability of the timber (is there a market for these species?)
- the operability of the site (can we afford to harvest it?)
- other resource values (visual quality objectives, wildlife considerations)
- the protection and silviculture objectives for the site
- the potential for windthrow
- the sensitivity of the site to degradation

The cutblock boundary should delineate an area that is considered appropriate as a management unit for the consistent application of treatments.

Developing the Prescription

Using the information and advice gathered from references, field assessment, and consultation with specialists, the forester develops a final prescription for the site.

Ecosystem units are transferred from photos to a base map and labelled. Any significant plot and transect information, such as soil characteristics and ecosystem associations, is also noted. From this information, treatment units are identified and plotted on the map. A final prescription is completed for each cutblock, and, where there is more than one unit per cutblock, prescriptions are modified by treatment unit.

In developing the pre-harvest prescription, the first things to be considered are the limiting factors on the site: the available light, moisture, and nutrients; the air and soil temperatures; and the potential for damage to seedlings from frost, wind, or other sources. The reforestation objectives for the site will play a central role in the prescription development, since they influence the choice of silvicultural system, harvesting method, site preparation, and planting stock, as well as the selection of planting season and the need for brushing. For each phase (e.g., site preparation) a preferred treatment is prescribed, with an alternative as backup where necessary. Alternative treatment methods should be selected according to how well they serve the specified treatment objectives, and considering any operational or administrative constraints.

Once the site-specific issues have been identified, along with the management options for dealing with them, various factors must be weighed. The best of these, and sometimes alternative management strategies, are then selected for each silviculture activity.

Pre-harvest prescriptions are site-specific and tied to the management objectives for an area. This means that the length and detail of a prescription will vary according to the complexity of the site. Where the site is simple, without major importance for non-timber resources, the prescription may be short. Where sites are more complex because of variation in terrain, vegetation, or other resource values, the prescription should be more detailed.

Obtaining approval

The existence of the pre-harvest prescription is advertised by the licensee to give the public a chance to comment on the prescription. The prescription, along with any comments received and the licensee's response to such comments, is submitted to the district manager for approval.

Following approval, the licensee must submit any revisions, in writing, to the district manager. The licensee is further obliged to submit an annual report on the performance of responsibilities under the pre-harvest prescription.

Accomplishment Monitoring and Feedback

Pre-harvest prescriptions provide a written record of the intent, actions, and results to be achieved in carrying out forestry operations on individual cutblocks. This makes it possible to monitor the effectiveness of various treatments, enhance feedback, and improve future prescriptions.

The real value of monitoring lies in the ecological basis of the pre-harvest prescription. Because prescriptions are tied to ecological units, it is possible to compare the results of different treatments on similar ecosystem units, and to evaluate the preferred treatment options for specific ecosystems. As well, the costs of prescribed treatments can be recorded and eventually assessed against the value of the returns. Though the systems for economic and growth modeling are still in development, in the future these tools will likely become part of the information base for developing pre-harvest prescriptions.

SUMMARY

The pre-harvest prescription is the framework by which the overall management objectives for an area are translated into site-specific operations. It sets out, before logging, the methods and schedule by which an area will be harvested, regenerated, and tended. The prescription process considers the management objectives for an area in the context of the sensitivity of the site and its resources to forestry operations. It then recommends forestry activities that will protect the long-term productivity of the site and its other resource values. The whole process relies heavily on the ability of the forester involved to assimilate information, to evaluate how activities affect each other, and to integrate these findings into a technically sound schedule of forest management activities.

In addition to its role as a plan of action for a site, the prescription is also a contract for good forest management. Legally, it binds the parties responsible for carrying out basic silviculture — either the licensee or the Forest Service — to the activities set out in the prescription.

The pre-harvest prescription stands as a key element in the process for regenerating British Columbia's forests. As the initial statement of the harvesting, regeneration, and silviculture plans that will be developed for each site, it represents both a tool and a philosophy for good forest management.

9 MONITORING REGENERATION PROGRAMS

C. Pearce

Monitoring is the operational practice of evaluating the outcome of activities to improve their effectiveness. Successful activities are identified so they can be repeated; failures are examined so the reasons they did not meet the objectives can be determined. A monitoring program must uphold this commitment to examining failures and changing treatments to improve the performance.

This chapter provides a practicing forester with the tools to develop a comprehensive regeneration monitoring program. It first reviews the characteristics of an effective monitoring program, and then discusses the major considerations that should be addressed when such a program is designed. Finally, it describes common monitoring practices for each step in the reforestation process.

CHARACTERISTICS OF A SUCCESSFUL MONITORING PROGRAM

To ensure a regeneration monitoring program achieves its purpose of improving reforestation results, it must have several simple, commonsense elements:

1. Incentives

There must be an incentive to improve regeneration results if a monitoring process is to be taken seriously. Without any benefits to be gained by improving regeneration performance, monitoring becomes inconsequential and inefficient.

For example, in a monitoring program for planting, the organization responsible for the planting project must have some reason for reforesting the area. On Crown land in British Columbia, the incentive is the continued right to harvest Crown timber. On private land, the incentive is usually monetary but may also reflect the desires of the landowner. For the project supervisor, the incentive to carry out the project successfully is continued employment; for the nursery grower to produce high quality seedlings, it is payment and future business; for the planters to handle the seedlings carefully and plant them according to the project specifications, it is monetary penalties and bonuses.

2. Linkages

Regeneration programs are carried out within complex physical and biological systems. Climate, site factors, and seedling condition can singly, or through interactions, influence the success of reforestation. A successful monitoring program evaluates how the interactions of these and timing factors affect the outcome of a combination of regeneration treatments.

As well, because regeneration programs involve reforestation activities that are often institutionally and organizationally separated, the individuals within each organization must share a common goal if the regeneration program is to be successful. Incorporating such linkages into the monitoring program will promote accountability for the success of activities, and hasten response to unacceptable treatment results.

In many operations, for example, the harvesting and site preparation are completed by a different person than the field forester who is responsible for the success of the subsequent plantation. In turn, the field forester relies on the nursery grower to provide healthy planting stock, and on the planters to handle and plant the seedlings carefully. Poor performance at any of these steps can lead to a failed plantation, with the cause of the failure being difficult to trace and rectify.

3. Stratification

Differences in site and stand conditions and in treatment characteristics should be distinguished to explain the effects of a treatment on a forest site. These differences influence all site management decisions. Stratification (i.e., defining homogeneous units) is a basic requirement for a successful monitoring program.

The ecosystem unit provides the basis for stratification on a specific site (see Chapter 6). Differences in vegetation cover, operational or administrative constraints, or other factors may mean smaller units should be defined.

Monitoring information for plantations, for example, should be stratified by the following factors:

- site conditions
    - ecosystem unit
    - vegetation cover
    - previous treatments (site history)
    - weather conditions (during treatment and immediately following)

- seedlings
    - species
    - stock type
    - age
    - nursery
    - handling practices

- planting practices
    - inter-tree distances
    - screefing requirements
    - planting quality requirements.

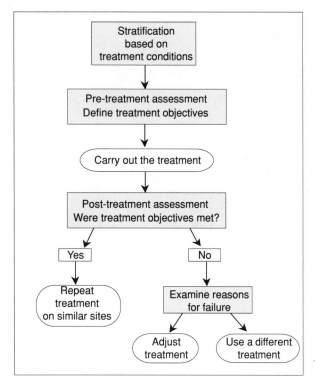

FIGURE 9.1. Components of an effective reforestation treatment monitoring system.

This level of stratification is often not feasible, but significant differences in the performance of two similar plantations are usually the result of one or a combination of the above factors. Without proper stratification, identifying the cause of the difference in performance may not be possible.

4. Objectives

The objectives of a program or treatment must be defined before the effectiveness of the activity can be evaluated. In a regeneration program, both short-term objectives for specific treatments and long-term objectives for the free-growing stand should be defined.

As Figure 9.1 shows, objectives are set during a pre-treatment assessment, when site conditions are evaluated and the biological, operational, and administrative constraints to managing the site are identified. For example, in preparing for a planting project, a pre-treatment assessment should be made to evaluate the number of plantable spots. A definition of what constitutes a plantable spot on this particular site — including duff depth, brush conditions, type of soil, and desired density at the end of the reforestation process — would be needed. The objective for the planting operation would then be the number of acceptably planted trees the planters are expected to plant, based on the number of spots found during the pre-treatment assessment. The contract specifications should include the size of screefs, the minimum inter-tree distance, the minimum distance from competing vegetation, and seedling handling requirements. These specifications ensure that both the quantitative and qualitative aspects of the treatment objective are stated.

5. Evaluation Procedures

Information must be collected and reviewed so the effectiveness of the treatment or series of treatments can be determined in light of the objectives that were set. If a treatment has failed, an attempt should be made to identify the reasons for failure.

In monitoring a planting project, for instance, post-planting assessments are needed to measure whether the project met its objectives. Planting quality and seedling handling should be checked soon after a planting project starts so that unacceptable practices can be changed immediately. For the next few years, plantation survival and growth should be reevaluated at regular intervals to ensure seedling performance meets expectations.

6. Records

The rapid turnover of forestry personnel in most organizations means that clear, concise, up-to-date records must be kept. These records should document the objectives of the treatments, the actual treatments that occurred, the timing of the treatments, and their outcomes. The information should be easy to obtain and understand, and in a form that allows comparative analyses to identify trends.

7. Feedback

The results of the monitoring program should be quickly passed on to the people responsible for setting the objectives and implementing the treatments. If monitoring indicates planting practices are contributing to failures for example, planters should be cautioned immediately about improper practices, and instructed how to change their techniques. This feedback should include a discussion of the possible causes of failure and the options that exist for altering the treatments. Research staff can often help identify the cause of a treatment failure, or suggest appropriate research to study the problem.

Data collection and analysis for monitoring should also be reviewed to ensure that the current design meets the needs of the existing program and will be effective for the revised treatments.

8. Flexible Design

Monitoring activities should be updated frequently as knowledge improves and objectives and treatments change. At the beginning of a program, all reforestation treatments should be closely monitored to identify the sources of failure. The emphasis of the program will change as monitoring is intensified to eliminate "trouble spots," and as spot checks replace regular monitoring of successful activities. It is not wise to stop monitoring a specific reforestation activity completely, because changes in personnel and practices may result in a successful treatment becoming a trouble spot.

9. Practical Procedures

Simple procedures are more likely to produce the desired results than are highly detailed, complicated procedures. Resource limitations — in budgets, equipment, or trained personnel — should be considered in the design of a monitoring program. For example, a post-treatment evaluation of a completed treatment and a pre-treatment assessment for the next step can usually be done simultaneously, reducing cost and personnel requirements.

DESIGNING A SUCCESSFUL MONITORING PROGRAM

Each activity in a monitoring program should be designed to ensure the appropriate information is collected using the most effective procedures. The appropriate procedures will depend on the objectives of the assessment, the information that is required, and the capabilities of the people doing the assessments. The observation skills of the surveyors, and their understanding of seedling physiology and the interactions within the seedling environment, are perhaps the most important factors in the success of a regeneration monitoring program. Excellent general references on monitoring program design are Society of American Foresters (1984) and Stein (1978, 1985).

Information Needs

The objectives of each monitoring activity should be clearly defined before specific information requirements are discussed. The following questions should be asked:

- Is a pre- or post-treatment assessment necessary?
- Are two assessments being done at the same time?
- Is this assessment for a single treatment, a series of treatments, or both?
- Should the treatment method be decided during the pre-treatment assessment?
- Are contract specifications required in a pre-treatment assessment?
- How should the possible cause of failure be recorded?
- Is this an assessment of the fulfillment of a legal obligation, requiring defensible information, or a less rigid organizational or personal requirement?

Inevitably, it will seem that a long list of information is required to answer the relevant questions. Data collection costs, however, and the availability of trained surveyors will require that the priority objectives for each assessment be defined. The information that is absolutely necessary to meet these objectives should be identified and listed, and its use in the monitoring process explained to the surveyors so they can appreciate the importance of each piece of information they record.

The appropriate level of detail for each type of information should also be defined, taking into consideration the difficulty of obtaining a statistically reliable measurement of each item. For example, it is relatively easy to measure the height of seedlings less than 1 m tall. Accurate estimates of seedlings between 3 and 5 m tall are more difficult and costly to obtain. A compromise between statistical perfection and operational reality must be reached.

As well, clear definitions of terms are necessary. For example, there must be a consistent definition of an "acceptable seedling" whether a sample is taken in the nursery, the planting bag, or 3 years after planting. This allows the sampling procedures to be streamlined and sampling results to be compared. Descriptions and definitions may change over time. For example, a seedling with a double top may be acceptable at the regeneration stage but may not be acceptable at the free-growing stage. Seedling condition (pest damage, color, form), size, species, and age may all at some time be part of the definition of an acceptable seedling (Ferguson 1984; Klinka and Feller 1984). Such elements will determine what data should be recorded. Beforehand, however, the practical implications of adopting certain definitions must be considered. For example, the cost of evaluating bud size and number as a measure of seedling condition may preclude the operational use of such characteristics in an assessment.

The minimum area that must be assessed and treated as a separate unit also affects the procedures and costs of monitoring regeneration treatments. This discussion usually centers around the need to identify voids in stocking, but the same concern applies to small areas where the best treatment is significantly different from the rest of the unit. The feasibility of carrying out alternative treatments and the cost associated with these treatments must be considered when defining minimum strata size. Even with voids in stocking there is a minimum size below which it is uneconomical to treat an area.

On most sites, a portion of the area cannot practicably be reforested — rock outcrops, swamps, or the wheel surface of skid trails, for example. Therefore, a definition of what constitutes a "nonstockable" or nonproductive spot should be provided, and steps for identifying and estimating such areas should be included in field survey procedures.

Once the specific data requirements and the desired detail for each item have been decided, the appropriate data collection procedures can be selected. Evaluating alternative procedures before the information requirements are clear will usually lead to either unnecessarily complicated procedures or inadequate data collection.

Sample Design

Data can be collected by informal reconnaissance surveys or formal sampling procedures. Reconnaissance surveys are used when ocular estimates of the sample characteristics are adequate. These surveys can be made from the air or roadside, or during a walk through the area. A visual check of the condition of seedlings is also a form of reconnaissance survey. A few formal samples may be taken to support the ocular evaluations. A reconnaissance may also be used to stratify an area in preparation for more intensive surveys. These surveys can be cost effective if they are completed by knowledgeable individuals who are experienced at assessing the conditions being evaluated.

More intensive surveys involving a standardized process of data collection to assess and document the required information can also be carried out. The distribution, size, timing, need for remeasurement, and survey method will depend on the information that is being collected and the resource constraints within the program (Kaltenberg 1978).

Sample pattern

A sample must represent the population being assessed. One way to ensure this is to sample the entire population — carry out a 100% sample. With few exceptions, this is not economical or practical in reforestation monitoring. Only a limited number of sites and seedlings can be inspected carefully during a monitoring program.

The diversity of site and seedling conditions makes it difficult to ensure that a monitoring sample is representative. The process used to select the individuals or sites that are assessed can have a significant effect on the accuracy of the results of a sample.

In *simple random sampling*, each sample has an equal chance of being selected. The surveyor must have a complete list of the samples that could be selected, and use a selection process that ensures each sample has an equal opportunity of being chosen. The time required to enumerate all the possible sample units, to randomly select the units that will be sampled, and to locate these units make this type of sampling infeasible for reforestation monitoring.

Stratified random sampling is also based on the principle that each sample in a population has an equal chance of being assessed, but the large population is subdivided into more homogeneous units before the samples are selected. This type of sampling is used to monitor seedling condition. The seedlings are first stratified according to species, stock type, seedlot, and the nursery that produced them; and then a sample of seedlings is selected at random from each stratum for testing. Stratified random sampling is also used during walk-through reconnaissance assessments. The surveyor stratifies the area into similar units, based on environmental conditions, vegetation cover, and operational or administrative constraints. Descriptions are then prepared for each unit from random observations.

Systematic sampling requires the surveyor to traverse the entire unit. Sample points are located at regular, predetermined distances along a grid pattern. A large number of samples are required if the population is highly variable, but these samples can be located quickly with the systematic approach.

Systematic stratified sampling combines the advantages of stratification and systematic sampling. The population is first subdivided into homogeneous units, and then samples are taken at regular intervals throughout each unit. This sampling pattern is used for most field surveys. The observations made by the surveyor travelling from plot to plot are as valuable in the sampling process as the data collected at the plot locations.

Sample size

The number of samples depends on the statistical accuracy wanted in the assessment, and the variability of the characteristics that are being measured. Precise assessments of characteristics that are extremely variable will require many samples. In some cases, the cost of obtaining statistically reliable samples may be prohibitive. With systematic stratified sampling, a minimum number of samples is often required — even in homogeneous units — to ensure the unit has been adequately assessed.

A form of sequential sampling can be used to define sample size. A minimum number of samples are established and the statistical variables are calculated. If a sample size decision can be comfortably made from this information, the assessment is complete. However, if these preliminary data show that the sample is highly variable and the statistical values do not support use of that sample size, further samples must be taken and the statistics recalculated. This process ensures the assessments are concentrated in areas that are highly variable, where decisions will be difficult to make.

Timing of samples

The appropriate time of the year for each type of sample should be considered. Post-treatment monitoring should begin shortly after the treatment starts. Unacceptable practices can be identified, discussed, and changed. Waiting until the end of the project to evaluate the treatment may result in the entire project being unsuccessful.

Seedling condition should be assessed at time intervals that will allow probable causes of reduced performance to be identified. Mortality within 4 weeks of the planting date is usually due to the condition of the stock at the time of planting. Mortality and poor condition later in the first growing season and in subsequent years are more likely due to poor planting practices or extreme weather or site conditions. Plantation failures should be identified as quickly as possible so that planting can be rescheduled, especially if vegetation competition is likely to be a problem on a site.

Stocking assessments of the number of acceptable seedlings on a site are best done in the early spring or late fall when conifer seedlings can be easily seen. Vegetation competition, however, will be underestimated in surveys taken during this time. Competition should be assessed in the middle of the growing season when the vegetation is fully developed.

Remeasurements

Samples can be taken at the same point during every monitoring event, or at locations that are most appropriate for each type of assessment. The location of a *temporary sample* is not permanently marked, as these sampling sites are not reassessed.

Semi-permanent samples, on the other hand, are remeasured over a defined period of time so that the changes in specific characteristics can be documented. For these assessments, the exact location of the sample and the individual sampled items must be established and mapped.

Semi-permanent samples are often maintained during a specific phase of the reforestation process, and their permanency depends on the length of the monitoring period. They are often used to assess plantation performance. In survival surveys, for example, the development of specific seedlings is monitored. This provides an accurate evaluation of their survival rate and an opportunity to document causes of seedling mortality.

Permanent samples are monitored throughout the life of a stand. This form of sampling requires an expensive, long-term commitment to data collection, and must be approved before initial establishment costs are incurred. It is crucial that these plots be marked boldly both in the field and on operating maps to ensure they are not altered or destroyed by forest management treatments.

Field survey methods

Most regeneration monitoring activities include field surveys. The uses, advantages, and limitations of several common field survey methods are reviewed here and summarized in Table 9.1.

Aerial.   Recent advances have been made in using aerial photography to assess reforestation activities. The advent of 70 mm photography (Hall 1984) and satellite imagery (Goba 1984) is providing many new options. In general, these methods are limited to assessing older stands where individual seedlings can be identified. They are not useful where microsite conditions or young seedlings have to be evaluated.

Small scale aerial photographs (1:10 000 - 1:15 000) should be used in conjunction with other surveying methods to perform an area reconnaissance or to pre-stratify a site in preparation for an intensive survey. Using air photos can improve the efficiency of most field surveys.

TABLE 9.1.   Summary of field survey methods

Survey method	Advantages	Limitations	Uses (less common uses)
Aerial	Inexpensive Fast	Cannot see seedlings less than 50 cm tall Cannot evaluate soil conditions Need trained surveyors	Reconnaissance (Free-growing surveys)
Ocular	Inexpensive Fast	Need trained surveyors No statistical verification possible	Reconnaissance Pre-harvest silviculture prescription Cone crop assessment (Brush encroachment)
Distance	Fast Little training required	Questionable accuracy	
Plot counts	Cost depends on the size of plot and data collected Statistical evaluations are easy Can provide detailed, statistically valid information	Can be slow if all trees must be tallied within a large plot Need method for defining acceptable distribution of crop trees	Stocking surveys Free-growing surveys Pre- + post-site preparation surveys Post-planting assessment (Planting quality plots) Pre- and post-spacing surveys
Stocked quadrat plots	Fast Little training required Simple statistical analysis	Does not provide detailed site information	(Stocking surveys outside B.C.)
Staked points	Remeasurement of the same attribute reduces sampling error Little training required Simple statistical analysis	Expensive to establish plots Can be difficult (time-consuming) to relocate samples	Plantation survival assessments Success of treatment combinations
Variable plots	Fastest way to sample pole size and mature stems Simple statistical analysis	Inefficient to use on stems less than 10 cm diameter	Pre-harvest silviculture prescription Stocking and free-growing surveys for selection and shelterwood cuts
Line intersect	Fast	Questionable statistical validity Data summary can be time-consuming if it is not computerized	All surveys with small unmappable types
Photopoints	Fast Visual presentation of information Easy to make comparisons of changes over time	No statistical validity Value depends on maintaining the same photopoints over time	

Ocular estimate.   A walk-through reconnaissance, or ocular estimate, is the most appropriate of the survey methods if the statistical accuracy of the information does not have to be proven, or the treatment recommendations or land status decision will not be significantly altered by sample data. The observation skills of the surveyor are critical to the accuracy of this method.

Ocular estimates are commonly used for pre-harvest silviculture prescriptions and for cone crop and brush encroachment assessments. They are also important for stratifying areas before formal surveys are completed.

Distance methods.   The density and distribution of seedlings or treated spots can be calculated from the distance between a sample point (plot center or previously selected seedling or spot) and the nearest seedling or spot. The average distance between these units is used to calculate the average density over the survey area. Distance methods are comparatively fast to complete and provide a good measure of the sizes of voids. However, because there is some controversy over the accuracy of density measurements, distance methods have had limited use in reforestation monitoring to date (Dennis 1984).

Plot counts. The characteristics of sample units that fall within the boundaries of a selected plot area can be assessed in a plot count sample (Stein 1984). The appropriate shape and size of the plot depends on the intensity of the sample, the distribution and size of the sample units, and the cost of establishing and assessing each type of plot. Circular plots are common for field surveys because the boundaries are easy to establish from a designated plot center.

The intensity of the survey defines the total percentage of the area and the number of plots that should be sampled. Each plot represents a percentage of the survey area. To achieve the required intensity, a few large plots or many small plots can be used. For example, if 1% of each hectare should be sampled, one 1/100th-ha plot (5.64-m radius), two 1/200th-ha plots (3.99-m radius), or five 1/500th-ha plots (2.52-m radius) could be established. Table 9.2 shows the characteristics of commonly used fixed area plots.

The appropriate plot size also depends on the size of the units being sampled. Large plots are needed for widely spaced sample units; small plots are acceptable for small units. For example, 1/100th-ha plots (5.64-m radius) are used to assess crop trees left after spacing projects, while 1/500th-ha plots (2.52 m radius) are used to assess mineral soil spots after site preparation.

A reliable estimate of the total number of stems per hectare can be calculated using fixed area plot counts. The plot size should be kept as small as possible in this type of survey to avoid spending time searching for seedlings within a large plot in understocked stands, or counting large numbers of stems in dense stands. The practical benefits of small plots must be balanced against need to assess the spatial arrangement of crop trees.

If plot counts are used to evaluate the stocking status of a site, a method for assessing the distribution of acceptable stems is needed. Stand density is the total number of stems on a site; stocking status is a measure of the number of acceptable seedlings on a site relative to the number needed to produce a desirable crop at rotation. In the plot count method, only some of the seedlings (or spots) will be spaced far enough apart to be counted for stocking. This spacing must be defined if plot counts are to be used to assess stocking status.

$1\ ha = 10^4\ m^2$

Stocked quadrat plots. Stocked quadrat plots have long been used to evaluate the effectiveness of a series of reforestation treatments at the establishment period — 2 or 3 years after planting, or when it is expected that natural regeneration will be established. Each stocked quadrat plot represents the area that would be occupied by a seedling if a unit were fully stocked; each plot in which an acceptable seedling is found is said to be stocked. To calculate the stocking level, the number of plots that are "stocked" is divided by the total number of plots that were established (Stein 1984). Stocking below a specified minimum is considered to be unacceptable, and further treatments are recommended for the area.

TABLE 9.2. Information for fixed area plots

Plot area (m²)	Per hectare factor[a]	Circular plot radius(m)	Square plot side (m)
500	1/20 ha	12.62	22.36
200	50	7.98	14.14
100	100	5.64	10.0
50	200	3.99	7.07
33.33	300	3.26	5.77
25	400	2.82	5.0
20	500	2.52	4.47
10	1000	1.78	3.16

[a] Each plot represents the fraction of a hectare. Each sample within the plot thus represents the listed number of units per hectare.

This procedure indicates the level of stocking, but not the total density of the stand. Density can be calculated if the total number of stems in each plot is tallied.

Staked points.   To measure changes in specific attributes over time, individual seedlings or sites can be staked in the field and relocated and remeasured at defined intervals. This method is common in research programs or operational trials.

Sample selection is important to ensure there is adequate representation of the variability in the population. The shape of the plot depends on the distribution of the item being sampled and the variability of the population. Circular, rectangular, or line samples have been used.

Staked points are regularly used to monitor plantation performance. Because the habits of each planter can influence seedling survival and growth, seedlings planted by a number of planters should be staked.

The cost of establishing and relocating these samples can become significant. Accurate mapping and record-keeping are vital if the benefits of this procedure are to be obtained.

Variable plots.   This survey method is commonly used to prism-cruise mature timber. Its application in reforestation monitoring is limited to conditions where trees greater than 15 cm diameter are being sampled. This occurs when reforestation in selection or shelterwood systems is being assessed. The number, size, and distribution of large stems may influence the success of the reforestation efforts. Large fixed area plots may be required to sample these trees, making variable plots more effective.

Line intersect.   A line intersect survey evaluates the amount and distribution of various forest types within a sample area (B.C. Forest Service 1987). The surveyor walks along a survey line in a pre-determined direction. The location of boundaries between different stands (stocked, not stocked, overstocked, etc.) is tallied along the survey strip. The length of the strip occupied by each type, divided by the total length of the strip, provides an estimate of the percentage of the occupied area by each type.

This method is useful for assessing stands where well-defined types exist, but the islands of each type are too small to map. Aggregating these islands may create a significant treatment area. The line intersect sample can be used to indicate the area and distribution of each type. Other survey methods should be used in conjunction with the line intersect method to describe each type.

The statistical accuracy of this method depends on the number of strip lines established and the correlation of the length of each island, measured along the strip line, with the width of the island.

Photopoints.   Although photographs are not commonly considered to be a sample, some silviculturists maintain photopoints in their monitoring program. A photopoint is selected in a representative location within a unit, and a photograph is taken. These photos are added to the data collected for that site. Further surveys include updated photos taken from the same photopoints. As well, photographic methods can be used to document seedling size and condition at the time of planting.

Photographic samples are particularly useful in demonstrating changes that occur in stands over time, but they rarely fulfill the needs of a monitoring program on their own.

Records and Analysis

Simplicity and ease of use should be the objectives when data collection forms are designed. The user should be prompted to consider a series of factors in the assessment, and should have enough space to record the required information as well as comments and visual impressions.

All field survey records should be accompanied by a map that identifies the units sampled, the location of sample lines (including walk-through reconnaissances), and a description of significant features on the site. This map can often be used to implement the next treatment.

Surveyors should be required to complete simple data analyses such as the calculation of averages and confidence intervals. Detailed analysis should be the responsibility of a trained statistician, or be conducted through standard procedures supported by computer programs. Computerized data collection and analysis procedures will improve the quality and detail of reforestation monitoring.

While the calculation of average or mean values is simple, this may not be adequate to illustrate the range of conditions that have been sampled. Measures of distribution such as standard deviations and confidence intervals should be incorporated when appropriate.

The Costs of Monitoring

The cost of a monitoring program must cover the design and implementation phase; the manpower, equipment, and supplies needed to carry out the monitoring activities; and the manpower and resources needed to evaluate the information collected and communicate the results to those responsible for improving the program. A simple, well-coordinated regeneration monitoring program can minimize costs significantly. Because travel costs often make up a major portion of field monitoring costs, assessments should be combined as much as possible. Carefully defining monitoring objectives and minimizing data analysis requirements and reducing the time between data collection and feedback will ensure that failures are identified quickly and practices are adjusted to avoid further losses.

Monitoring costs should be evaluated in relation to the benefits that are expected from the program. Consider, for example, a jurisdiction where 200 ha are not successfully restocked annually, and these areas must be retreated at a cost of $400/ha. This represents an annual cost of $80 000. A successful monitoring program, which identified the causes of failure and provided incentives to improve the regeneration practices, would therefore be appropriate. A total cost of $40 000 could be justified if the failure rate was reduced by 50% as a result of the monitoring information. For this amount, a large monitoring program could be developed.

REGENERATION MONITORING PRACTICES IN BRITISH COLUMBIA

Regeneration monitoring practices in the province can be divided into two categories: program and treatment level. Program level monitoring activities are designed to assess combinations of reforestation treatments. These assessments include pre-harvest silviculture prescriptions, stocking surveys and free-growing surveys. Pre- and post-treatment evaluations are also completed for individual treatments. Figure 9.2 shows the relationship of program and treatment monitoring activities in British Columbia. More information on each type of survey is available in the Silviculture Manual of the B.C. Forest Service.

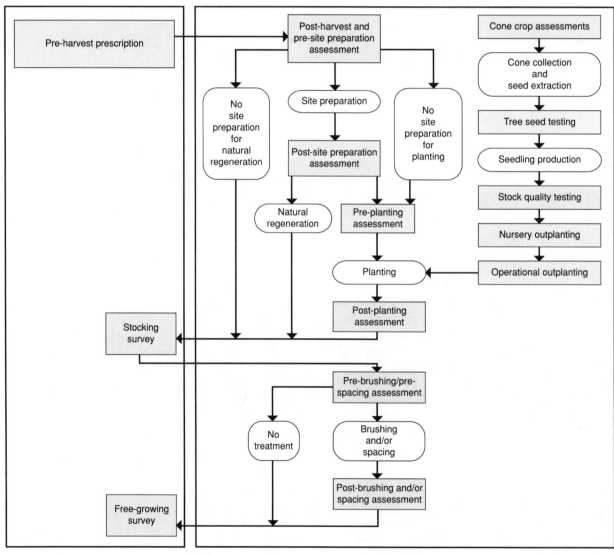

Program Level   **Treatment Level**

FIGURE 9.2.   Program and treatment reforestation monitoring activities in British Columbia.

Program Monitoring

Pre-harvest silviculture prescription

A pre-harvest silviculture prescription (PHSP) defines objectives for a number of phases in the reforestation process (see Chapter 8). The sampling procedures for PHSP's vary widely. The observation skills and knowledge of the surveyor are important in this assessment. A systematic walk-through with data collected by ocular estimation, or the appropriate type of plots located in representative areas, are the most effective sampling methods.

Stocking survey

Forest sites are assessed within the regeneration delay period to define the stocking status of each site. A stocking survey, as this assessment is called, is the most common element of all regeneration monitoring programs. It is a legislated requirement in British Columbia to confirm the restocking of public lands.

A stocking survey is a post-treatment assessment of harvesting, site preparation, and natural regeneration or planting treatments. Ideally, the objectives for this stage of the reforestation process have already been defined in the PHSP, or they can be calculated from other objectives stated in the PHSP or other guidelines.

The primary focus of this survey is the stocking status of the site. If the area is not acceptably stocked, the reasons for this failure should be identified. Whether the area is stocked or not stocked, a pre-treatment assessment to define the objectives for future treatments should be prepared.

The appropriate survey methods depend on the desired accuracy of the sample and the additional information needed. Stocked quadrat surveys are popular because they are fast, but they do not provide information about the overall condition of the stand. Distance methods are also fast, but they provide limited information. Ocular estimates are common in jurisdictions where statistical accuracy is not important or where stocking condition is obvious. Aerial methods have been used where the regeneration is large enough to be identified on small scale aerial photographs. Fixed radius count plots are preferred where statistical accuracy is important and additional quantitative site information is required for further decisions.

In British Columbia, systematically established fixed radius count plots replaced stocked quadrat plots for stocking surveys in 1981 (Wyeth 1984). The surveyor conducts a reconnaissance of the site using aerial photos and a walk-through to stratify the area and set the survey parameters. The total number of stems and the number of acceptable, well-spaced stems are tallied using 1/200th-ha plots. "Acceptable, well-spaced" stems must meet species, size, age, condition, and distribution criteria set out in the PHSP or defined for the site based on regional stocking standard guidelines. Descriptions of the total stand and the well-spaced stems are required. A minimum number of plots must be established to meet the statistical requirements of the survey.

The number of well-spaced stems per hectare is calculated and compared to a minimum stocking standard to define the stocking status for the site. Pre-treatment information is collected to support recommendations for future treatments or surveys.

Free-growing survey

Objectives are defined in the PHSP for the free-growing stage of stand development. This stage is defined as the time from the start of harvesting until a minimum number of acceptable, well-spaced, free-growing stems are established on a site. The free-growing period is defined in the PHSP for each site according to the site conditions, the characteristics of the crop tree species that are to be established, and the time period during which non-crop vegetation may threaten crop tree success. It ranges from 6 to 15 years for most sites.

Free-growing surveys are post-treatment assessments of the entire reforestation process. They measure the success of the reforestation process in creating a stand that meets the objectives defined in the PHSP. They may also be pre-treatment surveys for brushing, if the stand has unacceptable levels of vegetation competition and thus too few free-growing seedlings.

These surveys are virtually the same as stocking surveys except they are carried out in older stands. Often the definition of an acceptable stem is different from that used during a stocking survey. More stringent size, age, and quality criteria may be used in these surveys. The assessment methods for the two survey types should be similar so that the stocking and free-growing survey results can be compared.

Success of treatment combinations

The success of particular combinations of treatments on specific forest sites should be evaluated. Permanently located sample plots should be established in representative ecological units so that a range of treatment combinations can be sampled. The survival and growth of these samples should indicate the comparative success of the tested treatment combinations.

Treatment Monitoring

Harvesting

How well the harvesting objectives have been attained should be evaluated during a post-harvesting assessment. These assessments can usually be completed with random or systematic walk-throughs of a site. If specific site conditions need to be evaluated, plots may be established. For example, a combination of a line intersect and plot count survey can be used to estimate site disturbance; fixed area count plots or variable plots can be established if the trees left standing on the site are being assessed.

A pre-treatment assessment for site preparation should be carried out in conjunction with the post-harvesting evaluation if site preparation is needed.

Site preparation

Pre-treatment assessments for site preparation can be random or systematic ocular estimates, or can include fixed area count plots. The latter should be established when the number of cones on the site (for natural lodgepole pine regeneration), the amount of exposed mineral soil, or the number of plantable spots is being estimated. If a site preparation treatment is needed, quantitative and qualitative goals should be defined, usually as the number of plantable or mineral soil spots to be created by the site preparation treatment. Without these goals, objectively evaluating the effectiveness of a site preparation treatment is difficult.

Systematically located fixed area count plots should be established during the site preparation project. Unacceptable results should be discussed with the individuals who are responsible for the treatment so that treatment practices can be adjusted. This evaluation can be used as the basis for paying a contractor or for defining the objectives for the next treatment. For example, a post-site preparation evaluation should show the actual number of plantable spots for the planting operation.

Cone collection

The existence of a collectable crop should be established before a cone collection project is started (see Chapter 15). The surveyor can do this by counting the number of trees with collectable crops, estimating the number of cones on a sample of these trees, and determining the number of viable seeds in cones taken from the sample trees. This pre-treatment assessment provides an estimate of the number and quality of cones that should be collected. The amount of seed and the number of seedlings that will likely be produced from these cones can also be calculated. If these estimates are exceeded or fewer cones, seeds, or seedlings are produced, the assessment and collection procedures should be examined to identify the reasons for the differences.

The post-treatment assessments may include tallying the number of sacks of cones that are collected, evaluating the germination potential of the seed, and counting the number of plantable seedlings that are finally produced from each collection. The long time periods between the cone collection assessment and the post-treatment evaluations often result in limited feedback to the collection personnel, and poor identification of causes of failure.

Seedling production

Monitoring the condition of seedlings effectively throughout the nursery, transportation, and planting processes is one of the greatest challenges in a regeneration monitoring program. The number of treatments the seedlings are subjected to, the usually disjointed responsibilities for each activity, and the ability of seedlings to appear healthy even when under severe stress emphasize the importance of having effective monitoring procedures (see Chapters 16 and 17).

Seedlings are evaluated frequently while they are in the nursery. Nutrient condition, moisture stress, and pest damage are checked regularly, and successful growers adjust their cultural practices rapidly in response to the monitoring information gathered.

The field forester wants to know the condition of the seedlings before they leave the nursery (or storage) gates and become the responsibility of the operational planting program. A variety of vigor tests (e.g., root growth capacity and Oregon State University vigor test) can be done at this time to evaluate the condition of the stock. It is also common practice to plant approximately 50 seedlings on the nursery grounds to evaluate their performance. The results of these nursery outplanting trials provide an estimate of the best performance that can be expected on the planting site.

Seedling transportation

After the seedlings leave the nursery, many factors may cause mortality or reduced growth. It takes a well-coordinated monitoring program to identify the causes of poor seedling performance. The monitoring process recommended has been developed by Weyerhaeuser Canada Limited.

Seedlings can be physically damaged during transportation or subjected to stress that leads to mortality and reduced growth. Carton temperatures should be monitored regularly throughout the transportation process. As well, planting project supervisiors can outplant a sample of 50 seedlings as soon as they arrive at the planting site, and evaluate their performance to determine the effects of transportation. These seedlings should be staked as semi-permanent samples so they can be reevaluated as needed. A significant difference in the performance of these trees compared to the nursery outplanted seedlings would show problems in the transportation phase.

Planting

In addition to the number of seedlings to be planted on a site (as determined by the post-site preparation assessment), specific planting conditions — such as screef size, planting depth, and acceptable fill material in the planting hole — are also important characteristics of acceptably planted trees (see Chapter 18). Systematically established fixed linear count plots (Planting Quality Plots) are used to assess these factors. The plots are established on most plantations in British Columbia during planting operations. Unacceptable planting can be identified and immediately discussed with the planters so the practices are changed quickly. The plots are also used for inspecting contracts and defining the payment due.

Seedling temperature, moisture status, and condition should be monitored and recorded throughout the planting process. Weather information at the time of planting and shortly afterwards may also help to identify causes of poor plantation performance.

Plantation performance. Staked, semi-permanent samples are commonly used for assessing plantation performance. Fifty to 100 operationally planted seedlings are staked in each stratum of a plantation for future evaluation. Monitoring the same seedlings removes the variation that would occur if different samples of the same plantation were taken. "Survival surveys," as these assessments are called, should focus on the growth and condition of the seedlings, as well as on mortality rates.

Post-planting assessments should be timed to provide information on the causes of reduced plantation performance. In the Weyerhaeuser program, the first assessment is completed 2-4 weeks after the plantation is established. Mortality during this time is usually due to nursery, transportation, or storage practices. If mortality has also occurred in the nursery outplanting, nursery practices should be investigated. Transportation and storage procedures should be checked if the nursery outplanted seedlings are healthy but the outplanted seedlings on the site experience significant mortality. If both the nursery and on-site outplanted seedlings are healthy, but operationally planted trees are unhealthy, on-site handling and planting practices are likely at fault.

The next assessment is completed at the end of the first growing season. If the plantation appeared healthy during the first month following establishment, but performance was poor at the end of the first growing season, the planting practices and the suitability of the species or stock type to the site should be examined. Weather records should also be examined so that stresses caused by severe conditions might be identified. The seedlings that were carefully outplanted on the site provide an estimate of the best that can be expected from the operationally planted seedlings. A large difference in the performance of the outplanted seedlings and the operationally planted seedlings indicates a problem with the planting procedures.

The staked seedlings can be reexamined at regular intervals for the next few years, if required. Most monitoring programs include a second- and fifth-year assessment.

Brushing

Pre-treatment evaluations for brushing treatments are often combined with stocking surveys and long-term plantation performance assessments. The species composition, cover, and stand structure of the non-crop vegetation should be described (see Chapter 19); and the condition of the crop trees should be assessed to evaluate their present response to competition. Treatment objectives should include the number of crop trees to be released from competition in the desired time span.

Many survey methods can be used for these assessments. Non-crop vegetation is often described by ocular estimates. A variation of the distance method, where the non-crop vegetation that is the "nearest neighbor" to a crop tree is described, has also been applied. Fixed area count plots are used to assess the number and condition of the crop trees. Photopoints provide visual records of treatment effects.

The number of crop trees that have been released should be evaluated immediately after a brushing treatment and any damage to the crop trees should be recorded. Non-crop vegetation that appears to be resistant to the treatment should also be noted. Fixed area count plots are commonly used for these post-treatment assessments. Semi-permanent fixed area plots in treated and untreated areas should be established to assess the longer term response of the vegetation community to the treatment. Short-term effectiveness may be overshadowed by vegetation regrowth the following year.

Juvenile spacing

A pre-spacing survey should be completed wherever a spacing treatment is considered. Stand density and stem distribution and size are important factors to evaluate in this survey. The condition of the stand, particularly of potential crop trees, should also be examined.

Systematically located fixed area count plots can be used for this type of survey. Where access and project size limits ground assessment, aerial methods or ocular estimates can be used. After the survey, the preferred species and the number of stems per hectare to be left following spacing should be stated as the objectives of the spacing project.

Post-spacing surveys usually involve systematically located fixed area count plots. Ocular estimates are used where statistically validated information is not required. These assessments should be established during the spacing operation so that the spacer can be notified of unacceptable performance and the spacing practices can be adjusted as required. Post-spacing surveys are often used as the basis for payment in contract projects. They also document the condition of the stand after treatment, and can be used for comparison with future assessment information.

SUMMARY

A successful regeneration monitoring program is built on the principles of accountability and incentives for improved performance. The objectives of the program and of each intermediate treatment must be stated and the evaluation procedures should measure the success of the treatments in achieving these objectives. Feedback to the responsible individuals is necessary so that unsuccessful treatments can be changed.

The procedures for collecting data should be designed to provide the necessary information in a simple, efficient way. Data analysis and records should be easy to use, and assessments of individual treatments should be linked, creating a comprehensive monitoring system.

In British Columbia, regeneration objectives are defined in the pre-harvest silviculture prescription. Stocking and free-growing surveys measure the success of the prescribed treatments in meeting these objectives. Pre- and post-treatment assessments are completed for each reforestation activity. These assessments define the objectives of the treatment and evaluate the outcomes.

Although a complex web of biological and institutional factors influence the success of regeneration treatments, with careful thought and planning, foresters can design successful regeneration monitoring systems.

SECTION THREE

10 NATURAL REGENERATION

G. Weetman and A. Vyse

Almost all of British Columbia's existing forests have regenerated naturally. Even plantations contain a proportion of naturally regenerated stems. With this apparent abundance of natural regeneration, why are forest regeneration programs so heavily committed to planting?

Traditionally, foresters were trained to value natural regeneration and to discover the factors that enhanced its success. The emphasis on natural regeneration, however, has changed as logging practices have been honed to a fine edge of efficiency — an efficiency that, for a long time, ignored concerns about seed availability, seed dispersal, seed bed, and microsite. Planting has offered a relatively simple solution to the problem of renewing forest productivity, and it has increasingly become an assured method of restocking.

The aim of this chapter is to encourage foresters to take another look at the natural regeneration option. There are two reasons in particular for considering it. First, public pressure is mounting to promote alternatives to the efficient but ugly practice of clearcutting. Alternative logging practices in the future may well keep disturbance to a smaller scale than presently occurs with progressive or large patch clearcutting. This will give foresters more chance to manipulate natural regeneration. The second reason is regeneration cost. Natural regeneration, although not without cost, offers the forester an opportunity to reduce forest renewal costs without sacrificing regeneration objectives.

The chapter is divided into five sections. The first two present a review of the principles of natural regeneration and a commentary on the special problems of such regeneration in the old-growth forests in British Columbia. The third section discusses the advantages and disadvantages of pursuing natural regeneration. A simplified guide to the silvicultural systems that might be used to enhance natural regeneration is covered in the fourth section. The last section concludes with some suggestions to foresters on how to refine that guide by observing and experimenting in their local forests.

PRINCIPLES OF NATURAL REGENERATION

The occurrence of natural regeneration depends on the scale and type of disturbance that initiates the regeneration cycle, and on the reproductive potential of trees and non-crop vegetation within, or on the edge of, the disturbance.

Disturbance

There are two main types of disturbance: *severe* disturbance, in which the forest stand and the vegetation are destroyed; and *releasing* disturbance, which kills or removes some or all of the trees in the forest canopy but does not disturb the understory vegetation (Smith 1986). Severe disturbances can vary in scale from small landslides of a hectare or less to vast expanses of the landscape cleared by fire or volcanic action. Releasing disturbances also vary in scale, from the death of a single tree to the death of many through agents such as insect, disease, or wind. Types of disturbance differ in the growing space that each allows for the regenerating species and in the regeneration mechanism that is favored.

Microsites created by severe disturbance often do not favor the survival of germinants of many tree species. The main reason is that high levels of solar radiation reach the soil surface, heating and drying it. In some cases, however, severe disturbances can be advantageous. With no existing vegetation on an otherwise favorable microsite, seedlings, once established, may thrive.

Severe disturbances favor species that store seed in the soil or disseminate their seed by wind. Larger disturbances favor lighter seeded species. If the disturbance does not kill belowground parts, species that can sprout from stem bases or sucker from roots will survive best.

Microsites created by releasing disturbance vary depending on the cause, size, and timing of the disturbance. Releasing disturbances generally favor species that germinate under shady conditions. Seed germination, however, may be reduced by pathogens in such cool, moist microsites. Regeneration may be suppressed and poorly formed if existing crop and non-crop species respond rapidly to the change of conditions and release of resources set off by the disturbance.

Regeneration Mechanisms and Reproductive Potential

The ability of plants to regenerate following disturbance varies among individuals of the same species, among species, and over time. All tree species of commercial interest in British Columbia reproduce by seed, although some, such as aspen, birch, and cottonwood, reproduce effectively by vegetative propagation.

Seed availability is a major limiting factor in achieving natural regeneration because annual seed production is highly variable within and between species (Daniels et al. 1979). If severe disturbances, such as extensive clearcutting or large wildfires, occur in a year of limited seed production in one species, the resulting pattern of regeneration will reflect the presence of other, more prolific seeders. Only lodgepole pine is able to store seed on the tree. This gives the species an enormous advantage following severe disturbance, as long as the disturbance is not so severe that the stored seed is destroyed. Vegetative propagation of a species such as aspen, with its ability to sucker after disturbance, has similar advantages and limitations.

Seed size also influences reproductive potential. Dispersal of large seed is limited. Most seed from white pine (*Pinus monticola*), for example, germinates within 6 m of the source, whereas the small seed from western hemlock (*Tsuga heterophylla*) and Douglas-fir (*Pseudotsuga menziesii*) may disperse 300 m or more (Hofmann 1911). Large seeds are also more subject to predation than small seeds and are usually produced in smaller quantities. In their favor, however, large seeds supply stored energy to the germinant, which may provide a competitive advantage. Ponderosa pine (*Pinus ponderosa*), for example, has a large seed that allows rapid extension of the radicle and root growth. Because of this root development, the seedling can often avoid drought conditions in the upper soil horizons by exploiting soil water at depth.

Simulating Natural Disturbances

To use natural regeneration successfully, a forester must first understand the reproductive potential of all plant species capable of regenerating on a given site, and then be able to manipulate the existing stand in a way that favors the desired species. As Smith (1986, p. 192) noted, "[If] one wants to create a certain kind of forest, the best point of departure is consideration of the natural disturbances that bring it into being in nature. Once this is known, it is possible to conjure up ways that simulate the appropriate disturbance."

This advice is not easy to follow, especially in the old-growth forests of British Columbia.

THE SPECIAL PROBLEM OF REGENERATING OLD-GROWTH STANDS

Old-growth coniferous ecosystems are common in parts of British Columbia, and many of them are unique (Waring and Franklin 1979). Using natural regeneration in old-growth ecosystems can be difficult.

Old-growth stands are highly variable in structure and age. Any one stand may include a mixture of species, sizes, and ages. In such stands, large volumes of woody detritus have amassed on the forest floor, and the process of decay may be well advanced in standing trees whether they are dominant or suppressed understory stems. Pathogens (e.g., dwarf mistletoe) may be abundant, and the old trees are less resistant to attacks by defoliating and bark-burrowing insects than younger trees (Waring and Schlesinger 1985). Certain unique plants and animals may also be found in some old-growth forests. Such distinctions in these old forests mean that managers are faced with managing a special type of ecosystem — one for which they have very few precedents.

The classical silvicultural texts, with their emphasis on silvicultural systems, have little to teach us in dealing with old growth. For example, the European silvicultural systems described by Troup (1952) relate to the management of forests that have been cut and regenerated many times in the long history of human occupancy. Much of the debate in European forestry over this condition turns to the question of whether, and how best, to create irregular stand structures with mixed species, as some representation of the former "natural" forest.

The experience gained by foresters working on the Pacific coast and in mountains of the western United States offers some guidance. From their knowledge and skills, the application of the principles of natural regeneration has been developed (see, for example, Alexander 1987). However, differences in climate, ecosystem structure, and — above all — management objectives cloud comparisons between U.S. conditions and those in British Columbia. Ultimately, we have to turn to our own experience and the record of our own successes and mistakes.

The first report on natural regeneration in British Columbia's forests appeared in 1915. It dealt with Douglas-fir reproduction. Many reports followed, emphasizing the ability of the species to restock severely disturbed areas if attention were paid to seed supply and protection of the regenerated stands. Efforts were made to modify the early progressive clearcutting of valley bottoms in railroad operations with patch clearcutting, fire breaks, seed blocks, and seed trees (Gorman 1955; UBC Forest Club 1959). Still, there were too many delays in stocking and too much variability in achieving acceptable stocking. By the 1960's, foresters had switched to planting as a surer and quicker way of regenerating the Douglas-fir forest. They justified the cost of planting on the grounds of improved early growth rates, consistent stocking levels, and reduced rotation lengths.

The same historical sequence of natural regeneration followed by planting has occurred in other coastal forest types. Western hemlock was shown to regenerate easily on many sites (Allen 1944), yet once stock production problems were overcome, planting expanded rapidly. Douglas-fir was often first planted in those sites, but when its unsuitability on certain sites became apparent, western hemlock was used. Extensive cutting at high elevations in the coastal mountains did not begin until the 1960's. At first, existing advance regeneration from previous release disturbances was relied on to restock sites, but it proved to be irregular in distribution and difficult to protect, especially during the harvest of large trees, which shattered from internal decay. Once stock of yellow-cedar, mountain hemlock, and Pacific silver fir became available, planting became the preferred option.

In the Interior, early uncontrolled harvesting prompted numerous studies aimed at understanding and improving natural regeneration. The extensive spruce-subalpine fir types were examined closely (e.g., Griffith 1931; Barnes 1937; Pogue 1946; Smith 1955; Stettler 1958). Years of removing low volumes of high grade logs in the sub-boreal forests around Prince George and in subalpine forests on the accessible high plateaus of the southern Interior led to an aggressive attempt to modify stand disturbance and to improve regeneration success. In the 1950's, the B.C. Forest Service produced a key to help foresters match disturbance type to stand and site conditions. Scarification studies were also conducted, to discover whether mineral seed beds provided improved conditions for the spruce regeneration; how best those seed beds could be created; and how cutting should be timed to coincide with seed production (Clark et al. 1954; Gilmour and Konishi 1965).

After almost 100 000 ha of spruce-subalpine fir were treated (Glew 1963), the log market changed. Small trees became more valuable to the establishing pulp industry, the economics of harvesting changed, and severe disturbances in the form of large scale clearcuts became the rule. The natural regeneration experiment was essentially abandoned. Many cutovers were left unregenerated and only one long-term experiment was in place (Smith and Clark 1974). Attention focussed on planting and site preparation operations. Interest in natural regeneration was relegated to the large areas of subalpine fir (*Abies lasiocarpa*) regeneration left after partial cutting or clearcutting operations (Smith and Craig 1968; Herring and McMinn 1980; Monchak 1982).

Elsewhere in the Interior, regeneration of Douglas-fir and lodgepole pine (*Pinus contorta*) stands are two examples of continued reliance on natural regeneration (Figure 9.1). Most Douglas-fir stands in the dry Interior have been partially cut once and others many times. Conscious efforts to manage these stands date back to the 1950's (Clark 1952). The B.C. Forest Service stand treatment guide called for light, medium, or heavy seed tree marking, depending on the stocking of advance regeneration from previous release disturbances. Glew and Cinar (1966) reported considerable success. Ironically, this was followed by a period of low cost high volume logging operations, particularly in the Cariboo. A concern grew over the quality and quantity of residual advance regeneration, however, harvesting practices reverted to partial cutting and management of advance regeneration (Vyse 1987). Concerns for wildlife habitat and summer forage have strengthened adherence to the natural regeneration option (Armleder 1986; Jeanes 1987).

Once extensive cutting of pine started in the late 1960's, foresters began to put into use their knowledge that lodgepole pine regenerates readily from stored seed following even the severest form of clearcutting. Pine regeneration is usually reliable following some seed bed manipulation and cone distribution by scarification (Navratil and Vyse 1985). Logging practices that reduce the amount of seed are a concern (Clark 1974), but the major problem remains the over-abundance of regeneration in portions of almost every cutblock.

ADVANTAGES AND DISADVANTAGES OF NATURAL REGENERATION

Experience with natural regeneration in British Columbia and other parts of the world identifies several key characteristics that must be considered before a natural regeneration program can be pursued. These are:

- regeneration cost
- species mix
- root form
- density control
- delayed regeneration and irregular stocking
- acceptability of advance regeneration

Regeneration cost

If natural regeneration can meet the prescribed stocking goals for a particular site within the acceptable regeneration delay period, costs associated with planting can be avoided. But natural regeneration is not without cost. Suitable conditions must be provided for both the germinant and the developing seedling, and density targets must be met. Controlling canopy opening to achieve the best environmental conditions for desirable species, or regulating logging operations to protect advance regeneration, is likely to cost more than standard operations. Low volume harvests or small

1

2

3

4

5

FIGURE 9.1. Natural regeneration of Douglas-fir in the dry Douglas-fir forests of the central and southern Interior. 1. Douglas-fir regenerating beneath a canopy of 20-m high lodgepole pine. The pine canopy is disintegrating due to a variety of causes including, mountain pine beetle attack. Douglas-fir growth is accelerating in response. 2. Douglas-fir regenerating under a canopy of fire-killed snags. Most of the snags had fallen by the time the photograph was taken, 27 years after the fire. 3. Douglas-fir regenerating in a small 0.1-ha clearing created by partial cutting. No special seedbed preparation was carried out. 4. Douglas-fir regenerating on the western edge of a large clearing created by road building. 5. Douglas-fir and interior spruce regenerating in the middle of a large clearing. The mineral soil seedbed with an easterly aspect was created by road building.

cutblocks also increase overhead costs associated with the extraction of set amounts of wood. Standard logging practices, however, can impose costs that are not borne by the logging contractor or the forest license holder. These external costs include the loss of mature forest wildlife habitat and scenic views. If harvesting practices aimed at natural regeneration also avoid or mitigate some of these costs, the arguments in their favor are strengthened (Jeanes 1987).

Species mix

It is usually assumed that plantations will result in uniform stands of single species. Often this is not the case but naturally regenerated stands are more likely to be well mixed. This may have long-term productivity advantages, because diverse forest stands provide greater management flexibility and a hedge against pest problems (Schowalter et al. 1986). The mixed stand also offers some protection against wood and fiber market trends.

Root form of natural stems

Many comparative examinations of natural and planted seedlings have shown that their root forms are different (Van Eerden and Kinghorn 1978). There have also been several reports of "toppling" (juvenile instability) in planted pines on several continents and with lodgepole pine in British Columbia (Burdett 1979a; Burdett et al. 1983). The concerns have been sufficient to prompt modifications in nursery practice with pine, but there is no evidence that the problem is sufficiently serious to warrant promoting natural pine regeneration.

Density control

The irregular spacing and timing of natural regeneration can be both an advantage and disadvantage. Naturally regenerated stands almost always require density reduction or spacing treatments to maximize early crop tree growth. Plantations, on the other hand, can be established at desired densities. The ingress of natural regeneration may, however, create a need for spacing treatments in plantations, though it might also replace mortality losses.

Profuse natural regeneration can be an advantage where fast early growth of crop trees is not wanted. Higher initial densities reduce the proportion of juvenile wood, promote early self-pruning, and reduce knot size in lower boles, potentially increasing the value of crop trees.

Regeneration delays and irregular stocking

Natural regeneration, even under favorable conditions, is usually slow and always less certain than planting. Studies of lodgepole pine, British Columbia's most prolific conifer, show that the annual recruitment of stems peaks 6-8 years after logging and still continues at a slow rate after 14 years (Crossley 1976; Johnstone 1976). At higher elevations in the southern Interior, the rates and amounts of Engelmann spruce (*Picea engelmannii*) and subalpine fir ingress are very much less than those recorded for lodgepole pine (Butt et al. 1989). Little ingress is expected after 7 years, possibly because of competition from non-crop vegetation.

The cost of regeneration delays in terms of wood production foregone is difficult to assess. Smith (1988) has produced estimates for untreated backlog forest land in the province. The differences in yield are substantial, but they do not represent the cost of well-planned and executed efforts to achieve natural regeneration. Much more information is needed on this subject.

Acceptability of advance regeneration

Substantial research has been aimed at answering questions from operational foresters about the value of advance regeneration, its release potential, and disease risk. Subalpine fir provides a good example. This species is present throughout the highly valued mature and overmature stands of Interior spruce (*Picea glauca* x *engelmannii*). Logging disturbance of any type results in many residual stems (mostly subalpine fir) of variable sizes from seedlings to merchantable stems, and of varying condition. Studies by Stettler (1958), Smith and Craig (1968), Herring (1977), Herring and McMinn (1980), and Monchak (1982) have shown that subalpine fir responds well to release, but that stems damaged during logging are highly susceptible to the decay fungi, *Stereum sanguinoletum* and *Amylostereum chailleti*. Large stems are also likely to be infected with *Echinodontium tinctorium*. The advance regeneration also tends to be clumped.

Sanitation spacing of subalpine fir, which involves the removal of damaged and diseased stems and the control of density, has been practiced to a very limited extent on old logged areas. More widespread activity has not followed because the dominant crop tree would be subalpine fir, which is regarded as lower in value than spruce. This assessment is questionable given that the two species have very similar wood qualities (Josza 1989).

The question of reserving advance regeneration exists for other species in different parts of the province. Herring and Etheridge (1976) have investigated Pacific silver fir; Mc-Caughey and Ferguson (1988) have more recently examined a wide range of western conifers. Table 10.1 summarizes the current acceptability of species by ecological zone.

REPRODUCTION METHODS

All British Columbia forests have regenerated repeatedly following disturbances of many origins. Many of these forests regenerated over long periods of time and, in many cases, stands show patchy stocking. Following the principles outlined earlier, however, the forester should be able to simulate disturbances to produce successful natural regeneration. These simulations are commonly referred to as reproduction methods.

Reproductive methods have the two-fold purpose of (1) harvesting mature even-aged forest stands or mature trees occurring singly or in small groups in uneven-aged forest stands, and (2) replacing them with young stands established either naturally, from seed or by vegetative regeneration, or artificially, from planted seedlings or sown seed.

TABLE 10.1. Summary of current silvicultural acceptance of advance regeneration by ecological zone

| Ecological Zone | Advance regeneration acceptability | | |
	Usually acceptable	Sometimes acceptable	Rarely acceptable
CDF		Fdc, Bg	
CWH		Ba, Cw	
MH		Ba, Cy, Hm	
PP	Py, Fdi		
IDF	Fdi	Sw	Pl, At
ICH		Cw, Sw, Fdi	Hw, Bl, At, Ac, Ep
MS		Sw, Fdi	Pl, At, Bl
SBS		Sw	Bl, Pl, At, Ac
ESSF		Se	Bl
SBPS		Sw	Pl
BWBS		At	

Species codes:

Ac	Poplar	Fdc	Coastal Douglas-fir
At	Trembling aspen	Fdi	Interior Douglas-fir
Ba	Amabilis fir	Hm	Mountain hemlock
Bg	Grand fir	Hw	Western hemlock
Bl	Subalpine fir	Pl	Lodgepole pine
Cw	Western redcedar	Py	Yellow pine
Cy	Yellow-cedar	Se	Engelmann spruce
Ep	Paper birch	Sw	White spruce

They include any subsequent cultural treatment used to ensure the harvested trees are replaced rapidly by adequately stocked stands of desirable tree species. Reproduction methods are one step in a silvicultural system. A silvicultural system is a long-term program of treatment including controling non-crop vegetation, thinning, harvesting, and reproduction.

Numerous methods have been applied to regenerate forest stands from seed, stump sprouts, root suckers, or layering. Any given method can usually be classified under one of the six standard regeneration methods, each of which reflects distinctly different principles. The following classification is after that provided by Smith (1986). An earlier and more detailed classification can be found in Troup (1952).

1. *Selection method*:   the removal of mature trees, usually the oldest and largest trees, either single or scattered individuals (single tree selection or thinning) or in small groups (group selection) from areas rarely exceeding 0.1 ha in size at relatively short intervals, repeated indefinitely. The selection method is the regeneration phase of the selection system. The selection system is applied to uneven-aged forests or even-aged forests being converted to an uneven-aged condition. Reproduction is achieved by natural regeneration in the openings created by mature tree removal, or by thinning and spacing operations. This method can and has been misused as a rationale for "high grading" a forest for low investment, extensive silviculture.

2. *Shelterwood method*:   the removal of all trees on an area to be regenerated in a series of cuttings extending over a period of years. Removal usually occurs over less than one-quarter to one-tenth of the rotation. Establishment of natural regeneration of desirable tree species is obtained under the partial shelter of the trees remaining after each cutting. Regeneration of a mature forest stand by the shelterwood method may involve a series of different kinds of cutting applied in order: preparatory cuttings that remove unwanted trees and improve the condition of the remainder; seed cuttings that create canopy openings and suitable forest floor conditions; and removal cuttings which remove the remainder of the stand when regeneration is established.

The number of cuttings required to regenerate a forest stand by the shelterwood method depend on the species composition, abundance, and distribution of advance regeneration present beneath the stand. For example, regeneration of a dense mature stand with no advance regeneration may require a preparatory cutting, a seed cutting, and several removal cuttings. At the other extreme, regeneration of an open stand with an abundance of well-distributed advance regeneration may require only one removal cutting to complete the regeneration process. This type of cutting is not clearcutting. In fact, the regeneration has become established under the partial shelter and protection of the parent stand, and so is properly classified as being the final removal cutting of the shelterwood method.

3. *Seed-tree method*:   the removal of all trees on an area to be regenerated in one cutting except for a small number of seed-bearing trees, usually less than 25 trees per hectare. Trees are retained either singly (single seed-tree method) or in small groups (group seed-tree method) to provide seed for the subsequent natural regeneration of the area. Following the establishment of adequate regeneration, the seed-bearing trees may be removed in a second cutting or left indefinitely.

4. *Clearcutting method*:   the removal of all trees on an area in one cutting, with regeneration of desirable species being subsequently obtained naturally from seed disseminated over the cutting area from adjacent forest stands, from trees removed in the harvesting operation, or from advance regeneration, or artificially from planted tree seedlings or sown seed.

5. *Coppice method*:   any type of cutting which relies primarily on vegetative regeneration (stump sprouts, root suckers).

6. *Coppice-with-standards method*:   the combination of coppice method with a method that reserves a few better trees to be grown through one or more cycles of coppicing.

Choosing a Regeneration Method

Table 10.2 provides a summary of the methods we know will work *where we wish to regenerate the same forest type.* If the management objective is to alter the forest type, the appropriate regeneration method will change. If the method is unacceptable for reasons other than meeting the regeneration objective (for example, for aesthetic considerations), then the forester must accept the consequent changes in forest type.

TABLE 10.2.   Recommended regeneration methods for reestablishing forest types

Region	Forest type	Old growth						Young natural					
		CCP	CCN	ST	SW	SE	CO	CCP	CCN	ST	SW	SE	CO
Coast	Cottonwood	R	F	F	n	n	F	n	n	n	n	n	R
	Red alder	n	R	F	n	n	n	n	R	F	n	n	n
	Douglas-fir	R	F	F	F	n	n	R	R	F	F	F	n
	Western hemlock	R	R	F	F	n	n	F	R	F	R	F	n
	Western redcedar/ Western hemlock	R	F	F	F	n	n	F	R	F	F	F	n
	Sitka spruce	R	F	F	F	n	n	R	R	F	F	n	n
	Mountain hemlock	F	R	F	F	n	n	F	R	R	R	F	n
	Yellow-cedar	R	F	F	n	F	n	R	F	F	F	F	n
	Pacific silver fir	R	F	n	F	n	n	R	F	n	R	F	n
S. Interior	Engelmann spruce/ Subalpine fir	R	F	n	n	F	n	F	F	n	R	F	n
	Lodgepole pine	F	R	n	n	n	n	F	R	n	n	n	n
	Western larch	F	F	R	F	n	n	F	F	R	F	n	n
	Douglas-fir - Dry Belt	n	n	n	R	F	n	n	n	n	R	F	n
	Douglas-fir - Wet Belt	R	F	F	n	n	n	R	F	F	n	n	n
	Ponderosa pine	F	F	R	F	n	n	F	F	R	F	n	n
	Western redcedar/ Western hemlock	R	F	n	n	n	n	F	R	n	n	n	n
	Montane spruce	R	n	n	n	n	n	F	F	F	F	F	n
N. Interior	Sub-boreal spruce	R	n	n	n	n	n	F	n	n	F	n	n
	Aspen	n	R	n	n	n	n	n	R	n	n	n	R
	Mixed wood	R	n	n	n	n	n	R	n	n	n	n	n
	Black spruce	R	n	n	n	n	n	R	n	n	n	n	n
	White birch	n	R	F	n	n	n	n	R	F	n	n	n

CCP	-	clearcut method with planting	R -	recommended
CCN	-	clearcut method with natural regeneration	F -	feasible
ST	-	seed tree method	n -	not feasible
SW	-	shelterwood method		
SE	-	selection method		
CO	-	coppice		

The six reproduction methods are categorized in the table as:

- - not feasible; that is, will not regenerate same forest types, or
- - feasible; that is, will regenerate same forest type but not recommended because of high cost (including social and economic costs);
- - recommended, given present social and economic conditions.

In addition, Table 10.2 lists methods of regenerating stands that do not have old-growth characteristics. Typically, this includes young natural stands that have developed after fire, or second-growth stands that have developed after clearcutting. In such stands, the lack of deadwood accumulations, reduced volume of standing unmerchantable materials, and lower insect and disease risks allow the forester more choice in selecting prescriptions for developing the future stand.

REFINING THE USE OF THE NATURAL REGENERATION OPTION

Table 10.2 is a guide to the difficult business of selecting the appropriate reproduction method for a particular forest type. But it is a crude and controversial device. It is offered less as a statement of knowledge than as a challenge to attempt new and unorthodox approaches. We expect to be proven wrong. We agree with David M. Smith who forecast that the realities of nature and of human need would lead to the evolution of methods of silvicultural treatments beyond the bounds of our present imagination (Smith 1972). To further the process of evolution we suggest that foresters should become more observant in the forest. It is our experience that careful observation of natural regeneration and successional trends can help a forester to build a great deal of local knowledge about regenerating stands. The following points may help others to follow suit:

- Use the ecosystem approach to classify forest sites, which provides a framework for assessing the effects of climate and site on the success of alternative reproductive methods.

- Note the occurrence and nature of regeneration on roadsides and landings and other types of disturbance; estimate the timing following disturbance; and investigate the nature and distance of the seed source. Remember that limbing of trees often occurs at roadside.

- Obtain local information on the periodicity of seed crops and the relationship between the abundance of seed produced and the resultant number of seedlings (seed:seedling ratios).

- Observe how long favorable seed bed conditions last following disturbance.

- Note the occurrence, type, and distribution of natural regeneration in routine regeneration surveys.

- Reexamine old cutblocks and natural disturbances for the quality and quantity of natural regeneration, the rate of ingress, and the development of advance growth.

- Note the influence of cutblock aspect, orientation, size, and shape on regeneration success.

- Examine old records, photos, and files and talk to people who know the history of cutting and other disturbances in the local forests. The forest survey reports produced in the 1920's and 1930's are a possible source of information and photographs.

- Compare growth and yield of natural stands and planted stands.

- Document your findings. Permanent regeneration sample plots in well-defined forest types can be invaluable and could lead to the development of a scheme for predicting regeneration. Ferguson et al. (1986), for example, developed such a scheme for the grand fir - cedar - hemlock ecosystem of the northern Rocky Mountains.

Once foresters have obtained a good basic knowledge about local natural regeneration, they can begin to determine what factors contribute to its success or failure. These ideas should be tested, and demonstration areas established so that further study of natural regeneration can take place. Foresters must always keep the principles of regeneration in mind and not let the European precedent of formalized "systems" of natural regeneration straitjacket their thinking about ways to obtain natural regeneration. Systems and methods developed for other species and climates are not readily portable. Blind testing of a reproduction method to find a solution to poor natural regeneration or failing plantations, without consideration of the silvics of the species and careful observation of local conditions, is unlikely to be successful.

SITE PREPARATION: INTRODUCTION

J. Otchere-Boateng and L.J. Herring

Forest site preparation for either natural regeneration or planting is a key step in the overall planned silviculture cycle which consists of harvesting, site preparation, reforestation (planting and seeding), brushing and stand tending. The ultimate goal of any site preparation is to create an environment that favors crop tree performance — from successful seedling survival and establishment, to rapid growth. Inadequate or improper site preparation can often result in regeneration failure.

Following harvesting or a wildfire, the forest manager may be faced with any of several impediments to regeneration efforts:

- logging slash that can be a fire hazard or hinder access to planting crews;
- residual and invading vegetation that can (1) compete with crop species for site resources (light, moisture, nutrients, and growing space) and thus reduce survival and growth of crop trees; (2) impose physical obstructions that hamper planting access; and (3) harbor tree-damaging small mammals;
- lack of an adequate mineral seedbed for natural regeneration or artificial seeding;
- disease and insect problems. For example, *Phellinus weirii* infection of stumps which may need removal to reduce future attack of the new crop trees.
- soil compaction on landings and skid trails, and other unfavorable microsite conditions which may need amelioration to improve soil physical properties, soil aeration, water relations and nutrient availability for seedling growth.

The immediate objective of the forest manager is to prepare the site so that these impediments are eliminated or reduced to a level not inimical to the attainment of the objectives of management. Also important is to select the appropriate site preparation method or technique that will have no significant long-term impact on the environment or on overall site productivity. A poor prescription can affect the chemical, physical, hydrological, and biological properties of the soil.

Measures commonly used in British Columbia to accomplish site preparation goals can be grouped into prescribed burning, mechanical, and chemical methods, and combinations of the three. Each method has advantages and limitations and therefore must be prescribed on a site-specific basis. To select the best option, the forester must weigh the available methods on the following merits:

- ability of the method to achieve the intended regeneration objectives with minimum impact on the site. This requires knowledge of the ecology of the vegetation species, and of the ecological possibilities and limitations of the available methods and physical site factors (e.g., terrain exposure, soil type, erosion hazard, size of the treatment area, and accessibility).
- available resources: time, money, labor, and equipment.
- law and policy relating to the methods available.

The following three chapters will discuss burning, mechanical, and chemical site preparation methods.

SITE PREPARATION: FIRE

11

B.C. Hawkes, M.C. Feller, and D. Meehan

Slashburning is used to remove organic materials from an area. There are several reasons for doing so:

- to reduce the fire hazard;
- to facilitate planting, surveys, and stand tending;
- to provide an environment favorable to seedling establishment and growth;
- to reduce brush competition or undesirable advance regeneration;
- to eliminate disease or insect problems;
- to enhance browse or grazing potential; and
- to improve an area for use by some wildlife species, primarily ungulates.

Organic material can also be reduced in several other ways besides burning. These include: burying, crushing, chipping, scarifying, or clearing the material (discussed in Chapters 12 and 13); increasing the decay rate of slash by using microorganisms; and increasing the intensity of use, thus decreasing the amount of residue left behind after logging. Each of these alternatives is economically and practically feasible in some ecosystems under certain conditions. It is the forest manager's responsibility to evaluate the comparative advantages and disadvantages of the alternatives before selecting the most appropriate treatment.

Numerous studies on the effects and desirability of slashburning report that the treatment has a wide range of effects, from beneficial to detrimental (see, for example, Feller 1982 and Loucks et al. 1987). For any effect reported in one study, it is usually possible to find the opposite effect reported in another study. Such apparent contradiction is due to the complexity and lack of documentation of the interacting factors that determine the effects of fire.

Reducing organic material generally maintains or even enhances the productivity of crop tree species. In some situations, however, burning might do the opposite, creating an environment that does not favor seedling establishment and growth. It might also increase brush competition, cause disease or insect problems, and create air pollution. Such problems have resulted in public demands for restrictions on burning.

This chapter presents information to help the forest manager maximize the beneficial effects of burning and minimize the detrimental ones. The first section describes general slashburning considerations that must be included in any decision about whether or not to burn. These include factors relating to ecological effects, smoke management, treatment combinations, and site sensitivity. The second and third sections detail the planning and operational factors that must be addressed once a decision has been made to conduct a slashburn. The last section describes monitoring and evaluation considerations.

THE EFFECTS OF SLASHBURNING ON FOREST PRODUCTIVITY

Several factors determine how prescribed burning will affect forest productivity: 1) soil properties; 2) the regeneration and growth of crop tree species; and 3) the presence of vegetation that can compete with the crop tree species. A brief summary of these factors follows. For more details, readers should consult Feller (1982) and Haeussler and Coates (1986).

Soil Properties

Soil erosion

Slashburning has a major effect on surface soil erosion. It may also affect mass wasting, though its influence is slight compared to that of tree removal. The following factors, then, relate to surface erosion alone.

- **Climatic characteristics.** Erosion due to fire-induced hydrophobicity of soils is more serious in drier than in wetter climates. Hydrophobicity occurs when organic chemicals, which are distilled off burning fuels during the fire, move down into the soil. As the temperature drops with depth, these chemicals condense onto the soil particles. A layer, composed of soil particles covered with organic compounds, can form beneath the soil surface. This layer can repel water and stop its downward percolation, causing it to run over the soil surface. In drier climates, vegetation may contain a relatively high amount of hydrophobicity-inducing chemicals and the thickness of the hydrophobic soil layer is greater (DeBano et al. 1976; Wells et al. 1979).

- **Intrinsic soil erodibility.** This depends mainly on soil aggregate stability (erodibility decreasing as aggregate stability increases); texture (silty and fine sandy soils being the most erodible); organic matter content (erodibility decreasing as organic matter content increases); parent material (erodibility being greater for soils derived from acid igneous rocks than from volcanics); and slope (erodibility increasing with slope).

- **Fire severity.** This is defined as the degree of removal of the forest floor. Fire severity influences the rate of revegetation, soil organic matter loss, and the degree of soil aggregate destruction. In general, the more severe the fire, the greater the likelihood of more erosion.

- **Rate of revegetation.** This depends on the phenological time, for example, spring versus fall (revegetation being slower for burns conducted at times when plant reserves are low); the severity of fire; and the moisture and nutrient status of the ecosystems present (revegetation being slower for drier and nutrient-poor sites).

Post-fire soil temperature

In the lower elevations and more southerly warmer soils, high surface temperatures increase the chance that maximum values might reach levels which can kill seedlings through root collar girdling. However, in the higher elevations and more northerly cooler soils, where low soil temperatures in the root zone may limit plant growth, increases in soil temperature following burning can have a strong beneficial effect.

The following factors, in addition to aspect and climate, influence post-fire soil temperatures.

- **Fire severity.** A blackened surface generally heats up more than an unburned forest floor or an exposed mineral soil surface. Unburned slash and vegetation will moderate temperature extremes by lowering surface temperatures during the day and increasing them at night.
- **Rate of revegetation.** The slower the rate, the greater the duration of high surface temperatures.

Soil moisture status

Fire destroys vegetation. This increases the quantity of water in the soil by reducing interception and decreasing transpiration. At the same time, fire destroys soil organic matter, which decreases the moisture-holding capacity of the soil surface. These opposing effects may result in either a moisture excess or deficit. Aspect, soil depth, coarse fragment content, and soil hygrotope all affect soil moisture status. Even more important, however, is the influence of soil organic matter content and distribution. There is greater likelihood of a moisture deficit when most of the organic matter is present in the forest floor and the mineral soil contains little incorporated organic matter.

Soil nutrient status

Burning usually increases the short-term (< 5 years) availability of nutrients in the soil, but may cause longer-term nutrient losses. It may also alter soil cation exchange capacity (CEC): by increasing the rate at which the colloidal component of the soil organic exchange complex forms; by increasing soil pH; and by decreasing soil organic matter (Grier 1972). The balance between the first two factors (which may increase CEC) and the third factor (which decreases CEC) determines whether burning will increase or decrease total soil CEC. Increases are most likely on soils high in organic matter or Kaolinite. Other factors influence soil nutrient status, as well.

- **Fire severity.** Severe fires increase nutrient losses because most nutrients are located in the organic matter.
- **Organic matter form and distribution.** Organic matter incorporated into the mineral soil is not usually burnt, so nutrients are not lost. Losses are potentially of concern where the organic matter accumulates on the mineral soil surface (mor humus forms) or where there is a layer of organic material over bedrock or parent material (terrestrial organic soils with mor humus forms).
- **Soil depth.** Nutrient losses are potentially more serious in soils with a smaller depth.
- **Slope.** Nutrient losses are potentially more serious as slope increases, because of the higher probability of surface erosion.

- **Rainfall following a fire.** Intense and prolonged rainfall after a fire can result in potentially serious nutrient losses because of leaching and surface erosion.
- **Parent material.** Nutrient losses are potentially more serious when soils have a high coarse fragment content or are derived from parent materials that are highly siliceous.

Soil organisms

Certain insects and disease organisms may be either promoted or retarded by slashburning (Harvey et al. 1976; Fellin 1980). The response to fire of most insect and disease organisms is not fully known. Some beneficial organisms, such as siderophore-producing fungi (important for tree iron nutrition) and nitrogen-fixing bacteria, appear to be retarded, particularly by severe fires. Mycorrhizal fungi appear to be initially retarded by burning, but recover relatively quickly (Harvey et al. 1976). Of the organisms that attack young trees, the weevil *Steremnius carinatus*, the black army cutworm (*Actebia fennica*) (Maher 1988), and the feeder root disease fungus *Rhizina undulata* tend to be promoted by burning.

TABLE 11.1. Summary of the likely regeneration and early growth response to slashburning of the major tree species in British Columbia

Tree species	Response to slashburning compared to no burning
Abies amabilis	Adverse on intermediate to dry, nutrient-poor sites; beneficial on others
Abies grandis	Insufficient information available but probably adverse on the driest sites; beneficial on others
Abies lasiocarpa	Adverse on intermediate to dry, nutrient-poor sites; beneficial on others
Chamaecyparis nootkatensis	Insufficient information available but probably adverse on the driest sites; beneficial on others
Larix occidentalis	Generally beneficial except for severe burns
Picea engelmannii	Variable effects depending on site factors and degree of forest floor removal
Picea glauca	Variable effects depending on site factors and degree of forest floor removal
Picea mariana	Adverse on the driest sites; beneficial on others
Picea sitchensis	Generally beneficial
Pinus contorta	Generally beneficial except severe burns
Pinus monticola	Adverse on the driest sites; beneficial on others
Pinus ponderosa	Generally beneficial
Populus tremuloides	Generally beneficial
Pseudotsuga menziesii	Generally adverse on the drier, nutrient-poor sites; beneficial on others except possibly for severe burns
Thuja plicata	Adverse on all but the wettest sites
Tsuga heterophylla	Generally adverse except in perhumid climates (CWvh and CWwh subzones)
Tsuga mertensiana	Insufficient information available, but probably adverse on the drier sites; beneficial on others

Regeneration and Growth of Crop Tree Species

All of the above changes in soil properties brought about by slashburning can influence the regeneration and growth of tree species. Shade-tolerant species are likely to be adversely affected by burning. The general response to prescribed burning of the major tree species in British Columbia is given in Table 11.1. This table applies to both planted and naturally regenerated seedlings and was adapted from information in Feller (1982) and Klinka et al. (1984). In general, if a species is adversely affected by burning, this is more likely to occur on drier sites and with more severe fires.

Competing Vegetation

The response of a plant species to fire depends on the resistance of its aboveground parts to fire damage; on its ability to reproduce vegetatively from underground rhizomes or roots; and later on its ability to reproduce from seed either stored in the forest floor or surface mineral soil, or dispersed into an area. The more severe the fire, the greater the consumption of the forest floor and accompanying seeds, roots, and rhizomes, and the more the heat will penetrate into the mineral soil, destroying buried seed and underground perennating organs. Heat penetration is facilitated by moisture and a lack of organic matter incorporated in the surface mineral soil layers. Water and organic matter are better conductors of heat than mineral soil. However, because water has a high heat capacity, moisture may restrict the actual increase in mineral soil temperature during the fire.

Table 11.2 shows the response to slash fire of some of the most important competing species in British Columbia.

TABLE 11.2.   Response of some important herb, shrub, and fern species to fire [a]

Species	General response to burning
Acer circinatum (vine maple)	Severe fires can kill plant. Otherwise, vigorous sprouting from basal portions of the stem and roots.
Acer glabrum (Douglas maple)	Moderate to severe fires can kill plant. Light fires promote sprouting and can increase cover.
Acer macrophyllum (bigleaf maple)	Severe burns can kill plants. Usually sprouts back vigorously.
Alnus incana ssp. *tenuifolia* (mountain alder)	Set back by moderate to severe fires.
Alnus rubra (red alder)	Fire can reduce stump sprouting and seedling establishment if mineral soil exposure is low. After fire, red alder invades primarily by seed dispersal. Seeding can be abundant if fire has created excessive mineral soil exposure.
Alnus viridis (Sitka or green alder)	Not readily burned, but can be set back by moderate to severe fires. General increases after fire. Seeds in and sprouts from root crowns after fire.
Athyrium filix-femina (lady fern)	Fire decreases cover and frequency on drier sites, but resprouting is likely on subhygric sites.
Betula papyrifera (paper birch)	Seedlings establish on exposed mineral soil left by fire. Severe burns may reduce sprouting.
Calamagrostis canadensis (bluejoint)	Increases in cover and frequency after fire. Sprouts and seeds-in vigorously.
Calamagrostis rubescens (pinegrass)	Increases in cover and frequency after fire. Sprouts and seeds-in vigorously.
Cornus sericea (red-osier dogwood)	Set back by severe fires. Favored by light fires. Usually increases after burns on subhygric sites.
Corylus cornuta (hazelnut)	Aerial parts easily killed by fire. Vigorous regrowth expected. Only the most severe fires will destroy underground parts.
Epilobium angustifolium (fireweed)	Promoted by fire. Much more abundant on burned areas.
Gaultheria shallon (salal)	Generally slow to recover to preburn levels. Fire can successfully control this species on dry sites but not usually on wet sites. Fire stimulates resprouting from roots and stem bases.
Lonicera involucrata (black twinberry)	Moderate to severe burns reduce abundance. Resprouting is vigorous after light burns. Slow to recover but can become abundant on subhygric Sub-Boreal Spruce sites.
Menziesia ferruginea (false azalea)	Fire-sensitive. Significantly reduced in abundance and slow to recover after fire.
Polystichum munitum (sword fern)	Burning has variable results depending on fire severity and soil moisture.
Populus balsamifera ssp. *balsamifera* (balsam poplar)	Fire stimulates suckering and may retard sprouting if severe.
Populus balsamifera ssp. *trichocarpa* (black cottonwood)	Fire stimulates sprouting. Severe burns may reduce sprouting vigor.
Populus tremuloides (trembling aspen)	Fire promotes suckering. Density can be dramatically increased. Severe fires kill plants and promote prolific sprouting.
Pteridium aquilinum (bracken)	Invades burned areas. Sprouts and suckers vigorously. Density increases after fire.
Rhododendron albiflorum (white-flowered rhododendron)	Susceptible to fires of moderate intensity. Slow to recover.
Ribes bracteosum (stink currant)	Sprouts after fire, but can take 2-3 years to recover.
Ribes lacustre (prickly gooseberry)	Often invades or increases in cover after fire. Sprouts from rhizomes and root crowns after light fires. After fire, seeds on-site and carried in by birds, can germinate.
Rosa spp. (roses)	Moderately fire resistant. Usually favored by fire. Sprout from root crowns and rhizomes and germinate from on-site and transported seeds.
Rubus idaeus (red raspberry)	Invades burned areas through buried and new seed. Sprouts and suckers after fire.

(Continued)

TABLE 11.2. (Continued)

Species	General response to burning
Rubus parviflorus (thimbleberry)	After fire it sprouts and suckers. Cover may increase. Can be set back on dry sites.
Rubus spectabilis (salmonberry)	After fire it sprouts, suckers, and seeds in often achieving maximum cover 3-5 years after fire. Cover increases, but can decline relatively early on dry sites.
Salix spp. (willows)	Sprout after fire. Greatly favored by fire in most habitats. Severity of burn significantly affects response. Different species also respond differently to fire.
Sambucus spp. (elderberries)	Response to fire variable. Sprout after fire. May seed-in. Severity of burn affects response, but buried seeds on subhygric sites are usually stimulated by fire to germinate.
Symphoricarpos albus (snowberry)	Cover often decreased by severe burns but increased by less severe burns. Suckers and sprouts after fire. Seed germination may be stimulated.
Vaccinium membranaceum (black huckleberry)	Sprouts and suckers after fire but recovery is slow. Severe fires cause mortality or greatly reduced sprouting.
Vaccinium ovalifolium (oval-leaved blueberry)	Abundance reduced and slow recovery after fire.
Valeriana sitchensis (Sitka valerian)	Recovery after light fires can take several years. Severely set back by severe fires that kill rhizomes and roots.
Viburnum edule (high cranberry)	Abundance may be initially reduced after fire causes sprouting, with a subsequent increase in abundance during the next 10 years or so.

[a] Extracted from Coates and Haeussler (1986) with additions by E. Hamilton (B.C. Ministry of Forests, Research Branch), J. Mather (Skyline Forestry Consultants), and M. Feller (University of British Columbia).

SITE SENSITIVITY TO SLASHBURNING

Different forest ecosystems or sites respond to a given slashburning treatment in different ways. The response depends on the characteristics of the ecosystem; the climatic conditions before, during, and after burning; and the characteristics — primarily the severity — of the fire (Feller 1982). If the most important factors influencing the effects of burning on forest productivity are known, then sites can be rated according to their relative sensitivity to fire. This has been done for the Vancouver Forest Region (Klinka et al. 1984), where the most important factors influencing the effects of burning on site forest productivity are those related to soil erosion and soil nutrient status. The sensitivity of a site in this region to fire can be estimated with the use of a key (Figure 11.1). Since this key is based on soil erosion and nutrient status factors, it cannot be used in areas where other factors are as important in controlling site productivity. It would have to be revised for much of interior British Columbia where other important factors, such as soil moisture and temperature, influence forest productivity.

THE EFFECTS OF SLASHBURNING ON AIR QUALITY

The smoke emitted from slashburns has several adverse effects, including those on human health and ripening orchard fruit. The major effect is probably the impairment of visibility, the extent of which is determined by the quantity of particulates emitted and the degree of particulate dispersion in the atmosphere. The following factors affect the quantity of particulates emitted during burning.

- **Quantity of fuel burned.** The quantity of particulates emitted during burning increases as the quantity of fuel burned increases.

Key to identification of site sensitivity to fire

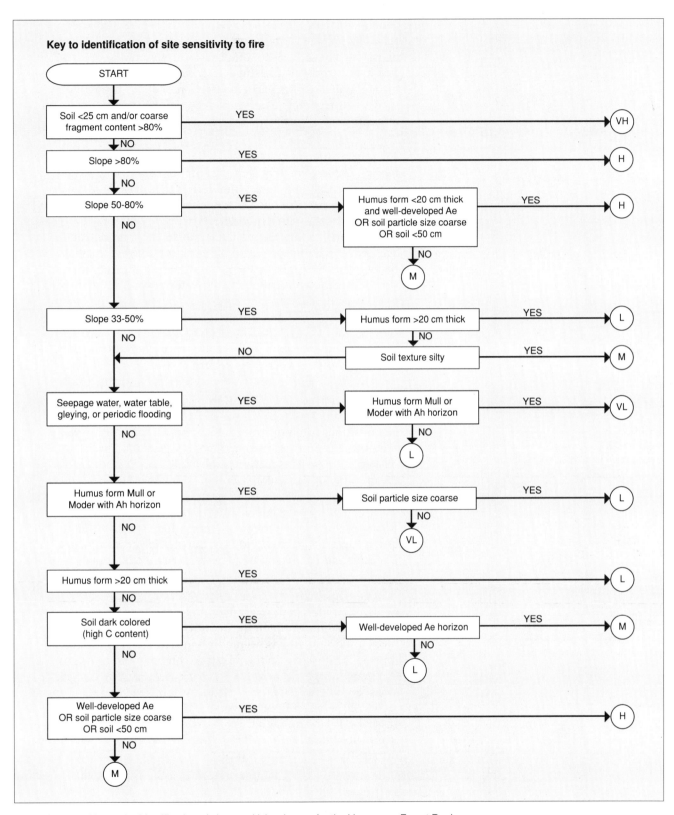

FIGURE 11.1. Key to the identification of site sensitivity classes for the Vancouver Forest Region.

- **Frontal fire intensity.** This is the rate at which heat energy is released per unit time per unit length of fire front. It depends on the heat of combustion, fuel consumption in the fire front, and rate of spread. The emission factor (the percentage of fuel burned that becomes particulates in smoke) has been found to increase as frontal fire intensity decreases because combustion is less complete at lower fire intensities.

- **Type of fire.** This influences the rate of combustion and the frontal fire intensity, both of which influence the emission factor. The key element is the amount of smoldering which occurs during a fire: more smoldering produces more particulates. The flame front in a heading fire moves rapidly with the wind and burns with a high intensity, but it does not completely consume fuel before the main combustion zone moves ahead. This leaves a large zone of smoldering fuel behind the main flame front. By contrast, the flame front in a backing fire moves slowly into the wind, allowing a greater proportion of the fuel to be consumed in the flaming zone. This reduces the amount of smoldering. Heading fires have been shown to produce significantly greater quantities (up to 2-3 times) of particulates than backing fires. Similarly, fuel consumption during the flaming period of a convection burn is relatively high, reducing the degree of smoldering (Cook et al. 1978; Sandberg 1983).

- **Fuel properties.** Several fuel properties influence the quantity of particulates emitted. The most important are compaction, composition, and moisture content. In general, very compact fuels burn slowly and incompletely because of a low rate of oxygen supply. This increases the likelihood of smoldering and the quantity of particulates emitted. On the other hand, if compaction is very low, then combustion may not be sustained at the optimum level and again considerable smoldering may occur. The best arrangement of fuel, which would result in the best balance of air, fuel, and heat transfer for maximum fire intensity and combustion efficiency, is not well defined.

  Fuel moisture content has a very important influence on particulate emissions. As it increases, so does the quantity of particulates emitted per kilogram of fuel consumed. However, the effect of fuel moisture on the quantity of fuel consumed is even more important. It has been found in western Washington that for each 1% increase in the moisture content of large woody fuel (8-23 cm diameter), there is a 3% decrease in particulate emissions (Sandberg 1985). As well, burning when the duff (F and H layers of the forest floor) is wet (e.g., Duff Moisture Code [DMC] < 15) (Van Wagner 1987) can decrease particulate emissions substantially (up to 25%) compared to burning when the duff is dry (e.g., DMC > 35).

Particulate dispersion in the atmosphere is influenced by the following factors.

- **Presence of a convection column above the fire.** High intensity fires with a good convection column take the smoke higher into the atmosphere. This decreases the likelihood of high particulate concentrations forming in the air near the ground, particularly if the convection column is able to break through the top of an inversion layer.

- **Atmospheric stability.**   The more stable the air near the ground and the greater the height of this stable layer, the greater the likelihood of high particulate concentrations occurring in the air near the ground. One important aspect of atmospheric stability is that it often has daily cycles in mountainous terrain. An unstable atmosphere during the day may be replaced by a surface inversion as the air cools at night. This surface inversion may be reinforced by cold air draining down slopes in mountainous terrain. Stable air above the ground is prevalent during autumn when high pressure systems with light winds stagnate over southern British Columbia.

  Occasionally, the air in a valley bottom is stable while above, separated by an inversion layer, the air is less stable. Fires on slopes above the inversion may not cause any visibility problems, as the particulates they emit can be widely dispersed well above the valley bottom.

- **Wind velocity and direction.**   The greater the wind velocity, the lower the particulate concentrations in the atmosphere. Wind direction is also important. Downslope and down-valley winds, which often occur in mountainous terrain during the night, can increase particulate concentrations in the air near the ground. Wind may also blow particulates toward or away from a smoke-sensitive area.

TABLE 11.3.   Numerical values of the Ventilation Index and their significance to smoke dispersal

Ventilation Index	Smoke dispersal
0 - 34	poor
35 - 44	marginal
45 - 54	fair
55 - 64	good
> 65	excellent

Wind velocity and atmospheric stability have been combined to produce a parameter known as the Ventilation Index. The greater the wind velocity and the greater the depth of the air layer above the ground in which smoke can mix (the mixing layer), the greater the Ventilation Index and the dispersion of particulates emitted from a fire (Table 11.3).

THE EFFECTS OF COMBINING FIRE WITH OTHER TREATMENTS

Prescribed burning for silvicultural purposes is often used after another treatment, such as herbicide application or mechanical clearing or piling, has prepared the fuels for burning. The full ecological ramifications of such combined treatments are still largely unknown, though several general concerns are clear.

One is whether the other treatment will reduce or increase any possible adverse effects of prescribed burning on forest productivity. For example, the other treatment might allow prescribed burning to be conducted under lower impact conditions, or it might help to reduce plant competition following burning. If smoke is a concern, the other treatment might reduce or enhance the likelihood of smoke pollution.

Piling (bunching) and burning is commonly used to remove slash. Piling concentrates fuels and results in a more severe burn. Fuel consumption in burns of piles occurs almost independently of fuel moisture (Blackwell et al. 1986), allowing piles to be burned under a wide range of conditions. Compared to broadcast burning, piling and burning usually results in greater fuel consumption, more smoke production, and more severe but more localized effects on the soil.

MAKING THE BURN DECISION

The decision to burn is usually based on a pre-harvest silvicultural assessment and prescription, and followed up with a post-harvest silvicultural and site preparation assessment.

The Pre-Harvest Silviculture Prescription (PHSP) is one of the most significant developments since the early 1980's (see Chapter 8). It helps forest managers in planning prescribed fires, making the initial burn decision, and setting burn objectives. It has also helped them to improve block layout, harvesting sequence, and choice of harvesting methods.

A follow-up assessment may be necessary after the PHSP is written, to address unanticipated changes in post-harvest conditions. A post-harvest site preparation guide, FS 117, is available in British Columbia and provides this needed feedback to the PHSP phase. The pre-harvest assessment should document overall management and silvicultural objectives, fire danger rating (hazard and risk), protection objectives, range assessment, post-logging silvicultural assessment (e.g., natural regeneration, planting, and site treatment objectives), burn impact objective, prescription and feasibility, and recommended site treatment. A rating or overall assessment helps the forest manager to decide what site preparation approaches to use and to determine what limitations there are to achieving the desired objectives.

The economic criteria used in making the burn decision are also incorporated into this prescription. A standard method for doing this evaluation is currently not available. The costs of site preparation are only part of the overall costs of regenerating the forest to rotation age. Although slash-burning may appear to be the least costly site preparation treatment, subsequent follow-up treatments or forest productivity losses could raise costs above those of other site preparation options.

SETTING THE BURN OBJECTIVE

Once the decision to burn has been made, a burn objective must be set to drive the planning process for prescribed fire. Many resource considerations — forest management, silvicultural, protection, ecological — must be evaluated and reflected in the burn objective. Simply translating silvicultural objectives into burn impact objectives is difficult because of the lack of information on what fire impacts are required to effect various silvicultural treatment objectives (such as reducing vegetative competition, increasing soil temperatures, or creating additional planting spots). In general, burn objectives are expressed in terms of slash fuel reduction (by size class), organic layer reduction, and mineral soil exposure.

These three factors are combined into an impact rank in the Prescribed Fire Predictor (PFP) (Muraro 1975) with a scale of 1 to 8, 1 being the lowest impact rank and 8 the highest. The Vancouver Forest Region fire sensitivity guidelines coupled with PFP impact ranks have helped in translating ecological constraints into burn impact objectives for coastal biogeoclimatic zones. Additional work is needed in the Interior of British Columbia to describe the most important ecological constraints to using fire and other site preparation techniques.

To meet silvicultural and protection objectives in areas currently being logged, several basic considerations must be addressed in setting the burn objectives.

- Improving planting access in recent logging slash (usually < 3 years since logging) can be accomplished with a low impact rank (< 3) because most slash fuels less than 7 cm will be consumed by the fire if coverage is adequate. This impact rank will not be high enough if significant duff reduction is required.

- If the organic layer must be reduced to improve ease of planting or soil temperature, then a higher impact rank will be required to achieve any significant reduction (usually > 3).

- Control of vegetation depends on the type of vegetation present. For example, *Rhododendron* and *Menziesia* can be controlled in a low impact rank, but lady fern (*Athyrium felix-femina*) must be controlled with a higher impact burn. If a systemic herbicide like glyphosate is used before or after burning, the impact rank can be lower.

- Hazard abatement requires an impact rank in the moderate range (3-5), so that enough fine and large slash is consumed.

These are general rules-of-thumb. They vary according to the differences in fuel and vegetation conditions and to the burn objective that has been developed.

DEVELOPING SLASHBURNING PRESCRIPTIONS

Once the burn objective has been set, the burning conditions must be decided so that the desired fire impact can be achieved with good ignition and spread and an acceptable risk of escape. The burn must also meet smoke management guidelines.

These burning conditions are referred to as the prescribed fire prescription. They include such items as fuel preparation criteria, fuel moisture requirements (in terms of the Canadian Fire Weather Index [FWI] System codes and indices), weather (wind speed and direction, upper air conditions, Ventilation Index), and ignition pattern, rates, and techniques (i.e., equipment and fuel). When burn prescriptions are described, fuel moisture and weather tend to receive the most attention.

The PFP is the principal aid for prescription selection in British Columbia. It provides fuel moisture codes of the FWI system which are required to achieve the desired impact, control, and spread ranks. An ignition rank (ease of ignition of slash fuels) is also predicted based on the desired spread rank. All of these ranks have a scale of 1 to 8, corresponding to verbal descriptions (control rank 1 is very easy and 8 is extremely difficult). Lawson (1981) describes the PFP's two distinct formats (planning and daily prediction) and shows how it is used to guide prescription selection.

TABLE 11.4.   Example of a moderate impact prescription for a British Columbia Interior site

Silvicultural Objectives:
1. Create 1200 plantable spots per hectare.
2. Eliminate the advanced regeneration of mistletoe-infested lodgepole pine on-site.
3. Reduce organic layer thickness to increase soil temperature.

Burn Objectives:
1. Reduce slash fuels less than 12 cm by 50%.
2. Reduce organic layer depths of 15 cm by 50%.

Impact Rank Required: I.R. 4 (logging completed less than two summers)

Slope: 15%   Control Rank Chosen: 5-6
Spread Rank Chosen: 4-6

Fire Weather Index Codes Required:
Fine Fuel Moisture Code: 76-88
Duff Moisture Code: 30-64
Drought Code: 151-400
Wind Speed (10 m): less than 10 km/h
Ignition Rank: 3-6

Applying prescribed fire guidelines (such as PFP) effectively depends on on-site weather. Adjustment procedures are available, but they are only approximations of the on-site burning conditions, made from off-site weather stations. Other tools, such as fuel moisture sticks and fuel moisture meters, can also give on-site information on slash moisture content.

The PFP can be used only if the decision to burn has been made and the forest officer has a stated burn impact objective, expressed in terms of duff and slash reduction and mineral soil exposure. Until recently, it had not been rigorously field-tested with various fuel types and conditions (slash age, loading, and arrangement), or with ignition techniques and patterns. Lawson and Taylor (1986) made the first attempt at testing the PFP quantitatively with operational, helicopter-ignited prescribed fires. Existing models are based on information from hand-ignited burns that show mainly strip or frontal ignition patterns. New models are being developed to predict fire impact from helicopter-ignited mass fires.

An example of a prescription for a moderate impact burn in the Interior of British Columbia is given in Table 11.4.

Prescriptions for backlog NSR fuel types do not have a prediction system such as the PFP. Preliminary prescription information on brush fields and NSR areas dominated by unmerchantable subalpine fir is provided by Taylor and Hawkes (1988), and for overstocked lodgepole pine by Blackwell et al. (1986). There is little information on aspen and decadent cedar/hemlock rehabilitation.

TESTING THE BURN PRESCRIPTION

Once a burn prescription has been developed, it should be tested against historical weather information for the area to be burned. The data and programs are available on the fire management system of the Protection Branch, B.C. Ministry of Forests. The system can be accessed by all the Ministry's district offices and some forest company divisional offices. If the prescription cannot be accomplished according to the test, the burner should adjust the burn objective and develop a different prescription. If the burn objective cannot be changed, other methods of site preparation might have to be considered.

A test of the prescription outlined in Table 11.4, which uses weather records from Prince George, showed that the prescription can be achieved on approximately 6 days during the average burning season, with the best months being June, July, and early August.

BURNING PLANS

The effective use of slashburning requires that the burner, the company management, and the government regulatory agencies be committed to allocating sufficient supervisory time, ignition and mop-up manpower, and equipment to the job. To be efficient, the burner must have developed a burn schedule of blocks that weighs the burn impact required against the risks associated with burning. Such risks are a function of:

- fuel type, and amount
- elevation, slope and aspect
- size and shape of block
- adjacent values
- amount and age of brush
- weather indices (a function of the season of burning and weather)
- weather forecast (both for the day and the 5-day outlook)
- smoke venting requirements

The slashburner must also know the limitations to effective burning as a result of geography. For example, burning opportunities on high elevation blocks in the Interior wet belt may be lost with the first rains at the end of August; and north slopes must be burned before late fall rains.

Between the local regulatory government agency and the forest company there should be a good joint understanding of, and commitment to, all aspects of the burning program. For the burning program to be successful, the lines of communication should be clearly identified and followed. As well, several other factors should be considered during preparation for a burn:

- **Block layout.** Block boundaries must be designed to facilitate burning. Where possible, the block layout should use as its boundaries natural topographic breaks, existing roads, swamps, creeks, and snow lines. Irregular boundaries should be avoided, and the burner should realize that fingers of timber jutting into the block will invariably be burned once the slash is lit on either side.

- **Fireguards.** Before a guard is built or installed, the burner should ask:

  - Is the guard really necessary? Unexposed block edges, such as the lower block boundary, may be low risk and would not need a constructed guard.
  - Will it help control the fire, considering the planned ignition method?
  - Can the guard be built within acceptable site disturbance guidelines?
  - Can access for mop-up equipment be improved concurrently?
  - Can the fireguard be water barred to prevent surface erosion after burning?

  Sprinklers are a cost-effective means of guarding difficult areas. They should be set up outside the guard and run for a period that will adequately wet the fuels of concern for fire control. Foam has short-term effectiveness (1-2 hours), but has proved useful for black-lining the upper edge of blocks on steep slopes. Retardant is expensive to buy, transport, and apply, and requires time to use. If the burn is postponed and it rains before another burn opportunity comes, all benefit will be lost.

FIGURE 11.2. On-site weather station.

- **Weather stations.**   Accurate, on-site weather information is vital for effective burning (Figure 11.2). Stations should be set up immediately after the snow leaves the block. If spring or summer burns are planned, daily readings should be taken. If late summer burning is planned, rain gauges should be set up as the snow leaves, and daily readings started 1-2 weeks before burning. Fuel moisture sticks and fuel moisture meters are also valuable tools in determining on-site fuel moisture. Sticks have tables for correlating their moisture readings to the Fine Fuel Moisture Code. Fuel moisture meters are currently being tested for accuracy and correlation to fuel moisture codes.

- **Public safety.**   Appropriate steps should be taken to ensure that the public is not put at risk when driving or walking unaware into an active burn area. This includes placing announcements on the local media about time and location of burns.

- **Selecting a helicopter company.**   A suitable helicopter company is one which has the resources (experienced pilots, helicopters, torches, barrels) to accomplish the program, and is available when needed.

IGNITION AND CONTROL OF SLASHBURNS

Ignition Tools

A range of ignition tools is available:

- **Hand-held drip torch.**   This can be a very cost-effective method on the appropriate block. Mobilization is quick, and low cost makes it attractive for small isolated blocks. Fire can be built up slowly. It is the best method of burning along a back line with down-flowing air.

  Drip torches must be used with helicopter burning so that the burn can be carried on if the helicopter breaks down or if it cannot light the edges of the block safely. They should also be used to burn off accumulations inside the guard during mop-up activities.

- **Terra torch.**   This is a truck-mounted torch which shoots ignited gelled fuels for a short distance from the side of a road or skid trail. The device has also been mounted on all-terrain vehicles for better access into the burn block.

- **Helicopter ignition.**   Helicopters allow greater control over speed of ignition, the pattern of light-up (and, thus, the fire intensity and fire control), and the amount of ignition done in a day.

  A number of helicopter drip torches are available. These require non-gelled fuel (gas, jet B, diesel), which can be used effectively when fines are abundant and the Fine Fuel Moisture Code is high. Because the fuels have a short burning time, the helicopter must fly low to minimize the fuel burning in the air. Logistics, supply, and cost often determine preference for these fuels. A crew is required under the helicopter to mount the fuel barrels on the torch and to remove them when they are empty.

The helitorch ignition system uses gelled fuel. Gelling agents hold the fuel together better and help it burn longer. This allows the helicopter to fly higher and faster when igniting the block, which provides more safety and control over the ignition rate (Figure 11.3). Slash penetration by the gelled burning fuel is much better than with non-gelled fuels. Varying the amount of gelling chemical gives control over the consistency of the mixture and results in different effects on fire spread. Gelled fuels give excellent burn coverage, although the gelling chemical adds additional cost ($5-15 per barrel).

- **Delayed aerial ignition device.** In this incendiary device, or "ping pong ball machine," the balls ignite after a predetermined elapsed time. The one used in British Columbia was initially developed by Forestry Canada in Victoria, B.C., in the 1970's, with a local company, Premo Plastics Eng. Inc.

FIGURE 11.3. Helicopter ignition using a helitorch.

Ground crews are not required to operate this device, so mobilization is fast and large areas can be ignited quickly. There is, however, a delay in fire coverage because of the spot ignition pattern. It works best in dry, fine fuels.

Seasonal Considerations

As the burning season progresses, the DMC and Drought Code (DC) usually rise. At any point in time, as elevation increases, however, these tend to fall. When they do rise, so does the impact of the burn, the risk of escape, and the cost of mop-up. This means that decisions on when to burn should be based on current DMC's and DC's and on expected changes in the short and long term.

Spring considerations
Advantages:
- longer daylight period than for fall burning, therefore more options of when to light
- winds generally more stable
- good for fast burns in fine fuels when desired impact is low
- usually good smoke venting
- easily mopped up.

Limitations:

- limited to sites with good road access
- limited to sites with fine fuels only. Large dead and down fuels, winter skid trail debris accumulations, decadent timber, slash and stumps, and unburned landings will all create difficult mop-up problems, especially if they are dry.
- mop-up must be total inside and outside the guard to prevent flare-ups later in the spring or summer. Thus, it will probably be very extensive and expensive.
- on Interior sites, the risk of ignition of adjacent timber is high if burning is done before soils have thawed and tree foliage has hydrated.

Summer considerations

Advantages:

- best time for achieving good results in wetter areas, at high elevations, and on north-facing slopes
- smoke venting good
- good, high impact burns resulting in less need for post-planting brush control
- good convections and ignition control
- weather patterns fairly predictable.

Limitations:

- serious potential for escape means the day's forecast as well as the indices must be considered for upslope winds, upper atmospheric winds, and air mixing. The 1- to 5-day weather outlook should also be considered.
- lower elevations with high DMC and DC pose difficult and expensive mop-up problems.
- mop-up must be extremely aggressive and efficient, the necessary resources must be available, and the supervision must be superior.

Fall considerations

Advantages:

- daylight period is shortening, temperatures begin to decrease, and relative humidities increase for greater percentages of the 24-hour period, with good overnight recoveries. These help to minimize escapes and mop-up activities.
- in favorable years, many burns can be done in a short period with little mop-up required if fall rains are adequate
- in many areas, fall burning is the least technically demanding for mop-up if there is an adequate moisture difference between adjacent fuels and the slash area
- mid- to high impacts are generally easy to achieve
- the fall usually brings a change to wetter weather conditions
- fall frosts kill and dry vegetation, allowing for good fine fuel burns.

Limitations:

- less daylight in which to burn
- the perceived advantage of "fall rains" may give a false sense of security. Significant damage can still be done if DMC's and DC's are still high.
- winds are commonly stronger in the fall, resulting in more difficult ignition and more mop-up
- higher humidities constrain ignition
- smoke dispersal is often poorer
- frost-killed fuels in adjacent plantations require special attention.

Time of Day

Understanding the weather changes within a day and between days can help the slashburner to control ignition and minimize escapes. This information can be obtained by:

- observing general changes throughout a day;
- monitoring an on-site weather station;
- holding detailed discussions with a local or regional weather officer; and
- maintaining contact with appropriate staff so that weather information can be updated as it is released.

Safety

Safe operating procedures around the helicopter, fuel, and gel chemicals must be clearly understood by all personnel involved — supervisors, ground crew, and pilots. Appropriate safety equipment is mandatory for head, ears, eyes, and hands. Good radio contact among staging crew, the supervisor, and the pilot must be maintained.

Ignition Patterns

There are two general burning patterns: the frontal, or strip-burning, method; and the convection burning method, where in generally favorable terrain sufficient heat is generated for continuous air drafting into the fire from all edges. Modifications to patterns can be used to control the rate of oxygen, fuel, and heat of the fire. With fire intensity built in appropriate areas of the block, the suction winds created by the fire can pull fire from subsequently lit strips, across or down slopes, thus "holding" it from running up slope.

It is important for the burn supervisor to establish the method of ignition, the standards, the types of fire laid down, and the sequence of burning, in consultation with the pilot and ground crews.

FIGURE 11.4.   Mopping up after a slashburn.

"MOP-UP" OF SLASHBURNS

"Mopping up" slashburns must be aggressive and efficient to reduce the risk and cost of escapes. Their objectives are first to contain the problem areas by mid-morning following ignition, and then to extinguish the fire to within pre-defined limits within a given time (Figure 11.4).

The resources to mop up must be estimated before light-up. These estimates should be based on the FWI System codes and indices, the size of the block, the forecast weather, and recent experience in similar burns. The resources must be on-site by 6:00 a.m. the following morning. As the risk drops during the fall, mop-up can be tapered accordingly.

Water delivery systems are crucial to good mop-up. They include:

- gravity-fed systems
- pressure pumps and hose
- skidder-mounted tanks
- water trucks
- sprinklers

Effective mop-up also relies on good supervision and well-trained, motivated crews. The work can be dangerous, and safe working practices must be emphasized in training and on the mop-up line.

SLASHBURN MONITORING AND EVALUATION

The purpose of monitoring is to evaluate whether the fire objectives were met. The improvement of slashburning in British Columbia is closely linked to a well-structured fire monitoring program. Detailed monitoring at all sites is neither necessary nor cost-effective, but for "selected" slash fires, quantitative estimates of vegetation and tree growth response and of fire behavior and impact are valuable. This information can be used to develop and test prescribed fire models and guidelines, and to run more detailed prescribed fire evaluations.

A field handbook for slashburning assessments in British Columbia (Trowbridge et al. 1986) was developed in 1985. It has been designed solely for voluntary operational assessments and is intended for use in documenting the prescribed fire treatment and assessing the success or failure of specific fire prescriptions. Procedures for making pre- and post-burn assessments, as well as, observations during the burn, are described. Along with information on the fire impact (slash consumption and organic layer reduction) and site (ecosystem) factors, all documented burns must include on-site weather so that a weather data base can be collected.

The assessments in the handbook are plot-based and sites must be stratified according to topography and ecosystem distribution, fuel type, and loading. A minimum of two plots per stratum are required for an assessment. One or more assessments may be done in any treatment site.

The handbook assessment program generated a data base for British Columbia of 40 burns in 1988. This will increase in the coming years. A prescribed fire information system gives foresters access to these data to help them in developing prescriptions for their own sites.

12 SITE PREPARATION: MECHANICAL AND MANUAL

R.G. McMinn and I.B. Hedin

In many areas of the province, conditions following harvesting or wildfire are rarely optimal for the survival and growth of germinants or planted seedlings. Moreover, after mature stands are harvested, slash loadings are commonly high enough to impede planter access. Mechanical and manual site preparation can produce favorable seedbeds or planting spots to improve the early performance of seedlings and aid planting efficiency.[1] This enhanced early performance may improve subsequent growth and shorten time to harvest. Where mechanical site preparation clears paths through the slash or organizes planting spots into discrete patches or rows, planter access and planting efficiency is also improved.

Mechanical site preparation implements can create a variety of *microsites* by manipulating the soil surface horizons (McMinn 1982; Scrivener and MacKinnon 1989). Microsites should be prepared to meet the specific requirements of each site and species. The following factors can be modified:

- soil temperature
- soil moisture
- soil aeration
- soil physical conditions
- soil nutrients
- competing vegetation
- light
- frost susceptibility
- insect and disease susceptibility
- small mammal damage susceptibility.

Surface organic matter (LFH[2] or duff layers) is generally the main obstacle to germination and survival of germinants. While planted seedlings may survive and grow satisfactorily in an undisturbed surface organic layer, they may still be adversely affected by its presence and by the competing vegetation rooted in uppermost soil horizons. Overnight re-radiation of heat accumulated by exposed mineral soil may also reduce frost damage to seedlings during the growing season, a protection not provided by undisturbed soil insulated by surface organic matter.

---

[1] For simplicity, only "mechanical site preparation" will be used throughout this chapter, although the method sometimes includes manual treatments where applicable.

[2] The litter, fermentation and humus layers consisting of undercomposed, partly decomposed, and highly decomposed organic materials, respectively.

From a biological perspective, the basic methods of modifying surface organic layers are *scalping*[3] (removing the surface organic layer to expose mineral soil), *mixing* (incorporating the surface organic layer into the underlying mineral soil), and *inverting* (turning the surface organic layer upside down; the inverted organic layer may be covered with mineral soil) (Figure 12.1).

Once seedlings are established, tree growth is responsive to the depth of the rooting zone. Growth, for instance, may be restricted by an impervious soil layer close to the surface. To ameliorate shallow soil depth, subsoil tilling has been used effectively to break up restrictive layers. Hardpans or clay layers may be shattered by subsoiling at the time of mechanical site preparation. Winged subsoilers shatter subsurface layers with little disturbance to surface layers. Deep plowing increases soil penetrability in subsurface layers, as well as modifying the surface organic and uppermost mineral layers. Initial trial results using these techniques have produced promising responses in tree growth. Information on the long-term effects on British Columbia soils will be gained as the performance of subsoiling is monitored.

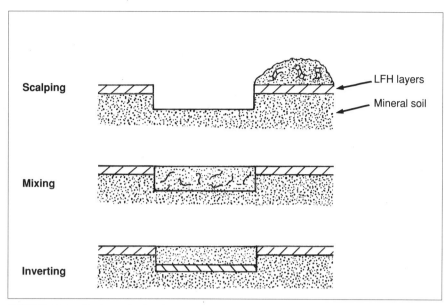

FIGURE 12.1. Basic methods of preparing soils by modifying LFH layers.

Seedbeds or planting spots formed by the three basic methods of modifying soil surface layers may be *raised* (elevated above the general ground line), *level* (at the general ground line), or *depressed* (below the general ground line). Raised or depressed planting spots can be formed to suit the particular characteristics of a site.

Mechanical site preparation may be in *continuous* or *semi-continuous* strips or *discontinuous* patches.

METHODS OF MODIFYING SURFACE ORGANIC LAYERS

Scalping

Scalping removes surface organic layers to expose the underlying mineral soil. Exposed mineral soil warms more rapidly than the undisturbed soil beneath the insulating organic layers. As well, removal of shading vegetation promotes warming of the soil surface. Increased soil temperature is generally beneficial because roots grow faster in warm soil than in cold soil. Warm soil also facilitates water uptake, and can reduce frost damage to seedlings through re-radiation of heat energy.

---

[3] Although *scalping* and *screefing* are commonly used as synonyms, screefing is commonly also used generically to cover any form of soil disturbance to facilitate regeneration; scalping is intended to mean removal of surface organic layers to expose subsurface mineral soil.

Seedlings in scalped soil do not initially have access to the nutrients in the relatively fertile surface layers removed by scalping. Seedling roots, however, stimulated by increased soil temperature, may rapidly grow beyond the scalped area to reach the nutrients in the surrounding undisturbed layers. Patch size should not be so large that the roots of seedlings planted in the middle of a patch take longer than the first growing season to reach the nutrients in the surrounding surface organic layers. Optimum patch size varies with site. Large patches are needed where surrounding vegetation may shade seedlings or the soil of patches excessively or may crush seedlings when the vegetation is pressed down by snow.

Soil texture is an important factor influencing the post-planting performance of seedlings planted in scalped soil. Medium and moderately coarse-textured soils generally do not inhibit root growth. However, fine-textured, compacted subsurface soil exposed in scalped patches may restrict seedling root growth sufficiently for seedlings to become chlorotic, because access to the nitrogen in adjacent surface organic layers is delayed for years. Deep scalping of fine-textured soil may result in waterlogged patches and in restricted root extension. Seedling root systems may be sufficiently shallow in scalped, fine-textured soil to cause sapling instability. Frost heaving can also be a problem for seedlings planted in exposed fine-textured mineral soil.

On sites where soil moisture deficits restrict seedling performance, removal of competing vegetation by scalping means that the moisture reaching the planting spot is available to the planted seedling. In dry climates, the benefits of shade cast by adjacent vegetation may be more than negated by the moisture it removes from the soil at the expense of seedlings. Only inanimate objects such as logs, stumps, or shade cards provide shade without consuming soil moisture. Mechanical site preparation can provide beneficial shade by aligning cull logs to shade germinants or planted seedlings.

Matching depth of scalping to the site is critical. If scalping is too shallow, competing vegetation may not be controlled because its roots are not removed. If scalping is too deep, the resulting depressed planting spot may become waterlogged, especially on wet sites or during wet periods. Consequently, scalping is most effective on well-drained sites with medium-textured soils, where such treatments can be deep enough to control vegetation, yet not result in other problems such as waterlogging or inhibition of seedling root growth.

Mixing

Mixing treatments incorporate surface organic layers with the underlying mineral soil, leaving the nutrients of the organic layers immediately available to germinants or planted seedlings. Mixing generally exposes mineral soil, which enhances soil temperature, much as scalping treatments do.

For fine-textured soils, mixing may be a more satisfactory treatment than scalping. Incorporating organic matter into the mineral soil produces planting spots that are less compact than those in exposed, fine-textured subsurface soil. Mixing also averts the problems of restricted root growth and waterlogging, which are commonly associated with scalping.

The effectiveness of mixing treatments for controlling competing vegetation depends on the intensity of mixing and the aggressiveness of the competing vegetation. Intense mixing can control competition where roots and other plant parts are chopped up small enough to inhibit resprouting. This requires high-speed or repeated mixing. Intense mixing is most suitable for fine-textured, relatively stone-free soils. Partial or coarse mixing is only effective in promoting seedling growth when competing vegetation is not aggressive. Otherwise, it may increase competition from weed plants because it improves soil fertility without sufficiently reducing resprouting potential.

There is some evidence that mixing may cause long-term depletion of nutrients by making them excessively available in the first few years after treatment. Nutrients not taken up by plants may be lost to the ecosystem through leaching. Mixing only the planting spots rather than the entire site appears to avoid this problem.

Inverting

Planting spots consisting of pads or strips of surface organic matter, turned upside down and covered with a mineral soil cap, can provide several benefits for germinants and planted seedlings. These include enhanced soil temperature, control of competing vegetation, and immediate access to the nutrients in surface soil layers.

Soil temperature is increased in the mineral soil cap because the exposed mineral soil surface absorbs the sun's radiation. Seedling roots can proliferate in this warm soil.

Mineral soil cappings, if deep enough, suppress resprouting so that competing vegetation is effectively controlled. Inverted organic layers with minimal soil cappings, however, may enhance competition rather than control it. Competing vegetation, as well as tree seedlings, can benefit from increased soil temperature and the improved access to nutrients provided by planting spots prepared by inverting.

Forming deep mineral soil cappings is difficult when surface organic matter is deep. Under these conditions, the resulting organic cappings may not control competing vegetation or enhance soil temperature as effectively as mineral soil cappings would.

Following inversion, soil nutrients in the inverted humus layer are uppermost, next to the warm mineral soil capping. In unprepared soil, the humus layer may remain cool on warm days because the litter and fermentation layers above it act as insulation. Seedling roots reaching the interface between the inverted mineral soil cap and the inverted humus layer have the benefit of both the nutrients in the humus layer and the warm mineral soil capping. Seedling roots must be long enough, and the seedling planted deeply enough, to reach the mineral/humus layer interface and so benefit from the nutrients in this zone.

The desiccation of mineral soil cappings in dry periods may be accentuated by the inverted surface organic layers acting as a capillary discontinuity. Seedling roots confined to the mineral soil cap may suffer moisture stress during droughty periods. This may be particularly serious on coarse-textured soils. On the other hand, roots reaching to the mineral soil beneath the inverted layers have access to an enhanced supply of moisture — the result of the capillary discontinuity. Moisture accumulates beneath the organic layers because evapotranspiration from the soil horizons under these layers is minimal when vegetation is controlled.

Frost heaving of seedlings, even when mineral soil cappings are fine textured, has not been a problem following site preparation by inversion in British Columbia. In Ontario, however, frost heaving in hand-simulated inverted humus mounds has been sufficiently severe to cast doubt on the suitability of such planting spots (Wood et al. 1988).

ELEVATION OF PREPARED PLANTING SPOTS

Raised Planting Spots

Raised planting spots are favorable on wet sites because elevation improves aeration and drainage. Soil temperature is enhanced because well-drained soil heats faster than waterlogged soil. Even on mesic and submesic sites, the enhanced soil temperature of elevated planting spots in zones with cool climates (e.g., SBSe or SBSk) may improve seedling performance. However, seedlings may be subject to moisture stress when elevated planting spots desiccate during dry periods. Seedlings should have sufficiently long roots (e.g., PSB 323 with 23 cm long root systems) and be planted deep enough to ensure that the roots have access to a continuous supply of soil moisture at the base of the elevated planting spot.

Raised planting spots may be formed as mounds or as continuous or discontinuous ridges or berms.

While all types of raised planting spots enhance soil temperature and aeration, their effectiveness in providing adequate soil water, nutrients, vegetation control, and light varies with site. The various types of raised seedbed or planting spot can be categorized as follows.

Inverted humus mounds or ridges

Inverted humus mounds or ridges are especially suitable for fine-textured soils. Seedling roots will extend and grow well in the friable mineral soil/ humus layer interface where the soil is warm and nutrients in the inverted organic layer are easily accessible.

It is important, however, that roots grow beyond the raised mound or ridge before nutrients in the raised area are depleted. Sapling vigor may decline when nutrients and moisture supply from the restricted soil volume within the mound or ridge are exhausted. The roots of some species experience difficulty in leaving raised planting ridges with vertical sides. These roots may extend along the ridge, developing two-dimensional root systems which make saplings vulnerable to toppling or larger trees susceptible to windthrow.

The roots of standard-length plugs (PSB 313) planted to the root collar in mounds or ridges with deep mineral soil cappings are not long enough to reach the moisture in the mineral soil beneath the organic layers. A deep capping, nevertheless, may be required to control competing vegetation. Planting at the edge of the ridge or mound is not a solution to this problem when tall vegetation surrounding the margin of the elevated planting spot is likely to smother seedlings. Another difficulty is that the double surface organic matter layer beneath the capping can act as a physical impediment to planting, resulting in seedlings being J-root planted, unless planters are alert to the problem. Such J-rooted seedlings, dependent on the mineral soil cap alone for moisture, may die or become stunted when the cap dries out.

With standard-length seedlings, a possible solution is to plant their roots deeply enough to reach the moisture beneath the organic layers, even though some needles may be buried. Another alternative, currently being tested, is the use of long-rooted seedlings.

Mineral mounds

Raised mineral soil planting spots (i.e., heaps of mineral soil) on mineral soil may be favorable for seedling growth. Mineral mounds are beneficial on dry sites where enhanced temperature is desired, but where soil moisture availability may be restricted by the presence of inverted humus layers (Orländer 1986). Capillarity helps to maintain soil moisture in mineral mounds even though the planting spot is an elevated site because there is no capillary discontinuity in this planting microsite. Nitrogen in the surrounding organic layers can quickly be reached by seedling roots because root growth is enhanced by the increased soil temperature on sites where soil texture does not inhibit root penetration. Mineral mounds may also be beneficial for seedling growth on cool, moist sites. At present, there are no comparative data to indicate whether mineral mounds are more or less favorable than inverted humus mounds on moist sites.

Mixed humus and mineral soil

Raised planting spots consisting of mixed humus and mineral soil elevate soil temperature, avoid capillary discontinuity, improve aeration, and provide access to the nutrients in the mixed organic layer. On sites where competing vegetation is not a problem, elevated planting spots consisting of coarsely chopped organic layers mixed with mineral soil may be favorable. However, elevated planting spots consisting of mixed surface organic matter and mineral soil have the same restriction previously referred to in the mixing section.

Peat mounds and ridges

In deep peat soils, mounds or ridges formed from peat may be the only way to increase soil temperature, improve drainage, and control competing vegetation. The initial chlorotic appearance of seedlings commonly apparent in peat soils suggests that the nutrient status of raised peat may initially be less than ideal. However, as the peat mound mineralizes, seedling color improves. To overcome the problem of desiccation, seedlings should be planted deeply or long-rooted seedlings used.

Depressed Planting Spots

Depressed planting spots — that is, those below the general level of the soil surface — may be beneficial in dry climates. Snow and rainfall accumulating in a depression can provide seedlings with an extended period of soil moisture availability. Seedlings can also be somewhat protected from desiccation by wind because of their slightly sheltered position.

During the growing season, however, frost resulting from overnight pooling of cold air may be accentuated when seedlings are in depressed rather than raised planting spots. As well, seedlings planted in depressions in fine-textured soils on wet sites may be adversely affected by accumulations of water. Consequently, depressed planting spots are better suited to medium-textured, well-drained soils than to fine-textured soils liable to seasonal moisture excess.

Level Planting Spots

The inverted furrow slice, made by a breaking plow, falls onto mineral soil exposed by the removal of the previous furrow slice. An inverted planting spot is thus formed, which is level with the surrounding terrain and which consists of mineral soil covering a layer of inverted organic matter resting on mineral soil. Such planting spots may be advantageous in dry climates. Seedlings are not elevated and are therefore not as subjected to wind desiccation as seedlings on raised planting spots. Capillary discontinuity is minimized because there is only a single organic layer above the mineral soil. This layer is also below general ground level, flanked by other furrow slices. In that position, the inverted organic layer is less exposed to drying than in a raised planting spot. This method of site preparation is likely to be favorable for fine-textured soils in dry climates.

CONTINUITY OF PREPARED PLANTING SPOTS

Preparing continuous strips rather than isolated spots provides planters with more choice in finding suitable planting spots. If locations at the desired spacing are unsuitable, appropriate spots may still be found within specified tolerance limits.

Where preparation causes continuous furrows, some drainage of the site may be an additional advantage. These furrows, however, should not extend uphill and downhill where there is a possibility of erosion. Recently developed implements allow automatic interruption of the furrow (trench), which reduces erosion potential without significantly sacrificing the increased planting spot selection afforded by essentially continuous preparation.

Exposure of mineral soil may provide sufficient heat from re-radiation to protect seedlings from frost during the growing season. Increased mineral soil exposure is more likely to occur with continuous or semi-continuous soil strips than with small patches. Patch length can be increased, however, by appropriate adjustments to patch scarifiers to give increased mineral soil

TABLE 12.1.   Relative effectiveness of various planting spot types in relation to site factors

Planting spot types	Soil temperature	Soil moisture	Soil aeration	Nutrient availability	Competition control
Undisturbed	0[a]	0	0	0	0
Bare mineral soil					
Depressed	+	+	0 to -[b]	- to --[b]	++
Level	+	0	0	- to --	+
Raised	+	0	++	- to --	++
Inverted LFH with mineral cap					
Level	+	-	0	+	+
Raised	++	- -[c]	++	+	++
Mineral on LFH					
Raised	++	- -[c]	+	0	0
Mixed LFH/ Mineral soil					
Level	+	+	++	+	- - to ++[d]
Raised	++	- -[c]	++	+	- - to ++[d]

[a]	++	strongly positive	[b] More negative	[c] Deep planting	[d] Depending
	+	positive	effect in fine-	may be used	on the degree
	0	no effect	textured soils.	to alleviate	of mixing.
	-	negative		moisture stress.	
	- -	strongly negative			

exposure. The minimum size of exposed patch needed to protect seedlings from growing season frost by re-radiation has not been established.

SITE PREPARATION IMPLEMENTS

The numbers and types of mechanical site preparation implements have increased in recent years (Thorsen 1978; CPPA/CFS 1984; Fryk 1986; Gorman 1985; C.R. Smith 1987a, 1987b; Hunt and McMinn 1988). Each implement may produce several types of planting spots, making the selection and use of site preparation equipment a complex decision. The following section describes the broad equipment types, the objectives of each treatment achieved by the equipment, and examples of the equipment and the models available. More detailed descriptions are given by Coates and Haeussler (1987).

Brush Blades and Rakes

Objectives of treatment

Brush rakes and blades are used primarily to rearrange slash material for hazard abatement and improvement of planter access. Disturbance by the implement will produce scalped or some incidental mixed spots in level positions, with minor improvement of soil temperature and moisture conditions and reduced vegetative competition. The treatment often includes the piling of slash and follow-up burning. Because site preparation treatments are facilitated by slash removal, brush blades and rakes are often used as a first-pass treatment before more microsite-specific preparation, such as mounding, is done.

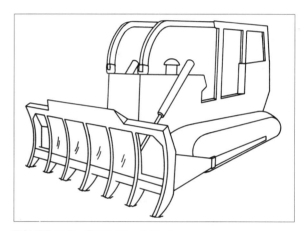

FIGURE 12.2. Beales' brush blade.

Models and types available

- fixed-tooth blades and rakes: Beales' brush blade (Figure 12.2), 4-way blade, 6-way blade
- flexible-tooth rakes: Eden piling rake, Raumfix, Force

Front-Mounted V-Blades

Objectives of treatment

Front-mounted V-blades are used to improve planter access by aligning slash and removing competing vegetation in appropriate sites. A level or depressed, scalped spot is produced by removing vegetation roots and reducing surface organic layer thickness. V-blades are suitable for areas with deeper organic layers and medium- to coarse-textured soils, and can be used in rehabilitating brushed-in blocks. Deep-blading can be detrimental where soils are fine-textured, and should be avoided on such sites. Blading is generally a first-pass treatment to improve the effectiveness of trenchers, mounders, and mixing implements, either before the second treatment or concurrently with it.

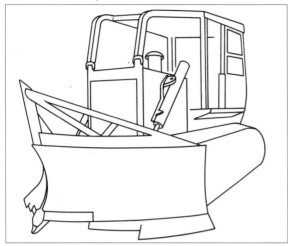

FIGURE 12.3. Sanders' V-blade.

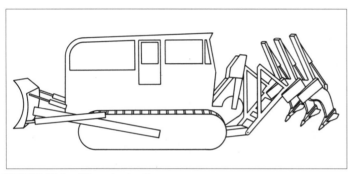

FIGURE 12.4. Winged subsoiler.

Models and types available

- Sanders' V-blade (Figure 12.3), V2000 slash rake, C&H V-plow

Rear-Mounted Plows and Rippers

Objectives of treatment

Rear-mounted plows are used to remove vegetation and organic layers where deep or extensive disturbance is required. Usually such implements create an overturned berm and trench, but the treatment profile depends on the individual attachment. Objectives vary with the implement and site. Planting spots can be prepared at the top of the overturned material (inverted, raised), on the scalped level portion, or in the scalped depressed trench, depending on the requirements of the site and the species.

Models and types available

- Marttiini plow
- ripper plows
- agricultural breaking plows
- winged subsoilers (Figure 12.4)

Drag Scarifiers

Objectives of treatment

Drag scarification is used primarily on lodgepole pine sites to create seedbeds and distribute cone material. Surface organic layers are removed and mineral soil is exposed (scalped, level). Serotinous cones close enough to the ground may experience temperatures high enough to release seed. In some cases, seedbeds are composed of combined organic/ mineral soil (mixed, level). Fire hazard is reduced because slash accumulations are redistributed.

Models and types available

- chain drags (Figure 12.5)
- sharkfin barrels

Shear Blades, Downing Chains, and Roller Drum Choppers

Objectives of treatment

This equipment is used primarily to flatten vegetation, snags, dense lodgepole pine, and aspen. In most cases, little soil disturbance is desired or achieved. Preparation of planting spots is often completed later by burning or by other mechanical or manual methods.

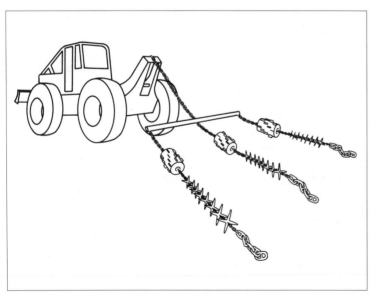

FIGURE 12.5. Chain drags.

Models and types available

- shear blades (Figure 12.6)
- downing chain
- drum choppers: Marden

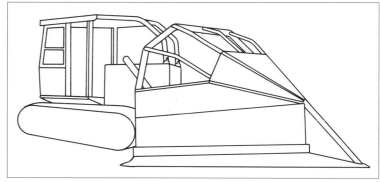

FIGURE 12.6.   Shear blade.

Patch Scarifiers

Objectives of treatment

Patch scarifiers create scalped, depressed prepared spots, a level hinge, and a raised loose mound. Removal of organic layers provides a microsite that promotes seedling survival and growth on mesic sites with uncompacted loamy soils. On drier sites, the preferred spot may be in the depression; on moister sites, the preferred spot may be at the hinge (level, i.e., at general ground line). Generally, this treatment does not provide adequate vegetation control where competition is serious, nor is it successful on wet or very dry sites where trenches or berms and mounds have been more effective.

Models and types available

Three types of patch scarifiers, imported from Sweden and Finland, have been used in British Columbia. Each has a pair of mattock wheels with tines. As the mattock wheels rotate, the tines drag and scrape away the surface organic matter and mineral soil. A scalped patch and an accumulation of surface material at the trailing end of the patch are produced. The equipment is used with rubber-tired or tracked prime movers and is rear-mounted. Slash conditions are limiting for all models, but V-blades may be used to improve the effectiveness of treatment.

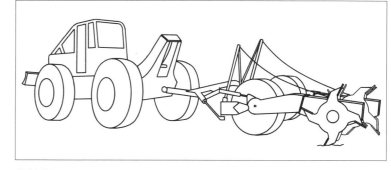

FIGURE 12.7.   Bräcke scarifier.

- Leno scarifier
- Bräcke scarifier (Figure 12.7)
- Sinkkilä HMF scarifier

Mounders

Objectives of treatment

Inverted humus mounds and mineral mounds provide raised, prepared spots. These may serve different biological purposes. Trials are currently being conducted to determine the range of sites that can be successfully treated by mounders, and the amount of mineral soil capping that is optimal on different sites.

Models and types available

- Bräcke mounder
- Sinkkilä HMF scarifier
- Ministry/Rivtow mounder (Figure 12.8)
- Donaren 870H
- Öje mounder (boom-mounted)
- Excavators

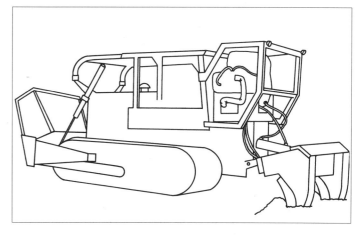

FIGURE 12.8.   Ministry/Rivtow mounder.

Disc Trenchers and Cone Scarifiers

Objectives of treatment

Disc trenchers and cone scarifiers create pairs of continuous trenches (or furrows) and berms, which offer a variety of planting positions. The mineral soil trench can be used when moisture conservation is required (scalped, depressed planting spot). The hinge position at the junction of the trench and berm is favorable on sites with intermediate moisture regimes. The mineral soil/surface organic matter berm provides a raised spot that may be partially mixed or generally inverted with a mineral soil capping. This raised microsite is suitable for moist sites. Powered trenchers are required for mineral soil exposure on sites with heavy slash and deep organic layers.

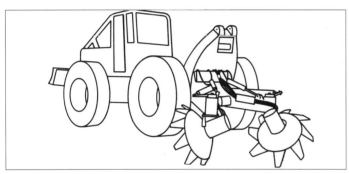

FIGURE 12.9. Disc trencher.

Models and types available

Passive disc trenchers:

- CFE disc trencher
- TTS-35 disc trencher

Powered disc trenchers: (Figure 12.9)

- TTS Delta, Donaren 180D, 180L, 280D, 870H

Powered cone scarifier:

- Silva Wadell

Mixing Equipment

Objectives of treatment

Mixing equipment is designed to incorporate surface organic matter into the mineral soil to improve nutrient status, to increase soil temperature, and to improve soil physical properties. Prepared spots may be raised or level. Raised spots may be created by a bedding attachment. Most soils would benefit from this treatment, but operational constraints restrict the applicability of mixing.

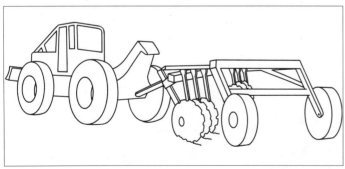

FIGURE 12.10. Eden bedding plow.

Models and types available

- agricultural and forestry discs: Rome, Crabe, Savannah
- bedding plow: Eden Relief Bedding Plow (Figure 12.10), Savannah Bedding Plow, Rome Bedding Plow
- Rotoclear (Figures 12.11 and 12.12)

Excavators

Objectives of treatment

Excavators are used as carriers for forks, rakes, and powered attachments mounted to the boom. Spot treatments remove heavy organic layers, often producing scalped, depressed planting spots. Exposure of mineral soil may improve soil temperature. Excavators may provide some degree of mixing. Mounds can also be produced (inverted, mixed).

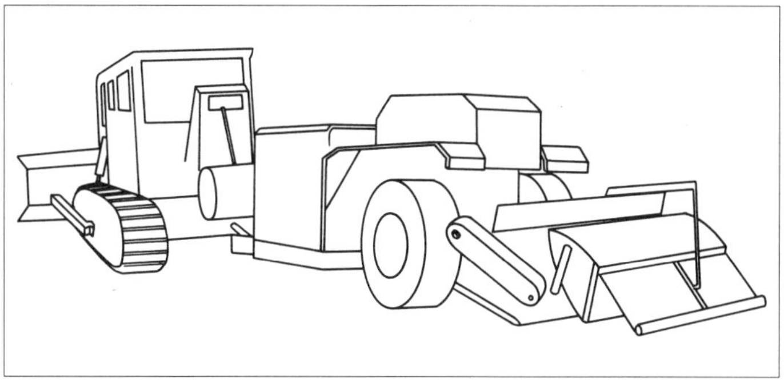

Models and types available

- Cat 180, 205, 219
- Hitachi Ex 200, Ex 270, UH 121, UH 16LC
- John Deere 490, 590, 790 (Figure 12.13)
- Powered attachments: Slashbuster, Mitsui Miike

Motormanual Scarification Tools

Objectives of treatment

These tools are used to remove fine slash and surface organic matter to provide scalped planting spots which may be level or depressed.

Models and types available

- chainsaw-based: "Hawk" Power Scalper
- brushsaw-based: La Taupe (Figure 12.14), Rippa, Eco, Scarri

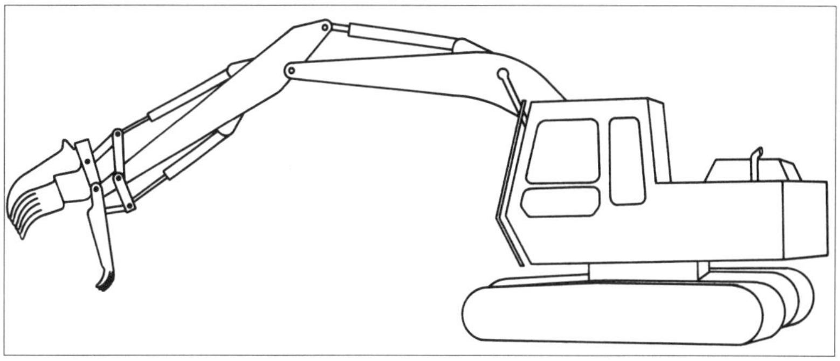

SUMMARY OF MECHANICAL SITE PREPARATION EQUIPMENT

The prepared spot types created by the site preparation equipment described in this section are summarized in Table 12.2. When the desirable spot type has been determined following assessment of the site, the equipment type can be chosen. Operational considerations of slope and ground roughness, soil and slash conditions, equipment availability, and cost influence choice of specific implement and prime mover.

CHOOSING MECHANICAL SITE PREPARATION EQUIPMENT

Two examples (page 163), representing contrasting ecological characteristics at two sites, are given to show the constraints and considerations at each site, the recommended mechanical site preparation methods, and the benefits anticipated.

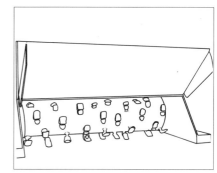

FIGURE 12.11. Rotoclear.

FIGURE 12.12. Close-up of Rotoclear drum.

FIGURE 12.13. John Deere 490 excavator.

FIGURE 12.14. La Taupe.

TABLE 12.2. Plantation spot types created by mechanical site preparation implements

	Bare mineral soil			Inverted LFH with mineral cap		Mineral on LFH	Mixed LFH/mineral soil		Planters access	Profile of planting spot type (planting spot ↓)
	Depressed	Level	Raised	Level	Raised	Raised	Level	Raised		
Brush blades	very	mod.	slight					slight	very	
V-blades	very	mod.	slight					slight	very	
Marttiini plow [a]	very	very	slight		very				very	
Ripper plow	mod.	mod.	mod.		slight			slight	mod.	
Breaking plow	slight			very	mod.				very	
Drags	slight	mod.						slight	slight	
Patch scarifier	very	mod.			mod.				slight	
Bräcke mounder [b]	very	mod.	very		very			slight	slight	
Sinkkilä	very	slight			very			slight	slight	
MOF/Rivtow mounder	very	slight			very			slight	slight	
Disc trenchers	very	very			slight	slight	slight	slight	mod.	
Cone scarifier	very	mod.						mod.	mod.	
Agricultural disc							slight		very	

● slightly effective   ⬤ moderately effective   ⬤ very effective

[a] referring specifically to current model AKLM 190
[b] including full range of options

	Bare mineral soil			Inverted LFH with mineral cap		Mineral on LFH	Mixed LFH/mineral soil		Planters access	Profile of planting spot type (planting spot ↘)
	Depressed	Level	Raised	Level	Raised	Raised	Level	Raised	Planters access	
Madge rotoclear							●	•	●	Fine mix
Excavator	●	•	●	•	●	●	•	•	•	Mineral patch / Mineral mound / Inverted mound
Motormanual scarifiers	●	•					•	•		Mineral
Bedding plow	•						●	●		Coarse mixed

Choosing mechanical site preparation equipment

Example 1.

ZONE: SBS

SUBZONE: SBSwk1

ASSOCIATION: SBSwk1/07(b) - Hybrid Spruce - Devil's club (fine-textured)

Constraints and Considerations:
- competition from shrubby and grassy vegetation
- low soil temperature
- poor microsite drainage and aeration
- compact subsoil
- competition from "weed" trees with airborne seed

Recommendation: Create inverted humus mound with thick (>10 cm) mineral soil cap using mounder capable of forming deep capping

Benefits:
- vegetation control by inverting and burying organic layers beneath deep mineral soil cap
- improved soil temperature in mineral soil cap and raised planting position
- improved drainage in raised planting spot
- seedling root growth unrestricted in friable interface between mineral soil cap and inverted organic layers
- access to fertility of organic layers

Caveats:
- avoid planting in exposed subsurface soil because root growth is restricted when subsurface soil is compact, waterlogging/poor aeration is probable, and nitrogen availability is low
- avoid excessive mineral soil exposure, which creates a seedbed for competing trees species with windborne seed (e.g., willow, birch)

Example 2.

ZONE: IDF

SUBZONE: IDFdk2

ASSOCIATION: IDFdk2/01 Douglas-fir - Lodgepole pine - Pinegrass - Feathermoss

Constraints and considerations:
- soil moisture shortage
- vegetation competing for soil moisture
- early season low soil temperature
- shading not necessary
- roots not impeded by loamy soil
- drainage adequate; no significant periods of waterlogging

Recommendation: Create depressed, scalped, planting spot with patch scarifier or intermittent trencher

Benefits:
- vegetation control leaves all available soil moisture for seedlings
- planting at bottom of scalped patch or trench puts seedling in moisture-accumulating position and may reduce transpiration
- mineral soil exposure facilitates early season soil warming

Caveats:
- avoid excessive soil disturbance because excessive rate of organic matter reduction could affect growth rates 15 - 25 years after planting
- avoid excessively deep gouging if subsurface soil is compact (high clay content), because compact soil restricts root growth

13 SITE PREPARATION: CHEMICAL

J. Otchere-Boateng and L.J. Herring

Chemical site preparation, which involves the use of herbicides, controls competing vegetation before planting or natural regeneration, and during the early stages of seedling establishment.

In general, herbicides are effective in suppressing most undesirable vegetation with minimum disturbance to the soil. They are therefore well suited for use on many sites where competing resprouting residuals or invading germinants pose a problem to reforestation (Walstad et al. 1987).

SUITABILITY OF HERBICIDES FOR SITE PREPARATION

For effective site preparation from chemical methods alone, the site must have the following characteristics:

1. Live vegetation species which are susceptible to the available registered herbicides. The vegetation must be scattered enough to allow planting to be done at a reasonable cost (Stewart 1978; Sutton 1985), since the interwoven dense stems of chemically killed vegetation make planting difficult. On a recently disturbed site, the herbicide should usually be applied after shrubs and hardwoods have sprouted.
2. Low density of logging residues and other debris.
3. Forest floor litter which is thin enough to permit seeding, where natural regeneration is planned or screefing, if artificial reforestation is needed.

If these criteria are met, then chemical site preparation may be the most appropriate option for achieving regeneration objectives, particularly where non-chemical methods would be detrimental, ineffective, unsafe, costly, or unpractical. Examples of such situations favoring chemical site preparation include:

- Where mechanical equipment cannot be used because the slope is very steep (greater than 35%), or the soil is easily compacted or eroded.
- Where non-chemical methods provide poor control of sprouting species, or where stored seed might be stimulated to germinate following burning or mechanical treatments.

- Where soil moisture stress is a problem. Site preparation techniques that remove shade cover will increase soil and air temperature extremes near the soil surface (especially in burned areas) and thus expose seedlings to unfavorable conditions. The dead vegetation left following a herbicide treatment may act as a mulch or shade for the seedlings (Heidmann 1969).

- Where burning can lead to loss of nutrients bound in slash and litter, or produce hydrophobic soils which can prevent natural regeneration (Kramme and DeBano 1965; DeBano et al. 1970).

- Where a pre-harvest assessment or survey prescribes control of advanced sprouting in hardwoods. A herbicide technique such as hack and squirt can be used.

- Where site preparation is to be done in poorly accessible and scattered locations in portions of plantations and natural stands which are understocked. Fire would not be practical and mechanical equipment would damage crop trees.

Even when the above conditions are met, however, several drawbacks to chemical site preparation must also be considered. For one, not all vegetation in forest communities can be controlled with the available registered herbicides (Newton and Knight 1981). Some minor herbicide-resistant species can develop into a major competition problem after a treatment. Burning or mechanical treatment may be needed as a follow-up. In some areas of the province, herbicides may not be effective in ameliorating unfavorable microsite conditions such as cold soils and frost problems (Stathers 1989) affecting regeneration. In these areas, site preparation techniques such as burning, scalping, trenching, mounding, and ripping may be more appropriate than chemical site preparation. Thirdly, herbicide application in most cases must wait until shrubs and hardwoods have sprouted to ensure maximum uptake and translocation. This can delay reforestation efforts.

Another problem is that herbicides are regulated and not allowed to be applied on all sites. Examples are sites close to sensitive areas, such as potable water sources and fish-bearing streams. Finally, there is growing public concern on the use of chemicals in the environment. This can have some impact on herbicide use for site preparation.

Ecological and Environmental Impacts of Herbicides in Site Preparation

Herbicides, applied according to the label recommendations, have little site impact, and therefore offer many ecological and environmental advantages over other site preparation alternatives. Unlike the non-chemical methods, herbicides are not directly capable of:

- removing or displacing moisture-conserving plant residues or nutrient rich topsoils;

- decreasing or increasing soil compaction, excessively exposing soils to erosion, puddling soils, or excessively disrupting normal drainage patterns;

- creating a preferred germination seedbed for invading undesirable vegetation seed;

- removing all aboveground plant parts and their beneficial shade; and
- destroying desirable advance regeneration when the crop species is tolerant or when a directed spray technique is used to prevent spraying over crop trees (Boyd 1982).

Non-persistent herbicides affect soil properties indirectly. Soil moisture content may increase as a result of vegetation reduction (Tarrant 1957; Heidmann 1969; Eckert 1979; Ross and Walstad 1986), and there may be greater nutrient losses by leaching, increased microbial activity, increased daytime temperatures, and decreased nighttime temperatures (Gregory 1981).

Using Herbicides with Other Site Preparation Alternatives

Where the objective of site preparation is not vegetation suppression alone, but includes, for instance, removal of flammable logging residues or mineral seedbed preparation, herbicides may be used in combination with mechanical and burning methods. Examples of such situations include:

- where a harvested area is invaded by herbaceous and brush species before logging slash treatment. The green (live) vegetation does not burn readily; it also tends to shade the logging residues and retard them from drying out enough to facilitate fire. A pre-burn herbicide application to desiccate, defoliate, or kill vegetation can allow the slash to warm and dry, thus allowing the burning to be done effectively. The competing vegetation is usually killed to the ground level by such spray and burn combinations. Without a herbicide pre-spray, such a site could be burned only under more hazardous conditions, or might not burn at all.
- where brush species on the site are susceptible to herbicide treatments, but removal of the standing dead vegetation is also required to reduce planting costs and minimize small animal damage.
- where resprouting brush species exist, but the presence of logging debris makes the site inaccessible for planting. A herbicide spray followed by mechanical or burning treatments would be required.
- where some of the competing vegetation is resistant to herbicides. Burning may be used as a follow-up treatment.

Herbicide/Mechanical Combination

Spray-crush and spray-scarify techniques are examples of herbicide/mechanical combination methods. These techniques can reduce resprouting and are particularly useful in dense stands of brittle evergreen species on gentle topography (Stewart 1978). However, they can also leave debris on the site, which may hinder planting activity or provide cover for small mammals.

Herbicide/Burning Combination

Applying herbicides as a precursor to prescribed burning is becoming an accepted site preparation method, as it prevents resprouting and facilitates burning. There are two techniques, spray-and-burn and brown-and-burn. The former uses systemic (translocated) herbicides such as glyphosate or 2, 4-D; the latter uses contact herbicides which are not registered in Canada. Some characteristics of these techniques are presented in Table 13.1.

The use of systemic herbicides before burning results in important changes in post-burning succession, which may affect the need for subsequent treatment. Sprouters are reduced or eliminated following the burn, thereby reducing the need for establishment release. However, herbs and shrubs of seed origin may survive, resulting in greater early competition to crop trees. Planting success without follow-up brushing would likely be low, especially if low vigor stock were planted.

TABLE 13.1. Characteristics of spray-and-burn and brown-and-burn techniques

Spray-and-burn	Brown-and-burn
1. Translocated (systemic) herbicide used.	1. Contact herbicide used.
2. Slower action. Burning can be delayed several months to a year or more after spraying, to achieve maximum root kill and stem desiccation. Minimum waiting period before burning is 4 weeks.	2. Fast action only. 10-14 days required between spraying and burning.
3. Defoliate and control vegetation before burning. Postburning respraying may be reduced. Greater flexibility of timing of burn than brown-and-burn.	3. Herbicide not translocated into roots. Vegetation frequently not killed, just desiccated. Respraying required if burning delayed.

PLANNING FOR A CHEMICAL SITE PREPARATION

Planning for chemical site preparation begins with problem identification or assessment of potential vegetation problems at the pre- and post-harvest stages. This is followed by selection of a treatment method. Other selection considerations include treatment cost, and effect of the method on workers, bystanders, crop trees, and the environment (water, fish and wildlife resources). Planning should also include during-treatment monitoring, post-treatment effectiveness assessment, and prescription examination or evaluation. The evaluation should assess whether reforestation objectives were met.

Problem Identification: Pre-Harvest Considerations

One of the criteria that must be met for chemical site preparation to be appropriate is the presence of herbicide-susceptible competing vegetation on the site. Predictions of the abundance and rate of growth of the potential vegetation expected during regeneration of the next stand must be made. This can be done before harvest and also at the post-harvest/pre-site preparation stages. Predictions made at the pre-harvest stage are particularly important. Until the competing vegetation appears in the next stand, the pre-harvest stage is the best time to assess the possible vegetation problems. With knowledge of the expected problem species, the forester can integrate harvest practices and site preparation activities to achieve management objectives.

While chance can play some role during the early successional process, the severity of disturbance — primarily from site preparation activities — affects the potential species distribution, establishment, and growth. Therefore, the potential impacts of the various harvesting and site preparation activities on, for example, seed germination and survival must be considered. The plan to use chemicals for site preparation, alone or in combination with other site preparation alternatives, may be identified at the pre-harvest stage.

In a pre-harvest survey, the ecosystem type and the existing vegetation (the plant community and the life history) of the most important species in the community must be known, as well as how these species respond to disturbance. For illustration, the establishment potential of selected competing species in British Columbia are described in Figure 13.1. More detailed autoecological information on 31 important competing species are described in Haeussler and Coates (1986).

A pre-harvest survey will identify species capable of regenerating from either seed or vegetative propagules, and vegetation that might invade from off-site seed sources. Knowing these, the forester can predict the potential problem vegetation species that would regenerate and dominate the site after harvest (Neuenschwander et al. 1986). This allows for pre-harvest treatments, such as herbicide tree injections, to control the problem in the new stand. If pre-harvest chemical treatments are prescribed, they should be scheduled so that enough time is allowed for the herbicide to act in the plant, but not too long so that the killed trees would present a hazard to workers during subsequent logging operations.

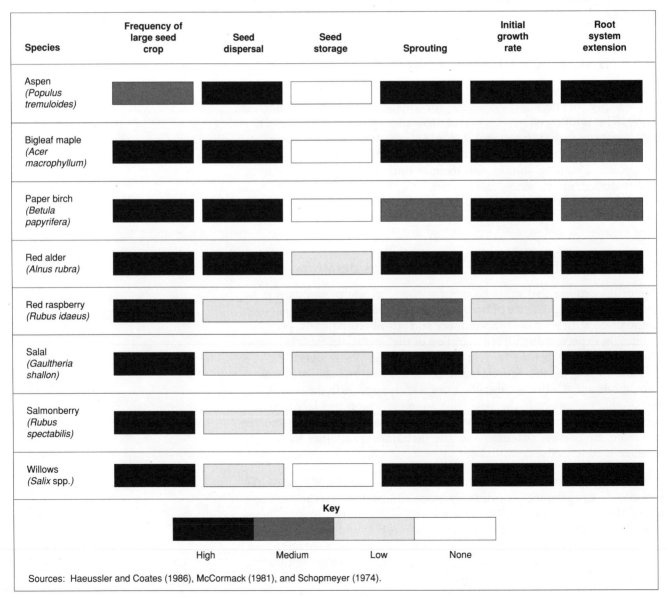

FIGURE 13.1. Establishment potential for selected competing species occurring in British Columbia.

Problem Identification: Post-Harvest Considerations

Post-harvest considerations for site preparation activities should include surveys to determine the composition, abundance, and distribution of sprouting or suckering vegetation species, non-crop germinants, and seed sources within or adjacent to the site. The decision to use herbicides, alone or in combination with non-chemical methods, must consider the overall impact of the methods on the site and the competing vegetation. The degree and duration of vegetation control by the herbicide, conifer tolerance (if treatment spots are within existing plantations or naturally regenerated areas), cost, and impact on the soil and future planted seedlings will determine treatment choice. Additional factors to consider are the registration status and use restrictions.

Before a translocated (systemic) herbicide is applied, the target vegetation must be assessed to determine whether it has recovered from harvesting damage. Adequate foliage must be present to absorb foliar herbicides, and plants must be actively growing to facilitate root absorption of soil-active herbicides.

Selecting Herbicides for Site Preparation

Miller and Kidd (1984) and D.L. Miller (1986) have described the prescription process for vegetation control with herbicides. Included in the process is treatment selection which involves determining, from the list of the registered herbicides, the chemicals (with the appropriate carriers and application rates) which are effective on the identified target species.

The selection of herbicides for the intended job can be simplified by using herbicide evaluation matrices ("checkerboards") as illustrated in Table 13.2. This interim chart was compiled from results of research and silvicultural trials, and operational work done in British Columbia.

Post-Treatment Effectiveness Evaluation

Following a herbicide treatment, site evaluations should be conducted to determine (1) whether the immediate objective of controlling vegetation (before planting) was satisfied; and (2) if the ultimate intent of reforesting the site was achieved. Post-treatment surveys provide the forester with decision-making information to determine whether further treatments are needed to ensure plantation success.

The results of chemical site preparation treatments should be actively evaluated and compared with those from untreated controls and other site preparation methods. The vegetation control evaluations should include assessment of percent target vegetation and resistant species, vegetation shifts, effect on young seedlings, and impact on other resource users. The information obtained from specific sites can be fed back to operational people, to improve future prescriptions. Data from treatment-effectiveness evaluations can be used to construct herbicide treatment matrices for operational use.

TABLE 13.2.   Effectiveness of herbicide treatments in British Columbia: interim charts.

Coniferous trees / Deciduous trees

Herbicide and application method [a]	Douglas-fir *Pseudotsuga menziesii*	Engelmann spruce *Picea engelmannii*	Grand fir *Abies grandis*	Lodgepole pine *Pinus contorta*	Sitka spruce *Picea sitchensis*	Subalpine fir *Abies lasiocarpa*	Western hemlock *Tsuga heterophylla*	Western redcedar *Thuja plicata*	White spruce *Picea glauca*	Bigleaf maple *Acer macrophyllum*	Bitter cherry *Prunus emarginata*	Black cottonwood *Populus balsamifera*	Douglas maple *Acer glabrum*	Red alder *Alnus rubra*	Paper birch *Betula papyrifera*	Sitka alder (green) *Alnus viridis*	Trembling aspen *Populus tremuloides*	Vine maple *Acer circinatum*	Willows *Salix* spp.
Vision® (glyphosate) Foliar (July–Sept.)	○	○	○	○	○	○	◉	◉	○	◕	●	◕	◕	◕	◕	◕	◕	●	◕
Vision® (glyphosate) Injection																	●		
Velpar L® (hexazinone) Spot (spring, fall)			◉	◉		○	◉	◉	◉	◕	◉	◉	◕	◕	◕		◕		◉
Velpar L® (hexazinone) Broadcast (spring)		○	◉			◉	◉	◉	◉	◉	◕		◉	◕		◕	⊘	◕
2,4-D amine Injection										◕			●			●		
2,4-D amine, Broadcast (April–June & Aug.–Sept.)							○			⊘			●	◕	◕		◉
Weedone CB® (2,4-D, 4-DP)										●[b]								

Shrubs

Herbicide and application method [a]	Devil's club *Oplopanax horridus*	Elderberry *Sambucus* spp.	False azalea *Menziesia ferruginea*	Falsebox *Paxistima myrsinites*	Hazelnut *Corylus cornuta*	Highbush-cranberry *Viburnum trilobum*	Honeysuckle *Lonicera utahensis*	Huckleberry *Vaccinium* spp.	Mountain ash *Sorbus sitchensis*	Oval-leaved blueberry *Vaccinium ovalifolium*	Raspberry *Rubus ideaus*	Red-osier dogwood *Cornus sericea*	Rhododendron *Rhododendron albiflorum*	Roses *Rosa* spp.	Salal *Gaultheria shallon*	Salmonberry *Rubus spectabilis*	Saskatoon berry *Amelanchier* spp.	Snowberry *Symphoricarpos albus*	Stink currant *Ribes bracteosum*	Thimbleberry *Rubus parviflorus*	Twinberry *Lonicera involucrata*	Twinflower *Linnaea borealis*
Vision® (glyphosate) Foliar (July–Sept.)	◉	◕	◕	⊘	◉	◉	●	◉	◕	◕	◕	⊘	◕	●	○	◉	◕	●	◕	◕	●	◕
Velpar L® (hexazinone) Spot (spring, fall)				⊘	◉			◉		◉	⊘		◕	○		◕	●	◉	◉	◕	
Velpar L® (hexazinone) Broadcast (spring)				⊘	◉			◉		◉	⊘		◕	○		◉		⊘	◉	◕	
2,4-D amine, Broadcast (April–June & Aug.–Sept.)							◕														
Asulox F® (Asulam)																					

Grasses / Ferns / Flowers

Herbicide and application method [a]	Grasses (general) *Graminae*	Bluejoint *Calamagrostis canadensis*	Pine grass *Calamagrostis rubescens*	Bracken fern *Pteridium aquilinum*	Lady fern *Athyrium filix-femina*	Oak fern *Gymnocarpium dryopteris*	Sword fern *Polystichum munitum*	False Solomon's-seal *Smilacina amplexicamlis*	Fireweed *Epilobium angustifolium*
Vision® (glyphosate) Foliar (July–Sept.)	●	◕	◕	◉	◕	◉	●	⊘	
Velpar L® (hexazinone) Spot (spring, fall)	◕	◕	◉						◕
Velpar L® (hexazinone) Broadcast (spring)	◕	◕	◉			◉			◕
2,4-D amine, Broadcast (April–June & Aug.–Sept.)	○								
Asulox F® (July) (Asulam)				●					

Injury

●	90 – 100% (very severe)	◉	25 – 60% (moderate)
◕	60 – 90% (severe)	⊘	< 25% (light)
☐	Insufficient data	○	No visible injury

[a]   Applications were made using the techniques, rates, and timing recommended on the labels.

[b]   Only above ground vegetation killed.

Sources: The matrices were constructed from the following sources: (a) Operational Treatment Evaluation reports supplied by B.C. Forest Service field staff (District and Regional offices); (b) Reports of various research and operational trials conducted in B.C.; (c) Annual Silviculture Abstracts reported in the Expert Committee on Weeds (ECW) Western Section Research Report for the years 1984 to 1989.

SITE PREPARATION CHEMICALS

Pesticide Laws and Regulations

The use of herbicides for site preparation, like all other pesticide use, is controlled by federal and provincial laws and regulations. These laws and regulations may be found in various manuals and publications (see, e.g., Henigman and Beardsley 1985 and B.C. Ministry of Forests 1989).

All pesticides are required to be registered by Agriculture Canada before they can be used. They must carry a manufacturer's label and be used according to the specific instructions on that label. It is illegal — and possibly hazardous—to use pesticides in a manner other than that specified on the label.

A provincial use permit is required for any pesticide to be applied in British Columbia forests. Any person applying a pesticide must have special training in pesticide application and be certified by the B.C. Ministry of Environment (Pesticide Control Branch), or be supervised closely by a certified applicator. It is the user's responsibility to adhere to the laws and regulations governing pesticide handling, storage, and application. Additional information on current herbicide registration status, label changes, and recommended uses may be obtained from the manufacturers and sources such as the Silviculture Manual (B.C. Ministry of Forests) and the Forest Pesticide Handbook of British Columbia (Henigman and Beardsley 1985).

Herbicides Registered for Site Preparation

Table 13.3 shows the herbicides and examples of their formulations that are registered for forest site preparation. However, only glyphosate (Vision®), 2,4-D amine, and 2,4-D ester have forest management registration and hence can be applied on a treatment site greater than 500 ha. The rest are registered solely for woodland use (< 500 ha). Triclopyr (Garlon®), a useful silviculture herbicide, is currently not registered in Canada. It is included here because forestry registration of triclopyr ester (Garlon 4®) is expected in Canada in the early 1990's. The most widely used herbicides in British Columbia forests are now glyphosate, hexazinone, and 2,4-D. Amitrol has not yet been used for forest site preparation in the province.

General requirements and characteristics of site preparation herbicides

A site preparation herbicide must not show extended residual activity in soil, which might damage crop trees planted in the future. Environmental effects on the site and other resources must be considered. The waiting periods needed for conifer establishment following site preparation herbicide treatment are presented in Table 13.4.

TABLE 13.4. Post-herbicide treatment[a] waiting period for conifer planting (modified from Contrell 1985 and manufacturers' labels)

Herbicide (Common name)	Herbicide (Trade name)	Rate used/ha (Product)	Waiting period
Amitrol	Amitrol-T®	8.5 - 22.5 L	6 months
Amitrol + Simazine	Amazine®[b]	7.75 kg	7-10 days
Asulam	Asulox F®	5.5 L	6 weeks
Glyphosate	Vision®	3 - 6 L	None
Hexazinone	Velpar L®	9 L	None
		9 - 18 L	12 months
Simazine	Simadex 80W®	5.5 - 8.25 kg	None
2, 4-D (amine)	2, 4-D Formula 40®	8 L	None
2, 4-D (amine)	Forestamine®	6 - 8 L	None
2, 4-D (ester)	Esteron 600®	5.5 - 8.5 L	None
2, 4-D (ester)	For-Ester®	6.6 -10.2 L	None
Triclopyr (ester)[c]	Garlon 4®	9.4 L	4 weeks
		9.4 -18.8 L	8 weeks

[a] Excludes stem injection (or frill), stump treatments, and stem basal treatments.
[b] Formulated as a mixture of 15% amitrol and 45% simazine.
[c] Currently not registered for forestry in Canada.

TABLE 13.3.   Registered herbicides for forest site preparation

Herbicide (common name)	Examples of formulation (Manufacturer) PCP No.	Guarantee % (a.i., a.e.)	Registration	Target vegetation group	Uptake route	Application method
Amitrol	Amitrol-T ® (Allied Chem.) 16548	20	W	Annual and perennial grasses, broadleaves	Foliage, roots	G
Amitrol + Simazine	Amizine Industrial WP ® (Union Carbide) 8655	15 + 45[a]	W	Annual and perennial grasses, broadleaves	Foliage, roots	G
Asulam	Asulox F ® (May & Baker) 11341	40	W	Bracken fern	Foliage	G
Glyphosate	Vision ® (Monsanto) 13644	35.6	F&W	Annual and perennial weeds, hardwood trees	Foliage, cut surface	G, A S, I
Hexazinone	Velpar L ® (Dupont) 18197	24	W	Annual, biennial and perennial weeds and grasses; hardwood trees	Foliage, roots	G; SP
Simazine	Simadex 80W ® (FBC) 13561	80	W	Grasses and broadleaves germinating plants	Roots	G
2, 4-D amine	Forestamine ® (U.A.P.)[b] 16995	47	F&W	Alder, willow	Cut surface	G; I
	Formula 40 ® (Dow) 16994	47	F&W	Alder, willow	Cut surface foliage	G, I, A
	Guardsman ® Silvamine 50 ® (VW&R)[c] 19385	48	F&W	Alder, willow	Cut surface	G,I
2, 4-D ester	Esteron 600 ® (Dow) 15981	60	F&W	Shrubs, broadleaved forbs, hardwood trees	Stem, foliage Cut surface	G, A; S, I, B
	For-Ester ® (U.A.P.)[b] 16675	47	F	Shrubs, broadleaved forbs, hardwood trees	Stem, foliage cut surface	G, A; S, I, B
2,4-D ester + 2,4-DP ester	Weedone CB ® (May & Baker) 19780	8 + 8	F&W	Woody plants	Stem, cut surface	G S, I, B
Triclopyr[d]	Garlon 4 ® (Dow)	44.3	F&W	Shrubs, broadleaved forbs, hardwood trees	Stem, foliage cut surface	G, A; S, I, B

[a] 15% amitrol + 45% simazine
[b] United Agri Products.
[c] Van Waters and Rogers Ltd.
[d] Currently not registered for forestry in Canada.

G = ground broadcast; A = aerial; S = stump treatment;
SP = spot treatment; I = stem injection; B = basal treatment;
F = forest management registration (> 500 ha of a treatment site);
W = woodland registration (< 500 ha of a treatment site)

Source: Canadian Pulp and Paper Association (CPPA) 1986 and manufacturers' labels.

Where there is no need for saving residuals or naturals, treatment windows can be wider than for release operations. The characteristics of the herbicides registered for site preparation are described below.

Amitrol (Amitrol-T®):　Amitrol is a foliar-applied systemic herbicide, which is similar to glyphosate in activity. Salmonberry and elderberry are extremely susceptible to it. As well, it is effective on grasses and moderately effective on several blackberry species (Newton and Dost 1984). Because most evergreen shrubs are tolerant, its use on mixed broadleaved evergreen/deciduous sites may increase dominance of the evergreen shrub component. Conifers are damaged by this compound at most seasons of the year, especially in spring and fall.

For site preparation, Amitrol-T® is applied in June or early July at application rates of 1.7 - 4.5 kg/ha (a.i.) in 93 L of water per hectare (Newton and Dost 1984). Amitrol is very soluble in water (28 g/100g at 25°C). It binds loosely to soils and so can leach readily (Ghassemi 1981). Persistence of this compound ranges from several days to 6 months or more (Ghassemi 1981). Livestock should be kept out of treated area during season of use.

Amizine, a registered formulation containing 15% amitrol and 45% simazine, is applied at the rate of 7.75 kg/ha in 800 L of water/per hectare.

Asulam (Asulox F®):　Asulox F® is registered in forestry for bracken fern control only. This limitation, and the fact that other herbicides such as glyphosate can provide some control of bracken fern (in addition to many other species), have made this chemical uneconomic to produce and market. Though registered, Asulox F® may not be available for purchase in Canada.

Asulam inhibits growth and chlorophyll synthesis. For best results it is applied in summer (July), or just before full frond (i.e., when leaves have fully unfurled) but before the leaves turn brown, at a rate of 5.5 L per hectare of Asulox F® in 200 L of water per hectare. Treated vegetation must not be disturbed (e.g., by cutting). The effect of asulam on target vegetation is not evident until a year later, when formation of new fronds is prevented. There is no residual effect on seedlings if they are planted 6 weeks after spraying.

Glyphosate (Vision®):　Glyphosate is a broad spectrum, foliar-active systemic herbicide, registered for both aerial and ground (broadcast, stem injection, or frill) applications. It primarily inhibits the formation of amino acids (phenylaline, tyrosine, and tryptophan), which are essential for protein synthesis (Cole 1985) leading to metabolic failure and death. At the rate of 3-6 L/ha of product, it is effective on deciduous hardwoods and shrubs, some ferns (e.g., bracken), grasses, and herbaceous broadleaf species. Some shrub species with thick, waxy leaves are tolerant to glyphosate. Conifers are moderately tolerant during fall and winter. When it is used for site preparation in existing plantations in the spring, the directed spray technique is recommended. In soil, glyphosate is bound tightly, has minimum mobility, and degrades very rapidly. Because it leaves no biologically active residue in soil, no post-treatment waiting period is required for planting. Glyphosate-treated areas are generally subject to reoccupation by competing herbs and woody species.

Glyphosate can be applied from the time target vegetation undergoes full leaf expansion until leaf color change (but before a major frost), provided no major leaf drop has occurred. Complete translocation of glyphosate in the plant happens between 6 and 8 weeks following application. Though vegetation can turn brown when treated from late spring to early summer, best results are obtained for woody species when treatment is done in late summer to early fall. The optimum time to control grasses and ferns, however, is the spring, but not late in the season (August) after the vegetation has curled out (Miller, D.L., 1986). Glyphosate may not be effective on damaged vegetation, such as that caused by logging activities. For effective glyphosate treatment results, a waiting period of up to 1 year may be needed in some cases for the target vegetation to recover. Since glyphosate is inactivated by soil particles, dusty vegetation (like that found along logging roads) should not be treated, nor should unclean water be used as a carrier. Effectiveness is also reduced when rainfall occurs within 6 hours following treatment.

When glyphosate-susceptible non-herbaceous vegetation is treated, browning of vegetation occurs generally within 30-60 days. The herbaceous vegetation normally turns yellow and brown about 10-30 days after treatment. "Browning" increases the fuel source, which greatly facilitates effective late summer burning, and also improves spring burns.

Hexazinone (Velpar L®): Hexazinone is primarily a residual soil-active herbicide. In the plant, it interferes with photosynthetic activity. It remains in the soil for more than 4 weeks. At the recommended rate of 9-18 L/ha product, Velpar® is effective on herbaceous broadleaves, grasses (principally), and some woody broadleaves (especially *Rubus* species). The legumes and some pines exhibit some tolerance to it. Usually it is applied in early spring up to the time of target vegetation bud swell, but not after budburst (De Yoe and White 1985) when leaves are fully formed.

Hexazinone is soluble in water (about 1 kg/100 L in cold water) and mobile, with mobility depending on the soil type. Adequate rainfall is required for its action in soil, but not so much to cause a saturated flow in soil. For efficacy and prevention of unplanned movement to non-target areas, this chemical is not recommended for use on: poorly drained soils (wet soils); soils high in organic matter and clays (approximately 45% clay content); gravelly or rocky soils; soils with greater than 85% sand content; sandy loam soils with less than 2% organic matter content; compacted areas; soils with hardpan close to the surface; frozen ground; and drainage channels.

To increase the effectiveness of hexazinone, the treated site should not be burned after the initial foliage browning because of the contact action of the chemical. Burning should be delayed (usually 60-90 days after adequate rainfall) to allow sufficient root uptake and translocation to the site of action. The general recommendation is to allow at least one defoliation to take place before burning.

Simazine (Simadex 80W®): Like hexazinone, simazine inhibits the photosynthetic process. It also affects nitrogen metabolism and controls herbaceous species, principally grasses. Simadex 80W®, a simazine formulation, is applied at the rate of 5.5-8.2 kg product in 350 L of water per hectare. Uptake of simazine is through the roots, and it is most effective when applied in late fall when root activity is at its maximum. Because of its residual activity (half-life of 4-6 months), it is effective on treated sites where there is a potential problem of re-invasion by seed germination. Its use, therefore, can prolong vegetation suppression beyond that provided by other site preparation treatments (Boyd 1982).

2,4-D: The phenoxy herbicide 2,4-D is effective on broadleaved-herbs and some deciduous species (e.g., alder, cherry), but not on grasses, sedges, or salmonberry. As a growth regulator, it interrupts the mechanism of cell wall formation and elongation. Sprouting is reduced when it is applied early in the season: spring and early summer. Conifers such as ponderosa pine (*Pinus ponderosa*) and Douglas-fir (*Pseudotsuga menziesii*) will also be damaged about this period (ponderosa pine: February to July; Douglas-fir: April to July).

The amine formulations are normally used for stem injection (e.g., hack-and-squirt) and stump treatments. The low volatile esters are broadcast-applied in water at the per hectare rate of 2.2-3.3 kg (a.e.) emulsified in 93 L of water. The 2,4-D esters are more effective on shrubs than amine formulations are. They can also be used for stump and stem injection or frill treatments.

When 2, 4-D is used as a spray-and-burn, at least 1 month should elapse between the chemical treatment and burning. In areas where vegetation species recover quickly, burning should be done by the end of the first summer; otherwise, it can be done after two growing seasons (Stewart 1978).

A ready-to-apply formulation of dichlorprop and 2,4-D ester (Weedone CB®) has recently been registered for forestry use in the control of undesirable woody species (e.g., aspen, alder, and birch) by basal, stump, or stem application.

Triclopyr (Garlon®):   This chemical is a growth-regulator (auxin type) selective herbicide, similar to the phenoxy herbicides (e.g., 2,4-D). It suppresses sprouting of many species well, and it is generally more effective when applied in the spring than the phenoxy herbicides are.

The ester formulation (Garlon 4®) is recommended for site preparation in the United States by aerial application at the rate of 1.1-1.7 kg/ha (a.e.) in 93 L/ha water-based spray. In the dormant season (spring), oil may be used as a carrier (Newton and Dost 1984).

APPLICATION OF HERBICIDES

For vegetation control through chemical means to be effective, the herbicides must be absorbed into plants (via leaves, stems, twigs, or roots) and subsequently translocated (in the case of systemic herbicides) to the site of action in appropriate form and quantity. Herbicide absorption is influenced by herbicide formulation, carrier and orientation, and chemical composition of plant surfaces. Two sets of factors control translocation: the inherent properties of the herbicide; and plant phenology and condition (e.g., plant vigor, water or drought stress, and damaged plant parts). The key to effective vegetation control therefore involves appropriate selection of the following: herbicide formulation, carriers, application rate and spray volume, application season, application method, and supervision.

Herbicide Formulations

The choice of herbicides or their formulations (e.g., 2,4-D ester, 2,4-D amine) depends on the user's knowledge of the vegetation species or plant type (annual or perennial grasses, herbaceous species) on the site needing control. The prescribed herbicide must be able to control the most common and dominant target species.

Carriers

Carriers (diluents) are mixed with herbicides to improve spray coverage, permit uniform distribution of the active ingredients over a large area, and enhance herbicide uptake. The common diluents are water, oil (diesel oil or No. 2 fuel oil), and oil-in-water emulsions. Water may be used to dilute herbicides for application on cut surfaces (hack-and-squirt, stump treatments), foliage (especially new leaves or deciduous species), or soil. Sprays containing oil are used as a dormant treatment to enhance wetting of surfaces, and provide improved herbicide penetration into bark and thick, waxy cuticle. Because oil in a mixture can contribute to rapid foliage kill, thus leading to reduced herbicide absorption and translocation, oil-herbicide sprays should not be applied on young and tender leaves. The oil-water emulsions can be applied on mature deciduous leaves and evergreen foliage that are resistant to water sprays.

Application Rate

For efficacy and economy, and to prevent undesirable effects on the site, proper application rates must be used. Too high a rate can kill plant parts (especially leaves), rapidly resulting in poor herbicide absorption and translocation within the plant. Since the density or the height of vegetation varies from site to site, the spray volume must be adjusted accordingly to improve coverage.

Application Seasons

Figure 13.2 summarizes the preferred seasons (periods of optimum species susceptibility) for applying herbicides in site preparation. Most foliar applied herbicides tend to move with carbohydrates, so the spray period for maximum species susceptibility is generally late spring to early summer when plants are actively growing. The soil-active herbicides such as simazine and hexazinone are generally applied in the spring.

Method of Herbicide Application

Herbicides may be applied for site preparation by broadcast aerial spraying (fixed-wing aircraft and helicopter) and various ground application methods: broadcast ground spraying, ground spot treatment, vehicle-mounted spraying, stem injection (hack-and-squirt), and basal spraying.

Table 13.5 presents a summary of some application methods and techniques for the commonly used herbicides in British Columbia. Details of herbicide application methods or techniques, as well as their advantages and disadvantages, can be found in sources such as the Silviculture Manual (B.C. Ministry of Forests 1987a), Henigman and Beardsley (1985), Newton and Knight (1981), and Edwards (1985).

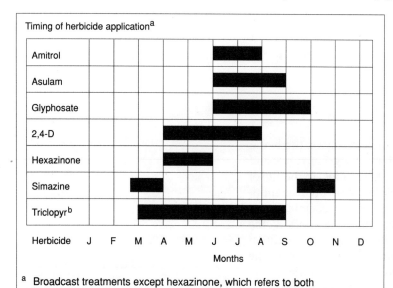

Timing of herbicide application[a]

[a] Broadcast treatments except hexazinone, which refers to both broadcast and spot treatment.

[b] Triclopyr is currently not registered for forestry use in Canada.

FIGURE 13.2.   Optimum herbicide application timing for site preparation.

TABLE 13.5.   Summary of some application methods and techniques for commonly used herbicides in British Columbia

Method	Herbicide	Technique
Aerial broadcast spraying (helicopter, fixed-wing aircraft)	Vision® (glyphosate)	3-6 L/ha in 30-100 L/ha of clean water. Higher volume for dense/multi-level vegetation. Average droplet size (or VMD) 250-500 micron diameter.
	Esteron 600®, For-Ester® (2, 4-D ester)	5.5-8.5L/ha Esteron 600® or 6.6-10.2 L ha For-Ester® in 30-100L/ha. Spray mixture. Carriers: water, oil, oil-water mixture; 10% oil solution best. Avoid spraying after prolonged dry period.
Bark treatment	Esteron 600® For-Ester® (2, 4-D ester) Weedone CB® (2, 4-DP)	Use 3% herbicide oil solution of 2, 4-D ester or full strength Weedone CB®. Treat stems to a height of 50 cm from the ground
Grid spot application	Velpar L® (hexazinone)	Apply 9-18 L full strength product per hectare using a spot gun. Direct application to soil. Lower rates for soils low in organic matter and clay. Spot should be placed 1 m from stem of desirable trees.
Ground broadcast spraying: backpack	Forestamine® (2, 4-D amine) Vision® (glyphosate)	6-8 L Forestamine® in 1000 L of water. Thorough foliage coverage; 3-6 L/ha of Vision® in 100-300 L/ha of clean water. Vegetation not taller than 2.5 m.
	Velpar L® (hexazinone)	9 -18 L/ha. Use at least 5L of water for each litre of Velpar L®.
Ground broadcast spraying: vehicle-mounted sprayers (power-operated hand gun)	For-Ester® Esteron 600® (2,4-D ester)	5-8.0 L (or 6-9 L For Ester®) in 1000 L of water. Vegetation up to 2.5 m tall. Well-developed foliage. Avoid spraying after prolonged dry period. Good coverage; spray to runoff.
Hack-and-squirt or frill	Formula 40F® Forestamine® Guardsman 500® (2, 4-D amine)	For trees > 15 cm dbh make complete frill. Trees < 15 cm dbh make one notch for every 3 cm dbh. All notches should angle downwards to hold herbicide solution. Add 1 mL undiluted product or up to 2:1 dilution per notch. For frill, add sufficient herbicide solution but without runoff. Use full strength for trees > 15 cm dbh.
	Vision® (glyphosate)	Apply 1 mL of undiluted (or up to 50% dilution of 1 mL) product for every 10 cm dbh. Tree > 20 cm dbh may not be controlled.
	Esteron 600® (2, 4-D ester)	Treat freshly cut frill with 3% oil solution (30 L/1000 L) of 2, 4-D Esteron 600®.
Stump treatment	Formula 40F® Forestamine® Guardsman 500® (2, 4-D amine) Vision® (glyphosate)	Cut stem close to ground, at least 50 cm with brush saw or chainsaw. Apply to freshly cut stumps and stubs, using brush or sprayer, immediately with full strength or up to 2:1 water: herbicide dilution. Ensure coverage of cambial layer.
	Esteron 600® (2, 4-D ester)	Mix 30 L Esteron 600® in 1000 L diesel oil, fuel oil, or kerosene. Apply to the freshly cut surface. Ensure coverage of cambial layer.
	Weedone CB® (2, 4-DP)	Apply full strength Weedone CB® to cut stump. Immediate treatment not required.

Sources: Herbicide manufacturers' labels.

TABLE 13.6.   Average costs[a] of herbicide treatments in British Columbia

Treatment	Average costs for 1987 treatments $/ha
Ground broadcast	490
Hack-and-squirt	260
Spotgun (Velpar L®)	320
Fixed-wing aircraft	165
Helicopter	255
[a] Total costs for one entry treatment.	

The choice of any of these methods is influenced by several factors: the allowable registered use as noted on the label; extent and nature of the treatment area; urgency of treatment; accessibility; availability of labor; cost; and sensitivity of the area. Ground application techniques are limited by the steepness or roughness of the terrain, by impediments such as logging residues and other debris, and by size of the target vegetation (in the case of broadcast backpack spraying). Compared to aerial application, ground spraying is less likely to cause chemical drift, and so may allow treatment closer to sensitive ares. Aerial spraying is best used in areas dominated by debris and tall shrubs, where the terrain is steep, or the area is very large or inaccessible.

Aerial herbicide treatments are more cost-effective than ground treatments. Recent average costs of herbicide treatments in British Columbia provided by the B.C Forest Service (Silviculture Branch) are presented in Table 13.6. These include direct on-site supervision costs, overhead and chemical costs. Vision® has been the chemical used except for Velpar L®in grid and spotgun treatments.

SUMMARY

When used properly, herbicides are effective site preparation tools where competing vegetation posses problems to reforestation. They can be used on many sites where burning or mechanical methods are less effective in suppressing resprouts or not feasible because of physical constraints on the site. Where other site preparation objectives are to be satisfied, herbicides combined with prescribed burning or mechanical methods provide the best results. Their use must always conform with laws, regulations, and policies. Follow-up evaluations can determine whether reforestation objectives were met through chemical site preparation or not.

SECTION FOUR

14 GENETIC CONTROL AND IMPROVEMENT OF PLANTING STOCK

D.T. Lester, C.C. Ying, and J.D. Konishi

In addition to appropriate site preparation, nursery culture, and storage, successful reforestation by planting depends on planting stock that contains, at a minimum, those genes which confer adaptation to the environments in which the trees are to grow. By adaptation we mean the genetically programmed responses of a plant to the environment (climate, soils, pests), anticipated as a result of the environments in which past generations of the plant have grown. Adaptation also suggests that the plant has some genetically controlled flexibility ("adaptability") in meeting less predictable environmental challenges.

In the absence of information on how trees grown from seed of various origins are adapted to a particular area, it has been assumed that seed should be collected and used locally. This was the predominant practice in British Columbia until the 1970's. The use of only local seed follows from the expectation that natural selection has resulted in trees that are well adapted within their area of origin but not necessarily in other areas. The same expectation guided early tree improvement efforts toward the selection of outstanding individuals within a relatively small geographic area, rather than the introduction of seed from distant locations. As tree improvement programs mature, the genetic quality of initial selections will become evident and, in some cases, the inclusion of non-local parents will significantly improve the gene pool.

Reforestation using planting stock only from local seed may minimize biological risk, but it also has several disadvantages. These include: the difficulty of delineating what constitutes local seed without reliable information on environmental variation within, as well as among, zones; the likelihood that each species may require a zone that is somewhat different in shape and size; and the administrative complexity in all phases of seed and seedling production. One detailed analysis of reforestation concluded that, for the area studied, the limiting factor in meeting reforestation objectives was not funding, but rather lack of seed from specific seed zones (Teeguarden and von Sperber 1968).

Along with efforts to develop genetic resources of local forests, tree breeders establish and evaluate plantations using seed collected from well-documented locations throughout most of a species' range. These experiments are called provenance tests. Performance of the different seedlots is then interpreted to establish geographic patterns of genetic variation and to estimate the effects of seed transfer. For some species, these tests have been showing that trees from local seed are not always the most productive. There are several possible explanations for the improved productivity of non-local seed: seasonal growth patterns that are overly conservative in relation to present day climate; economic emphasis on stem volume (which removes reproductive ability as a strong element in selection); adaptability to environments created by current harvesting practices (especially for clearcutting followed by planting of species common to later stages of succession); and other genetic changes caused by gene migration or mutation.

PROVENANCE SELECTION

After a species has been chosen, identifying the best available provenance is next. The word "provenance" refers to the geographical origin of seed from native forests. Although the precise area represented by any given provenance is not usually known, provenance tests reveal general patterns of genetic variation associated with geography. As well, documentation for seed collections used in provenance testing is also usually adequate for relocating the sampled area. Provenance tests established in British Columbia during the 1960's and 1970's (Illingworth 1978a,b) are yielding a wealth of information about geographic variation, and providing the basis for continued refinement of seed transfer guidelines. Although the older provenance tests are now only about one-quarter of rotation age, they identify seed transfers that are clearly to be avoided and suggest other seed transfers that promise significantly increased productivity.

A decision to use the best available provenances sometimes involves seed transfers over substantial distances and may entail risks. Provenance tests can only illustrate responses to environments in which they are grown. Rare events, such as historic freezes and droughts, may not be experienced during the test period. Integrated laboratory and field testing, however, can markedly reduce risks, and confidence grows as the understanding of geographic patterns of genetic variation evolves.

The main features of provenance variation for the major native conifers in British Columbia are outlined as follows:

Lodgepole pine

The pattern of provenance variation is complex, but four geographic regions can be readily detected in measurements of provenance responses to environments throughout interior British Columbia. Table 14.1 lists some of the distinguishing features of trees from each region.

The central and southern British Columbia-southern Alberta region is of most practical interest to reforestation in British Columbia (Figure 14.1). Within this region, no clear latitudinal and longitudinal pattern has been evident, although there is large variation among provenances. Generally, trees grown from seed collected at high elevations (above 1500 m) are slow growing and susceptible to needle cast (*Lophodermella concolor*) when grown at low to mid-elevations.

Seed collections containing genes from coastal environments are poorly adapted to interior (continental) environments. Introducing seed with any trace of coastal genes into interior forests must be avoided. The extent

TABLE 14.1. Features of lodgepole pine trees grown in interior British Columbia from seed collected in the indicated geographic region

Geographic region	Features
Pacific Coast	Least frost-hardy; dark green needles
Coast-Interior transition	Susceptible to frost and needle cast
Yukon-northern B.C.	Frost-hardy, susceptible to needle cast, slow growing; yellowish foliage
Central and southern B.C. southern Alberta	Frost-hardy, fast growing

FIGURE 14.1. Provenance variation in lodgepole pine at the Prince George Tree Improvement Centre in central British Columbia. Taller trees are from the Nechako River provenance. Shorter trees are from the Nanaimo provenance and show the reduced vigor and winter injury typical of coastal provenances transferred to the Interior.

of genetic differentiation between coastal and interior lodgepole pine is recognized taxonomically in the designation var. *contorta* for the coastal variety and var. *latifolia* for the interior variety.

Interior spruce

In the central and southern interior of British Columbia, spruce has shown no clear pattern of genetic variation associated with latitude or longitude. However, genetic differences are associated with elevation, and trees grown from seed collected at high elevations are slow growing. Fast-growing provenances develop rapidly in a variety of environments.

Interior Douglas-fir

In the southern Interior, seed collected in the southern coastal-interior transition area has produced the most vigorous trees. This result is markedly different than that described above for lodgepole pine. In the central Interior, near the northern limit of Douglas-fir, movement of seed north from the southern Interior has resulted in poorer survival and growth as compared to that for more local provenances. Provenance testing for both interior spruce and interior Douglas-fir has been much less thorough than for lodgepole pine.

Coastal Douglas-fir

Genetic differentiation associated with geography in coastal Douglas-fir parallels the major climatic regions and is much more clearly defined between maritime and subcontinental climate than from north to south along the coast. Biological risk in seed transfer is thus much higher in an east-west direction than in a north-south direction. Both natural selection and random genetic changes seem to have played a role in genetic differentiation of coastal Douglas-fir.

Sitka spruce

Sitka spruce shows strong north-south and coast-inland trends in growth and hardiness. Provenances from latitudes to the south and from outer coastal areas are faster growing but less hardy than northern and inner coastal provenances. Near the coast, the transfer of seed from more southern latitudes can result in growth rates that are substantially greater than those from local seed; and risk from poor hardiness is low as long as the trees are planted in areas with a strong maritime climate. In contrast, genetic changes from coastal to inland climates are rapid and complex, especially where Sitka spruce hybridizes freely with white spruce (e.g., in the Skeena and Nass valleys) and where coast-inland seed transfers involve high risk.

Sitka spruce provenances vary not only in growth and hardiness, but also in their ability to tolerate attack by the spruce weevil (*Pissodes strobi*). Two provenances, Kitwanga and Big Qualicum, have shown a high degree of tolerance. The former is from the inland portion of the Skeena River and is believed to be an introgressed population of Sitka and white spruce. The latter provenance is from the southeastern coast of Vancouver Island.

These results illustrate the potential of using non-local seed in reforestation. Table 14.2 summarizes some of the more promising opportunities for seed transfers in British Columbia.

TABLE 14.2. Seed transfer opportunities in British Columbia as indicated by provenance testing

Species	Provenance	New environment
Lodgepole pine	Interior wet belt	Interior, south of 55° N
Interior spruce	Interior wet belt	Interior, south of 55° N
Interior Douglas-fir	Southern coast - interior transition	Southern interior - moist and wet zones
Coastal Douglas-fir	Western Washington	Vancouver Island and lower coast
Sitka spruce	Oregon-Washington coast	Western Vancouver Island, Queen Charlotte Islands

SEED PLANNING ZONES AND SEED TRANSFER GUIDELINES IN BRITISH COLUMBIA

The delineation of geographic zones by which seed movement is controlled evolves with our increasing knowledge of genetics and ecology for each species. Sometimes the nomenclature used in identifying these geographic zones also changes. The term "seed zone" refers to a somewhat arbitrarily designated geographic area. Seed zones were identified for the purpose of ensuring that reforestation stock was planted within the same general area in which seed was collected from wild stands. A "seed orchard planning zone" delineates an area within which parent trees have been selected and propagated for the purpose of producing seed. The selected parents often represent a broader sample of the zone than do wild stand seed collections. Orchard seed is to be used only within the zone from which the parents came. In some zones, orchard seed use is further constrained by elevation. For the practical purpose of controlling seed transfer, the two types of seed zones can be combined and designated by the term "seed planning zone," although it should be remembered that seed from wild stands is expected to be different from orchard seed in both genetic quality and physiological quality (orchard seed benefiting from the better nutrition and more available moisture achieved through orchard management). Seed planning zones for the major reforestation species are based largely on results of seed source testing.

The initial seed zones for British Columbia were delineated only for Vancouver Island and the south coast mainland in the 1940's (B.C. Forest Service 1946). As reforestation practices expanded into the Interior, and initial

FIGURE 14.2. Forest tree seed zones of British Columbia: 1974 - 1982.

biogeoclimatic classification identified different environments for tree planting, 67 numbered seed zones within 8 regions were designated to control the movement of seed (Figure 14.2). As additional information on provenance performance and biogeoclimatic zoning became available, seed planning zones were reduced in number to 37 in the late 1970's and early 1980's. For most seed planning zones, from 50 to several hundred parent trees were selected to establish the initial gene pool for orchards. The selected trees were distributed throughout each planning zone and covered the elevational distribution for the species to be planted. For some orchards, genetic differences associated with elevation were known or suspected to be large enough to require elevational limits on seed transfer within a planning zone.

For interior British Columbia, the current seed planning zones are shown in Figure 14.3 are unchanged. For the coast, there has been a major reduction in the number of zones (Figure 14.4).

Where provenances have been evaluated in extensive comparative tests over several years, detailed rules for seed transfer can be developed. Examples of current rules for three species follow.

Lodgepole pine

1. As a general rule, seed collected in a zone should be used in that zone with the following elevational constraints:

	Maximum transfer (m)	
Latitudinal range	Upward	Downward
49 - 56°	300	100
56 - 60°	100	50

2. Transfer between zones is allowed with the following constraints:

- Latitude: no more than 2° northward; no more than 1° southward from origin.
- Longitude: no more than 3° eastward; no more than 2° westward from origin.
- Elevation: as in (1) above
- Seed transfer from the coast or coastal-interior transition into the interior is **prohibited**.
- Seed transfer across major biogeoclimatic subzones (e.g., from dry to moist or wet zones and vice versa) is **prohibited** in the absence of substantial test results indicating minimal risk and significant potential for gains in productivity.

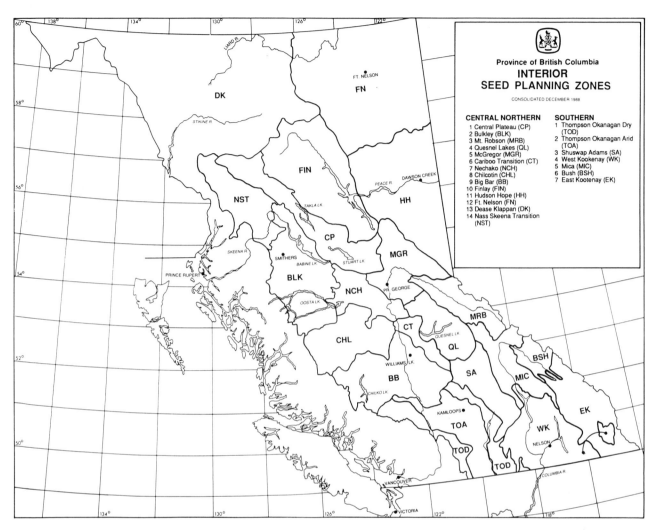

FIGURE 14.3. Interior seed planning zones: 1988.

Interior spruce

1. Seed transfer guidelines are similar to those of lodgepole pine except for elevational constraints for transfer both within and between seed planning zones. The guidelines are as follows:

	Maximum transfer (m)	
Latitudinal range	**Upward**	**Downward**
49 - 53° (Nelson Forest Region only)	400	200
49 - 56°	300	100
56 - 58°	200	100
58 - 60°	100	50

Coastal Douglas-fir

1. There are three seed planning zones: Georgia Lowland, Maritime, and Submaritime (Figure 14.4).

2. Within the Georgia Lowland, there are no elevational limits to seed transfer. Seed cannot be transferred out of the zone. Seed transfer into the zone is limited by the transfer distances indicated for the other two zones.

3. Seed transfer for the Maritime and Submaritime Zones is controlled only by the following geographic limits which apply both within and between zones.

Seed planning zone	North	South	Maximum transfer Upward (m)	Downward (m)
Maritime	3°	2°	300	100
Submaritime	2°	1°	200	100

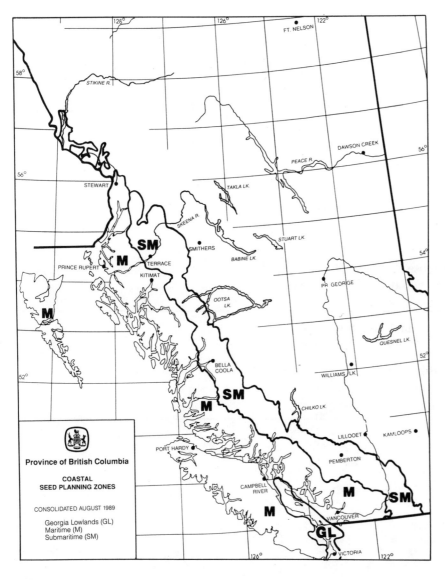

FIGURE 14.4. Coastal seed planning zones: 1989.

For other species, seed transfer guidelines are based on provenance information available from British Columbia, provenance information from elsewhere, general patterns of genetic variation associated with geography, and biogeoclimatic classification. As contrasting examples, the only restriction on transfer of western white pine seed on the coast is movement east of a planning zone boundary; most other species have limits comparable to those for Douglas-fir.

Because of the environmental complexity of British Columbia, it is not feasible to develop guidelines that would be applicable to all situations. Seed planning zones and transfer guidelines provide a broad framework for control of seed movement. Guidelines are reviewed at 5-year intervals. Local discretion is encouraged where there is evidence favoring minor variances to these guidelines.

SELECTION OF INDIVIDUAL TREES

Silviculture, without genetic improvement, cannot expect to achieve maximum productivity. It is equally true that the benefits of planting genetically improved stock are likely to be diminished without appropriate silvicultural practices. Where intensive silviculture is warranted, genetic improvement and stand management prescriptions should be complementary. Where stand management is expected to be of low intensity, genetic improvement may represent a major contribution to the success of future forests (in disease resistance or early plantation survival), or may be a practice that is very difficult to justify from an economic perspective.

The initial cycle of genetic improvement for the major conifers of British Columbia has concentrated on the selection and testing of individual trees from native forests. The heterogeneity of these forests has made it difficult to apply methods in which candidate trees are carefully compared with adjacent trees of similar age and position in the stand. Inaccessibility has further complicated the selection process, and in some cases, selection has emphasized geographic representation more than physical traits of the selected tree. Nevertheless, large numbers of trees have been selected and most are now represented in clone banks, seed orchards, and progeny tests. An example of one selected parent is shown in Figure 14.5. The result of selection efforts can be summarized in terms of numbers of selected trees (Table 14.3). This represents an enormous amount of work by many people over the last 20 years.

Volume growth rate has been the primary trait of interest, although selected trees were also required to be free of disease. For some species, straightness, branch angle, and branch diameter were additional selection criteria. The

TABLE 14.3. Summary of selected trees by species and by status of progeny testing

Species	Number of selected trees		Number of parents in progeny tests	
	Coast	Interior	Coast	Interior
Douglas-fir	968	1532	372	1316
Lodgepole pine				
var. *contorta*	0	134	0	0
var. *latifolia*	—	1352	—	1150
Western hemlock	1404	0	170	0
Mountain hemlock	5	0	0	0
Western white pine	168	135	0	0
Sitka spruce	706	—	0	—
Interior spruce	—	3209	—	1850
Engelmann spruce	171	0	0	0
Pacific silver fir	422	—	0	—
Western redcedar	453	0	0	0
Yellow-cedar	269	—	0	—
Grand fir	53	0	0	0
Larch	0	50	0	0
Cottonwood	13	0	0	0

realization that the second-growth forest might produce wood with qualities that differ from those in wood traditionally produced in British Columbia has prompted increased interest in the potential of tree breeding to influence wood quality. Relative density, as a major factor in strength of wood used for structural purposes and in cellulose yield, may become an important trait. Pest resistance, currently of interest in weevil-infested spruce and because of rust-induced losses in lodgepole and white pine, is likely to receive more emphasis in future breeding efforts.

METHODS TO ACHIEVE GENETIC IMPROVEMENT

Seed

Seed currently represents nearly the only form in which improved genes can be packaged. Although significant progress continues to be made in various techniques of vegetative propagation – including the rooting of cuttings, and tissue and cell culture – it is unlikely that large-scale clonal propagation will soon be a dominant method of producing planting stock for reforestation in British Columbia.

Seed may be obtained in a variety of ways, each of which has its own combination of cost and potential genetic benefit. From natural stand collection to the production of highly selected full-sib families, opportunities exist for obtaining seed that will be at least as good as, and often remarkably better than, seed resulting from seed acquisition practices of the past. The more common seed production practices are reviewed below.

FIGURE 14.5. A parental selection of lodgepole pine from interior British Columbia.

Natural stand seed collections

Although many seed orchards are now reaching high levels of production, seed collection in unimproved natural stands remains the common source of tree seed in Canada (Schooley and Mullin 1987). At best, natural stand collections offer only limited opportunities for genetic improvement. Even here, however, control of seed collection is important to minimize the risk of using seed that has **less** genetic potential than seed from the forest being replaced.

Without information showing that seed of non-local origin is reliably better than local seed, the seed transfer guidelines presented earlier should be used to guide location of stands which are healthy, vigorous, of above-average stem quality, and representative of the area to be reforested. Such stands may produce large quantities of seed at very low cost. One good seed year may meet seed requirements for several years.

The principal disadvantages are lack of any control over the genetic and physiological quality of seed, and no influence on the periodicity or size of seed crops. For interior spruce at high elevation, the long periods between flower crops, aggravated by the effects of spruce budworm and severe weather, offer little promise that unmanaged natural stands will provide reliable seed crops. For most other species, wild stand collections remain as one way to obtain seed.

Where provenance information is available, natural stand collections or seed production areas may offer opportunities for substantial genetic gains. Table 14.2 shows some examples for British Columbia. Unfortunately, where the indicated provenances are outside local jurisdiction, access to genetically better seed may be complicated or impossible. In addition, some of the best provenances may no longer be available as a consequence of harvesting.

Seed production areas

One step beyond opportunistic seed collection in natural stands is the designation of certain stands as seed production areas. These can be managed to an intensity that ranges from no management for seed production, to selection of crop trees, culling of non-crop trees, and use of fertilization, root pruning, and other cone promotion techniques that enhance seed production.

Seed collected in unmanaged seed production areas has the same advantages and disadvantages as seed collected in natural stands, except that a seed production area, if withdrawn from harvesting plans, can provide a continuing source of seed whose quality will be somewhat known from repeated use.

Through managed seed production areas, modest improvements can be made in the size and quality of seed crops. Removal of non-crop trees will promote larger cone crops and reduce the potential for inbreeding, and may provide small genetic gains. These gains will be predictably small in most cases because an appropriate density for the residual stand will limit the intensity with which crop trees can be selected. The most substantial genetic gains are likely where a trait, such as disease resistance, is strongly inherited and more than one-half of the prospective seed production area is infected. Unlike in unmanaged seed production areas, cultural treatments in the managed area can significantly increase the size of seed crops and, often, reduce their periodicity.

In British Columbia, seed production areas represent only an interim source of seed, although seed needs for species of lesser economic importance could be met for decades in such areas. Presently, seed production areas are being developed for western white pine and western larch. An additional opportunity would be in provenances identified (by provenance testing) as having high genetic potential.

Seed orchards

Seed orchards are the principal way in which genetically improved seed is being produced for the conifers of major economic importance in British Columbia. Seed orchards are collections of individuals selected for specific traits. These individuals usually represent the seed zone in which orchard seed will be used. The trees are brought together in one location by the grafting or rooting of many shoots from the selected parent to produce a clone. For Douglas-fir, some early orchards included seedlings from open-pollinated parents because graft incompatibility resulted in the loss of many orchard trees.

Trees in seed orchards are arranged randomly to produce a thorough mixing of genes in orchard seed. Between 30 and 100 clones or progenies are included. For most species, progeny tests have been established to evaluate the genetic worth of each parental clone. Clones with poor genetic value are being removed from orchards to raise the amount of genetic gain.

Choosing the site for a seed orchard is one of the most critical activities in a successful seed orchard program. Experience accumulated from many parts of the northern hemisphere shows that moving orchard trees into environments which are warmer and drier than their native habitat results in large increases and reduced periodicity in cone production. Most orchards are now located to the south of seed planning zones. However, establishing seed orchards outside seed planning zones has created a problem of genetic contamination from local pollen. Research into this problem may influence seed orchard location in the future (El-Kassaby et al. 1986).

Most orchards are managed intensively with irrigation, pest control, crown control (to facilitate cone collection), and treatments to promote seed production. The ease with which seed can be produced by chemical treatment on small trees of some species (e.g., western hemlock) has stimulated interest in large-scale seed production on potted trees. Seed orchards in pots would allow a high degree of control in orchard management and require much less land.

Seed orchard planning, like much of forestry, is an exercise in predicting the future. Seed orchards require several years after establishment before they produce seed crops large enough to warrant cone collection. This means that estimates of seedling needs for periods of 10 - 30 years ahead are required. These estimates are matched with seed yield estimates for orchards 10 - 15 years after establishment to produce a "target date" by which an orchard is expected to produce the required amount of seed. For orchards in British Columbia, seed yield estimates have generally been conservative and many orchards are producing large quantities of seed earlier than expected. Progress in identifying treatments that promote seed production has helped to shorten the time to full production, as well as to reduce the periodicity that characterizes seed production of most conifers in forest environments.

In British Columbia, the current status of seed orchard establishment reflects the variety of priorities influencing the allocation of limited resources. It also points up the differences in the speed with which different species can be induced to produce seed. The provincial goal is to produce enough orchard seed for 120 million seedlings by the year 2000. This represents about one-half of the anticipated demand for planting stock. The status of seed orchard development over the last two decades is summarized in Table 14.4.

Seed orchards usually have a planned life of about 30 years. With crown control, seed production can probably be extended for a longer period. For orchards not supported by a breeding program, an extended life may be appropriate. Where provenance and progeny testing are identifying greater genetic potential, orchards may be

TABLE 14.4. Summary of current status for seed orchards in British Columbia (from B.C. Ministry of Forests 1986 a,b)

Species	Orchard status (ha)		
	Developing	Established	Producing
Douglas-fir (coastal)	2.8	17.4	35.6
Lodgepole pine (interior)	16.0	13.9	4.2
Western hemlock	3.8	16.8	.7
Sitka spruce	2.7	0	4.7
Interior spruce	7.4	36.4	0
Engelmann spruce	3.6	0	0
Pacific silver fir	2.0	8.6	0
Western redcedar	0	1.6	0
Yellow-cedar	0	1.8	0

replaced at younger ages. Coastal Douglas-fir will be the first species for which selections made in first-generation progeny tests will be used to produce a new orchard. This will contain genetic gains both from the progeny-tested parents and from within-progeny genetic variation.

Clonal Propagation

Using seed to deliver genetic improvement is not without disadvantages. Useful gene combinations are lost as genes recombine and interact in the sexual process. As a consequence, the progeny are somewhat genetically different than the parents. Clonal propagation offers several advantages, a major one being that the parental genotype is duplicated in clonal progeny. As well, it allows improved genotypes to be used more quickly; it eliminates inbreeding in planting stock; it offers access to gene combinations which may occur only in one or few individuals; it allows the mass production of valuable but expensive genotypes; it allows the close control of genetic diversity in plantations; and it simplifies management of production orchards (hedge orchards or stoolbeds).

Unfortunately, routine use of clonal propagation is not yet possible for more than a few species. Cottonwoods and willows have been produced clonally for centuries and some conifers are clonally propagated by cuttings or grafts, mainly for the woody ornamentals trade. For most conifers, however, rooting ability, growth rate, and growth form are closely related to age of the parent tree. The ease with which clonal stock can be produced declines rapidly after the first few years of seedling life. Similarly, sophisticated techniques of cell and tissue culture have not yet made mass propagation of desirable conifer genotypes common.

Despite the difficulties in clonally propagating most conifers on a large scale, a few programs of conifer mass propagation by vegetative techniques are currently in operation. Two of the best known have produced millions of rooted cuttings of Norway spruce for forest plantation establishment in West Germany and Sweden (Kleinschmidt 1983) and of cryptomeria in Japan (Toda 1974). The Japanese experience with reforestation by rooted cuttings extends over several centuries. In Canada, rooted cuttings of spruces are expected to have a place in reforestation (Armson et al. 1980).

For forest regeneration in British Columbia, it seems likely that clonal propagation will be restricted in the immediate future to a few special situations. For yellow-cedar, 400 000 rooted cuttings are being produced annually with cuttings taken from seedlings or from hedges kept physiologically juvenile by severe shearing. The appeal of clonal propagation in yellow-cedar is heightened by problems of seed supply from natural stands. Clonal propagation also has promise for the mass production of plants from the few seeds obtained by crossing parents shown in progeny tests to have outstanding genetic potential for growth. In the latter case, multiplication by seed may be more economical when seed orchards containing the outstanding parents reach a productive age.

Use of Genetically Improved Planting Stock

Large quantities of orchard seed will soon be available for most of the important conifers in British Columbia. As a result, decisions will have to be made about how best to use this new resource. How genetically improved seed will affect silviculture is not known. Interest in maximizing the establishment of improved seedlings will prompt reappraisals of current practices, including seed processing, nursery activities, site preparation, and planting density. In some cases, greater care with certain practices may be required; in other cases, less.

Until orchards reach their full productive potential, too little improved seed will be available to cover all hectares needing reforestation. Allocating what is available to higher quality lands will be the most likely practice, but the assumptions underlying this should be checked. Another question will be whether mixtures of orchard seed should be planted, or family blocks.

Similar issues will arise if large numbers of clonally propagated trees become available. The higher cost of clonal material means that even closer attention will have to be paid to ensure that genetically improved stock is used appropriately.

The need to maintain a level of genetic diversity commensurate with risk is an increasingly important issue as tree breeders continue to refine genetic variation. Keeping track of source identity and establishing an adequately broad genetic base are of major importance when plantations can be established with clonally propagated stock. Legislated regulations in some countries specify how clones should be used, in terms of minimum numbers to be maintained in production, minimum numbers to be planted per unit area, and minimum distance between plantings of the same clone. Such regulations are under consideration in some parts of Canada. Less restrictive regulations may result if plantations begin to use the greater genetic potential (but reduced genetic diversity) inherent in seedlings where half- or full-sib progenies are established in family blocks rather than in intimate mixtures.

SUMMARY

The opportunity to use genetic variation in British Columbia reforestation is great. With a current planting program of 200 million trees annually, relatively small genetic gains can result in significant benefits.

Options for applying genetic principles include the following: eugenic practices in seed collection from natural stands; using non-local provenances where provenance test data indicate a high benefit:risk ratio; capturing, through seed orchards, genetic variation among individual trees; and, perhaps in time, achieving the mass multiplication of outstanding individuals through techniques of vegetative propagation. In the immediate future in British Columbia, seed production areas will provide seed for western white pine; untested seed orchards will supply seed for Sitka spruce, western hemlock, Pacific silver fir, western redcedar, and yellow-cedar; and progeny testing will provide genetic gains from seed orchards of lodgepole pine, interior spruce, and coastal and interior Douglas-fir.

As the quantity and genetic quality of improved planting stock increase, the next challenge will be to determine how forest regeneration systems and stand management practices should be modified so that projected genetic benefits are assured.

SEED BIOLOGY, COLLECTION AND POST-HARVEST HANDLING

15

C.L. Leadem, R.D. Eremko, and I.H. Davis

An important element of forest renewal in British Columbia is the availability of high quality seeds. Such seeds are clean and sound, store well, and retain a high capability to produce healthy seedlings. At present, more than 95% of the seeds used for reforestation are obtained from natural forest stands. The remainder are produced in seed orchards. The size of seed crops and the interval between them in natural stands are highly variable, and dependent on a large number of interrelated biological and environmental factors. When a good crop occurs, enough cones must be collected and placed in storage to meet the province's requirements through years of poor production. The capability of stored seeds to produce vigorous seedlings is affected by seed quality at the time of collection, and the care with which seeds are handled during collection, transport, processing, and storage.

This chapter discusses the development of seed crops, the assessment of crop quality and maturity, cone collection and handling procedures, and seed extraction and storage. Emphasis is placed on the maintenance of seed quality, not only in the field, but throughout all seed-handling processes.

SEED BIOLOGY

The following discussion of seed biology is a synthesis of material obtained from several sources: Allen and Owens 1972; Schopmeyer 1974; Dobbs et al. 1976; Puritch and Vyse 1972; Eis and Craigdallie 1981; Huber 1981; Miller et al. 1984; Owens and Molder 1984 a,b,c,d; Alden 1985; Edwards 1986; Miller 1986; Owens 1986; and Sutherland 1986.

Seed Formation and Development

A mature seed is essentially a dormant, living organism (the embryo) surrounded by food storage tissue (megagametophyte) and a protective covering (the seedcoat) (Figure 15.1). The initiation, development, and maturation of cones and seeds are collectively referred to as the reproductive cycle. In British Columbia conifers, the reproductive cycle varies by species and can take anywhere from 17 to 28 months.

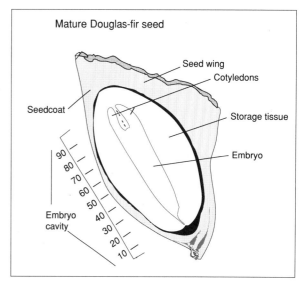

FIGURE 15.1. The structure of a seed.

In the earliest stages of the reproductive cycle, buds are formed on elongating vegetative shoots. Differentiation into vegetative and reproductive buds begins in spring, and by midsummer anatomical differences are apparent when buds are dissected and observed with a hand lens. When buds become dormant in the late summer or early fall, reproductive buds contain recognizable pollen cones or seed cones, and are protected by tightly overlapping scales. A pollen cone consists of an axis bearing leaf-like structures (microsporophylls). Each microsporophyll has two to several pollen sacs (microsporangia) attached to its lower surface. Within the pollen sacs, pollen mother cells form. After dormancy, each pollen mother cell produces four microspores by meiotic division. Meiosis is a sequence of complex nuclear changes which results in haploid cells that contain only half the original number of chromosomes. The microspores separate and develop into pollen grains through a series of non-meiotic divisions. The sequence of pollen development is illustrated for Douglas-fir in Figure 15.2.

A seed cone also consists of an axis bearing bracts. An ovuliferous scale, supporting two ovules on its upper surface, is attached to the axis above each bract. Each ovule is surrounded by a covering called the integument, which later becomes the seedcoat. A single mother cell in the central tissue of each ovule undergoes meiotic division to produce four haploid megaspores (Figure 15.3). As the ovule matures, only one of the megaspores remains functional while the other three degenerate. This megaspore develops into the large megagametophyte which contains the eggs within the ovule. Each haploid megagametophyte normally contains several eggs, which are also haploid.

In the spring of the second year, the pollen cones elongate, causing the rapidly enlarging pollen sacs to separate. At the same time, the internodes of the seed cones elongate, separating the bracts so that the pollen can enter. During warm weather, the pollen sacs dry out, break open, and release the pollen. The pollen is transported by wind and drifts down among the bracts and scales of the seed cones to the ovules at their bases. This transfer of pollen from the male cone to the receptive female cone is referred to as pollination.

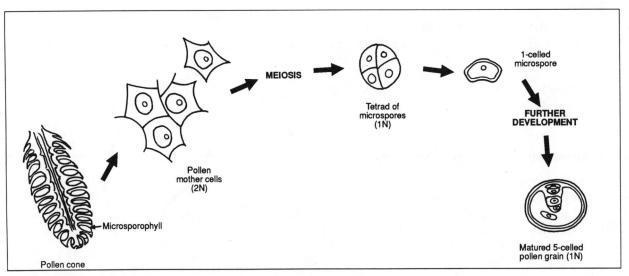

FIGURE 15.2.   Pollen development in Douglas-fir (after Allen and Owens 1972).

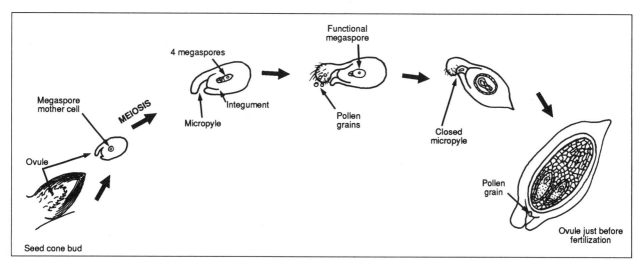

FIGURE 15.3. Ovule development in Douglas-fir (after Allen and Owens 1972).

There are four basic mechanisms by which pollen is drawn into the ovule. In species such as western redcedar (*Thuja plicata*), yellow-cedar (*Chamaecyparis nootkatensis*), pines (*Pinus* spp.), and spruces (*Picea* spp.), the receptive ovule secretes a pollination drop, a watery drop containing sugars (Figure 15.4). Pollen lands on this drop and as the drop evaporates it recedes into the ovule, pulling the pollen grain down into the micropyle, a small opening at the narrow end of the ovule.

The true firs (*Abies* spp.) and mountain hemlock (*Tsuga mertensiana*) have a different pollination mechanism. Instead of a pollination drop, many microscopic droplets are secreted on arm-like or funnel-like extensions of the ovule, and pollen is collected on these droplets. The extensions then collapse inward, carrying the pollen into the micropyle. In western hemlock (*Tsuga heterophylla*), the pollen has small spines which attach to the waxy cuticle of the bract. The pollen then forms long pollen tubes which grow into the micropyle. In Douglas-fir and larch (*Larix* spp.), long hairs around the micropyle—rather than secretions—trap the pollen. The hairs then grow into the micropyle carrying the pollen with them.

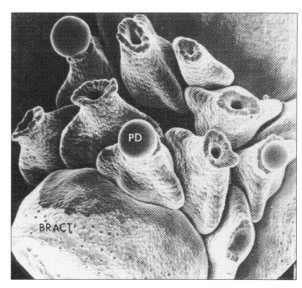

FIGURE 15.4. Secretion of a pollen drop (PD) by a receptive ovule (Owens and Molder 1984).

After pollination, the cone scales close rapidly. Within a short time the pollen grains germinate and a pollen tube develops and penetrates the inner tissue of the ovule. A sperm cell from the pollen tube fuses with an egg cell of the ovule. The fusion of the sperm nucleus with the egg nucleus is referred to as fertilization. This fusion doubles the chromosomes, restoring their number to that characteristic of the species. The time between pollen tube growth and fertilization may vary greatly, from 1 week in Douglas-fir to 1 year in pines.

The fertilized egg cell divides and differentiates to form a recognizable embryo. Ovules of many conifers do not require pollination for seed development to continue, but lacking fertilization, these seeds will not contain an embryo. Pines and most spruces, however, do require a pollen stimulus for seeds to develop.

TABLE 15.1. Origin and composition of seed tissues

Period	Tissue	Chromosome number	Origin
Pre-fertilization	Pollen cone	2 N	Male
	Pollen	1 N	Male
	Seed cone	2 N	Female
	Egg	1 N	Female
Post-fertilization	Storage tissue	1 N	Megagametophyte
	Embryo	2 N	Fusion of egg and sperm
	Seedcoat	2 N	Integument of ovule (female parent tissue)

The fully developed seed is composed of several types of tissue (Table 15.1). As each seed matures, the haploid megagametophyte and the diploid embryo undergo a series of physiological changes, part of which is an increase in levels of carbohydrates, nitrogenous compounds, fats and organic acids. The embryo contains some nutrients, but the major food storage function is assumed by the megagametophyte. Also associated with maturation is a natural decrease in seed moisture content.

Factors Influencing Seed Formation and Development

For most coniferous species found in British Columbia, the entire reproductive cycle takes approximately 17 months (Figure 15.5). The time between pollination and fertilization is several weeks. Subsequent seed development is continuous over several months. Release of mature seeds begins in late summer/early fall of the same year as pollination, and may continue into late winter/early spring.

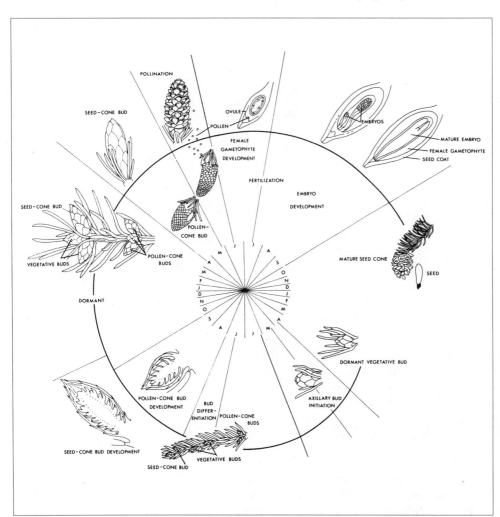

For species such as pine and yellow-cedar, reproductive cycles are approximately 26 and 28 months, respectively (Figures 15.6 and 15.7). In pines, pollination occurs in the spring of the second year of development, but the process stops once pollen tubes and ovules have partially developed. Development resumes in the third year, with fertilization in the spring and seed maturation by fall. Yellow-cedar exhibits another variation in this longer cycle. Fertilization occurs shortly after pollination in the second year, but seed development slows down and stops in late summer. The seeds overwinter, complete their development in the spring of the third year, and mature in the fall.

In addition to interspecies differences, variations in the length of the reproductive cycle may occur among individual trees of the same species. Geographic location and local climate may

FIGURE 15.5. A common reproductive cycle of spruce in British Columbia (after Owens 1986).

also affect the length of the cycle. The stages and sequence of development, however, are consistent among all coniferous trees.

Because of these biological and environmental factors, seed crops do not necessarily develop successfully every year. The time between seed crops, referred to as crop periodicity, varies with the species, tree nutrition, weather, pollination failure, insects, and disease. Good seed crops are generally followed by either poor or very light crops, since seed production is a major drain on the tree's metabolic resources. Consequently, several years of reduced production are necessary to replace depleted reserves, restore foliage, and produce potential cone buds.

The initiation of reproductive buds is also thought to be influenced by variations in climate. In the year prior to seed maturation—or 2 years before in pines—warm, sunny, summer weather is

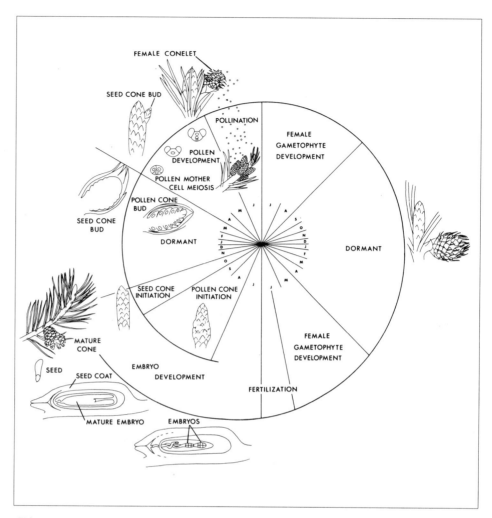

FIGURE 15.6.   The reproductive cycle of pine (after Owens 1986).

thought to promote bud initiation. Low spring temperatures and high rainfall in the year of seed production may adversely affect pollination and, therefore, fertilization. Seed cone abortion as a result of low temperatures soon after pollination can be common. Frost may kill pollen and ovules without leaving any external signs of injury. As well, post-fertilization seed losses may be caused by early summer moisture deficits.

Insects and disease may affect seed development and maturation, although their impact varies among sites and over time. When heavy cone crops follow light crops, insect damage is generally minimal because insect populations, governed by the availability of food, are low. The occurrence of several medium or good crops in succession allows insect populations to build up again, thus causing serious damage. When light crops follow heavy crops, the light crops are virtually destroyed.

Insects affect seed production either directly by destroying or damaging developing cones, or indirectly by attacking other parts of the tree (see Chapter 21). Diseases generally cause seed failure in the infected cones, or may result in abnormal germination. Some diseases such as sirococcus (*Sirococcus strobilinus*) blight may not immediately affect seed production, but the infection may be carried within the seeds to impede later stages of

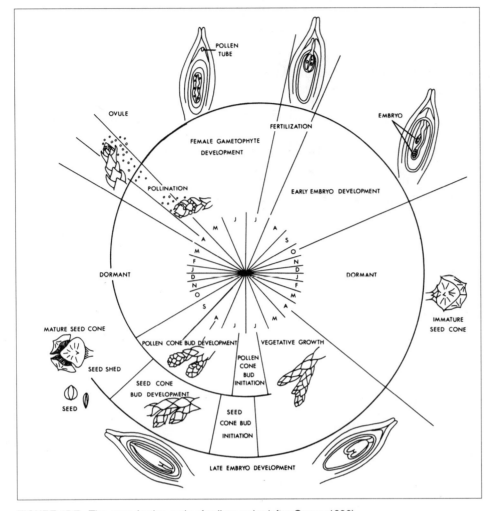

FIGURE 15.7. The reproductive cycle of yellow-cedar (after Owens 1986).

the reforestation process (see Chapter 20). Since sirococcus blight infects the current shoots and needles, it can seriously damage spruce, lodgepole pine (*Pinus contorta*), and ponderosa pine (*Pinus ponderosa*) seedlings in the nursery. Chapter 21 provides a summary of common British Columbia cone and seed pests and their damage.

Predation by birds and squirrels can cause additional seed losses. Birds may eat reproductive buds, and may attack mature cones to obtain the seeds. Squirrels usually begin cutting cones in late summer and continue harvesting until seed fall.

Man can also impede seed development, especially by collecting cones prior to seed maturation, so that poor seed quality results. On the other hand, man can enhance the production of mature, viable seeds by correctly manipulating the variables that influence the reproductive cycle. Seed orchard treatments, such as thinning to increase light and reduce moisture stress, management of tree-crown form, fertilization, girdling, root pruning, hormone application, branch pruning, grafting, supplemental pollination, and insect and disease control, have been developed to enhance cone crops in seed orchards. Some of these treatments may have application in natural stands.

SEED COLLECTION

Seed maturity has been defined as the stage at which seeds are capable of germination and successful storage (Edwards 1981). The actual date of maturation varies with species, location, and year. Maturity also varies between individual trees in the same stand, and the position of cones on the same tree. The degree of maturity at the time of cone collection affects seed extractability, the storability of cones before they are processed, the susceptibility of the seeds to damage during processing, and the long-term storage of extracted seeds. The range of effects related to seed maturity emphasizes the importance of collecting cones at the peak of their development. Seed maturity has ramifications throughout all subsequent steps of seed processing and use, and ultimately will affect the potential of the seeds to produce healthy, vigorous seedlings.

Cone Crop Monitoring

The decision of whether or not to collect cones is based on a systematic monitoring process which is carried out annually in all forest stands. A detailed description of this process is provided in the Silviculture Manual (B.C. Ministry of Forests), as well as in Eremko et al. (1989).

The monitoring process involves locating and assessing the size of developing cone crops. The relative abundance of cones observed in the cone-bearing portion of dominant and co-dominant trees in a stand are assessed and recorded by species and location. Surveys are made when cones are readily visible but not fully mature, usually throughout late July to early August. Additional monitoring to determine the timing of collections is conducted from August to early September. For yellow-cedar, and western hemlock, crop assessment may continue through September into October.

The number of cones and their distribution throughout the crown varies with species. For example, in redcedar, yellow-cedar, hemlock and lodgepole pine, cones occur over the entire crown. In other species, such as white pine (*Pinus monticola*) and the true firs, cone production is limited to the top five to eight whorls. Consequently, the cone production characteristics of each species should be considered when the actual numbers of cones contained in a heavy crop are estimated.

Cone crop ratings are compiled for each crop production area, by species, and may range from nil to very heavy. The reliability of these estimates depends on the number of trees observed and how well these trees represent the overall stand condition. This procedure is subjective, and dependent on the observer's local experience. For example, the size of crops may be overestimated through the inclusion of old cones as part of the current crop, or if only roadside trees are evaluated, since they often produce heavier crops because of increased exposure to sunlight.

Properly done, such crop surveys provide a mechanism for assessing the size of crops, comparing potential collection areas, and planning cone collection programs. In general, medium to heavy crops are considered collectable, but when severe seed shortages exist, crops with light ratings may be collected.

Seed Crop Evaluation

Based on the survey results, potential cone collection areas can be selected. Seed development in these areas is then reassessed throughout the rest of the maturation period, by means of a process referred to as seed evaluation. This intensive examination of potential crops provides an estimate of the quantity, maturity, and overall condition of seeds in the cones. Seed evaluation guides all final decisions as to when and where seed collections will take place.

Seed evaluation is carried out on representative samples of cones from all potential cone collection areas. To estimate the seed content of sample cones, the cones are sectioned or, in the case of lodgepole pine, the seeds are extracted, and the number of filled seeds are counted. Averages are calculated and compared to acceptable filled seed content standards to determine whether seed yields are adequate to warrant collection. These standards are described in the Silviculture Manual (B.C. Ministry of Forests).

During seed evaluation, cones should also be examined for color, general condition, and moisture level. Insect activity is indicated by premature browning, cone disfigurement, frass, pitch, bore holes, or larvae in the cones or seeds. Damage may also be caused by cone rusts, particularly in spruce, which can be detected by orange-yellow spore masses on the cone scales. Such rusts result in premature cone opening, reduced viability, or abnormal germination. In general, if over 50% of the seeds examined are damaged, collection of the crop is not considered worthwhile. However, where seeds are in short supply or are unavailable for reforesting a particular area, cone crops that show signs of disease or insect infestation may have to be collected.

If potential yields are considered adequate, seed maturity must be frequently monitored to determine when collections should start. Seed maturity is assessed with the cutting test, which involves sectioning and examining individual seeds. In most species, seeds are considered mature when the embryo fills at least 90% of the embryo cavity, the storage tissue is firm, and the embryo has turned yellowish. In lodgepole pine and western redcedar, embryos are white when mature. A simple test for maturity is to examine seeds that have been sliced in half longitudinally and left at room temperature for several hours or overnight. If the seeds are mature, the storage tissue will have shrunk very little, and there will be a slight gap between it and the seedcoat.

Other maturity indicators, such as cone condition and the ease with which the seeds separate from the cone scale, should also be checked. Seed evaluation techniques are described more fully in the Silviculture Manual (B.C. Ministry of Forests) and in Eremko et al. (1989). Species-specific maturity indicators are also in Eremko et al. (1989). The crop is collectable when all the conditions listed above have been met.

Seeds of most species are generally shed within 2 weeks of maturation (Edwards 1986). This provides a fairly narrow cone collection window, but the period can be extended by the collecting of cones prior to full maturity, as is done with *Abies*. In general, however, cones should be collected as close to full maturity as practical considerations will allow. It is believed that seed quality is at a maximum when seeds are mature and still on the tree (Edwards 1986), so care should be taken during subsequent collection and handling procedures to ensure that this level of quality is maintained. If cones are collected early they should be stored in a cool site to allow further seed maturation to occur.

Collection Methods

Various techniques, including felling, climbing, and aerial, are available for collecting cones. The choice of technique depends on species characteristics, the number and density of cone-bearing trees, access, and costs. The objective of all techniques is to collect cones in the most efficient and safe manner while minimizing damage to the seeds. Whichever method is used, cones that show signs of heavy damage, seem unusually small, or have opened prematurely should be avoided.

POST-HARVEST HANDLING

Field Handling of Collected Cones

Following collection, cones should be kept well ventilated and dry. The presence of debris in the cone sacks may result in seed abrasion, bruising, and tissue damage, all of which may lead to decreases in viability. Excess moisture promotes mold which may hamper seed extraction, and poor ventilation may result in overheating that increases mold or direct damage to the seeds. These problems are particularly prevalent in immature collections, but may also occur in mature collections of hemlock, true firs, redcedar, and yellow-cedar. Allowing western redcedar and hemlock cones to remain warm and moist often leads to the germination of seeds in the cone.

Since freshly harvested seeds are perishable, they must be handled carefully at all times. It may be necessary to clean, air-dry, and re-sack cones at the interim storage facility, particularly if there is a lot of debris among the cones, or if the cones are very moist. Cone sacks should be loosely filled to allow for the expansion that occurs as further drying takes place, and storage at the interim storage facility should be on racks surrounded by air space. Good ventiliation not only aids cone drying, but also helps reduce overheating created by the respiration of moist seeds and cones. Sacks should be turned regularly to further reduce the risk of overheating and mold (temperatures inside the sacks should never exceed 25°C). As well, cones should also be protected against predation by squirrels and rodents. Periodic cone and seed cutting tests performed on random samples of stored cones will give an estimate of seed quality and help the detection of potential problems.

Cone Shipment to the Processing Plant

Cones must be kept dry, cool, and well ventilated during shipment to the processing plant. Pallets placed between layers of cone sacks, and air spaces between the cones and walls of the truck will help promote air circulation. Refrigerated trucks, maintained at 5-10°C, are generally the most appropriate means of transport, and travel times to the processing plant should be as short as possible. Good communication between the collection agency and processing facility will ensure prompt unloading and proper storage before processing begins.

Cone Processing

On arrival at the processing facility, cones may or may not be processed immediately. Cones can be stored for different periods, with minimal reductions in seed quality (Leadem 1982). The length of storage varies between species, ranging from a few weeks for western redcedar and hemlock (which may pre-germinate in the cones if improperly handled) to several months for species such as lodgepole pine.

After the cones have arrived at the processing facility, an assessment is made of seed maturity, potential yield, insects and disease, mold and fungal activity, pre-germination, and overheating. This provides the basis for determining the most appropriate extraction and processing procedures. Cones that are still wet may be dried and resacked before being placed in the cone storage shed.

For most species, cone and seed processing involves several steps (Figure 15.8): kiln drying, seed extraction, initial cleaning, dewinging, intermediate cleaning, drying, and final seed cleaning and sizing.

Kilning is the first step in extracting seeds from cones. During this drying process, temperature, relative humidity, and air flow are carefully controlled. Although the amount of kilning varies with cone condition and species, most cones require 16-18 hours of drying before they will open completely. Wet cones, when encountering excessive temperatures in the kiln, may sometimes case harden. This condition occurs as a result of the outer layers of a cone drying out more quickly than the moist interior. Drying of the outer cone blocks water movement away from the interior layers and prevents the cone scales from opening. This makes seed removal virtually impossible. True fir cones are not kiln-dried, since they naturally disintegrate when they are stored for 2-3 months at 5-10°C. After drying, remains of these cones are mechanically screened to remove the cone axis, scales, and other large debris. The remaining extraction and processing procedures for true firs are similar to those for other species.

Dry cones are tumbled in rotating mesh drums to shake the seeds free. Seeds and fine debris fall through the screen walls of the drum into a collector. Tumbling must take place soon after kilning, since the scales may close again if cones are exposed to cool, moist air. Prolonged tumbling should be avoided because it often results in the increased release of poorly developed seeds and debris from broken cones.

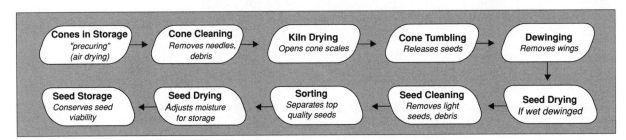

FIGURE 15.8.   Steps in the seed extraction process.

Seed Processing

Once extracted from the cones, the mixture of seeds and debris is passed over a series of progressively finer mesh screens for separation. Screen sizes are varied to suit the species and type of debris to be removed. This initial cleaning step is usually referred to as scalping.

During dewinging, seeds are separated from the seedwings. In some species, such as Douglas-fir, the seedwings are part of the seedcoat and must be broken off mechanically. Small seedwings are impractical to remove without damaging the seeds; for this reason, seeds of western redcedar and yellow-cedar are not dewinged. In pine and spruce, the wings are attached to seeds by means of the integument. To remove seedwings in these species, a small amount of water is added to the seeds, causing the (hygroscopic) wings to expand and the integument to release its grip on the seed. Care must be taken with all species to avoid excessive abrasion during dewinging, since such damage will result in poor germination and increased susceptibility to fungal attack.

At the B.C. Ministry of Forests Seed Centre, dewinged seeds are placed in a water bath to remove resin particles, debris, and damaged seeds. Debris and damaged seeds are easily separated because they remain submerged while the intact seeds float. Intact seeds are dried to reduce their moisture content to 5-10%, and then sorted to remove empty and poorly developed seeds. At the time that processed seeds are put into extended cold storage, they are at least 98% free of non-seed impurities. For more detailed descriptions of cone and seed processing, refer to Edwards (1981, 1986).

The quality of stored seeds is influenced by seed maturity and post-collection handling as well as seed moisture content, storage temperature, and storage method (Wang 1974). Generally, seeds are stored in sealed containers at low temperatures (-18°C). Even under optimum storage conditions, the lower the seed quality the more rapid the deterioration of the seeds (Justice and Bass 1978). When initial viability is high, seeds can be stored for 10 years or more with little change in their ability to produce seedlings (Edwards 1981).

Seed Testing

Since seed quality can change at any point from cone collection and the time the seeds are used in the nursery, seed quality must be monitored regularly. Seed quality tests, generally repeated every 2 years for stored seeds, include the determination of moisture content, seed purity, and germinability (Association of Official Seed Analysts 1981; International Seed Testing Association 1985; Stein et al. l986). Seed moisture is determined by weight after several seed samples are dried in an oven, and is expressed as the difference between the fresh weight and dry weight of seeds, as a percentage of the fresh weight. Seed purity tests determine the composition of the seedlot in terms of seeds and impurities. Samples are separated into pure seeds and inert matter, and each fraction is weighed and its relative percentage calculated based on the total weight of the sample. The number of pure seeds per unit weight of the seedlot is also determined. Purity and seed weight are essential parameters for calculating the number of seeds required for nursery sowing.

Germination tests determine the number of usable seedlings that can be produced from a seedlot under favorable environmental conditions (Stein et al. 1986). The seeds of British Columbia species (except western redcedar) are considered to be dormant because they do not germinate rapidly and completely unless they have received a dormancy-breaking treatment. The most effective method for releasing seeds from dormancy is stratification, a process in which moist seeds are refrigerated at 2-5°C for several weeks to several months. Generally, paired germination tests are run simultaneously with stratified and unstratified seeds. The difference between the two results is an indication of the dormancy of the seedlot. In some instances, stratified seeds germinate less than those not stratified, a sign that the seeds may not have been fully mature at the time of collection, were damaged during processing, or have deteriorated in storage (Cleary et al. 1978). Seed germinability is a function of many variables, including genetic variation among species and seed sources, seed maturity and dormancy, and growing environment (Copeland 1976). These differences will exist even if all seedlots have been optimally treated and contain only filled seeds.

The vigor of seeds is reflected in the speed at which seeds germinate, their ability to germinate under adverse environmental conditions, their susceptibility to disease, and their viability over long-term storage (Bonner 1974). Reliable, standardized techniques for estimating tree seed vigor have not yet been established, but differences in vigor among seedlots may explain the inconsistencies that are sometimes observed between laboratory and field germination results.

Preparing Seeds for Sowing

Under natural conditions, dormancy is an attribute which ensures continuation of the species under a range of environmental conditions (Copeland 1976). However, in artificial reforestation programs, dormancy must be overcome to enhance rapid and uniform germination in the nursery. Stratification is commonly used to prepare seeds for nursery sowing. It is an effective dormancy-release treatment because it mimics conditions under which seeds might naturally overwinter in the field, but the requirements among species may vary. Table 15.2 shows the stratification regimes recommended for seed sown in warm environments such as a greenhouse. Seed for bareroot nurseries benefit from longer stratification periods (see Chapter 16). Damaged seeds, or those that have low viability, may deteriorate during stratification (Cleary et al. 1978; Leadem 1986). In those instances, stratification may not be advantageous and the seeds should be used without treatment or discarded.

Moisture, oxygen, and favorable temperatures are all essential for germination. Water is needed to activate physiological processes; oxygen is required for respiration, to supply energy for germination. For most British Columbia conifers, optimal temperatures for germination are in the range of 15 - 30°C. The rate of germination is inhibited when temperatures fall below 10°C. Some species are reportedly capable of germinating in the snow pack, but temperatures just above freezing do not favor germination as a whole. Temperatures of 35°C or higher are usually lethal to germinating conifer seeds.

Light is known to enhance germination of many genera—true firs, larch, spruce, pines, Douglas-fir, and hemlock—but there is little documented evidence specific to British Columbia conifers. The light response is affected by stratification and environmental parameters such as temperature and, sometimes, moisture. In general, light will promote germination without stratification, while increasing the length of stratification will enhance the ability of seeds to germinate in darkness.

SUMMARY

The identification and monitoring of developing cone crops is the first step in obtaining high quality seeds for reforestation. Seed quality levels are more assured if cone crops are harvested when they are fully mature and collections are properly tended in the field. Appropriate handling of cones at the collection site, as well as during temporary cone storage and shipment to the extractory, is also critical to maintaining seed quality. Seed extraction and cleaning are more efficient when cones have been harvested and handled with due care and attention in the field: seeds from carefully

TABLE 15.2. Stratification[a] of British Columbia conifer seeds

Species name	Common name	Current practice[b] Soak	Current practice[b] Stratification	Alternate method Soak	Alternate method Stratification
Abies amabilis	Pacific silver fir	48 h[c]	4 + 8 wk[d]	48 h[c]	4 + 12 wk[e]
Abies grandis	grand fir	24 h	4 wk	48 h[c]	4 + 12 wk[e]
Abies lasiocarpa	subalpine fir	48 h[c]	4 + 8 wk[d]	48 h[c]	4 + 12 wk[e]
Abies procera	noble fir	48 h[c]	4 wk	48 h[c]	4 + 12 wk[e]
Chamaecyparis nootkatensis	yellow-cedar	48 h[c]	4 W + 8 C[f]	10-28 da[g]	16-20 wk
Picea glauca	white spruce	24 h	3 wk	24 h	3 wk
Picea sitchensis	Sitka spruce	24 h	3 wk	24 h	3 wk
Pinus contorta	lodgepole pine	24 h	4 wk	24 h	3 wk
Pinus monticola	western white pine	48 h[c]	4 W + 8 C[f]	48 h[c]	4 W + 8 C[f]
Pinus ponderosa	ponderosa pine	24 h	4 wk	24 h	3 wk
Pseudotsuga menziesii	Douglas-fir	24 h	3 wk	24 h	3 wk
Thuja plicata	western redcedar	0 h[c]	0 wk	0 h[c]	0 wk
Tsuga heterophylla	western hemlock	24 h	4 wk	24 h	3 wk
Tsuga mertensiana	mountain hemlock	24 h	4 wk	24 h	4 wk

[a]   Chilling of moist seeds at 2-5°C.

[b]   Stratification procedures currently used by B.C. Ministry of Forests Seed Centre (R. Bowden-Green per. comm.,1989).

[c]   Seeds which are soaked for 48 h receive a water change after the first 24 h.

[d]   Modified stratification-redry treatment (see note e): Seeds are soaked for 48 h, stratified for 4 wk, dried to 30 to 35% moisture content, and stratified for 8-12 wk.

[e]   Stratification-redry treatment: Seeds are soaked for 48 h and drained to remove excess water. They are then placed, with no surface drying, at 2°C for 4 wk. After stratification for 4 wk, the seeds are dried to 30-35% moisture content, and chilled for an additional 12 wk.

[f]   Warm/cold stratification: Seeds are soaked, drained and kept at 20°C for 4 wk, then stratified for 8 wk at 2-5°C.

[g]   Water should be changed every second day.

handled cones are less susceptible to processing damage and are more likely to store well. The amount of attention paid to seed quality during all stages of collection, processing, storage, and preparation is especially evident in the nursery. When high quality seeds are used for reforestation, fewer seeds are required and more vigorous seedlings are produced at lower cost.

Although by some estimates seed costs appear to represent only a small portion of the total cost of producing a seedling, such estimates do not take into account the many nursery costs that are directly attributable to the quality of seeds. These include: high thinning costs because of greater than predicted germination; disease problems arising from high seedling densities when seeds have been oversown; high overheads associated with empty greenhouse space when germination is lower than expected; poor performance of seedlings produced from seeds which have received inadequate stratification; the costs of maintaining high greenhouse temperatures when lower temperatures would be adequate for properly stratified seeds (Allen 1960; Leadem 1986); and the costs of culling seedlings that result from seeds with low vigor. If all these factors were considered, the real costs associated with poor seed performance would be much higher than is often estimated (see Chapters 16 and 17).

With our current knowledge of seed biology and technology, the maintenance of adequate supplies of high quality seeds can be ensured.

16

SEEDLING PRODUCTION AND PROCESSING: BAREROOT

T.G. Daniels and D.G. Simpson

The task of forest nurseries is to produce, by set dates, required numbers of seedlings that meet predetermined morphological and physiological specifications. For bareroot stock, a 2-year production cycle is generally required so that the seedlings can achieve adequate size for establishment on average sites.

Seed is sown in early spring, cultured for two growing seasons, and harvested in the fall of the second year. Graded and packaged stock is overwintered in cold or freezer storage and shipped to planting sites following snowmelt in spring. Several other combinations of seedling age, date of lifting, and date of planting are also used.

Whatever the production technique followed, the forester should have an understanding of seedling growth cycles and of how cultural practices affect those cycles. This chapter gives an overview of the requirements and steps involved in the production and processing of bareroot seedlings. For detailed accounts of production technique, the reader is referred to van den Driessche (1969), Aldhous (1972), Duryea and Landis (1984), and Lantz (1984).

SEED FOR REFORESTATION

Seed used for the reforestation of provincial Crown land must be registered and stored at the B.C. Ministry of Forests Seed Centre in Surrey, B.C. It is obtained by the nursery after authorization is received from the seed owner.

Delivery of seed must be scheduled carefully. The Seed Centre and the nursery need to work closely to ensure that seed is delivered when required and in the proper quantity. The Seed Centre will prepare and process seed as instructed, delivering it to the nursery 6-12 weeks before the planned sowing date if seed stratification (dormancy release) or additional processing is to be carried out.

Quantity of Seed

To optimize the number of plantable seedlings (those that have desirable attributes) per area of bed space, the proper quantity of seed must be sown.

Determining how much seed to sow for a particular combination of nursery environment, species, and stock type is not an easy task. Sowing too many seeds in a given length of bed may result in a high proportion of small (cull) seedlings. Sowing too few seeds may result in insufficient seedlings to fill the order. These fundamental data may take years to develop and refine as cultural activities are modified to account for changes in grading standards and for genetic differences between seedlots.

Sowing density is the number of viable seeds specified for sowing to produce a certain number of plantable seedlings. A unit area of nursery bed space tends to produce a constant biomass when moisture and nutrients remain constant. The biomass may be in the form of many small seedlings or fewer large seedlings (Wakeley 1948). The number of seedlings competing for the same growing space will determine the size distribution of the seedling population.

Sowing and recovery densities are based on morphological selection criteria for a plantable seedling. Primary criteria are stem caliper, total height, and root mass. Seedlings are usually graded to minimum size specifications. The minimum acceptable stem caliper for many species is 3.0 mm. Recently, target size specifications have been developed by the Ministry of Forests to encourage nurseries to increase quality by producing larger stock.

TABLE 16.1. Typical sowing and recovery factors, seed characteristics, and bed space requirements for 2+0 bareroot species

Species	Sowing density (seeds/m²)	Recovery density (seedlings/m²)	Viable seeds/g (vs/g)	Viable seeds/ plantable seedlings	Viable seed (g)/ 1000 plantable seedlings	Bed space(m²)/ 1000 plantable seedlings
Ponderosa pine	300	150	20	2.00	100.0	6.7
Interior Douglas-fir	350	150	100	2.33	23.3	9.1
Western larch	360	180	250	2.00	8.0	5.6
Lodgepole pine	350	200	310	1.75	5.6	5.0
Interior spruce	500	180	420	2.78	6.6	5.6
Coastal Douglas-fir	240	120	100	2.00	20.0	8.3

Nurseries develop their own set of sowing and recovery densities for each species and stock type produced. Sowing densities in British Columbia range from 240 to 500 viable seeds per square meter and recovery densities from 120 to 200 seedlings per square meter (Table 16.1). The ratio between sowing and recovery density indicates the number of viable seeds required to produce one plantable seedling. This ratio is highest for spruce (*Picea* spp.) and lowest for lodgepole pine (*Pinus contorta*).

Sowing density, recovery density, and the number of viable seeds per gram are part of the formula used to calculate the amount of seed and bed space required for production.

The difference between sowing density and recovery density is due to the loss of seed and seedlings during the production cycle. This may reflect nursery site characteristics, both physical and environmental, including losses due to diseases, pests, lifting damage, grading standards, and management practices. The relationship between the number of seeds sown and the number of plantable seedlings produced for several interior British Columbia species is shown in Figure 16.1. These data illustrate 2+0 crops established between 1985 and 1987 in southern British Columbia and

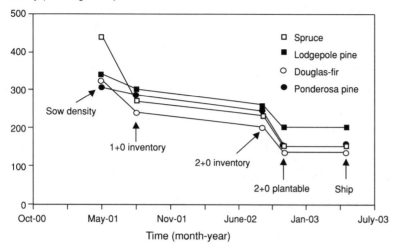

Density (seedlings/LBM)

FIGURE 16.1. Seed and seedling density trends from sowing to shipping for 2+0 spruce, lodgepole pine, Douglas-fir, and ponderosa pine crops grown at Grandview Nursery between 1985 and 1987. (LBM = lineal bed meter)

graded to a 3.0 mm caliper standard. Similar historical data are kept by all nurseries to help fine-tune seedbed density relationships and account for losses during the production period. These trends show species differences and production phases that require additional protection or modified culture.

Most crop losses occur during the first growing season and the grading operation (Figure 16.1). For example, the large decline in ponderosa pine (*Pinus ponderosa*) density between 2+0 inventory and recovery shows that approximately 30% of the total seedlings harvested were not packed. If records indicate seedlings attained adequate height and caliper but lacked root fibrosity, the nurseryman might modify root culture treatments in future ponderosa crops to try to increase recovery. Figure 16.2 shows the factors contributing to the decline in density between each stage of crop development, and the falldown percentage associated with the density changes. In the above example, no losses were incurred during storage. Seedlings leaving storage are either suitable or unsuitable for outplanting based on physiological testing or the extent of storage mold.

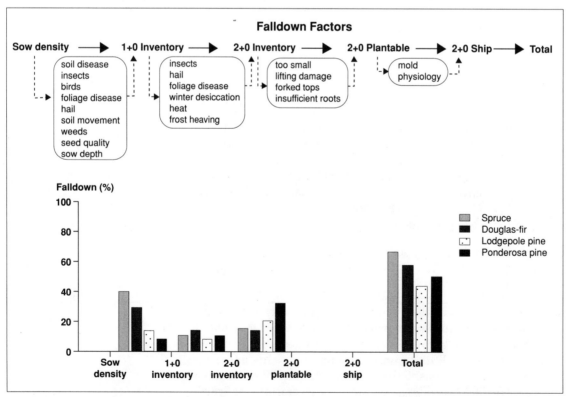

FIGURE 16.2. Falldown factors affecting crop density between successive stages of crop production and actual falldown percentages for trends shown in Figure 16.1 for crops sown between 1985 and 1987. No losses were experienced between 2+0 plantable and shipping.

Seed Quality Information

Several sources of information are available to nurseries to help them determine seedlot quality. The seed register is the main source for new collections or for collections not grown at the nursery before. It provides origin, elevation, germination, total seeds per gram, and number of viable seeds per gram. Nurseries frequently sow the same seedlot over a 2- to 3-year period and can judge quality based on field germination and seedling recovery. At the end of each season, nurseries are asked to identify atypical seedlots. A list of these and the problems encountered are compiled and distributed to all nurseries by the Ministry of Forests.

Seedlots with high germination values ($\geq$ 90%) are preferred by growers because of their quicker, more complete development. A seedling "underrun" will result if the nursery is unaware of low quality seed and does not compensate for reduced field germination by sowing more seed.

Seed Stratification

Most nurseries request that seed be stratified before delivery. However, there are several advantages to a nursery carrying out stratification treatments itself. The risk of damage occurring through mishandling is reduced when unstratified (dormant) seed is shipped. The dry weight of seed can be checked to verify that the correct amount of seed has been withdrawn.

Bareroot crops are sown in early spring when cool soil and air temperature are frequently encountered. Recent work by Tanaka et al. (1986) may explain why laboratory germination rates are often lower than those of field germination. They found that longer stratification generally improved the rate and completeness of Engelmann spruce (*Picea engelmannii*) and lodgepole pine germination, especially under a cool (15°C/5°C) rather than standard (30°C/20°C) temperature regime. Surface drying before stratification under cool test conditions retarded speed and completeness of germination. A 6- to 8-week stratification period was recommended for spruce and pine, with seeds surface-dried at the end rather than the beginning of stratification treatment.

SEEDBED PREPARATION

Nurseries producing 2+0 stock use a 3-year production cycle. Each production field is occupied with seedlings for 2 years. During the third year, either the field is bare-fallowed or a green manure crop is established. If the nursery is producing 2+0 stock and operating at capacity, usable bed space will be divided into three equal areas: one-third designated for first-year seedlings, one-third for second-year seedlings, and one-third for fallow. Nurseries producing transplant stock may have longer periods between fallow phases, provided soil chemical and biological factors can be satisfactorily maintained between seedling crops.

Bed preparation for seeding a new crop begins in the fallow phase. During this period, soil pH and fertility levels are determined and adjusted if required. Soil pH should be maintained between 5.2 and 5.8, with organic matter kept between 3 and 8% for most conifer species (Table 16.2). This is also the time when weeds and some insect populations are controlled; when

TABLE 16.2. Range of soil nutrient levels recommended prior to sowing or transplanting in British Columbia nurseries (adapted from Maxwell, 1988)

Soil constituents	Range	
pH	5.2 - 5.8	
% organic matter	3 - 8	
% total nitrogen[a]	0.20 - 0.25	
	meq/100 g	**ppm**
CEC	15 - 20	
P[b]		100 - 250
K	0.20 - 0.30	78 - 117
Ca	5.0 - 8.0	1000 -1600
Mg	< 1.4	< 340

[a] Determined by Kjeldahl method.
[b] Determined by Bray I method.

land levelling to smooth out depressions and subsoiling to break up compacted areas are performed; and when the presence of harmful soil fungi are determined. Soil assays are carried out by the Plant Diagnostic Clinic at the Pacific Forestry Centre in Victoria, and by other private laboratories.

New nursery fields established on old agricultural land frequently have high pathogen levels. Green manure crops grown on the nursery fields are also considered to be pathogen hosts (Davey and Krause 1980).

When a pathogen population reaches a level that cannot be controlled through cultural techniques, a soil fumigant is used. Fumigants are injected as a gas or incorporated as granules into the soil. The most frequently used fumigant is a mixture of 67% methyl bromide and 33% chloropicrin. It is extremely volatile and must be held in place by covering the soil surface with plastic sheeting. Treatment is very expensive and requires highly trained personnel familiar with specialized equipment and safety procedures.

Bed preparation is usually unique at each nursery site because of the different soil characteristics and machinery availability or preference. The main objective is to develop a well-aerated bed of uniformly mixed soil that has a flat surface. Before the beds are prepared, fertilizers are added to bring soil nutritional status within the recommended range (Table 16.2). Soil cultivation equipment is used to incorporate fertilizer and prepare soil for bed shaping. Equipment that preserves soil structure and prevents development of a plow layer is preferred. For this reason, harrows and spring-tooth cultivators are used more often than rototillers or disks.

SOWING OPERATION

Seed stratification and bed preparation are scheduled to coincide with environmental conditions to enable rapid seed germination and early growth. Critical elements in the sowing operation include controlling the amount of seed planted, planting at the proper depth, and sowing on the proper date for each species and stock type required.

Sowing Equipment

There are two basic types of seeding machines used in bareroot nurseries: those which employ a vacuum system for sowing individual seed, and those which employ a non-vacuum system. Most crops in British Columbia are sown with vacuum seeders, often referred to as precision seeders.

Both vacuum and non-vacuum seeders are capable of achieving target seed density. However, seed bounce and irregular spacing within drill rows are common with non-vacuum machines. Vacuum seeders control interseed spacing within drill rows. Such precision sowing has been found to increase greatly the uniformity of interseed spacing of Douglas-fir (*Pseudotsuga menziesii*) by reducing the number of missed and multiple sown planting spots (Dooley 1982) (Figure 16.3).

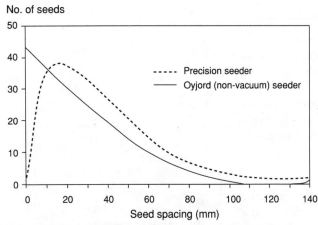

FIGURE 16.3. Generalized distribution of vacuum- and non-vacuum-sown Douglas-fir seed. Target interseed spacing was 27 mm (adapted from Dooley, 1982).

Vacuum seeders have also been successful with a wide variety of other species including ponderosa pine, western larch (*Larix occidentalis*), lodgepole pine, white spruce, and Engelmann spruce. Small, light seed such as western redcedar (*Thuja plicata*) may require pelleting to achieve seed singularity.

Bed density is the term used to describe numbers of seedlings per unit area, but it does not indicate how seedlings are distributed within that area. Several spacing configurations will result in a similar bed density, yet produce seedling populations with different size distributions. Most nurseries in British Columbia sow seven rows of seed spaced 15 cm between rows on a 1.1 m wide seedbed. When the objective is to maximize the number of packable seedlings per square meter, achieving uniform interseed spacing is an important goal. High quality seed and sowing equipment capable of distributing seed evenly are essential in this regard. In one study, a vacuum drum seeder reduced cull rates of loblolly pine by 4% over conventional seeders as a result of more uniform interseed spacing (Boyer et al. 1985).

Non-vacuum seeders are preferred at low sowing densities or with low quality seedlots because they can operate at twice the speed of vacuum seeders. The latter are also susceptible to pitch and other seed debris which plug seed orifices and require frequent cleaning to prevent skipped planting spots.

Sowing Date

Bareroot crops in British Columbia are generally sown between April 15 and May 15 when soil temperature is at least 6 °C at 5 cm. Nurseries avoid sowing seed in cold, wet soil or when the probability of frost damage to young germinants is high. Sowing in cold soil decreases speed of germination and exposes seed to soil pathogens for a longer period. Late sowing may also result in spotty germination caused by excessive heat or disease.

Early sowing enhances crop development in several ways. More size is achieved when seedlings have the benefit of a longer growth period (Rowan and Marx 1976) (Figure 16.4). Spruce species, for example, should be sown before pine and Douglas-fir. Spruces, which are slower to germinate, prefer cooler temperatures and take longer to reach plantable size. Early sowing of spruce allows seedlings to develop size and resistance to heat before high summer temperatures occur.

Another important benefit of early sowing is associated with seedling physiology and the dormancy cycle. Early-sown crops are able to complete the height growth cycle early in the season and therefore initiate the hardening-off process sooner. This earlier development and hardening carries over into the second season as well. Seedlings that achieve frost hardiness early in the fall can be lifted earlier, when soil conditions are usually drier and more favorable. This can result in less mechanical damage to root systems, and higher recovery rates.

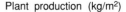

Plant production (kg/m²)

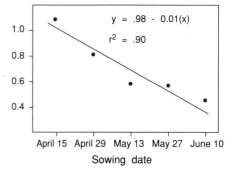

$y = .98 - 0.01(x)$

$r^2 = .90$

FIGURE 16.4. Effect of sowing date on loblolly pine biomass production (adapted from Rowan and Marx, 1976).

Sowing Depth

Each operation in the establishment phase of a new seedling crop is critical. Few, however, have more impact on seedling emergence and early development than that of achieving correct, uniform sowing depth. It is disheartening for the nurseryman to observe a new crop of ponderosa pine, exposed to the surface after a moderate rain, being devoured by birds, or to find a new spruce crop germinating vigorously 1.5 cm below the surface, with little chance of successful emergence.

Optimum sowing depth depends on seed size and the type of material used for covering. British Columbia nurseries use either coarse, river-washed sand or native sandy soil to cover seed. A general rule is to cover seed to a depth equal to the seed length. This ranges from about 0.3 cm for small seeded species such as spruce, to 0.7 cm for large seeded species such as ponderosa pine. Deeper sowing to discourage birds is only recommended for large seeded species – for example, ponderosa pine and, to a lesser extent, Douglas-fir. These species are quick to germinate, have large food reserves, and are capable of overcoming significant mechanical resistance. In one study, increasing sowing depth of Douglas-fir seed from 0.3 to 0.6 cm reduced total germination and decreased height and diameter after the first growing season (Guariglia and Thompson 1985) (Table 16.3).

TABLE 16.3. Bed germination and 1+0 density, height, and diameter of Douglas-fir seed sown at 0, 0.3, and 0.6 cm (adapted from Guariglia and Thompson, 1985)

Sowing depth	Germination %	Density m²	Height (cm)	Diameter (mm)
Surface	60.7	287 ab	14.0 a	3.22 ab
0.3 cm	65.8 a[a]	339 a	14.1 a	3.26 a
0.6 cm	52.5 b	253 b	12.5 b	3.09 b

[a] Values with the same letter are not significantly different at p = 0.05.

SEED GERMINATION

The most critical period in the production phase of bareroot crops occurs during the 3- to 4-week period after sowing, when seed germination and seedling emergence take place. The first visible sign of germination is swelling of the seed, followed by cracking of the seedcoat. Radicle emergence and development into the primary root takes 3-5 days for ponderosa pine and Douglas-fir, and 7-10 days for spruce.

Once the radicle appears, maintaining adequate soil moisture is critical. On sunny, warm days, two to three short irrigation treatments may be required. Hot weather aggravates a situation caused by uneven sowing depth. If moisture conditions are maintained for shallow-sown seed, deep-sown seed will be exposed to excess moisture and may rot.

The period between sowing and emergence may be as short as 10 days for ponderosa pine and as long as 20 days for spruce. Speed of germination is influenced by soil temperature. The germination phase is considered to be complete when the seedling has produced enough photosynthetic surface to supply itself with food (Kramer and Kozlowski 1960). Conditions that reduce the speed of germination — whether caused by improper sowing depth, lack of stratification, or soil disease — will result in reduced crop uniformity and increased cull rate.

SEEDLING PROTECTION

Seedlings are sensitive and vulnerable to many factors: temperature extremes; attack by soil pests including nematodes, fungi, and insects;

damage by birds and other animals; mechanical disturbance; and competition with weeds.

Temperature Extremes

After germination has occurred, irrigation treatments change from maintaining moist surface conditions to protecting seedlings from extreme temperatures. When seedlings are emerging in early May at coastal nurseries, and in late May at south-central nurseries, air temperatures frequently reach 30 °C. Surface soil temperatures may exceed 45 °C. Because any surface temperature of 40 °C or more is considered to be lethal to young seedlings (McDonald 1984), nurseries use an irrigation regime that recognizes seedling sensitivity to heat damage (Morby 1982). In British Columbia, surface soil temperature is gradually allowed to increase as the seedling develops a woody stem and sufficient foliage for shading (Table 16.4). Cooling treatments during the second growing season may be required for heat-sensitive species such as spruce, to prevent foliage damage caused by soil radiation.

TABLE 16.4. Recommended cooling irrigation regime for 1+0 spruce seedlings in relation to stage of seedling development[a]

Stage of development	Approximate month	Critical temperature	Treatment
Time of emergence	May	27° C at soil surface	10 min. every 30 min.
Self shade (primary needles)	June	32° C in canopy	10 min. every 30 min.
Stem lignification	July	32° C in canopy	10 min. every 30 min.
Target 1+0 ht. reached	August		Normal deep irrigation

[a] The information presented is based on the operational experience of John Maxwell, bareroot seedling specialist with the B.C. Ministry of Forests' Surrey Nursery.

Protection from low temperatures is most critical during stages of active shoot elongation. Young germinants and flushing 2+0 seedlings require protection from light frosts (-1 to -2 °C). Seedlings are less vulnerable in fall and can often safely withstand -3 to -5 °C. Sprinkling protects the seedlings with heat, released when the water changes state from a liquid to a solid. Seedling temperature will not fall below freezing as long as new ice formation is taking place. Plant temperature declines immediately if sprinkling stops (Chang 1968). For this reason, sprinkling must continue until air temperature has reached 0 °C.

Nurseries located in the Interior rely on winter snow cover to protect seedlings from arctic cold fronts. Winter temperatures can fall to -40 °C in central British Columbia.

Exposed seedlings may suffer winter desiccation damage ranging from foliage injury to mortality. A few inches of snow can provide complete protection. Artificial snow-making equipment has been used successfully to protect container-grown seedlings in outside compounds, although it has not been tested operationally in bareroot nurseries. Some nursery soils experience repeated freeze-thaw cycles during winter, which results in frost-heaving damage in 1+0 crops. Low-density spruce crops seem particularly vulnerable to this type of injury. Frost-heaving damage is often reduced or prevented by the application of 1-2 cm of sawdust mulch to seedbeds before winter freeze-up.

Diseases

A survey of 21 Northwest bareroot nurseries (Sutherland 1984) revealed that charcoal root disease (*Macrophomina phaseoli*), cortical rot (*Fusarium* spp.), and Phytophthora root rot (*Phytophthora* spp.) were the most serious diseases. Another root rot on conifers in British Columbia nurseries is caused by *Phythium* spp. All of these are soil-borne root diseases which are controlled by soil fumigation or, occasionally, by fungicides applied as a soil drench. In coastal nurseries, corky root disease caused by the plant parasitic nematode *Xiphinema bakeri*, may be a problem on Douglas-fir (Sutherland and van Eerden 1980; Sutherland et al. 1989). A needle and stem disease, Sirococcus blight (*Sirococcus strobilinus*) is spread by water splash. It is frequently mistaken for frost damage, as it affects new growth in early spring. To control it, surrounding diseased trees can be removed and fungicide sprays applied to seedlings. Storage molds are seldom a problem provided stock is dormant when lifted, its foliage is clean, and it is stored at -2 °C (see Chapter 20).

Few fungicides are registered for nursery use in British Columbia. Emphasis is placed on managing disease through cultural techniques. Many disease problems are promoted by excessive soil moisture, or by foliage that remains wet for long periods of time. Judicious use of irrigation is often a good preventive measure against soil and foliage disease. Damping-off disease in 1+0 Douglas-fir has been associated with the application of ammonium nitrate fertilizer, and many nurseries limit the use of this form of nitrogen during the first growing season.

Insects

Insects have much wider host ranges than diseases do (see Chapter 21). Nurseries adjacent to agricultural land or forest communities may be affected by insect population surges. In recent years, significant damage to British Columbia's nursery crops has been caused by several insect types. The one posing the most widespread problem is the tarnished plant bug (*Lygus lineolaris*), a sucking insect which attacks all species and causes stem and bud deformities. This insect prefers alfalfa and is thought to move into young seedling crops when adjacent hayfields are harvested. Another localized pest is the western spruce budworm (*Choristoneura occidentalis*), which enters into nurseries from surrounding forest stands. The larvae feed on Douglas-fir and spruce seedlings during shoot elongation.

Larvae of the strawberry root weevil (*Otiorhynchus ovatus*) feed on roots late in the summer and damage can go undetected until seedlings are harvested. The marsh crane fly (*Tipula paludosa*) has caused problems at some nurseries, as has the springtail (*Bourletiella hortensis*), the variegated cutworm (*Peridroma saucia*), and the cranberry girdler (*Chrysoteuchia topiaria*).

Various insecticides are used to control these pests when the population or damage is considered to be a significant risk. Accurate identification of pests and diseases is essential if suitable control measures are to be devised. The Ministry of Forests Nursery Pest Officer at Surrey and the Plant Diagnostic Clinic in Victoria provide an identification service. As well, timing sprays properly is critical, as certain stages of insect development are more effectively controlled than others.

Birds and Other Animals

Birds and other animals may cause damage during early crop development (Chapter 22). Birds are particularly fond of ponderosa pine and Douglas-fir seed, probably because of the seed's large size and easy availability.

Damage to lodgepole pine has also been observed. Deeper sowing discourages birds during the early stages of germination, but seeds are easily found as soon as they begin to crack the soil surface. Covering beds with a spun polyester screen shortly after sowing has been effective in southern British Columbia. Nurseries with severe, recurring bird problems should consider screening beds with a netting material.

Mechanical Disturbance

Mechanical damage caused by hail, heavy rain, and strong wind can be devastating to new crops. Soil-binding agents can be effective in preventing bed deterioration during heavy rains and the sand blasting that occurs during wind storms (Armbrust and Dickerson 1971). Windbreaks can help reduce wind velocity. Other sources of damage point out the importance of quality control in cultural operations. For example, seedlings may be uprooted during hand-weeding operations or their stems cut during lateral pruning; roots may be undercut too short and sections of seedbeds damaged by excessive wrenching treatments.

Weeds

Weeds are the most frequent pests found in nurseries. If left unmanaged, they compete for water, nutrients, and light, reducing seedling growth and yield. Weeds also attract insects that may feed on seedlings. All nurseries have a weed prevention and control program that combines mechanical, chemical, and hand-weeding methods. Few herbicides are registered for use in forest nurseries in Canada. The high cost of registration for the relatively small number of hectares under production is economically unattractive for herbicide manufacturers. One report estimated that proper herbicide use could reduce total weed control costs by up to 34% (Maxwell 1984).

SEEDLING CULTURE

Nurserymen manipulate nutritional status, plant water relations, root structure, and growing space to produce healthy seedlings. An additional technique, day length modification, is also being tested but has not been used on an operational scale. Increased height growth has been observed in bareroot crops growing adjacent to outside container crops supplemented with extended photoperiod. The successful use of these cultural techniques can only be achieved if nursery seedlings remain synchronized with the natural environment.

Growth Trends

Under natural conditions, seedlings germinate in early spring and complete height growth in early summer. For many conifers a small resting bud usually forms in response to moisture stress, and seedlings develop resistance to drought stress and frost damage. During the second growing season, height growth results from elongation of bud primordia formed during the first year. The amount of growth is determined by the number of bud primordia formed the previous year, as well as by the nutritional state and available soil moisture. The height growth period is generally short and only one flush of growth occurs. Once the terminal bud is formed, shoots generally do not resume growth in the fall even though soil moisture is replenished.

Roots normally begin to grow in early spring in response to the soil warming. Root growth declines when plant hormones trigger shoot growth, but continues at a low level during the summer months. It increases again in the fall when soil moisture increases, then declines as soil temperatures cool. If the soil has not frozen, some root growth may occur during the entire year.

Nurserymen must be aware of these natural growth cycles, and must apply cultural practices at the proper time and frequency to minimize their disruption. As well, they must recognize species differences and genetic variation within species. For example, high-elevation sources initiate shoot growth later but complete it sooner than do low-elevation sources. If necessary, only the amplitude of the growth cycle should be influenced, not its timing.

TABLE 16.5.   Recommended seasonal applications of N, P, and K during 1+0, 2+0, and transplant production phases (adapted from van den Driessche, 1983a)

Stage of crop development	Element	Pre-plant incorporation (kg/ha)	Post-plant top dressing (kg/ha)		Total year application (kg/ha)
			No. applications	Rate	
1+0	N	30	4	22	118
	P	134			134
	K	50	1	25	75
2+0	N		7	23	161
	P		1	67	67
	K		3	25	75
Transplant	N		4	45	180
	P	67			67
	K	50	2	25	100

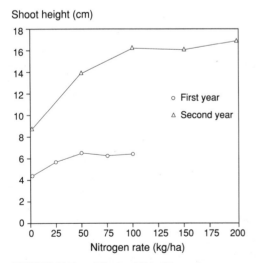

FIGURE 16.5.   Effects of N fertilizer rates on first- (a) and second- (b) year shoot length of Douglas-fir seedlings (adapted from van den Driessche, 1980).

Fertilization

Seedling crops remove elements from soil faster than the elements are replenished through natural mineralization. Fertilizers are applied to maintain a proper level and balance between elements (see Chapter 4). The nutrient levels in seedling tissue are also monitored (see Chapter 17, Table 17.3).

Nitrogen, phosphorous, and potassium are the primary elements applied by all nurseries. Frequency and rate of application of these elements have been developed for bareroot crops grown in British Columbia (van den Driessche 1983a) (Table 16.5). Nitrogen can be used early in the season to stimulate the height growth of slow-growing species or to achieve a specific height standard (Figure 16.5). With some species, growers prefer limiting N application during the growing season. This allows them to reduce the risk of damping-off disease (Sinclair et al. 1975), or to reduce height growth and therefore create a more balanced root:shoot ratio. During the summer, nitrogen is usually withheld or greatly reduced so that bud formation will be induced. Nurseries must be particularly careful in the summer to avoid combining high moisture levels with high N, to prevent seedlings from initiating a second flush of growth (Cleary et al. 1978). A second flush delays the hardening process, making seedlings more susceptible to early frost.

Late season N applications can benefit a crop's subsequent field survival and growth by increasing the availability of nutrient reserves the following growing season. Fall fertilization has been found to enlarge bud size of Douglas-fir, and to increase bud burst following planting (Thompson 1983; Margolis and Waring 1986). Late fall fertilizer studies support the concept that foliar nutrient concentration at the time of outplanting influences field performance. Van den Driessche (1980, 1988b) showed that 2% foliar N resulted in the highest field survival of Douglas-fir.

Phosphorous fertilizers are generally insoluble and must be incorporated into the soil close to the seedling roots. A standard practice in many nurseries is to band ammonium phosphate (11-55-0) 3-5 cm below seed drills before sowing. This greatly improves growth of white and Engelmann spruce seedlings on many nursery sites in British Columbia. Although growth responses to P fertilizers are seldom observed if maintenance dressings are applied at each rotation, one study found that the dry weight of 2+0 Douglas-fir seedlings fertilized at 400 kg/ha P was 50% greater than for those seedlings receiving only 100 kg/ha P (van den Driessche 1984a) (Figure 16.6).

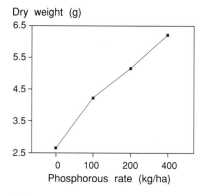

Dry weight (g)

Phosphorous rate (kg/ha)

FIGURE 16.6.   Total dry weight of 2+0 Douglas-fir seedlings for four top dressing rates of P (adapted from van den Driessche, 1989a).

Potassium fertilizers are very soluble and top dressings are recommended after June of the first growing season and throughout the second year (Table 16.5). Evidence of K deficiency has often been noted in 2+0 white spruce seedlings and transplants.

In some British Columbia nurseries, copper, zinc, iron, and boron deficiency symptoms have also been observed. Only small supplemental applications (3-10 kg/ha) of these micronutrients are required. Care must be taken in such applications to avoid toxic levels.

Irrigation

Managing the amount of water supplied to seedlings is based on an understanding of soil characteristics, species requirements, and stage of plant development. Other factors such as weather conditions and the integration of cultural practices, including fertilization and root culture, must also be considered. Because these factors differ from one nursery to another, standard irrigation regimes do not exist. However, each nursery should be able to quantify available soil water and internal seedling moisture stress (McDonald and Running 1979). Soil moisture retention curves or soil tensiometers are good for measuring soil moisture; pressure chambers are best for measuring seedling moisture stress.

High plant stress conditions may not be recognized by nurserymen who rely on visual or tactile methods to assess moisture conditions. Early in the growing season when rapid shoot elongation is taking place, bright, warm days can easily increase seedling moisture stress to levels that limit photosynthesis, even though the soil appears moist.

Irrigation should not be used to promote additional shoot growth beyond early July. Some northwest conifer species must experience *mild* moisture stress for the dormancy process to begin. Dormancy must be initiated by early July so that trees can become frost hardy before the onset of freezing weather, and can develop sufficient resistance to withstand harvesting, overwinter storage, transportation, and planting.

The dormancy process may take 5-6 months from the induction stage to the harvest stage. Nurseries that experience frozen soil conditions in the winter must ensure that crops are ready for harvest 3-4 weeks before freeze-up. Interior nurseries can expect frozen soil by late November, so dormancy must be initiated by early June. This situation stresses further the importance of accelerating growth early in the season, rather than "pushing" for extra growth late in the season. In southern Oregon, an irrigation regime designed to induce seedling dormancy was developed for Douglas-fir (Zaerr et al. 1981). After testing several watering regimes, the authors found that moderate moisture stress (1 megapasquel) during summer months allowed seedlings to achieve the required size standard and stage of dormancy.

Root Culture

Nurseries use three techniques – undercutting, wrenching, and lateral cutting – to modify seedling root form and growth during the production cycle. Root systems may be either severed or greatly disturbed through seedbed agitation for several reasons: 1) to promote a fibrous root system; 2) to control height growth; 3) to encourage dormancy by increasing moisture stress; 4) to prevent development of long roots (tap root and laterals) that would be damaged during lifting and planting; and 5) to reduce intertwining of adjacent root systems, and so increase speed of grading and reduce root damage during sorting.

Undercutting

Undercutting severs the tap root and other long roots which have developed beyond a desired depth. A thin, sharp blade is drawn beneath the seedbed at a depth of 10-15 cm, and is either fixed or reciprocating. The aim is to restrict root development to the upper zone of soil and to stimulate a more fibrous root system. In one study, undercutting notably reduced top growth of ponderosa pine and Douglas-fir seedlings, although its effects on root system morphology were less apparent (Hobbs et al. 1986). No differences in field performance were found 4 years after outplanting on a droughty site.

Undercutting is usually the first root culture activity carried out by a nursery. Species that form a tap root (pines) are usually undercut during the first growing season, in late summer or early fall. Shallow-rooted species (spruce) are undercut during the second year if required. Most nurseries perform undercutting only once. It is a slow process and, when the length of the root has been established, subsequent horizontal root culture involves wrenching.

Wrenching

Wrenching is a much more severe treatment than undercutting. It involves drawing a thicker, broader blade tilted at a 30% angle just beneath the undercut level (Figure 16.7). This treatment tears rather than cuts any new, long roots and disturbs the entire root system by loosening and aerating the soil. The blade is drawn under the seedbed at a faster speed than in undercutting, causing a wave action as it passes. Proper soil moisture is required to

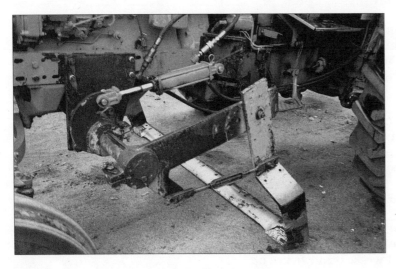

FIGURE 16.7. Wrenching bar mounted beneath tractor.

prevent bed damage. Nurseries may wrench as often as 4-6 times during the summer of the second year. Care must be taken to prevent overstressing stock, as continued high moisture stress levels will limit root growth as well as shoot growth.

Reported effects of wrenching on seedling morphology, physiology, and field performance are very inconsistent. The likely reason is the variations in nursery culture, soil, and climate; in season, depth, and frequency of root culture regime; and in species, variety, and seed source. A thorough review of root culture effect (Duryea 1984) reported the following general results and recommendations about root wrenching:

- Wrenching during the growing season results in early budset and small seedlings.

- Wrenching before the crop has achieved its size specifications may result in a final crop that is small and therefore has a low yield.

- Wrenching when the soil is dry or when the weather is hot, without immediate irrigation, can greatly increase seedling moisture stress. To reduce the risk of seedling damage in the beds and growth loss in outplanted seedlings, wrenching under such conditions should be avoided.

- Wrenching that causes mild seedling moisture stress can help induce budset and hardening and may aid field growth and survival.

- Late summer or fall wrenching may promote root fibrosity.

Several studies indicate that the timing of wrenching treatments is important. Treatments in late summer are most likely to increase field survival without reducing height growth. Since wrenching increases seedling moisture stress, the number of needle primordia developed and the seedling's subsequent height growth may be reduced if wrenching is carried out during bud formation. Van den Driessche (1983b) found that wrenching improved the root:shoot ratio over that in controls, but only late summer wrenching (from August 7 until September 11) resulted in both higher survival and increased shoot growth 2 years after outplanting (Figure 16.8). These results substantiate those of Tanaka et al. (1976) who found that wrenching from July 30 to October 22 increased survival of Douglas-fir. However, in his last study, control seedling survival was depressed because these were growing actively in September, just prior to outplanting.

Lateral pruning

Lateral root pruning cuts roots growing across seedbeds by passing colters, disks, or blades centered between seedling rows at a cutting depth of 12-15 cm. Seedling rows spaced closer than 15 cm make this operation difficult without damaging seedlings. Lateral pruning is done in the second growing season, usually once in the spring before crown closure and then again in the fall if required. It facilitates lifting and minimizes the stripping of fine roots during the grading operation when seedlings are separated from one another.

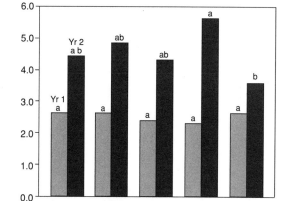

New shoot growth (cm)

FIGURE 16.8.   Effect of wrenching treatment on first- and second-year height growth of 2+0 Douglas-fir seedlings. Values within the same year followed by the same letter are not significantly different at p = 0.05 (adapted from van den Driessche, 1983b).

A modified lateral pruning and undercutting technique is used in some British Columbia nurseries. It involves passing a disk, angled 20-30° from vertical, between each seedling row. In one operation, the angled disks cut lateral roots on one side of each seedling row. The alternate side of each row and tap root is cut after 2-3 weeks. This technique results in a wedge-shaped root mass with most of the roots contained in the top 5 cm. It also reduces the amount of root trimming required during the packing operation.

Control of Bed Density

Much research effort and expense has been devoted to investigating the relationships among bed density, seedling morphology, seedling physiology, and outplant performance. It is generally accepted that seedlings grown at lower densities have greater mass, more vigor, and larger stored nutrient reserves. These characteristics are known to result in better survival and growth after outplanting. Control of growing density through seeding rates or by transplanting are the most effective cultural techniques used by nurserymen to achieve desired caliper and root mass specifications.

For each species, stock type, cultural regime, and nursery environment, there is an optimum growing density which maximizes the number of plantable seedlings for a given size specification. The density that maximizes the number of acceptable seedlings, however, may not always be the most economical, as the cost of harvesting and handling cull seedlings must also be considered. Selecting a growing density is often a compromise between maximizing the number of plantable seedlings and minimizing the number of culls. To meet target size specifications, many 2+0 seedling crops are grown at densities below 250 per lineal bed meter (Figure 16.1).

Tanaka and Kleyn (1987) found that when a minimum stem caliper of 3.5-4.0 mm was sought, yields of 2+0 Engelmann spruce and lodgepole pine were greatest when the seedlings were grown at a density between 200 and 300 per lineal bed meter (LBM). Their data further showed that the percent of packable yield was higher at lower densities than at higher densities, and that Engelmann spruce produced more acceptable seedlings than lodgepole pine at comparable growing densities (Table 16.6).

Lowering seedbed density usually results in larger stem diameter and heavier roots. Seedling height and the root:shoot ratio of some species are also affected by growing density. For coastal and interior varieties of Douglas-fir, lodgepole pine, and Sitka spruce grown 1, 2, 4, 8, and 12 cm apart, wider spacing has been found to increase 2+0 seedling dry weight, diameter, and shoot height (van den Driessche 1982). Strong correlations between seedling size (diameter and dry weight) and subsequent height growth after planting have also been found for all species (Figure 16.9).

In other experiments, van den Driessche (1984b) demonstrated that increases in spacing from 0.5 to 2.0 cm increased the number of needle primordia within the

TABLE 16.6. Number of acceptable 2+0 Engelmann spruce and lodgepole pine seedlings in relation to caliper standard and growing density (adapted from Tanaka and Kleyn, 1987)

Engelmann spruce yield				
Minimum caliper pack standard (m)	Growing density (no./LBM)			
	666	587	451	231
3.0	330	281	261	177
3.5	156	157	167	157
4.0	57	74	99	121
4.5	10	26	42	72
5.0	2	10	12	38

Lodgepole pine yield				
Minimum caliper pack standard (m)	Growing density (no./LBM)			
	770	455	331	207
3.0	154	212	238	169
3.5	52	78	133	141
4.0	12	15	50	90
4.5	1	1	10	35
5.0	0	0	0	10

bud. This could result in greater photosynthetic surface and therefore more growth after planting. In addition, 2+0 Douglas-fir seedlings grown at close spacing tended to develop shade-type needles (large area per unit dry weight), whereas those grown at wide spacing developed sun-type needles (small area per unit dry weight). Seedlings with the latter needles might be better adapted to the high light intensity normally encountered on new planting sites. In the same study, white spruce and Sitka spruce achieved greater stem diameter, total height, and survival when grown at wider spacing in the nursery (van den Driessche 1984b).

Despite the many advantages, there are also several negative aspects of wide spacing and large seedlings. Winter freeze-thaw cycles prohibit the low-density sowing of interior spruce in some nurseries, because widely spaced 1+0 crops are vulnerable to frost heaving. Larger seedlings also cost more to produce. Many expenses at bareroot nurseries are a function of area (hectares, lineal bed meters), and lower seedling yields per area result in higher seedling costs. In such cases, increased field performance of large stock should be weighed against higher production and planting costs.

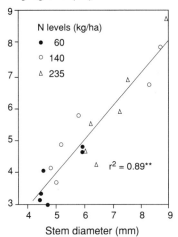

Height growth (cm)

N levels (kg/ha)
● 60
○ 140
△ 235

$r^2 = 0.89^{**}$

Stem diameter (mm)

FIGURE 16.9. Relationship between first season height growth and nursery stem diameter of 2+0 Sitka spruce seedlings. Symbols relate to N fertilizer levels in the nursery (adapted from van den Driessche, 1982).

Transplanting

Providing seedlings with more room in transplant beds or altering production cycles are two other methods of achieving desired seedling morphology or physiology. Transplant seedlings generally have a more fibrous root system, larger stem diameter, and higher root:shoot ratio than seedlings of the same age grown at standard densities. These characteristics are preferred for planting sites having heavy competition, animal pressure, and winter snow press. Interior spruce is the species most often transplanted, followed by Douglas-fir and lodgepole pine. Spruce is produced in a variety of stock types originating from bareroot and container seedlings. Transplanting can be done in the spring, summer, or fall, provided stock is handled carefully and sufficiently irrigated to reduce moisture stress. July transplanting of freshly lifted spruce is done once new height growth has lignified and terminal bud formation has begun. Transplants are grown at bed densities between 60 and 70 per square meter.

Transplant systems using small containerized seedlings (mini-plugs) have gained much interest in recent years. These systems incorporate a short greenhouse production phase of 2-3 months with one or more growing seasons in transplant beds. The two phases are merged by automated transplanting equipment, which extracts seedlings from containers and then transplants them in one operation. Benefits of this system include increased nursery production, a shorter production cycle, better seed use, and improved nursery efficiency through reduced transplanting costs and faster harvesting rates (Hee et al. 1988; Klapprat 1988). Increased stock uniformity and fewer culls increase the possibility of bed-run harvesting.

Other stock types

Regeneration success on high-elevation spruce sites has been increased through the use of summer hot-lifted stock rather than overwinter stored stocks. Stock lifted in November must remain in storage for 8-9 months before high-elevation sites are accessible. The long storage period depletes food reserves, resulting in outplant shock. This delays the height growth cycle and the development of cold hardiness. Summer lifting usually occurs

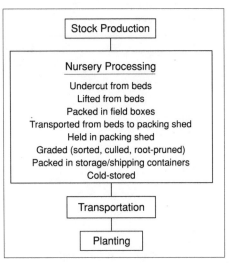

FIGURE 16.10. Sequence of steps during nursery processing of bareroot seedlings for field planting.

after trees have completed height growth and bud formation. Outplanted seedlings continue root growth and caliper development during the remainder of the growing season. At high elevations, however, frost can occur at any time during the year and may severely damage seedlings that have terminal buds which have not become cold hardy.

Sites where there is heavy brush competition or where winter snow press is a concern may require large transplant stock. However, on lodgepole pine sites where competition is low, or on shallow soils where planting is difficult, 1+0 stock has been successful.

HARVESTING PROCESS

When a crop of seedlings is fully grown, it must be removed from nursery beds and prepared for outplanting. Because seedling vigor is constantly at risk during the harvesting process (Figure 16.10), all aspects of harvesting are designed to minimize any negative effects on vigor.

Lift Date

The choice of lift date depends on the time of the year the seedlings are to be outplanted. Bareroot seedlings can be successfully planted provided they are handled carefully, are not in a stage of active height growth, and are not planted into frozen soil (Revel and Coates 1976). Summer- and fall-planted seedlings should be lifted at a stage when no additional height growth will occur after planting, and when they have some cold hardiness to tolerate frost at the planting site. Bareroot seedlings are only moderately resistant to the stresses associated with handling and storage at this point in their growth cycle. The time between removal from the nursery bed and planting should not exceed 3 days. Cool (2-5°C) storage with 95% relative humidity should be provided to minimize loss of vigor during this short period.

Seedlings for spring planting (up to June 15) can be harvested from the nursery in spring shortly before field planting, or harvested the previous fall and stored at cold (2°C) or frozen (-2°C) temperatures. Spring-harvested seedlings are usually very vigorous but have little resistance to stress. As they are post-dormant, the onset of shoot and root growth depends only on warming temperatures.

Planting sites in British Columbia tend to be out of phase seasonally with forest nurseries because of the sites' higher elevations or northern latitudes. Spring at nurseries occurs as early as March to April, yet some planting sites are snow-covered until May and June. The probability of maintaining vigor in spring-lifted stock which has been stored for more than 2 months is low (Ritchie et al. 1985). A more desirable alternative is to fall-harvest just before freeze-up at Interior nurseries and during January at coastal nurseries, combined with frozen (-2°C) storage. Long periods of storage for fall-harvested stock, however, may deplete seedling carbohydrate reserves (Ritchie 1982) (Figure 16.11).

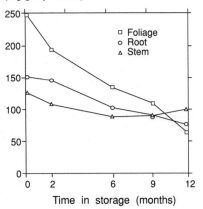

Total nonstructural carbohydrate (mg/g dry matter)

FIGURE 16.11. Changes in total nonstructural carbohydrate concentrations in foliage, stems, and roots of 2+0 Douglas-fir seedlings lifted January 27, 1978, and stored at -1°C. Vertical bars ± 1 standard error (after Ritchie, 1982).

Several studies have compared field performance of spring-lifted and –planted seedlings to fall-lifted, winter-stored, and spring-planted seedlings (van den Driessche 1977; van den Driessche and Cheung 1979; Burdett et al. 1983; Ritchie et al. 1985; Mattsson and Troeng 1986). Properly implemented, either approach is successful provided storage of spring-lifted stock is minimized and fall-lifted stock is planted in late spring.

For each harvest and plant option, the period of storage should be kept short. In practice, large reforestation programs use the fall-lift/winter-store option. Spring lifting is practiced when frozen nursery soil prevents fall lifting or when the nursery environment is in close synchronization with the planting site. This is usually only possible for low-elevation sites, which are a small portion of current planting programs. For small-scale programs where nursery and planting sites are in proximity, the spring-lift/spring-plant option can work well.

Success of fall-lift/winter-store harvesting programs depends on harvesting the seedlings when they have developed resistance to stresses associated with harvesting and long-term cold storage (+2 to -2 °C). Determining when seedlings are ready to lift is therefore critical. Three approaches are generally used. The first one relies on the nurseryman's past experience and the calendar date. Recent weather conditions and the absence of white root tips are typical indicators. The second approach presumes that some measurable aspect of the seedlings' natural environment related to storability can be used to predict lift date. The most commonly used aspect is the number of cumulative chilling hours below a threshold temperature (e.g., chilling hours < 5 °C) for the shoots or roots. This type of approach has been successfully used on Douglas-fir (Ritchie 1984b) and other species (Mullin and Parker 1976). Chilling hour accumulation varies from year to year (Figure 16.12) but can be used to estimate the time that seedlings are ready to harvest if correlations are developed between chilling hours and frost hardiness.

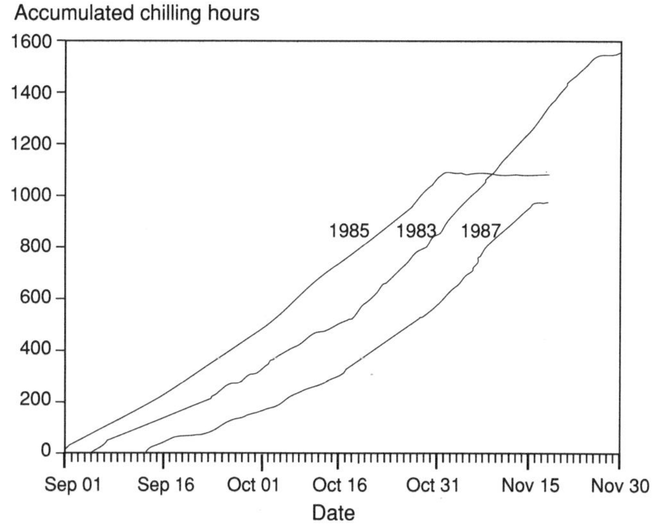

The third type of approach used to predict storability presumes that maximum stress resistance can be measured directly, or at least estimated by some aspect of the seedlings' physiology. Of the many aspects of seedling physiology that have been considered, foliage cold hardiness seems to be an easily measured factor and a good predictor of storability (Colombo et al. 1984; Burr and Tinus 1989). Current practice in British Columbia is to begin lifting for overwinter storage when seedlings exposed to -18 °C sustain less than 25% foliage damage.

Accumulated chilling hours

FIGURE 16.12.   Accumulation of chilling hours (0-10 °C) at Grandview Nursery near Armstrong, B.C., during 1983, 1985, and 1987.

Mechanics of Harvesting

Removal of seedlings from the nursery bed quickly and with minimal physical damage, drying, or temperature stress is required to maintain seedling vigor. Once seedlings are lifted, moisture stress increases to a level governed by atmospheric demands unless foliage and root systems are prevented from drying. Cold storage rooms in which stock is held before grading should be capable of cooling stock to 2 °C and maintaining a relative humidity of 95%.

FIGURE 16.13. Example of harvesting equipment: Fobro lifter and combine.

A variety of machines has been developed for lifting seedlings from nursery beds (Figure 16.13). The choice of machine is usually based on operational considerations which include capital and operating costs, ability to operate in changing soil conditions, degree of physical damage to seedling roots, production rate, seedling size, and species. Most machines lift seedlings into large bins that are used for short-term (1-5 days) storage before grading and packaging. Hand lifting is used at some nurseries when wet soil prohibits machinery access. However, because of lower production rates, high labor costs, and increased risk of employee injury, hand lifting is seldom used for large-scale harvest volumes in British Columbia nurseries.

Grading

Grading is a selection process which presumes that significant morphological variation exists, that it can be detected, and that it can be the basis for separating good from poor seedlings. In forest nurseries, grading is done either on a batch basis or on a single tree basis. Batch grading, in which entire units of planting stock are evaluated as a whole, is little used. It is limited to situations where most of the individuals in a seedlot or stock type are unsatisfactory because of disease or insect damage, or, conversely, where almost all individuals exceed minimum acceptable standards. More commonly, single tree grading is used. The presumption is that the population variance can be reduced by eliminating individuals which fall below some minimum level, and that the graded, more uniform population will have a better quality or field performance potential. The idea is open to some debate and has recently been the subject of a IUFRO symposium (Mason et al. 1989).

There is no doubt that single tree grading on the basis of characteristics such as height, stem diameter, and root fibrosity increases the uniformity of planting stock. It is less clear, however, that increased uniformity actually represents an increase in quality that will result in improved plantation performance. Economic analysis such as that undertaken by Blake et al. (1989) should accompany any decision to grade planting stock to specific size standards.

Storage

Seedlings destined for field planting must be packaged in a container that gives protection from moisture loss and mechanical damage, and that is easily transported from the nursery to the planting site. Moisture loss is minimized by the use of either polyethylene bags or polyethylene-coated, multi-walled, kraft paper bags. Physical protection and handling ease are provided by cardboard or plastic storage cartons. When mechanical damage can be avoided, seedlings may be shipped in storage bags alone.

Seedlings spring-lifted or actively growing (with swelling or flushing buds and white root tips) should be stored at in-carton temperatures between 2 and 4°C. At these temperatures, storage mold can be a problem, particularly if seedlings have dead or soil-covered foliage. Duration of storage should be no greater than 30 days for spring-lifted stock that has not begun to grow. Actively growing, spring-lifted stock should be planted within 2 weeks and the period of dark storage should be limited to 5 days. Fall- and winter-lifted seedlings scheduled for spring planting should be stored at in-carton temperatures between -1 and -3°C. This slows seedling respiration and reduces mold development.

Seedlings can be held in frozen storage for 6-7 months. All species grown in British Columbia can be stored at frozen temperatures if the seedlings have been harvested at their optimum stage of storability. Fluctuating in-carton temperatures must be avoided, as freeze-thaw cycles can result in seedling dehydration or initiate premature growth. To avoid loss of vigor and prevent growth of storage molds, seedlings should be kept frozen until no more than 1 week before field planting. Ideally, seedlings should be allowed to thaw gradually at 2°C in a controlled storage room. The moisture-proof storage bags should not be opened to speed the thawing process, as excessive moisture loss by seedlings will hurt field performance potential.

Forest nurseries work to provide vigorous seedlings that can survive and grow when planted on forest sites. Foresters must understand seedling growth cycles and the role of nursery culture in those cycles if they are to be successful in managing the transport, field handling and planting of seedlings.

17 SEEDLING PRODUCTION AND PROCESSING: CONTAINER

E. Van Eerden and J.W. Gates

Following the lead of Jack Walters, former Professor of Forestry at UBC, who invented and developed the Walters' bullet (Walters 1961, 1963, 1969) for mechanized planting, foresters from the Pacific Forestry Centre, Forestry Canada, and the B.C. Ministry of Forests, Silviculture Branch undertook, in 1967, to develop an operational container seedling system for the province (Kinghorn 1970, 1974; Arnott 1973; Sjoberg 1974). As a result of their efforts, container seedling techniques had been adopted on a wide scale in the province by the early 1970's.

There were a number of reasons for this success:

- The favorable climate of southern British Columbia permitted the production of relatively vigorous stock in small volume containers in simple facilities. Earlier efforts to introduce container-grown stock in British Columbia and Ontario (McLean 1959) depended on rapid production (8-10 weeks) of very small seedlings.
- It was recognized that the very small seedlings that had been produced in containers in the past would not be able to compete with the vegetation on many sites in the province.
- A combination of container culture, engineering expertise, and operational successes was in place when funds were made available for a rapid expansion in the provincial planting program.
- Container seedling production and planting costs were competitive with bareroot stock.

This chapter describes how the container production practices now used in British Columbia came about.

DEVELOPMENT OF THE BC/CFS STYROBLOCK REFORESTATION SYSTEM

Early trials with bullet seedlings had shown that removing seedlings from their container just before planting resulted in increased survival and growth (Arnott 1972, 1974; Van Eerden 1972; Gardner 1981). In the Walters' bullet, however, designed with a slit down one side and drainage holes at the tip (Walters 1961, 1963, 1969), plug seedlings could not be extracted easily because the roots became stuck. To address the problem, a new container — the "BC/CFS Styroblock" — was developed in 1969-70. A design modification 2 years later, aimed at preventing the spiralling of roots (especially of the pines), resulted in vertical ribs being incorporated into the styroblock containers.

TABLE 17.1. Styroblocks commonly used in British Columbia

Styroblock		No. of cavities/ block	Gross cavity volume (mL)	Cavity diam. (cm)	Cavity depth (cm)	No. of cavities/ m²
211A	(2A)	240	39	2.5	11.4	1130
211	(2)	192	39	2.5	11.4	1055
313A	(4A)	198	62	2.8	13.3	936
313B	(4)	160	65	3.0	12.7	764
415B	(8B)	112	106	3.6	14.9	527
415	(8)	80	133	4.1	15.2	441

Initially, the choice of container sizes was limited to two blocks, the "Styro 2" and the "Styro 8", designating container volumes of approximately 2 and 8 in.^{3}, respectively. These containers are now known as "PSB 211" and "PSB 415", indicating plugs (P) in styroblocks (SB) with, respectively, a diameter of approximately 2 and 4 cm and depths of 11 and 15 cm. Experience with these two containers led to the development and use of several others, the most common of which are shown in Table 17.1.

The increase in seedling density (no. of cavities/m²) achieved by converting from styroblocks 313B to 313A and 415 to 415B resulted from management pressure to increase seedling output under limited budgets. Experience has shown that output is not raised because of increased problems with disease and the production of larger numbers of seedlings below target size.

The first operationally planted styroblock seedlings were grown at the Pacific Forestry Centre in Victoria and planted near Houston, B.C., as part of a planting productivity trial in 1970 (Vyse et al. 1971). The trial used an original approach to styro-plug planting that was founded on the concept that seedlings should be left in their containers until time of planting, to minimize the potential for seedling disturbance and damage to the root system during handling. However, transporting seedlings in their containers, including cull seedlings and empty cavities, proved to be logistically difficult and costly. No evidence has been found to suggest that seedlings that have been extracted, graded, and packaged at the nursery show any detrimental effects of the nursery packaging procedure. As a result, the combination of improved logistics and favorable field results precipitated the move towards the shipping of graded and packaged container seedlings in British Columbia.

Styroblocks have remained the most popular containers used in British Columbia. In addition to being lightweight, relatively inexpensive, reuseable, and precisely modular (which makes automated processing easier), they are available with a number of specialized features. These include copper coating for chemical root pruning to prevent root spiralling, and holes between the cavities to permit better airflow through the seedling canopy and so reduce disease. There are also some disadvantages with styroblocks: they are bulky; they are not easily disposable; and contamination of the container surface by disease or weeds is difficult to eradicate. However, as work with the containers continues, improvements in design will likely address these problems.

THE EARLY APPROACH TO CONTAINER SEEDLING PRODUCTION

Because of the favorable climatic conditions of southern coastal British Columbia, initial production of container seedlings in the province was limited to the Pacific Forestry Centre in Victoria, the Koksilah Nursery at Duncan on Vancouver Island, and, starting in 1971, the Surrey Nursery in the Lower Mainland.

Seedlings were generally grown in open compounds or shade-frames. The quality and size of seedlings produced in such containers in single crop rotations were superior to that of container seedlings produced as multiple crops elsewhere. Open compound PSB 211 spruce (*Picea*) usually attained root weights of only 180-230 mg. Although this small container stock showed good initial survival, such seedlings were ill-equipped to cope with competing vegetation. Lodgepole pine (*Pinus contorta*), however, produced as PSB 211 in open compounds, performed favorably at all stages of establishment, and continues to be produced this way today.

During the mid-1970's, the B.C. Ministry of Forests established test greenhouses at Skimikin, Vernon, Red Rock, and Telkwa. Since then, greenhouse use has resulted in a rapid increase in the container production of all species except lodgepole pine.

British Columbia's approach to container seedling production has emphasized single-crop, low-risk rotations, largely during the normal growing season (Van Eerden 1974, 1981). As a result, the container stock is relatively large, and outdoor overwintering — the single most significant risk associated with container production — has been avoided. These two factors, the size of the stock and the minimal overwinter losses, account largely for the dominant position of container seedling production in the province.

CURRENT CONTAINER PRODUCTION TECHNIQUES

Seedlings are grown in facilities ranging from highly sophisticated greenhouses to open compounds (Matthews 1971; Brix 1972; Tinus and McDonald 1979; Scarratt et al. 1982; Carlson 1983). The stock standards achieved depend on factors such as sowing date, type of facility, and cultural program. Strict adherence to sowing dates that have been shown to produce a satisfactory species/stock type is important regardless of the production facility.

The choice of block in which the crop is to be grown is a major factor determining the final morphology of the trees. High seedling density blocks such as the PSB 211 are commonly used for lodgepole pine or species that are being grown for transplant purposes. The seedlings grown in these containers must be relatively small if they are to be of high quality. The most commonly used blocks in British Columbia are the PSB 313A and 313B. These are capable of producing seedlings suitable for many of the planting stock needs in the province. Rather than adopting lower densities at the outset, some growers have elected to start with a higher cavity density, and to reduce seedling spacing to a lower density by rogueing. This technique is especially appropriate for the PSB 313A, which has a cavity volume that is essentially the same as the lower density PSB 313B.

The largest seedling stock types, suitable for regenerating brush sites or for achieving rapid regeneration, are grown in the PSB 415B. On occasion, other block configurations are used to meet specialized needs.

Greenhouses

Generally speaking, the practice in British Columbia is to produce one crop per production area per year rather than to produce multiple crops, as is done elsewhere. This single crop production is relatively costly but ensures a higher quality tree than is grown under multiple cropping regimes.

January to early February sowing dates permit the development of large, vigorous stock that is suitable for planting in the summer and fall of the same year. A small portion of the spruce production is now grown this way. If the stock is properly treated to ensure dormancy before planting and if the sites are suitable, this stock will establish a good root system on the site before winter and will develop in physiological synchronization with the following season. The advantage of these trees over summer-planted 2+0 containerized seedling stock is the shorter planning time that is required, and the elimination of the overwintering risk associated with the 2+0 production.

Later sowing dates, ranging from late February through April, are commonly used for the more conventional 1+0 stock. In most instances, this stock will have achieved the required standards by the fall of the year it is planted and will be frozen-stored for spring planting.

Open Compound

Open compound crops are grown without overhead protection. The choice of nursery site is therefore a vital consideration if the stock is to be successful. Hot Interior sites are suitable for growing 1+0 lodgepole pine, but the stock must be lifted into storage before cold weather. Where the stock is to be grown on the site for more than one season (thus being exposed through the winter), milder coastal climates are the preferred locations. Severe winter losses have occurred when improperly hardened or protected stock has been subjected to extreme cold (Green and Fuchigami 1985) in Interior as well as coastal locations.

Given the significance of weather conditions for the overwintering of open compound crops, the recent introduction of 2+0 container stock reflects economic and logistic necessity rather than biological desirability. The increasing demand for larger stock, including bareroot and container seedling transplants, and the associated high costs of producing such stock, led to the search for lower-cost alternatives (Errico and Pelchat 1984). From various projects and data collected during summer planting studies near Prince George, 2+0 container stock appeared to offer an option, as long as it was summer-planted in the second season (Revel and Coates 1976). However, experience has since shown that this stock may not be a viable alternative for spring planting in the third season. Overwintering during two consecutive winters poses a very high risk of loss as stock can become pot-bound and may store poorly. Meeting the requirements for somewhat larger-than-average-size container stock can still be done through the use of early-sown 1+0 stock that has been carefully manipulated and conditioned through environmental control. In addition to cost, the logistics of handling a very large spring planting program (Prince George) was another consideration in the adoption of the 2+0 container stock type.

When successfully produced, open compound-grown 2+0 spruce is a large, stress-resistant, woody stock which will withstand severe site conditions of drought, snow, and brush press. Budset generally occurs late in the spring of the second year. By early summer, the seedling tops are dormant but root growth is rapid. If planted at this time, the seedling will establish new well-developed roots on the planting site. As with the early-sown greenhouse crop, this crop is in physiological synchronization with season, though it has a greater amount of wood. However, the open compound stock type is much less suitable for winter storage and planting the next spring. By fall, the understory needles are senescent and may be affected by foliar diseases. In addition, the roots will have become lignified within the container and subsequent establishment and growth may be handicapped.

More vigorous species, such as western redcedar (*Thuja plicata*) and Douglas-fir (*Pseudotsuga menziesii*), grown as 2+0 are less successful than spruce because nutrition and disease are hard to control in the second year. Size becomes excessive, and crops require large amounts of water and nutrients if they are to be kept healthy. These same conditions produce an ideal environment for foliage disease to develop. Lodgepole pine is particularly unsuitable for this stock form, because roots become lignified in the plugs and pot-bound in the containers. This results in poor development on the site and the occurrence of toppling years after planting.

Seed and Seeding

The vast bulk of the seed sown in British Columbia forest nurseries is obtained from wild collections. This raises the question of quality in all its aspects. The B.C. Ministry of Forests has a world-class center for seed preparation in Surrey. Processes such as extraction, cleaning, testing, storage, and stratification are carried out at this facility. Germination and vitality, two measures that are used to indicate whether seed is of suitable quality for containers, are relatively easy to determine.

An area of increasing concern to nurseries is that of seed-borne diseases (Chapter 20). *Fusarium* and *Sirococcus*, for example, are known to be present on the collected seed. In many instances, the affected seedlots are flagged for the growers' attention. Another disease recently identified as being present on some seed is *Cylindrocarpon*. This has caused severe root rot in some container-grown crops. As well, seed collected from squirrel caches is often infested with *Caloscypha fulgens* which may reduce germination, and which can make seeding difficult because of the clumping of seeds by mycelia (Sutherland et al. 1989).

Sowing rules based on probabilities and local experience have been developed to aid nurseries in determining the number of seeds that must be sown to grow the requested number of seedlings (Table 17.2) (Vyse and Rudd 1974; Matthews 1981).

TABLE 17.2. Present B.C. Ministry of Forests sowing rules for container sowing

Germination rate	Seeds/ cavity	Oversow factor[a]
100-96	2	1.25
95-93	2	1.30
92-90	2	1.35
89-86	2	1.40
85-81	3	1.30
80-76	3	1.35
75-71	3	1.40
70-66	3	1.45
65-61	4	1.50
60-56	4	1.55
55-51	4	1.60
50-46	4	1.65

[a] Number of extra containers sown.

The table shows a dramatic increase in seed requirements when seed of low germination capacity is used. Using seed with a high germination capacity translates into cost savings at every step in the system. Less labor is involved in collecting the seed and in processing, sowing, thinning, and grading the crop. Oversow factors are also lower, and space requirements are, therefore, reduced.

Seeding has been mechanized with a rotating vacuum drum system developed in British Columbia (Nyborg and Shikaze 1974).

Media

The growing medium used in container production has no soil and is made up primarily of peat. The chemical and physical properties of the components are closely monitored (Baker 1957; Lucas and Davis 1961). The peat goes through standardized testing procedures (Carlson 1983) and the bulk density of the medium is controlled during block-filling. Poor quality peat or improper filling of the blocks leads to water drainage and aeration problems, and predisposes crops to serious root disease such as *Pythium* and *Cylindrocarpon* (Sutherland et al. 1989). Work is currently under way to improve the characterization of a desirable medium, and to correlate this with irrigation management.

Cultural Management

The program for outside-grown crops is based on the local climate. Because temperature control or modification is limited to heat and frost protection using irrigation, site environmental characteristics become overriding factors in the success of the crop. Whether grown outdoors or in the greenhouse, crops undergo many of the same initial problems. The seed must be kept moist under temperatures conducive to germination. In open compounds, this means that the seeding date must be late enough to reduce the risk of cold temperatures and frost while still allowing for adequate growth in the season. In the greenhouse, low temperatures are eliminated. High temperatures are harmful to the germinants and require lowering through mist or light irrigations in both open compounds and greenhouses. Unfortunately, water applications of this nature produce conditions that can lead to the development of a number of serious diseases. The management skill of the nurseryman is important in achieving successful germination of the crops.

Environmental factors tend to limit growth of outside-grown crops. The predominant problem is the lack of control over heat. Physiological processes are temperature-dependent, with growth slowing when the temperatures are above or below an optimum. Thus, most crops that are grown out-of-doors require two seasons to reach the desired size. In the protection of a greenhouse, the temperature can be held closer to the optimum, which allows growth to proceed at a faster pace.

In both open compounds and greenhouses, water and nutritional management can be kept close to the needs of the crop. This results in more rapid growth than is generally achieved in soil-grown crops. Watering practices are designed to keep stress levels low, while permitting adequate root aeration and allowing the foliage to dry. Successful water management during crop growth is a key factor in reducing or eliminating disease and weed problems. Some programs use drought stress to cause budset and harden the crop in preparation for winter. This practice is becoming less common in light of new findings on its effect on the health and vigor of the seedling. When drought becomes severe in containers, roots can die. Dead roots become a point of entry for disease, and nutrient uptake is reduced. There is some evidence that terminal bud damage or death can occur. In spruce this may result in rosetting, the development of numerous buds in a "rosette" where there should be a single terminal bud. Research on Douglas-fir has shown that the use of drought to cause budset also results in abnormal terminal bud development in that species, and can inhibit the frost-hardening process (MacDonald and Owens 1987).

The goal of fertilizer programs in the nursery is to achieve balanced growth and ensure that trees leaving the nursery have a balanced complement of nutrients. Root development can be improved at the expense of some shoot growth if the nutrition is manipulated to reduce a nutrient, such as nitrogen, below the optimum level (Ingestad 1962). In this case, the seedling allocates more of its carbon resources to root development. Properly applied, the feeding program will result in a seedling with a desirable shoot:root ratio and suitable size, health, and vigor. Open compound crops rely on both a slow release fertilizer incorporated into the medium and a soluble feed in the water. With a better understanding of the nutritional needs of the crop, nurseries are reducing their dependence on incorporated fertilizers and are managing well with solubles in the greenhouse-grown crops. Nevertheless, in recognition of the potential benefits that slow release fertilizers may have on performance after outplanting (Brockley 1988), efforts are continuing to develop slow release fertilizer formulations and applications that will not jeopardize control over seedling growth in the nursery.

Nursery nutrition is known to have an impact on date of bud burst, duration of leader growth, and other growth factors that affect the seedling after it has left the nursery (Ballard and Carter 1985). Tissue nutrient analysis is widely used to monitor the plants, and tissue nutrient levels have been developed for producing high quality seedlings that grow rapidly after outplanting. The levels currently deemed satisfactory are shown in Table 17.3.

Carbon dioxide (CO_2) feeding, which has been common in horticultural practice for many years, is also being incorporated into feeding programs of forest seedling crops. The CO_2 is injected into the greenhouse environment (from CO_2 burners) at or above the ambient level of about 350 ppm.

TABLE 17.3.   Recommended tissue nutrient levels

Element	Target %	Current range %
Nitrogen	2.0	1.5 - 3.5
Phosphorus	0.25	0.2 - 0.4
Potassium	1.0	0.8 - 2.0
Calcium	0.35	0.2 - 1.0
Magnesium	0.15	0.12 - 0.3
Sulphur	10% of nitrogen	Minimum 0.15
Iron	100	80 - 600
Copper	8	4 - 20
Zinc	30	25 - 80
Manganese	100	>80
Boron	30	20 - 50

During their early juvenile phase (i.e., in the nursery), conifer seedlings respond to photoperiodic control. Under long nights (short days), whether naturally or artificially induced, seedlings cease vegetative growth and often set a bud. In many nurseries the prevailing day length is too short to allow continuous growth. The day is therefore artificially lengthened to 19 hours with low intensity light during the vegetative growth phase. When the seedlings have reached the desired size, the lights are turned off, effectively shortening the day and causing budset (Arnott 1974). Where the day is long enough to cause growth to continue, blackout systems have been installed in some greenhouses. This allows the nurseryman to extend the nights (shorten the days) artificially on the crop, and thus limit height growth (Dormling et al. 1968; Heide 1974a, 1974b).

Under long nights, the processes leading to dormancy and frost hardiness also begin. The first stages of frost hardiness are hastened by short days and warm conditions. During this treatment period, a significant amount of root and root collar diameter development can occur if the trees are not under stress. For further hardiness to develop, cooler conditions and, ultimately, temperatures near freezing are required. These processes must develop sequentially if stock quality is to attain the maximum cold hardiness possible (Heide 1974a). Frost hardiness testing is carried out to ensure that the trees are suitable to be lifted for cold storage. When subjected to controlled freezing to -18 °C, no more than 25% foliage damage is allowed. Testing has shown that trees meeting this criterion retain their quality when cold-stored (Dureya 1985; Simpson, 1990).

Stock may be lifted during the summer and early fall for planting at that time. Later lifted stock going to cold storage must satisfy the freezer test criteria. All stock must meet stringent morphological specifications when it is lifted. The specifications vary according to species and to the planting window for which they are intended.

Crop Monitoring

All aspects of the production cycle are monitored. Monitoring begins with ensuring that the quality of components such as peat and vermiculite used to grow the crop meet specific quality requirements before they are mixed. As the crop develops, tissue and morphological analyses are used to guide the grower in the nutritional and environmental programs needed to meet the final quality objectives for the crop. Growth is monitored on the basis of "standard" growth curves, developed for species, provenances, and nursery locations and facilities. Morphological readiness for lifting and packaging is determined on the basis of scatter diagrams which estimate the proportion of seedlings that have attained the morphological standards.

Lifting and Packaging

As stock is lifted, it is generally bundled in groups of 20 to 25 and the roots are wrapped with a thin plastic film. The bundles are placed in kraft paper bags, coated with a polyethylene film in waxed cartons. Lifting, grading, and packaging are largely limited to manual operations. Recently, the Ministry of Forests has made significant progress in developing a fully automated processing system, which includes computer vision grading.

Cold Storage

Stock destined for high elevations or Interior locations is generally frozen. A temperature of -3 °C will usually maintain the stock temperature at -2 °C. If conditions are carefully controlled, stock may be stored for prolonged periods with very little deterioration.

Coastal species are mostly stored at +2 °C. Because stock quality deteriorates more rapidly at temperatures above freezing, storage periods are short. In addition, some foliage and root diseases grow well at this temperature, and therefore the stock must have a very low incidence of disease if storage is to be successful. Several nurseries, however, have recently managed to freeze-store coastal species at -2 °C.

Container Stock Quality Considerations

Although there is much research under way on the relationship between various physiological characteristics and the performance of container stock after outplanting, no combination of physiological traits yet predicts adequately potential field performance for the wide variety of site conditions normally encountered in British Columbia. Neither are any of the current parameters suitable for practical and cost-efficient assessment on an operational basis. Field foresters are left largely to rely on morphological measurements and intuition.

Nevertheless, some tests are able to show how stock may perform under controlled conditions. Seedling quality, defined as "fitness for purpose" by Sutton (1980), can be measured in terms of root growth capacity (RGC), dormancy and hardiness, bud size and morphology, tissue nutrient levels, and stress. Recent work by Binder et al. (1988) has brought the reliability of the RGC test into question. At best, the test serves to separate live from dead seedlings, although modifications to the testing methodology (Haywood-Farmer 1989) have improved its utility. The Oregon State University stress test (McCreary and Dureya 1985) is probably the most reliable one now available, but it is very time consuming. A promising new development, a method which measures variable chlorophyll fluorescence (Vidaver et al. 1988), may provide a superior test. It is likely, however, that a combination of tests will be required to predict seedling performance adequately (Lavender 1989).

FUTURE TRENDS

Given current indications and past performance, it is likely that the demand for container stock will grow. Increasing knowledge, better seed quality, and the introduction of computerized, environmentally controlled production techniques will result in greater improvements in stock quality. As well, the trend towards larger containers and larger stock types will continue as the forest industry's responsibility for reforestation grows.

High priorities in improving nursery efficiency include developing techniques for separating low vigor, non-viable seeds from vigorous seeds with high germination capacities, and for automating the harvesting process. The use of expensive plug transplants can probably be avoided through improved site preparation. Also a high priority is the development of a fully automated "mini-transplant" system (Van Eerden 1981) — one that will eliminate empty cavities and facilitate the production, everywhere in the province, of large container stock at reasonable cost and without significant risk.

The increasing reliance of the forest industry on private sector seedling producers and the transfer of much of the reforestation responsibility to the forest industry has brought the producer and the customer closer together. This greater cooperation and contact will ultimately benefit reforestation in British Columbia.

PLANTING AND SEEDING

18

W.K. Mitchell, G. Dunsworth, D.G. Simpson, and A.Vyse

Planting in British Columbia is big business. The Ministry of Forests indicates that the rapid rise in numbers of trees planted through the 1970's and 1980's will peak in 1991 at 320 million per year, and then decline, as basic silviculture requirements are met on backlog areas, to a steady state of 210 million per year by the end of the century (Figure 18.1). The Ministry expects that approximately 65% of all denuded areas will be planted then, and that the cost of planting and associated site preparation, seed collection, and seedling production activities will be about $150 million annually.

The planting program has reached such a large size, and achieved such a dominant position in British Columbia silviculture, because it produces acceptable results much more frequently and faster than does natural regeneration under present day harvesting conditions. Average survival from 1981 to 1987 is shown in Figure 18.2. These numbers indicate that even with the massive expansion in planting activity, performance has managed to rise steadily. This is a tribute to the many people who work in the planting industry, from cone pickers and planters to supervisors. Provincial survival figures tell only part of the story, of course, because such averages hide a great deal of variation due to site, species, and stock differences. Nevertheless, the fact that only one in eight plantations requires replanting across the province supports the claims for success.

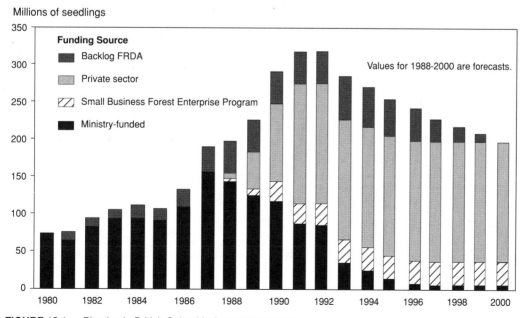

FIGURE 18.1. Planting in British Columbia from 1980 to 2000.

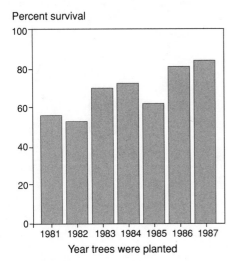

FIGURE 18.2. Average plantation survival for 1981 to 1987.

This chapter explains how this level of success can be maintained and even improved. The reasons for good performance are many: the benefits of seed selection, site preparation, and post-planting vegetation control are explained in other chapters. This chapter focuses on appropriate stock type selection, stock handling, and storage, and on the many guidelines developed from countless planting operations. It concludes with a short section on direct seeding. Many trials of direct seeding have been carried out in the province, with mixed success. The experience is reviewed here for those readers who might wish to consider seeding as an alternative to what is sometimes the high cost of planting.

STOCK TYPE SELECTION

Stock type selection requires the silviculturist to have an understanding of seedling morphology and physiology so that the seedling can be matched to the most stressful microclimatic conditions on the site. This choice is constrained by the biology of the species being planted and by the ability to control nursery culture, or the sources of stress from the nursery gate to the planting site.

Hobbs (1984) has suggested that, on most sites, a single factor can usually be identified as the primary cause of seedling mortality or growth reduction. Thus, effective stock type selection requires site-specific assessments of what those factors are, when they occur, and how long they last. This information must then be related to the expected phenology of the available stock types.

Primary Sources of Seedling Stresses

There are five primary sources of seedling stress in most regeneration environments which may first affect seedling establishment and then growth performance:

- drought
- flood
- frost
- heat
- mechanical

Other stresses, such as limited nutrient availability, are unlikely to affect seedling establishment though they may influence growth over a longer time. On sites where the primary sources of stress are the same, differences can often be found in the duration, intensity, and seasonal timing of the stress. Site conditions that influence these aspects of primary stresses are:

- soil type (texture, organic matter, and coarse fragment content), which can affect temperature (surface and depth) and seasonal water budget;
- soil rooting depth which can affect moisture and nutrient availability;
- slope and aspect, which can affect duration and intensity of solar radiation, in turn affecting temperature and site moisture;

- elevation, which can affect length of growing season, seasonal temperature, and patterns of precipitation;

- vegetation, which can affect light intensity and quality, temperature, soil moisture availability, and nutrient availability; and

- latitude, which can affect length of growing season, temperature, and seasonal precipitation.

Table 18.1 lists the conditions under which risk of stress and lethal damage is high, and the potential lethal effect. Information on these conditions can be obtained from the Research Sections of the Ministry of Forests. Records from the Atmospheric Environment Service or local fire weather station can also be used. All sources are limited in extent and their use requires careful extrapolation.

TABLE 18.1. Primary stresses and associated lethal effects

Primary stress	High risk condition	Lethal effect[a]
1. Drought		
Winter	- soil temperature < 4˚C - high evaporative demand due to warm air temperatures and low snow cover	- cell/tissue dehydration - turgor loss - cell membrane lysis
Summer	- soil moisture tension > 1.5 MPa - high evaporative demand	
2. Flood	- depressed planting microsites - prolonged soil flooding - prolonged root dipping	- root die-back - carbohydrate depletion - top desiccation
3. Frost	- frost pockets - air temperature below cold hardiness capabilities of the chosen species	- cell membrane lysis
4. Heat	- surface temperature > 50˚C - needle temperature > 30˚C	- protein and enzyme destruction in stem cells at or near soil surface
5. Mechanical	- animals - handling abuse - ravel - snow - vegetation	- physical impact - pressing - carbohydrate depletion

[a] These stresses can be additive and even synergistic (see Chapter 4 on seedling physiology).

Morphological and Physiological Features

Site-specific design of seedlings is a silvicultural ideal. Practically, however, this is not possible and flexibility in the stock type selected is necessary. Nurseries produce standard stock types that meet a variety of needs, and the forester is generally best varying the stock types chosen rather than trying to specify extraordinary morphological or physiological characteristics outside the stock type norm.

Morphological features

Once the primary stress has been identified, the next step is to select morphological minimums which will produce a seedling capable of tolerating the stress. In general, the emphasis should be on selecting stock with suitable root collar calipers and good shoot:root balance. These are the morphological features most likely to affect seedling response to drought and heat stress. It is unlikely that any variation in morphological features can overcome frost when it is the major cause of mortality, but larger seedlings are more likely to recover if the stress is sublethal.

What is a desirable shoot:root balance? That depends on the physiological capabilities of the species to deal with the primary stress. Species that have drought tolerance or avoidance mechanisms will require a small shoot (transpirational surface) area relative to their root area. Species with better water management capabilities can carry larger shoots for the same absorptive root area (Hennessey and Dougherty 1984).

Balance can be measured in a number of ways: height:caliper (where caliper is measured at the root collar); caliper:root dry weight; shoot dry weight:root dry weight; or shoot volume:root volume. The measures that tend to be the best predictors of survival and growth are the first two (Cleary et al. 1978; Chavasse 1980; Thompson 1985). Good balance for most container-grown species and sites in British Columbia is height:caliper of less than 80;

caliper:root dry weight of less than 4.0; and shoot dry weight:root dry weight of less than 2.0 (Dunsworth 1988b). On hot, dry sites, higher calipers are desirable (> 4 mm) and the ratios should be closer to 65, 3.0, and 1.5, respectively.

Good form and structure can significantly help seedlings endure the stress imposed by environmental factors. However, it is now well recognized that the best-looking seedling will only function as well as its physiological vigor will allow. Thus, the final step in stock type selection is to specify suitable levels of vigor.

Physiological tests of seedling vigor

Physiological tests differ from morphological targets in that the tests provide information about the ability of a seedling to function. Ritchie (1984a) calls the results of such tests "performance attributes," as distinct from material or morphological attributes.

Information on root growth capacity (RGC), frost hardiness, and nutritional status can be obtained within a reasonable time (1-2 weeks). Dormancy intensity and stress resistance can also be tested, but over a longer period (1-2 months). New tests are being developed which will allow a quicker assessment (1 day to 1 week) of the photosynthetic mechanism (chlorophyll fluoresence), whole plant stress and damage (gaseous test), and carbohydrate levels.

Minimum levels of RGC and frost hardiness have been defined for British Columbia conifers. In general, RGC should be greater than 1.0 at the time of planting as measured by Burdett's (1986) Index of Root Growth (IRG). Higher indices should provide relatively greater absorptive capacity. This would be most beneficial on sites with large seasonal soil moisture deficits or high evaporative demand conditions following planting. The IRG minimums for these kinds of conditions should be 2.0.

Frost hardiness minimums should be established according to the minimum temperature the silviculturist wishes to avoid and the level of risk he or she is willing to accept. Present operational practice requires lifting at the nursery to be delayed until the seedlings can withstand a freezing test down to -18°C. This emphasizes the need for site-specific information on duration, intensity, and timing of frost events. Because of the theoretical association of increased drought resistance with frost hardiness, it may soon be feasible to establish drought tolerance minimums according to frost hardiness in some species.

STOCK HANDLING, FIELD STORAGE, AND TRANSPORTATION

Ideally, seedlings should be moved from nursery to planting site and planted by the same person within a single day. This would be similar to the level of care given to garden plants. Unfortunately, circumstances conspire against this ideal and compromises must be made. These compromises often have a negative effect, but experience has shown that the effect can be minimized if the people involved in the care of handling, storage, and transportation activities are well informed about the seedlings' needs and the best field procedures to use.

The goal of good handling, storage, and transportation is to ensure that the full growth potential of the seedling at the point it leaves the nursery bed or container is present when it is planted. All stress and physical damage contribute to triggering a shock or survival response in the seedling. Instead of committing all its resources to growth, the seedling shifts its priorities to adjustment and repair and its growth slows. All seedling damage is cumulative; each occurrence adds to the effect of previous damage or stress if full recovery has not been achieved before subsequent stress. Severe damage or stress may result in mortality.

Stock handling guidelines are designed to prevent the circumstances that put seedlings under stress and result in damage. These circumstances include:

- heat, frost, and rapid temperature change;
- excessive moisture (if too wet for too long the seedling will drown) and excessive dryness (if too dry the seedling cells will desiccate);
- excessive radiation (the evaporative energy of radiation quickly dries the seedling and damages the root hairs);
- physical damage; and
- molds and fungi.

Information on long-term storage can be found in Chapters 16 and 17. Field storage, transportation, and handling procedures should be simple and direct. Seedlings should be stored for as short a time as possible and the number of steps from nursery to planting site minimized. This requires careful coordination of activities, and cooperation and understanding between the shippers and the planters. Shipments of seedlings that sit on site in less than perfect storage conditions must be avoided.

Handling Boxes and Containers

Seedling containers should be handled like boxes of eggs, not bales of hay. Dropping and slamming the boxes, sitting on tree bags, and driving fast on rough roads will all contribute to triggering shock or survival responses in the seedling.

Tests in Britain comparing seedlings that were dropped from a height of 3 m, one to fifteen times, showed that seedling survival and performance declined dramatically as the energy absorbed from the impact increased (Tabbush 1986). The trauma of the physical abuse results in a typical shock response from the seedling. Similar effects may be seen if boxes and seedlings are crushed by compaction. Boxes, therefore, should never be piled more than three high.

In caches, boxes should be stacked so that there are air spaces between them. Unless the seedling boxes and the ground are very cold, the boxes should be set up (on logs or two-by-fours) above the ground. Seedling metabolism generates heat, even during cold storage, and this heat must be dissipated. Seedling temperatures within a center box in a pallet, if there is no circulation, will be considerably higher than those at the outside of the box. If the stock is frozen, the reverse may be true, and air spaces will be needed to ensure uniform thawing.

Container-grown seedlings still in their containers (such as Spencer-Lemaire and paperpot), with seedling tops exposed, must never be piled on top of each other. This is also true of summer-planted stock where boxes may be left open for several days on site. In this case, the seedlings must be exposed to sunlight to permit photosynthesis.

On-Site Storage

Refrigerated vans

Refrigerated vans are commonly used for transportation and on-site storage. These cooling units are complicated and many things can go wrong. Even when the thermostat is connected to an alarm that goes off when the temperature is too high or too low, the units need constant monitoring. The temperature in the boxes should be checked daily with a probe thermometer. Stored trees should be maintained at 2-4°C.

Most cooling systems dehydrate the seedlings. For this reason, plastic-lined sealed bags should be used. If this is not possible, the seedlings should be misted frequently.

Root cellars and bunkers

Root cellars and bunkers are effective temporary storage facilities, but they usually have poor ventilation. Heat from respiring seedlings can then lead to higher storage temperatures. To avoid this problem, only dormant seedlings should be stored in them and only for brief periods.

Temporary seedling caches

Seedling caches are best set up on the edge of the planting block in the shade of standing timber, preferably on snow or near streams. Shaded areas under bridges may form perfect caches, but sudden runoff from rain or heat may cause a river to rise, with potentially disastrous results.

Silver-white or heat shield tarps are by far the best covers for seedling caches. They should always be used with the white side up or out and the silver side down or in. The white surface is highly reflective, absorbing little radiation, as well as being highly emissive, allowing for a quick release of heat buildup. The mylar-coated aluminum inner surface is not very emissive, and thus acts as a barrier to outside heat.

If a silver-white tarp is not available, then other tarps may be used, provided they are suspended 30-50 cm above the seedling boxes to ensure adequate air circulation. Canvas tarps trap heat effectively and should not be used unless the canvas can be kept moist so that evaporation cools the tarp.

Watering, dipping, and soaking

Seedlings that have been shipped in the containers in which they have been grown must be watered both morning and evening. Neither light rain nor cloudy weather prevents transpiration and evaporation from active seedlings. Large volumes of water are needed to keep container seedlings moist. Portable water pumps with hose and sprinkler systems should be used for this purpose.

Bareroot seedlings should always be dipped in a peat slurry to minimize exposure of fine roots and root hairs to dry air. Dipping should last for no more than 1 minute to avoid restricting the supply of oxygen to roots. During this procedure, planters should wear waterproof gloves, as they could contract a severe skin rash called Sporotrichosis. This is caused by the spores of a fungus (*Sporothrix schenckii*) which may be present on the peat moss used to produce the slurry.

Thawing frozen container stock

Generally, all stock arrives from storage properly thawed and ready to plant. However, if bundles are frozen, the seedlings must be thawed before planting. Bundles are generally frozen at the roots even though the shoots are actively metabolizing and transpiring. This can lead to a severe dehydration because the transpired water cannot be replaced by frozen roots.

Thawing should be done slowly, at temperatures not above 10 °C. Seedlings should never be put in the sun or wind to thaw. Bundles of frozen stock must never be broken apart, as this damages the brittle roots, needles, and branches.

PLANTING: FIELD OPERATIONS

Well-planned and carefully supervised planting operations carried out by motivated employees and contractors are crucial to the success of reforestation programs. Much can be done to minimize the stress imposed on seedlings between the time when boxes are broken open and the tree is planted. Planting spot selection can have a strong effect on future plantation performance.

Checking Seedling Quality

When planting stock is received at the planting site the condition of the contents of each box should be assessed. The first most probable cause of plantation failure is the planting of trees that, although they appear to be alive, are already dead.

The planting boxes should be opened and the following checks carried out:

- No "sour" odor should rise from the newly opened box. A sweet fermenting smell is a sure sign of heating during storage or the stock being packed when excessively wet. Both conditions lead to rapid degradation of stock and eventual death.
- If the needles in a bundle of plants are discolored (dark blotchy gray), the plants have been heated or stored for too long without ventilation.
- The seedlings must be dormant; buds should be firm with no evidence of new growth.
- The seedlings should be cool, preferably no warmer than 2-3 °C, and the roots moist.
- The seedlings should be free of molds. Presence of molds indicates warm storage temperatures, or incorrect pre-packaging conditions. Mold is not necessarily a reason for discarding the planting stock, but if an experienced opinion is not immediately available, a sample of the stock should be returned to the nursery for assessment.

- The root collar should be checked for cambial damage. The bark should be firm and of uniform color. To assess the condition of the conducting tissue, a section of the bark can be stripped off to reveal the tissue. It should appear moist and, for most species, white. If there is discoloration (brown or a "dirty color" such as a brownish yellow), the stock should be discarded as it is in poor condition and has little chance of survival. A similar test should be done to the roots.

- Bundles should be turned upside down and checked for broken roots, which are generally white. These indicate root tearing (and associated "rough" handling) that may have occurred during lifting operations. If roots appear to be excessively damaged, the other items listed above should be checked. Poor lifting techniques reflect a general disregard for stock handling in the nursery.

Bagging Up

All bags and boxes should be closed after a planter is loaded up. Seedlings in open boxes outside dehydrate quickly, whether sunlight is direct or diffused. Cloudy days are no excuse for leaving boxes uncovered or sorting trees in the open. Bareroot seedlings should always be loaded in the shade, even if all that is available is the shadow cast by the planter's body and the box. Planters should also disentangle and separate seedlings in the shade. Seedling roots should be exposed to the sunlight and dry air, only when they are taken from the planting bag to the planting hole. Bundles of container seedlings should be left wrapped until needed. Unwrapped seedling plugs may disintegrate in the bag, and fragile root tips can be damaged. Rigid tree bag inserts protect the seedlings from the buffeting of planter's legs and slash.

Seedling sacks

The purpose of the sealed seedling sacks is to keep the trees cool and moist during the planting process. The silver-white material acts in the same way as the tarp to keep the seedling cool, and the seal of the sack retains moisture. The sacks should be carefully pressed onto the seedling tops to minimize the air mass inside and maximize contact between the seedlings and the mylar or aluminized inner heat conductor.

Bareroot seedlings, soaked and slurried in the seedling sacks, are then set directly into the tree bags, thus reducing stock handling.

If seedling sacks are not available, the seedlings in the planter's bag should be sprinkled with water after being loaded. Covering the open top of the planters' bag with a shirt, raincoat, or cut-up space blanket will help protect the seedlings on hot days.

Culling and Root Pruning

The nursery culls the stock. Culling should not be carried out by the planters without the express consent of the project supervisor.

Severe root pruning has been discouraged in British Columbia nurseries since 1984. One of the authors (D. Simpson) found that a 5 cm root trim reduced root growth potential of spruce and pine by 50%. Field pruning by planters is not recommended.

Planting Flushed Seedlings

Flushing is the emergence of growth from the seedling bud. If flushing is observed, the seedlings must be planted quickly because the nutrient and moisture demands of the new growth can quickly deplete the reserves stored in the seedling. This is particularly important for bareroot stock which, unlike container stock, does not have an available nutrient supply in the plug. Despite this urgency, flushed buds must be handled with care, as the new growth in both bareroot and container stock is extremely tender and easily damaged.

Monitoring Quality

Quality standards must be set and maintained throughout the entire storage, handling, and planting process. The most important function of monitoring the quality of planting is to give the planters feedback on the planting and let them know directly the quality requirements for the planting project. Site-specific standards for planting quality should be stated at the site viewing and then reconfirmed at the pre-work conference.

Pattern, Density, and Spot Selection for Planting

The planting pattern, and how this pattern is interrupted by slash, rock, naturals, debris, deep duff, and competition, alters the spacing required to stock each hectare to the target density. The need to meet density targets, though, should never override the need to plant seedlings in spots that are biologically desirable. Better to have a few more or a few less well-planted seedlings than regimented rows of sickly plants. The spot chosen for a planted tree can have a profound influence on its future growth. Site preparation is based on this experience. However, with or without site preparation, the tree planter must make spot selections. In general, the following conditions are desirable:

- Microsites with a mixture of well-decomposed organic matter and well-aerated mineral soil from the A and upper B horizons supply both moisture and nutrients to seedlings. Sites composed entirely of organic matter can dry up in dry periods, although if moisture is plentiful, organic spots resemble the growing medium in container nurseries. Sites with no organic matter may be deficient in available nitrogen.
- The side of depressions rather than the bottom of hollows or the tops of hummocks should be selected. There are exceptions: on arid sites, depressions maximize moisture; and on wet sites, hummocks maximize soil warmth and drainage.
- Shaded locations behind logs or stumps should be selected to minimize evaporative demand and reduce transpiration from the foliage of newly planted seedlings.

Trees will not grow well in:

- mass-wasted sites where lower B or C horizons are exposed. These areas are usually devoid of nutrients.

- seepage areas with year-round flowing water. The water will be cold, retarding root development.

- areas subject to flooding or standing water.

- loose soil, which cannot be compacted or firmed around the roots of a newly planted tree.

- roadways, landings, and well-defined game trails, where the ground surface has been well compacted or subject to prolonged traffic (foot or vehicular).

In addition, there are a number of local conditions for which only experience can tell whether or not the planting site is unsuitable. Local knowledge should be used wherever possible.

Planting Tools

Manual tools

Planting spades and mattocks are the primary hand tools for tree planting in British Columbia. The spade, the most versatile of all the planting tools, is used for both bareroot and container stock. The mattock is used on steep hillsides and where heavy screefing is required. The dibble is used exclusively for planting container stock — a specific-sized dibble has been designed for each container size (the 211 dibble has a 2-cm top diameter, and an 11-cm length). While there are a variety of styles in all planting tools, recent studies (e.g., T.J. Smith 1987) show that injury to planters can be reduced when a straight-handle tool is used.

Mechanical planting

One aspect of mechanized silviculture that has been pursued for many years is the development of a reliable mechanical planting system. The first attempts at mechanized planting in British Columbia were conducted in the early 1950's with a hand-held planting "gun" and specially designed hardwalled seedling containers (Walters 1961). This system was intended to speed the planting process. While much effort went into developing this system, it was ultimately abandoned because of concerns about the long-term performance of seedlings planted in the "bullet" container and about the high cost of the expendable bullets. Biodegradable containers, to enhance productivity savings in the nursery and during planting while not restricting seedling growth, have been investigated, but a suitable lowcost container has not yet been developed. Emphasis has shifted towards developing a planting machine that will plant container stock.

Bareroot transplanting machines are used extensively in the United States and other countries. Several operational trials have compared various planting machines in an attempt to find one that will reliably plant seedlings across a range of British Columbia's very diverse terrain and site conditions. During the mid-1970's, sites in the Mackenzie, Vanderhoof, and Quesnel Forest Districts were operationally planted with the Caze and Heppner (C&H) tree planter (B.C. Ministry of Forests 1988). This planter was towed by a crawler tractor prime mover to which a C&H Reforestation Plow was attached for removing debris and creating a furrow. Sitting in the tree planter, an operator manually puts seedlings into a slit opened by a coulter wheel mounted at the front of the planter. The seedling is held firmly in place when the slit is closed by two packing wheels mounted at the back of the planter.

Assessments of these trials were carried out in 1987. Differences in performance between hand and mechanical planting methods were noted, but these were due to the differences in the choice of microsites rather than the method of planting. The mechanically planted seedlings were planted at the bottom of a continuous furrow and the hand-planted seedlings were planted on the adjacent raised berm. Thus, mechanically planted seedlings generally performed better in drier, coarse-textured soils, and hand-planted seedlings were superior on fine-textured, wetter soils where the seedlings benefited from the increased drainage and temperatures associated with a raised microsite. Excavations showed that mechanically planted seedlings had a higher incidence of basal sweeping and perhaps a more asymmetrical root system compared to hand-planted seedlings. This was often due to the predominance of roots oriented initially along the planting slit. Over time the root system is expected to become more normal as the roots grow away from the planting slit.

Further trials with three mechanical planters were carried out in 1987. Machines tested were the C & G planter (Arkansas), the Quickwood planter (Austria), and again the C&H tree planter (British Columbia). Neither the C&G nor the Quickwood could meet the existing operational standard for a well-planted seedling. Therefore, only the C&H tree planter underwent a full operational trial. The cost of mechanical planting with the C&H tree planter proved to be comparable to the cost of hand-planting on flat, easily accessible, windrowed sites.

The use of mechanical planting in the province is very limited at present, mainly because the present generation of mechanical planters are only able to plant the most accessible sites. Sites that are steep or rocky, or are covered with slash or stumps, must still be planted by hand. As well, no machine can consistently select the best planting microsite when there are a number of acceptable options. However, there may be a future for machines that can prepare and plant in one pass of the site. Such machines will have to be reliable, versatile and rapid to overcome the disadvantage of high capital cost and the competition from agile, energetic, and trained tree planters.

PLANTING GUIDELINES

The objective of any planting program is to achieve high rates of seedling survival and growth performance with the most efficient use of resources. This requires a careful assessment of site-specific factors that might limit seedling performance, followed by the development of an overall program that will optimize biological demands with operational constraints.

Site Constraints

In coastal, high elevation and southern interior environments, silviculturists encounter cases where interactions of low soil moisture and high soil temperature (particularly with late spring planting) can create plantation establishment problems. Seedlings need to transpire to remain cool and to capture carbon dioxide, but low soil moisture conditions significantly reduce the period of stomatal opening. Heat build-up then occurs as a cost of plant moisture retention. Planting earlier in the spring or deeply (up to and including burying the bottom whorl of the seedling branches) may be warranted on these sites.

Similarly, cold soils in northern environments can inhibit root development and hydraulic conductivity. Conditions can occur where air temperature and evaporative demand are high, yet the soils are cold. This creates a combined heat and moisture stress effect ("physiological drought") because the rate of water loss is greater than the rate of water uptake. Moisture stress can also combine with nutrient deficiencies and frost damage, having lethal consequences.

Effective site preparation will have modified much of the site constraints to plantation performance. It is critical that seedlings be planted in appropriate microsites, either produced by site preparation or selected from existing microsites. Where microsite selection alone will not adequately address the stresses, artificial protective measures should be considered (Table 18.2).

Timing of Planting

Choosing the best operational time to plant means juggling several factors which limit the length of the planting season and influence the suitability of time periods within that season. These factors include:

- environmental conditions leading directly to plant stress;
- stress resistance in planting stock;
- environmental conditions influencing the physical plantability of site; and
- availability of planting contractors and planters.

Ultimately, sites must be planted within the available early or late season planting windows. Within these windows, timing for specific sites must be arranged to minimize stress (during and after planting) and to use planting resources efficiently.

Seasonal Constraints to Planting

Spring planting on the coast

In coastal British Columbia, several problems are associated with late spring planting programs. Dunsworth's (1987) stock handling survey for MacMillan Bloedel indicated that a significant proportion of operational plantation failures during 1984-86 occurred after March 15 planting dates. This problem has become more prevalent in recent years because of increases in the size of planting programs and the increased proportion of higher elevation projects.

Late spring planting is characterized by two high-risk conditions: the rapid onset of moisture stress, and the planting of stock of lowered stress resistance (i.e., with out-of-phase phenology, carbohydrate depletion, low IRG, or storage mold infection). Dunsworth (1988b) has shown that dormancy intensity at the time of planting influences the pattern of seasonal biomass allocation for containerized Douglas-fir (*Pseudotsuga meniesii*) and western hemlock (*Tsuga heterophylla*). Seedlings with low dormancy burst bud rapidly, and expand their transpirational surface area before they have developed an ade-

TABLE 18.2. Examples of cases where protective measures should be considered

Site conditions	Protective measures
Low soil moisture and high air temperature	Shade cards or high, large organic debris
Small and large mammal damage	Deer browse tubes, mice and rabbit guards
Low soil moisture	Mulching, vegetation control
High soil moisture, low oxygen, and cold soils	Trenching/furrowing
Periodic low soil moisture, unusually acid soils and low fertility	Fertilization

quate absorptive volume of roots. The resulting moisture stress reduces photosynthesis and may lead to mortality. Early lifting (by January 15) and planting (by March 15) maximized seedling volume growth for both species on moist and dry regimes. If planting had to be delayed, early lift and storage (up to 4 months) were always better than later lifts. Cold storage acts to delay the rate of dormancy release, as has been shown in other recent studies with white spruce (*Picea glauca*) and lodgepole pine (*Pinus contorta*) (e.g., Ritchie 1985).

To achieve a low risk planting, spring programs should be completed within 2-3 weeks of starting, with a minimum requirement of 3-5% of the program planted per day. All planting should be completed before March 15, whenever possible.

Fall planting on the coast

Coastal fall planting has a history of variable success. Some research plantings indicate that fall may be an effective planting period for many coastal species. However, operational fall plantings have been less successful than the research trials. This discrepancy is related to the differences in seedling quality, handling, and soil climate conditions at the time of planting.

Variable stock quality in coastal bareroot stock results from variable late summer and fall climate. Drought stressing is the common dormancy induction method. If the nursery summer climate has been moist, the stock will be less dormant than stock produced in a drier year. DeYoe et al. (1989) have shown that short-day treated, containerized Douglas-fir had significantly better bud development than did drought-stressed stock. Short-day treatment allows finer control over the development of caliper, root mass, and frost hardiness, and over the timing of bud development.

Variable soil climate conditions are the rule rather than the exception for coastal sites. Proximity to the ocean and sharp relief lead to different patterns of precipitation. In general, soil should be sufficiently warm and moist to stimulate root development. The planting stock must also be sufficiently dormant that it will not prematurely burst bud following outplanting, and sufficiently frost hardy to avoid early fall frost events.

Dunsworth (1988a) has shown that natural seedling root phenology for Douglas-fir and western hemlock is linked to soil moisture and soil temperature. The highest levels of root activity were under 0.1 MPa soil moisture tension and over 4 °C. These soil climate conditions can be used to define a preliminary fall planting window. The effective window will vary with the physiological characteristics of the planting stock.

Spring planting in the Interior

Spring planting in the interior of British Columbia experiences the same sorts of problems as coastal spring planting. The greatest distinction is that the planting environments cover a wider range of latitude. The persistence of cold, wet soils in northern latitudes is a major impediment to planting. Cold soils effectively narrow the operational planting window and may significantly reduce root development over the growing season. Alternative site preparation (mounding or trenching) and careful selection of planting microsites can mitigate this problem on some sites.

The 0.1 MPa soil moisture tension and 4 °C planting window criteria provide a conservative estimate of the conditions required for Interior planting sites and species. In some areas this condition will not exist for long enough periods to allow for a complete planting program. Serious consideration should be given in these cases to a summer planting program. Site conditions will be less stressful and planting stock more stress-resistant than with late spring planting.

Stock that has been stored up to or beyond 8 months should not be outplanted even if the site appears suitable. In the Interior, therefore, the spring planting program should be completed by the end of June. For northern latitudes in the Prince George Forest Region, the program may be extended because of the operational constraints of a restricted planting season. This may be at a risk to plantation performance.

Summer planting in the Interior

Summer planting in the Interior overcomes many spring planting problems: the planting load is spread out; the warm soils increase root development following planting; there is no storage period because the stock is hot-planted directly from the nursery; and there is an on-site period of acclimation before peak stress exposure.

Summer planting is not without its risks, and is not feasible on all Interior sites. Candidate sites are usually north- and west-facing aspects that remain moist through the growing season. These sites are brush-prone and usually at higher elevations. Through increasing experience with summer planting, however, Interior silviculturists are finding that the range of candidate sites may be much more extensive.

Several risks with summer planting should be noted, too, including growing season frosts, late summer drying, potentially rapid brushing-in of sites, and increased logistical problems due to the short turnaround of planting stock. In spite of these risks, summer planting is now being prescribed extensively throughout the Interior.

Judicious selection of the appropriate season of planting can minimize the risks for the overall planting program. This requires a good understanding of the nature of the planting sites and of the planning required to meet the timing identified. The biological advantages of planting hot-lifted stock without a cold storage period should outweigh the logistical problems.

Daily weather considerations

Weather conditions at the time of planting directly affect a seedling's level of moisture stress. To maintain healthy seedlings, moisture loss to the atmosphere should be limited as much as possible. The rate of water loss from an exposed seedling is a function of the moisture gradient between the seedling and surrounding air. This moisture gradient, or vapor pressure gradient, is the driving force for water loss: the greater the gradient, the faster the water loss. The vapor pressure gradient is determined by subtracting the actual amount of water in the air (e_a) from the potential maximum amount of water the air could hold (e_s) at that temperature ($e_s - e_a$). (The relation expressed in this equation assumes that the air and seedling are at the same temperature. If the seedling temperature is greater than the air temperature, water loss will be greater. If the seedling temperature is less than the air temperature, water loss will be less.) Figure 18.3 shows the relation between e_s and temperature. As air temperature increases, air can hold more water. Relative humidity (RH) by itself cannot be used to estimate the moisture content of the air. Using RH to characterize

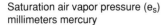

Saturation air vapor pressure (e_s)
millimeters mercury

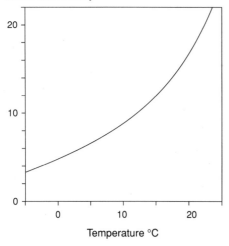

FIGURE 18.3. The relation between saturation air vapor pressure (e_s) and temperature. The air can hold more water as temperature increases.

Example 1

Suppose you must plant on one of two days and atmospheric conditions for each are:

Day 1: Air temperature 4.5°C, 6% RH

Day 2: Air temperature 21°C, 66% RH

On which day is the risk higher for water loss and moisture stress in exposed seedlings?

Step 1. Determine e_s from Figure 18.2.

Day 1: e_s = 6.4 mm Hg

Day 2: e_s = 18.0 mm Hg

Step 2. Determine e_a from the equation below that relates RH to e_a and e_s.

Day 1:	Day 2:
RH = e_a/e_s * 100	RH = e_a/e_s * 100
6 = e_a/6.4 * 100	66 = e_a/18 * 100
e_a = 6 * 6.4/100	e_a = 66 * 18/100
e_a = 0.384 = 0.4 mm Hg	e_a = 12. mm Hg

Step 3. Finally, determine the vapor pressure gradient (VPG).

Day 1: VPG = e_s - e_a = 6.4 - 0.4 = 6.0 mm Hg

Day 2: VPG = e_s - e_a = 18 - 12 = 6.0 mm Hg

Answer: In this example, even though the RH is 11 times greater the second day, the vapor pressure gradients are identical. Since it is the vapor pressure gradient that determines water loss, the risk of water loss is the same on both days.

Example 2

Which of the following days is best for planting to minimize moisture loss from exposed seedlings?

Day 1:   4.5°C air temperature, 50% RH

Day 2:   8°C air temperature, 60% RH

Day 3:   13°C air temperature, 75% RH

Step 1. Determine e_s from Figure 18.2.

Day 1: e_s = 6.4 mm Hg

Day 2: e_s = 8.0 mm Hg

Day 3: e_s = 11.0 mm Hg

Step 2. Determine e_a (RH = e_a/e_s * 100).

Day 1: e_a = 3.2 mm Hg

Day 2: e_a = 4.8 mm Hg

Day 3: e_a = 8.3 mm Hg

Step 3. Determine the vapor pressure gradient (e_s - e_a).

Day 1: 3.2 mm Hg

Day 2: 3.2 mm Hg

Day 3: 2.7 mm Hg

Answer: The vapor pressure gradient is lowest on Day 3. Therefore, Day 3 is the best planting day because moisture loss is slowest in exposed seedlings. The vapor pressure gradient and, therefore, the risk of moisture loss, are equal on Day 1 and Day 2. All three days in this example were better than the days in Example 1.

From: Cleary et al. (1978)

Note: mm Hg equals millimeters of mercury (Hg), the pressure of water in the air (1013 mm = 1 bar of pressure).

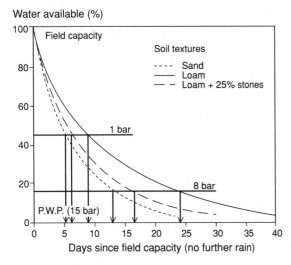

Water available (%)

FIGURE 18.4. The influence of soil texture on soil water depletion.

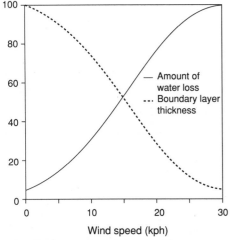

Water vapor loss and boundary layer thickness (%)

FIGURE 18.5. Thickness of the boundary layer (a layer of still or quiet air that surrounds needles, stem, and exposed roots) decreases as wind increases, thereby proportionately increasing the rate of water vapor loss from the seedling.

the relative driving force of water loss can be even more misleading. The following example from Cleary et al. (1978) shows why.

Ultimately, the most critical constraint to planting is the availability of adequate soil moisture at the time of planting. Figure 18.4 shows how soil water availability in different soils decreases over time when there is no recharge from precipitation. Field capacity is defined as the amount of water that a soil retains after enough water is applied to produce drainage so that the drainage becomes negligible. At this point, water availability to a seedling is 100%. The 1-bar reference line should be used as a guideline to show when the soil is becoming unacceptably dry for planting if the weather forecasts are predicting no rain in the near future. The 8-bar reference line is where severe stress for moisture is likely to be apparent.

Wind speed is another factor that influences the rate of water loss from exposed seedlings. Increasing the wind speed accelerates water loss from a seedling for all vapor gradients. Wind reduces the layer of quiet or dead air (boundary layer) surrounding the seedling (Figure 18.5). Thus, the pathway that water vapor must travel to leave the root or needle surface is shortened. Water vapor flows relatively faster across the shorter distance.

Both wind speed and vapor pressure gradient influence the rate of water loss in seedlings. As a general rule, air temperature should be between 0 and 18 °C and wind speed should be less than 30 km/hr (disregarding occasional higher gusts) for planting trees.

The principles for minimizing water loss during seedling planting also apply to lifting, cold storage, and transportation. Both moisture gradient and wind speed must be minimized with practical constraints throughout these operations. The potential moisture gradient is smallest under cold storage conditions (between about 4 and 6 mm Hg), even when relative humidity varies from 50 to 100 %. Thus, cold storage conditions are safest for seedlings out of the ground — which is one reason seedlings should be left in cold storage until they are planted.

Weather guidelines for safe lifting and planting have been developed according to physical laws that govern seedling moisture loss. When there are high risk weather conditions on one site, differences in local terrain and daily fluctuations in wind and temperature may allow planting of a nearby site instead, or even the same site after a few hours delay. The decision to suspend planting because of adverse weather must be made on site by an experienced silviculturist who has considered the existing site conditions, the likelihood of more favorable weather occurring, and the impact of prolonged field storage on the seedlings. Generally, the most critical factor to consider is soil moisture. As long as there is adequate moisture available to a seedling's roots, even immediately after planting, then it is probably wiser to plant than to suspend the operation. Of course the supervisor should ensure that special care is taken during adverse weather conditions to minimize seedling exposure during storage and handling. Roots, especially, must not be allowed to dry, as the delicate tips are easily damaged.

DIRECT SEEDING

Direct seeding is a method of artificial regeneration in which seeds, rather than seedlings, are planted in a microsite. In British Columbia, direct seeding has not been an important regeneration technique, its use in the past 15 years being limited to experimental trials on less than 1500 ha.

Methods of Direct Seeding

Broadcast seeding

In Ontario, large scale (15 000 - 30 000 ha) direct seeding of jack pine (*Pinus banksiana*) and to a lesser extent black spruce (*Picea mariana*) uses fixed-wing aircraft (Piper Supercub) with a Brohm seeder. Seeding rates recommended are 50 000 seeds per hectare for jack pine (Riley 1980) and 125 000 seeds per hectare for black spruce (Fleming et al. 1985). The importance of equipment calibration and flying methods in controlling the quantity and uniformity of seed distribution has been emphasized by several authors (Foreman and Riley 1979; Silc and Winston 1979; B.W. Smith 1984). In Alberta, a disk-type seeder mounted on a Bell 206 helicopter has been used to seed at rates of 300 000 - 400 000 seeds per hectare (C.R. Smith 1984). In British Columbia, the B.C. Ministry of Forests recommends a range of aerial seeding rates for several species (Table 18.3). However, because there have been few reported aerial seeding projects in the province, it is unclear if these seeding rates are appropriate.

Furrow and spot seeding

In conjunction with row site preparation equipment, such as Sharkfin barrels, seed can be distributed onto the prepared seedbeds. Scarifying equipment that produces a planting/seeding spot, such as the Bräcke, can be equipped with a seeder. The success of furrow and spot seeding is closely related to the ability of various harvesting and scarification methods to produce suitable, well-distributed seedbeds. Clark (1984) and Fleming et al. (1987) discuss these methods for direct seeding jack pine and black spruce, respectively. Although slower and more labor-intensive than aerial seeding, furrow and spot seeding offer greater control of spacing, better microsite selection, and a reduced seed requirement (Table 18.3).

Shelter cones

Various designs of bio- and photodegradable plastic cones have been evaluated in British Columbia and elsewhere in Canada (Wood and Jeglum 1984; Dominy and Wood 1986). The potential benefits from using these seed-covering devices include a reduced seed requirement, better germination from improved microsite environment, reduced seed losses from predation, and better control of spacing. However, the high costs of the cones themselves, the labor requirement to place the seed and cones properly, and the generally poor results experienced in trial plantations make this method of direct seeding of limited practical value. If the cones are used, they must be anchored securely, since both wind and predators may overturn them, reducing or eliminating their effectiveness.

TABLE 18.3 Direct seeding rates (viable seed)

Species	Broadcast (seed/ha)	Furrows (seed/ha)	Spots (2500 seeds/ha)
Lodgepole pine	70 000 - 80 000	16 000	5-8
Interior spruce	100 000 - 200 000	20 000 - 24 000	7-10
Douglas-fir	50 000 - 70 000	12 000 - 16 000	6-10
Ponderosa pine	18 000	8 000 - 12 000	4-8
Western larch	90 000 - 140 000	16 000 - 24 000	7-10

Seed

The quantity of seed required for direct seeding varies with the method of delivery. Aerial methods use relatively large amounts of seed, whereas spot seeding with shelter cones uses more modest amounts.

The quality of seed used for direct seeding, while perhaps not necessarily the high quality required for nursery sowing, still must be good. A minimum of 80% germination has been suggested as appropriate. Stratification of seed is usually not required for aerial seeding onto snow in late winter. However, late spring and summer seedings should use stratified seed where the species will benefit from this treatment.

Seed losses from small mammal predators such as deer mice (*Peromyscus maniculatus*) or voles (*Phenacomys intermedius*) can be substantial. Before direct seeding is carried out, a trapping program to check rodent populations should be done. The B.C. Ministry of Forests recommends 50 traps be set for three nights (=150 trap nights). A capture of one rodent per 10 trap nights indicates a high population and one rodent per 5 traps indicates there are too many rodents to permit successful direct seeding. The use of toxic chemicals is neither successful, because of rodent migration, nor permitted under British Columbia laws. An alternative food supply of sunflower seeds or oats may be a successful (although costly) means of reducing predation losses (Sullivan and Sullivan 1982b). Plastic shelter cones may, in some instances, provide a physical barrier to predation, but cones currently used have openings that permit rodent entrance.

Site Preparation

Direct seeding without preparation of suitable germination microsites is not likely to be successful. Seedbed microsite requirements for good germination vary with species. For jack pine in Ontario, receptive substrate includes mineral soil and shallow (10 mm) F- or H-horizons (Riley 1980). Although germination and establishment of jack pine may be good on C-horizon mineral soil, growth rates tend to be poor and seedlings chlorotic. Black spruce seeded on upland sites (less than 40 cm of organic material) establishes best on the Ah-Horizon or within 10 mm of the Ah/Ae interface. Establishment success declines rapidly above or below this stratum (Fleming et al. 1987). On black spruce, lowland sites (more than 40 cm organic material), some winter sheared conditions, and some mosses can provide successful establishment.

Direct seeding of jack pine on recently burned sites resulted in best stocking where mineral soil exposure was between 20 and 40%; seeding onto burned sites with more than 60% mineral soil exposed resulted in poor stocking (Brown 1984). The B.C. Ministry of Forests recommends 40% mineral soil as a suitable seedbed for direct seeding. Little research or operational experience, however, confirms this guideline. As the success of direct seeding is substantially influenced by both seeding rate and site preparation, installation of trials such as those described by Riley (1980), and development of models such as that described by Regniere (1982), should be undertaken before large scale direct seeding is considered. In general, successful direct seeding in Canada has been accomplished only with jack pine.

Season

Although direct seeding can usually be done at a faster rate than planting, the timing of seeding is often more critical. Direct seeding of jack pine is expected to be most successful in the spring or early fall (Clark 1984). It may, however, be possible to aerial seed in late winter onto fresh snow, thus protecting seed from temperature fluctuations and predation. Because seeding in conjunction with scarification limits the seeding window to the times suitable for mechanical site preparation, these times may not be best for seeding.

Shelter cones can be set out at any time the site is receptive, but spring establishment when there is adequate soil moisture and warm temperatures without frost may be best for seed germination. In this case, only stratified seed should be used to ensure rapid germination.

Species

Although attempts have been made to regenerate a number of species by direct seeding, the pines have been regenerated most successfully. In British Columbia, a large number of logged areas are managed to promote natural regeneration of lodgepole pine. In areas where logging slash has insufficient seed-bearing cones, it may be possible to direct seed this species. Direct seeding of spruce species in the province, however, seems an unlikely option because of the very slow growth of germinants, which predisposes them to drought and competition. The *Abies* species may be suitable for direct seeding with shelter cones, but there is no research or operational evidence to support this.

Cost Consideration

At first glance, direct seeding, particularly aerial seeding, seems inexpensive compared with planting as a means to regenerate an area. The costs of regenerating a lodgepole pine stand by aerial seeding, shelter cones, and planting are shown in Figure 18.6. This example illustrates that the cost advantage of direct seeding using aerial or shelter cone methods compared to planting is influenced by the relative success rates. Vyse (1973) offers a wider perspective on the economics of direct seeding.

As the limited experience in British Columbia with direct seeding has not indicted better than 25% success and planting success rates are much higher, pursuing large scale seeding at this time is not wise.

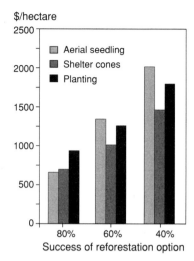

FIGURE 18.6. Cost comparison of regenerating a lodgepole pine stand using various regeneration methods.

SECTION FIVE

19 CONTROL OF COMPETING VEGETATION

M. Newton and P.G. Comeau

To be effective, vegetation control must reduce current vegetation, minimize future competition, and result in negligible damage to crop species. Release improves tree growth by providing increased solar radiation (see Chapter 5), water, and nutrients; or by reducing physical damage. It may also influence wildlife or fisheries habitat — positively for some species (Newton et al. 1989) and negatively for others (Santillo et al. 1989). Vegetation control is part of the overall silvicultural system.

Each method of control — chemical, manual, motor-manual, or mechanical — has specific effects and its own set of advantages and limitations. The appropriate choice of method is that one which has the ability to improve crop tree growth safely on a scale and at a cost compatible with need. This chapter outlines the principles of vegetation management in young conifer stands, and discusses the tools presently and potentially available for forest vegetation control in British Columbia.

EFFECTS OF NON-CROP VEGETATION

In British Columbia, 22 major vegetation complexes have been recognized on harvested sites and plantations (Table 19.1). These complexes include more than 30 species that have the potential to interfere with conifer growth. Each species or group of species has some effects on ecosystem function that may be beneficial or detrimental to crop tree growth.

Beneficial Effects

The rapid establishment of vegetation cover following disturbance may have important benefits:

- Non-crop vegetation captures, stores, and recycles considerable quantities of micro- and macronutrients that might otherwise be lost from the ecosystem. Fireweed (*Epilobium angustifolium*), for example, can effectively hold and recycle large amounts of nutrients.

- Non-crop vegetation can improve soil physical and chemical properties by adding organic matter and nitrogen. Nitrogen-fixing plants, such as alders (*Alnus* spp.), soopolallie (*Shepherdia canadensis*), lupines (*Lupinus* spp.), and snowbrush (*Ceanothus* spp.), may contribute to site nitrogen capital and long-term productivity.

TABLE 19.1. Major complexes of competing vegetation in British Columbia (modified from Conard, 1984)

Complex	Major species	Biogeoclimatic zone	Sites
Cottonwood	*Populus balsamifera* *Lonicera involucrata* *Cornus sericea* *Sambucus racemosa* *Rubus parviflorus* *Alnus viridis* ssp. *sinuata* *Alnus incana* ssp. *tenuifolia* *Calamagrostis canadensis* *Cinna latifolia*	IDF, ICH, MS, SBS, BWBS	Floodplains
Cottonwood-alder	*Populus balsamifera* *Alnus rubra* *Rubus spectabilis* *Cornus sericea* *Oplopanax horridus* *Sambucus racemosa* *Rubus parviflorus*	CDF, CWH	Floodplains
Bigleaf maple	*Acer macrophyllum*	CDF, CWH	Moist
Mixed hardwood	*Populus tremuloides* *Populus balsamifera* *Betula papyrifera* *Salix* spp. *Alnus incana* ssp. *tenuifolia* *Alnus viridis* ssp. *sinuata*	IDF, ICH, MS, SBS, BWBS	Various
Aspen	*Populus tremuloides*	IDF, ICH, MS, SBS, BWBS	Various
Boreal poplar	*Populus tremuloides* *Populus balsamifera*	SBS, BWBS	Fresh to moist
Red alder - shrub	*Alnus rubra* *Acer circinatum* *Rubus parviflorus* *Rubus spectabilis* *Sambucus racemosa* *Oplopanax horridus* *Ribes* spp. *Polystichum munitum*	CDF, CWH	Fresh to wet
Salmonberry	*Rubus spectabilis* *Rubus parviflorus* *Acer circinatum* *Ribes* spp.	CDF, CWH	Fresh to wet
Salal	*Gaultheria shallon*	CDF, CWH	Very dry to wet
Mixed shrub	*Rubus parviflorus* *Rubus idaeus* *Lonicera involucrata* *Acer glabrum* *Alnus viridis* ssp. *sinuata* *Paxistima myrsinites* *Sambucus racemosa* *Oplopanax horridus* *Menziesia ferruginea* *Salix* spp. *Cornus sericea* *Epilobium angustifolium* *Athyrium filix-femina* *Pteridium aquilinum*	ICH, MS, ESSF, SBS	Fresh to wet
Ericaceous shrub	*Rhododendron albiflorum* *Menziesia ferruginea* *Vaccinium* spp.	ICH, ESSF	Dry to moist
Dry alder	*Alnus viridis* ssp. *sinuata* *Epilobium angustifolium* *Calamagrostis rubescens*	IDF, ICH, MS, SBS	Dry to fresh

TABLE 19.1.   (Continued)

Complex	Major species	Biogeoclimatic zone	Sites
Wet alder	*Alnus viridis* ssp. *sinuata* *Alnus incana* ssp. *tenuifolia* *Rubus parviflorus* *Lonicera involucrata* *Calamagrostis canadensis* *Athyrium filix-femina* *Dryopteris assimilis*	ICH, MS, SBS, BWBS, ESSF	Wet
Dry shrub	*Amelanchier alnifolia* *Ceanothus* spp. *Paxistima myrsinites* *Shepherdia canadensis* *Symphoricarpos albus* *Holodiscus discolor* *Physocarpus malvaceus*	IDF, ICH, MS, SBS	Dry to fresh
Willow	*Salix* spp.	IDF, ICH, MS, ESSF, SBS, BWBS	Moist to wet
Pinegrass	*Calamagrostis rubescens*	PP, IDF, ICH, MS, ESSF, SBS, BWBS	Dry to fresh
Reedgrass	*Calamagrostis canadensis*	SBS, BWBS, (ICH, ESSF)	Moist to wet
Fern	*Athyrium filix-femina* *Dryopteris assimilis*	ICH, ESSF, SBS, BWBS	Fresh to wet
Bracken	*Pteridium aquilinum*	ICH, ESSF, SBS	Dry to wet
Fireweed	*Epilobium angustifolium*	CDF, CWH, IDF, ICH, MS, ESSF, SBS, SBPS, BWBS	Dry to wet
Subalpine herb	*Valeriana sitchensis* *Senecio trangularis* *Veratrum viride* *Luzula* sp. *Epilobium angustifolium*	ESSF	Fresh to wet
Introduced grasses	Domestic grasses	PP, IDF, ICH, MS, ESSF, SBS, BWBS	Various

- Plant cover and root systems aid in preventing soil erosion, soil puddling, and mass wasting on disturbed or unstable sites. Ground cover, litterfall, and root systems help protect and stabilize mineral soil surfaces.

- Some non-crop vegetation interferes with the movement of insects (e.g., willow and alder interfere with spruce weevil searches for suitable feeding sites on conifer leaders). Some plants may also serve as alternate hosts for desirable mycorrhizal fungi and therefore maintain mycorrhizal populations on site.

- Vegetation can protect seedlings from browsing animals such as deer, elk, and cattle by providing an alternative food source. Desirable species, however, such as domestic grasses, may attract cattle during the vulnerable early stages of plantation establishment.

- In turn, many non-crop species are important food sources for wildlife and domestic livestock. Salal (*Gaultheria shallon*) is important winter forage for mule deer. Moose browse extensively on willows (*Salix* spp.) and red-osier dogwood (*Cornus sericea*). Best browse conditions are often found where crop species are well spaced and preferred browse species have been maintained at an accessible height.

- Stream-side vegetation is very important to fisheries resources. Vegetation provides shade that moderates water temperatures and oxygen content, and organic debris that supports invertebrate and fish populations. Nutrient and fry productivity in cold streams can be enhanced by removing some stretches of cover (Holtby 1987). Productivity of warm streams can be maintained by leaving dense cover directly over the water. Cover, either coniferous or deciduous, also stabilizes stream banks.

Detrimental Effects

Non-crop vegetation cover can interfere with the establishment, survival, and growth of desired tree species by reducing the availability of light, water, and nutrients to crop seedlings, or by interfering with seedlings physically, chemically, or through indirect effects on microclimate. Several studies in the Pacific Northwest have shown that conifers perform best when competing vegetation is minimized (Walstad and Kuch 1987; Walstad et al. 1987).

How vegetation will affect tree survival and early growth depends on site factors, the abundance and competitive ability of non-crop species, and the silvical characteristics and vigor of the crop trees. Several negative effects are possible:

- Under well-developed canopies, light levels may be sufficiently low to result in very low rates of seedling photosynthesis. Seedlings on such sites show poor survival and grow slowly. As vegetation cover increases, the amount of light reaching overtopped seedlings declines (Figure 19.1). In some thimbleberry communities in the CWH and ICH zones, less than 1% of the photosynthetically active radiation may penetrate the brush canopy to reach overtopped seedlings.

- Salal (Price et al. 1986), grasses (McDonald 1986), and other species can capture a large proportion of available water. On some sites, reductions in the water available to crop tree seedlings may lead to substantial reductions in their survival and growth. Controlling competing vegetation addresses this problem by reducing seedling water stress (Barber 1984; Price et al. 1986; Petersen et al. 1988). The intensity of competition for water is determined by the availability of water on the site, the distribution of root systems in the soil, and the cover (or leaf area) of the vegetation. As well, the effect of any level of vegetation cover depends on the water deficits encountered on the site (Klinka et al. 1984). When climatic water deficits are large, even small amounts of vegetation may significantly reduce water availability to crop trees.

- Rapidly growing non-crop vegetation competes with conifer seedlings to capture nutrients. A well-developed fireweed community, for example, can contain more than 70 kg/ha of nitrogen in aboveground biomass. Where par-

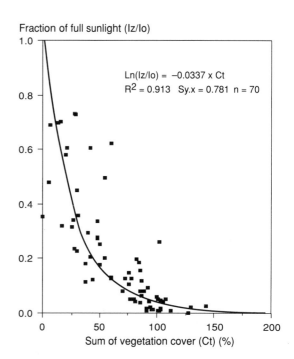

FIGURE 19.1. The fraction of full sunlight which penetrates vegetation canopies decreases as cover increases. Results shown are from mixed-shrub and fireweed communities of southern British Columbia.

ticular nutrients are in limited supply, vigorous growth of non-crop vegetation may substantially reduce the availability of nutrients to crop seedlings.

- Falling or bending vegetation may deform, crush, or break crop tree seedlings. This vegetation press is especially damaging to small-diameter seedlings and is commonly encountered in bracken, fireweed, thimbleberry, and reedgrass communities. Smothering of spruce seedlings (*Picea* spp.) by fireweed appears to be most common on cool, moist sites which have been burned. On these sites, fireweed may achieve 75% coverage and heights exceeding 1 m. Competition for light results in crop seedlings with a high height:diameter ratio, which increases their susceptibility to physical damage. Wet, heavy snow on its own may have similar crushing effects. This problem is minimized by planting stock with large caliper (low height:diameter ratio). Physical damage may also result from windwhip as conifers grow through hardwoods.

- Dense canopies of non-crop vegetation may reduce air and soil temperatures during the growing season. In some cold environments, this may shorten the length of the effective growing season by delaying bud burst. Vegetation cover also influences other aspects of seedling microclimate (Chapter 5), and may increase or decrease the risks of nighttime radiation frost (Stathers 1989).

- Suppression for more than 1 or 2 years leads to decreased numbers of buds (Tappeiner et al. 1987) and eventually to thin crowns with reduced leaf area and a high height:diameter ratio. Reduced leaf area leads to reduced seedling vigor, growth, and competitive ability. Ultimately, high levels of competition will result in the death of crop seedlings.

- Vegetation may provide protective cover for small mammals, which can cause substantial damage to crop seedlings (see Chapter 22).

COMPETITION ASSESSMENT

Vegetation control is undertaken when growth loss or mortality is anticipated to exceed some economic threshold. This threshold occurs where the cost of treatment is less than the value of the increased yield. The presence of particular shrub or herb species does not, in itself, provide a useful measure of whether or not that threshold will be exceeded. Combined with local experience and an understanding of species autecology and secondary succession, however, a quantitative assessment can be used to predict when serious problems will develop.

The best results from release treatments are realized when remedial measures are applied before competition becomes a problem (Newton and Preest 1988; Petersen et al. 1988). Early or preventative treatment is almost always less costly, and tree responses nearly always better where conifers remain dominant and vigorous. However, managers are generally faced with an inventory of plantations at varying levels of competition, and they must allocate resources where they are likely to provide the greatest return. For this reason, techniques are required for quantifying competition and assessing its effect on crop seedlings.

One of the first visual signs of significant competition in plantations is an increase in height:diameter ratios above those of open-grown trees. These ratios vary by species and by provenance in response to site factors. In Douglas-fir, ratios of 45-55 are normal for plantations of 2-10 years of age. Greater crowding leads to greater ratios (Cole and Newton 1987). Long-term height, diameter, and volume increment are jeopardized when the height:diameter ratio of Douglas-fir exceeds 60 before release.

To date, there are no comprehensive quantitative indexes available for assessing competition in conifer plantations in British Columbia. However, results from work in the province (Brand 1986), Oregon (Howard and Newton 1984; Wagner and Radosevich 1987), and elsewhere indicate that percent cover of overtopping vegetation can be used to estimate the intensity of competition for light. Physical damage to seedlings is generally evident where windwhip and vegetation- and snow-press are occurring. At present, predicting the development of these problems depends on local knowledge and experience, and on an understanding of the successional patterns occurring on particular sites.

Avoiding the Need for Release

Control measures are generally most effective when applied to prevent competition. The need for release can be reduced substantially if healthy, vigorous seedlings of the appropriate stock type and correct species are planted promptly after harvesting, before competitors are established. Delaying planting beyond the first year after harvest compromises the competitive position of seedlings by allowing site resources to be pre-empted before planting.

Site preparation often provides sufficient control, allowing seedlings to remain vigorous for 2 or more years after proper planting. Burning, for example, can effectively reduce shrub cover and, where the organic layer is maintained, reduce ingress from species (such as alder and birch) that require a mineral seedbed. Furthermore, using herbicides for site preparation rather than for conifer release avoids problems with crop tolerance and permits the use of higher application rates.

Planting large stock is another method of preventing competition early on, especially when it is combined with appropriate site preparation. Such stock is often successful at remaining above competing vegetation and can be used effectively for regenerating some sites (Dobbs 1976; Howard and Newton 1984; McMinn 1985).

TOOLS FOR CONIFER RELEASE

Vegetation management is aimed at redirecting resources to crop trees. The treatment method depends on the target species, crop species, site characteristics, other resource values, and environmental and social constraints. No vegetation management treatment can increase total resources, but it can increase the availability of resources to the crop species. If the treatment damages the crop tree so that it cannot respond to release, however, treatment will be ineffective.

Tools available for crop release can be chemical, manual, motor-manual, or mechanical. Grazing, although less commonly used, can also reduce competitive vegetation. Each approach has different risks, costs, feasibility, and effectiveness, and each is perceived differently by the public.

Chemical

Five herbicides are registered for conifer release in British Columbia: 2,4-D, 2,4-DP, glyphosate, hexazinone, and simazine. Triclopyr ester, although registered for industrial use (including on roadside right-of-ways), is still under review for forestry. Because all of these chemicals are systemic herbicides, the forester using them must ensure there is:

- uniform delivery to all target species;
- uptake by the target vegetation, but not by the crop tree;
- translocation to the site of action;
- enough chemical at the site of action to disrupt metabolism; and
- dosage low enough to avoid serious injury to desirable species.

Foresters make decisions that affect each of these points. Delivery and uptake are closely integrated, so the choice of chemical formulation is related to the application method. The application method also depends on the target vegetation – its species, size, and distribution on-site. For example, large hardwoods (> 5 m tall) are often not readily controlled with aerial applications, but are most effectively controlled on an individual-tree basis. Uptake and translocation are both related to the timing of application.

Foliar uptake

Foliar herbicides (glyphosate and esters of 2,4-D and triclopyr) are generally applied as broadcast sprays. Glyphosate is applied in water at rates of 1.1 to 2.1 kg ai/ha; 2,4-D ester may be applied in water, oil, or an oil-in-water emulsion at rates of 2.2-3.3 kg ai/ha. Oil, however, increases uptake through small branches, twigs, and the waxy cuticle, and this may result in unacceptable crop injury.

Broadcast sprays are most effective when applied to a relatively uniform canopy. Multistoried canopies may require more than one treatment. It is generally more cost-effective to treat a site before the overstory develops to a level of closure that interferes with chemical delivery to the shrub layer.

All foliar herbicides should be applied after conifers have completed active growth: mid- to late August in the northern Interior, late August to September in the southern Interior, and September on the coast. In the spring, 2,4-D ester and triclopyr are often used effectively before conifer bud break but after leaf-out of deciduous competitors. Western redcedar and western hemlock are especially susceptible and may sustain injury from most broadcast treatments unless products are applied without surfactants. Caution is required with 2,4-D and triclopyr emulsions, especially on western redcedar.

Stem uptake

To control hardwood species, stem application may be by individual stem injections (e.g., hack and squirt), cut-surface treatments, or dormant season basal sprays or thinline treatments. Dormant sprays require oil-soluble formulations to ensure penetration of bark tissues. For this purpose, 2,4-D and triclopyr esters are most effective in a diesel oil carrier. In contrast, stem injections require water-soluble formulations (glyphosate or 2,4-D amine) for effective uptake and translocation. Applications of water-soluble products to cut surfaces must be made soon after cutting has taken place, before exposed vessels occlude. On surfaces cut for more than 2 hours, undiluted esters may be more effective.

Root uptake

Delivery of the herbicide for root uptake occurs in two stages: first, the herbicide is applied to the soil surface; then it moves downward to the roots. Soil-active chemicals (hexazinone and simazine) may be applied by broadcast spray or spot treatment. The targets for their delivery include both soil and plant tissue. Simazine is absorbed relatively poorly by foliage so that the product is used when plants are small and their roots are near the surface. Hexazinone has more foliar activity and can reach roots 15-30 cm deep.

Movement to the rooting zone depends on: water solubility of the chemical; binding capacity of the chemical with soil particles; soil texture; and amount of water percolating into the soil. Simazine is strongly bound to clay or organic matter, which may restrict its movement to roots. Simazine has relatively low water solubility, and downward movement tends to be restricted to the top 5 cm of soil.

Hexazinone is more mobile. It is usually applied in the spring after non-crop species have emerged but before coniferous bud burst. Fall applications are less effective and may lead to off-site movement. Flow in the surface layers of the soil from heavy rains and snow melt may carry hexazinone off-site (Expert Committee on Weeds 1989).

Pines, larch, and Douglas-fir are susceptible to damage from hexazinone, especially on coarse-textured soils.

Application methods and guidelines for all of the above herbicides are found in the Silviculture Manual (B.C. Ministry of Forests) and the Forest Pesticide Handbook of British Columbia (Henigman and Beardsley 1985). Treatment efficacy is discussed in Chapter 13.

Manual and Motor-Manual

Cutting and knocking down

Machetes, brush hooks, handsaws, brush saws, chainsaws, and even hockey sticks may be used to cut, remove, or knock down vegetation. Such a treatment generally provides only short-term release of crop species, and cutting some shrubs, such as thimbleberry or salmonberry, may actually increase competition during subsequent years because the density of stems increases. Deciduous trees, such as bigleaf maple, aspen, birch, and red alder, usually resprout vigorously following cutting. The best control of red alder stems larger than 5 cm dbh has been achieved by cutting during the growing season, done as close to the ground as possible (Harrington 1984). In coastal British Columbia, D'Anjou (unpublished data) found late-summer was the most effective period to reduce alder resprouting.

Repeat treatments may be necessary to release conifers from competition by species which resprout rapidly from stumps or root systems. Manual removal of slow-growing species such as white-flowered rhododendron, false azalea, or salal may be very effective.

Manual and motor-manual methods may be combined with herbicides. Birch may be cut one year, allowed to resprout, and then treated with foliar herbicides. Cutting provides a uniform canopy which is more effectively controlled.

The extent of area cleared generally ranges from 100% to just a small area around the crop tree. This area should be of sufficient size to provide free growing space for the seedling. The actual size will depend on the height and rate of sprouting or suckering in the vegetation complex being controlled.

Timing of control by cutting or knocking down is important to maximize control effectiveness and minimize conifer injury. Because cutting and knocking down expose conifers suddenly to wind, sun, and snow, some conifers show stress response. Newton (1981) observed decreased rates of height growth with no accompanying increase in diameter growth in 10-year-old Douglas-fir on dry sites. The loss of physical protection may induce exposure stress in conifers, similar to that resulting from thinning. This can lead to the loss of old needles, sunscald, and the production of reaction wood; and to a shortening of leader growth for 2-5 years (Newton 1981; Petersen et al. 1988).

Conifers, when surrounded by vegetation in full leaf, are especially vulnerable to physical damage from workers. When workers cannot see crop seedlings, up to 25% of the crop may be damaged (Roberts 1980; Holmsen and Whitehead 1988). Care must be taken to identify suppressed trees and to avoid cutting them with brushsaws or chainsaws or toppling cut brush onto them.

Girdling

A number of hand and power tools can be used to girdle hardwood trees: axes, hatchets, sandviks, machetes, chainsaws, and specialized girdling devices such as the chain-girdler for large stems or the Vredenberg for 6- to 15-cm stems.

The effectiveness of girdling for controlling deciduous species has been variable. Much success has been achieved in controlling aspen when relatively isolated stems in a predominantly coniferous forest are treated several years before harvest. Species such as aspen, red alder, and maple may resprout vigorously following girdling unless other species provide sufficient cover to inhibit growth and survival of sprouts. Girdling scattered large red alder and aspen when conifers are above the surrounding shrub layer has also been a successful and economical treatment.

Mechanical

Mechanical release is primarily used to control intraspecific competition in dense lodgepole pine stands in the Interior. The only machine regularly operated is a rubber-tired Hydro-Ax®, which uses rotary horizontal double bars (Hedin 1987). Weyerhaeuser Canada tested a rolling drum-chopper, but discontinued its use because of limited success except under very cold or very dry conditions. These and other machines are described by Ryans (1988). The Forest Engineering Research Institute of Canada is working with Weldco to design a new cutting head to solve problems with stem breakage, live lower limbs remaining on cut stems, and damage to residual stems.

Grazing

Use of livestock to control herbaceous vegetation requires careful management to minimize trampling and browsing damage to crop trees (Chapter 22). In some areas of the province, predator control conflicts may arise between livestock and wildlife management.

ENVIRONMENTAL IMPACTS OF VEGETATION RELEASE

Vegetation management restructures the plant community to ensure the crop species will dominate. The choice of tools influences the short-term impact of the release on other components of the ecosystem.

Manual and motor-manual techniques, for example, reduce the stature of shrubs and non-crop tree species. This may result in a temporary increase in fine woody fuels, raising the fire hazard. As well, heavy slash may present an obstacle to wildlife and livestock movement.

After herbicides are used for control, chemical residues may remain on-site. Soil-active herbicides such as hexazinone are designed to stay active after application. They have a reported half-life from 1 month to 1 year or longer in cold, wet soils. Hexazinone may move off target areas with particles of soil and organic material dislodged by snow melt or intense rains. Avoiding fall application or treatment of scarified sites will reduce risks. Glyphosate and 2,4-D, however, are rapidly degraded in soils by microbial and, for 2,4-D, chemical processes. In one study, glyphosate residues 29 days after application were less than 1% of that originally applied (Feng and Thompson 1989).

The effect of glyphosate on the forest ecosystem – in particular on fish and fish habitat – has been intensively researched since 1983 at Carnation Creek on Vancouver Island. Results of the interdisciplinary studies (Reynolds 1989) showed no glyphosate residue in buffered streams, and no fish mortality in streams oversprayed with glyphosate; tributary sediments provided a sink for herbicide residues in the oversprayed streams; and, although litter fall was severely reduced, recovery occurred within 2-3 years after applications.

Other British Columbia studies on the environmental impact of herbicides include Balfour (1989), Beaudry (1989), and Pollack (1989). Beaudry summarized the fate in the forest environment of herbicides commonly used in British Columbia. None of the herbicides registered for conifer release in Canada has the potential for bioaccumulation.

In addition to environmental risks, Newton and Dost (1984) also recognized personal risk. Physical impacts of vegetation management was the cause of most medical problems for field personnel.

20 DISEASES IN REFORESTATION

J.R. Sutherland and R.S. Hunt

A plant disease can be defined as an unfavorable change of a plant's function or form from normal. Pathological (biotic) diseases are caused by pathogens such as fungi, while non-pathological (abiotic) diseases result from factors such as unfavorable environment and phytotoxic chemicals. Both types of disease can affect reforestation programs by severely damaging or killing cones and seeds, nursery or recently outplanted seedlings, or trees in both young and established stands. Only pathological diseases are covered in this chapter. Other publications give detailed information on non-pathological diseases such as nutrient deficiencies (Benzian 1965; Carter et al. 1986), air pollution and natural stresses (Malhotra and Blauel 1980), and red belt, a cold weather problem (Robins and Susat 1974). Other, more limited descriptions of abiotic diseases that may occur locally are given in publications by the U.S. Department of Agriculture (1983), Riffle and Peterson (1986), Hagle et al. (1987), and Hiratsuka (1987). Funk (1985b) gives a brief overview of definitions and principles of pathogens and plant diseases.

For a disease to develop, a pathogen, a susceptible host, and a suitable environment must be present. Because reforestation foresters frequently monitor the growing and planting of stock and the growth of plantations, they can often make decisions that will minimize the incidence and severity of both non-pathological and pathological diseases affecting the crop. For example, the incidence of western gall rust (*Endocronartium harknessii*) on lodgepole pine (*Pinus contorta* var. *latifolia*) or other hard pines can be greatly reduced by the removal of diseased (inoculum-producing) trees for about 300 m around the nursery. This simple procedure reduces seedling losses in the nursery, prevents introduction of the disease into new areas by infested nursery seedlings, and minimizes losses in plantations where the pathogen already occurs.

Treatment of another disease, laminated root rot (caused by the fungus *Phellinus weirii)*, shows how the reforestation specialist can prevent future plantation losses, by knowing whether or not pathogen inoculum is present and how susceptible the host plant is. Pre-harvest surveys can be used to determine the presence of *P. weirii* inoculum in existing trees and blowdown, and, if the pathogen is present, the site can be planted to a resistant host such as *Pinus* spp.

This chapter describes some of the more common plant diseases that may jeopardize successful reforestation in British Columbia and, where possible, it outlines management practices that can minimize the effects of these diseases.

DISEASES AFFECTING CONES, SEEDS, AND SEEDLINGS

Cone Diseases

Inland spruce cone rust, *Chrysomyxa pirolata*, is the only disease that consistently causes serious losses of cones in British Columbia. Although it occurs throughout the province, major damage only results in the Interior where the disease's principal conifer hosts — white spruce and Engelmann spruce — and alternate non-conifer hosts — species of *Pyrola, Orthillia*, and *Moneses* — are found.

Diseased cones first become noticeable in mid- to late summer, as they dry out, open prematurely, and shed massive amounts of yellow-orange spores (Figure 20.1). They should not be included in cone collections because they yield few seeds or seeds that germinate abnormally. No practical methods have been developed for managing cone rust in the forest. However, the disease is less prevalent in areas where the alternate hosts are absent either naturally or as the result of widespread forest fires. Seed orchard cones can be protected by the application of one or two sprays or fungicides (such as ferbam) to the cones at pollination, the time when the pathogen enters cones.

FIGURE 20.1.   White spruce cones affected by inland spruce cone rust.

Another rust affecting spruce cones is coastal spruce cone rust (*C. monesis*), which to date has only damaged cones of Sitka spruce in the Queen Charlotte Islands. The effects of the disease on Sitka spruce cones and seeds and the recommendations for disease management are similar to those for *C. pirolata*. Again, diseased cones should not be collected.

Other rusts, such as spruce shoot rust (*C. woroninii*) and American spruce - raspberry rust (*Pucciniastrum americanum*), affect needles and occasionally cones. These diseases can sometimes be destructive, particularly if both hosts are abundant and if cool, wet conditions prevail in the spring when cones are young.

Molding is the only other problem that regularly appears on cones. Normally it can be traced to storage of green or wet cones. Moldy cones sometimes generate heat, which can reduce seed viability; and the molds (several species might be involved), either alone or with accompanying pitch, can hinder seed extraction. Although not all cone molds adversely affect seed viability, some, including species of *Fusarium* that become seed-borne, can cause seed rot, damping off, or root rot in nurseries. Reforestation specialists can prevent the occurrence of molding by picking mature, dry cones; properly air drying the picked cones; and storing the cones under well-ventilated, cool, dry conditions for as short a period as is practical. Detailed information on the cone diseases of North American conifers is given in Sutherland et al. (1987).

Seed Diseases

The two major diseases presently known to affect seeds in British Columbia are the seed or cold fungus, *Caloscypha fulgens*, and *Sirococcus* blight, *S. strobilinus*. The former is so named because it is seed-borne and spreads under cool, moist conditions. This pathogen is most prevalent in the seeds of spruce (all species) and *Abies* (within infested seedlots, 1-30% of the seeds can contain it). It can, however, occur in seeds of all species with serotinous cones. The pathogen, which inhabits forest litter in small localized areas throughout the province, invades cones that contact the litter.

The longer the exposure, the higher the incidence of the pathogen in seedlots. Thus, cones collected from squirrel caches are most likely to contain the pathogen. Cones picked from the ground or from logging slash may also contain it, but at lower levels. Only cones picked from trees in the forest or seed orchard do not harbor *C. fulgens*.

In the field, the pathogen can hamper reforestation by killing seeds from seed trees or direct-sown seeds. It is of greater concern, however, in the artificial reforestation process because infection acquired before cone collection can spread on cones stored under cool, moist conditions. Further spread can occur during seed stratification, during cold storage before sowing, or during the period after sowing if cool, wet conditions prevail.

Diseased and healthy seeds are difficult to distinguish as the pathogen does not rot seed contents (i.e., the seeds remain firm). Sometimes *C. fulgens* can be detected as patches of hard, whitish mycelium on seed coats. Its presence can also be determined by laboratory isolation. To prevent the problem, cones should be picked directly from trees; ground-collected cones should not be included, especially those from squirrel caches. Dusting seeds with a fungicide before sowing reduces losses when infested seedlots are sown. Sowing seeds when temperatures are warmer (to speed up germination) also helps because seeds are not affected by the pathogen once germination begins.

The second seed-borne pathogen of concern in the province is *Sirococcus* blight. In the forest it is confined mainly to western hemlock, Sitka spruce, and lodgepole pine. On the first two species, the disease is most likely to occur in dense stands of trees before they reach pole size.

In container nurseries the pathogen is known to be seed-borne, mainly on spruce (all species). Spruce seedlots apparently become contaminated with diseased seeds when old cones, on which the fungus often grows and sporulates, are inadvertently included in cone collections. In the nurseries, disease centers develop from these seeds and secondary spread occurs from there. Small, dark spore bodies of *S. strobilinus* are fairly common on old spruce cones. However, since other fungi produce similar structures, *S. strobilinus* spores must be confirmed by microscopic examination. Diseased seeds, which have shrunken contents, can be detected by X-ray examination or the isolation of the fungus on a culture medium in the laboratory.

As seed orchards begin to produce, *Sirococcus* blight that results from seed-borne inoculum should eventually disappear because orchard collections will not contain old cones. Although in bareroot nurseries, where spruces, Douglas-fir, and lodgepole pine seedlings are commonly affected, some losses may still occur as the result of wind- and rain-borne inoculum from nearby diseased trees. Managing *Sirococcus* blight in the nursery includes removing diseased windbreaks and other trees nearby, applying fungicides, and, where practical, reducing watering, as moisture favors *Sirococcus* infection and spread. Consult Sutherland et al. (1987) for a more detailed discussion of *C. fulgens*, *Sirococcus* blight, and other potential pathogens of conifer seeds.

Nursery Diseases

Diseases of nursery seedlings can seriously hinder reforestation efforts. Outright killing of seedlings by diseases reduces the availability of planting stock, which in turn means another seedling crop must be grown. A more subtle effect of these diseases is that they lower seedling quality and thus reduce performance of outplanted stock. In addition to these problems is the concern of nursery workers and tree planters in handling fungicide-treated seedlings.

Some diseases, such as damping-off, kill seedlings only in the nursery; others, such as gray mold (*Botrytis cinerea*), damage seedlings during their growing phase in the nursery and can then be carried over to affect seedlings in storage and even afterward, during transit and handling at the planting site.

The recent trend in British Columbia of producing more seedlings in container nurseries and the gradual de-emphasis of bareroot production have resulted in a shift in the occurrence and importance of certain nursery diseases. For example, soil-borne damping-off and root rots which were major problems in bareroot culture have been surpassed in importance by shoot and foliage diseases, particularly gray mold. This disease, which damages both growing and stored seedlings, poses a special threat because seedlings are now often stored for longer periods than before.

Although numerous diseases affect seedlings in nurseries (see Sutherland et al. 1989), only gray mold on container-grown seedlings and storage molds are covered here. They are the main diseases that field foresters are most likely to encounter.

Gray mold

Gray mold is the most serious disease on container-grown seedlings in the province. Although numerous species of seedlings are susceptible to the disease, it is most severe on Douglas-fir, western hemlock, and spruce (all species). The disease symptoms become most conspicuous following seedling canopy closure and the onset of cool, often wet, autumn weather (Figure 20.2). They include masses of light-gray mold growth, which usually starts on the lowermost needles and spreads upward on the shoot. If not controlled, the disease can kill the needles on the lower half of the shoot and, when advanced, penetrate the bark, killing the woody lateral branches and the seedling's main stem.

In certain cases, root regeneration capacity or stress tests may be justified to determine seedling condition. If the foliage of seedlings is severely damaged or defoliated — and certainly if the vascular tissues are rotted — the seedlings should be culled.

FIGURE 20.2.   Gray mold on a container-grown seedling.

Nursery temperatures of 15-20° C, high humidities or free water, and the presence of senescent or dead needles where the pathogen becomes established all favor the disease. Therefore, nursery practices to use against the disease include: reducing or withholding irrigation; rearranging styroblocks to improve ventilation and reduce humidity; and applying fungicides before seedling canopy closure and again before the stock is lifted for storage. Where possible, removing the polyethylene/fiberglass cover of covered growing houses during the summer also alleviates gray mold by exposing seedlings to full sunlight.

Gray mold causes direct damage on growing seedlings and, if uncontrolled or undetected, it can also lead to further damage during or after storage. Indeed, some of the most serious losses to gray mold have occurred on stored stock. There are many reasons for this: the long storage period for certain species or seedlots favors the disease, even at cold temperatures; stored seedlings are not easily accessible for frequent inspections; and the fluctuating temperatures of some storage facilities, or the placing of warm seedlings into cold storage, results in water condensation which enhances gray mold.

Gray mold symptoms on stored seedlings are usually the same as those on growing seedlings, except that the disease can originate and spread from any portion of the shoot. It has not been seen to damage seedling roots. Managing this disease on stored seedlings involves: 1) applying a pre-storage fungicide to seedlings; 2) storing stock with a nursery history of the disease (even incipient disease) for the shortest time possible; 3) storing stock that will withstand frozen storage at -1 to -2° C; and 4) inspecting stored seedlings frequently for the disease and outplanting the stock as quickly as possible when gray mold is first noticed.

When seedlings are shipped from storage, the responsibility for minimizing gray mold damage and ensuring the physiological well-being of the seedlings transfers to the field personnel, including tree planters. After reaching the planting site, seedlings must be planted as soon as possible. Interim, on-site measures that should be taken include keeping the seedlings cool by storing the boxes in the shade under thermal blankets or by placing them in snow. It may sometimes be advisable to place the boxes in the shade with their tops open to improve ventilation around the seedling shoots. Seedlings with severe gray mold should be checked to determine if they are alive. See Sutherland et al. (1989) for a detailed discussion of gray mold in local nurseries.

Storage mold of bareroot seedlings

While molding of stored, container-grown seedlings is invariably caused only by gray mold, numerous fungi (e.g., species of *Penicillium*, *Fusarium*, and *Rhizoctonia*-like fungi) are responsible for causing molding of bareroot stock. Many of these fungi are soil-borne and get onto the foliage of seedlings during lifting and handling at the nursery. Symptoms, which appear after the seedlings have been in storage, include watery or dry molding of the foliage in localized areas or in patches over the entire shoot. The molds themselves vary in color: black, orange, blue, white, and gradations or mixtures of colors are common. A moldy odor may also be noticeable when boxes of seedlings are first opened. If string is used to tie seedlings together in bundles, molding may start and spread from around the string.

All species and age classes of seedlings can be affected, with the exception of lodgepole pine and ponderosa pine, which seem to be less prone than other conifers to storage molds. Transplanted seedlings are particularly vulnerable to storage molding, especially if they are stored for a long time before being transplanted and are then transplanted late and re-stored. This is thought to occur because the short growing season in the transplant bed restricts the seedlings' accumulation of photosynthates. The procedures for determining the severity and prevention of storage molds on bareroot seedlings are the same as those for assessing gray mold on container-grown stock. The recent publication by Sutherland et al. (1989) contains an in-depth section on storage molds.

Some fungi frequently seen on roots of stored seedlings may be beneficial mycorrhizae that have proliferated during storage. Identification should be verified by laboratory observation.

DISEASES OF YOUNG-GROWTH CONIFERS

Any stand entry ignoring a root disease will frequently exacerbate the disease problem. The symptoms of root disease — growth loss, butt rot, blowdown, and mortality — usually occur in patches or in scattered infected trees in the mature forest. Before harvest, the mature stand should be surveyed to determine the incidence, extent, distribution, and cause of root disease. In spruce and hemlock stands, however, such surveys may grossly underestimate the incidence and extent of Tomentosus and Annosus root rot, respectively, compared to the decay that will typically be found in the stumps after harvest.

Annosus Root Rot

The "S" strain of the fungus, *Heterobasidion annosum*, responsible for Annosus root rot in British Columbia, is found in the wet areas of the Vancouver, Prince Rupert, and Nelson Forest Regions. It causes butt rot in managed stands of western hemlock and true firs.

The fungus lives saprophytically in woody food bases such as stumps. Tree roots are attacked when they grow into contact with the woody food base. *Heterobasidion annosum* may then spread from tree to tree through root contacts, but it is a poor competitor with other fungi and does not spread from stump to stump. Fresh wounds (up to about 1 month old), such as stump tops in thinned stands and root wounds from skidders, are readily colonized by air-borne spores. Small food bases, spaced stumps for example, are exhausted as a food supply in a few years and the small roots of the stumps are readily invaded by competing fungi. The roots of large stumps, on the other hand, may be colonized internally from a large stump food base and the fungus may live for a long time there. For more information on *H. annosum*, see Wallis and Morrison (1975).

FIGURE 20.3.   *Armillaria* root rot. Note the white mycelium under the bark.

Armillaria Root Rot

The fungus responsible for Armillaria root rot, *Armillaria ostoyae*, is found throughout British Columbia south of Quesnel, along the 53° N latitude. It can cause extensive mortality to Douglas-fir, spruce, subalpine fir, lodgepole pine, western hemlock, and western redcedar, particularly in the Interior.

The fungus lives saprophytically in woody food bases, such as stumps and killed trees (Figure 20.3). Tree roots are attacked when they come into contact with the woody food base, or fungus rhizomorphs may grow out about 30 cm from the food base to attack tree roots. It can pass from tree to tree or stump to stump along root systems. Small food bases may be exhausted by *A. ostoyae* in a few years, while large food bases may support it for a long time. Similarly, small potential food bases such as root pieces are more readily colonized by competing fungi (which may exclude *A. ostoyae*) than are large potential food bases such as stumps. See Morrison et al. (1988) for additional information on *A. ostoyae*.

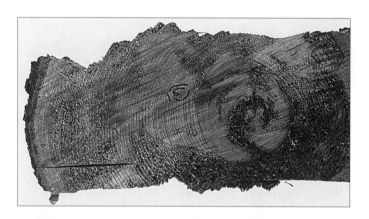

FIGURE 20.4.   Tomentosus root rot decay in stump top.

Tomentosus Root Rot

The fungus responsible for Tomentosus root rot is *Inonotus tomentosus*. It is reported south of 55° N latitude, into the United States, but occurs primarily as a root and butt rot of interior spruce north of about Williams Lake, along the 52° N latitude.

The fungus can live saprophytically in woody food bases, such as stumps and killed trees, for more than 25 years (Figure 20.4). It attacks tree roots that come into contact with woody food bases and it spreads from tree to tree by grafts and root contacts. The function of spores is currently being investigated. If they are capable of invading wounds, the biological situation may be similar to that of *H. annosum* and management practices may have to be similar to those for Annosus root rot. For more information on *I. tomentosus,* see Whitney (1977).

Black Stain Root Disease of Douglas-fir

The fungus responsible for black stain root rot, *Leptographium* (*Verticicladiella*) *wageneri* var. *pseudotsugae,* is found largely throughout the range of Douglas-fir. It causes patch mortality in young-growth Douglas-fir, particularly in stands with bedrock near the surface and on well-drained, coarse-textured (gravelly) soils that have been disturbed.

The fungus is initially vectored into tree roots by root-feeding beetles, which may be particularly attracted to trees under moisture stress or to dying root systems of stumps and older trees afflicted with other root diseases. Insects in their search for weakened roots may bite and inoculate both healthy and weakened roots. The fungus spreads rapidly in living roots and from tree to tree through grafts and sometimes root contacts. Other root-feeding insects, such as weevils, may spread the disease below ground. The fungus cannot rot wood, so its food source is exhausted quickly. It is also a poor competitor with other fungi, and so does not usually persist in stumps for more than 2 years. Sites can therefore be reforested with susceptible Douglas-fir. More detailed information on black stain root disease in British Columbia is included in Morrison and Hunt (1988).

Laminated Root Rot of Douglas-fir

FIGURE 20.5. Laminated root rot. Note the external mycelium growing along the root.

Phellinus weirii var. *pseudotsugae* is the fungus responsible for laminated root rot. It causes growth loss, butt rot, mortality, and proneness to windthrow throughout the Douglas-fir range south of about Williams Lake, along the 52° N latitude.

It lives saprophytically in woody food bases such as stumps and killed trees. Spores are rarely produced and are not known to have any function. Tree roots are attacked when they grow into contact with the woody food base. The fungus grows on the surface and in the bark scales of living roots, and thus spreads from tree to tree by grafts and root contacts (Figure 20.5). The surface growth penetrates into the wood and rots the roots. Eventually the fungus may extend up the tree as a butt rotter. It is a poor competitor with other fungi and does not readily colonize dead roots. As a result, it does not survive long in small food bases such as root pieces, though it may survive 100 years in large food bases such as old-growth stumps. For more information on *P. weirii*, see Morrison et al. (1988) and Wallis (1976).

Rhizina Root Disease

The fungus causing *Rhizina undulata* is primarily found in the wet areas of the Vancouver, Prince Rupert, and Nelson Forest Regions and sporadically in other areas of the province. High temperatures are necessary for spore germination, so the fungus occurs on newly planted sites that have been slashburned.

Germinating spores penetrate seedling roots and cover the root system with a white mycelium. Mycelial strands transmit the fungus from seedling to seedling or (though rarely) to larger unharvested conifers (Figure 20.6). The resulting patch mortality resembles drought death, but in the first year after planting, fungus fruit bodies can be found.

Controlling Root Disease

If infection centers are common or extensive, then control is warranted unless black stain root disease is the sole disease present. Inoculum in the soil may be reduced if the trees are pushed over at the time of logging, or the stumps are removed from the ground

FIGURE 20.6. *Rhizina* root disease. Seedling showing wilt symptoms, with fruit bodies at base.

and the roots raked so they are readily colonized by soil fungi. The root disease fungus then dies. On many sites, however, soil type or topography may preclude treatment. The alternative is to plant a less susceptible species. Once the disease is identified, a species susceptibility chart (Table 20.1) should be consulted and a less susceptible species planted (provided it is suited to the site). Hardwoods are either immune or more resistant to these fungi.

TABLE 20.1. The relative susceptibility of forest trees to six of the most serious root diseases in British Columbia. This list is based largely on observations and on a few experimental results, and should therefore be used with caution. All conifers are highly susceptible to Armillaria root rot (RR) for about the first 30 years.

	Root disease					
Susceptibility	*Armillaria* RR *ostoyae*	*Tomentosus* RR	Laminated RR var. *pseudotsugae*	*Annosus* RR "S"	Black stain var. *pseudotsugae*	*Rhizina*
Most resistant		Hardwoods	Hardwoods		Hardwoods, pines, spruce, *Abies* spp.	Hardwoods
Somewhat susceptible	Hardwoods, western larch	Western white pine	Western redcedar	Douglas-fir pines	Western hemlock	
Moderately susceptible	Spruce, ponderosa pine, western white pine, western redcedar	Subalpine fir, Douglas-fir	Pines	Western redcedar, hemlock		
Most susceptible	*Abies* spp., lodgepole pine, Douglas-fir, western hemlock	Spruce, lodgepole pine	*Abies* spp., spruce, Douglas-fir, western larch, hemlocks	*Abies* spp., Sitka spruce	Douglas-fir	Conifers

If the site has been burned, Rhizina root disease may attack newly planted seedlings. If the disease has occurred in the area in the past 2 years, then spore loads on the site may be high. Where site preparation by burning cannot be avoided, planting should be delayed for 2 years.

In stands slated for spacing (pre-commercial thinning), the incidence of infections should be determined beforehand. The rule of thumb is that if there are 10 or more infection centers per hectare, thinning should not be tried. In sites where mortality is extensive, as often occurs in *A. ostoyae* centers in the Interior, replacing the disease centers with a less susceptible species may be necessary. However, the food bases in such sites are plentiful and considerable mortality will continue unless the inoculum is reduced mechanically. If it is suspected that black stain root disease may increase following spacing, spacing is best done after the spring flight of the vectoring beetles. Late fall, winter, and spring felling produces stumps that are attractive to the insects.

If a stand is proposed for a commercial thinning or partial cut harvest, and if the incidence of root disease is high, it should probably be clearcut. This may be especially true if the root disease is caused by *A. ostoyae*, since this fungus can rapidly colonize the new stumps and then readily attack the leave trees. In the case of Annosus or Tomentosus root rot, symptoms may not be evident until decay is noted in the stumps. In true fir and hemlock stands, great care must be taken to avoid wounding leave trees and damaging roots. This can be done by selecting a proven crew, logging on snow, using rubber-tired skidders, and using bumper trees for skidding, felling them at the end of the operation. Stump tops of true fir and hemlock should be treated with a registered pesticide. Wounds and untreated stump tops are readily invaded by *H. annosum*, which leads to Annosus root and butt rot in leave trees of these species.

Stem Rusts

Pines are the only conifers subject to attack by stem rusts caused by *Cronartium* spp. All of these rusts have alternate hosts, and the incidence of rust on trees is higher when both hosts are growing in close proximity. The important stem rusts and their hosts are listed in Table 20.2. Rusts caused by *Cronartium* spp. produce elongate cankers on pines and can be recognized by the orange spores they produce on canker margins in the spring.

TABLE 20.2. Important stem rusts of pine and their hosts in British Columbia

| Stem rusts | Hosts | |
	Pines	Alternate
Cronartium coleo-sporioides Arth.	Lodgepole	Paintbrush, cow-wheat, yellow owl's clover, louse wart, and yellow-rattle
C. comandrae Peck	Lodgepole and ponderosa	Comandra
C. ribicola J.C. Fischer	White pines	(Ribes sp.) Currants and gooseberries
Endocronartium harknessii (J.P. Moore) Y. Hiratsuka	Lodgepole, ponderosa, Scots	None

Some alternate hosts such as comandra, paintbrush, flowering red currant, and sticky currant may be more abundant if the forest litter is greatly disturbed during road building, harvesting, or site preparation. Such disturbance should be minimized. If alternate hosts become abundant, herbicides may need to be applied in some instances. In British Columbia, the alternate hosts of white pine blister rusts are currants and gooseberries, and these grow mostly along stream banks. Maintaining dense vegetation cover over streams will impede spread of rust spores between these alternate hosts and white pines. For more information on managing white pine, see Hunt (1988).

Western gall rust, produces spherical galls on branches and stems of hard pines, particularly lodgepole pine, and is caused by *Endocronartium harknessii* . Because this rust lacks an alternate host, clean stock must be planted. Nurseries growing such stock should have all adjacent infected trees removed. Likewise, planting sites should not be flanked with severely infected stands. The earlier the rust becomes established, the more damage it does. Young stems are killed outright; older stems become deformed and, during wind storms, frequently break at stem cankers.

Opening up a stand during a pre-commercial thinning operation gives rust spores access to the remaining pines, and thus infection may intensify. Stands slated for pre-commercial thinning should be surveyed for the presence of rust and alternate hosts. Since many lodgepole pine stands lack both, thinning has no effect on intensifying the disease. If a stem rust or its alternate hosts are present, the stocking targets should be increased to allow for future mortality, with spacing removing the stem-infected trees. Properly trained crews are essential to carry out this work effectively.

Pruning all lower branches during spacing is a good control of western white pine rust, but preliminary evidence suggests it is not as effective with rusts of lodgepole pine. Pruning (complete branch removal) is recommended when the trees can be safely pruned to 1.25 m, and again as soon as the trees can be pruned to 2.5-3.0 m. Infected branches above the pruning height should also be removed. All infested western white pine stands, particularly those on slopes, should be examined at the commercial thinning stage to determine if a harvest cut is warranted. Many infected trees may develop topkill or infestations of secondary insects, and are best removed.

Hiratsuka and Powell (1976) and Ziller (1974) provide in-depth information on pine stem rust and other conifer rusts. Hunt (1988) has compiled the most up-to-date knowledge on white pine blister rust.

Needle Diseases

Little can be done to control needle diseases in plantations. The occurrence of many needle diseases is sporadic. They are epidemic for 1-3 years and then absent for many years. The most practical control would be to use resistant stock, which in most cases is yet to be selected. However, for one widespread and frequent needle disease of lodgepole pine, *Lophodermella concolor*, there are some simple rules to maximize resistance. High elevation seed sources should not be transferred to lower elevations, and the most susceptible sites of moist and relatively mild valleys in the Interior should be planted with resistant provenances native to these sites. These rules have been incorporated into the seed transfer rules for lodgepole pine.

For more information on needle diseases and cankers, consult Funk (1981 and 1985a).

DISEASES AFFECTING TREES OF ALL AGE CLASSES

The root diseases, stem rusts, and needle diseases discussed above usually start on young trees and continue to be a problem throughout stand rotations. As well, there are a multitude of diseases that affect trees regardless of age class. Their incidence and severity often vary according to numerous factors, including host species, locality, and long-term weather. Some of these diseases that appear to be severe, such as those on needles, may in fact not harm either height or volume growth of the tree. Other times, again as exemplified by needle diseases, damage may be related to the frequency with which the disease occurs.

Because space does not permit a discussion of each of these diseases individually, we have listed the more common ones that occur in young forests, along with a brief description of the damage they cause and some forest management practices that can be used to minimize that damage (Table 20.3). The information in the table should be used only as a general guide, as many of the symptoms (e.g., for die-back and needle diseases) are similar. To identify a particular disease correctly, a pathologist or mycologist should be consulted.

TABLE 20.3. Some common diseases of young forest trees in British Columbia

Disease or pathogen	Host(s)	Signs or symptoms	Damage	Forest management practice(s)
Dwarf mistletoe *Arceuthobium* spp.	Conifers, but certain mistletoes have specific hosts	Light green mistletoe shoots grow out of branch swellings or brooms.	Growth and vigor are reduced, which may lead to attack by secondary organisms.	All diseased trees should be removed at harvest or destroyed before planting.
Spruce needle rust *Chrysomyxa* spp.	All spruces	Orange spore pustules in white membranes of current year's needles.	Incidence only high in swampy habitats where the alternate host, Labrador tea, is abundant.	Avoid monoculture of spruce where alternate host is abundant.
Spruce-broom rust *Chrysomyxa arctostaphyli* Diet.	Spruce	Yellow brooms which bear fungus fruiting structures on short needles.	Brooms act to decrease increment. Decay fungi are associated with dead brooms. Most severe in northwestern B.C.	Particularly severe near kinnikinnick, the alternate host. Try to eliminate alternate host during site preparation. Sites with brooms on the tree stems should be spaced; otherwise, prune off brooms during pre-commercial thinning.
Fir blight *Delphinella abietis* (Rostr.) E. Muell.	Interior subalpine fir	New foliage looks burned or blighted.	Extensive and severe every 3-7 years.	No practical controls known.
Derma pseudotsugae Funk	Douglas-fir, grand fir	Bark necrosis, cankering and die-back.	Associated with early frosts and summer drought.	Remove seriously damaged trees during spacing operations.
Phomopsis canker *Diaporthe lokayae* Funk	Douglas-fir, western hemlock, and western redcedar	Annual stem cankers and die-back.	Associated with frost damage or summer drought.	Remove seriously damaged trees during spacing operations.
Dichomera gemmicola Funk and Sutton	Douglas-fir and spruce	Buds fail to flush, and develop black spore bodies.	Deformation or, if all buds are killed, death may occur.	Disease usually localized and trees often recover, thus no controls recommended.
Dime canker *Durandiella pseudotsugae* Funk	Douglas-fir	Dime-sized, raised cankers of the outer bark, usually many on a stem.	Usually associated with shallow soils or dense stands.	Increase vigor by spacing or fertilization.
Elytroderma deformans (Weir) Darker	Ponderosa and lodgepole pines	Dark red needles in the early spring, usually on brooms.	Early infection in lodgepole pine may cause dwarfing and death. Extensive brooming in ponderosa pine may lead to bark beetle attack.	Promote vigorous growth which can shade out infections, particularly in lodgepole pine. Space severely infected trees and prune off brooms.
Encoeliopsis laricina (Ettl.) Groves	Western larch	Shoot blight and cankering.	Can be severe on young larch.	None known.
Black stain root disease *Leptographium* (*Verticicladiella*) *wageneri* (Kendr.) Wingf.	Lodgepole pine, occasionally spruces and western white pine	Mortality in typically small (less than 0.2 ha) contiguous patches, with declining trees having thin foliage; often abrupt reduction in incremental growth. In the root collar there are black stains coming from the roots, which are in the spring wood only.	The disease is associated with dense old-growth stands growing at high elevation which are often attacked by *Ips*.	Stands can be harvested and replanted to any conifer suitable to the site, including lodgepole pine.
Leptomelanconium pinicola (Berk.& Curt.) R.S. Hunt	Ponderosa and lodgepole pines	Blight of all ages of foliage, particularly severe in lower crowns and saplings. Easily confused with redband needle blight.	Increment loss if repetitive. Areas of infestation often extensive, particularly in ponderosa pine.	None known.
Lirula macrospora (Hartig) Darker	Spruce	Longitudinal, black fruiting bodies on discolored 2-year-old and older needles.	Occasionally epidemic, increment loss if repetitive.	None known.

TABLE 20.3.   (Continued)

Disease or pathogen	Host(s)	Signs or symptoms	Damage	Forest management practice(s)
Meria blight *Meria laricis* Vuill.	Western larch, occasionally Douglas-fir	Scattered blighted needles which become yellow, then brown, and are shed.	Frequently epidemic. Increment loss if repetitive.	None known.
Swiss needle cast *Phaeocryptopus gaeumannii* (Rohde) Petr.	Douglas-fir	Current year needles healthy, some older needles yellowing and being cast. "Fly specks" at stomata on under-side of older needles.	Needle casting more pronounced on trees in dry habitats or following dry summers. Lasting effects are negligible. Often looks severe when it is not.	Plant proper seed source for site. No other controls known.
Potebniamyces die-back *Phacidium balsamicola* Smerlis	*Abies* spp.	Die-back of small branches, often with a pronounced swelling at the girdling point.	Common in some stands, but does not cause significant losses.	Severely infected trees should be spaced in pre-commercial thinnings. Pruning the die-back is not necessary.
Abies rust *Pucciniastrum* spp.	*Abies* spp., particularly subalpine fir	Orange spore pustules in white membranes on the underside of current or 1-year-old needles.	Incidence high in association with alternate hosts (fireweed or huckleberries). No severe losses known.	Minimize alternate hosts during site preparation. No forest controls known.
Douglas-fir needle cast *Rhabdocline* spp.	Douglas-fir	Infected needles develop yellow, then red blotches; epidermis splits open, usually on the lower needle surface, releasing spores. Lower branches most severely defoliated.	Some genotypes and some habitats, such as moist depressions, are chronically infected. Epidemics occasionally develop from these. Repeated defoliation results in loss of vigor and increment.	Plant proper seed source for site and discriminate against highly susceptible genotypes in seed orchards and during pre-commercial spacing.
Redband needle disease *Scirrhia pini* Funk & A.K. Parker	Pines	Blight on all ages of foliage; particularly severe in lower crowns and saplings. Red bands sometimes prominent on straw-colored needles.	Increment loss if repetitive. Areas of infestation often extensive, particularly in lodgepole and western white pines.	None known.
Sclerophoma spp.	Conifers	Die-backs.	Frequently associated with frost, drought, or off-site plantings.	Plant proper species and seed source for site. No other forest controls known.
Sirococcus strobilinus Preuss	Western hemlock, spruce, pines, and Douglas-fir	Blighted tip usually in a "shepherd's crook."	Blighting sometimes extensive in coastal stands of hemlock and Sitka spruce. Damage frequently unsightly but not considered severe. Important in nurseries.	None known.
White-spored rusts of *Abies* *Uredinopsis* spp.	*Abies* spp.	Tongue-shaped white membranes with white spores on the underside of chlorotic or green needles.	Damage usually minor, unless the alternate hosts (ferns) are abundant. Can be severe and stunting to bracken.	Avoid site preparation methods that encourage the growth of alternate hosts. If severe, herbicide application to alternate hosts may be necessary.
Venturia blight *Venturia* spp.	Poplar and aspen	New foliage looks burned or blighted; die-back and shepherd's crooking may occur. Black spots develop olive green mat of mycelium.	Damage more severe in moist sheltered areas, particularly along stream banks. Blighting is common. Regeneration may be delayed several years.	Plant resistant clones and use sites with good air drainage.
Virgella robusta (Tub.) Darker	Amabilis fir	Two-year-old and older foliage with small black fruiting bodies on the upper surface and long dark brown fruiting bodies on the lower surface of reddish-brown to straw-colored needles.	Unsightly loss of older foliage can be intensive, but effects on growth are probably minor.	None known.

INSECT PESTS IN REFORESTATION

21

K.E. Finck, G.M. Shrimpton, and D.W. Summers

Insects are a basic part of the forest ecosystem. Often what man perceives as being insect *damage* to the forest is really part of the ecological cycle. An example is the damage in overmature forests caused by the mountain pine beetle (*Dendroctonus ponderosae*) and western hemlock looper (*Lambdina fiscellaria lugubrosa*). The mortality that results in decadent stands, which these insects primarily attack, allows young and vigorous trees to establish. To man, however, overmature stands are often highly valuable and insect attacks on them are usually considered to be undesirable and costly.

Forest management itself may be responsible for many insect problems. Forest seed orchards, nurseries, and plantations do not occur naturally. As a result, they are subject to the consequences that manipulating nature often brings. Forest insect management tries to moderate these consequences.

Forest insects can be controlled in several ways:

- with silvicultural methods to alter stand composition, stocking density, site conditions, and stand vigor;
- with mechanical methods to trap or physically destroy insects or their habitat;
- with biological methods to control insects through the introduction of pathogens, parasites, and predators;
- with regulations such as quarantine to restrict the movement of infested material or prevent the introduction of new species of forest insects; and
- with insecticides to kill insects directly.

Before any form of insect control is attempted, the causal organism must be identified and the damage, or potential damage, assessed. Once this information is known, all consequences of the insect attack should be weighed against the added cost and other implications of insect control. An insect management regime should be followed only when it is considered to be economically and biologically sound — and socially acceptable.

This chapter describes the insects by setting (i.e., seed orchard, nursery, and plantation) that are the most damaging to seedling production and development. As well, it describes the damage they cause, and briefly discusses possible control options. For operational control information, the reader should consult specialists.

SEED ORCHARD INSECTS

Seed orchards are unique in that they are plantations of genetically selected stock, specifically designed for seed production. The trees are of high value because scion collection, propagation, planting, and maintenance represent a considerable investment. Each tree is also important because of its contribution to the genetic balance of the orchard. For these reasons, tolerance thresholds for pests in orchards are lower than in forest plantations.

Insects directly and indirectly affect seed orchards throughout the stages of orchard development and production. Indirect effects occur when defoliators, gall aphids, twig miners, and root weevils reduce tree growth and vigor or cause outright mortality. This increases the length of time required for the desired number of trees to reach a size large enough for full seed production. Direct damage by cone and seed insects after the orchard has reached full production can keep seed yields well below target.

Insects Affecting Seed Production Directly: Cone and Seed Insects

All conifers have an insect complex that attacks reproductive structures. Table 21.1 shows the British Columbia pest complexes and the damage they do to conifers.

The relative importance of each pest in the complex can vary from year to year, with crop size or location. Western spruce budworm populations, for example, periodically fluctuate from endemic to epidemic levels. Damage during an epidemic year can be devastating to cone crops. Cone and seed insects often do more damage to small cone crops than to large ones, because competition for resources is much more intense in the smaller crops. Some insect species may also be more damaging in one part of the province than in another. In spruce, the seed moth (*Cydia*) is more common in the southern Interior, while the cone maggot (*Strobilomyia*) is prevalent in the north of the province.

At the same time, members of a pest complex can be ranked as major or minor pests. For spruce, the cone maggot (*S. anthracinum*) and the seed worm (*C. strobilella*) are classed as major pests. They commonly destroy large amounts of seed. Most others are usually minor pests and only sporadically cause significant damage.

While cone and seed insects have several natural enemies, the primary factor limiting populations seems to be the cyclical nature of their food supply (cone crops). To overcome this, a portion of most cone and seed insect populations will enter a resting state called diapause for one to several years before adult emergence. This ensures that some of the population will survive a year of famine.

Regular cone crops, such as those in seed orchards, may result in less insect mortality and allow cone and seed insect populations to build up to the point where damage is consistently greater than in other areas. If seed is to be collected, some form of control measure may be necessary.

TABLE 21.1. Common insect pests of conifer cone and seed orchards

Insect name, distribution and references	Species affected	Potential for damage	Signs and symptoms
Moths *(Lepidoptera)*			
Ponderosa pine seed moth *Cydia piperana* Occurs throughout the range of its hosts in California, Oregon, Washington, Idaho, Montana, and the southern Interior of B.C. Hedlin (1974) Furniss and Carolin (1977)	Ponderosa pine	Especially destructive to pine seeds; in one study, nearly half of the total seeds per cone were destroyed by an average of 14 larvae per cone. There is no external evidence of damage to the cones.	Larva is off-white and 16 mm long, and has a brown head. The pupa is white, but turns very dark before the adult emerges. The moths are small, 16 mm long, and dark brown. The larva feeds inside young second-year cones from June to September, leaving the seeds full of frass. It constructs a silken tunnel between pairs of seeds and fuses them together. In late July, the larva burrows through to the cone axis and begins to spin a cocoon in which to over-winter and pupate the following April. (Figure 21.1)
Pine coneworm *Dioryctria auranticella* Distributed throughout the drier regions of the Western United States and B.C. Hedlin (1974) Furniss and Carolin (1977) Hedlin et al. (1980)	Second-year ponderosa pine	When present in large numbers, the insects can destroy a large amount of seed. By feeding on seeds and scales from a cavity inside the cone, the larvae severely distort the inside of the cone, making seed dispersal impossible.	Larvae are about 26 mm long, dark, and active. The adult has rust forewings with white markings and a wingspan of about 30 mm. The life cycle is not completely understood. The larvae appear in the cone in late spring, when they tunnel cavities within the cone, destroying seeds and scales. Fecal pellets and webbing are left behind in the cavities, and cone scales begin to brown and shrivel.
Fir coneworm *Dioryctria abietivorella* Occurs throughout B.C. and the Western United States. Hedlin (1974) Hedlin et al. (1980) Ruth (1980)	Douglas-fir, grand fir, subalpine fir, spruce, pine	A single larva can completely destroy all seeds within a cone by damaging both scales and seeds. Ponderosa pine is less severely affected. Damage ranges from light in years of good cone crops to almost total destruction of cones in poor years.	Larvae are reddish brown with brown heads, and are about 20 mm long when mature. The adult is a mottled, gray moth with brown and silver forewings and unmarked gray hindwings having a wingspan of 28 mm. From June to September, larvae feed and tunnel through scales and seeds. Several large holes with coarse frass on the surface of the cone indicate the presence of the larvae.
Spruce seedworm *Cydia strobilella* Most commonly found in northern coastal and interior areas of B.C. Hedlin (1974) Hedlin et al. (1980) Ruth et al. (1982)	White, Engelmann, Sitka, black spruce	One larva can destroy 40% of the seed in a cone; more than two can destroy 100%. Usually no more than three larvae are present in one cone. They mine through the cone but only feed on seeds.	Larvae are cream-colored with dark heads. They measure about 10 mm when mature. The adult is a small, smoky-brown moth with a wingspan of about 9 mm. Young larvae enter the seeds and feed on their contents from June to September, filling the empty shells with frass and leaving no external signs of damage. The larva burrows into the cone axis to overwinter, and pupates the following spring.
Douglas-fir cone moth *Barbara colfaxiana* Occurs in California, Washington, Montana, Colorado, and B.C., where it is more serious in interior than in coastal areas. Hedlin (1974) Hedlin and Ruth (1974) Furniss and Carolin (1977) Hedlin et al. (1980) Ruth (1980)	Douglas-fir	Larvae first feed on the scales and then seeds of young cones. A single larva will destroy about 65% of the seed in the cone, while two or more will destroy 100% of the seeds in a cone.	Larvae are cream-colored, with black heads that turn brown during development. The adult is a small, gray moth with speckled forewings and a wingspan of 15-20 mm. It lays its eggs on the outer edge of bracts of young, erect conelets during early spring. Larvae mine through the seeds and scales, making a resinous tunnel. On small cones, frass and resin may be visible, which allows damage to be detected. Feeding also causes the cone scales to wither and brown. Infested cones remain on the tree over the winter because of the heavy flow of resin that fuses the bracts together and prevents degradation. (Figure 21.2)

TABLE 21.1.   (Continued)

Insect name, distribution and references	Species affected	Potential for damage	Signs and symptoms
Flies (*Diptera*)			
Red-cedar cone midge *Mayetiola thujae* Distributed throughout Oregon, Washington, and B.C. Hedlin (1974) Furniss and Carolin (1977) Hedlin et al. (1980)	Western redcedar	The larva is capable of damaging more than one seed in a cone. There may be up to 150 larvae per cone; they usually destroy all seeds in the cone.	Larva is small and orange with a distinct spatula. The adult is 3 mm long. It lays egg clusters beneath cone scales and eggs hatch in mid-April. Larvae move from cone scale to cone scale, damaging scales and seeds, but they do not tunnel. The larvae feed during the summer and then overwinter in the cone in a gray cocoon, pupating in February. Damage is often evident after a few weeks of larval feeding by the splitting and browning of the outer scales.
Spiral spruce-cone borer *Strobilomyia neanthracinum*	White, Engelmann, Sitka, black spruce	Single larva can destroy up to 50% of the total seeds in a cone. Where infestations are severe, the total seed crop may be destroyed.	Larva is 8 mm long and has white and black mouth hooks. Pupa is smooth and brown. Adult is a small black fly, similar to a housefly, about 6 mm long. Eggs are laid singly between cone scales. Larvae hatch and feed in a spiral around the cone axis, damaging scales and seeds. Feeding continues from early June to July, leaving clean tunnels that later fill with pitch. Larva leaves the cone by way of an exit hole to the surface of the cone, and overwinters in the litter. (Figure 21.3)
Fir cone maggot *Earomyia aquilonia* Occurs across Canada from Newfoundland to the interior of B.C., from the Yukon along through the Western United States. Hedlin (1974) Hedlin et al. (1980)	Douglas-fir, subalpine fir, tamarack	Total destruction of all seeds may result if there are more than four larvae per cone.	Larva is white with black mouth parts. It is 6-7 mm long. Adult is a small black, velvety fly about 4 mm long. In late spring, adults lay individual eggs on the inner surface of the cone scale. Within a month, the larvae hatch and feed on seeds throughout the cone. They finish feeding in late summer and drop to the ground to pupate and overwinter.
Douglas-fir cone gall midge *Contarinia oregonensis* Occurs throughout the range of its host but is more common in coastal areas than in the Interior. Hedlin (1974) Hedlin et al. (1980) Ruth (1980)	Douglas-fir	All seeds may be destroyed if there are several hundred larvae present in a cone.	Larvae are orange and about 2.8 mm long when mature. The adult is mosquito-like with an orange abdomen. Eggs are frequently laid in clusters at the base of the cone scales in erect female flowers around the time of pollination (April to May). Larvae form galls in the cone scales by burrowing into the scales and inducing swelling of the surrounding tissue. Cone scales will turn a reddish brown in late summer due to premature death if the cone is severely infested.
Beetles (*Coleptera*) **Pine cone beetle** *Conophthorus ponderosae* Ranges from B.C. to Idaho and California. Hedlin (1974) Furniss and Carolin (1977) Hedlin et al. (1980)	Second-year cones of western white, lodgepole and ponderosa pine	The burrowing done by the adult female into the cone to lay its eggs severs the vascular tissue and kills the cone. The larvae then feed in galleries in the dead or dying cone. Damage to ponderosa, western white, and sugar pines is often very severe.	Larvae are small, white, and curled, and have light brown heads; they feed in galleries in the cone tissues. Adult is a small, shiny, cylindrical beetle 2.4-4 mm long. In late spring, after tunnelling to the axis of the immature cone, the female lays its eggs and the tunnel becomes an egg gallery. All of the seeds are destroyed by the developing larvae. Damage is indicated by dry, withered, half-grown pine cones that either stay on the tree blighted, or drop to the ground prematurely. (Figure 21.4)

TABLE 21.1. (Continued)

Insect name, distribution and references	Species affected	Potential for damage	Signs and symptoms
Sawflies, bees, wasps, ants (*Hymenoptera*)			
Douglas-fir seed chalcid *Megastigmus spermatrophus* Occurs in the Western United States and Canada. Hedlin (1974) Furniss and Carolin (1977) Hedlin et al. (1980) Ruth (1980)	Douglas-fir	Seed loss ranges from 2 to 15% of total seed crop. Reports of much bigger damage in literature. Stopping the spread of the insect is difficult because there is no external difference between infested and normal seeds.	The adult female is amber, wasp-like, and about 4 mm long, with a long, thin ovipositor. The adult male is yellow and 3 mm long. In late May and June the adult lays up to 150 eggs into the immature Douglas-fir seeds, normally one egg per seed. The larva feeds on the seed contents, and remains there until it pupates and emerges as an adult the next spring. The curled white larvae feeds during June, July, and August, leaving no external signs of seed damage. The insect can be detected only by seed dissection, X-rays, or evidence of an emergence hole through the seed coat, left as the adult emerges the next year. (Figure 21.5)
Bugs (*Hemiptera*)			
Western conifer seed bug *Leptoglossus occidentalis* Occurs from B.C. and Alberta to Mexico and from California to Colorado. Hedlin 1974 Hedlin et al. (1980) Ruth (1980)	Douglas-fir, grand fir, incense cedar, lodgepole, Monterey, ponderosa, and western white pine	Large populations and heavy feeding by this insect result in reduced quality of seed. Up to 41% seed loss has been recorded in Douglas-fir and 26% seed loss in western white pine.	Nymphs are orange to reddish orange. Adult is large, 15-18 mm long, 4-6 mm wide, with an elongate body that is reddish brown to gray. It has dense, white hairs and fore-wings marked with white zigzag lines. Barrel-shaped eggs are laid on the host's needles from early June until mid-August. Damage to the seeds by shrivelling of the endosperm can be detected only by seed dissection or X-rays. The nymphs initially feed on foliage. Subsequently they and adults feed on the juices of young seeds by piercing through the cone scales into the developing seed. The adults overwinter and feed on 1-year-old cones and emerging male flowers the next spring. (Figure 21.6)

Control of cone and seed insect pests

The intensity and frequency of insect damage, and therefore the need for control measures, vary with the conifer species, orchard location, crop frequency, and long- and short-term weather patterns. For instance, seed orchards should be located away from natural stands of the same species. This isolation can preclude many pest problems and, if coupled with a quarantine system for new stock coming in, it can minimize the need for direct pest controls. In time, many pests will inadvertently become established as endemic residents in an orchard. With proper sanitation and occasional chemical intervention, however, populations may be kept to a minimum.

The management of cone and seed insect pests in seed orchards requires a complex series of decisions by the orchard manager. The manager must consider several factors when assessing the need for direct control measures. The pest management system in place for coastal Douglas-fir seed orchards in British Columbia illustrates many of these considerations. In these orchards the major pest is the Douglas-fir cone gall midge (*Contarinia oregonensis*). This insect causes galls to form on cone scales or on the ovule. Seeds either do not develop or are fused inside the cone by the gall.

D.S. Ruth, Forestry Canada

FIGURE 21.1. *Cydia piperana* (ponderosa pine seed moth) larva burrows through cones to feed on seeds.

D.S. Ruth, Forestry Canada

FIGURE 21.2. *Barbara colfaxiana* (Douglas-fir cone moth) larva on Douglas-fir cone.

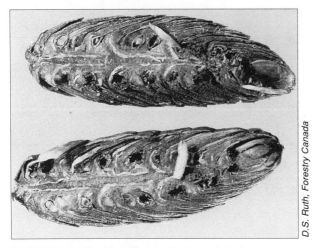

D.S. Ruth, Forestry Canada

FIGURE 21.3 *Strobilomyia neanthracinum* (spiral spruce-cone borer) on spruce cone.

D.S. Ruth, Forestry Canada

FIGURE 21.4. *Conophthorus ponderosae* (pine cone beetle) larvae in western white pine cone.

D.S. Ruth, Forestry Canada

FIGURE 21.5. *Megastigimus* sp. (seed chalcid) larva feeding inside seed.

D.S. Ruth, Forestry Canada

FIGURE 21.6. *Leptoglossus occidentalis* (western conifer seed bug).

To address the problem, many Douglas-fir orchards employ management techniques that are aimed at eliminating the need for insect management to protect a crop. For example, overhead irrigation is used to cool the trees during warm spells in the late winter and early spring. This often delays the flowering period, puts the trees out of synchrony with trees surrounding the orchard, and reduces pollen contamination from outside sources. The delay may also put the gall midge population out of synchrony with the flowers. The oviposition period for gall midge coincides with the pollination period for Douglas-fir and, if an adequate delay is obtained in seed orchards through cooling, midge damage is reduced. This process of cooling is too expensive for cone and seed insect management alone and it periodically fails to do the job. When it does work, however, its successes can be outstanding.

The size and quality of the orchard crop should have a bearing on how much effort goes into managing it. A small or poorly pollinated Douglas-fir crop may not be worth the costs involved to protect it from cone and seed insect attack, or to collect it when it matures in the fall. Likewise, trees with few cones in an otherwise medium or heavy orchard crop may not produce enough seed to be worth protecting. However, treatment of these trees may be warranted as a sanitation measure if cones cannot be picked before insect emergence. Sanitation cone picking can help keep resident orchard pest populations to a minimum, although the procedure may not always be practical. The costs of sanitation can outweigh the benefits in cases where most of the pest population migrates into the orchard each year from surrounding stands.

If a Douglas-fir cone crop is worth protecting, monitoring techniques and damage prediction models are essential to the pest management program. The system for *C. oregonensis* begins with the collection of young conelets in the spring and a laboratory examination of the scales for midge eggs. If the average number of egg-infested scales per conelet indicates seed loss of 10% or more, a review of seed production targets may be needed. In a heavy crop, 10-20% seed loss may be acceptable because the annual seed production target can be met without intervention. Similarly, if an orchard has overproduced in the past and seed supply in storage is adequate, treatment may not be worthwhile. Lighter crops offer fewer options, but the decision-making process is the same. In British Columbia, this monitoring system has resulted in 30-40% savings in treatment costs, compared to those incurred from using regular annual sprays.

Once the decision has been made to protect a seed crop, an acceptable insecticide and the appropriate application equipment must be selected. With Douglas-fir, systemic rather than purely contact insecticides are used because the gall midge egg sampling system precludes prophylactic spraying against adults. By the time gall midge oviposition is completed and the pest population has been assessed, the conelets have closed around the eggs. Systemic insecticides are absorbed by the cones and foliage and translocated to actively growing sites. As a result, when the gall midge larvae begin to feed on the inside of the cone, they consume the insecticide and are killed. A single spray applied to runoff when the conelets are horizontal is usually sufficient to provide control. Prophylactic calendar spraying to kill adults during the oviposition period would require at least two to three sprays with a contact insecticide, whether it was needed or not.

Federal and provincial regulations should be consulted during insecticide selection. Only registered insecticides can be used. As of this writing, only azinphosmethyl (Guthion®), dimethoate (Cygon®), and oxydemeton-methyl (Metasystox-R®) are registered as foliar sprays for cone and seed insects in Douglas-fir seed orchards. Dimethoate is also registered for spruce. No registrations exist for other conifers. Of the three registered products, only Metasystox-R® and dimethoate are systemic. (Note: In general, insecticides have a high toxicity to humans and should be handled appropriately.)

Proper pesticide application is essential for a successful control program. For large numbers of crop trees, air-blast sprayers or mist blowers may be more efficient than truck- or tractor-mounted hydraulic sprayers. If individual crop trees are spread throughout an orchard, hydraulic sprayers can be efficient. If used with an orchard type manlift, sprays can be applied directly to the cone-bearing portion of the trees. This minimizes the amount of pesticide required. By comparison, air-blast sprayers and mist blowers tend to wet more of the tree and also result in more drift — an important consideration in treating seed orchards located in urban areas.

Insects Affecting Seed Production Indirectly: Aphids, Defoliators, and Twig Miners

Conifers set their reproductive buds on vegetative growth in the year before cone and pollen production. Insects attacking new vegetative growth therefore have the potential to reduce seed production the following year. Twig miners, such as *Pitophthorous orarius*, *Argyresthia pseudotsuga* on Douglas-fir, or gall aphids (*Adelges cooleyi*, *Pineus* spp.) on spruce, terminate new shoots and reduce the number of potential cone-producing sites. It is conceivable that a heavy attack in a year conducive to cone initiation could limit the subsequent crop. If cones themselves are attacked by gall aphids, seed yield can be reduced substantially. In addition, defoliators such as spruce budworms (*Choristoneura*) and tussock moths (*Orgyia*) can reduce tree vigor. This in turn reduces the ability of the tree to produce and carry a healthy cone crop.

These defoliating insects are often more harmful in developing seed orchards than cone and seed insects are because, at this stage, vegetative growth is important for future cone production sites. Once trees attain sufficient size and the orchard enters the production phase, tolerance thresholds for these insects increase. As in a forest plantation where occasional defoliation can be tolerated, the loss of some vegetative production in a producing orchard is often not critical in meeting seed production targets.

Control of pests indirectly affecting seed production

In seed orchards, the management techniques for pests other than cone and seed insects are much the same as those used in Christmas tree plantations or ornamental nurseries (B.C. Ministry of Agriculture and Fisheries 1987, 1988; Wallner and Butcher 1973). Economic thresholds are seldom defined and control measures are applied when damage begins to exceed some arbitrary level set by the orchard manager. In most cases this approach is successful and seldom receives detailed economic consideration.

As the material and labor costs of applying control measures increase, however, more elaborate pest management systems are needed. Ideally, some form of monitoring will indicate when treatment is necessary and, subsequently, how effective that treatment has been. Green spruce aphid (*Elatobium abietinum*) and spruce spider mite (*Oligonychus ununguis*), for example, can cause serious defoliation in coastal spruce seed orchards. Both insects must be constantly monitored during their active periods because numbers can increase dramatically in a few weeks. Control measures must be applied early as symptoms are often not apparent until after the damage is done. Subsequent assessments can determine the efficacy of treatment and the need for further control measures during the rest of the season.

Recommendations for using appropriate pesticides and application equipment to deal with pests indirectly affecting seed production can be found in various forestry and agricultural guides (B.C. Ministry of Agriculture and Fisheries 1987, 1988).

Insect management is an integral part of seed orchard management. Potential losses in current and near-future seed production must be weighed against seed production goals and past seed yields. As orchards develop and the investment in them increases, pest management will also need to evolve so that losses can be kept to acceptable levels.

NURSERY INSECTS

Conifer seedling nurseries have a unique complex of insect pests because young and succulent seedlings can be hosts to a number of insects that would not normally feed on mature trees. Many of these insects are general feeders and often attack agricultural crops. They directly affect the quantity and quality of nursery stock. Monetary losses include the cost of producing dead or culled seedlings, as well as the cost of control procedures. Complications arise when planting sites have been prepared in the field and the seedlings are not available. In addition, infested stock can disseminate pests to new areas, reducing the survival of the stock.

Foliage Feeders

Most insect pests in conifer nurseries feed on the needles and shoots of seedlings. General feeders will readily attack young seedlings before the stems become woody and the needles become resinous. These insects are the most easily detected because pest presence or damage can be seen on inspection. They are also relatively easily controlled. In small infestations, the insects can be removed by hand and destroyed. In large infestations or when damage is severe, foliar applications of pesticides may be necessary.

Root Collar Feeders

Conifer seedlings can sustain girdling damage from several insects. Although the damage from different insects often looks similar, type of stock, time of damage, and some characteristics of the girdle can help to distinguish the culprits. For example, Figure 21.7 shows damage caused by adult root weevils and Figure 21.8 illustrates the mode of action of the cranberry girdler (*Chrysoteuchia topiaria*) larvae.

FIGURE 21.7. Damage to seedlings caused by adult weevils.

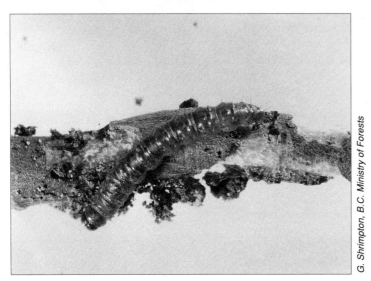

FIGURE 21.8. *Chrysoteuchia topiaria* (cranberry girdler) and damage caused from feeding.

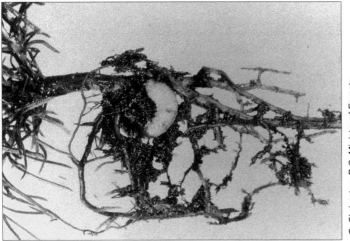

FIGURE 21.9. *Otiorhynchus sulcatus* (blackvine weevil) larva and feeding damage.

G. Shrimpton, B.C. Ministry of Forests

Girdling damage or presence of the insects is not easily detected. Most of these pests are soil or surface dwelling; some are nocturnal. Often their presence is not noted until major feeding damage to the root collar has caused the shoot to turn chlorotic. Seedlings girdled late in the season will not turn chlorotic, and damage will still appear fresh when seedlings are lifted. If the damage occurs before the seedlings have hardened off for the winter, callous tissue may develop along the edges of the feeding injury. Adventitious roots may grow on some seedlings that have been attacked.

Partial girdling probably does reduce seedling vigor, especially when seedlings are planted in reforestation sites. However, under current grading standards, all such seedlings are automatically culled and should not reach planting sites.

Root Feeders

Soil-dwelling insects that feed on the roots of conifer seedlings are the most difficult to detect and control. Unless the seedlings are lifted during routine surveys, infestations are not noticed until the supply of water and mineral nutrients to the seedling shoot is reduced, resulting in foliar symptoms. By this time, damage is usually too severe to save the seedling. Figure 21.9 shows the damage on container stock caused by blackvine weevil (*Otiorhynchus sulcatus*) larvae.

Root feeders cause further problems by opening infection courts for soil-dwelling pathogens. Pesticides must be applied as a soil drench, and contacting all pests can be difficult. As well, the chemical used must be carefully chosen because many compounds are inactivated in the soil. Often control programs for larval stages are aimed at preventing the mobile adults from ovipositing on the conifer seedlings.

Control Considerations

Insect control in nurseries is practised at all phases of production and begins with the selection of the nursery site. Factors to be considered include: the incidence of pests in the surrounding areas; the presence of plants that could serve as alternative hosts, such as spruce or Douglas-fir for the Cooley spruce gall aphid; and the existence of established quarantine zones for insects such as the balsam woolly aphid.

General year round maintenance of the site is crucial for reducing and controlling many insect populations. For example, grasses in and around the nursery can serve as alternate hosts for both the cranberry girdler and the European marsh crane fly. Removal of weeds in general can help reduce endemic populations of cutworms, lygus bugs (Figure 21.10), and root weevils. Populations of fungus gnats can build up in pools of standing water, so greenhouse facilities should have adequate drainage. The build-up of algae, moss, and liverworts in container culture can also encourage fungus gnats and springtails.

Monitoring programs have been developed for several nursery insect pests. Pheromones are used to trap the spruce budworm, European pine shoot moth, and cranberry girdler moth. Yellow-colored sticky traps are used to monitor fungus gnats, and board traps are used for root weevils. Light traps are occasionally used to reduce and monitor populations of moths in greenhouses.

Current control procedures are de-emphasizing the use of pesticides. Many insect pests such as cutworms and tussock moth larvae are hand-picked and destroyed. Some pests are physically excluded from greenhouses for part of the season by closed doors and screens placed over the fans. Several biological control agents have also been tested. Nematodes have been used against root weevil larvae, viruses against rusty tussock moth larvae, and *Bacillus thuringiensis*s against cutworms.

Pest management in British Columbia conifer seedling nurseries is a relatively new field. As nurseries are becoming established in new areas and as stock types change, new insects are becoming pests. When discovered, the pests are identified, their biology is investigated, and management programs are developed. An active program to gain new registrations for safer and more effective pesticides has also been established in the province.

Table 21.2 describes the major nursery insect pests and their damage, and outlines recommended control procedures. The insects are grouped by feeding habits: chewing, sucking, girdling, and root feeding.

Further information on all insect pests mentioned can be found in the references provided here, notably Sutherland et al. (1989).

Specific control recommendations, including pesticide application rates and timings, can be found in the *Nursery Production Guide for Commercial Growers* published annually by the B.C. Ministry of Agriculture and Fisheries.

PLANTATION INSECTS

The job of regenerating British Columbia's forests is not complete once seedlings are planted. Infancy for forest trees is a perilous time, when the young trees may fall prey to injury, growth reduction, or death caused by environmental stresses, diseases, and insects. To ensure that a site becomes reforested, foresters must monitor and protect forest regeneration from these damaging agents. This section describes insects that feed primarily on young conifers, and other insects that attack forest plantations secondarily when their normal food supply is depleted. Three groups of insect management approaches, both direct and indirect, are also discussed. (The discussion is restricted to those insects affecting conifer trees from newly planted

TABLE 21.2.   Common insect pests of conifer nurseries

Insect name, and references	Species affected	Potential for damage	Signs and symptoms	Management
Chewing insects				
Cutworms, especially **variegated cutworm** *Peridroma saucia* Palmer and Nichols (1981)	All species of conifers in both bareroot and container culture	Greatest losses occur in 1+0 stock; several seedlings can be destroyed by a single larva each night. Larvae shelter in 2+0 stock in open compounds, causing minimal damage, but may then also accompany stock to planting sites. There are probably populations at all nurseries in every growing season, but the severity of the infestation varies greatly.	During growing season, larvae grow up to 4 cm long; large, soft, fat caterpillars, hairless bodies, and shiny heads. Feed on foliage. Symptoms that may indicate presence of cutworms: stems without needles, depressed area on stems that look like fungal lesions, stems cut off below the soil so it appears that the seedling did not germinate, stems cut off at ground level. Adult cutworm moths are thick-bodied, dull-colored, mostly nocturnal, and about 18 mm long. They fold their wings in a tent fashion when at rest.	Permethrin is effective when applied under warm, moist conditions in the evening when activity is highest. Adult moth population can be reduced by the use of light traps, closed doors, and screens placed over fans in greenhouses. Keeping nursery site weed-free reduces cutworm populations because many moths are attracted to certain weeds when ovipositing. Applications of bait reduce cutworms in 2+0 stock.
Needle tiers *Choristoneura rosaceana* and *Archips rosanus* Furniss and Carolin (1977)	Infestations often occur in spruce, but most sp. of seedlings have been attacked	Spotty distribution throughout the crop, usually solitary; most infestations are incidental.	Larvae web the top needles of the seedlings together early in the season when the seedlings are about 5-8 cm tall.	Can be controlled physically by the removal of caterpillars. Applications of insecticides are seldom necessary. Larvae are green with black heads.
Spruce budworm *Choristoneura occidentalis* Unger (1986)	Douglas-fir and spruce seedlings. Do not feed significantly on pine.	Larvae are voracious feeders and cause severe damage to small seedlings. Adult moths may oviposit on nursery seedlings. Resulting larvae can accompany stock from the nursery to reforestation sites.	In spring, nursery stock can become infested by larvae that have overwintered in small, silken cocoons in mature trees in and around the nursery site. The larvae spin long silken threads which get caught in the wind and carry the larvae into nursery stock. Full-grown larvae are 30 mm long, with brownish heads and bodies and prominent ivory-colored spots.	Applications of sevin are often necessary to protect seedlings from larvae in the spring. Pheromone traps are used to monitor adult moths. If warranted, diazinon sprays will discourage oviposition on the seedlings.
European pine shoot moth *Rhyacionia buoliana* Harris and Ross (1975)	Most two- and three-needle pines are affected. Mugho and Scots pine preferred over ponderosa or lodgepole pine. Container and bareroot 2+0 stock are infested, but not 1+0 bareroot stock.	Has predominantly been a pest of newly established plantings, parks, gardens, and commercial nurseries. Very few infestations in nursery production stock.	Adult moths have a wingspan of about 2 cm; the orange forewings are marked with irregular silvery lines and gray hindwings. Adult moths lay their eggs near buds, and the dark brown larvae feed on the needles and later bore into buds and shoots where they overwinter. Shoots are either killed or distorted.	Three applications of diazinon directed at adult moths, eggs, and the young larvae before they burrow into the buds is successful. Also, moth populations can be monitored by pheromone traps which indicate when and if sprays should be applied.

TABLE 21.2.   (Continued)

Insect name, and references	Species affected	Potential for damage	Signs and symptoms	Management
Rusty tussock moth *Orgyia antiqua* Erickson (1978)	All species of seedlings can be attacked. Infestations occur mostly in container stock but some bareroot seedlings have also been affected.	Larvae have been collected from several nurseries in the province, but have only been a chronic problem at one nursery in the Lower Mainland.	Adult male moth is rusty brown, with a white dot and light brown band on each forewing. The female is flightless and sedentary, with a body covered in light tan hairs. The female moths cement their white egg masses to the sides and bottoms of styroblocks, and these eggs survive block-washing. Around May of the next year, larvae emerge in groups, denuding seedlings. The caterpillars are hairy, up to 28 mm long. They have two black hair pencils projecting forward and one to the rear, four golden brushes of hair on the back, and eight warty protuberances on each segment, with yellow and black hairs.	Because of their bright color, the larvae are easily noticed and can be squashed. When infestations become too large to be manually controlled, orthene sprays can be applied.
Spruce spider mite *Oligonychus ununguis* Doidge and Marshall (1971)	Douglas-fir, true firs, hemlock, larch, spruce, and pine	Sporadic pests at some nurseries, particularly in the interior of B.C., but infestations are usually not severe. Low host vigor, host crowding, and the absence of natural enemies will enhance outbreaks; damage usually occurs near the end of the growing season when seedlings are being stressed for water and nutrients to induce bud set.	The mites feed on needles, causing them to become dry, mottled, and bleached. First there is a chlorotic stippling of the foliage; later a fine silk webbing develops which eventually covers the foliage. Severely affected foliage turns dingy yellow to dull rusty brown and the needles drop off.	A proper miticide must be used; applications must often be repeated because the eggs are resistant to pesticides, and several different life stages are usually present simultaneously.
Grasshoppers Banham and Arrand (1970)	All seedlings of all ages	Have occasionally become pests at nurseries located in the interior of the province. Can invade the nursery at any time during the growing season.	Nymphs emerge in May or June from overwintering eggs, and reach the adult stage in July or August. When the seedlings are young, grasshoppers will bite the stems off at the soil line. On older seedlings, foliage can be partially or wholly stripped, and the bark is often chewed.	Treating infested areas in and around the nursery site with an approved pesticide will reduce the population. Insecticides are most effective against young nymphs.
Sucking insects				
Giant conifer aphids *Cinara* spp. Furniss and Carolin (1977)	All species of seedlings can be hosts for at least one species of *Cinara*	Usually do not cause damage until they have reached high numbers, but population build-up is fast and erratic. They are	Aphids are 3–5 mm long, dark-colored and long-legged. They feed gregariously, usually on the stem of the seedlings. Heavy infestations severely	Wasps feed on the honeydew the aphids produce, as well as on the aphids themselves, and can be used to control small populations. Larger

TABLE 21.2.   (Continued)

Insect name, and references	Species affected	Potential for damage	Signs and symptoms	Management
Giant conifer aphids (Cont'd)		a particular problem on stock grafted for seed orchards.	reduce growth and vigor of seedlings and may cause foliage chlorosis. Often *Cinara* infestations are detected by the presence of wasps or ants. Eggs, the overwintering stage in the aphid life cycle, are about 1 mm long, black, and oval, usually one per needle.	infestations may require an insecticide. At the end of the growing season, aphids may lay overwintering eggs on the seedlings. Once present, eggs are hard to control and stock will leave the nursery infested with aphids.
Cooley spruce gall aphid *Adelges cooleyi* 1st life stage Woolly stage Wood (1977)	Douglas-fir, white, Engelmann, or Sitka spruce seedlings	The woolly stage can be a serious pest on nursery stock, being present all year round. The white, woolly covering makes them harder to control.	Aphids appear as little white balls of fluff approx. 1 mm long on the lower surface of needles and shoots. (Figure 21.11) Feeding on the needles causes them to be mottled or twisted and severe infestations can cause stunting or needle drop.	Small infestations can be successfully treated with Safer's soap; large infestations can be treated with diazinon. Mature spruce trees host the alternate stage of the life cycle and should be removed from the nursery site.
2nd life stage Gall stage	Spruce transplant or grafting stock that is at least 3 years old	Seedlings are seldom killed, but heavy infestations can reduce growth and vigor and cause deformation in small trees.	Cone-shaped galls form on spruce.	Galls may be clipped off and destroyed. Removing Douglas-fir, the alternate host, will help to reduce populations.
Green spruce aphid *Elatobium abietinum* Koot (1983)	Most spruce species, particularly Sitka spruce, may occur on pine and Douglas-fir.	Initial feeding results in mottled needles, followed by chlorosis and needle drop. Severe infestations can lead to complete defoliation and seedling death.	Aphids are 1 mm long, and dark green with long cornicles. They are usually found on lower shaded needles rather than on the leader or growing tip.	Populations overwinter as adults on foliage and, under mild conditions, will continue to reproduce and feed. Nursery personnel must be aware of populations throughout the year. Control is often necessary.
Woolly aphid *Mindarus obliquus*	Spruce	Has been a problem at several nurseries across the province. Capable of killing the terminal of the seedling and causing deformation.	Aphids appear as a white woolly mass at the tip of the seedling.	Widespread infestations may require treatment with an insecticide.
Balsam woolly aphid (adelgid) *Adelges piceae* Harris (1978)	Several species of true fir	Feeding on stems, branches, and twigs causes calluses and gall-like formations. Gouting progressively weakens and may kill trees. Infestations have spread throughout the Lower Mainland and half way up Vancouver Island.	Aphids are often difficult to detect until symptoms of injury appear. In summer they can be found by their tufts of white wool. In winter no wool is present and a microscope or hand lens may be necessary to see those aphids less than 2 mm long.	Although this pest has never been found on *Abies* spp. in conifer seedling nurseries, infestations would pose a threat to forested areas if contaminated stock were to be established in reforested sites. Therefore, nurseries inside the quarantine zone may not grow *Abies* spp.

TABLE 21.2.   (Continued)

Insect name, and references	Species affected	Potential for damage	Signs and symptoms	Management
Tarnished plant bug *Lygus lineolaris* Schowalter et al. (1986)	Preference for 1+0 stock. Most damage has occurred on pine and spruce; Douglas-fir, cedar, and larch have also been attacked. Up to 50% of some stock types can be attacked.	Lygus bug damage has been found at almost every nursery. Lygus populations invade the nurseries throughout the growing season from mid-May to late September.	Adults are mottled yellowish or reddish brown, 7 x 3.5 cm, with flat, oval bodies (Figure 21.10). The five nymphal instars are greenish and resemble aphids. Feeding on the apical meristem causes an initial distinctive terminal distortion. Needles are thicker, shorter, and twisted; adult foliage may develop in pine. An elongate scar may appear on the stem; later a multiple leader develops.	One application of Cymbush during the first week of June, July, and August has reduced damage significantly.
Girdling insects **Cranberry girdler** *Chrysoteuchia topiaria* Kamm et al. (1983)	Most damage has occurred on bareroot 2+0 Douglas-fir and true firs; 2+0 spruce and Douglas-fir container stock have been attacked	In severe infestations, losses can exceed 25% of the seedlings in a bed; damage generally occurs in scattered patches where almost all seedlings are injured.	Larvae are up to 1.5 cm long and dirty white, with tan head capsules. They feed on stock from late August to mid-November. Larvae eat the bark and chew into the wood. (Figure 21.8) The area, approx. 2.5 cm above and below the soil line is attacked; major damage to the root collar will cause the seedling to turn chlorotic. Adults are 1-2 cm long moths with a protruding snout. They have pale forewings with touches of brown, silver, and black. Hindwings are gray.	Pheromone traps are used to monitor moth populations and diazinon spray is applied to protect the crop, acting as an insecticide and repellent. Reducing the amount of grass also works by limiting the alternate host for populations.
Adult weevils *Otiorhynchus rugosostriatus, Otiorhynchus ovatus, Otiorhynchus sulcatus* Suspect *Trachyphloeus bifoveolatus,* Suspect *Strophosoma melanogrammus* Gerber et al. (1974)	Container seedlings 8-15 cm in height. Spruce preferred but cedar, larch, fir, and pine attacked.	Seedlings at the edges of greenhouses and on the outsides of styroblocks are most frequently attacked. Usually one seedling is girdled at one time.	Damage consists of a uniform 1-cm wide ring below the point at which foliage begins in the fleshiest part of the stem. (Figure 21.7) Damage usually occurs in June and July.	Applications of Belmark as a foliar spray during the second week of May followed by a second application 3 weeks later.
European marsh crane fly (leather jackets) *Tipula paludosa* Wilkinson and Gerber (1983)	Any stock present in the nursery in early spring may be attacked	Limited to coastal areas. Chronic pests at several coastal nurseries for the past 10 years. Common and damaging pests of lawn and turf.	Adults resemble large mosquitoes, 2.5 cm long, and have 2 cm wings and long spindly legs. Legless larvae are a grayish color, with tough leather-like skin. They are 4 cm long in older instars. Damage occurs in the spring and consists of a uniform ring 3 cm wide at soil line; only the bark is consumed. Spotty distribution of damage with one to seven seedlings attacked by one larva.	Best control is achieved by drenching for larvae with insecticides in October.

TABLE 21.2.   (Continued)

Insect name, and references	Species affected	Potential for damage	Signs and symptoms	Management
Springtails *Bourletiella hortensis* Marshall and Ilnytzky (1976)	Conifer seedlings in bareroot	Most feed on decaying material but if in large numbers will feed on conifer seedlings.	Small, less than 6 mm long, often gray-colored insects, with an appendage-like structure on the abdomen that allows them to jump. Attack hypocotyle area between the needles and the roots, after seedling emergence for about 3 weeks, producing small lesions which may result in deformation or mortality of seedlings.	Once the seedling stems become woody, springtails are no longer a problem. Routine pre-emergence applications of the herbicide A W K reduce numbers. If large populations persist, Diazinon may be applied.
Root feeding insects **Black vine weevil** *Otiorhynchus sulcatus* Nielsen et al. (1978)	Conifer seedlings in container culture, Douglas-fir and hemlock	Larvae can cause considerable damage to container stock, especially at coastal nurseries enhanced by 2+0 container rotation. Also a serious problem in grafting houses.	Adults are 9 mm long and brownish black, with patches of yellow hair on abdomen. Larvae are white, C-shaped, and legless, with brown-headed capsules. They consume roots and girdle the stem below the ground line throughout the fall and winter. (Figure 21.9) Adults girdle seedlings from late May to July.	Can be physically excluded by placing stickem on table legs or placing each table leg in a bucket of soapy water. Applications of Belmark for recurring infestations are recommended, applied after adult emergence but before egg-laying begins.
Strawberry root weevil *O. ovatus* Shrimpton (1985)	Predominantly 2+0 bareroot stock	Damages conifer seedlings in the Pacific Northwest, but has only been a serious problem in one Lower Mainland nursery. Damage usually occurs in patches because weevils are somewhat gregarious.	Adults are dark brown to black, 6 mm long, and egg-shaped. Larvae are white, C-shaped, and legless, with brown-headed capsules, smaller than those of black vine weevil larvae. Larvae eat roots of seedlings, stripping most laterals. In heavy concentrations, may girdle root collar. Seedlings may become chlorotic in the fall, indicating root damage.	Populations are monitored using board traps to determine the length of the adult emergence period, the distribution of weevils throughout the nursery, and the effectiveness of control programs. Surface application of Orthene or Belmark is recommended. First spray applied 2 weeks after the adult population starts to emerge in the spring; later applications may be necessary.
Fungus gnats family *Sciariadae* Lindquist (1983)	Container seedlings, all species	Larvae normally feed on soil fungi and organic matter but will be attracted to seedlings if they have been predisposed by stress. Infestations often accompany infections of root pathogens.	Adults are small, 2.5 mm, dark-colored, mosquito-like flies, with clear wings, long legs, segmented antennae. Larvae are legless, semi-transparent, milky-white worms with black heads. They range up to 0.5 cm in length. Larvae consume root hairs and small rootlets, but in heavy concentrations will strip main roots and sometimes girdle the stem just below and at soil line. Symptoms include wilting and loss of vigor.	General greenhouse sanitation: removing moss and algae, and ensuring good drainage to remove puddles of water. After stock has been lifted, styroblocks should be washed and greenhouses cleaned. If larvae become established and damage is evident, drenching with diazinon may be necessary. Populations of adult flies can be monitored with the use of yellow-colored sticky traps.

TABLE 21.2. (Concluded)

Insect name, and references	Species affected	Potential for damage	Signs and symptoms	Management
June beetle *Polyphylla crinita* Sutton and Stone (1974)	All ages and species of bareroot seedlings	Have occasionally become pests in bareroot panels. Most damage has occurred in nurseries recently established in areas that were once grassy fields.	Larvae have thick-curved, milky white bodies with a dark head, three pairs of prominent legs, and can be up to 8 cm long. Larvae remove most of the seedling root system, frequently cutting the main stem off slightly below soil surface. Most feeding occurs in late spring to summer.	Frequent discing and shallow ploughing of fallow panels in early summer will help to reduce populations. Infestations in established seedling beds can be spot-drenched with sevin.
Conifer root aphid *Pachypappa tremulae* Shrimpton (1985)	Container spruce, spruce potted for grafting stock; also pine, larch, and Douglas-fir	Has infested stock at several nurseries, particularly in the Prince George area. Those that have been infested report no damage. Damage will be minimal if seedlings are growing in ideal conditions with ample nutrients.	Aphids are detected by secretions of white, waxy filaments, and infestations are usually on the surface of the plug between the roots and the container wall. An alternative life cycle occurs on the leaves of *Populus tremuloides*, where aphids form leaf nest structures.	No control measures recommended to date.

G. Shrimpton, B.C. Ministry of Forests

FIGURE 21.10.   *Lygus lineolaris* (tarnished plant bug).

G. Shrimpton, B.C. Ministry of Forests

FIGURE 21.11.   *Adelges cooleyi* (Cooley spruce gall aphid) covered in "wool."

or naturally regenerated seedlings, to trees of approximately 20 years of age.)

Forest seedlings represent a considerable economic investment by the time they are outplanted. Losses caused by insects can therefore be very costly. Insect-caused mortality of planted seedlings carries the direct cost of replanting, in addition to many indirect costs such as loss of fiber production. Non-fatal injury from insect activity has indirect negative effects because trees deformed by insect attack are often of lower quality and value. Injuries can also cause growth reduction and may predispose trees to physiological stresses and attacks by secondary insects or pathogens, or to overtopping by competing vegetation.

Foresters can minimize the effects of plantation insects. Pest control in a plantation offers several options not available for a mature stand. Before planting, tree species can be altered or mixed, stock size and type can be selected, and the site can be prepared specifically with plantation insects in mind. These activities are relatively inexpensive and less controversial than the mechanical, chemical, or biological methods that are often the only means of controlling insects attacking more mature forests. However, before foresters can control losses from plantation insects, they must be aware of potential problems. They must, therefore, develop the ability to identify major plantation insects, and to acquire information that will allow them to consider these insects when making forest management prescriptions during reforestation and stand tending.

The insect descriptions presented here concentrate on the most damaging stage of the insects' life cycle and the resulting symptoms that will assist in field identification. Insect activity is usually slow in the winter. In the spring, insects become active; later in the growing season the symptoms of their feeding become visible. Insects included in this section are presented in three groups: defoliators, inner bark feeders, and sucking insects. A brief introduction to each group follows. A table of relevant information on specific insects follows the introduction.

Defoliators

Insects that consume tree foliage are called "defoliators." Outbreaks of these insects often appear to develop suddenly, but usually populations are cyclic and build over several years before becoming epidemics. The effects of defoliation on forest plantations vary from no noticeable detriment, to growth reduction, topkill, and direct mortality. Most of the major defoliators, such as budworms and sawflies, attack any age stand. Plantations can be defoliated by these insects, but they are not singled out. Some species of defoliators, such as the blackarmy cutworm (*Actebia fennica*) (Figure 21.12) however, primarily attack conifers that are of seedling to juvenile age.

Defoliation disrupts a tree's normal growth process by reducing available photosynthetic leaf area, and thus interfering with normal transpiration and translocation of water, nutrients, and food. Vulnerability to damage from defoliation varies among tree species, and among individuals of a host species. Deciduous trees, including larch, are relatively tolerant of defoliation. Most evergreen conifers are less tolerant, although several complete defoliations are usually required to cause death. Some species, such as western hemlock, are very intolerant of defoliation and can be killed from one complete defoliation. Fortunately, many insects prefer to feed on either current or old foliage and will only completely defoliate trees during heavy infestations.

The timing of defoliation also influences the degree of damage that will result from an attack. The loss of foliage is more damaging to the tree early in the growing season, because at this point a tree's food reserves are low. As well, tree age has a bearing on defoliation damage. Young and suppressed trees have less-developed root systems compared to those in more mature trees, and are, therefore, more vulnerable to such damage.

Individual hosts of the same species also respond differently to defoliation. This variation in damage from the same level of defoliation results from a combination of genotype and environmental conditions, such as growing site and weather. For example, a drought-stressed tree is less likely to recover from severe defoliation than a similarly defoliated, unstressed tree. Some individuals, however, are better equipped genetically to tolerate drought and defoliation. Therefore, variation in host response will be seen even though the level of defoliation appears to be uniform.

Sucking Insects

A large group of insects has adapted to feeding on the sap of living trees. They accomplish this by inserting tube-like mouth parts through outer bark tissues or leaf epidermis into the tree's sap stream. Damage to the host tree results from disruption of the conductive tissue at the feeding site, which interferes with translocation. These insects also deprive the hosts of food by removing it directly from the sap stream. Sucking insects are typically very small and their feeding does not always produce conspicuous symptoms. Populations of sucking insects must, therefore, be very high before a host is damaged significantly. Young and suppressed trees are more vulnerable to damage.

Sucking insects are abundant in conifer plantations. In general, they are less destructive than other insects, but they do have the potential to inflict appreciable damage. One species of sucking insect, the balsam woolly adelgid (*Adelges piceae*), can cause extensive mortality in *Abies* species, but it usually attacks mature trees.

Inner Bark Feeders

The inner bark (phloem and cambium tissues) of trees is a very nutritious food source. Consequently, many insects feed in this area during some portion of their life cycle. Damage to these tissues disrupts the translocation of the basic life-supporting compounds, sugars, nutrients, and water. Young trees, from seedling to juvenile age, are particularly susceptible to attack by inner bark feeders because they have less-developed root systems and storage capacities, and their protective bark layers are not fully developed. Since the entire tree is covered by inner bark, attacks by these insects can occur anywhere from the terminal shoot to the root system, depending on the species of the attacking insect.

Damage from attacks by inner bark feeding insects ranges from insignificant lesions to direct mortality. A complete stem girdle of the inner bark within the crown will result in mortality above the girdle. If a complete stem

FIGURE 21.12. *Actebia fennica* (black army cutworm) on spruce seedling.

E. Chatell, Forestry Canada

FIGURE 21.13. *Hylobius warrenii* (Warren's root collar weevil) larvae.

FIDS, Forestry Canada

FIGURE 21.14. *Pissodes strobi* (white pine weevil) damage to spruce. Note that 2 years of terminal growth are affected.

FIDS, Forestry Canada

girdle occurs anywhere between the bottom of the crown and the root collar, tree mortality usually results. Complete girdling of a root by larvae such as those of the Warren's root collar weevil (*Hylobius warrenii*) (Figure 21.13) will kill the root beyond the injury. Terminal weevils girdle the inner bark of terminal shoots, which causes shoot mortality and possible crown deformation (Figuers 21.14 and 21.15).

Partial girdles are less damaging but can be significant. They often cause crooks, which may weaken the stem and cause breakage during adverse weather. As well, they can provide an entry point for pathogenic fungi. Stem deformations may lower timber quality. Partial girdles may also disrupt translocation sufficiently to retard growth and cause physiological stress. This can reduce tree growth and increase susceptibility to secondary pathogens and insects.

A diverse group of insects feeds on the inner bark of plantation trees. Table 21.3 describes the most damaging insects occurring on the terminal shoot, stem, and roots of plantation-aged conifers.

FIGURE 21.15. *Pissodes strobi* (white pine weevil) larvae in dead spruce leader.

J. Harris, Forestry Canada

FIGURE 21.16. *Cinara* spp. (giant conifer aphids) on seedlings.

J. Sutherland, Forestry Canada

TABLE 21.3. Common insect pests of forest plantations

Insect name, distribution, and references	Species affected	Potential for damage	Signs and symptoms	Management
Defoliators				
Black army cutworm *Actebia fennica* May occur province-wide but in damaging levels in central and south-eastern Interior Ross and Ilnytzky (1977) Maher (1989)	Conifer seedlings, esp. white spruce and lodgepole pine. Herbaceous vegetation is preferred.	High seedling mortality if conditions are favorable, but damage seldom occurs for more than one season.	Larvae 0.5 - 4.0 mm long. Upper surface is velvety black, with two pairs of fine white double lines along the length of each side. (Figure 21.12) Defoliation of needles and some buds of seedlings occurs.	Outbreaks last 1 year. Adult moths are attracted to areas burned up to 1 year previous. Larvae feed on seedlings the following year. Planting should be delayed until the larvae complete their feeding in mid-June.
Pine needle sheath miner *Zelleria haimbachi* Throughout southern British Columbia Stevens (1971)	Juvenile lodgepole pine, ponderosa pine, and occasionally white pine	Tree mortality has not been associated with this insect, but growth reduction from defoliation has been documented. All new growth may be destroyed over hundreds of hectares.	Larvae 1.5 mm-1.4 cm long, tan-colored with two dull orange stripes running the length of the body. Color changes to a greenish hue before pupation. Current year's foliage appears faded. Growth of needles terminates early. Needles may droop back or hook towards the needle base. A small hole may be noted in the sheath surrounding an attacked fascicle.	Control measures have not been developed. Juvenile spacing of defoliated stands does not increase defoliation of remaining trees.
Sucking insects				
Giant conifer aphid *Cinara* spp. Throughout British Columbia Johnson (1965)	All native conifers except cedar	Can cause growth reduction in young conifers. May predispose a tree to secondary insects, pathogenic fungi, or drought stress.	Adults are 2-5 mm in length, dark colored. The body is pear-shaped and may have a dusting of powdery material. They have long, slender legs and may have wings. (Figure 21.16) The aphids feed in stationary groups on branches, roots, or main stem. Ants are often associated with feeding groups.	Control measures are seldom necessary and have not been developed.
Cooley spruce gall aphid *Adelges cooleyi* Throughout the province where Douglas-fir is established Wood (1977)	Douglas-fir, and Sitka, Engelmann, and white spruce	ON Douglas-fir: Light infestations are common, though not seriously damaging. Significant damage occurs sporadically when young trees are severely attacked. ON Spruce: Repeated attacks can produce stunted, deformed trees, but normally it is not a concern on spruce plantations.	This insect has a complex life cycle involving two hosts, spruce and Douglas-fir. Insect identification and damage are addressed separately for the two hosts. ON Douglas-fir: Adults are about 1 mm long, oval and light to dark brown in color. At maturity they are covered with white, waxy wool and appear as stationary wool tufts on the underside of needles from spring to fall. Needles of infested trees are twisted and mottled with chlorotic spots; severely	The cause of severe attacks on young Douglas-fir is not known; however, it has been suggested that nitrogen-fertilized sites are attacked more frequently than unfertilized sites. *Adelges cooleyi* can be reduced if the planting of Douglas-fir and spruce in close proximity is avoided.

TABLE 21.3. (Continued)

Insect name, distribution, and references	Species affected	Potential for damage	Signs and symptoms	Management
Cooley spruce gall aphid (Cont'd)			infested foliage may be completely chlorotic and drop prematurely. ON Spruce: Adult similar to those found on Douglas-fir. Infested spruce displays cone-like or "pineapple" galls at the ends of branches. Galls are 1-8 cm long with needles extending perpendicular to the gall. New galls are green, pink, or purple and flexible, but as they age they become brown, hard, and brittle. Old galls can persist for several years.	
Inner bark feeders of terminal shoots **Terminal weevils** *P. strobi:* Throughout the ranges of spruce, south of 56° N latitude, except Queen Charlotte Islands Duncan (1986)	Sitka, white, and Engelmann spruce and occasionally lodgepole pine. Usually trees from 1.5 to 10 m in height are attacked.	These weevils prefer vigorous, open-grown trees and have been reported to attack greater than 50% of a stand in 1 year. In addition to growth loss, attacks reduce timber quality by inducing forked and crooked stems. *Pissodes strobi* causes terminal dieback of 2 years' growth. (Figure 21.14)	Larva is yellow-white with a light brown head and reaches 6 mm in length. (Figure 21.15) The first sign of attack occurs in spring, when small punctures appear near tips of previous year's leaders. Resin droplets are associated with these wounds. By midsummer, the current year's leader will be distorted and wilted and its color changed from yellow to red to brown. In late summer to fall, large holes made by emerging adults will be noted midway down the previous year's leader. Signs of previous attacks may remain for several years and include deformed or multiple leaders, dead stubs along the main stem, and crooked or forked main stems.	Numbers of this insect can be reduced through a comprehensive clipping of infested leaders after they show symptoms of attack and before the adult weevils have emerged from the leader. In high hazard areas, the creation of extensive stands of host trees should be avoided and alternate species should be considered where possible.
P. terminalis Throughout the range of lodgepole pine Duncan (1986) Wood and McMullen (1983)	Lodgepole pine, of same height	*P. terminalis* attack results in the loss of 1 year's terminal growth.	The basic description is the same ; however, the small punctures appear in late spring to early summer and are located near the base of the current year's leader.	Similar to *P. strobi*
Inner bark feeders of stems **Pith moths** *Petrova* spp. Throughout British Columbia following range of host species	Lodgepole pine, usually 0.3-3.0 m in height and occasionally larger trees	Feeding larva can kill the tips of branches or terminal shoots by girdling the inner bark. Occasionally, nodules on the main stem become large enough to girdle	The larva are about 1.5 cm long. The color of the body varies from yellow to orange-brown, and the head is reddish-brown. Characteristic pitch nodules occur near terminal buds,	Where pine is regenerated, damage may be reduced if entire cutovers are planted the same year rather than in blocks over several years. The stocking of pine

TABLE 21.3. (Concluded)

Insect name, distribution, and references	Species affected	Potential for damage	Signs and symptoms	Management
Pith moths (Cont'd) * Note: *Synanthedon sequoiae* and *Dioryctria abietivorella* are similar in appearance and cause damage similar to *Petrova* spp. Duncan (1982)		and thus kill the tree. Damaged areas are weakened and, therefore, subject to wind and snow breakage. Larval feeding reduces timber quality by inducing crooked leaders.	at the crotch of branch junctions, or at the crotch of the main stem and branches. These nodules are lined with silk, pitch, and frass, and conceal a single feeding larva. The nodules produced at branch or stem crotches are usually 4 cm or more in diameter; those occurring at terminal buds are usually less than 1 cm in diameter.	plantations should be kept high because the insects prefer open-grown trees. It is possible to control the insect by crushing the pitch nodules, thus killing the developing larvae. This treatment should be done in May for 2 consecutive years.
Plantation weevil *Steremnius carinatus* The coast and interior wet belt of British Columbia Condrashoff (1968)	Seedlings of Douglas-fir and Sitka spruce are preferred. Hemlock, true firs, and redcedar seedlings are also attacked.	Partially girdled seedlings may recover, but a complete girdle will result in mortality. Damage is most extensive in first-year plantations and, since older stock is less likely to be girdled, damage is negligible after seedlings have survived one growing season.	Damage is caused by adult weevils which are 0.75 -1.0 cm long. Young adults are brick red, becoming brown to yellowish as they age. Sections of bark are stripped from attacked seedlings; some may be completely girdled at the stem. The injuries usually occur near the root collar, but can extend several centimeters up the stem. Attacked seedlings can appear normal after recent attack and change to yellow or red, later in the season. Not all seedlings are attacked; therefore, symptoms will appear randomly throughout an infested site.	Several methods can be used to control *Steremnius carinatus*: 1) Plant cutovers immediately after logging and site preparation. This will allow one growing season before weevil populations build up in slash. 2) Plant larger stock where weevil populations build up in slash. 3) Plant in late spring to allow one growing season before weevil attack. 4) Plant to a higher stocking to allow for losses from weevil attacks.
Inner bark feeders of roots **Warren's root collar weevil** *Hylobius warreni* Throughout British Columbia, following the range of its hosts. Optimal conditions for this weevil occur on moist sites with coarse-textured soils and a heavy duff layer. Cerezke (1970)	Lodgepole pine, Engelmann spruce, and white spruce; also reported on true firs and larch. Usually only trees over 1.5 m are attacked.	The feeding larva tunnels into the phloem, cambium, and slightly into the wood. Young trees may be completely girdled at the root collar; complete girdling on older trees is usually confined to main and secondary roots. Mortality occurs only in young trees. In addition to direct mortality, trees suffer growth loss and increased susceptibility to root rotting and blue stain fungi.	The larvae are approximately 2 cm long and creamy white, with a brown head capsule (Figure 21.13). The adult insect is a typical weevil with a prominent curved snout. It is 1.0 -1.5 cm long and 0.6-0.7 cm wide, with dull black-flecked coloring and gray-white scales. Infested plantations display random mortality of single or small groups of trees. Damaged trees exhibit straw-colored to deep red foliage and stunted terminal growth. Damaged trees are often easily pushed over or have an obvious lean. Positive identification requires checking around the root collar and noting either the insect or evidence of tunnelling in the cambium and phloem of the roots.	Extremely heavily infested plantations should be cut, leaving no residuals. Scarification or prescribed burning should follow in an effort to reduce the duff layer. Manually scraping the duff layer from the bases of trees reduces attacks, as does pruning the lower branches. Planting alternative species is another option. Resistant species are Douglas-fir, hemlock, cedar, and true firs.

22 CONTROL OF MAMMAL DAMAGE

T.P. Sullivan, A.S. Harestad, and B.M. Wikeem

Herbivorous mammals are a major cause of damage in British Columbia forests. Birds such as grouse contribute to the overall damage, but are less of a problem.

All stages of forest regeneration, from direct seeding and planting to free-growing plantations, are vulnerable to feeding attacks by one or more mammalian species. Such attacks cause reforestation failures, result in the death of some trees, and inhibit the growth of other trees. As well, sublethal injuries can increase the susceptibility of trees to diseases and to overtopping by competing vegetation.

Rodents were first recognized as pests in British Columbia because of their consumption of coniferous seed sown on cutover areas. However, since the demise of direct seeding and the advent of intensive regeneration and silvicultural practices in the province, many more species have created pest problems.

In general, most outbreaks of mammal damage can be related to the population fluctuations in various species. These cycles in the numbers of animals can occur annually or over several years, with the result that some species may cause a damage problem every year (e.g., deer mouse), while others (e.g., snowshoe hare) may be a problem only every 9-10 years. In other situations, it is the favorable habitats — such as those arising from certain combinations of logging, site preparation, and planting practices, or from poor management — that can encourage the increase of a population and subsequently hamper regeneration. Most damage by wild mammals occurs during feeding activity; most damage by domestic livestock is the result of trampling.

This chapter discusses the three main types of mammal damage affecting British Columbia's regenerating forests: seed predation; browsing of plantation seedlings; and barking and girdling of saplings. Under each category is a description of the damage (adapted, in part, from Lawrence et al. 1961 and Harestad et al. 1986); a summary of the population and habitat conditions under which the damage occurs; and a list of management recommendations for reducing damage.

CONIFER SEED

Seed Predation by Rodents

For almost half a century, foresters in North America have used direct seeding as a method of regenerating cutover forestlands. Destruction of the seed by small mammals has had adverse effects on the success of these reforestation projects (Black 1969; Radwan 1970; Radvanyi 1973). The deer mouse (*Peromyscus maniculatus*) is the most important seed predator in British Columbia. Chipmunks (*Eutamias townsendii* on the coast and *E. amoenus* in the Interior) and voles (*Microtus* and *Clethrionomys spp.* in the Interior) have also contributed to the problem. The deer mice and chipmunks have annual cycles of abundance and can be a problem every year. The meadow vole (*M. pennsylvanicus*) and long-tailed vole (*M. longicaudus*) have 3- to 4-year population cycles, with increased seed predation occurring during peak periods.

The inconsistency of direct seeding to establish uniform stands of seedlings may be directly related to seed predation by rodents. Seeding Douglas-fir (*Pseudotsuga menziesii*) on cutover areas in coastal British Columbia was tried up to the late 1960's with little success. Before a planting regime was implemented, several control techniques — primarily poison baits and seed repellents — were tried to eliminate the rodent problem. However, these control programs generally failed. Poison baiting did not completely eliminate the resident rodent population and could not prevent the rapid reinvasion of animals from surrounding regions (Sullivan 1979a). Commercial seed repellents tended to reduce seed germination and were not durable enough to withstand adverse weather conditions.

Another control technique, however, involving the use of alternative foods, has successfully reduced rodent predation of Douglas-fir seed on the coast (Sullivan 1979b) and lodgepole pine seed (*Pinus contorta*) in the Interior (Sullivan and Sullivan 1982) under experimental conditions. Future direct-seeding projects may use some version of this technique, particularly for establishing lodgepole pine on burned areas in the Interior. The method may be adapted for both aerial and mechanized ground row-seeding applications on an operational basis.

Cone Cutting by Tree Squirrels

Two species of tree squirrels inhabit the coniferous forests of British Columbia. The Douglas squirrel or chickaree (*Tamiasciurus douglasii*) lives in the south coastal part of the province west of the Cascades. The red squirrel (*T. hudsonicus*) lives in the rest of the province except the south coast, and on Vancouver Island. Both squirrels have similar habits and are active throughout the winter.

The occurrence of scattered cut cones and an accumulation of cone scales in midden piles indicate squirrel activity. Heavy cone cutting begins with the ripening of seed in late summer. Occasionally, squirrels have been a problem in seed orchards on Vancouver Island.

On a local basis, the provision of alternative foods such as sunflower seeds can help reduce cone cutting. Shooting or trapping individuals also offers a temporary solution, but removed squirrels are usually quickly replaced by others.

PLANTATION SEEDLINGS

Browsing by Deer, Elk, and Moose

Browsing damage to conifer seedlings by black-tailed deer (*Odocoileus hemionus columbianus*) and Roosevelt elk (*Cervus elaphus roosevelti*) is the most common type of mammal damage in coastal forests of the province. Some browsing damage from Rocky Mountain elk (*C. e. canadensis*) and moose (*Alces alces*) also occurs in the Interior, but is minor and localized compared with that on the coast. Browsing of terminal and lateral shoots by these ungulates leaves a ragged, splintered break, and seedlings may be uprooted. As well, antler rubbing in the fall and scraping from incisors may strip bark from the trunk and branches of saplings. Deer feed on both dormant seedlings (winter browsing) and growing seedlings (summer browsing). The latter is generally light the first year after outplanting, when seedling growth is slow. Thereafter it becomes heavy, until seedlings are tall enough to "escape" from the deer.

Deer browsing of plantation seedlings is severe on the west coast of Vancouver Island and near deer winter ranges. In a survey in the Vancouver Region, 43 of 51 (84.1%) plantations sampled had deer damage (Howard 1982). However, perhaps the most serious example of overbrowsing and habitat alteration by deer exists on the Queen Charlotte Islands, where the introduced deer have reached high population densities because they have no natural predators. Western redcedar (*Thuja plicata*) has been seriously depleted on the Islands and sometimes eliminated as regeneration in mature forests and on cutovers. Serious silvicultural impacts of this continued overbrowsing include the probable elimination of *T. plicata* and yellow-cedar (*Chamaecyparis nootkatensis*) as commercial timber species on the Islands and the increase in damage to young Sitka spruce (*Picea sitchensis*) and western hemlock (*Tsuga heterophylla*).

In a 10-year study of deer damage to Douglas-fir seedlings in Oregon and Washington, browsing significantly reduced survival during the first 5 years after planting (Black et al. 1979). In the subsequent 5 years, frequent injury continued but there was little difference in survival between browsed and unbrowsed trees.

In terms of height growth, damaged trees sustained a 41% loss, compared with controls, in the first 5 years after planting (Black et al. 1979). This loss declined to 24% in the next 5 years, and height suppression was generally minimized after the eighth year.

Several attributes tend to make plantations susceptible to deer damage:

- small area (< 20 ha)
- broadcast burning and scarification, which improve access for deer
- Douglas-fir and cedar species
- small stock types
- particular combinations of site quality, aspect, slope, and elevation, which may influence deer use (e.g., near a south-facing, low-elevation winter range).

Management recommendations to reduce damage include:

- identifying areas with a high hazard before logging so that harvest plans can be adjusted or prepared to protect subsequent plantations.

- using mechanical barriers over the seedlings, such as Vexar tubing and milk cartons. These methods tend to be expensive and are not practical over large areas.

- using commercial repellents. Drawbacks to these preventive methods are their lack of durability and their anthropomorphic origins. Encapsulated predator odor repellents are currently being developed.

- planting less susceptible species (e.g., western hemlock), resistant genotypes if available, or jumbo stock (3-year-old bareroot).

- increasing harvest and enhancing predator pressure within particularly susceptible areas.

- using herbicides for conifer release to enhance tree growth beyond the critical size (2-m height). This may also make the habitat less attractive to deer in some situations.

Browsing/Clipping by Snowshoe Hares

Damage to coniferous plantations by snowshoe hares (*Lepus americanus*) has been reported in many areas of Canada (especially northern Alberta and central British Columbia). Hares damage seedlings by clipping the leader and lateral shoots. The extent and economic significance of this browsing damage to reforestation has been clearly shown in Washington and Oregon (Black et al. 1979), but few surveys have been done to assess the damage in British Columbia.

A characteristic feature of the snowshoe hare is its 9- to 10-year cyclic fluctuation in abundance (Figure 22.1). The historical record of these fluctuations goes back at least 200 years. This cycling occurs throughout much of Canada, but the most dramatic changes in numbers of hares occur in central and northern regions. During peak years of abundance, hares severely browse seedlings in plantations during winter months when their alternative preferred foods (various deciduous plant species) are scarce.

Feeding damage is usually most severe in areas having sufficient cover to provide suitable habitat for hares. In the U.S. Pacific Northwest, for example, plantations overgrown with deciduous brush suffer from a serious damage problem. It is not clear whether outbreaks of damage in these areas coincide with cycling populations or the availability of favorable habitat adjacent to and in the plantations. Habitat manipulation by scarification or herbicides is considered to be the best approach to reducing the suitability of habitats that lead to hare population buildups (Sullivan and Moses 1986a).

Recommended management techniques to achieve restocking of conifers in northern and central British Columbia include:

- planting mainly during the predictable 5- to 6-year period (between peaks) of relatively low hare populations.

- using larger stock for planting.

- using nursery seedlings with a reduced fertilization regime, which may make seedlings less susceptible to severe browsing.

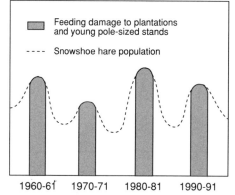

Feeding damage to plantations and young pole-sized stands

- - - - Snowshoe hare population

1960-61   1970-71   1980-81   1990-91

FIGURE 22.1. Conceptual model of the 10-year population cycle of snowshoe hares in boreal and sub-boreal forests of British Columbia.

- selecting tree species based on hare preference for seedlings: Douglas-fir > lodgepole pine > white spruce > subalpine fir.

- keeping the site clear of brush by using an appropriately timed application of a herbicide.

- using a repellent system during the 1-3 years when peak populations of hares exist.

These recommendations are designed to allow plantation seedlings (particularly pine and spruce) to gain enough growth so they can survive beyond the stage of critical hare damage during the second peak (12-15 years) after planting. Such trees should probably be at least 2 m in height. Population reduction by poison, shooting, and trapping has also received much attention, but these methods are not as effective when practiced at operational scales because of the rapid colonization of depopulated areas by hares (Figure 22.2) (Sullivan and Sullivan 1986b). Of the above recommendations, only the last two are practical alternatives for reforestation programs.

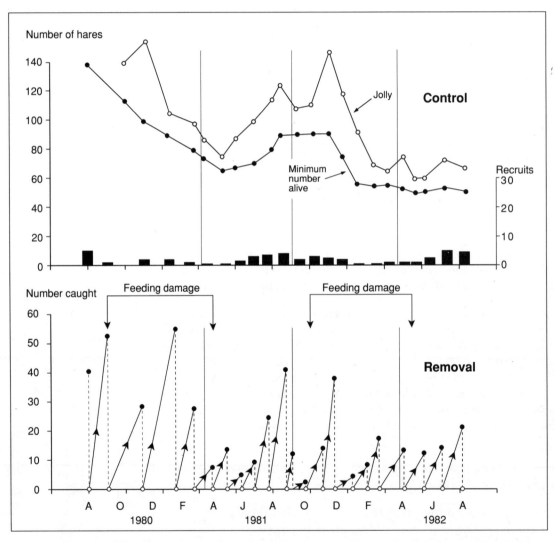

FIGURE 22.2.   Population densities of snowshoe hares (estimation techniques of minimum number alive and Jolly) on control and removal areas during the study (note difference in scale). Histograms indicate number of new hares recruited into the control population. All hares captured during each trapping period on the removal grid were permanently removed. Periods of feeding damage (removal of bark and vascular tissues) by hares to coniferous trees are represented between arrows. Vertical lines mark the limits of summer and winter periods (from Sullivan and Sullivan 1986b).

Barking and Clipping by Voles

Damage to plantations by voles (*Microtus* spp.) has been documented in the south coastal region of British Columbia for the Townsend vole (*M. townsendii*) and in the northern Interior for the meadow vole (*M. pennsyl-vanicus*). Voles clip terminal and lateral shoots of small seedlings. They usually have to make several cuts to sever the stem, and this action leaves a rougher oblique cut than that made by snowshoe hares. Basal debarking and girdling of seedlings also occur, leaving a gnawed surface of exposed sapwood. Irregular patches of gnawed bark may appear on the lower bole, low branches, root collar, and roots. Indistinct toothmarks average 1.5 mm in width and resemble light scratches or small grooves approximately 8 mm long.

Most species of *Microtus* have a 2- to 5-year cyclic fluctuation in abundance. Seedlings associated with grass habitats and with areas having a heavy shrub or post-harvest slash cover are especially vulnerable to vole attack. Such habitats are preferred by voles and result in population buildups and consequent damage to seedlings.

A high incidence of feeding damage by meadow voles and brown lemmings (*Lemmus sibiricus*) has been observed in various forest plantations in the Prince Rupert Region. Incidence of damage to lodgepole pine seedlings, in particular, may be as high as 70-80% in susceptible plantations. In general, plantations in which broadcast burning has reduced post-harvest debris and vegetation experience a lower incidence of damage than those with high levels of logging debris.

There is currently no information available on the cyclic phases or habitat preferences of meadow voles and lemmings in the Prince Rupert Region.

Management recommendations to reduce seedling damage from voles include:

- controlling grasses and associated vegetative cover by applying herbicides or using scarification to prevent population buildups.
- reducing ground cover (post-harvest debris) wherever possible.
- using synthetic predator odor (mustelids) repellents (see Sullivan et al. 1988a).
- using mechanical protection with tree guards, as described for deer.
- providing alternative foods.

As discussed for snowshoe hares, the use of toxicants to reduce vole populations is not considered to be a viable means of control because of the resiliency of voles to depopulation.

Stem and Root Clipping by Pocket Gophers

Pocket gopher (*Thomomys talpoides*) damage to young plantations (up to 10 years) has received much attention in the ponderosa pine (*P. ponderosa*) and lodgepole pine areas of the Pacific Northwest. Damage is most severe east of the Cascade Range in Washington and Oregon, as well as in some areas of Idaho. Because lodgepole pine is now the dominant commercial timber species in the southern Interior of British Columbia, the potential for major damage there by pocket gophers is also high.

These burrowing rodents damage seedlings by root pruning and by a combination of stem girdling and clipping. Seedlings are frequently clipped at or near the ground surface and the roots or stems are taken. Damage occurs year-round but is most frequent in winter. Root cutting in plantations sometimes goes unnoticed until foliage turns brown from summer drought.

Burrowing animals are very difficult to eliminate by conventional means (Barnes 1973). Pocket gophers are no exception, although some success has been achieved with poison placed in their burrows. However, such positive results are usually overshadowed by the hazard of poison to non-target animals which frequent the same habitat. Another method of avoiding gopher problems involves minimizing the disturbance of understory during harvesting. This practice helps control growth of herbaceous vegetation that enhances gopher habitat (Crouch 1982). Herbicide applications to remove undesirable vegetation have reduced gopher populations in eastern Oregon (Crouch 1979).

Other recommendations include using shelterwood harvesting to protect advanced regeneration wherever possible, and preparing plantation hazard assessments before logging (Crouch 1982). Predator odor repellents placed in a burrow system have also shown potential for excluding gophers from treated areas (Sullivan et al. 1988b).

Barking and Clipping by Pikas and Mountain Beavers

The American pika (*Ochotona princeps*) and the snowshoe hare clip terminal and lateral shoots of seedlings in similar ways.

Small seedlings may be completely consumed; larger seedlings may have their bark removed. Damage tends to occur near talus slopes, the preferred habitat for pikas. This species is present in all forest regions in British Columbia, but damage incidence is very localized and of minor significance.

The mountain beaver (*Aplodontia rufa*) cuts terminal and lateral shoots of larger seedlings, leaving short projections from the main stem. Small seedlings may completely disappear. The cutting marks are indistinguishable from those made by hares. Basal girdling of saplings and seedlings and cutting of roots may occur. These animals also pull bark in strips from trees, leaving scattered horizontal toothmarks and irregular claw marks. Mountain beavers have been reported in Manning Park and the Chilliwack River Valley. The incidence of damage is minor.

Budding and Clipping Injuries by Grouse

Bud removal and needle clipping by blue grouse (*Dendragapus obscurus*) in young plantations occur in Pacific coast forests. Budding has often been overlooked or misidentified as deer browsing. Small shoots may be clipped off in a manner similar to that of deer. Portions of needles may be removed or needles may be plucked from the stem altogether. No bark is removed. Newly planted seedlings may occasionally be uprooted as needles are pulled off. Grouse injury appears to be most severe in the spring, from March to June.

In a survey in the Vancouver Forest Region, grouse damage and bud loss was observed in 23 of 51 plantations (Howard 1982). The impact of such bud removal on small Douglas-fir seedlings can suppress height growth significantly. On the coast, the most serious recorded grouse damage occurs on Vancouver Island (Howard 1982) and in the Coast Range of Washington (Black et al. 1979). In the interior of British Columbia, grouse damage is common in young Douglas-fir plantations in the wet belt of the Cariboo Region. Plantations at Niquidet Lake (northwest of Horsefly) and Gavin Lake (west of Likely) have had up to 20% of seedlings experience some degree of bud loss .

Planting large stock seedlings and using plastic netting or screening are two suggested control techniques.

Grazing and Trampling by Livestock

Forest land accounts for nearly 8.3 million ha, or 80%, of the total area grazed by cattle in British Columbia. Until the early 1960's, there were few conflicts between range and forestry users on mid- and high-elevation forests in the southern Interior. Most of these areas were unlogged and offered limited value as range. Clearcut logging, however, improved access to new areas and provided opportunities for multiple use of forest land that were not previously available to cattle.

Browsing

Livestock browsing does not appear to be a significant factor affecting conifer growth and survival, except when browsing animals uproot seedlings. Similarly, conifer mortality resulting from cattle browsing is negligible. Pearson (1987), in a review of cattle grazing on southern U.S. pine plantations, concluded that not all injury necessarily affects survival and growth of southern pine seedlings.

Numerous studies indicate that repeated browsing of terminal shoots may reduce height growth increment (Hill 1917; Pearson 1931; Tustin et al. 1979; Sharrow and Leininger 1983b) or deform the conifer seedling (Currie et al. 1978). Nonetheless, Heerwagen (1954) found that ponderosa pine seedlings regained their normal shape and vigor within a few years of being released from repeated browsing. As well, other studies have shown that Douglas-fir (Cleary 1978), ponderosa pine (Sparhawk 1918), and longleaf pine (*P. palustris*) (Maki and Mann 1951) all produce growth rates similar to that in unbrowsed trees once they are freed from terminal damage.

Browsing on lateral shoots by cattle and sheep appears to have little effect on conifer seedlings if the terminal bud remains intact (Sharrow and Leininger 1983a). Even when the terminal shoots were removed, however, Cassady et al. (1955) reported that lateral buds almost always developed. Furthermore, Edgerton (1971) found that, in ponderosa pine, laterals would assume dominance when the terminal shoots were removed.

Trampling

Livestock trampling may directly affect conifer seedlings by removing bark, bending or breaking the stem, and exposing the root collar and roots. Indirectly, bark removal can expose the cambium which may interrupt nutrient or water flow and can provide entry for pathogens, parasites, and disease. Soil compaction may restrict water penetration and create conditions that accelerate soil erosion. Although these indirect effects are possible, there are no data to substantiate their impacts.

Conifer seedlings appear to be most susceptible to trampling damage during the first 5 years after planting and especially in the first year (Pearson 1974; Lewis 1980b; Krueger 1983) (Figure 22.3). It is also during this period, from planting to the free-growing stage, that the greatest opportunities are available for establishing a domestic forage crop for livestock.

Undoubtedly, the most significant effect of livestock trampling on forest regeneration may be to kill trees outright. Study estimates of mortality to different conifer species as a result of trampling damage range from less than 10% (Krueger 1983; McLean and Clark 1980) to more than 30% (Cassady et al. 1955; McLean and Clark 1980). Eissenstat et al. (1982), in a Douglas-fir plantation in Idaho, found that survival of trampled seedlings equalled only 36% compared to 77% survival for untrampled seedlings.

Little information is available on the proportion of the stem diameter scarred by livestock trampling or the effects of this girdling on survival and growth of conifer seedlings. In their study, Eissenstat et al. (1982) observed few scars exceeding 30% of the stem's diameter.

Factors determining livestock damage

Numerous factors undoubtedly combine to determine if, when, and to what extent livestock and forest regeneration may be incompatible. Factors that may affect the occurrence and degree of conifer damage by livestock include:

- **Livestock preferences.**   Both cattle and sheep have variable preferences for different conifer species. Sheep generally cause more browsing damage to conifers than do cattle and horses (Hill 1917; Pearson 1950). Most livestock species tend to prefer deciduous trees to conifers (Biswell and Hoover 1945; Smith et al. 1958).

- **Forage abundance and variety of forage choices.**   Conifer damage is generally low when adequate forage is available to livestock using the site (Cassady et al. 1955; Edgerton 1971). Such forage abundance appears to promote better animal distribution. Similarly, the incidence of browsing may be reduced when a variety of forage choices are available (Hall et al. 1959).

- **Livestock numbers and forage utilization.**   The correlation among seedling damage or mortality, livestock numbers, and the degree of forage use has been poorly documented. Bennett and Halls (1954) and Monfore (1983) concluded that there is no relationship between forage use and conifer seedling damage. On the other hand, Pearson (1974) showed that although slash pine and longleaf pine survival was unaffected by light and moderate grazing, it was reduced by 18-20% after 5 years of heavy grazing.

- **Tree phenology.**   Conifers are generally most palatable during the period of terminal elongation when the trees are succulent (Pearson 1950; Hall et al. 1959; Monfore 1983; Sharrow and Leininger 1983a). Browsing is generally confined to current

FIGURE 22.3.   Scarred bark on seedling from animal trampling.

annual growth. Seedlings may be more susceptible to trampling damage during the active growth phase when sap is flowing freely.

- **Animal distribution.** Poor animal distribution has often been cited as an important factor determining the extent of livestock damage on forest regeneration. Seedling losses from trampling have tended to be greatest in areas where livestock congregate and overgraze (Nordstrom 1984). Despite this widespread acknowledgment that poor animal distribution may affect forest regeneration, little has been published documenting the specific factors contributing to conifer damage by livestock on forest range.

The amount and location of water and salt blocks are perhaps the most important factors determining livestock distribution on dry sites when animals are left unherded. Even though cattle on one Oregon plantation congregated around watering points, the animals were well distributed on the site because the water points were well dispersed (Krueger 1983). Also, when livestock are thirsty, they are more likely to browse seedlings than when they are well watered (Cassidy 1937a, 1937b).

Krueger (1983) found that models to predict cattle distribution on forest range in Oregon were of limited value. Nonetheless, factors such as distance to salt, distance to water, soil depth, and canopy cover accounted for 99% of the forage use pattern by cattle. Other factors that may contribute to poor animal distribution are slope (Krueger 1983), animal learning (Krueger 1983; Monfore 1983), and the amount and distribution of logging slash (Edgerton 1971). Furthermore, silvicultural treatments such as burning, disking, scalping, brush control, or trenching may modify livestock behavior and result in higher levels of seedling damage (Cassady et al. 1955).

Benefits of livestock grazing

Unsuccessful forest regeneration resulting from livestock damage has most often been attributed to poor livestock management rather than to an inherent incompatibility between livestock and crop trees. Any forest management practice, however, may be used inappropriately, restricting forest regeneration. In the past, perhaps too much effort has been focused on quantifying damage rather than on developing strategies which use domestic livestock to accomplish forest management goals.

Several studies, over a wide range of environmental conditions, indicate that livestock grazing may: 1) have minimal or no effect on forest regeneration (Kosco and Bartolome 1983); or 2) promote seedling growth (Sharrow and Leininger 1983a; Nordstrom 1984; Doescher et al. 1987) and enhance long-term forest production (Krueger 1987; Pearson 1987). For example, improvements in height growth increments between 7 and 27% have been reported for Douglas-fir seedlings (Ingram 1931; Hedrick and Keniston 1966; Cleary 1978; Richmond 1983) and 3-10% for ponderosa pine seedlings (Edgerton 1971) on grazed areas compared to ungrazed controls. These gains have generally been attributed to a reduction in competition between crop trees and associated vegetation as a result of livestock grazing.

Similar increases have been reported in juvenile stands that have been grazed for long periods of time. Krueger (1987) reported that both height growth and diameter for ponderosa pine, Douglas-fir, western white pine (*P. monticola*), and western larch (*Larix occidentalis*) were significantly larger on grazed areas compared to the ungrazed controls after 20 years of cattle and wildlife grazing. Indeed, height increases ranged from 17 to 50%, and diameters were from 9 to 61% larger among tree species. Similarly, Douglas-fir trees were 20% taller on grazed compared to ungrazed areas on an Oregon plantation 10 years after planting, even though the initial height growth was lower on the grazed areas until the trees were about 1 m high (Cleary 1978).

Management Recommendations

Management practices that may reduce seedling damage and enhance forest production include:

- **Planning.** Integrated forest/range resource management can only be accomplished when resource managers and users are committed to planning for integrated use together. Both the Five-Year Development Plan and the Pre-Harvest Silviculture Prescriptions (Chapter 8) should aim for integrated resource management, rather than range and forest management planning being conducted in isolation.

- **Inventory.** The biological and physical conditions within the planning unit should be assessed before the plan is implemented. This assessment should include a review of the harvesting plan and current range management system; an evaluation of the short- and long-term livestock forage requirements and availability in the area; an evaluation of the physical site conditions that may impede or promote livestock distribution; an estimate of the amount and distribution of water; and an appraisal of the current and future range and forest management improvements necessary to meet management goals.

- **Livestock preferences.** Although cow/calf operations are most prevalent on British Columbia rangelands, grazing preferences should be taken into consideration on areas where livestock are being introduced as a vegetation management tool. Sheep, for example, generally prefer fireweed and browse more than cattle do.

- **Time of grazing.** For livestock to be effective as a vegetation management tool, grazing should be timed to coincide with forage availability and the phenological development of trees. Although it has often been recommended that grazing not coincide with the flush of annual conifer growth, Doescher et al. (1987) suggest that grazing may be possible during this period if adequate forage is available and animal distribution can be controlled.

  Although livestock grazing may affect seedling survival until the free-growing stage, generally the worst damage occurs in the first year. Consideration should be given to deferring grazing for the first year after planting, on sites where forage is limited or where domestic forage seedings are establishing. On the other hand, controlled grazing can also be prescribed to control competing vegetation (Doescher et al. 1987). Animals should be removed from plantations at the first sign of problems with regeneration or when forage becomes limiting.

- **Animal distribution.** Good animal distribution is essential for ensuring proper forage use and minimal damage to conifer seedlings. Animal distribution should be controlled through well-distributed water developments and strategically located salt. Herding is strongly recommended in areas where natural barriers, water, and salt cannot adequately spread animals about. Furthermore, herding can have important secondary benefits by conditioning animals to positive distribution patterns (Monfore 1983; Krueger 1987), particularly when new animals are introduced onto a range unit. Where feasible, fencing should be considered to control animal movements.

- **Animal numbers.** Animal numbers should be set in relation to forage availability, but adjusted to account for distribution factors that may result in conifer damage. Stocking rates that use 40-60% of the forage have often been recommended to ensure compatibility with forest regeneration (Cassady et al. 1955; Pearson 1974; Currie et al. 1978). However, higher levels of use may be possible with adequate animal distribution (Doescher et al. 1987).

- **Silvicultural treatments.** Silvicultural treatments such as disposal of logging slash, site preparation, fertilization, and herbicide control should be cooperatively planned with the range users. Poorly planned silvicultural treatments may affect forage availability, water distribution, fencing, and animal distribution, thus altering livestock use patterns and indirectly contributing to seedling damage and survival.

- **Monitoring and re-evaluation.** Management units should be monitored regularly to ensure that the goals of the Pre-Harvest Silviculture Prescription are being met. The planning team should meet at regular intervals to update all users on progress, identify problems, and alter the plan where necessary to meet management goals.

POLE-SIZED (SAPLING) STANDS

Barking and Girdling by Snowshoe Hares

Snowshoe hares remove bark from the base of stems and low branches of large seedlings and sapling trees up to 6.0 cm dbh, in addition to damaging young seedlings (Figure 22.4). Feeding damage may occur higher on the stem and branches, depending on snow depth. The gnawed sapwood has a shaggy or ragged appearance and complete girdling of the stem may occur. Toothmarks are indistinct, with an average width of 2 mm in a horizontal or diagonal configuration on exposed sapwood. Fecal droppings, which are slightly flattened spherical pellets 10 mm in diameter, are

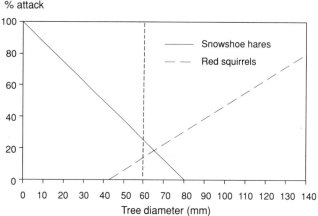

FIGURE 22.4. Conceptual model of percentage of lodgepole pine trees attacked by snowshoe hares and red squirrels by tree diameter. Vertical dashed line represents the tree diameter that usually separates snowshoe hare and red squirrel feeding.

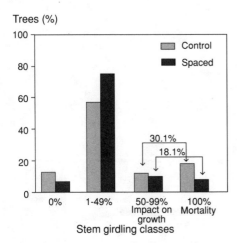

Trees (%)

FIGURE 22.5. Impact of percentage of stem circumference girdled, from feeding by snowshoe hares, on tree growth and survival in natural (control) and spaced stands of lodgepole pine.

usually present at feeding sites. Barking and girdling injuries occur mainly in winter and early spring (November to April). A detailed description of hare (and red squirrel) barking injuries to lodgepole pine in central British Columbia is discussed in Sullivan and Sullivan (1982c).

In general, overstocked pine stands provide optimum habitat for snowshoe hares. It is during the peak in abundance every 9-10 years when hares cause serious damage to crop trees in natural and thinned stands of lodgepole pine. If spacing is to be successful, damage due to hares must be taken into account.

Complete girdling of the stem of a crop tree by hare feeding clearly leads to mortality. However, even partial girdling (> 50% of stem circumference) can significantly suppress diameter and height growth (Sullivan and Sullivan 1986a) (Figure 22.5). In general, width (circumference) of a given wound has a greater effect on tree growth than does surface area of bark and tissue removed. Paradoxically, there tends to be a rapid growth of trees that have large areas of damage. This relationship is most likely a result of hare preference to feed on faster growing (and presumably more nutritious) pine. This conclusion is supported by one study which found that fertilization significantly increased hare damage to lodgepole pine (Sullivan and Sullivan 1982d) (Figure 22.6).

Recommendations to alleviate damage from snowshoe hares in juvenile stands (Sullivan 1984) include:

- delaying the juvenile spacing of overstocked stands of lodgepole pine (> 15 000 stems per hectare) that are susceptible to hare damage until the potential crop trees are > 60 mm average diameter. Overstocked stands (< 15 000 stems per hectare) may be spaced without concern for potential hare damage.

- spacing stands with potential crop trees of average diameter < 60 mm during the peak year or first year of the decline in the hare population cycle. One year with minimal damage will follow because the fallen pine foliage acts as an alternative food source. However, crop trees must be of sufficient initial size to reach > 60 mm diameter during the 6-7 years before the next hare population increase.

- in stands with a wide range of size classes, choosing large diameter (> 60 mm) crop trees and, if necessary, leaving smaller diameter stems as sacrifice food for hares.

- adopting a two-step spacing program. After an initial close-spacing treatment, small mammal damage in the stands could be assessed, and the level of treatment in the second stage adapted to compensate for tree mortality. This second-stage thinning assumes that stems have grown beyond susceptibility to hare damage before the stand is treated, and that other potential mortality factors such as disease or insect attack do not appreciably lower the final crop tree density.

- ensuring that spacing operations cover as large an area (> 50 ha) as possible to make the spaced stand habitat less attractive to hare populations.

These recommendations cannot be applied to coniferous plantations in the central and northern regions of British Columbia which, in most cases, must outgrow and survive two and probably three peaks of snowshoe hare populations. After this time, trees will presumably have reached a stage where they could be spaced on the basis of crop tree selection.

Barking and Girdling by Red Squirrels

The red squirrel is another small mammal species that may seriously damage crop trees in spaced stands of lodgepole pine. Squirrels strip bark from a stem to feed on the cambium and exposed sapwood. Characteristics of squirrel barking are the indistinct toothmarks on the sapwood and the presence of bark strips (3 x 8 cm) which accumulate on the ground under the injured tree. These bark strips are often the only evidence that distinguishes squirrel work from similar crown girdling injuries by porcupines. Because squirrels climb, they can also damage any part of a tree. Most of the damage they cause occurs in spring and early summer (May and June), during the early part of the growing season. Damaged stems are usually > 60 mm dbh.

Squirrel damage to lodgepole pine is locally present in most British Columbia Forest Regions, but attention has largely been focused on the problem in the Prince George, Cariboo, and Kamloops Regions. In general, these rodents damage larger crop trees and remove greater amounts of bark per attack than do hares. Squirrel population fluctuations tend to coincide with cone crops (Halvorson 1984; Sullivan 1987).

Their abundance in a mature stand peaks in the year after a substantial cone crop, and a surplus of squirrels appears in juvenile stands in subsequent years (Figure 22.7). Incidence of damage and feeding intensity generally tends to be associated with high densities of squirrels, although local exceptions to this pattern may occur (Sullivan 1987).

Unfortunately, the red squirrel population cycle does not have the consistent long-term periodicity of the snowshoe hare 10-year cycle. This factor, and the preference by squirrels to attack vigorous, large-diameter (>60 mm) stems, means that spacing operations cannot be timed with population cycles as is recommended for snowshoe hares.

Juvenile pine stands appear to act as marginal habitat for the surplus of squirrels from population increases in mature forest. Since spaced stands have significantly fewer squirrels than unspaced, it is possible that stand thinning over a large area (e.g., > 100 ha) might reduce immigration from surrounding areas and so help alleviate damage (Sullivan and Moses 1986b). However, it must be noted that even low numbers of squirrels can evidently cause high levels of damage to juvenile trees, particularly in fertilized stands. As discussed by Sullivan and Moses (1986b), a population reduction program with toxicants or trapping would likely be ineffective because of the difficulty in achieving complete removal of all animals. In addition, the resiliency of squirrels to depopulation would result in available habitat being rapidly filled.

Recommendations to alleviate damage from red squirrels in juvenile stands include, as for hares, spacing over a large area and using a two-step spacing program. Other recommendations include:

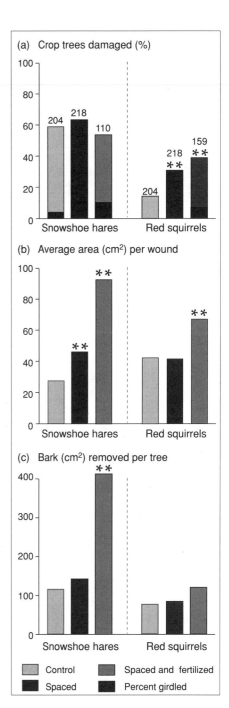

FIGURE 22.6. Influence of fertilization on feeding attacks on lodgepole pine by snowshoe hares and red squirrels. Variables measured include (a) percentage of crop trees damaged, (b) average area of bark and vascular tissues removed per attack, and (c) average area of bark and vascular tissues removed per tree (**p<0.01) (from Sullivan 1985).

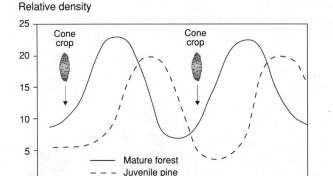

FIGURE 22.7. Population cycle of the red squirrel in stands of mature white spruce/lodgepole pine and juvenile lodgepole pine from 1978 to 1986. Populations were monitored from 1981 to 1986 with heavy cone crops recorded in 1979 and 1983 (from Brockley and Sullivan 1987).

- monitoring conifer (interior spruce and Douglas-fir) cone crops to predict future outbreaks of squirrel populations and damage. After a substantial cone crop there may be up to a 2- to 3-year delay before squirrel populations increase in juvenile stands.

- developing a diagnostic system to identify those stands susceptible to squirrel attack. This should be done on a region-wide basis. In stands where the risk of squirrel damage is high, fertilization of spaced stands should be delayed until risk potential is reduced. Spaced trees can be expected to remain responsive to fertilizer application as long as the live crown ratio is favorable and inter-tree competition is not severe.

- installing direct control methods, such as predator odor repellents (and perhaps systemic repellents), in susceptible stands before predicted outbreaks of damage.

- providing alternative foods (e.g., sunflower seeds) during the May-June damage period.

Barking and Girdling by Porcupines

The porcupine (*Erethizon dorsatum*) injures the bark of coniferous saplings. It gnaws bark from stems, leaving broad (2.5 mm), prominent vertical and diagonal incisor marks on the exposed sapwood. Basal girdling is common on smaller trees, while debarking is common on the upper bole and major branches of larger trees. Top girdling produces a characteristic bushy crown and spike top. Occasional porcupine damage has been reported for lodgepole pine in the central Interior and ponderosa pine and larch in the southern Interior, but the most widespread incidence of attack is in the Kalum and North Coast Districts of the Prince Rupert Forest Region.

Porcupines are particularly abundant in second-growth western hemlock - Sitka spruce stands of northwestern British Columbia. Sullivan et al. (1986) reported on the incidence of damage and its potential impact on growth and yield in the forest stands of Khutzeymateen Inlet northeast of Prince Rupert. Western hemlock, which composed 67% of sampled stands, was the most severely (52.7%) damaged species, followed by Sitka spruce with 7.8% of trees attacked. The less frequent amabilis fir (*Abies amabilis*) and western redcedar were not attacked. In general, porcupines have been found to prefer large-diameter stems for feeding.

A major method of porcupine control in Washington and Oregon was the use of strychnine salt blocks, although this technique has not been effective in western forests (Anthony et al. 1986) and there is no quantitative evidence relating population reduction to damage reduction (Evans 1987).

In the absence of definitive research, management recommendations to reduce porcupine damage include:

- for thinning programs, selecting tree species that are not readily attacked by porcupines (e.g., amabilis fir, western redcedar).

- managing fisher (*Martes pennanti*) as a biological control technique to reduce porcupine abundance.

- using sheet metal collars or sleeves (87.5 cm in length) around lower boles of susceptible trees to prevent porcupines from climbing the stems.

- initiating a bounty system or live-trapping by fur trappers as a means of lowering population density of porcupines.

Barking and Girdling by Voles

In addition to attacking seedlings, voles also debark and girdle sapling-size trees. The gnawed surface of the exposed sapwood is fuzzy, with irregular patches of gnawed bark on the lower bole, low branches, root collar, and roots. Spaced and natural stands of Douglas-fir have been attacked by Townsend voles on Texada Island (Harper and Harestad 1986), and western hemlock and grand fir (*A. grandis*) have been attacked on Vancouver Island. In general, vole damage is related to heavy post-thinning slash cover and to a lack of preferred alternative foods during the winter period (Harper and Harestad 1986). Management recommendations (where required) to reduce vole damage to saplings are the same as those made to reduce damage to seedlings.

Barking and Girdling by Black Bears

Barking and girdling injuries by black bears (*Ursus americanus*) and grizzly bears (*U. arctos*) to pole-sized and larger trees is common in the Pacific Coast and Kootenay forests of British Columbia. The animals strip bark from young trees during the spring and early summer months to feed on new sapwood. In doing so, they leave large strips of bark around the base of trees that they peel and long vertical grooves in the sapwood from their incisors or claws. This is in contrast to the short horizontal or diagonal grooves left by rodents and hares in barked stems.

Damage by bears in British Columbia tends to be minor and localized. Where damage is common in the U.S., it occurs on trees in thinned rather than unthinned stands (Mason and Adams 1987; Schmidt 1987) that are preferentially attacked.

Management recommendations to reduce black bear damage include organizing spring harvests of timber and providing supplemental food (Flowers 1987).

SUMMARY

Animal damage to the regenerating forests in British Columbia tends to be localized. The intensity and distribution of the damage is generally related to habitat conditions within and near the plantation or site to be regenerated. Outbreaks of small mammal damage may be predicted on the basis of population cycles, particularly the multi-annual cycling species such as snowshoe hares and voles.

Summary – Management Recommendations

1. Plantation Seedlings

- Pre-harvest/pre-planting surveys
  - hazard assessment
- Plant more seedlings/unit area
- Vegetation control   – scarification
  - herbicides
- Repellent system

2. Juvenile Stands

- Strategic timing of spacing/thinning + fertilization
  - snowshoe hare cycle
  - red squirrel fluctuation
- Greater number of crop trees/unit area
- Tree species selection
- Repellent system
- Alternative foods   – red squirrel
- Predator management and bounty
  - porcupine

FIGURE 22.8.   Summary of management recommendations to alleviate feeding damage by mammals to plantations and juvenile stands.

Improperly managed livestock may severely damage forest plantations by trampling and, to a lesser degree, by browsing. Factors that contribute to poor animal distribution and encourage animals to congregate are most often associated with livestock damage. Under proper management, however, domestic livestock can potentially improve forest regeneration. Good management practices should be encouraged to ensure compatibility between forest and range users of British Columbia's forestland.

Where regeneration has been delayed and conversion of backlog land to forest plantation is planned, increasing problems with mammal damage may be expected. Accurate identification of the potential pest species and knowledge of the population cycle, habitat preferences, and damage control methods are critical for successful regeneration of a given forest site. A general summary of management recommendations for plantations and juvenile stands is given in Figure 22.8.

Wherever possible, forest and wildlife resource managers should conduct trials of various damage control techniques to determine which methods will help reduce animal damage in their respective areas. This approach provides a data base that managers can rely on for future recommendations. It also provides information on the efficacy of damage control techniques conducted both operationally and in small-scale experiments.

REFERENCES

Adams, S.N. 1975. Sheep and cattle grazing in forests: a review. J. Appl. Ecol. 12:143-152.

Agriculture Canada Expert Committee on Soil Survey. 1987. The Canadian system of soil classification. 2nd ed. Supply and Services Can., Ottawa, Ont. Agric. Can. Publ. 1646. 164 p.

Alden, J. 1985. Biology and management of white spruce seed crops for reforestation in subarctic taiga forests. Univ. Alaska. Fairbanks, Alaska. Agric. For. Exp. Sta., Bull. 69. 51 p.

Aldhous, J.R. 1972. Nursery practice. For. Comm. Bull. 43, Her Majesty's Stationery Office, London. 184 p.

Alexander, R.R. 1987. Ecology, silviculture, and management of the Engelmann spruce-subalpine fir type in the central and southern Rocky Mountains. U.S. Dep. Agric. For. Serv., Washington, D.C. Agric. Handb. 659.

Allen, G.S. 1944. Management recommendations for the Hemlock and associated forest types of the Juan de Fuca region of southwestern Vancouver Island. B.C. For. Serv., Victoria, B.C. Res. Note 11.

_____. 1960. Factors affecting the viability and germination behavior of coniferous seed. IV. Stratification period and incubation temperature, *Pseudotsuga menziesii* (Mirb.) Franco. For. Chron. 36:18-29.

Allen, G.S. and J.N. Owens. 1972. The life history of Douglas-fir. Environ. Can., Can. For. Serv., Victoria, B.C. 88 p.

Anderson, M.L. 1950. The selection of tree species. Oliver and Boyd Ltd., Edinburgh and London. 151p.

Anderson, R.F. 1960. Forest and shade tree entomology. J. Wiley and Sons, Inc., New York, N.Y.

Annas, R. M. and R. Coupé (editors). 1979. Biogeoclimatic zones and subzones of the Cariboo Forest Region. B.C. Min. For., Victoria, B.C. 101p.

Anthony, R.M., J. Evans, and G.D. Lindsey. 1986. Strychnine-salt blocks for controlling porcupines in pine forests: efficacy and hazards. *In* Proc. 12th Vertebrate Pest Conf., San Diego, Calif., pp. 191-195.

Archibold, W.O. 1980. Seed input into a postfire forest site in northern Saskatchewan. Can. J. For. Res. 10:129-134.

Armbrust, D.V. and J.D. Dickerson. 1971. Temporary wind erosion control: cost and effectiveness of 34 commercial materials. Soil and Water Conserv. 26:154-157.

Armleder, H.M., R.J. Dawson, and R.N. Thompson. 1986. Handbook for timber and mule deer management co-ordination on winter ranges in the Cariboo Forest Region. B.C. Min. For., Victoria, B.C. Land Manage. Handb. No. 13.

Armson, K.A., M. Fung, and W.R. Bunting. 1980. Operational rooting of black spruce cuttings. J. For. 78: 341-343.

Arney, J.D. 1986. User's guide for the Stand Projection System. J.D. Arney, Lewiston, Idaho.

Arnott, J.T. 1972. Influences affecting container seedling performance on Vancouver Island, British Columbia. *In* Proc. Workshop on Container Planting in Canada. R.M. Waldron (editor). Can. Dep. Environ., Can. For. Serv., Inf. Rep. DPC-X-2, pp. 84-91.

_____. 1973. Evolution of the styroblock reforestation system in British Columbia. Commonwealth For. Rev. 52(1): 72-78.

_____. 1974. Performance in British Columbia. *In* Proc. N. Am. Containerized Forest Tree Seedlings Symp. R.W. Tinus, W.I. Stein, and W.E. Balmer (editors). Great Plains Agric. Counc. Publ. 68, pp. 283-290.

Arnott, J.T. and A. N. Burdett. 1988. Early growth of planted western hemlock in relation to stock type and controlled-release fertilizer application. Can. J. For. Res. 18 (6):710-717.

Association of Official Seed Analysts. 1981. Rules for testing seeds. J. Seed Technol. 6:1-162.

Atkinson, W.A. and R.J. Zasoski. 1976. Proceedings of western hemlock management conference. Univ. Wash., Coll. For. Resources, Seattle, Wash. 317 p.

Baker, K.F. (editor). 1957. The U.C. system for producing healthy container-grown plants. Univ. Cal., Div. Agric. Sci., Agric. Exp. Sta. Exten. Serv., Berkeley, Cal. 332 p.

Balfour, P.M. 1989. Effects of forest herbicides on wildlife forage. For. Can. and B.C. Min. For., Victoria, B.C. FRDA Rep. No. 020. 58 p.

Ballard, T.M., T.A. Black, and K.G. McNaughton. 1977. Summer energy balance and temperatures in a forest clearcut in southwestern British Columbia. Proc. 6th B.C. Soil Sci. Workshop, Richmond, B.C., B.C. Min. Agric., Victoria, B.C., pp. 74-86.

Ballard, T.M. and R.E. Carter. 1985. Evaluating forest stand nutrient status. B.C. Min. For., Victoria, B.C. Land Manage. Rep. No. 20. 60 p.

Banham, F.L. and J.C. Arrand. 1970. Recognition and life history of major insect and allied pests of vegetables in British Columbia. B.C. Dep. Agric., Victoria, B.C. Bull. 70-9.

Barber, A. 1977. Nutrients in the soil and their flow to plant roots. *In* The belowground ecosystem: a synthesis of plant-associated processes. J.K. Marshall (editor). Colo. State Univ., Range Sci. Dep., Fort Collins, Colo. Sci. Ser. No. 26, pp. 161-169.

Barber, H.W. 1984. Effects of site preparation on survival and moisture stress of interior Douglas-fir seedlings planted in grass. Tree Planters Notes, Fall 1984: 7-10.

Barnes, G.H. 1937. The development of uneven-aged stands of Engelmann spruce and probable development of residual stands after logging. For. Chron. 13:417-457.

Barnes, V.G. 1973. Pocket gophers and reforestation in the Pacific Northwest: a problem analysis. U.S. Dep. Int., Fish Wild. Serv., Special Scientific Rep., Wildl. No.155. 50 p.

Baumgartner, D.M., R.G. Krebill, J.T. Arnott, and G.F. Weetman (editors). 1985. Lodgepole pine: the species and its management. State Univ., Coop. Exten., Pullman, Wash. 381 p.

Baylis, G.T.S. 1974. The evolutionary significance of phycomycetous mycorrhizae. *In* Mechanisms of regulation of plant growth. R.L Bielski, H.R. Ferguson, and M.M. Creswell (editors). R. Soc. N.Z. Bull. 12, Wellington, N.Z., pp. 191-193.

Beaudry, P. 1989. The fate of herbicides in the forest environment. For. Can. and B.C. Min. For., Victoria, B.C. FRDA Res. Memo No. 74. 6 p.

Bennett, F.A. and L.K. Halls. 1954. The effect of grazing on slash pine seedling survival. U.S. Dep. Agric. For. Serv., SE For. Exp. Sta., Res. Note 58. 2 p.

Benzian, B. 1965. Experiments on nutrition problems in forest nurseries. Vol. 1. For. Comm. Bull. No. 37, Her Majesty's Stationery Office, London. 251 p.

Binder, W.D., R.K. Scagel, and G.J. Krumlik. 1988. Root growth potential: facts, myths, value? *In* Proc. Meet. of the Western Forest Nursery Assoc. U.S. Dep. Agric. For. Serv., Rocky Mtn. For. Range Exp. Sta., Gen. Tech. Rep. RM-167, pp. 111-118.

Biswell, H.H. and M.D. Hoover. 1945. Appalachian hardwood trees browsed by cattle. J. For. 43:675-676.

Black, C.A. 1968. Soil-plant relationships. John Wiley & Sons, Inc., New York, N.Y. 792 p.

Black, H.C. 1969. Fate of sown coniferous seeds. *In* Wildlife and reforestation in the Pacific Northwest. H.C. Black (editor). Oreg. State Univ., School of Forestry, Corvallis, Oreg., pp. 42-51.

Black, H.C., E.J. Dimock II, J. Evans, and J.A. Rochelle. 1979. Animal damage to coniferous plantations in Oregon and Washington. Part I. A survey, 1963-1975. Oreg. State Univ., For. Res. Lab., Corvallis, Oreg. Res. Bull. 25. 44 p.

Blackwell, B., M.C. Feller, and R. Trowbridge. 1986. Rehabilitation of densely stocked lodgepole pine stands in the Lakes Forest District, west-central B.C. *In* Proc. NW For. Fire Council Ann. Meet., Nov. 18-19, 1986, Olympia, Wash.

Blake, J., J.B. Zaerr, and S. Hee. 1979. Controlled moisture stress to improve cold hardiness and morphology of Douglas-fir seedlings. For. Sci. 25 (4):576-581.

Blake, J.I., L.D. Teeter, and D.B. South. 1989. Analyses of the economic benefits from increasing uniformity in Douglas-fir nursery stock. *In* Forestry Vol. 62 Supplement. pp. 251-262.

Blatchford, O.N. 1978. Forestry practice. For. Comm. Bull. No. 14, Her Majesty's Stationery Office, London. 138 p.

Bonner, F.T. 1974. Seed testing. *In* Seeds of woody plants of the United States. C.S. Schopmeyer (technical coordinator.) U.S. Dep. Agric. For. Serv., Washington, D.C. Agric. Handb. No. 450, pp. 136-150.

Boyd, R. J. 1982. Chemical site preparation treatments for herbaceous plant communities. *In* Site preparation and fuel management on steep terrain. D. M. Baumgartner (editor). Wash. State Univ., Coop. Exten., Pullman, Wash., pp. 46-53.

Boyer, J.N., D.B. South, D.A. Muller, and H. Vanderveer. 1985. A comparison of nursery sowers. Tree Planters Notes:20-24

Brand, D.G. 1986. A competition index for predicting the vigour of planted Douglas-fir in southwestern British Columbia. Can. J. For. Res. 16: 23-29.

Breadon, R. E. 1987. Site preparation equipment in British Columbia: current availability and future needs. For. Eng. Res. Inst. Can., Vancouver, B.C., Spec. Rep. SR-46. 106 p.

British Columbia. 1910. Report of the Royal Commission on Timber and Forestry, 1901-1910. F.J. Fulton, Chairman. Victoria, B.C. 117 p.

_____. 1912. Forest Act. *In* Statutes of the Province of British Columbia. Chap. 17. Victoria, B.C.

_____. 1945. Report of the Royal Commission on The Forest Resources of British Columbia. Hon. G. McG. Sloan, Commissioner. Victoria, B.C. 195. p.

_____. 1956. Report of the Royal Commission on The Forest Resources of British Columbia. Hon. G. McG. Sloan, Commissioner. Victoria, B.C. 2 vols. 888 p.

_____. 1976. Report of the Royal Commission on Forest Resources, Timber rights and forest policy in British columbia. P.H. Pearse, Commissioner. Victoria, B.C. 2 vols. Vol. 1, 395 p. Vol. 2, mult. pag.

B.C. Forest Service. 1946. Cone collections. *In* Reforestation manual: with instructions to forest officers on seed collections and planting practice. Economics Div., Victoria, B.C., pp. 7-8.

B. C. Ministry of Agriculture and Fisheries. 1987. Nursery production guide for commercial growers. Victoria, B.C. 78 p.

_____. 1988. Nursery, greenhouse vegetable and ornamental 1988/89 production guide for commercial growers. Co-sponsored by Coop Protection Institute of Canada (B.C. Council). Co-published by Coast Agri-Coop Products Division. Victoria, B.C.

B.C. Ministry of Environment. 1980. Guidelines for watershed management of Crown lands used as community water supplies. Victoria, B.C.

B.C. Ministry of Forests. Protection manual. Victoria, B.C. Updated regularly.

B.C. Ministry of Forests. Silviculture manual. Victoria, B.C. Updated regularly.

B.C. Ministry of Forests. 1981. Forest landscape handbook. Recreation Manage. Branch, Victoria, B.C. 100 p.

B.C. Ministry of Forests. 1986a. British Columbia Coastal Tree Improvement Council: First progress report: 1981 - 1984. J. Konishi, I. Karlsson, and J. Woods (editors). Victoria, B.C. 46 p.

_____. 1986b. British Columbia Interior Tree Improvement Council: Second Progress Report: 1981 - 1984. J. Konishi, I. Karlsson, and J. Woods (editors). Victoria, B.C. 39 p.

_____. 1987. A field guide for the identification and interpretation of ecosystems of the Cariboo Forest Region. Williams Lake, B.C.

_____. 1988a. Annual report 1987/88. Victoria, B.C. 84 p.

_____. 1988b. Assessment of mechanical planting trials in North Central British Columbia. Silv. Branch, Victoria, B.C. 25 p.

_____. 1989. A quick guide to pesticides: use and regulations in B.C. forest management. Victoria, B.C. 51 p.

B.C. Ministry of Forests and Lands. 1987a. Ground skidding guidelines. Engineering and Silviculture Branches, Victoria, B.C. 58 p.

B.C. Ministry of Forests and Lands, B.C. Ministry of Environment and Parks, Federal Department of Fisheries and Oceans, and Council of Forest Industries of B.C. 1987. British Columbia coastal fisheries forestry guidelines. Victoria, B.C.

B.C. Ministry of Forests and Lands, Timber Harvesting Methods Committee, and Terry Lewis. 1988. Guidelines for timber harvesting prescriptions for Interior sites of various degradation sensitivities. Available from B.C. Ministry of Forests, Victoria, B.C. 65 p.

Brix, H. 1972. Growth response of Sitka spruce and white spruce seedlings to temperature and light intensity. Environ. Can., Can. For. Serv., Victoria, B.C. Inf. Rep. BC-X-74. 17 p.

Brockley, R.P. 1988. The effects of fertilization on the early growth of planted seedlings: a problem analysis. For. Can. and B.C. Min. For., Victoria, B.C. FRDA Rep. 011. 16 p.

Brockley, R.P. and T.P. Sullivan. 1988. Impact of feeding by small mammals on cultural treatments in young stands of lodgepole pine. *In* Proc. Symp. on Future Forests of the Mountain West: A Stand Culture Symp. U.S. Dep. Agric. For. Serv., Int. For. Range Exp. Sta., Ogden, Utah. Tech. Pap. INT-243, pp. 322-329.

Brown, G. 1984 Aerial seeding of wildfire areas in the northwestern region. *In* Proc Jack Pine Symp. C.R. Smith and G. Brown (co-chairmen). Can. Dep. Environ., Can. For. Serv., Sault Ste. Marie, Ont. COJFRC Symp. Proc. O-P-12, pp. 93-101.

Brumelle, S.L., J.S. Carley, I.B. Vertinsky, and D.A. Wehrung. 1988. Evaluating silvicultural investments: an analytic framework. Forest Economics and Policy Analysis Research Unit, Univ. B.C. Working Pap. 116.

Burdett, A.N. 1979a. Juvenile instability in planted pines. Irish Forestry 36:36-47.

_____. 1979b. New methods for measuring root growth capacity: their value in assessing lodgepole pine stock quality. Can. J. For. Res. 9:63-67.

_____. 1987. Understanding root growth capacity: theoretical considerations in assessing planting stock quality by means of root growth tests. Can. J. For. Res. 17:768-775.

Burdett, A.N., D.G. Simpson, and C.F. Thompson. 1983. Root development and plantation establishment success. Plant and Soil 71:103-110.

Burr, K.E. and R.W. Tinus. 1989. Effect of the timing of cold storage on cold hardiness and root growth potential of Douglas-fir. *In* Proc. Meet. of the Western Forest Nursery Assoc., Vernon, B.C., Aug. 8-11, 1988. U.S. Dep. Agric. For. Serv., Fort Collins, Colo. Gen. Tech. Rep. RM-167, pp. 133-138.

Butt, G. 1988. Backlog forest land rehabilitation in the SBS and BWBS zones in the northern interior of British Columbia. For. Can. and B.C. Min. For., Victoria, B.C. FRDA Rep. No. 023.

Butt, G., B. Bancroft, and R. Folk. 1989. Ingress of Engelmann spruce and subalpine fir in the Southern Interior ESSF. For. Can. and B.C. Min. For., Victoria, B.C. FRDA Rep. Proj. 3.61.

Canadian Pulp and Paper Association (CPPA). 1986. Herbicides registered for forest and woodlands management. Forest Protection Committee, CPPA. Montreal, Que. 6 p.

Canadian Pulp and Paper Association and Canadian Forest Service (CPPA/CFS). 1984. Mechanization of silviculture: increasing quality and productivity. Proc. CPPA/CFS Seminar on Mechanization of Silviculture, Thunder Bay, Ont., Sept. 17, 1984. 89 p.

Cantrell, R. L. 1985. A guide to silvicultural herbicide use in the Southern United States. Auburn University, Auburn, Tex. Chap. 2, pp. 2-1 to 2-15.

Carlson, L.W. 1983. Guidelines for rearing containerized conifer seedlings in the prairie provinces. Environ. Can., Can. For. Serv., Edmonton, Alta. 64 p.

Carr, W.W. 1980. A handbook for forest roadside erosion control in British Columbia. B.C. Min. For., Victoria, B.C. Land Manage. Rep. No. 4. 43 p.

Carter, R.E. and K. Klinka. 1986. Symptoms and causes of distorted growth in immature forest stands in coastal British Columbia. B.C. Min. For., Victoria, B.C. Land Manage. Rep. No. 39. 61 p.

Carter, R.E., A.M. Scagel, and K. Klinka. 1986. Nutritional aspects of distorted growth in immature forest stands of southwestern coastal British Columbia. Can. J. For. Res. 16:36-41.

Cassady, J.T., W. Hopkins, and L.B. Whitaker. 1955. Cattle grazing damage to pine seedlings. U.S. Dep. Agric. For. Serv., South. For. Exp. Sta., Occas. Pap. 141. 14 p.

Cassidy, H.O. 1937a. How cattle may use cut-over ponderosa pine-bunchgrass ranges with minimum injury to reproduction. U.S. Dep. Agric. For. Serv., SW For. Range Exp. Sta., Res. Note No. 15. 3 p.

_____. 1937b. How to handle sheep on cut-over ponderosa pine-bunchgrass ranges to keep injury to reproduction at a minimum. U.S. Dep. Agric. For. Serv., SW For. Range Exp. Sta., Res. Note No. 16. 2 p.

Cerezke, H.F. 1970. A method for estimating abundance of the weevil, *Hylobius warreni* (Wood), and its damage in lodgepole pine stands. For. Chron. 46:392-396.

Cerezke, H.F. and R.E. Holmes. 1986. Control studies with carbofuran on seed and cone insects of white spruce. Environ. Can., Can. For. Serv., Edmonton, Alta. Inf. Rep. NOR-X-280. 10 p.

Chang, J. 1968. Climate and agriculture: an ecological survey. Aldine Publishing Co., Chicago, Ill. 296 p.

Chavasse, C.G.R. 1980. Planting stock quality: a review of factors affecting performance. N. Z. J. For. Res. 25:144-171.

Chung, H.H. and P.J. Kramer. 1975. Absorption of water and ^{32}P through suberized and unsuberized roots of loblolly pine. Can. J. For. Res. 5:229-235.

Clark, A. 1984. Ground seeding requirements for jack pine regeneration. *In* Proc. Jack Pine Symp. C.R. Smith and G. Brown (co-chairmen). Can. Dep. Environ., Can. For. Serv., Sault Ste. Marie, Ont. COJFRC Symp. Proc. O-P-12, pp. 87-92.

Clark, J.D., L.W.W. Lehrle, and S.H.G. Smith. 1954. Scarification in Engelmann spruce-Alpine fir forests. B.C. For. Serv., Victoria, B.C. Res. Note No. 25.

Clark, M.B. 1952. A preliminary study of growth and development of some Douglas-fir-Ponderosa pine types. B.C. For. Serv., Victoria, B.C. Tech. Publ. 38.

_____. 1974. Effect of cutting method, slash disposal treatment seedbed preparation and cone habit on natural regeneration of lodgepole pine in the south central Interior of British Columbia. B.C. For. Serv., Victoria, B.C. Res. Note 67.

Clark, M.B. and A. McLean. 1974. Compatibility of grass seedling and coniferous regeneration of clearcuts in the south central interior of British Columbia. B.C. For. Serv., Res. Note 83. 25 p.

Cleary, B.D. 1978. Vegetation management and its importance in re-forestation. Oreg. State Univ., For. Res. Lab., Corvallis, Oreg. Res. Note 60. 4 p.

Cleary, B.D., R.D. Greaves, and R.K. Hermann. 1978. Regenerating Oregon's forests: a guide for the regeneration forester. Oreg. State Univ., Exten. Serv., Corvallis, Oreg. 286 p.

Cleary, B.D., R.D. Greaves, and P.W. Owston. 1978. Seedlings. *In* Regenerating Oregon's forests: a guide for the regeneration forester. B.D. Cleary, R.D. Greaves, and R.K. Hermann (editors). Oreg. State Univ., Exten. Serv., Corvallis, Oreg., pp. 63-97.

Coates, D. and S. Haeussler. 1987. A guide to the use of mechanical site preparation equipment in North Central British Columbia. 2nd ed. Revised by A. MacKinnon, L. Bedford, and J. Maxwell. May 1989. B.C. Min. For., Victoria, B.C. FRDA Handb. No. 002. 63 p.

Cole, D.J. 1985. Mode of action of glyphosate: a literature analysis. *In* The herbicide glyphosate. E. Grossbard and D. Atkinson (editors). Butterworths Ltd., Toronto, Ont. Chap. 5, pp. 48-74.

Cole, E.C. and M. Newton. 1987. Fifth-year responses of Douglas-fir to crowding and non-coniferous competition. Can. J. For. Res. 17(3):181-186.

Colombo, S.J., D.P. Webb, and C. Glerum. 1984. Frost hardiness testing: an operational manual for use with extended greenhouse culture. Ont. Min. Nat. Resources, For. Res. Rep. No. 110. 11 p.

Conard, S.G. 1984. Forest vegetation management in British Columbia: problem analysis. B.C. Min. For. Res. Rep. RR84001-HQ.

Condrashoff, S.F. 1968. Biology of *Steremnius carinatus* (Coleoptera: Curculionidae), a reforestation pest in coastal British Columbia. Can. Entomol., Vol. 100, pp. 386-394.

Cook, J.D., J.H. Himel, and R.H. Moyer. 1978. Impact of forestry burning upon air quality: a state-of-the-knowledge characterization in Washington and Oregon. Geomet Inc. U.S. Nat. Tech. Inf. Serv., Rep. No. EPA 910/9-78-052.

Copeland, L.O. 1976. Principles of seed science technology. Burgess Publ. Co., Minneapolis, Minn. 369 p.

Coulson, R.N. and J.A. Witter. 1984. Forest entomology-ecology and management. John Wiley & Sons, Inc., New York, N.Y.

Crossley, D.I. 1976. The ingress of regeneration following harvest and scarification of lodgepole pine stands. For. Chron. 52:17-21.

Crouch, G.L. 1979. Atrazine improves survival and growth of ponderosa pine threatened by vegetative competition and pocket gophers. For. Sci. 25:99-111.

_____. 1982. Pocket gophers and reforestation on western forests. J. For. 80:662-664.

Currie, P.C., C.E. Edminster, and F.W. Knott. 1978. Effects of cattle grazing on ponderosa pine regeneration in central Colorado. U.S. Dep. Agric. For. Serv., Rocky Mtn. For. Range Exp. Sta., Res. Pap. RM 201. 7 p.

Daniels, T.W., J.A. Helm, and F.S. Baker. 1979. Principles of Silviculture. 2nd ed. McGraw Hill, New York, N.Y. 500 p.

Davey, C.B. and H.H. Krause. 1980. Functions and maintenance of organic matter in forest nursery soils. *In* Proc. N. Am. Forest Tree Nursery Soils Workshop. L.P. Abrahamson and D.H. Bickelhaupt (editors). State Univ. New York, Coll. Environ. Sci. For., Syracuse, N.Y., pp. 130-165.

Davis, L.S. and K.N. Johnson. 1987. Forest management. 3rd ed. McGraw Hill Book Co., Toronto, Ont.

DeBano, L.F., L.D. Mann, and D.A. Hamilton. 1970. Translocation of hydrophobic substances into soil by burning organic litter. Soil Sci. Soc. Am. Proc. 34:130-133.

DeBano, L.F., S.M. Savage, and D.A. Hamilton. 1976. The transfer of heat and hydrophobic substances during burning. Soil Sci. Am. J. 40:779-782.

DeByle, N.V. and R.P. Winokur (editors). 1985. Aspen: ecology and management in the western United States. U.S. Dep. Agric. For. Serv., Rocky Mtn. For. Range Exp. Sta., Fort Collins, Col. Gen. Tech. Rep. RM-119. 283 p.

Decima Research Ltd. 1986. Study on forestry issues. Study done for Can. For. Serv., Victoria, B.C. June, 1986. No. 1643.

Delong, C., S. Jenvey, and A. McLeod. 1986. A field guide for the identification and interpretation of ecosystems of the SBSjl in the Prince George Forest Region. B.C. Min. For., Prince George, B.C. 47 p.

Dennis, B. 1984. Distance methods for evaluating forest regeneration. *In* New forests for a changing world. Proc. 1983 Tech. Sessions of the Inventory, Remote Sensing and Photogrammetry, and Biometrics Working Groups, 1983 Convention of the Soc. Am. For., Portland, Oreg., pp. 14-19.

DeYoe, D.R., J.E. MacDonald and J.N. Owens. 1989. Culturing and preconditioning that improve bud development and cold hardiness of containerized Douglas-fir seedlings. *In* Proc., 10th N. Am. Forest Biol. Workshop, Physiology and Genetics of Reforestation. J. Worrell, J. Loo-Dinkins and D.T. Lester (editors). U.B.C. Vancouver, B.C., pp. 254

DeYoe, D.R. and D. White. 1985. Site preparation for woodland managers. III. The use of herbicides. Unpublished report. Oreg. State Univ., Corvallis, Oreg.

Dobbs, R.C. 1976. Effects of initial mass of white spruce and lodgepole pine planting stock on field performance in the British Columbia interior. Environ. Can., Can. For. Serv., Victoria, B.C. BC-X-149.

Dobbs, R.C., D.G.W. Edwards, J. Konishi, and D. Wallinger. 1976. Guidelines to collecting cones of B.C. conifers. B.C. For. Serv. and Environ. Can., Can. For. Serv., Joint Rep. No. 3. 98 p.

Doescher, P.S., S.D. Tesch, and M. Alejandro-Castro. 1987. Livestock grazing: a silvicultural tool for plantation establishment. J. For. 85:29-37.

Doidge, D.F., and V.G. Marshall. 1971. Spruce spider mite in British Columbia. Dep. Fish. For., For. Res. Lab., For. Pest Leafl. No. 33.

Dominy, S.W.J. and J.E. Wood. 1986. Shelter spot seed trials with jack pine, black spruce and white spruce in Northern Ontario. For. Chron. 62:446-450.

Dooley, J.H. 1982. Precision sowing - west; First season experience with the 816 precision sower. Weyerhaeuser Co. Tech. Rep. Proj. 050 - 1607. Tacoma, Wash. 31 p.

Dormling, I., A. Gustafsson, and D. von Wettstein. 1968. The experimental control of the life cycle in *Picea abies* (L.) Karst. Silvae Genet. 17:44-63.

Doumas, P. and J.B. Zaerr. 1988. Seasonal changes in levels of cytokinin-like compounds from Douglas-fir xylem extrudate. Tree Physiol. 4:1-8.

Draper, D., W. Binder, R. Fahlman, and D. Spittlehouse. 1985. Post-planting ecophysiology of interior spruce. *In* Proc. Symp. Interior Spruce Seedling Performance. North. Silv. Committee, Prince George, B.C.

Duncan, R.W. 1982. Common pitch moths in pine in British Columbia. Environ. Can., Can. For. Serv., Victoria, B.C. For. Pest Leafl. No. 69.

_____. 1986. Terminal and root-collar weevils of lodgepole pine in British Columbia. Environ. Can., Can. For. Serv., Victoria, B.C. For. Pest Leafl. No. 73.

Dunsworth, B.G. 1987. Stock handling survey 1983-1985. MacMillan Bloedel Internal Rep., Project 312.13. 18 p.

_____. 1988a. Fall and spring root phenology for Douglas-fir and western hemlock: a bioassay approach to defining planting windows. Proc. 10th N. Am. For. Biol. Workshop. D.T. Lester and J.G. Worrell (editors). Univ. B.C., Vancouver, B.C. pp. 295-307.

_____. 1988b. Impact of lift date and storage on field performance for containerized coastal Douglas-fir and western hemlock. Proc. West. For. Nursery Assoc. Meet., Vernon, B.C. 14 p.

Duryea, M.L. (editor). 1985. Evaluating seedling quality: principles, procedures, and predictive abilities of major tests. Oreg. State Univ., Coll. For., Corvallis, Oreg.

_____. 1984. Nursery cultural practices: impacts on seedling quality. *In* Forestry nursery manual: production of bareroot seedlings. M.L. Duryea and T.D. Landis (editors). Oreg. State Univ., For. Res. Lab. Martinus Nijhoff/ Dr. W. Junk Publishers. Corvallis, Oreg., pp. 143-164.

Duryea, M.L. and T.D. Landis (editors). 1984. Forest nursery manual: production of bareroot seedlings. Oreg. State Univ., For. Res. Lab., Corvallis, Oreg. 385 p.

Eckert, R.E. 1979. Establishment of pine (*Pinus* spp.) transplants in perennial grass stands with atrazine. Weed Sci. 27:253-257.

Edgerton, P.J. 1971. The effect of cattle and big game grazing on a ponderosa pine plantation. U.S. Dep. Agric. For. Serv., Pac. NW For. Range Exp. Sta., Res. Note PNW-172. 8 p.

Edwards, D.G.W. 1981. Cone collection and processing: effects on seed quality and yield. *In* Proc. Workshop on High-Quality Collection and Production of Conifer Seed. Edmonton, Alta. R.F. Huber (compiler). Nov. 1979, Environ. Can., Can. For. Serv., Info. Rep. NOR-X-235: 12-37.

_____. 1986. Cone prediction, collection and processing. *In* Proc. Symp. on Conifer Tree Seed in the Inland Mountain West. Missoula, Mont., Aug. 1985. R.C. Shearer (compiler). U.S. Dep. Agric. For. Serv., Gen. Tech. Rep. INT-203: 78-102.

Edwards, J.C. 1985. Herbicide applications technology in forestry: an analysis for British Columbia. Environ. Can., Can. For. Serv., Victoria, B.C. 73 p.

Eis, S. 1980. Effect of vegetative competition on regeneration of white spruce. Can. J. For. Res. 11:1-8.

Eis, S. and D. Craigdallie. 1981. Reproduction of conifers: a handbook for cone crop assessment. Environ. Can., Can. For. Serv., Victoria, B.C. Info Rep. BC-X-219. 32 p.

Eissenstat, D.M., J.E. Mitchell, and W.W. Pope. 1982. Trampling damage by cattle in northern Idaho forest plantations. J. Range Manage. 35:715-716.

El-Kassaby, Y.A., R. Davidson, and J.E. Webber. 1986. Genetics of seed orchards: Douglas-fir case study. *In* Tree improvement: theory and practice. Proc. IUFRO Working Parties on Breeding Theory, Progeny Testing, and Seed Orchards. Williamsburg, Va., Oct. 13-17, 1986. R.J.Weir (editor), pp. 440-456.

Eremko, R.D., D.G.W. Edwards, and D. Wallinger. 1989. Guide to collecting cones of British Columbia conifers. For. Can. and B.C. Min. For., Victoria, B.C. FRDA Rep. 055. 114 p.

Erickson, R.D. 1978. The Douglas-fir tussock moth. Environ. Can., Can. For. Serv., Victoria, B.C. For. Pest Leafl. No.9.

Errico, D. and M.K. Pelchat. 1984. An investigation of nursery operations for interior spruce. B.C. Min. For., Victoria, B.C. Res. Rep. RR 84009-HQ. 24 p.

Evans, J. 1987. The porcupine in the Pacific Northwest. *In* Proc. Symp. on Animal Damage Management in Pacific Northwest Forests. Spokane, Wash., pp. 75-78.

Expert Committee on Weeds. 1989. Research report. Vol. 3. West. Can. Section Meet.,Banff, Alta., Nov. 28-Dec. 1, 1989.

Feller, M.C. 1982. The ecological effects of slashburning with particular reference to British Columbia: a literature review. B.C. Min. For., Victoria, B.C. Land Manage. Rep. No. 13.

Fellin, D.G. 1980. A review of some interactions between harvesting, residue management, fire, and forest insects and diseases. *In* Environmental consequences of timber harvesting in Rocky Mountain coniferous forests. U.S. Dep. Agric. For. Serv., Gen. Tech. Rep. INT-90, pp. 335-414.

Feng, J.C. and D.G. Thompson. 1989. Persistence and dissipation of glyphosate in foliage and soils of a Canadian coastal forest watershed. *In* Proc. Carnation Creek Herbicide Workshop. P.E. Reynolds (editor). For. Can. and B.C. Min. For., Victoria, B.C. FRDA Rep. No. 063. pp. 65-87.

Feret, P.P., R.C. Freymans, and R.E. Kreh. 1985. Variation in root growth potential of loblolly pine from seven nurseries. *In* Internat. Symp. on Nursery Manage. Southern Pines. D. South (editor). Auburn Univ., Ala. Exp. Sta., Montgomery, Ala., pp. 317-328.

Ferguson, D.E. 1984. Needed: guidelines for defining acceptable advance regeneration. U.S. Dep. Agric. For. Serv., Intermtn. For. Range Exp. Sta., Ogden, Utah. Research Note INT-341. 4 p.

Ferguson, D.E., A.R. Stage, and R.J. Boyd. 1986. Predicting regeneration in the grand fir-cedar-hemlock ecosystem of the northern Rocky Mountains. Soc. Am. For., Washington, D.C. For. Sci. Monogr. 26.

Fleming, R.L., F.F. Foreman, and J. Regniere. 1985. Black spruce seed distribution with the Brohm seeder/Piper PA-18A aircraft combination. Environ. Can., Can. For. Serv., Sault Ste. Marie, Ont. Inf. Rep. O-X-370. 24 p.

Fleming, R.L., D.S. Mossa, and T.R. Burns. 1987. Scarification trials for direct seeding on upland black spruce sites in northwestern Ontario. Environ. Can., Can. For. Serv., Inf. Rep. O-X-385. 47 p.

Flowers, R.H. 1987. Supplemental feeding of black bear in tree damage areas of western Washington. *In* Proc. Symp. on Animal Damage Management in Pacific Northwest Forests. Spokane, Wash., pp. 147-148.

Foreman, F.F. and L.F. Riley. 1979. Jack pine seed distribution using the Brohm seeder/Piper PA-18A aircraft combination. Environ. Can., Can. For. Serv., Sault Ste. Marie, Ont. Inf. Rep. O-X-294. 33 p.

Forest Engineering Research Institute of Canada (FERIC). 1980. Site classification system promises reduced costs, efficient logging. Can. Pulp and Paper Industry 1980 (6):26-29.

Fowells, H.A. (editor). 1965. Silvics of forest trees of the United States. Revised ed. U.S. Dep. Agric. For. Serv., Washington, D.C. Agric. Handb. No. 271. 762 p.

Fraser, G.A. 1985. Benefit - cost analysis of forestry investment. Environ. Can., Can. For. Serv., Victoria, B.C. BC-X-275.

Fryk, J. 1986. Adapted site preparation in Sweden. Forskningsstiftelsen Skogsarbeten. Results presented at IUFRO 1986 Workshop S1.05.12, Dawson Creek, B.C. Aug. 14, 1986. 19 p.

Funk, A. 1981. Parasitic microfungi of western trees. Can. Dep. Environ., Can. For. Serv., Victoria, B.C. Inf. Rep. BC-X-222. 189 p.

_____. 1985a. Foliar fungi of western trees. Environ. Can., Can. For. Serv., Victoria, B.C. Inf. Rep. BC-X-265. 159 p.

_____. 1985b. Introduction to forest diseases. Environ. Can., Can. For. Serv., Victoria, B.C. For. Pest Leafl. 54. 15 p.

Furniss, R.L. and V.M. Carolin. 1977. Western forest insects. U. S. Dep. Agric. For. Serv., Washington, D.C. Misc. Publ. No. 1339.

Gardner, A.C. 1981. Field performance of containerized seedlings in Interior British Columbia. *In* Proc. Can. Containerized Tree Seedlings Symp. J.B. Scarratt, C. Glerum, and C.A. Plexman (editors). COJFRC Symp. Proc. O-P-10, pp. 299-306.

Garner, W.W. and H.A. Allard. 1920. Effect of the relative length of day and night and other factors of the environment on growth and reproduction in plants. J. Agric. Res. 18:553-606.

Gerber, H.S., N.V. Tonks, and D.A. Ross. 1974. The recognition and life history of the major insect and mite pests of ornamental shrubs and shade trees of British Columbia. B.C. Dep. Agric., Victoria, B.C. Bull. 74-13. 47 p.

Ghassemi, M. 1981. Environmental fates and impacts of major forest use pesticides. Report prepared for U.S. Dep. of Commerce, Environ. Protection Agency, Washington, D.C. 41 p. + 436 p. (Appendix).

Gilmour, J.D. and J. Konishi. 1965. Scarification in the Spruce Alpine fir type of the Prince George Forest District: preliminary evaluation of methods and resulting regeneration. B.C. For. Serv., Victoria, B.C. For. Manage. Note 4.

Glew, D.R. 1963. The results of stand treatment in the white spruce-alpine fir type of the Northern Interior of B.C. B.C. For. Serv., Victoria, B.C. Manage. Note 1.

Glew, D.R. and S.Z. Cinar. 1966. The results of stand treatment following seed tree marking in dry belt fir types. B.C. For. Serv., Victoria, B.C. For. Serv. Manage. Note 5.

Goba, N.L. 1984. Regeneration success survey aided by aerial infrared photography. *In* New forests for a changing world. Proc. 1983 Tech. Sessions of the Inventory, Remote Sensing and Photogrammetry, and Biometrics Working Groups, 1983 Convention of the Soc. Am. For., Portland, Oreg., pp. 8-13.

Gorman, E.H. 1955. Regeneration problems and their silvicultural significance in the coastal forests of B.C. B.C. For. Serv., Victoria, B.C. Tech. Publ. 41.

Gorman, J. R. (compiler). 1985. Proceedings of the 1984 mechanized silviculture workshop. Environ. Can., Can. For. Serv., Edmonton, Alta. Inf. Rep. NOR-X-272. 47 p.

Green, J.L. and L.H. Fuchigami. 1985. Overwintering container grown plants. Ornamentals NorthWest Newsletter. Vol. 9, No. 2, pp. 10-23.

Green, R.N., P.J. Courtin, K. Klinka, R.J. Slaco, and C.A. Ray. 1984. Site diagnosis, tree species selection, and slashburning guidelines for the Vancouver Forest Region. B.C. Min. For., Victoria, B.C. Land Manage. Handb. No. 8. 143 p.

Gregory, J.D. 1981. Impact of forest weed control on soils. *In* Weed control in forest management. H.A. Holt and B.C. Fischer (editors). Purdue Univ., Dep. For. Natural Resources, West Lafayette, Ind., pp. 231-236.

Grier, C.C. 1972. Effects of fire on the movement and distribution of elements within a forest ecosystem. Ph.D. thesis. Univ. Wash., Seattle, Wash.

Griffith, B.G. 1931. The natural regeneration of spruce in Central B.C. For. Chron. 7:204-219.

Guariglia, R.D. and B.E. Thompson. 1985. The effect of sowing depth and mulch on germination and 1+0 growth of Douglas-fir seedlings. *In* Proc. Meet. Western Forest Nursery Council and Intermountain Nurserymen's Assoc., Coeur d'Alene, Ind., Aug. 14-16, 1984. U.S. Dep. Agric. For. Serv., Ogden, Utah. Gen. Tech. Rep. INT-185, pp. 88-90.

Gunter, J.E. and H.L. Haney. 1984. Essentials of forestry investment analysis. OSU Bookstores Inc., Corvallis, Oreg.

Haeussler, S. and D. Coates. 1986. Autecological characteristics of selected species that compete with conifers in British Columbia: a literature review. B.C. Min. For., Victoria, B.C. Land Mange. Rep. No. 33. 180 p.

Hagle, S.K., K.E. Gibson, and C.J. Gilligan. 1987. Field guide to diseases and insect pests of Idaho and Montana forest. U.S. Dep. Agric. For. Serv., Missoula, Mont. 123 p.

Haley, D. 1972. The economic analysis of activities designed to accelerate stand growth in the context of the managed forest. Paper prepared for the Stand Management Committee, Western Forestry and Conservation Assoc., Seattle, Wash.

Hall, F.C., D.W. Hedrick, and R.E. Keniston. 1959. Grazing and Douglas-fir establishment in the Oregon white oak type. J. For. 57:98-105.

Hall, R.J. 1984. Use of large-scale aerial photographs in regeneration assessments. Environ. Can., For. Serv., Edmonton, Alta. Inf. Rep. NOR-X-264. 31 p.

Halvorson, C.H. 1984. Long-term monitoring of vertebrates: a review with suggestions. *In* Proc. Symp. on Research Natural Areas: Baseline Monitoring and Management, March 21, 1984, Missoula, Mont. J.L Johnson, J.F. Franklin, and R.G. Krebill (editors). U.S.Dep. Agric. For. Serv., Int. For. Range Exp. Sta., Ogden, Utah. Gen. Tech. Rep. INT-173.

Hamilton, E.H. and H.K. Yearsley. 1988. Vegetation development after clearcutting and site preparation in the SBS zone. For. Can. and B.C. Min. For., Victoria, B.C. FRDA Rep. No. 018. 66 p.

Harestad, A.S., F.L. Bunnell, T.P. Sullivan, and L. Andrusiak. 1986. Key to injury of conifer trees by wildlife in British Columbia. B.C. Min. For., Victoria, B.C. WHR-23. 37 p.

Harley, J.L. 1974. Mycorrhizae. Oxford Biology Readers, Oxford Univ. Press, Oxford, England. 16 p.

Harper, P.A. and A.S. Harestad. 1986. Vole damage to coniferous trees on Texada Island. For. Chron. 62:429-432.

Harrington, C.A. 1984. Factors influencing initial sprouting of red alder. Can. J. For. Res. 14:357-361.

Harris, J.W.E. 1978. Balsam woolly aphid. Environ. Can., Can. For. Serv., Victoria, B.C. For. Pest Leafl. No. 1.

Harris, J.W.E. and D.A. Ross. 1975. European pine shoot moth. Environ. Can., Can. For. Serv., Victoria, B.C. For. Pest Leafl. No. 18.

Harvey, A.E., M.F. Jurgensen, and M.J. Larsen. 1976. Intensive fibre utilization and prescribed fire: effects on the microbial ecology of forests. U.S. Dep. Agric. For. Serv., Gen. Tech. Rep. INT-28.

Haywood-Farmer, S. 1989. Ministry root growth capacity testing. *In* Seed and seedling extension topics. B.C. Min. For., Silv. Br., Victoria, B.C., pp. 4-5.

Hedin, I. 1987. Strip thinning trials in British Columbia - 1986. FERIC, Vancouver, B.C. Tech. Note, TN112.

Hedlin, A.F. 1974. Cone and seed insects of British Columbia. Environ. Can., Can. For. Serv., Victoria, B.C. BC-X-90. 63 p.

Hedlin, A.F. and D.S. Ruth. 1974. *Barbara colfaxiana siskiyouana* (Kft.). A pest in cones of *Abies grandis*. J. Entomol. Soc. B.C. 71:13.

Hedlin, A.F., H.O. Yates III, D. Cibrian Tovar, B.H. Ebel, T.W. Koerber, and E.P. Merkel. 1980. Cone and seed insects of North American conifers. Environ. Can., Can. For. Serv./U.S. Dep. Agric. For. Serv./Secret. Agric. Recur. Hidraul., Mexico. Victoria, B.C. 122 p.

Hee, S.M., T.S. Stevens, and D.C. Walch. 1988. Production aspects of mini-plug transplants. *In* Proc. Meet. of the Western Forest Nursery Assoc., Vernon, B.C., Aug. 8-11, 1988. U.S. Dep. Agric. For. Serv., Fort Collins, Colo. Gen. Tech. Rep. RM-167, pp. 168-171.

Heerwagen, A. 1954. The effect of grazing use upon ponderosa pine reproduction in the Rocky Mountain area. Proc. Soc. Am. For. 1954:206-207.

Heide, O.M. 1974a. Growth and dormancy in Norway Spruce ecotypes (*Picea abies*). I. Interaction of photoperiod and temperature. Physiol. Plant. 30:1-12.

_____. 1974b. Growth and dormancy in Norway Spruce ecotypes (*Picea abies*). II. After-effects of photoperiod and temperature on growth and development in subsequent years. Physiol. Plant. 31:131-139.

Heidmann, L.J. 1969. Use of herbicides for planting site preparations in the Southwest. J. Forestry 67:506-509.

Helgerson, O. 1988. Heat damage in seedlings and its prevention. FIR Report 10 (2):6-7.

Hendrick, D.W. and R.F. Keniston. 1966. Grazing and Douglas-fir growth in the Oregon white-oak type. J. For. 64:735-738.

Henigman, J.F. and J.D. Beardsley. 1985. Forest pesticide handbook of British Columbia. Council of Forest Industries of B.C. and B.C. Min. For. 7 volumes.

Hennessey, T.C. and P.M. Dougherty. 1984. Characterization of the internal water relations of Loblolly Pine seedlings in response to nursery cultural treatments: implications for reforestation success. *In* Seedling physiology and reforestation success. M.L. Duryea and G.N. Brown (editors). Martinus Nijhoff/Dr. W. Junk Publishers, Boston, Mass., pp. 225-247.

Hermann, R.K. and D.P. Lavender. 1979. Testing the vigor of coniferous planting stock. Oreg. State Univ., For. Res. Lab., Corvallis, Oreg. Res. Note No. 63. 4 p.

Herring, L.J. 1977. Studies of advance subalpine fir in the Kamloops Forest District. B.C. For. Serv., Victoria, B.C. Res. Note 80.

Herring, L.J. and D.E. Etheridge. 1976. Advance amabilis-fir regeneration in the Vancouver Forest District. Can. For. Serv. and B.C. For. Serv., Victoria, B.C. Joint Rep. 5.

Herring, L.J. and R.G. McMinn. 1980. Natural and advance regeneration of Engelmann spruce and sub-alpine fir compared 21 years after site treatment. For. Chron. 56:55-57.

Hill, R.R. 1917. Effects of grazing upon western yellow-pine reproduction in the national forests of Arizona and New Mexico. U.S. Dep. Agric., Bull. No. 580. 27 p.

Hiratsuka, Y. 1987. Forest tree diseases of the prairie provinces. Environ. Can., Can. For. Serv., Edmonton, Alta. Inf. Rep. NOR-X-286. 126 p.

Hiratsuka, Y. and J.M. Powell. 1976. Pine stem rusts of Canada. Can. Dep. Environ., Can. For. Serv., Ottawa, Ont. For. Tech. Rep. 4. 83 p.

Hobbs, S.D. 1984. The influence of species and stock type selection on stand establishment: an ecophysiological perspective. *In* Seedling physiology and reforestation success. M.L. Duryea and G.N. Brown (editors). Martinus Nijhoff/Dr. W. Junk Publishers, Boston, Mass., pp. 179-224.

Hobbs, S.D., D.P. Lavender, and K.A. Wearstler. 1982. Performance of container-grown Douglas-fir on droughty sites in southwest Oregon. *In* Proc. Symp. Canadian Containerized Tree Seedling. J.B. Scarrett, C. Glerum, and C.A. Plexman (editors). COJFRC Symp. Proc. 0-P-10, Can. For. Serv., Sault Ste. Marie, Ont., pp. 373-378.

Hobbs, S.D., S.G. Stafford, and R.L. Slagle. 1986. Undercutting conifer seedlings: effect on morphology and field performance on droughty sites. Can. J. For. Res. 17:40-46.

Hoffman, J.V. 1911. Natural reporduction from seed stored in the forest floor. J. Agric. Res. 11:1-26.

Holmsen, S.D. and R.J. Whitehead. 1988. Comparison of clearing-saw cutting attachments for weeding young conifer plantations. For. Can., Victoria, B.C., FRDA Rep. No. 028. 21 p.

Holtby, L.B. 1987. The effects of logging on the coho salmon of Carnation Creek, British Columbia. *In* Proc. of the Workshop: Applying 15 years of Carnation Creek Results. Carnation Creek Steering Committee, Nanaimo, B.C., pp. 159-174.

Howard, D. 1982. 1982 status report: wildlife damage to forests in the Vancouver Forest Region. B.C. Min. For., Victoria, B.C. WHR-3. 21 p.

Howard, K.M. and M. Newton. 1984. Overtopping by successional Coast Range vegetation slows Douglas-fir seedlings. J. For. 82(3):178-180.

Huber, R.F. (compiler). 1981. High quality collection and production of conifer seed. Proc. Workshop, Edmonton, Alta., Nov. 1979, Environ. Can., Can. For. Serv., Inf. Rep. NOR-X-235. 88 p.

Hunt, J. A. and R. G. McMinn. 1988. Mechanical site preparation and forest regeneration in Sweden and Finland: implications for technology transfer. B.C. Min. For., Victoria, B.C. FRDA Rep. 031. 58 p.

Hunt, R.S. (compiler). 1988. Proceedings of a western white pine management symposium. Westar Timber, B.C. Min. For. Lands and Can. For. Serv., Victoria, B.C. 92 p.

Husted, L. and D.P. Lavender. [1990]. Effect of soil temperature upon the root growth and mycorrhizae formation of white spruce (*Picea glauca* (Moench) Voss.) seedlings grown in controlled environments. Annales de Science Forestière. In press.

Illingworth, K. 1978a. Douglas-fir provenance trials in coastal British Columbia: results to six years after planting. Proc. IUFRO Working Parties S2-02-05, S2-02-06, S2-02-12, and S2-02-14. B.C. Min. For., Victoria, B.C. Vol. I: 411-425.

_____. 1978b. Sitka spruce provenance trials three years after planting in British Columbia. Proc. IUFRO Working Parties S2-02-05, S2-02-06, S2-02-12, and S2-02-14. B.C. Min. For., Victoria, B.C. Vol. II: 311-326.

Ingestad, T. 1962. Macro element nutrition of pine, spruce, and birch seedling in nutrient solutions. Meddelanden fran statens skogsforskning institut band 51. nr7. 133 p.

Ingram, D.C. 1931. Vegetative changes and grazing use on Douglas-fir cut-over land. J. Agric. Res. 43(5):387-417.

International Seed Testing Association. 1985. International rules for seed testing. Seed Sci. Technol. 13(2):299-513.

Jeanes, T.G. 1987. Multiple use in the man-made forest. For. Chron. 63:108-111.

Johnson, N.E. 1965. Reduced growth associated with infestations of Douglas-fir seedlings by Cinara species (Homoptera: Aphidae). Can. Entomol. Vol. 97, No. 2.

Johnson, W. and G.V. Wellburn (editors). 1976. Handbook for ground skidding and road building in British Columbia. FERIC, Vancouver, B.C. FERIC Handb. No. 1.

Johnstone, W.D. 1976. Ingress of lodgepole pine and white spruce following logging and scarification in West Central Alberta. Environ. Can., Can. For. Serv., Edmonton, Alta. Inf. Rep. NOR-X-170.

Jozsa, L.A. 1989. Subalpine fir, a B.C. Interior wood. Forintek Canada Corp. Vancouver, B.C. Report prepared for B.C. Min. For., Res. Br., Victoria, B.C. 22 p.

Justice, O.L. and L.N. Bass. 1978. Principles and practices of seed storage. U.S. Dep. Agric. Handb. No. 506. 289 p.

Kaltenberg, M.C. 1978. Evaluation of regeneration sampling methods: a Monte Carlo analysis using simulated stands. Dep. Nat. Resources, State Wash., Olympia, Wash. DNR Rep. No. 39. 50 p.

Kamm, J.A., P.D. Morgan, D.L. Overhulser, L.M. McDonough, M.E. Triebwasser, and L.M. Kline. 1983. Management practices for cranberry girdler (Lepidoptera: Pyralidae) in Douglas-fir nursery stock. J. Econ. Entomol. 76(4):923-926.

King, D.R., R.L. Bailey, and P.W. Walston. 1978. Predicting cattle damage in first-year loblolly pine plantations. J. Range Manage. 31:234-235.

Kinghorn, J.M. 1970. The status of container planting in Western Canada. For. Chron. 48:235-239.

_____. 1974. Principles and concepts in container planting. *In* Proc. N. Am. Containerized Forest Tree Seedling Symp. R.W. Tinus, W.I. Stein, and W.E. Balmer (editors). Great Plains Agric. Counc. Publ. 68, pp. 8-18.

Klapprat, R.A. 1988. Techniculture transplants: an innovation in planting stock production. *In* Taking stock: the role of nursery practice in forest renewal. Ont. For. Res. Committee Symp. Proc. 0-P-16. Can. For. Serv., Sault Ste. Marie, Ont., pp. 31-33.

Kleinschmidt, J. 1983. Concepts and experiences in clonal plantations of conifers. *In* Proc. 19th Meet. Can. Tree Improvement Assoc. Part 2:26-56.

Klinka, K. and M.C. Feller. 1984. Principles used in selecting tree species for regeneration of forest sites in southwestern British Columbia. For. Chron. 60(2):77-85.

Klinka, K., R.N. Green, P.J. Courtin, and F.C. Nuszdorfer. 1984. Site diagnosis, tree species selection, and slashburning guidelines for the Vancouver Forest Region, British Columbia. B.C. Min. For., Victoria, B.C. Land Manage. Rep. 25. 180 p.

Klinka, K., R.N. Green, R. L. Trowbridge, and L. E. Lowe. 1981. Taxonomic classification of humus forms in ecosystems of British Columbia. B.C. Min. For., Victoria, B.C. Land Manage. Rep. No. 8. 54 p.

Klinka, K. and V.J. Krajina. 1987. Ecosystems of the University of British Columbia Research Forest. Univ. B.C., Fac. For., Vancouver, B.C. 123 p.

Klinka, K., V.J. Krajina, A. Ceska, and A.M. Scagel. 1989. Indicator plants of coastal British Columbia. Univ. B.C. Press, Vancouver, B.C. 288 p.

Knight, F.B. and H.J. Heikkenen. 1980. Principles of forest entomology. McGraw-Hill, Inc., New York, N.Y.

Koot, H.P. 1983. Spruce aphid in British Columbia. Environ. Can., Can. For. Serv., Victoria, B.C. For. Pest Leafl. No. 16.

Kosco, B.H. and J.W. Bartolome. 1983. Effects of cattle and deer on regenerating mixed conifer clearcuts. J. Range Manage. 36(2):265-268.

Krag, R.K. and S.R. Webb. 1988. Cariboo Lake logging trials: production, performance and costs of rubber tired skidder, small crawler tractor and cable yarding systems on steep slopes in the central interior of British Columbia. FERIC, Vancouver, B.C. 48 p.

Krajina, V.J. 1969. Ecology of forest trees in British Columbia. Ecol. West. N. Am. 2(1):1-146.

_____. 1972. Ecosystem perspectives of forestry. H.R. MacMillan Forestry Lecture Series. Univ. B.C., Cent. for Continuing Education, Vancouver, B.C., pp. 1-11.

_____. 1977. On the need for an ecosystem approach to forest land management. *In* Ecological classification of forest land in Canada and Northwestern U.S.A. Can. Inst. For., For. Ecol. Working Group, Univ. B.C., Vancouver, B.C., pp. 1-11.

Krajina, V.J., K. Klinka, and J. Worrall 1982. Ecological characteristics of trees and shrubs of British Columbia. Univ. B.C., Vancouver, B.C. 131 p.

Kramer, P.J. and T.T. Kozlowski. 1960. Physiology of trees. McGraw-Hill Book Co., New York, N.Y. 642 p.

Kramme, J.S. and L.F. DeBano. 1965. Soil wettability: a neglected factor in watershed management. Water Resources. Br. 1(2): 283-286.

Krueger, W.C. 1983. Cattle grazing in managed forests. *In* Proc. Forestland Grazing Symp., Spokane, Wash., Feb. 23-25, 1983.

_____. 1987. Pacific Northwest forest plantations and livestock grazing. J. For. 85:30-31.

Krutilla, J.V. 1986. Multiple use forest economics. Starker Lectures. Oreg. State Univ., Corvallis, Oreg., pp. 29-38.

Lantz, C.W. (editor). 1984. Southern pine nursery handbook. U.S. Dep. Agric. For. Serv., South. Region, Atlanta, Ga. 224 p.

Lavender, D.P. 1964. Date of lifting for survival of Douglas-fir seedlings. Oreg. State Univ., School For., Corvallis, Oreg. Res. Note No. 49. 20 p.

_____. 1981. Environment and shoot growth of woody plants. Oreg. State Univ., For. Res. Lab., Corvallis, Oreg. Res. Paper No. 45. 47 p.

_____. 1989. Characterization and manipulation of the physiological quality of planting stock. *In* Proc. 10th N. Am. For. Biol. Workshop. D.T. Lester and J.G. Worrall (editors). Univ. B.C., Vancouver, B.C., pp. 32-58.

_____. 1990. Dormancy. *In* Techniques and approaches in forest tree ecophysiology. J.P. Lassoie and T.M. Hinckley (editors). CRC Press, Boca Raton, Fla. In press.

Lavender, D.P. and S.N. Silim. 1987. The role of plant growth regulators in dormancy in forest trees. *In* Hormonal control of tree growth. S.V. Kossuth and S.D. Ross (editors). Martinus Nijhoff, Boston, Mass., pp. 171-192.

Lavender, D.P. and R.B. Walker. 1979. Nitrogen and related elements in nutrition of forest trees. *In* Proc. For. Fertilization Conf. S.P. Gessel, R.M. Kenady, and W.A. Atkinson (editors). Inst. For. Resources, Univ. Wash., Seattle, Wash., Contribution No. 40, pp. 15-22.

Lawrence, W.H., N.B. Kverno, and H.D. Hartwell. 1961. Guide to wildlife feeding injuries on conifers in the Pacific Northwest. West. For. Conserv. Assoc., Portland, Oreg. 44 p.

Lawson, B.D. 1981. Prediction of prescribed fire behavior and effects on forest fuels. *In* Proc. NW For. Fire Council Ann. Meet., Portland, Oreg., Nov. 23-24, 1981. West. For. Conserv. Assoc., Portland, Oreg., pp. 79-93.

Lawson, B.D. and S.W. Taylor. 1986. Preliminary evaluation of prescribed fire impact relationships and predictors for spruce-balsam slash. *In* Proc. Symp. on Fire Management. Sponsored by Central Interior Fire Protection Committee, Prince George, B.C., April. 8-9, 1986, pp. 48-68.

Leadem, C.L. 1982. Seed viability of *Abies*, *Picea* and *Tsuga* after storage in the cones. *In* Proc. IUFRO WP S2.01.06 (Seed Problems) Intl. Symp. on Forest Tree Seed Storage, Sept. 1980. B.S.P. Wang and J.A. Pitel (compilers and editors) Environ. Can., Can. For. Serv., Petawawa, Ont., pp. 57-67.

_____. 1986. Stratification of *Abies amabilis* seeds. Can. J. For. Res. 16(4):755-760.

Lewis, C.E. 1980a. Simulating cattle injury to planted slash pine: defoliation. J. Range Manage. 33:345-348.

_____. 1980b. Simulated cattle injury to planted slash pine: combinations of defoliation, browsing and trampling. J. Range Manage. 33:340-344.

Lindquist, R.K. 1983. Fungus gnats becoming a pest. Greenhouse Manager 2:66-71.

Loucks, D.M., S.R. Radosevich, T.B. Harrington, and R.G. Wagner. 1987. Prescribed fire in Pacific Northwest Forests: an annotated bibliography. Oreg. State Univ., Coll. For., For. Res. Lab, Corvallis, Oreg. 185 p.

Lousier, J. D. and G. Still (editors). 1988. Degradation of forested lands: forest soils at risk. Proc. 10th B.C. Soil Science Workshop. B.C. Min. For., Victoria, B.C. Land Manage. Rep. No. 56.

Lucas, R.E. and J.F. Davis. 1961. Relationships between pH values of organic soils and availability of twelve plant nutrients. Soil Sci. 92:172-182.

Lyr, H. and G. Hoffmann. 1967. Growth rates and growth periodicity of tree roots. *In* International review of forestry research. Vol. 2. J.A. Romberger and P. Mikola (editors). Academic Press, New York, N.Y., pp.181-236.

McCaughey, W.W. and D.E. Ferguson. 1988. Response of advance regeneration to release in the Inland Mountain West: a summary. *In* W.C. Schmidt (ed.) Proc. Future Forest of the Mountain West: A Stand Culture Symp. U.S. Dep. Agric. For. Serv., Gen. Tech. Rep. INT - 243, pp. 255-266.

McCormack, M.L. 1981. Chemical weed control in Northeastern forests. *In* Weed control in forest management. H.A. Holt and B.C. Fischer (editor). Purdue Univ., Dep. For. Nat. Resources, West Lafayette, Ind., pp. 108-115.

McCreary, D.D. and M.L. Duryea. 1985. OSU vigor test: principles, procedures and predictive ability. *In* Evaluating seedling quality: principles, procedures and predictive ability of major tests. M.L. Duryea (editor). Oreg. State Univ., For. Res. Lab., Corvallis, Oreg., pp. 85-92.

_____. 1987. Predicting field performance of Douglas-fir seedlings: comparison of root growth potential, vigor and plant moisture stress. New Forests 3:153-169.

McCreary, D.D. and J. B. Zaerr. 1987. Root respiration has limited value for assessing Douglas-fir seedling quality. Can. J. For. Res. 17:1144-1147.

MacDonald, J. and J.N. Owens. 1987. Effect of dormancy induction treatments on terminal bud formation in coastal Douglas-fir seedlings. Proc. 7th Ann. Meet., For. Nursery Assoc. B.C., Smithers, B.C.

McDonald, P. 1986. Grasses in young conifer plantations: hindrance and help. Northwest Sci. 60(4): 271-278.

McDonald, S.E. 1984. Irrigation in forest tree nurseries: monitoring and effects on seedling growth. *In* Forest nursery manual: production of bareroot seedlings. M.L. Duryea and T.D. Landis (editors). Oreg. State Univ., For. Res. Lab. Martinus Nijhoff/ Dr. W. Junk Publishers. Corvallis, Oreg., pp. 107-121.

McDonald, S.E. and R.W. Running. 1979. Monitoring irrigation in western forest tree nurseries. U.S. Dep. Agric. For. Serv., Rocky Mtn. For. Range Exp. Sta., Fort Collins, Colo. Gen. Tech. Rep. RM-61. 8 p.

McLean, A. and M.B. Clark. 1980. Grass, trees, and cattle on clearcut-logged areas. J. Range Manage. 33:213-217.

McLean, M.M. 1959. Experimental planting of tubed seedlings 1958. Ont. Dep. Lands For., Div. Res., Rep. 39. 13 p.

McMinn, R. G. 1982. Ecology of site preparation to improve performance of planted white spruce in northern latitudes. *In* Forest regeneration at high latitudes: experiences from northern British Columbia. U.S. Dep. Agric. For. Serv., Pac. NW For. Range Exp. Sta., Misc. Rep. No. 82-1:25-32.

_____. 1985. Successful spruce stock types and sizes. *In* Interior spruce seedling performance: state of the art. North. Silv. Committee Seminar, Northern Silviculture Committee, Prince George, B.C.

Maher, T.F. 1988. The effects of black army cutworm on backlog regeneration efforts in the north Thompson Valley. For. Can. and B.C. Min. For., Victoria, B.C. FRDA Rep. 022. 21 p.

Major, J. 1951. A functional factorial approach to plant ecology. Ecology 32:392-412.

_____. 1963. A climatic index to vascular plant activity. Ecology 44:485-498.

Maki, T.E. and W.F. Mann. 1951. Some effects of sheep grazing on longleaf pine. J. For. 49:278-281.

Malhotra, S.S. and R.A. Blauel. 1980. Diagnosis of air pollutant and natural stress symptoms on forest vegetation in western Canada. Can. Dep. Environ., Can. For. Serv., Edmonton, Alta. Inf. Rep. NOR-X-228. 84 p.

Margolis, H.A. and R.H. Waring. 1986. Carbon and nitrogen allocation patterns of Douglas-fir seedlings fertilized with nitrogen in autumn. I. Overwinter metabolism. Can. J. For. Res. 16:897-902.

Marshall, P.L. 1988. A decision analytic approach to silvicultural investment decisions. Univ. B.C., Forest Economics and Policy Analysis Research Unit, Vancouver, B.C. Working Pap. 110.

Marshall, V.G. and S. Ilnytzky. 1976. Evaluation of chemically controlling the collembolan *Bourletiella hortensis* on germinating Sitka spruce and western hemlock in the nursery. Can. J. For. Res. 6:467-474.

Mason, A.C. and D.L. Adams. 1987. Black bear damage to managed timber stands in northwest Montana. *In* Proc. Symp. on Animal Damage Management in Pacific Northwest Forests. Spokane, Wash. Abstract.

Mason, W.L., J.D. Deans and S. Thompson. 1989. Producing uniform conifer planting stock. Forestry Vol. 62 Supplement. 314 p.

Matthews, R.G. 1971. Container seedling production: a provisional manual. Environ. Can., Can. For. Serv., Victoria, B.C. Rep. BC-X-58. 57 p.

_____. 1981. Contrasting approaches to containerized seedling production. I. British Columbia. *In* Proc. Can. Containerized Tree Seedlings Symp. J.B. Scarratt, C. Glerum, and C.A. Plexman (editors). COJFRC Symp. Proc. O-P-10, pp. 115-122.

Mattsson, A. and E. Troeng. 1986. Effects of different over winter storage regimes on shoot growth and net photosynthetic capacity in *Pinus sylvestri's* seedlings. Scand. J. For. Res. 1:75-84.

Maxwell, J.W. 1984. Weed control and current practises and problems in British Columbia. *In* Proc. Workshop on Weed Control in Tree Nurseries, July 17-18, 1984. G.B. Neill (editor). PFRA, Indian Head, Sask., pp. 45-47.

Mayer, H. 1977. Waldbau aus soziologisch-okologischer. Grundlang. Gustav Fischer Berlag, Stuttgart. 483 p.

Megahan, W.F. and R. Steele 1987. An approach for predicting snow damage to ponderosa pine plantations. For. Sci. 33:485-503.

Mengel, K. and E. A. Kirkby. 1978. Principles of plant nutrition. Internat. Potash Inst., Berne, Switzerland. 593 p.

Middleton, G.R., R. E. Carter, B. D. Munro, and J.F.G. MacKay. 1989. Losses of timber values associated with distorted growth in immature Douglas-fir. For. Can. and B.C. Min. For., Victoria, B.C. FRDA Rep. No. 050. 20 p.

Miller, D.L. 1986. Conifer release in the inland northwest: chemical methods. *In* Weed control for forest productivity in the interior west. D.M. Baumgartner, R.J. Boyd, D.W. Breuer, and D.L. Miller (editors). Wash. State Univ., Coop. Exten., Pullman, Wash., pp. 109-113.

Miller, D.L. and F.A. Kidd. 1984. How to write an herbicide prescription for shrub control. For. Tech. Paper TP-82-4. Potlatch Corp., Lewiston, Ind. 22 p.

Miller, G.E. 1983. Evaluation of the effectiveness of cold-water misting of trees in seed orchards for control of Douglas-fir cone gall midge (Diptera: Cecidomyiidae). J. Econ. Entomol. 76:916-919.

_____. 1986a. Damage prediction for *Contarinia oregonensis* Foote (Diptera: Cecidomyiidae) in Douglas-fir seed orchards. Can. Ent. 118:1297-1306.

_____. 1986b. Insects and conifer seed production in the Inland Mountain West: a review. *In* Proc. Symp. on Conifer Tree Seed in the Inland Mountain West. Missoula, Mont. R.C. Shearer (compiler). Aug. 1985. U.S. Dep. Agric. For. Serv., Gen. Tech. Rep. INT-203: 225-237.

Miller, G.E., A.F. Hedlin, and D.S. Ruth. 1984. Damage by two Douglas-fir cone and seed insects: correlation with cone crop size. J. Entomol. Soc. B.C. 81:46-50.

Minore, D. 1979. Comparative autecological characteristics of northwestern tree species: a literature review. U.S. Dep. Agric. For. Serv., Pac. NW For. Range Exp. Sta., Portland, Oreg. Gen. Tech. Rep. PNW-87. 72 p.

_____. 1983. Western redcedar: a literature review. U.S. Dep. Agric. For. Serv., Pac. NW For. Range Exp. Sta., Portland Oreg. Gen. Tech. Rep. PNW-150. 70 p.

Mitchell, R.W. and R. N. Green. 1981. Identification and interpretation of ecosystems of the western Kamloops Forest Region. B.C. Min. For., Victoria, B.C. Land Manage. Handb. No. 2.

Monchak, D.K. 1982. Factors affecting the growth performance and management of subalpine fir advance regeneration in the Kamloops Forest Region. B.C. For. Serv., Silv. Sect., Kamloops, B.C. 131 p.

Monfore, J.D. 1983. Livestock: a useful tool for vegetation control in ponderosa pine and lodgepole pine plantations. *In* Proc. Forestland Grazing Symp., Spokane, Wash., Feb. 23-25, 1983. 4 p.

Morby, F.E. 1982. Irrigation regimes in a bareroot nursery. *In* Proc. Meet. Intermountain Nurserymen's Assoc. R.F. Huber (editor). Can. For. Serv., Edmonton, Alta., Inf. Rep. NOR-X-241, pp. 55-59.

Morrison, D.J. and R.S. Hunt. 1988. *Leptographium* species associated with root disease of conifers in British Columbia. *In Leptographium* root diseases on conifers. T.C. Harrington and F.W. Cobb, Jr. (editors). APS Press, St. Paul, Minn., pp. 81-95.

Morrison, D.J., G.W. Wallis, and L.C. Weir. 1988. Control of *Armillaria* and *Phellinus* root diseases: 20-year results from the Skimikin stump removal experiment. Environ. Can., Can. For. Serv., Victoria, B.C. Inf. Rep. BC-X-302. 16 p.

Mueller-Dombois, D. 1964. Effect of depth to water table on height growth of tree seedlings in a greenhouse. For. Sci. 10 (2): 306-316.

Mullin, R.E. and J.D. Parker. 1976. Provisional guidelines for fall lifting for frozen overwinter storage of nursery stock. For. Chron. 52: 22-25.

Muraro, S.J. 1975. Prescribed fire predictor. Environ. Can., Can. For. Serv., Victoria, B.C.

Navratil, S. and A. Vyse. 1985. Advances in lodgepole pine regeneration *In* Proc. Symp. on Lodgepole pine: the species and its management. D.M. Baumgartner, R.G. Krebill, J.T. Arnott, and G.F. Weetman (editors). Wash. State Univ., Pullman, Wash., pp. 173-186.

Nawitka Resource Consultants. 1987. Impact of intensive forestry practices on net stand values in British Columbia. For. Can. and B.C. Min. For., Victoria, B.C. FRDA Rep. 014.

Neilsen, W.A. 1981. Effects of simulated browsing on survival and growth of *Pinus radiata* (D. Don) seedlings. Aust. For. Res. 11:47-53.

Neuenschwander, L.F., H.L. Osborne, and P. Morgan. 1986. Integrating harvest practices and site preparation activities to manage competing vegetation. *In* Weed control for forest productivity in the interior west. D.M. Baumgartner, R.J. Boyd, D.W. Breuer, and D.L. Miller (editors). Coop. Exten., Wash. State Univ., Pullman, Wash., pp. 29-34.

Newton, M. 1981. Chemical management of herbs and sclerophyll brush. *In* Reforestation of skeletal soils. S.D. Hobbs and O.T. Helgerson (editors). Oreg. State Univ., For. Res. Lab., FIR Program, Corvallis, Oreg., pp. 50-65.

Newton, M., E.C. Cole, R.A. Lautenschlager, D.E. White, and M.L. McCormack, Jr. 1989. Browse availability after conifer release in Maine's spruce-fir forests. J. Wildl. Manage. 53(3):643-649.

Newton, M. and F.N. Dost. 1984. Biological and physical effects of forest vegetation management. Final report submitted to Wash. Dep. Natural Resources, Olympia, Wash. 423 p.

Newton, M. and F.B. Knight. 1981. Handbook of weed and insect control chemicals for forest resource managers. Timber Press, Beaverton, Oreg. 213 p.

Newton M. and D.S. Preest. 1988. Growth and water relations of Douglas-fir (*Pseudotsuga menziesii*) seedlings under different growth regimes. Weed Sci. 36:653-662.

Nielsen, D.G., M.J. Dunlap, and J.F. Boggs. 1978. Controlling black vine weevils. Am. Nurseryman 147:12, 13, 89-92.

Nitsch, J.P. 1957. Photoperiodism in woody plants. Proc. Am. Soc. Hort. Sci. 70:526-544.

Nooden, L.D. and J.A. Weber. 1978. Environmental and hormonal control of dormancy in terminal buds of plants. *In* Dormancy and developmental arrest. M.E. Clutter (editor). Academic Press, New York, N.Y., pp. 221-268.

Nordstrom, L.O. 1984. The ecology and mangement of forest range in British Columbia: a review and analysis. B.C. Min. For., Victoria, B.C. Land Manage. Rep. No. 19. 91 p.

Nyborg, E.O. and G. Shikaze. 1974. Development of high-capacity precision seeding, loading and handling equipment for container nurseries. *In* Proc. N. Am. Containerized Forest Tree Seedlings Symp., Denver, Colo., pp. 146-157.

Oliver, C.D., D. P. Hanley, and J. A. Johnson (editors). 1986. Douglas-fir: stand management for the future. Univ. Wash., Coll. For. Resources, Seattle, Wash. Contribution No. 55. 388 p.

Oliver, C.D. and R.M. Kenady (editors). 1982 Proceedings of the biology and management of true firs in the Pacific Northwest symposium. Univ. Wash., Coll. For. Resources, Seattle, Wash. Contribution No. 45. 344 p.

Orländer, G. 1986. Effect of planting and scarification on the water relations of planted seedlings of Scots pine. Studia Forestalia Suecica 173. 17 p.

Owens, J.N. 1986. Cone and seed biology. *In* Proc. Symp. on Conifer Tree Seed in the Inland Mountain West, Missoula, Mont., Aug. 1985. R.C. Shearer (compiler). U.S. Dep. Agric. For. Serv., Gen. Tech. Rep. INT-203:14-31.

Owens, J.N. and M. Molder. 1984a. The reproductive cycle of interior spruce. B.C. Min. For., Victoria, B.C. 30 p.

_____. 1984b. The reproductive cycle of lodgepole pine. B.C. Min. For., Victoria, B.C. 29 p.

_____. 1984c. The reproductive cycles of western and mountain hemlock. B.C. Min. For., Victoria, B.C. 34 p.

_____. 1984d. The reproductive cycles of western redcedar and yellow-cedar. B.C. Min. For., Victoria, B.C. 28 p.

Packee, E.C. 1976. An ecological approach toward yield optimization through species allocation. Ph.D. thesis. Univ. Minn., Minneapolis, Minn. 740 p.

Palmer, M. and T. Nichols. 1981. How to identify and control cutworm damage on conifer seedlings. U. S. Dep. Agric. For. Serv., N. Central For. Exp. Sta., Leafl. No. 767-160.

Payandeh, B. and J.E. Field. 1985. FIDME: Forestry Investment Decisions Made Easy. Environ. Can., Can. For. Serv., Sault Ste. Marie, Ont. Inf. Rep. 0-X-364. 22 p.

Pearse, P.H. 1976. Timber rights and forest policy in British Columbia. Report of the Royal Commission on Forest Resources, Victoria, B.C.

Pearse, P.H., A.J. Lang, and K.L. Todd. 1986. Economic priorities for reforesting unstocked forests in British Columbia. Univ. B.C., Forest Economics and Policy Analysis Project, Vancouver, B.C. Inf. Rep. 85 - 14.

Pearson, G.A. 1931. Recovery of western yellow pine seedlings from injury by grazing animals. J. For. 29:876-894.

_____. 1950. Management of ponderosa pine in the Southwest. U.S. Dep. Agric., Agric. Monogr. 6. 218 p.

Pearson, H.A. 1974. Utilization of a forest grassland in southern United States. Proc. Int. Grass. Congress. 12:409-415.

_____. 1987. Southern pine plantations and cattle grazing. J. For. 85:36-37.

Petersen, T.D., M. Newton, and S.M. Zedaker. 1988. Influence of *Ceanothus velutinus* and associated forbs on the water stress and stemwood production of Douglas-fir. For. Sci. 34(2):333-343.

Pirozynski, K.A. 1981. Interactions between fungi and plants through the ages. Can. J. Bot. 59:1824-1827.

Pogue, H.M. 1946. Regeneration and growth of white spruce after logging. B.C. For. Serv., Victoria, B.C. Tech. Publ. 29.

Pojar, J. (editor and compiler). 1983. Forest ecology. *In* Forestry handbook for British Columbia. S.B. Watts (editor). Univ. B. C., Fac. For., The Forestry Undergraduate Society, Vancouver, B.C., pp. 221-318.

Pojar, J., K. Klinka, and D. V. Meidinger. 1987. Biogeoclimatic ecosystem classification in British Columbia. For. Ecol. Manage. 22:119-154.

Pojar, J., R. Trowbridge, and D. Coates. 1984. Ecosystem classification and interpretation of the Sub-Boreal Spruce Zone, Prince Rupert Forest Region, British Columbia. B.C. Min. For., Victoria, B.C. Land Manage. Rep. No. 17. 319 p.

Pollack, J.C. [1990]. Some effects of different forest herbicides on upland *Salix* spp. Can. J. For. Res. Submitted.

Pollard, D.F.W. and C.C. Ying. 1979. Variation in response to declining photoperiod among families and stands of white spruce in southeastern Ontario. Can. J. For. Res. 9:443-448.

Pons, T.L. 1983. Significance of inhibition of seed germination under the leaf canopy in ash coppice. Plant, Cell and Environment 6:385-392.

Price, D.T., T. A. Black, and F.M. Kelliher. 1986. Effects of salal understory removal on photosynthetic rate and stomatal conductance of young Douglas-fir trees. Can. J. For. Res. 16:90-97.

Puritch, G.S. and A.H. Vyse. 1972. Cone production in conifers: a review of the literature and evaluation of research needs. Environ. Can., Can. For. Serv., Victoria, B.C. Inf. Rep. BC-X-65. 56 p.

Radvanyi, A. 1973. Seed losses to small mammals and birds. *In* Direct Seeding Symp. J.H. Cayford (editor). Can. Dep. Environ., Can. For. Serv., Ottawa, Ont. Publ. No. 1339, pp. 67-75.

Radwan, M.A. 1970. Destruction of conifer seed and methods of protection. Proc. 4th Vertebrate Pest Conf., Sacramento, Calif., pp. 77-82.

Reed, F.L.C. 1984. The case for investing in forestry. Can. Pulp and Paper Assoc., Policy Committee. 25 p.

Regniere, J. 1982. A probabilistic model relating stocking to degree of scarification and aerial seeding rate. Can. J. For. Res. 12:362-367.

Revel, J. and H. Coates. 1976. Planting of white spruce throughout the growing season on high site areas in the Sub-Boreal Forest Region of British Columbia. B.C. Min. For., Res. Div., Victoria, B.C. Final Rep. 37 p.

Revel, J., D.P. Lavender, and L. Charleson. [1990]. Summer planting of coniferous seedlings in British Columbia. For. Can. and B.C. Min. For., Victoria, B.C. FRDA Rep. In press.

Reynolds, P.E. (editor). 1989. Proceedings of the Carnation Creek herbicide workshop. For. Can. and B.C. Min. For., Victoria, B.C. FRDA Rep. No. 063. 349 p.

Richmond, R.M. 1983. Problems and opportunities of forestland grazing in the Pacific Northwest. *In* Proc. Forestland Grazing Symp., Spokane, Wash., Feb. 23-25, 1983.

Riffle, J.W. and G.W. Peterson (technical coordinators). 1986. Diseases of trees in the Great Plains. U.S. Dep. Agric. For. Serv., Fort Collins, Col. Gen. Tech. Rep. R-M-129. 149 p.

Riley, L.F. 1980. The effect of seeding rate and seedbed availability on jack pine stocking and density in northeastern Ontario. Can. Dep. Environ., Can. For. Serv., Sault Ste. Marie, Ont. Inf. Rep. O-X-318. 36 p.

Ritchie, G.A. 1982. Carbohydrate reserves and root growth potential in Douglas-fir seedlings before and after cold storage. Can. J. For. Res. 12:905-912.

_____. 1984a. Assessing seedling quality. *In* Forest nursery manual: production of bareroot seedlings. M.L. Duryea and T.D. Landis (editors). Oreg. State Univ., For. Res. Lab. Martinus Nijhoff/Dr. W. Junk Publishers. Corvallis, Oreg., pp. 243-259.

_____. 1984b. Effect of freezer storage on bud dormancy release in Douglas-fir seedlings. Can. J. For. Res. 14:186-190.

_____. 1985. Root growth potential: principles, procedures and predictive ability. *In* Evaluating seedling quality: principles, procedures and predictive abilities of major tests. M.L. Duryea (editor). Oreg. State Univ., For. Res. Lab., Corvallis, Oreg., pp. 93-107.

Ritchie, G.A., J.R. Roden, and N. Kleyn. 1985. Physiological quality of lodgepole pine and interior spruce seedlings: effects of lift date and duration of freezer storage. Can. J. For. Res. 15:636-645.

Roberts, C. 1980. Cooperative brush study. Second-year report. Oreg. State Univ., For. Res. Lab., FIR Program, Corvallis, Oreg. 29 p.

Robins, J.K. and J.P. Susat. 1974. Red belt in Alberta. Can. Dep. Environ., Can. For. Serv., Edmonton, Alta. Inf. Rep. NOR-X-99. 6 p.

Ross, D.A. and S. Ilnytzky. 1977. The black army cutworm in British Columbia. Environ. Can., Can. For. Serv., Victoria, B.C. Inf. Rep. BC-X-154.

Ross, D.L. and J. D. Walstad. 1986. Vegetative competition, site preparation and pine performance: a literature review with reference to Southcentral Oregon. Oreg. State Univ., College For., For. Res. Lab., Corvallis, Oreg. Res. Bull. 58. 21 p.

Rowan, S.J. and D.H. Marx. 1976. Ectomycorrhizae and planting date affect rust incidence in forest tree nurseries. *In* Proc. 1976 Southeastern Area Nurserymen's Conf., Charleston, S.C., pp. 107-109.

Ruth, D.S. 1980. A guide to insect pests in Douglas-fir seed orchards. Environ. Can., Can. For. Serv., Victoria, B.C. BC-X-204. 19 p.

Ruth, D.S., G.E. Miller, and J.R. Sutherland. 1982. A guide to common insect pests and diseases in spruce seed orchards in British Columbia. Environ. Can., Can. For. Serv., Victoria, B.C. BC-X-231. 26 p.

Ruth, R.H. and A.S. Harris. 1979. Management of western hemlock-Sitka spruce forests for timber production. U.S. Dep. Agric. For. Serv., Pac. NW For. Range Exp. Sta., Portland, Oreg. Gen. Tech. Rep. PNW-88. 197 p.

Ryans, M. 1988. Mechanized pre-commercial thinning methods: experience to date. FERIC, Vancouver, B.C. Special Rep. 56.

Sandberg, D.V. 1983. Research leads to less smoke from prescribed fires. *In* Proc. NW For. Fire Council Ann. Meet., Olympia, Wash., 1983, pp. 107-121.

_____. 1985. Scheduling prescribed fires for wetter periods reduces air pollutant emissions. *In* Proc. 8th Conf. on Fire and Forest Meteorology, Soc. Am. For., 1985, Detroit, Mich., pp. 132-138.

Santillo, D.J., D.M. Leslie, Jr., and P.W. Brown. 1989. Responses of small mammals to glyphosate application on clearcuts. J. Wildl. Manage. 53(1):164-172.

Scarratt, J.B., C. Glerum, and C.A. Plexman (editors). 1982. Proc. Canadian Containerized Tree Seedlings Symp. Can. Dep. Environ., Can. For. Serv., Sault Ste. Marie, Ont. COJFRC Symp. Proc. O–P–10.

Schmidt, W.C. 1987. Bear damage: a function of stand density in young larch forests? *In* Proc. Symp. on Animal Damage Management in Pacific Northwest Forests. Spokane, Wash. Abstract.

Schooley, H.O. and T.J. Mullin. 1987. Seed production strategies: current vs. future. *In* Proc. 21st Meet. Can. Tree Improvement Assoc. Part 2:155-169.

Schopmeyer, C.S. (technical coordinator). 1974. Seeds of woody plants of the United States. U.S. Dep. Agric. For. Serv., Washington, D.C. Agric. Handb. No. 450. 883 p.

Schowalter, T.D., W.W. Hargrave, and D.A. Crossley Jr. 1986. Herbivory in forested ecosystems. Ann. Rev. Entomol. 31:171-196.

Schowalter, T.D., D.L. Overhaulser, A. Kanaskie, J.D. Stein, and J. Sexton. 1986. *Lygus hesperus* as an agent of apical bud abortion in Douglas-fir nurseries in Western Oregon. New Forests 1:5-15.

Scrivener, B.A. and J.A. MacKinnon (editors). 1989. *In* Learning from the past, looking to the future. Proc. North. Silv. Committee's 1988 Winter Workshop, Feb. 2-3, 1988, Prince George, B.C. For. Can. and B.C. Min. For., Victoria, B.C. FRDA Rep. 030. 140 p.

Sharrow, S.H. and W.C. Leininger. 1983a. Forage preferences of herded sheep as related to brush control and seasonal browsing damage to Douglas-fir regeneration. Alsa Ranger District, Siuslaw National Forest, USFS Contract No. 53-04T0-0-296N. 187 p.

_____. 1983b. Sheep as a silvicultural tool in coastal Douglas-fir forest. Proc. Foothills for Food and Forest, an International Hill Land Symp. Oreg. State Univ., Corvallis, Oreg.

Shrimpton, G.M. 1985. Four insect pests of conifer nurseries in British Columbia. Western Forest Nursery Council - Intermountain Nurseryman's Assoc., U. S. Dep. Agric. For. Serv., Gen. Tech. Rep. INT-185.

Silc, T. and D.A. Winston. 1979. Recommendations for calibrating mechanical seeders. Tree Planters Notes 30:22-24.

Silen, R. A. 1982. Nitrogen, corn and forest genetics: the agricultural yield strategy implications for Douglas-fir management. U.S. Dep. Agric. For. Serv., Pac. NW For. Range Exp. Sta., Portland, Oreg. Gen. Tech. Rep. PNW-137. 20 p.

Simpson, D.G. [1990]. Frost hardiness, root growth capacity and field performance relationships in interior spruce, lodgepole pine, Douglas-fir and western hemlock seedlings. Can. J. For. Res. In press.

Sinclair, W.A., D.P. Cowles, and S.M. Hee. 1975. Fusarium root rot of Douglas-fir seedlings: suppression by soil fumigation, fertility management, and inoculation with spores of the fungal symbiont *Laccaria laccata*. For. Sci. 21:390-399.

Sjoberg, N.E. 1974. The styroblock container system. *In* Proc. N. Am. Containerized Forest Tree Seedlings Symp. R.W. Tinus, W.I. Stein, and W.E. Balmer (editors). Great Plains Agric. Counc. Publ. 68, pp. 217-228.

Smith, B.W. 1984. Aerial seeding requirements for jack pine regeneration. *In* Proc. Jack Pine Symp. C.R. Smith and G. Brown (co-chairmen). Can. Dep. Environ., Can. For. Serv. COJFRC Symp. Proc. O-P-12, pp. 78-86.

Smith, C.R. 1984. Status of mechanization of silviculture in Canada. *In* Mechanization of silviculture: increasing quality and productivity. Proc. CPPA/CFS Seminar on Mechanization of Silviculture, Thunder Bay, Ont., pp. 41-49.

_____. 1987a. Silviculture equipment reference catalogue for southern Ontario. Revised. Ont. Min. Nat. Resour., For. Resources Br., Toronto, Ont.

_____. 1987b. Silviculture equipment reference catalogue for northern Ontario. Revised. Ont. Min. Nat. Resour., For. Resources Br., Toronto, Ont.

Smith, D.M. 1972. The continuing evolution of silvicultural practice. J. For. 50:89-92.

_____. 1986. The practice of silviculture. 8th ed. J. Wiley & Sons, New York, N.Y. 527 p.

Smith, J.H.G. 1955. Some factors affecting reproduction of Engelmann spruce and alpine fir. B.C. For. Serv., Victoria, B.C. Tech. Publ. 43.

Smith, J.H.G. and M.B. Clark. 1974. Results of methods of cutting and related studies initiated in Engelmann Spruce-sub-alpine fir forests near Bolean Lake B.C. in 1950. Prog. Rep. EP 371. B.C. For. Serv., Res. Div., Victoria, B.C.

Smith, L.F., R.S. Campbell, and C.L. Blout. 1958. Cattle grazing in longleaf pine forests of south Mississippi. U.S. Dep. Agric. For. Serv., South. For. Exp. Sta., Occas. Pap. 162. 25 p.

Smith, N.J. (N.Y. editor) 1988. Western redcedar — does it have a future? Proc. Conf. Univ. B.C., Fac. For., Vancouver, B.C. 177 p.

Smith, R.B. and H. R. Craig. 1968. Decay in advanced alpine fir regeneration in the Kamloops District of British Columbia. For. Chron. 46:217-220.

Smith, S.M. 1988. Regeneration delays and natural yields on untreated backlog forest land in British Columbia. Can. For. Serv., Victoria, B.C. FRDA Rep. 43. 204 p.

Smith, T.J. 1987. Occupational characteristics of tree planting work. Silv. Magazine, Jan./Feb. 1987. MacLean Hunter Ltd., Toronto, Ont.

Smith, W.C., R.C. Shaerer, and A.L. Roe. 1976. Ecology and silviculture of western larch forests. U.S. Dep. Agric. For. Serv., Intermtn. For. Range Exp. Sta., Ogden, Utah. Tech. Bull. No. 1520. 96 p.

Society of American Foresters. 1984. Proc. 1983 Tech. Sessions of the Inventory, Remote Sensing and Photogrammetry, and Biometrics Working Groups, 1983 Convention of the Soc. Am. For., Portland, Oreg. 48 p.

Soil Survey Staff. 1975. Soil taxonomy. U.S. Dep. Agric., Soil Conserv. Serv., Washington, D.C. Handb. No. 436. 754 p.

Sparhawk, W.N. 1918. Effect of grazing upon western yellow pine reproduction in central Idaho. U.S. Dep. Agric. Bull. No. 738. 31 p.

Spittlehouse, D.L. and R.J. Stathers. 1990. Seedling microclimate. Land Manage. Rep. 65. B.C. Min. For., Victoria, B.C.

Spurr, J.E. and B.V. Barnes. 1980. Forest ecology. John Wiley & Sons, Inc., New York, N.Y. 687 p.

Stathers, R. J. 1989. Summer frost in young forest plantations. For. Can. and B.C. Min. For., Victoria, B.C. FRDA Rep. No. 073. 24 p.

Stein, J.D. and G.P. Markin. 1986. Evaluation of four chemical insecticides registered for control of the Douglas-fir cone gall midge, *Contarinia oregonensis* (Diptera: Cecidomyiidae), and the Douglas-fir seed chalcid, *Megastigmus spermotrophus* (Hymenoptera: Torymidae) in Douglas-fir seed orchards. Can. Ent. 118:1185-1191.

Stein, W.I. 1978. Reforestation evaluation. *In* Regenerating Oregon's forests. B.D. Cleary, R.D. Greaves, and R.K. Hermann (editors). Oreg. State Univ., Exten. Serv., Corvallis, Oreg.

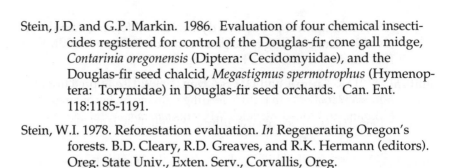_____. 1984. Fixed-plot methods for evaluating forest regeneration. *In* New forests for a changing world. Proc. 1983 Tech. Sessions of the Inventory, Remote Sensing and Photogrammetry, and Biometrics Working Groups, 1983 Convention of the Soc. Am. For., Portland, Oreg., pp. 20-26.

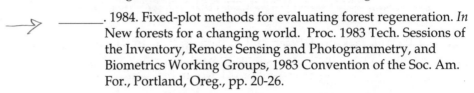_____. 1985. Designing preharvest and postharvest stocking surveys. *In* Proc. Workshop on the Shelterwood Management System. Oreg. State Univ., For. Res. Lab., Corvallis, Oreg. 7 p.

Stein, W.I., R. Danielson, N. Shaw, S. Wolff, and D. Gerdes. 1986. Users guide for seeds of western trees and shrubs. U.S. Dep. Agric. For. Serv., Gen. Tech. Rep. PNW 193. 45 p.

Sterling Wood Group Inc. 1988. Analysis of changes in timber values due to silviculture treatments under the Canada - British Columbia Forest Resource Development Agreement. For. Can. and B.C. Min. For., Victoria, B.C. FRDA Rep. 041. 67 p.

Stettler, R.F. 1958. Development of a residual stand of interior spruce-alpine fir during the first 28 years following cutting to a 12 inch diameter limit. B.C. For. Serv., Victoria, B.C. Res. Note 24.

Stevens, R.E. 1971. Pine needle-sheath miner. U.S. Dep. Agric. For. Serv., For. Pest Leafl. No. 65.

Stewart, R.E. 1978. Site preparation. *In* Regenerating Oregon's forests. B.D. Cleary, R. D. Greaves, and R.K. Hermann (editors). Oreg. State Univ., Exten. Serv., Corvallis, Oreg. pp. 99-129.

Stone, E.C., J.L. Jenkinson, and S.L. Krugman. 1962. Root-regeneration potential of Douglas-fir seedlings lifted at different times of the year. For. Sci. 8:288-297.

Sullivan, T.P. 1979a. Repopulation of clear-cut habitat and conifer seed predation by deer mice. J. Wildl. Manage. 43:861-871.

_____. 1979b. The use of alternative foods to reduce conifer seed predation by the deer mouse (*Peromyscus maniculatus*). J. Appl. Ecol. 16:475-495.

_____. 1984. Effects of snowshoe hare damage on juvenile lodgepole pine: implications for spacing natural stands. B.C. Min. For., Victoria, B.C. Res. Note 94. 27 p.

_____. 1985. Small mammal damage agents which affect the intensive silviculture of lodgepole pine. Proc. Lodgepole Pine Symp. Spokane, Wash. and Vancouver, B.C., pp. 97-105.

_____. 1987. Red squirrel population dynamics and feeding damage in juvenile stands of lodgepole pine. Can. For. Serv. and B.C. Min. For. Lands, Victoria, B.C. FRDA Rep. 019. 20 p.

Sullivan, T.P., D.R. Crump, and D.S. Sullivan. 1988a. Use of predator odors as repellents to reduce feeding damage by herbivores. III. Montane and Meadow voles (*Microtus montanus*) and *Microtus pennsylvanicus*). J. Chem. Ecol. 14:363-377.

_____. 1988b. Use of predator odors as repellents to reduce feeding damage by herbivores. IV. Northern pocket gophers (*Thomomys talpoides*). J. Chem. Ecol. 14:379-389.

Sullivan, T.P., W.T. Jackson, J. Pojar, and A. Banner. 1986. Impact of feeding damage by the porcupine on western hemlock - Sitka spruce forests of north-coastal British Columbia. Can. J. For. Res. 16:642-647.

Sullivan, T.P. and R.A. Moses. 1986a. Demographic and feeding responses of a snowshoe hare population to mechanical habitat alteration. J. Appl. Ecol. 23:53-63.

_____. 1986b. Comparison of red squirrel populations in natural and managed stands of lodgepole pine. J. Wildl. Manage. 50:595-601.

Sullivan, T.P. and D.S. Sullivan. 1982a. The use of alternative foods to reduce lodgepole pine seed predation by small mammals. J. Appl. Ecol. 19:33-45.

_____. 1982b. Reduction of conifer seed predation by use of alternative foods. J. For. 80:499-500.

_____. 1982c. Barking damage by snowshoe hares and red squirrels in lodgepole pine stands in central British Columbia. Can. J. For. Res. 12:443-448.

_____. 1982d. Influence of fertilization trials on feeding attacks to lodgepole pine by snowshoe hares and red squirrels. For. Chron. 58:263-267.

_____. 1986a. Impact of feeding damage by snowshoe hares on growth rates of juvenile lodgepole pine in the central interior of British Columbia. Can. J. For. Res. 16:1145-1149.

_____. 1986b. Resiliency of snowshoe hares to population reduction. J. Appl. Ecol. 23:795-806.

Summers, D. and G.E. Miller. 1987. Experience with systemic insecticides for the control of cone and seed insects in Douglas-fir seed orchards in coastal British Columbia, Canada. *In* Proc. 2nd Conf. Cone and Seed Insects Working Party S2.07-01. IUFRO. Sept. 3-5, 1986. Briançon, France. A. Rogues (editor). U.S. Dep. Agric. For. Serv.

Sutherland, J.R. 1984. Pest management in Northwest bareroot nurseries. *In* Forest nursery manual: production of bareroot seedlings. M.L. Duryea and T.D. Landis (editors). Oreg. State Univ., For. Res. Lab. Martinus Nijhoff/Dr. W. Junk Publishers. Corvallis, Oreg., pp. 203-210.

_____. 1986. Influence of diseases on seed production. *In* Proc. Symp. on Conifer Tree Seed in the Inland Mountain West., Missoula, Mont., Aug. 1985. R.C. Shearer (compiler) U.S. Dep. Agric. For. Serv. Gen. Tech. Rep. INT-203: 14-31.

Sutherland, J.R., T. Miller, and R.S. Quinard (editors). 1987. Cone and seed diseases of North American conifers. N. Am. For. Commission, Publ. No. 1. Victoria, B.C. 77 p.

Sutherland, J.R., G.M. Shrimpton, and R.N. Sturrock. 1989. Disease and insects in British Columbia forest seedling nurseries. Can. For. Serv. and B.C. Min. For., Victoria, B.C. FRDA Rep. 065. 85 p.

Sutherland, J.R., and E. Van Eerden. 1980. Diseases and insect pests in British Columbia forest nurseries. Can. For. Serv. and B.C. Min. For., Victoria, B.C. Joint Rep. 12. 55 p.

Sutton, R.F. 1980. Planting stock quality, root growth capacity, and field performance of three boreal conifers. N.Z. J. For. Sci. 10(1):54-71.

_____. 1983. Root growth capacity: relationship with field root growth and performance in outplanted jack pine and black spruce. Plant and Soil 71:111-122.

_____. 1985. Vegetation management in Canadian forestry. Can. For. Serv., Sault Ste. Marie, Ont. Inf. Rep. 0-X-369. 34 p.

_____. 1988. Planting stock quality is fitness for purpose. *In* Proc. Symp. on Taking Stock: the Role of Nursery Practice in Forest Renewal. Can. For. Serv., Sault Ste. Marie, Ont., Ont. For. Res. Commitee O-P-16, pp. 39-43.

Sutton, R.F. and E.L. Stone. 1974. White grubs: a description for foresters, and an evaluation of their silvicultural significance. Environ. Can., Can. For. Serv. Inf. Rep. 0-X-212.

Tabbush, P.M. 1986. Rough handling, soil temperature and root development in outplanted Sitka spruce and Douglas-fir. Can. J. For. Res. 16:1385-1388.

Tanaka, Y., and N.J. Kleyn. 1987. Final report of the 1984 growing density and seed-bed covering trials at Weyerhaeuser Grandview Nursery. Weyerhaeuser Co., Tacoma, Wash. Tech. Rep. 050-9011/1.

Tanaka, Y., N.J. Kleyn, and L.M. Harper. 1986. Seed stratification of Engelmann spruce and lodgepole pine: the effect of stratification duration and timing of surface drying. For. Chron. 62:147-151.

Tanaka, Y., J.D. Walstad, and J.E. Borrecco. 1976. The effect of wrenching on morphology and field performance of Douglas-fir and loblolly pine seedlings. Can. J. For. Res. 6:453-458.

Tappeiner, J.C., T.F. Hughes, and S.D. Tesch. 1987. Bud production of Douglas-fir (*Pseudotsuga menziesii*) seedlings: response to shrubs and hardwood competition. Can. J. For. Res. 17:1300-1304.

Tarrant, R.F. 1957. Soil moisture conditions after chemically killing manzanita brush in central Oregon. U.S. Dep. Agric. For. Serv., Pac. NW For. Range Exp. Sta., Portland, Oreg. Res. Note 156. 4 p.

Taylor, S.W. and B.C. Hawkes. 1988. Site rehabilitation burning considerations in North Central B.C. *In* Learning from the past, looking to the future. B.A. Scrivener and J.A. MacKinnon (editors). Proc. North. Silv. Meet., Feb. 9-10, 1988, Prince George, B.C., For. Can. and B.C. Min. For., Victoria, B.C. FRDA Rep. 030. pp. 121-125.

Teeguarden, D. E. and H.L. von Sperber. 1968. Scheduling Douglas-fir reforestation investments: a comparison in methods. For. Sci. 14:354-368.

Thompson, B. 1983. Why fall fertilize? *In* Proc. Conf. of the Western Nurserymen's and Western Forest Nursery Council, Medford, Oreg., Aug. 10-12, 1982. South. Oreg. State Coll., Ashland, Oreg., pp. 85-91.

Thompson, B.E. 1985. Seedling morphological evaluation: what can you tell by looking. *In* Evaluating seedling quality: principles, procedures and predictive abilities of major tests. M.L. Duryea (editor). Oreg. State Univ., For. Res. Lab., Corvallis, Oreg., pp. 59-73.

Thorsen, A. (editor). 1978. Scarification. Forskningsstiftelsen Skogsarbeten Manual. Tryckeri AB Knappen, Karlstad, Sweden. 32 p.

Timmis, R. and Y. Tanaka. 1976. Effects of container density and plant water stress on growth and cold hardiness of Douglas-fir seedlings. For. Sci. 22 (2):167-172.

Tinus, R.W. and S.E. McDonald. 1979. How to grow tree seedlings in containers in greenhouses. U.S. Dep. Agric. For. Serv., Rocky Mtn. For. Range Exp. Sta., Gen. Tech. Rep. RM 60.

Toda, R. 1974. Vegetative propagation in relation to Japanese forest tree improvement. N. Z. J. For. Sci. 4:410-417.

Toewes, D.A.A. and M.J. Brownlee. 1981. A handbook for fish habitat protection on forest lands in British Columbia. Can. Dep. Fish. Oceans, Ottawa, Ont. 166 p.

Trewartha, G.T. 1968. An introduction to climate. 4th ed. McGraw-Hill, New York, N.Y. 408 p.

Troup, R.S. 1952. Silviculture system. 2nd ed. Oxford Univ. Press, London.

Trowbridge, R., B. Hawkes, A. Macadam, and J. Parminter. 1986. Field handbook for prescribed fire assessments in B.C.: logging slash fuel. B.C. Min. For., Victoria, B.C. Land Manage. Handb. No. 11. 63 p.

Tustin, J.R., R.L. Knowles, and B.K. Klomp. 1979. Forest farming: a multiple land-use production system in New Zealand. For. Ecol. Manage. 2:169-189.

Unger, L.S. 1986. Spruce budworms in British Columbia. Environ. Can., Can. For. Serv., Victoria, B.C. For. Pest Leafl. No. 31.

U.S. Department of Agriculture. 1983. Forest management disease notes. For. Serv., For. Pest Manage., Portland, Oreg.

University of British Columbia Forest Club. 1959. Forestry handbook for British Columbia. 2nd ed. Vancouver, B.C.

Utzig, G.F., P.G. Comeau, D.L. MacDonald, M.V. Ketchison, T.F. Braumandl, A.R. Warner, and G.W. Still. 1986. A field guide to the identification and interpretation of ecosystems in the Nelson Forest Region. B.C. Min. For., Victoria, B.C. 82 p.

Utzig, G.F. and M.E. Walmsley. 1988. Evaluation of soil degradation as a factor affecting forest productivity in British Columbia: a problem analysis. Phase I. Can. For. Serv., Pac. Yukon Region, Victoria, B.C. FRDA Rep. 25. 111 p.

van den Driessche, R. 1969. Forest nursery handbook. B.C. For. Serv., Victoria, B.C. Res. Note 48. 44 p.

_____. 1977. Survival of coastal and interior Douglas-fir seedlings after storage at different temperatures, and effectiveness of cold storage in satisfying chilling requirements. Can. J. For. Res. 7:125-131.

_____. 1980. Effects of nitrogen and phosphorus fertilization on Douglas-fir nursery growth and survival after outplanting. Can. J. For. Res. 10:65-70.

_____. 1982. Relationship between spacing and nitrogen fertilization of seedlings in the nursery, seedling size, and outplanting performance. Can. J. For. Res. 12:865-875.

_____. 1983a. Soil fertility in forest nurseries. *In* Forest nursery manual: production of bareroot seedlings. M.L. Duryea and T.D. Landis (editors). Oreg. State Univ., For. Res. Lab. Martinus Nijhoff/ Dr. W. Junk Publishers. Corvallis, Oreg., pp. 63-74.

_____. 1983b. Growth, survival, and physiology of Douglas-fir seedlings following root wrenching and fertilization. Can. J. For. Res. 13:270-278.

_____. 1984a. Response of Douglas-fir seedlings to phosphorous fertilization and influence of temperature on this response. Plant and Soil 80:155-169.

_____. 1984b. Seedling spacing in the nursery in relation to growth, yield, and performance of stock. For. Chron. 60:345-355.

_____. 1988a. Response of Douglas-fir (*Pseudotsuga menziesii* (Mirb.) Franco) to some different fertilizers applied at planting. New Forests 2: 89-110.

_____. 1988b. Seedlings using fertilizers of different solubilities and application time, and their forest growth. Can. J. For. Res. 18:172-180.

van den Driessche, R. and K.W. Cheung. 1979. Relationship of stem electrical impedance and water potential of Douglas-fir seedling to survival after cold storage. For. Sci. 25:507-517.

Van Eerden, E. 1972. Influences affecting container seedling performance near Prince George, British Columbia. *In* Proc. Workshop on Container Planting in Canada. R.M. Waldron (editor). Can. Dep. Environ., Can. For. Serv., Inf. Rep. DPC-X-2, pp. 92-100.

_____. 1974. Growing season production of western conifers. *In* Proc. N. Am. Containerized Forest Tree Seedlings Symp. R.W. Tinus, W.I. Stein, and W.E. Balmer (editors). Great Plains Agric. Counc. Publ. 68, pp. 93-103.

_____. 1981. The fundamentals of container seedling production. *In* Proc. Can. Containerized Tree Seedlings Symp. J.B. Scarratt, C. Glerum, and C.A. Plexman (editors). COJFRC Symp. Proc. O-P-10, pp. 83-90.

Van Eerden, E. and J. M. Kinghorn (editors). 1978. Proc. Symp. on Root Form of Planted Trees. B.C. Min. For. and Can. For. Serv., Victoria, B.C. Joint Rep. 8. 357 p.

Van Wagner, C.E. 1987. Development and structure of the Canadian Forest Fire Weather Index System. Environ. Can., Can. For. Serv., Ottawa, Ont. For. Tech. Rep. 35.

von der Gonna, M. and D. P. Lavender. 1989. Root egress of white spruce (*Picea glauca*) seedlings after outplanting as affected by patch and mound site preparation. *In* Learning from the past, looking to the future. B.A. Scrivener and J.A. MacKinnon (editors). For. Can. and B.C. Min. For., Victoria, B.C. FRDA Rep. No. 30., pp. 76-80.

Vyse, A.H. 1973. Economics of direct seeding versus other regeneration techniques. *In* Proc. Direct Seeding Symp. J.H. Cayford (editor). Can. Dep. Environ., Can. For. Serv., Ottawa, Ont. Publ. No. 1339, pp. 35-48.

_____. 1987. A review of silvicultural principles for dry belt fir management. Proc. of Dry-belt Fir Timber Management Conf.: A review for practitioners. F. Barber (editor). B.C. Min. For. Lands, Silv. Br., Victoria, B.C.

Vyse, A.H., G.A. Birchfield, and E. Van Eerden. 1971. An operational trial of the styroblock reforestation system in British Columbia. Environ. Can., Can. For. Serv., Victoria, B.C. Inf. Rep. BC-X-59. 34 p.

Vyse, A.H. and J.D. Rudd. 1974. Sowing rules for container nurseries. *In* Proc. N. Am. Containerized Forest Tree Seedlings Symp. R.W. Tinus, W.I. Stein, and W.E. Balmer (editors). Great Plains Agric. Counc. Publ. 68, pp.164-169.

Wagner, R.G. and S. Radosevich. 1987. Interspecific competition indices for vegetation management in young Douglas-fir stands on the Siuslaw National Forest: Rep. No. 1. Oreg. State Univ., For. Sci. Dep., Corvallis, Oreg. 108 p.

Wakeley, P.C. 1948. Physiological grades of southern pine nursery stock. *In* Proc. Soc. Am. For., Washington, D.C., pp. 311-322.

Wallis, G.W. 1976. *Phellinus (Poria) weirii* root rot, detection and management proposals in Douglas-fir stands. Can. Dep. Environ., Can. For. Serv., Victoria, B.C. For. Tech. Rep. 12. 16 p.

Wallis, G.W. and D.J. Morrison. 1975. Root rot and stem decay following commercial thinning in western hemlock and guidelines for reducing losses. For. Chron. 51: 203-207.

Wallner, W.E. and J.W. Butcher. 1973. Christmas tree insect management. Mich. State Univ., Coop Exten. Serv. Exten. Bull. E353. Farm Sci. Series.

Walmsley, M.G., G. Utzig, T. Vold, D. Moon, and J. van Barneveld (editors). 1980. Describing ecosystems in the field. B.C. Min. Environ., RAB Tech. Pap. 2, and B.C. Min. For., Land Manage. Rep. No. 7. 225 p.

Walstad, J.D. and P.J. Kuch (editors). 1987. Forest vegetation management for conifer production. John Wiley & Sons, New York, N.Y. 523 p.

Walstad, J.D., M. Newton, and R.J. Boyd, Jr. 1987. Forest vegetation problems in the Northwest. *In* Forest vegetation management for conifer production. J.D. Walstad and P.J. Kuch (editors). John Wiley & Sons, New York, N.Y., pp. 15-54.

Walstad, J.D., M. Newton and D. H. Gjerstad. 1987. Overview of vegetation management alternatives. *In* Forest vegetation management for conifer production. J.D. Walstad and P.J. Kuch (editors). John Wiley & Sons, New York, N.Y. 523 p.

Walters, J. 1961. The planting gun and bullet: a new tree-planting technique. For. Chron. 37:94-95, 107.

_____. 1963. An improved planting gun. U.S. Dep. Agric., Washington, D.C. Tree Planters Notes 57: 1-3.

_____. 1969. Container planting of Douglas-fir. For. Prod. J. 19:10-14.

Wang, B.S.P. 1974. Tree-seed storage. Can. Dep. Environ., Can. For. Serv., Ottawa, Ont. Publ. No. 1335. 32 p.

Waring, R.H. and J.F. Franklin. 1979. The evergreen coniferous forests of the Pacific Northwest. Science 204:1380-1386.

Waring, R.H. and W.H. Schlesinger. 1985. Forest ecosystems: concepts and management. Orlando Academic Press, Orlando, Fla.

Weetman, G.F., R.C. Yang, and I.E. Bella. 1984. Nutrition and fertilization of lodgepole pine. *In* Proc. Symp. on Lodgepole pine: the species and its management, May 1984. D.M. Baumgartner, R.G. Krebill, J.T. Arnott, and G.F. Weetman (editors). Wash. State Univ., Pullman, Wash., pp. 225-230.

Weiser, C.J. 1970. Cold resistance and injury in woody plants. Science 169:1269-1278.

Wells, C.G., R.E. Campbell, L.F. DeBano, C.E. Lewis, R.L. Fredriksen, E.C. Franklin, R.C. Froelich, and P.H. Dunn. 1979. Effects of fire on soil. USDA For. Serv. Gen. Tech. Rep. W0-7. 34 p.

Whitney, R.D. 1977. *Polyporus tomentosus* root rot of conifers. Can. Dep. Fish. Environ., Can. For. Serv., Sault Ste. Marie, Ont. For. Tech. Rep. No. 18. 11 p.

Wilford, D.J. 1987. Watershed workbook: forest hydrology sensitivity analysis for coastal British Columbia watersheds. Interim ed. B.C. Min. For. Lands, Smithers, B.C. 33 p.

Wilkinson, A.T.S. and H.S. Gerber. 1983. Description, life history, and control of leatherjackets. B.C. Min. Agric. Food, Victoria, B.C.

Wood, C. 1977. Cooley spruce gall aphid. Can. Dep. Fish. Environ., Victoria, B.C. For. Pest Leafl. No. 6.

Wood, J.E. and J.K. Jeglum. 1984. Black spruce regeneration trials near Nipigon, Ontario: planting versus seeding, lowlands versus uplands, clearcut versus strip cut. Can. Dep. Environ., Can. For. Serv., Sault Ste. Marie, Ont. Inf. Rep. O-X-361. 19 p.

Wood, J.E., R. F. Sutton, T.P. Weldon, and H. Rissanen. 1988. Jack pine establishment: effect of stock type, Bräcke scarification, mounding, and chemical site preparation. Three-year results. Environ. Can., Can. For. Serv., Sault Ste. Marie, Ont. Inf. Rep. O-X-393. 16 p.

Wood, R.O. and L.H. McMullen 1983. Spruce weevil in British Columbia. Environ. Can., Can. For. Serv., Victoria, B.C. For. Pest Leafl. No. 2.

Wyeth, H.H. 1984. British Columbia Ministry of Forests regeneration survey system. *In* New forests for a changing world. Proc. 1983 Tech. Sessions of the Inventory, Remote Sensing and Photogrammetry, and Biometrics Working Groups, 1983 Convention of the Soc. Am. For., Portland, Oreg., pp. 40-43.

Yates, H.O. III (editor). 1984. Proceedings of the cone and seed insects working party conference. Working Party S2.07-01. IUFRO, Athens, Ga., 1983. U.S. Dep. Agric. For. Serv., SE Exp. Sta. 214 p.

Zaerr, J.B., B.D. Cleary, and J. Jenkinson. 1981. Scheduling irrigation to induce seedling dormancy. *In* Proc. Meet. of the Intermountain Nurserymen's Assoc. and Western Forest Nursery Council, Boise, Idaho, Aug. 12-14, 1980. U.S. Dep. Agric. For. Serv., Intermtn. For. Range Exp. Sta., Ogden, Utah. Gen. Tech. Rep. INT-109, pp. 74-78.

Ziller, W.G. 1974. The tree rusts of western Canada. Can. Dep. Environ., Can. For. Serv., Ottawa, Ont. Publ. No. 1329. 272 p.

LIST OF SPECIES

Scientific name	Common name	Abbreviation
Trees		
Abies amabilis (Dougl. *ex* Loud.) Forbes	Pacific silver fir	Ba
Abies grandis (Dougl. *ex* D. Don) Lind.	grand fir	Bg
Abies lasiocarpa (Hook.) Nutt.	subalpine fir	Bl
Abies procera A. Nobilis	Noble fir	
Acer glabrum Torr.	Douglas maple	
Acer macrophyllum Pursh.	bigleaf maple	
Alnus rubra Bong.	red alder	Dr
Betula papyrifera Marsh.	paper birch	Ep
Chamaecyparis nootkatensis (D. Don) Spach	yellow-cedar	Cy
Larix laricina (Du Roi) K. Koch	tamarack	
Larix occidentalis Nutt.	western larch	Lw
Picea engelmannii Parry *ex* Engelm.	Engelmann spruce	Se
Picea glauca (Moench) Voss	white spruce	Sw
Picea mariana (P. Mill.) B.S.P.	black spruce	Sb
Picea sitchensis (Bong.) Carr.	sitka spruce	Ss
Pinus albicaulis Engelm.	whitebark pine	
Pinus contorta Dougl. *ex* Loud.	lodgepole pine	Pl
Pinus monticola Dougl. *ex* D. Don *in* Lamb.	western white pine	Pw
Pinus palustris Mill.	longleaf pine	
Pinus ponderosa Dougl. *ex* P.&C. Lawson	ponderosa pine/yellow pine	Pp/Py
Pinus radiata Dougl. *ex* Loud.	radiata pine	
Pinus sylvestris L.	Scots pine	
Populus balsamifera L. ssp. *balsamifera*	balsam poplar	Ac
Populus balsamifera L. ssp. *trichocarpa* (Torr. & Gray *ex* Hook.) Brayshaw	black cottonwood	
Populus tremuloides Michx.	trembling aspen	At
Pseudotsuga menziesii (Mirb.) Franco	Douglas-fir	Fdc/Fdi
Thuja plicata Donn *ex* D. Don *in* Lamb.	western redcedar	Cw
Tsuga heterophylla (Raf.) Sarg.	western hemlock	Hw
Tsuga mertensiana (Bong.) Carr.	mountain hemlock	Hm
Other plants		
Acer circinatum Pursh	vine maple	
Alnus incana ssp. *tenuifolia* (L.) Moench Nutt. Breitung	mountain alder	
Alnus viridis (Chaix) DC.	Sitka or green alder	
Cornus sericea L.	red-osier dogwood	
Corylus cornuta Marshall	hazelnut	
Athyrium filix-femina (L.) Roth	lady fern	
Calamagrostis canadensis (Michx.) Beauv.	bluejoint	
Calamagrostis rubescens Buckley	pinegrass	
Ceanothus spp.	Snowbrush	
Epilobium angustifolium L.	fireweed	
Gaultheria shallon Pursh	salal	
Lonicera involucrata (Richards.) Banks *ex* Spreng.	black twinberry	
Lupinus spp.	Lupines	
Menziesia ferruginea Sm.	false azalea	
Polystichum munitum (Kaulfuss) Presl	sword fern	
Pteridium aquilinum (L.) Kuhn in Decken	bracken	
Rhododendron albiflorum Hook.	white-flowered rhododendron	
Ribes bracteosum Dougl. *ex* Hook.	stink currant	
Ribes lacustre (Pers.) Poir. *in* Lam.	prickly gooseberry	
Rosa spp.	roses	
Rubus idaeus L.	red raspberry	
Rubus parviflorus Nutt.	thimbleberry	
Rubus spectabilis Pursh	salmonberry	
Salix spp.	willows	
Sambucus spp.	elderberries	
Symphoricarpos albus (L.) Blake	snowberry	
Vaccinium membranaceum Dougl. *ex* Hook.	black huckleberry	
Vaccinium ovalifolium Sm. *in* Rees	oval-leaved blueberry	
Vaccinium parvifolium Sm. *in* Rees	red huckleberry	
Valeriana sitchensis Bong.	Sitka valerian	
Viburnum edule (Michx.) Raf.	high cranberry	

INDEX